THE SEASONS

The earth revolves around the sun once a year in an anti-clockwise direction. The earth is tilted at an angle of 66½ degrees to the plane of its orbit and always points into space in the same direction. In June the northern hemisphere is tilted towards the sun and it is the northern summer – days are longer and it is generally warmer. The southern hemisphere is pointing away from the sun. It is cooler and the days are shorter – the southern winter. In December the reverse is the case.

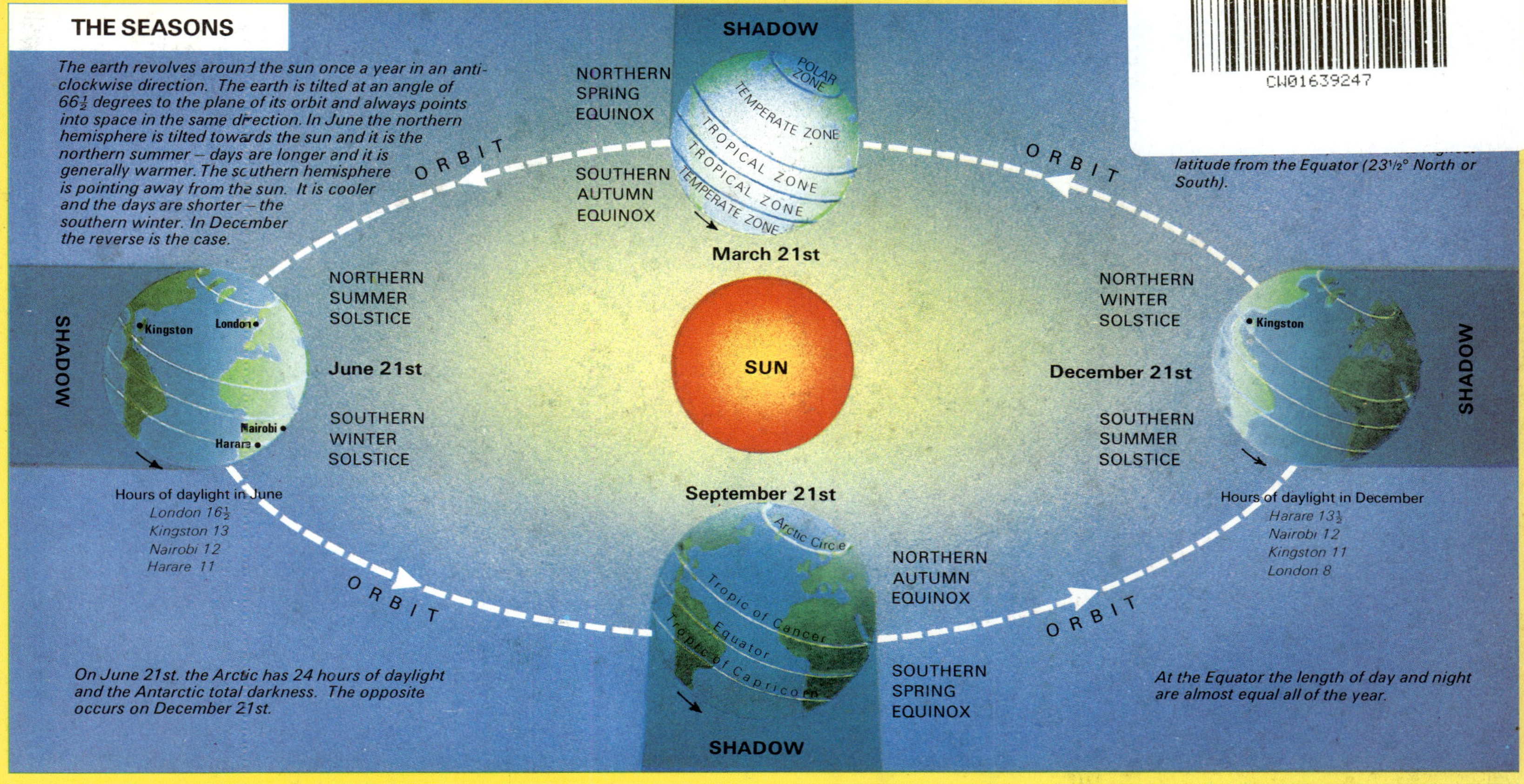

latitude from the Equator (23½° North or South).

On June 21st. the Arctic has 24 hours of daylight and the Antarctic total darkness. The opposite occurs on December 21st.

At the Equator the length of day and night are almost equal all of the year.

LENGTH OF DAY AND NIGHT ON THE EARTH

TIME

The Year *– the time taken by the Earth to revolve around the Sun, or 365¼ days.*

The Month *– the approximate time taken by the Moon to revolve around the Earth. The twelve months of the year in fact vary from 28 (29 in a Leap Year) to 31 days.*

The Week *– an artificial period of 7 days, not based on astronomical time.*

The Day *– the time taken by the Earth to complete one rotation on its axis.*

The Hour *– 24 hours make one day. Usually the day is divided into hours A.M. (ante meridiem or before noon) and P.M. (post meridiem or after noon), although most timetables now use the 24-hour system, from midnight to midnight, for example, 1p.m. = 13.00 hours.*

SUNRISE AND SUNSET

From the diagrams below it is possible to find out the time of sunrise or sunset on a given date and for latitudes between 60°N and 60°S.

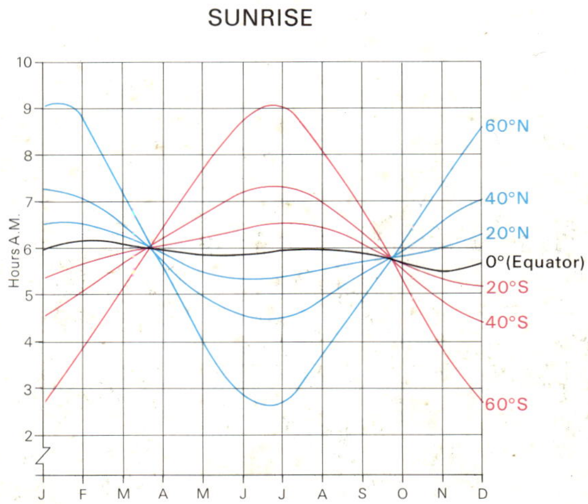

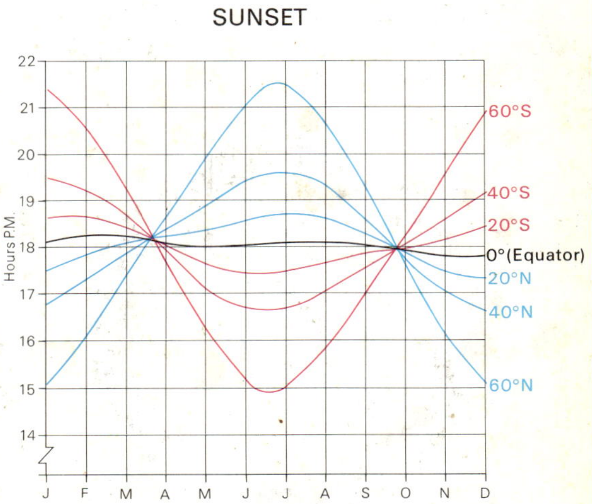

PHILIPS' MODERN SCHOOL ATLAS

Contents

Front Endpaper: Astronomical Geography

British Isles

4	Physical ~ 1:4M Geology ~ 1:16M
5	Administrative ~ 1:4M
6	Climate
7	Transport
8	Population
9	Agriculture
10	Energy and Industry
11	Employment, Leisure and Trade
12-13	Climate Graphs
14-15	South and South-East England ~ 1:1M
16	South-West England ~ 1:1M
17	Wales ~ 1:1M
18-19	Northern England ~ 1:1M
20-21	Scotland: South ~ 1:1M
22-23	Scotland: North ~ 1:1M
24-25	Ireland ~ 1:1,25M

Europe

26	Physical ~ 1:20M
27	Political ~ 1:20M
28	Climate and Natural Vegetation ~ 1:40M
29	Economic ~ 1:20M
30-31	Themes
32-33	Statistics
34-35	France and Western Europe ~ 1:4M
36	Low Countries and Lower Rhine ~ 1:2M
37	Spain and Portugal ~ 1:5M
38-39	Mediterranean Lands ~ 1:10M
40-41	Italy and the Balkan States ~ 1:5M
42-43	Central Europe ~ 1:5M
44-45	Scandinavia and the Baltic Lands ~ 1:6M
46-47	European Russia and Turkey ~ 1:10M
48-49	Union of Soviet Socialist Republics ~ 1:20M

Asia

50	Physical ~ 1:50M
51	Political ~ 1:50M
52	Climate and Natural Vegetation ~ 1:100M
53	Economic ~ 1:50M
54-55	Statistics (*including Oceania*)
56-57	South-West Asia ~ 1:15M The Holy Land ~ 1:1,5M
58-59	South Asia ~ 1:10M
60-61	China and Korea ~ 1:15M
62	Japan ~ 1:7,5M
63	South-East Asia ~ 1:15M
64-65	Pacific Ocean ~ 1:54M

Australia and New Zealand

66-67	Australia ~ 1:12M Political ~ 1:80M
68	Climate and Natural Vegetation ~ 1:60M
69	Economic ~ 1:20M
70	South-East Australia ~ 1:4,5M
71	New Zealand ~ 1:6M Samoa, Fiji and Tonga Islands ~ 1:12M

Africa

72	Physical ~ 1:40M
73	Political ~ 1:40M
74	Climate and Natural Vegetation ~ 1:80M
75	Economic ~ 1:40M
76-77	Statistics
78-79	Northern Africa ~ 1:15M
80-81	Central and Southern Africa ~ 1:15M

Edited By

B.M. Willett, *Cartographic Editor*

D. Gaylard, *Assistant Cartographic Editor*

and L. Prince-Smith, J. Russell, R. Smith and A. Wells

George Philip Ltd., London

Maps prepared by

George Philip Cartographic Services Ltd., London under the direction of A.G. Poynter, *Director of Cartography*.

Eighty-sixth Edition

ISBN 0 540 05598 0 (Paperback Edition)
0 540 05585 9 (Hardback Edition)

Printed in Great Britain by Redwood Offset

Contents

North America

82 Physical ~ 1:35M
83 Political ~ 1:35M
84 Climate and Natural Vegetation ~ 1:70M
85 Economic ~ 1:32M
86-87 Statistics (*including South America*)
88-89 Canada ~ 1:15M
Alaska ~ 1:30M
90-91 United States ~ 1:12M
Hawaiian Islands ~ 1:10M
92-93 Basin of the St Lawrence and North-East United States ~ 1:6M
94-95 Mexico, Central America and the West Indies ~ 1:15M
Panama Canal ~ 1:1M
Jamaica, Trinidad and Tobago, Leeward and Windward Islands ~ 1:5M

South America

96 Physical ~ 1:30M
97 Political ~ 1:30M
98 Climate and Natural Vegetation ~ 1:70M
99 Economic ~ 1:30M
100-101 South America: North ~ 1:16M
102 South America: South ~ 1:16M

The World

103 Polar Regions ~ 1:50M
104-105 Physical ~ 1:80M
106-107 Structure, Volcanoes and Earthquakes
108-109 Climatic Regions, Soils and Vegetation
110-113 Climate Statistics
114 Temperature and Ocean Currents
115 Pressure, Winds and Annual Precipitation
116-117 Density of Population
118-119 Population of Cities
120 Languages and Religions
121 International Organisations
122-123 Population Trends
124-125 Quality of Life
126-127 Economic Facts of Life
128-129 Political ~ 1:80M
130-131 Time and Distance

Index

Back Endpaper: Map Projections

General Reference

SETTLEMENTS

Settlement symbols in order of size

LONDON — Osaka — Venice — Andropov — *Toledo* — *Cromer* — *Interlaken*

Settlement symbols and type styles vary according to the scale of each map and indicate the importance of towns on the map rather than specific population figures.

ADMINISTRATION

International Boundaries

International Boundaries
(Undemarcated or undefined)

Internal Boundaries

International boundaries show the 'de facto' situation where there are rival claims to territory.

COMMUNICATIONS

Motorways in UK
Principal Roads
Tracks and Seasonal Roads
Road Tunnels
Principal Railways
Railways under construction
Railway Tunnels
Passes
Principal Canals
Principal Oil Pipelines
Principal Airports

PHYSICAL FEATURES

Perennial Streams
Seasonal Streams
Seasonal Lakes and Salt Flats
Swamps and Marshes
Permanent Ice and Glaciers
Wells in Desert
▲ 8848 Elevations in metres
▼ 8050 Sea Depths in metres
1134 Height of Lakes

BRITISH ISLES : Physical

1: 4 000 000

Projection: Conical with two standard parallels

Projection: Conical with two standard parallels

January Temperature

Actual surface temperature

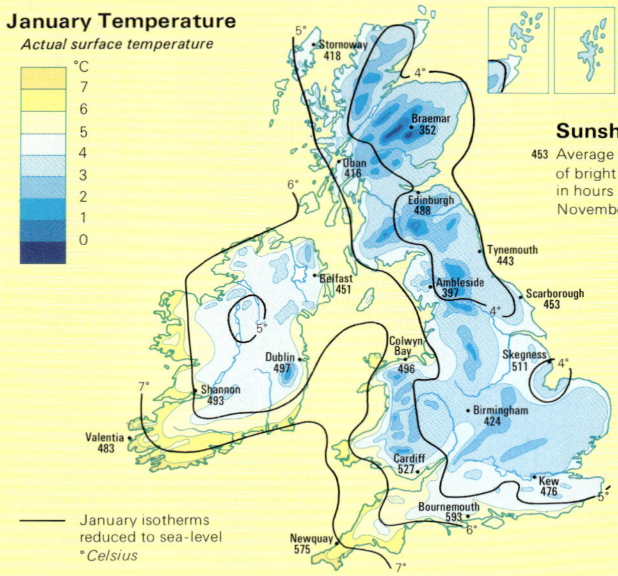

July Temperature

Actual surface temperature

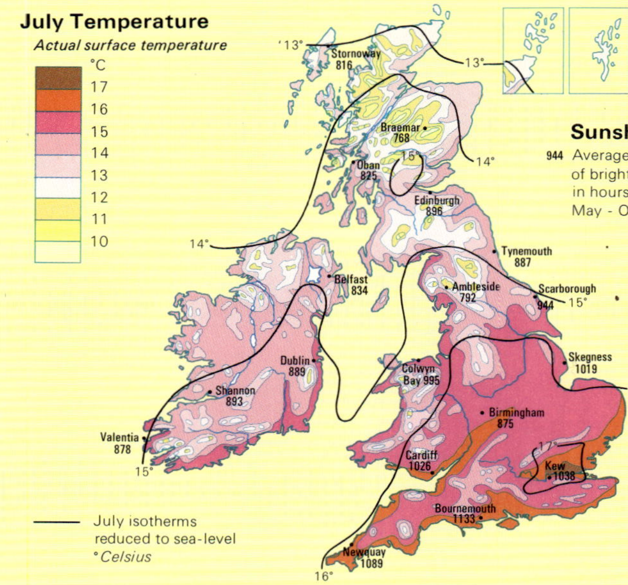

Annual Rainfall

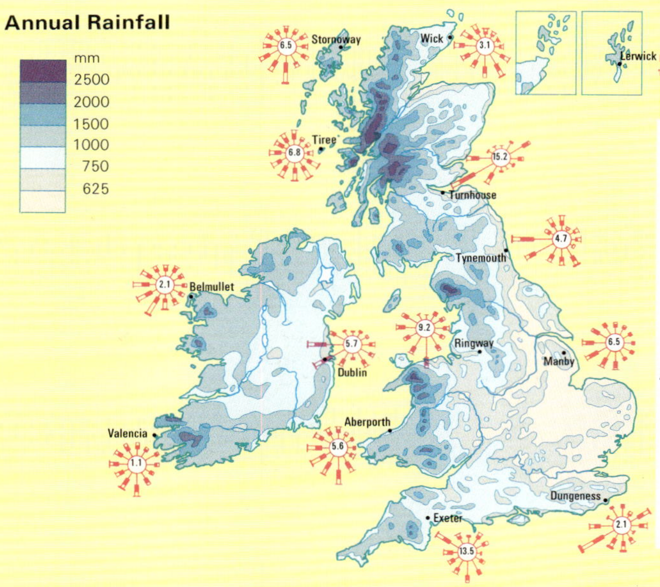

Wind

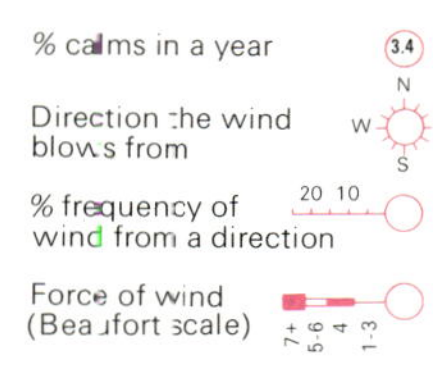

BEAUFORT FORCE	SPEED (K.P.H.)	CATEGORY
1-3	1-20	*Light breeze*
4	21-29	*Moderate breeze*
5-6	30-50	*Fresh to strong wind*
7	51-61	*Moderate gale*
8-12	over 62	*Gale, storm or hurricane*

Snow

Average number of mornings with snow cover per year

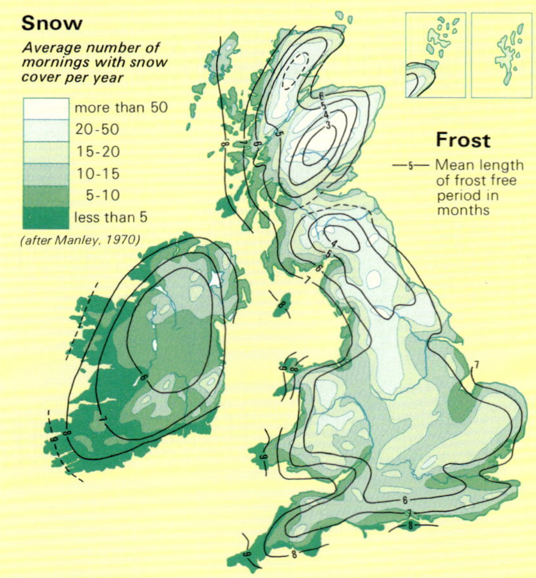

Variability of Rain

The percentage frequency with which rainfall varies from the normal rainfall regime in an area: the higher the percentage figure, the more variable the rainfall.

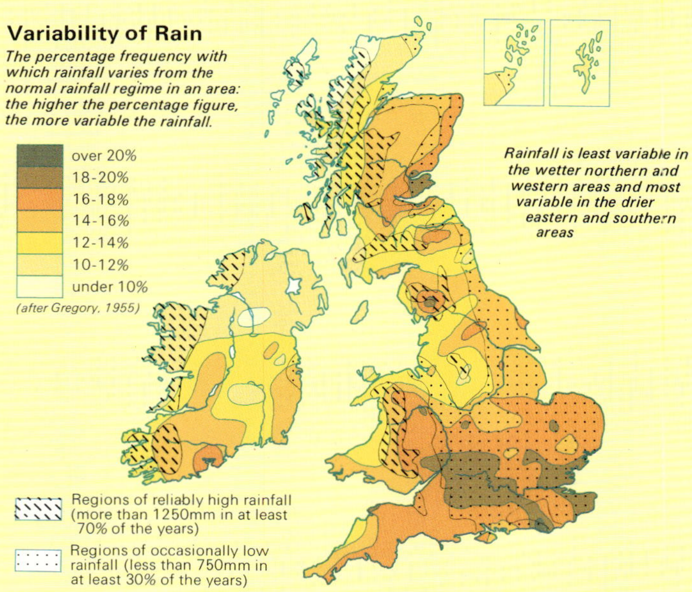

Synoptic Chart for a Typical Winter Depression

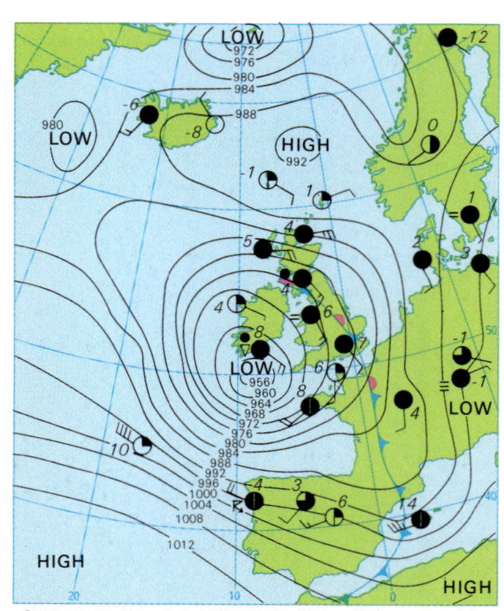

Based upon the Meteorological Office Weather Charts, with the sanction of the Controller of H.M. Stationery Office

HOUR OF OBSERVATION
06h00 GREENWICH MEAN TIME

PRESSURE
Isobars are drawn at intervals of 4 mb.

WIND
Arrows fly with the wind. A full length feather represents 18 k.p.h. and a short feather 9 k.p.h. A solid pennant represents 90 k.p.h. Calm is indicated by a circle outside the weather symbol

TEMPERATURE
Given in °C and is shown on the charts by a figure alongside the station circle.

CLOUD SYMBOLS
Clear sky; Sky ⅛ covered; Sky ⅛ covered; Sky ⅛ covered; Sky ⅛ covered; Sky ⅛ covered; Sky ⅛ covered; Sky ⅛ covered; Sky ⅛ covered; Sky obscured

WEATHER SYMBOLS
Rain; Hail; Drizzle; Shower; Snow; Thunderstorm; Rain and Snow; Fog; Mist

FRONTS
Warm front on the surface
Cold front on the surface
Occluded front

Roads and Ferry Routes

Motorways
Main primary routes
Average 24 hour flow of vehicles at a selected point on a motorway. Figures are given in thousands

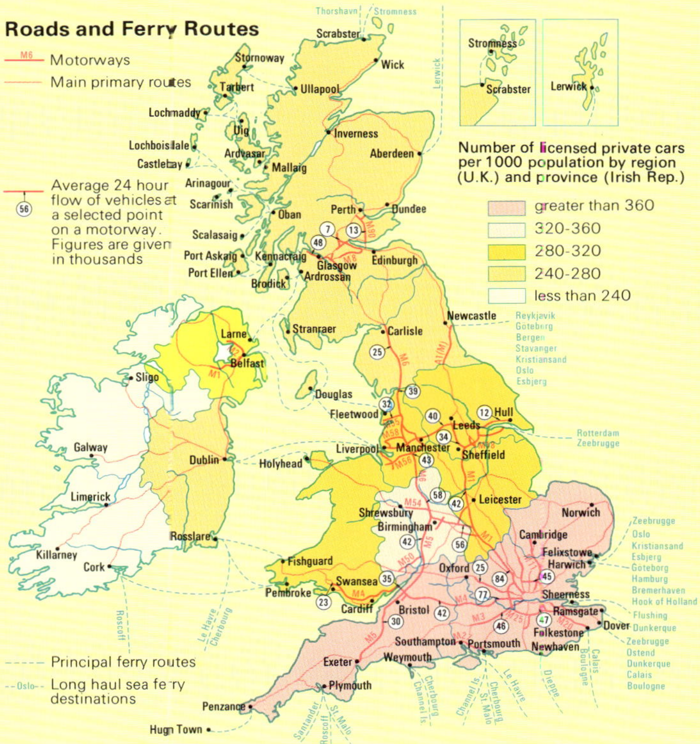

Number of licensed private cars per 1000 population by region (U.K.) and province (Irish Rep.)

- greater than 360
- 320-360
- 280-320
- 240-280
- less than 240

Principal ferry routes
--Oslo-- Long haul sea ferry destinations

Railways

Electrified lines
Other main lines

Furthest distances from London reached within a journey time of

	3 hours	6 hours
1950	▲	●
1982	▲	●

The electrification of the London-York-Newcastle and Edinburgh section of the East Coast Main Line is due for completion in May 1991.

Means of Transportation Within the U.K.

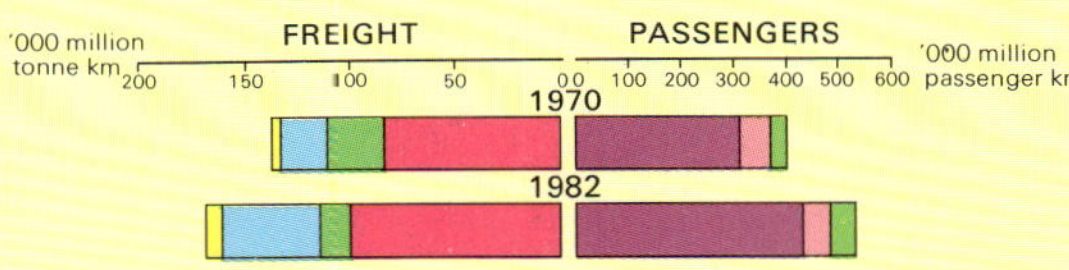

- Road
- Rail
- Pipeline
- Coastal shipping
- Private transport (Road)
- Public transport (Road)
- Rail

(Air transport accounted for only 2000 million passenger km in 1970 and 3000 million in 1982)

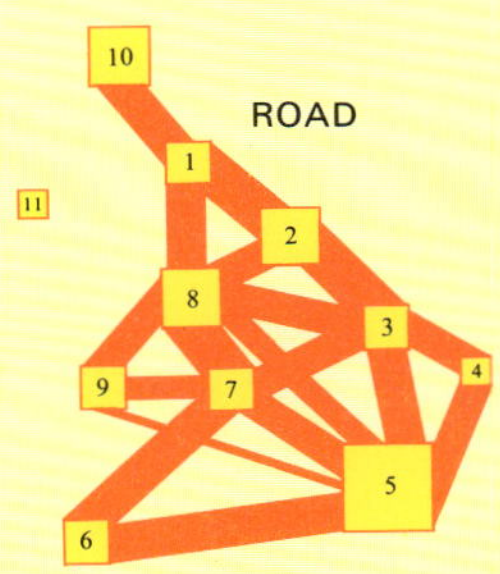

Regional Freight Movement

Within regions
million tonnes

200-250
100-150
0-50
150-200
50-100

Between regions
million tonnes

- less than 2·5
- 2·5-5
- 5-7·5
- 7·5-10
- 10-20
- 20-30
- 30-40

1. North
2. Yorkshire & Humberside
3. East Midlands
4. East Anglia
5. South East
6. South West
7. West Midlands
8. North West
9. Wales
10. Scotland
11. Northern Ireland

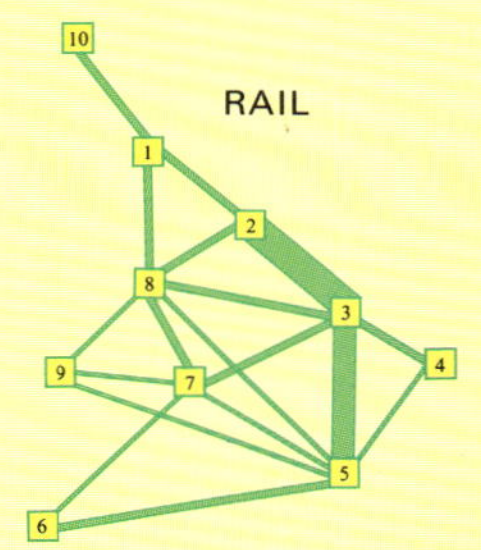

Rail freight movement is negligible within Northern Ireland

Ports

Goods traffic by port group
Foreign and domestic traffic
million tonnes
120 / 90 / 60 / 30
Fuel
Other goods

Ports handling over 1 million tonnes of goods traffic
million tonnes

- ■ 50-60
- □ 40-50
- ◉ 30-40
- ◎ 20-30
- • 10-20
- · 1-10

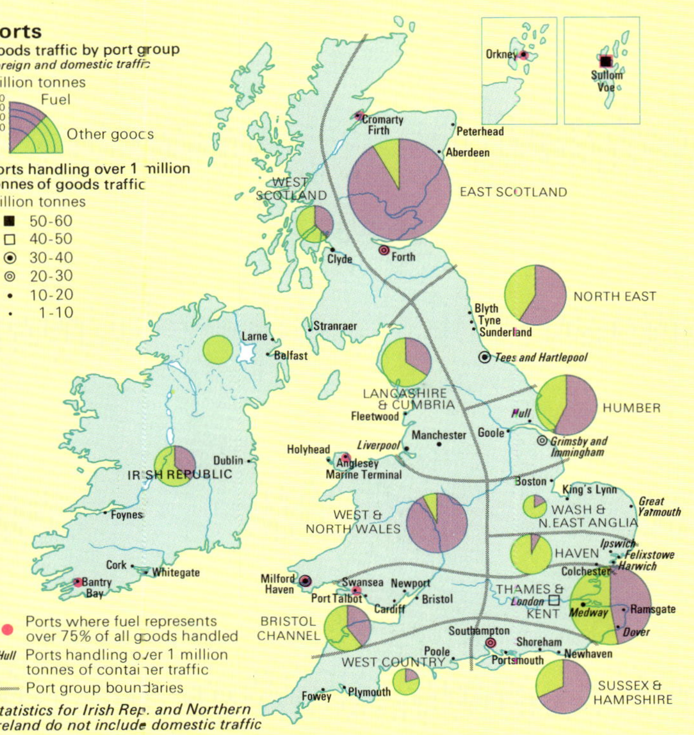

● Ports where fuel represents over 75% of all goods handled
Hull Ports handling over 1 million tonnes of container traffic
— Port group boundaries

Statistics for Irish Rep. and Northern Ireland do not include domestic traffic

Airports

Passenger traffic
'000 passengers

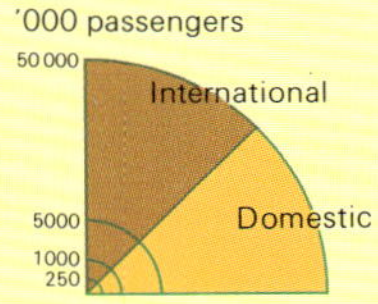

• Less than 200 000 passengers

Domestic flows of greater than 25 flights per week

- 100-150 flights
- 50-100 flights
- 25-50 flights

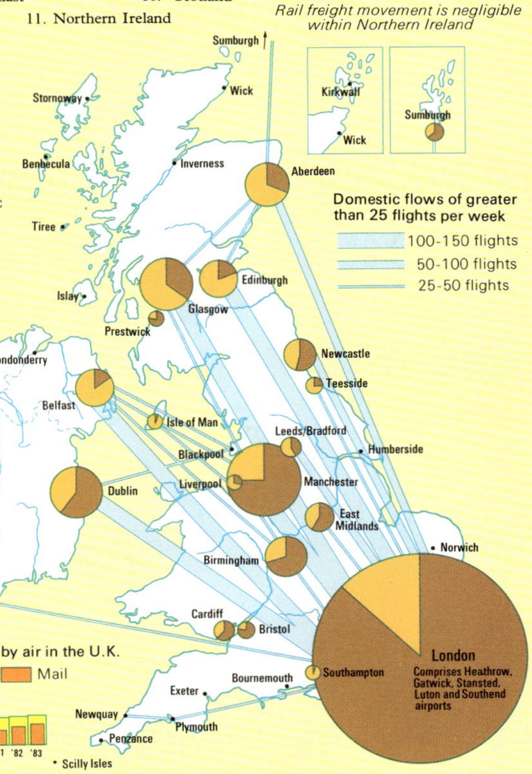

Domestic freight carried by air in the U.K.

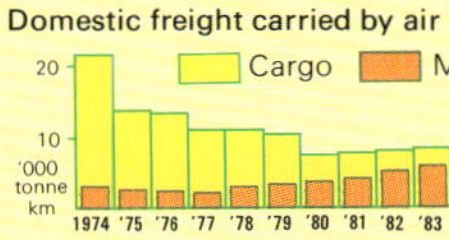

Population Density and Principal Towns

1:8 500 000

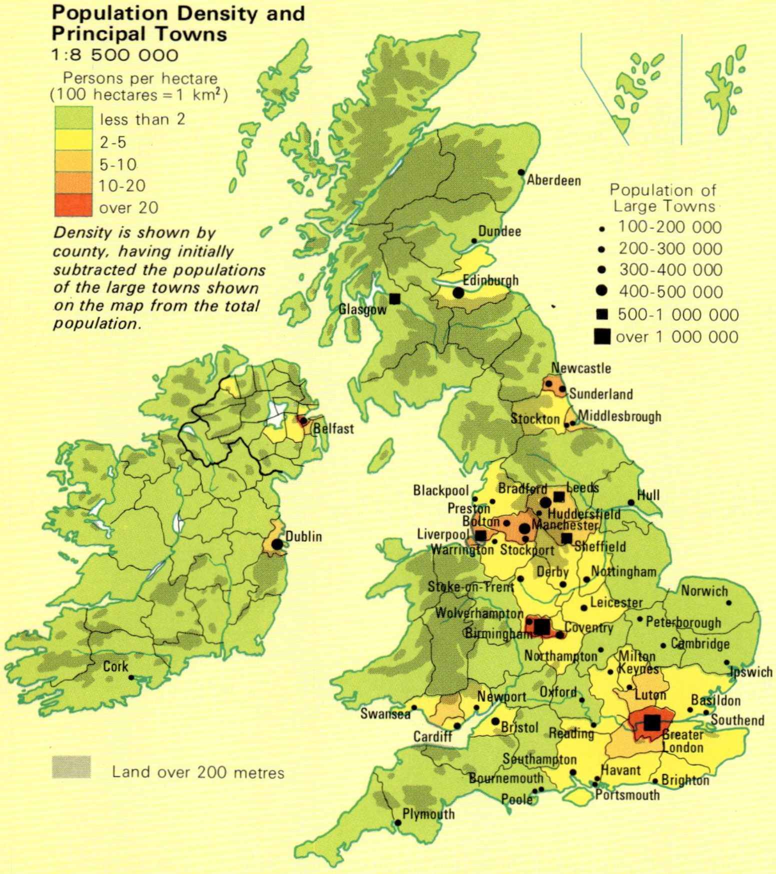

Population Change 1961-1981

1:8 500 000

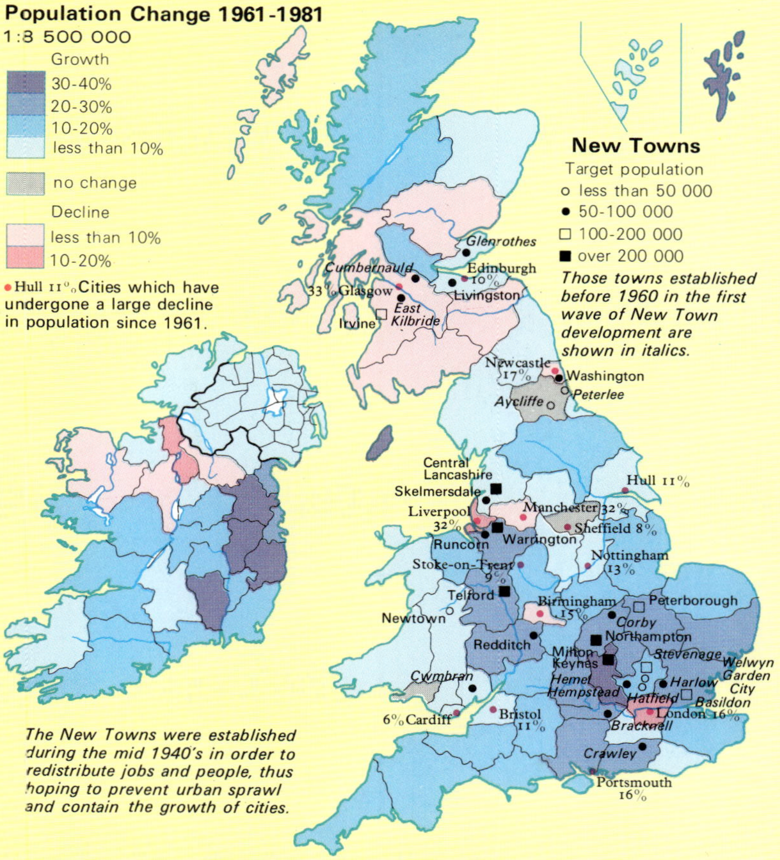

Dependency Ratio

1:10 000 000

The dependency ratio is the number of people aged under 15 years plus those of retiring age (60 and over for females, 65 and over for males) per 100 people of working age.

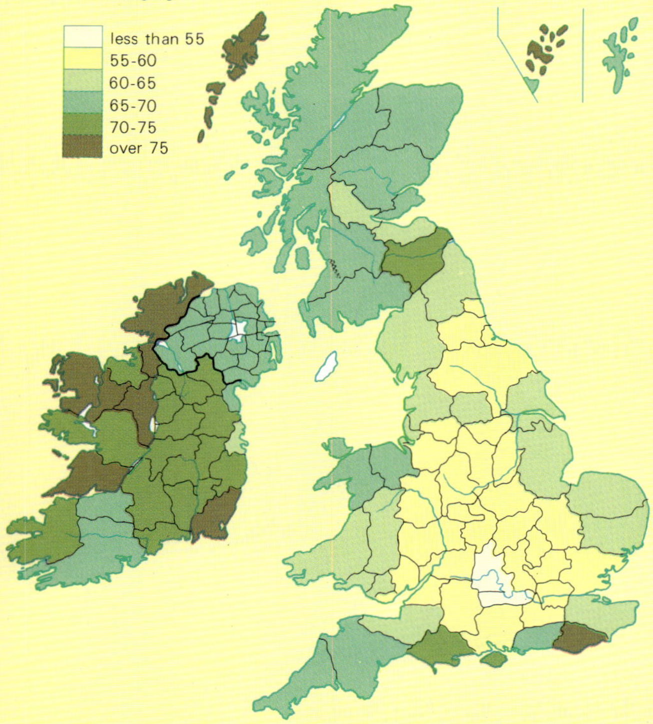

Age Structure of the U.K. in 1901, 1983 and Projected to 2051.

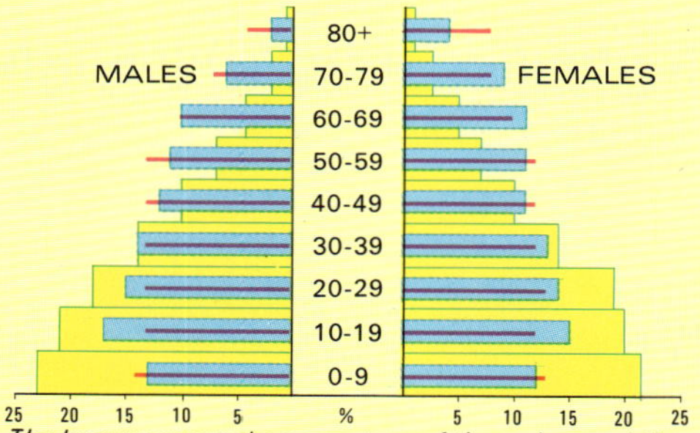

The bars represent the percentage of the male population and the percentage of the female population in the age group shown. 1901 1983 2051

Age Group Distribution Within the Population of the U.K.

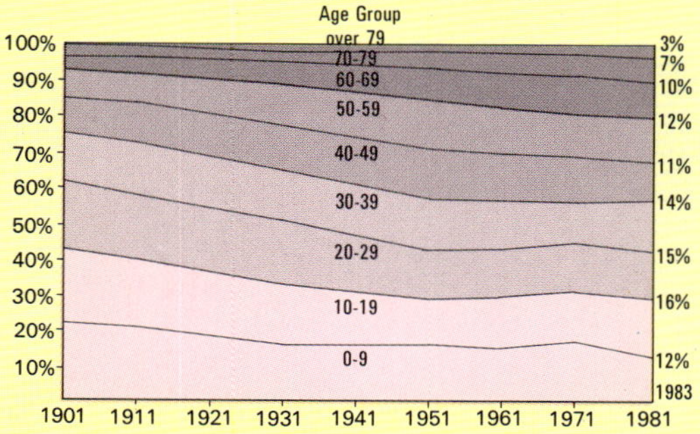

U.K. Vital Statistics, 1900-2000

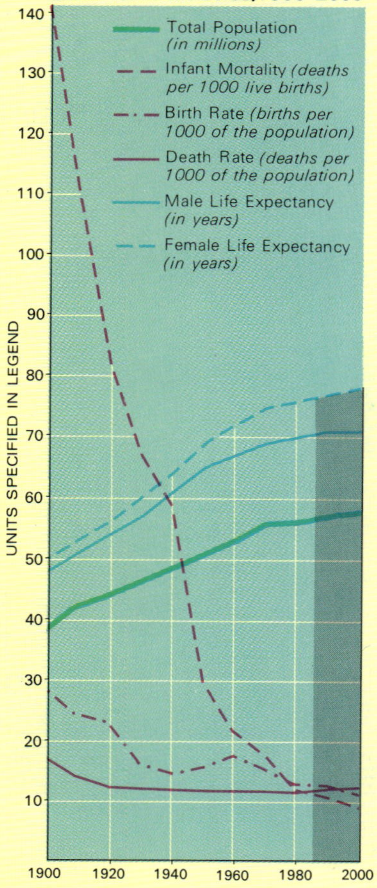

Agricultural Land Use Capability
1: 10 000 000

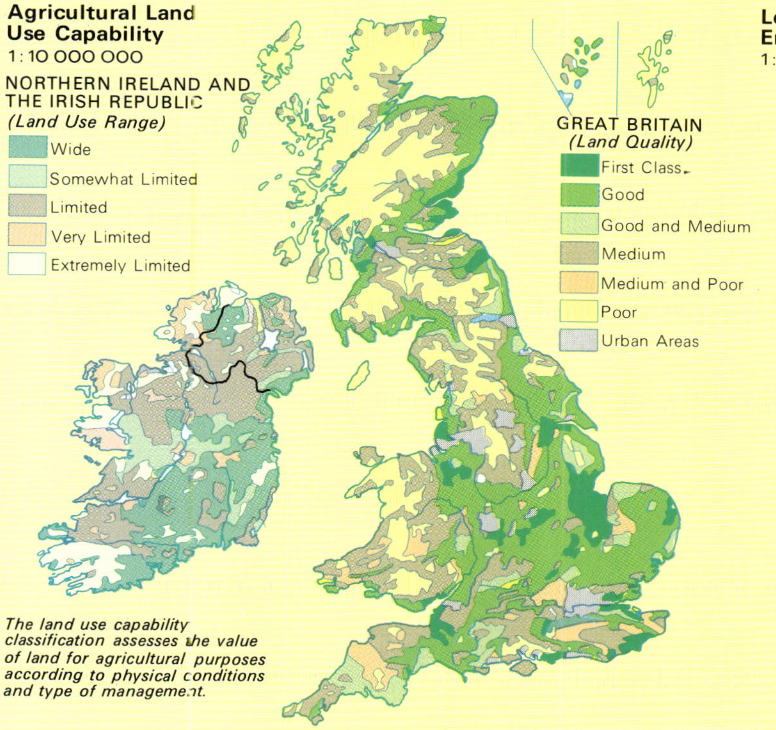

The land use capability classification assesses the value of land for agricultural purposes according to physical conditions and type of management.

Leading Agricultural Enterprises
1: 10 000 000

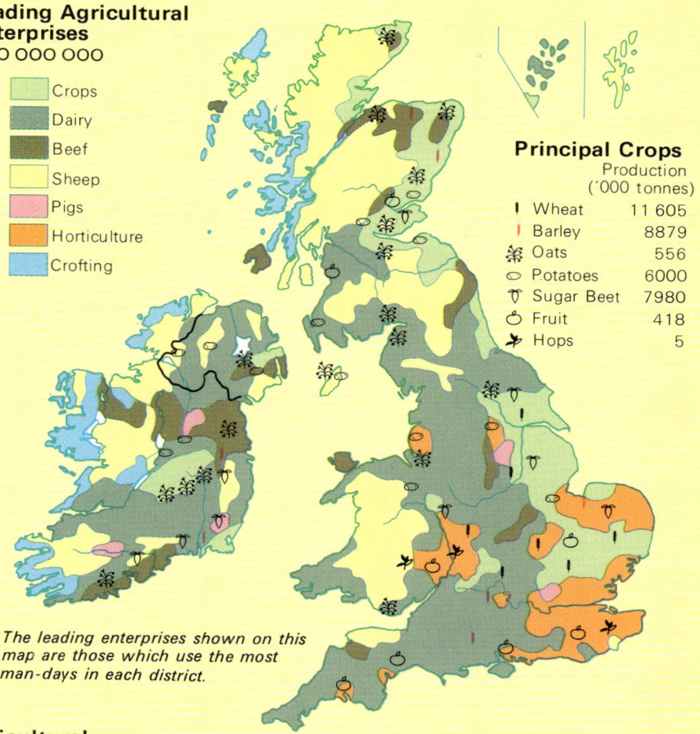

The leading enterprises shown on this map are those which use the most man-days in each district.

Yield of Selected Crops in the U.K.

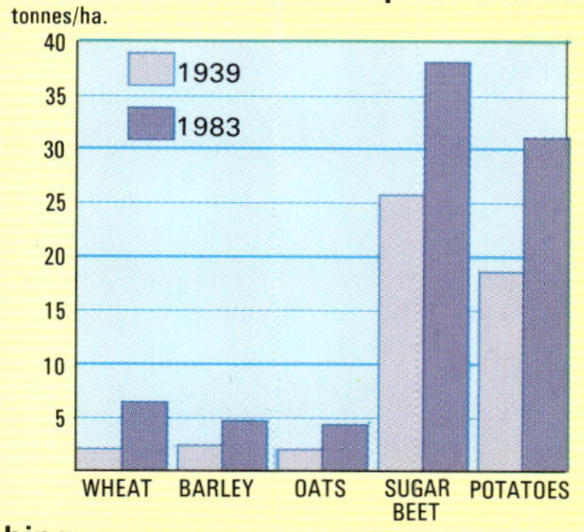

Number and Size of Agricultural Holdings in the U.K.

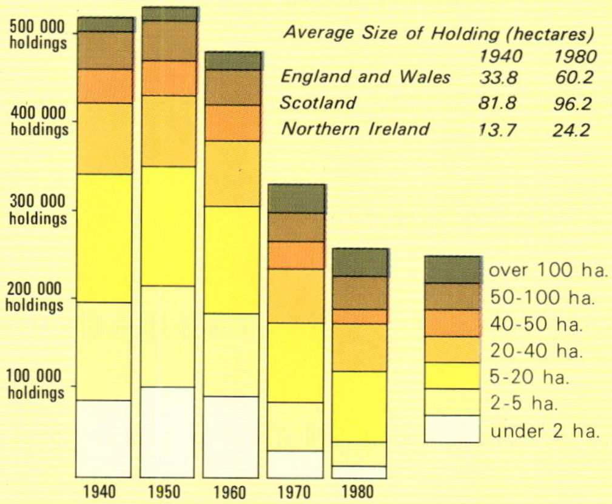

Self-Sufficiency of the U.K. in Agricultural Production
(home production given as a percentage of total consumption)

PRODUCT	1969	1977	1987
Wheat	42%	61%	79%
Barley	90%	121%	114%
Potatoes	91%	95%	95%
Sugar	33%	40%	53%
Cheese	45%	67%	67%
Butter	12%	40%	63%
Beef	77%	72%	99%
Pork	101%	62%	127%
Poultry	100%	100%	98%

Fishing
1:10 000 000

Quantity of fish landed by domestic vessels at major ports, (port districts in Scotland.)

Forestry

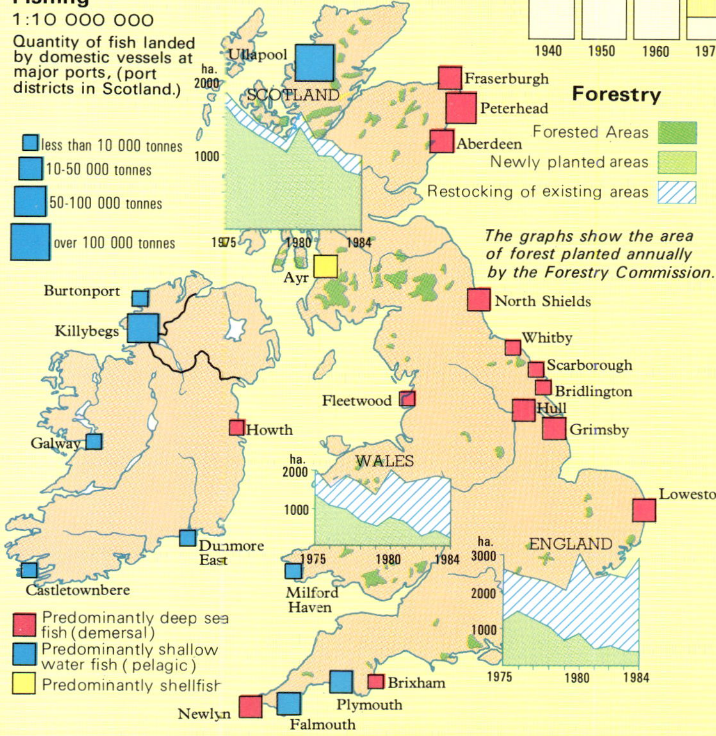

Area of Agricultural Land Under Selected Enterprises

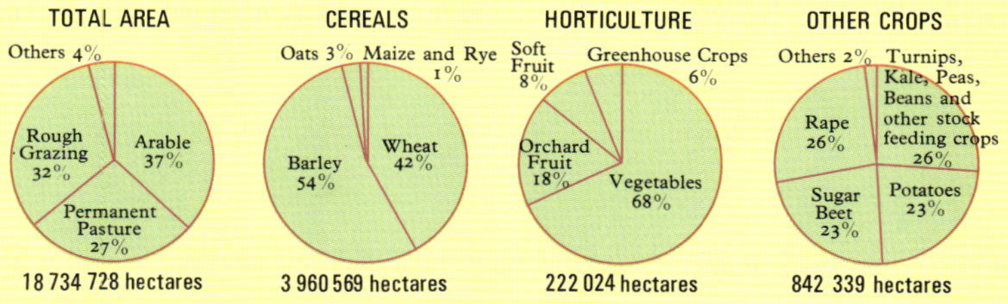

Quantity of Fish Landed by British Vessels in all Fishing Areas

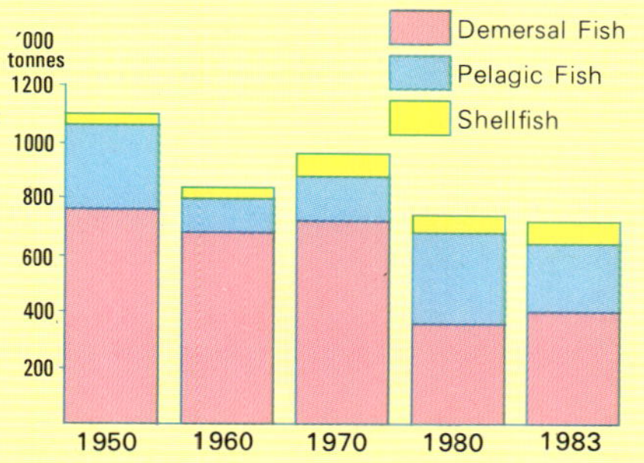

Number and Size of Livestock Holdings in the U.K.

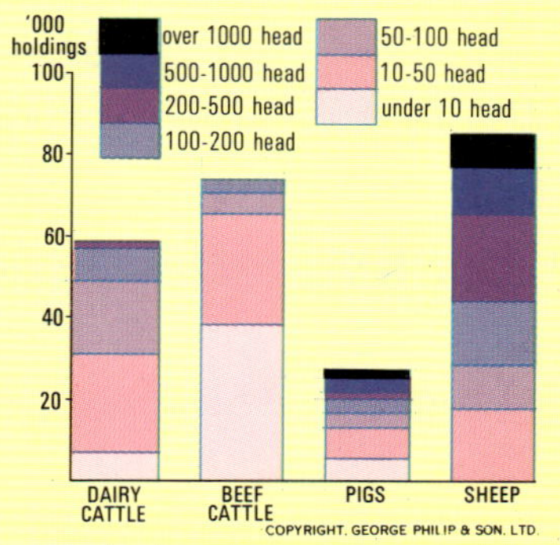

Coal and Power 1:8 500 000

Coalfields 1988-89	Saleable Output (million tonnes)	Output per Manshift (tonnes)
1 Scottish	1.9	10.1
2 North East	10.3	18.7
3 North West	9.8	24.2
4 South Wales	5.0	15.3
5 North Yorkshire	16.1	29.9
6 South Yorkshire	13.3	17.6
7 Nottinghamshire	17.2	17.2
8 Kent	0.4	14.1
9 Central	10.8	16.9

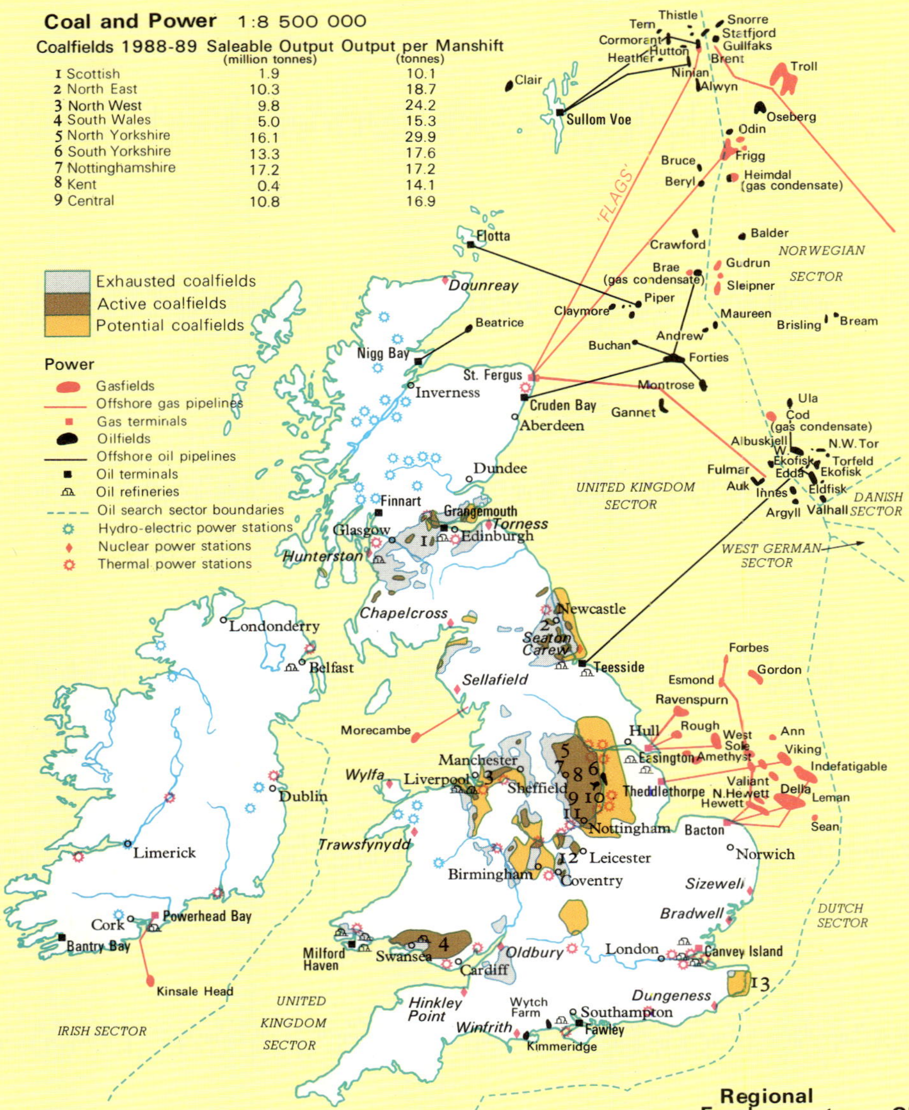

Production of Primary Fuels in the U.K.

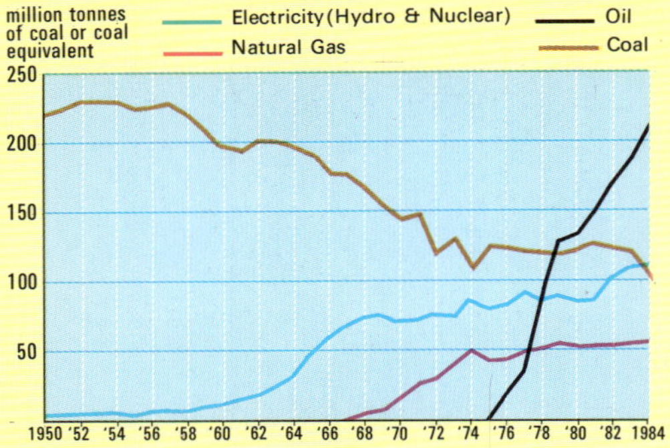

Consumption of Primary Fuels in the U.K.

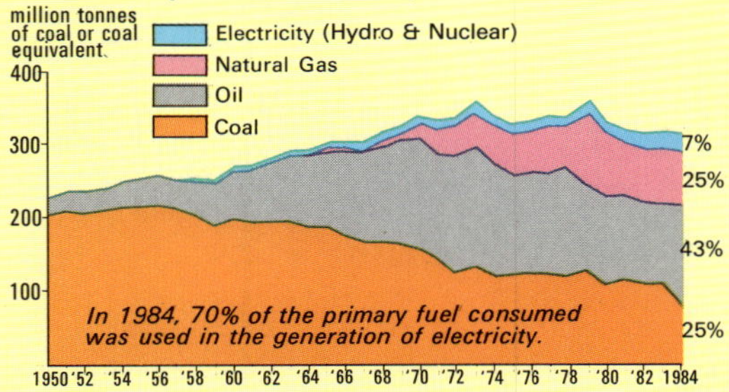

Coal Consumption in the U.K.

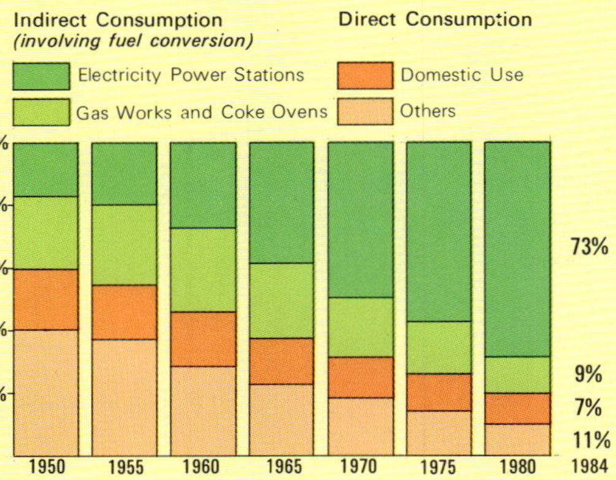

Minerals
1:10 000 000

Basic Industries

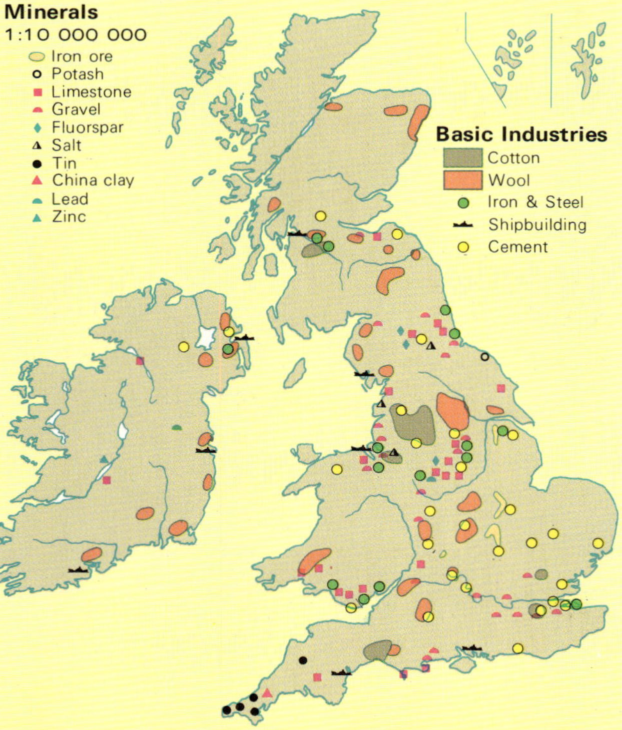

Regional Employment by Industry

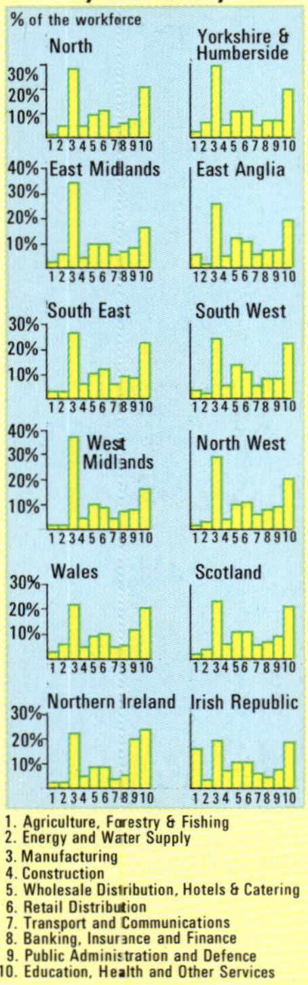

1. Agriculture, Forestry & Fishing
2. Energy and Water Supply
3. Manufacturing
4. Construction
5. Wholesale Distribution, Hotels & Catering
6. Retail Distribution
7. Transport and Communications
8. Banking, Insurance and Finance
9. Public Administration and Defence
10. Education, Health and Other Services

Change in Manufacturing Employment by County 1961-1981
1:10 000 000

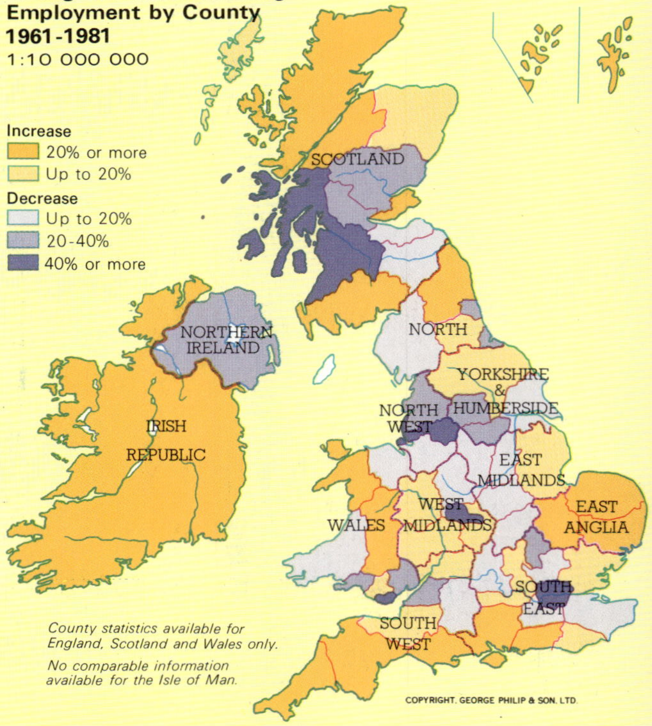

County statistics available for England, Scotland and Wales only.

No comparable information available for the Isle of Man.

EMPLOYMENT

Employment in the U.K. by Industry

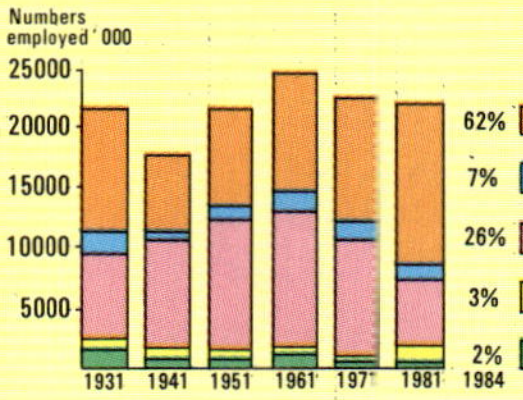

Employment by County

£ Over 75% employed in Services

Over 30% employed in Manufacturing

Over 5% employed in Agriculture

County statistics available for England, Scotland and Wales only.

UNEMPLOYMENT

1:10 000 000

Unemployment Rate by County, 1985

- over 20%
- 16-20%
- 12-16%
- 8-12%
- less than 8%

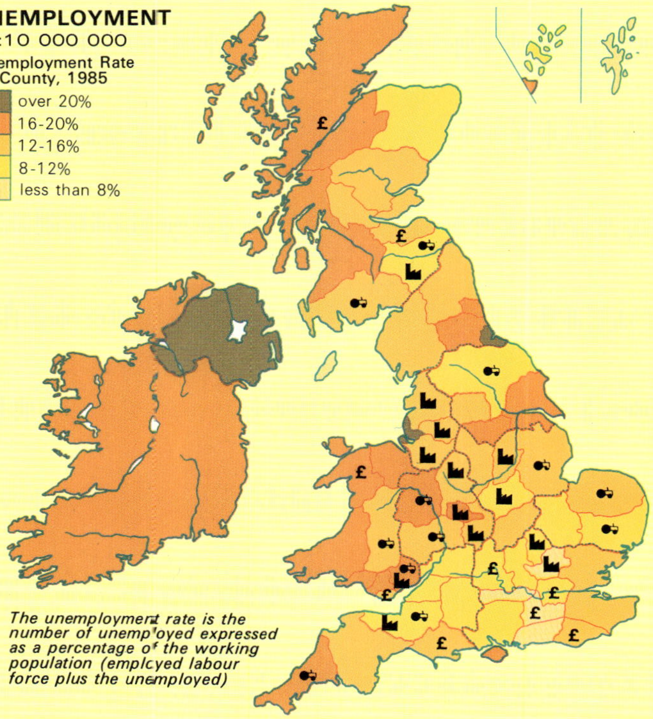

The unemployment rate is the number of unemployed expressed as a percentage of the working population (employed labour force plus the unemployed)

Leisure

1:8 500 000

- National Parks
- National Park Direction Areas (Scotland)
- National Forest Parks
- Areas of Outstanding Natural Beauty (England & Wales)
- National Scenic Areas (Scotland)
- Coastal Conservation Zones (Scotland) / Heritage Coasts (England & Wales)
- Long Distance Footpaths
- Navigable Waterways
- Canals

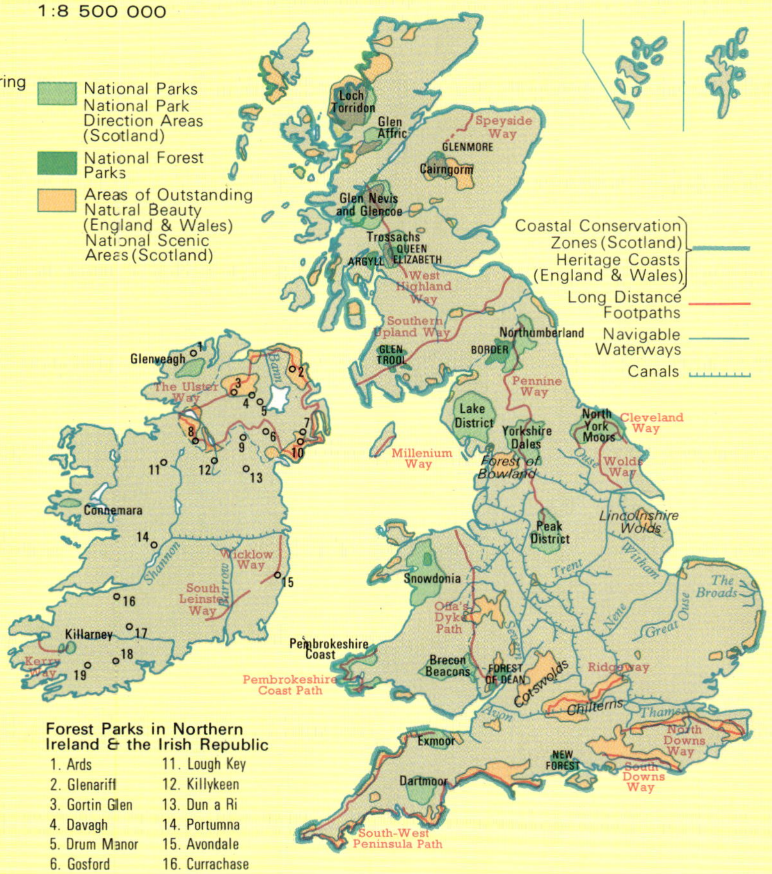

Forest Parks in Northern Ireland & the Irish Republic

1. Ards
2. Glenariff
3. Gortin Glen
4. Davagh
5. Drum Manor
6. Gosford
7. Castlewellan
8. Florence Court
9. Rossmore
10. Tollymore
11. Lough Key
12. Killykeen
13. Dun a Ri
14. Portumna
15. Avondale
16. Currachase
17. Doneraile
18. Farran
19. Gougane Barra

Top Ten Trading Partners with the U.K. by Value of Goods

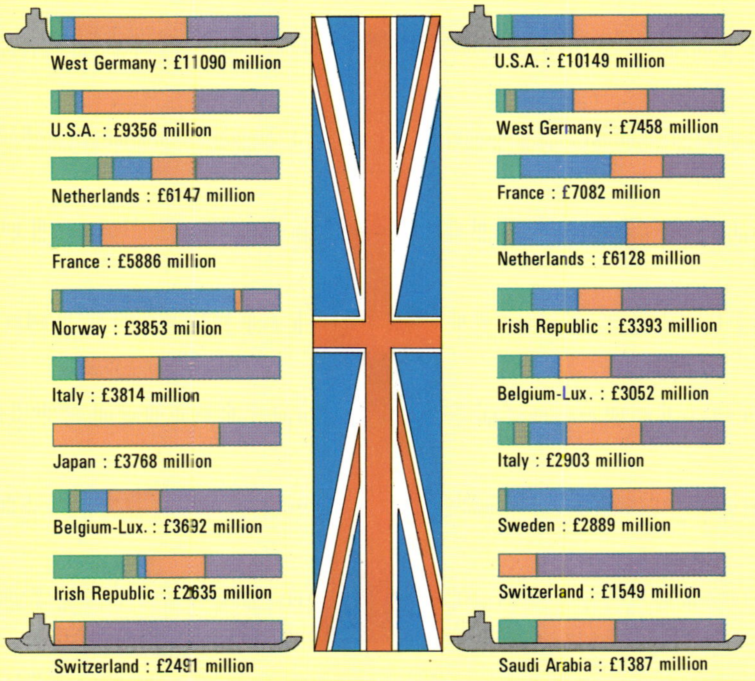

- Food and drink
- Raw materials
- Fuel
- Machinery and equipment
- Manufactured goods

U.K. Trade by Country Group and Commodity Type

(percentages are given by value of trade)

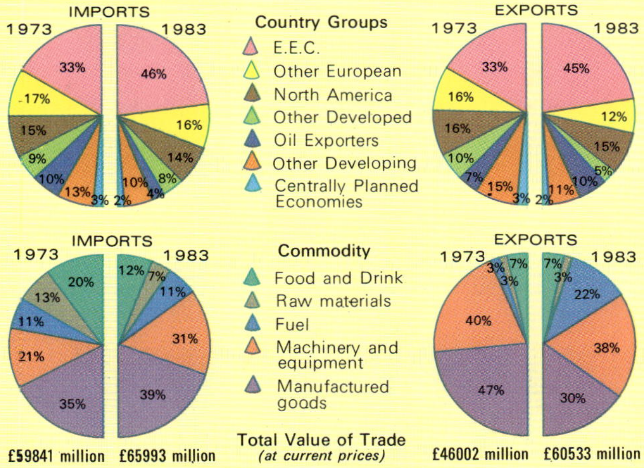

Balance of Payments (£ million)

		1967	1977	1987
CREDITS	Visibles *(Exports)*	5241	31682	79422
	Invisibles	3310	21351	80010
	Total	8551	53033	159432
DEBITS	Visibles *(Imports)*	5840	34006	89584
	Invisibles	2992	19177	72352
	Total	8832	53183	161936
BALANCE		−281	−150	−2504

Visible trade involves transactions of goods while invisible trade involves transactions of money and services.

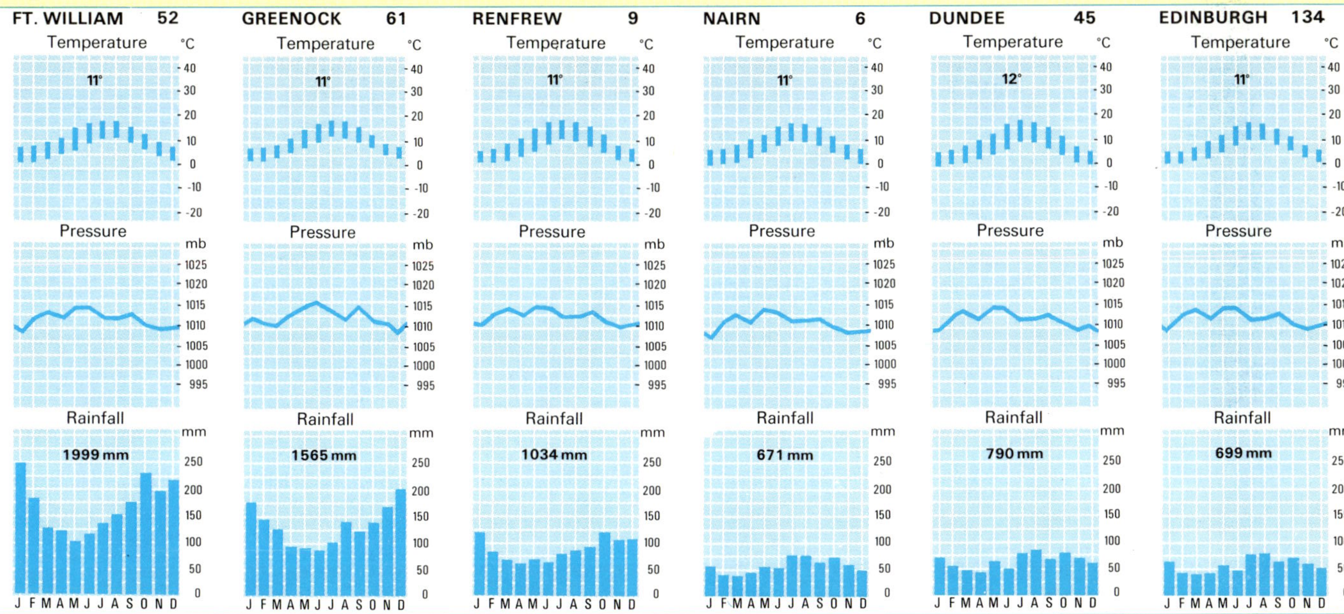

The climate graphs should be used in conjunction with the maps illustrating the climate of the British Isles on page 6. The stations have been selected to show climatic variations throughout the British Isles. On each graph the name of the station is followed by its height in metres above sea level, so that comparisons between stations can be made allowing for elevation. Temperature is shown by a bar, the top of the bar representing the mean monthly maximum and the bottom of the bar the mean monthly minimum temperature. A mid point between these is the mean monthly temperature; the mean annual range of temperature (in degrees Celsius) is given above the graph. The line on the pressure graphs shows the mean monthly pressure (in millibars and reduced to sea level). The rainfall graphs show the average monthly rainfall and above them is given the average total annual rainfall (in millimetres).

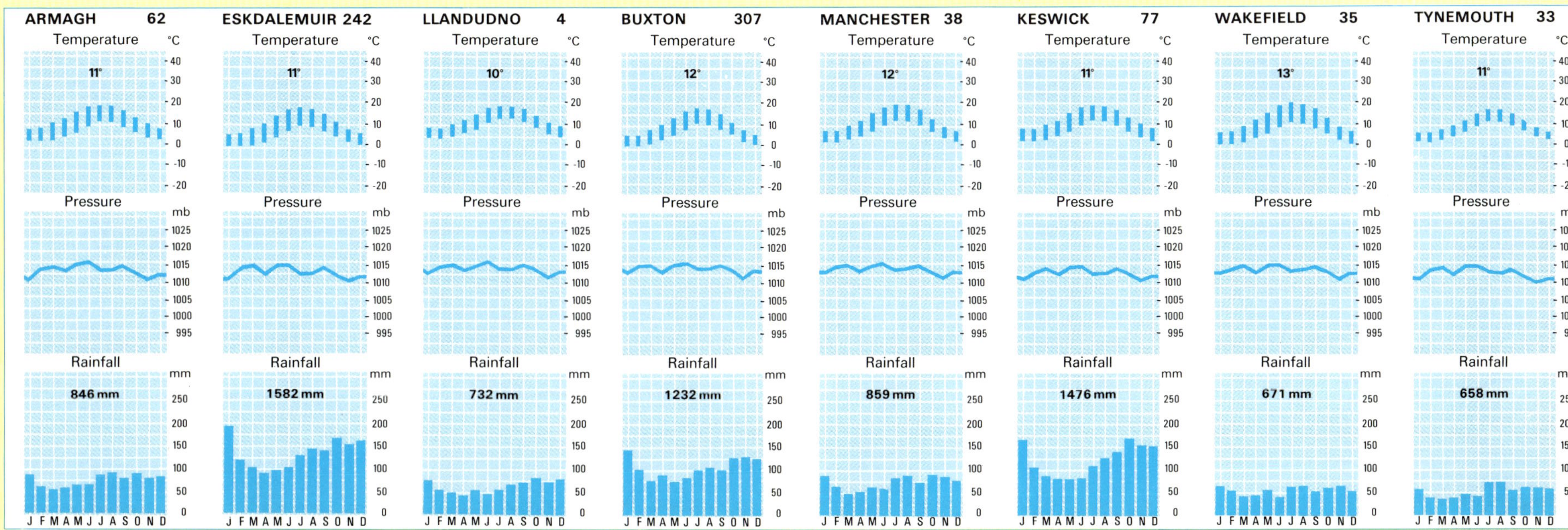

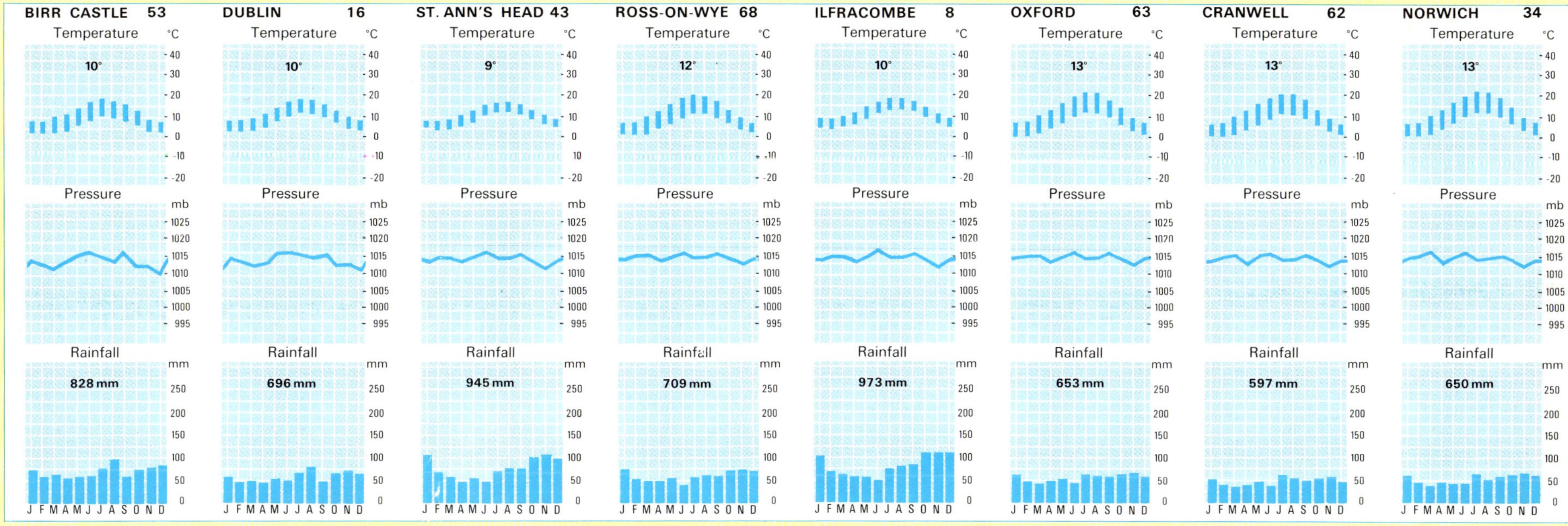
BIRR CASTLE 53
Temperature °C
10°
Pressure mb
Rainfall mm
828 mm
DUBLIN 16
10°
696 mm
ST. ANN'S HEAD 43
9°
945 mm
ROSS-ON-WYE 68
12°
709 mm
ILFRACOMBE 8
10°
973 mm
OXFORD 63
13°
653 mm
CRANWELL 62
13°
597 mm
NORWICH 34
13°
650 mm
J F M A M J J A S O N D

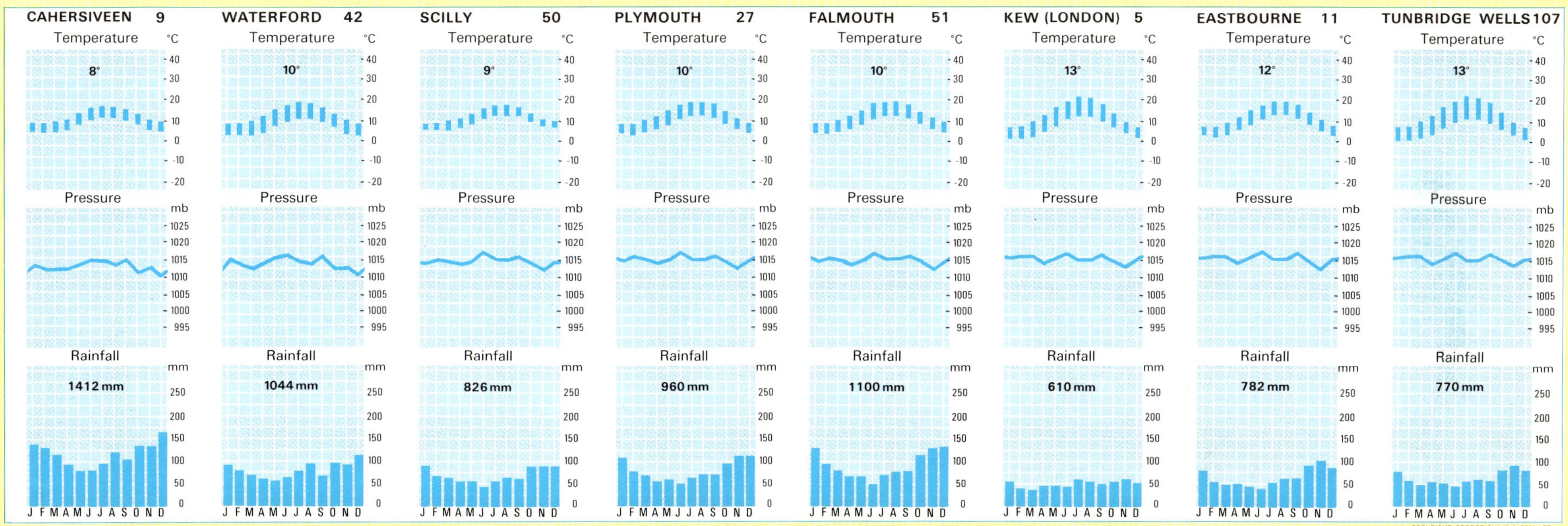
CAHERSIVEEN 9
Temperature °C
8°
Pressure mb
Rainfall mm
1412 mm
WATERFORD 42
10°
1044 mm
SCILLY 50
9°
826 mm
PLYMOUTH 27
10°
960 mm
FALMOUTH 51
10°
1100 mm
KEW (LONDON) 5
13°
610 mm
EASTBOURNE 11
12°
782 mm
TUNBRIDGE WELLS 107
13°
770 mm
J F M A M J J A S O N D

SOUTH AND SOUTH-EAST ENGLAND

1:1 000 000

10 0 10 20 30 40 km

Based upon the Ordnance Survey Map with the permission of the Controller of Her Majesty's Stationery Office. Crown Copyright Reserved.

1:1 000 000

Based upon the Ordnance Survey Map with the permission of the Controller of Her Majesty's Stationery Office. Crown Copyright Reserved.

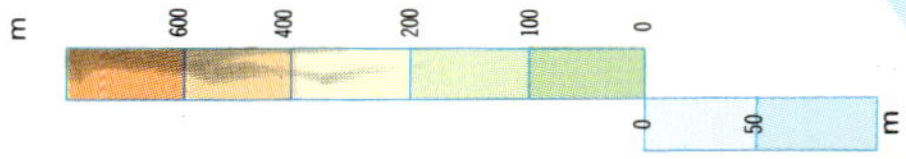

1:1 000 000

10 0 10 20 30 40 km

Projection: *Conical with two standard parallels*

West from Greenwich

60' 50' 40' 30' 20' 10' 0'

DUMFRIES AND GALLOWAY
NORTHUMBE
Dumfries
Annan
Gretna
Carlisle
Brampton
Haltwhistle
Hexham
Prudhoe
Consett
Solway Firth
HADRIAN'S WALL
Newton Stewart
Wigtown
Wigtown Bay
Luce Bay
Kirkcudbright
Castle Douglas
Maryport
Workington
Whitehaven
Cockermouth
Keswick
Penrith
Appleby
Bishop Au
Barnard Castle
Cumbrian Mountains
Lake District
Windermere
Kendal
Ambleside
Ulverston
Barrow-in-Furness
Morecambe
Morecambe B.
Lancaster
Heysham
Fleetwood
Blackpool
Preston
Southport
Wigan
Bolton
Blackburn
Burnley
BRADFORD
Huddersfield
Rochdale
Oldham
MANCHESTER
Salford
Stockport
Warrington
Widnes
Runcorn
LIVERPOOL
Birkenhead
Wallasey
Bootle
St. Helens
Chester
Crewe
Macclesfield
Congleton
Newcastle-under-Lyme
STOKE ON TRENT
Wrexham
Oswestry
Llangollen
Rhyl
Prestatyn
Colwyn Bay
Llandudno
Conwy
Bangor
Caernarfon
Holyhead
Anglesey
Menai Str.
Caernarfon Bay
Lleyn Peninsula
Pwllheli
Porthmadog
Bala
Ffestiniog
Snowdon 1085
GWYNEDD
CLWYD
CHESHIRE
MERSEYSIDE
GREATER MANCHESTER
LANCASHIRE
CUMBRIA
STAFFORDSHIRE
SHROPSHIRE
ISLE OF MAN
Douglas
Ramsey
Peel
Castletown
Calf of Man
Snaefell 620
IRISH SEA
Liverpool Bay
Pennines
Wensleydale
Weardale
Teesdale
Forest of Bowland
Skipton
Keighley
Settle
Lytham St. Anne's
Leyland
Chorley
Knutsford
Wilmslow
Nantwich
Winsford
Middlewich
Northwich
Ellesmere Port
Flint
Mold
Denbigh
Ruthin
Holywell
Projection: Conical with two standard parallels

1:1 000 000

10 0 10 20 30 40 km

Projection: Conical with two standard parallels

West from Greenwich

1:1 000 000

10 0 10 20 30 40 km

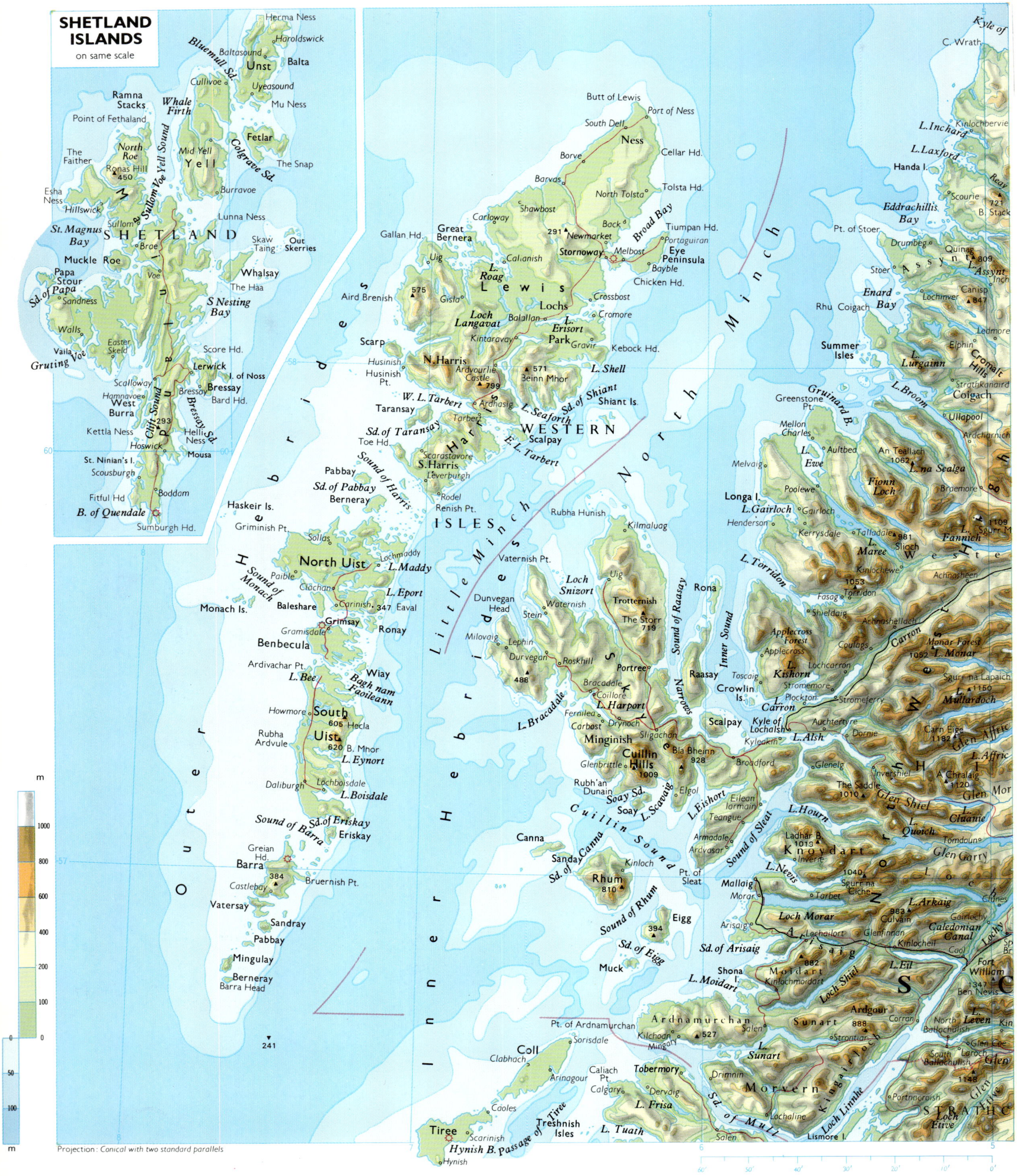
SHETLAND ISLANDS
on same scale
Herma Ness
Haroldswick
Bluemull Sd.
Baltasound
Unst
Balta
Cullivoe
Uyeasound
Ramna Stacks
Whale Firth
Mu Ness
Point of Fethaland
North Roe
Fetlar
The Faither
Yell Sound
Mid Yell
Yell
Colgrave Sd.
The Snap
Ronas Hill 450
Esha Ness
Burravoe
Hillswick
Sullom Voe
Lunna Ness
St. Magnus Bay
Sullom
SHETLAND
Skaw Taing
Out Skerries
Brae
Muckle Roe
Voe
Whalsay
Papa Stour
The Haa
Sd. of Papa
Sandness
S Nesting Bay
Mainland
Walls
Vaila
Easter Skeld
Score Hd.
Gruting Voe
Lerwick
I. of Noss
Scalloway
Bressay
Hamnavoe
West Burra
Bard Hd.
Clift Sound
Bressay Sd.
293
Kettla Ness
Helli Ness
Hoswick
Mousa
St. Ninian's I.
Scousburgh
Fitful Hd
Boddam
B. of Quendale
Sumburgh Hd.
Kyle of
C. Wrath
Butt of Lewis
Port of Ness
South Dell
Ness
Cellar Hd.
Borve
Barvas
North Tolsta
Tolsta Hd.
Shawbost
Carloway
Back
Broad Bay
291 Newmarket
Tiumpan Hd.
Great Bernera
Gallan Hd.
Stornoway
Melbost
Portaguiran
Eye Peninsula
Uig
Callanish
Bayble
L. Roag
Chicken Hd.
Lewis
575
Gisla
Aird Brenish
Lochs
Crossbost
Loch Langavat
Balallan
L. Erisort
Cromore
Kintaravay
Park
Gravir
Kebock Hd.
Scarp
Husinish
Husinish Pt.
N. Harris
Ardvourlie Castle
799
571 Beinn Mhor
L. Shell
Taransay
W. L. Tarbert
Ardhasig
Sd. of Shiant
Shiant Is.
L. Seaforth
Tarbert
Harris
Scalpay
Sd. of Taransay
E. L. Tarbert
WESTERN
Toe Hd.
Scarastavore
S. Harris
Leverburgh
Sound of Harris
Pabbay
Sd. of Pabbay
Berneray
Rodel
Renish Pt.
ISLES
Haskeir Is.
Griminish Pt.
Sollas
Lochmaddy
North Uist
L. Maddy
Paible
Sound of Monach
Clachan
L. Eport
Monach Is.
Baleshare
Carinish
347 Eaval
Grimsay
Gramisdale
Ronay
Benbecula
Ardivachar Pt.
Wiay
L. Bee
Bagh nam Faoileann
Howmore
South Uist
605 Hecla
Rubha Ardvule
620 B. Mhor
L. Eynort
Daliburgh
Lochboisdale
L. Boisdale
Sound of Barra
Sd. of Eriskay
Eriskay
Greian Hd.
Barra
384
Castlebay
Bruernish Pt.
Vatersay
Sandray
Pabbay
Mingulay
Berneray
Barra Head
241
Outer Hebrides
North Minch
Little Minch
Inner Hebrides
Rubha Hunish
Kilmaluag
Vaternish Pt.
Loch Snizort
Uig
Rona
Dunvegan Head
Waternish
Trotternish
Stein
The Storr 719
Sound of Raasay
Inner Sound
Milovaig
Lephin
Dunvegan
Roskhill
Portree
Raasay
488
Bracadale
Toscaig
Crowlin Is.
L. Bracadale
Coillore
Fernilea
L. Harport
Carbost
Drynoch
Narrows
Skye
Scalpay
Kyle of Lochalsh
Minginish
Sligachan
Kyleakin
L. Alsh
Bla Bheinn 928
Cuillin Hills
Glenbrittle
1009
Broadford
Rubh'an Dunain
Soay Sd.
Soay
Elgol
L. Scavaig
L. Eishort
Eilean Iarmain
Teangue
Cuillin Sound
Armadale
Ardvasar
Sound of Sleat
Canna
Sanday
Sd. of Canna
Kinloch
Rhum
810
Pt. of Sleat
Mallaig
Morar
Sound of Rhum
Eigg
394
Sd. of Eigg
Muck
Sd. of Arisaig
Arisaig
Shona I.
L. Moidart
Pt. of Ardnamurchan
Ardnamurchan
Kilchoan
Mingary
527
Salen
Sorisdale
Coll
Clabhach
Arinagour
Caliach Pt.
Tobermory
Calgary
Dervaig
L. Frisa
Cooles
Tiree
Scarinish
Passage of Tiree
Treshnish Isles
L. Tuath
Hynish B.
Hynish
Sd. of Mull
Salen
Lochaline
Morvern
Loch Linnhe
Lismore I.
Drimnin
L. Sunart
Sunart
Strontian
888
Kinlochbervie
L. Inchard
L. Laxford
Handa I.
Scourie
Eddrachillis Bay
721
B. Stack
Pt. of Stoer
Drumbeg
Quinag 809
Stoer
Assynt
Enard Bay
Lochinver
Canisp 847
Rhu Coigach
Ledmore
Summer Isles
Elphin
L. Lurgainn
Cromalt Hills
Gruinard B.
Greenstone Pt.
L. Broom
Coigach
Ullapool
Mellon Charles
Aultbea
An Teallach 1062
L. Ewe
L. na Sealga
Melvaig
Fionn Loch
Poolewe
Longa I.
L. Gairloch
Gairloch
Henderson
Kerrysdale
Talladale
881 Slioch
L. Maree
Fannich
Kinlochewe
L. Torridon
1053 Torridon
Achnasheen
Fasag
Shieldaig
Achnashellach
Applecross Forest
Applecross
Coulags
Carron
1052
Monar Forest
L. Monar
Lochcarron
L. Kishorn
Stromemore
Plockton
Stromeferry
L. Carron
1150
L. Mullardoch
Auchtertyre
Dornie
Carn Eige 1182
Glen Affric
Glenelg
Inversheil
A'Chralaig 1120
The Saddle 1010
Glen Shiel
L. Cluanie
L. Hourn
Ladhar B. 1015
Knoydart
L. Quoich
Tomdoun
Inverie
Glen Garry
L. Nevis
1040
Sgurr na Ciche
Tarbet
Loch Morar
L. Arkaig
983 Gulvain
Caledonian Canal
Gairlochy
Lochailort
Glenfinnan
Kinlocheil
Arisaig
882
Moidart
Kinlochmoidart
Loch Shiel
L. Eil
Fort William
1347 Ben Nevis
Ardgour
Corran
North Ballachulish
South Ballachulish
L. Leven
Glen Coe
1148
Glen Etive
Portnacroish
Loch Etive
Projection: Conical with two standard parallels
m
1000
800
600
400
200
100
0
50
100
m

1:1 000 000

10 0 10 20 30 40 km

Based upon the Ordnance Survey Map with the permission of the Controller of Her Majesty's Stationery Office. Crown Copyright Reserved.

DISTRICTS IN NORTHERN IRELAND
1 Londonderry
2 Limavady
3 Coleraine
4 Ballymoney
5 Moyle
6 Larne
7 Ballymena
8 Magherafelt
9 Cookstown
10 Strabane
11 Omagh
12 Fermanagh
13 Dungannon
14 Craigavon
15 Armagh
16 Newry and Mourne
17 Banbridge
18 Down
19 Lisburn
20 Antrim
21 Newtownabbey
22 Carrickfergus
23 North Down
24 Ards
25 Castlereagh
26 Belfast
NORTHERN IRELAND
ULSTER
CONNACHT
LEINSTER
DONEGAL
LONDONDERRY
ANTRIM
TYRONE
FERMANAGH
ARMAGH
DOWN
MONAGHAN
CAVAN
LOUTH
MEATH
WESTMEATH
LONGFORD
ROSCOMMON
SLIGO
LEITRIM
MAYO
BELFAST
DUBLIN
Lough Neagh
Donegal Bay
Sligo Bay
Clew Bay
Dundalk Bay
Blue Stack Mts
Sperrin Mts
Mourne Mts
Nephin Beg Range
Ox Mts
Inishowen
Connemara

1:1 250 000

10 0 10 20 30 40 50 km

COPYRIGHT GEORGE PHILIP & SON, LTD

West from Greenwich

Projection: Conical with two standard parallels

1: 20 000 000

200 0 200 400 600 800 km
NORWEGIAN SEA
NORTH SEA
BALTIC SEA
BLACK SEA
CASPIAN SEA
ADRIATIC SEA
MEDITERRANEAN SEA
ATLANTIC OCEAN
Bay of Biscay
Tyrrhenian Sea
Ionian Sea
Aegean Sea
Ligurian Sea
White Sea
G. of Bothnia
G. of Finland
G. of Riga
Irish Sea
English Channel
Skagerrak
Kattegat
Str. of Gibraltar
Str. of Otranto
Str. of Messina
Str. of Kerch
Sea of Azov
S. of Marmara
Bosporus
Ural Mountains
Tundra
Obshchiy Syrt
Volga Uplands
Central Russian Uplands
Ukraine
Pripyat Marshes
North European Plain
Finland
Lapland
Scandinavia
Kola Peninsula
Kanin Peninsula
Caucasus
Anatolia
Taurus
Crimea
Carpathians
Transylvanian Alps
Wallachia
Balkan Peninsula
Balkans
Rhodope
Pindus
Morea
Plain of Hungary
Dinaric Alps
Alps
Apennines
Sudetes
Erz Geb.
Harz 1142
Jura
Vosges
Black For.
Ardennes
Massif Central
Cevennes
Pyrenees
Iberian Peninsula
Old Castile
New Castile
Sierra Morena
Andalusia
Sa. Nevada
Cantabrian Mts.
Atlas
Iceland
British Isles
Great Britain
Ireland
Brittany
Jutland
Corsica
Sardinia
Sicily
Crete
Cyprus
Malta
Balearic Is.
Shetland Is.
Orkney Is.
Faroe Is.
Hebrides
Lofoten
Vesterålen
North Cape
Nordkinn
Volga
Don
Dnepr (Dnieper)
Dnestr (Dniester)
Danube
Rhine
Elbe
Weser
Odra (Oder)
Wisła (Vistula)
Niemen
Loire
Seine
Garonne
Rhone
Po
Tagus
Douro
Ebro
Kama
Pechora
Mezen
N. Dvina
Onega
Oka
Bug
Prut
Tisza
Sava
Drava
Morava
Kuban
Manych
Terek
Kura
Araks
Tigris
Euphrates
L. Ladoga
L. Onega
Rybinsk Res.
L. Chudskoye
Vänern
Vättern
Mälaren
Gotland
Dogger Bank
Rockall
Fisher Bank
Arctic Circle
Mt. Elbrus 5633
Ararat 5165
L. Van
L. Urmia
L. Tuz
Mt. Blanc 4807
Etna 3263
Vesuvius 1277
Gran Sasso 2914
Pico de Aneto 3404
Mulhacén 3478
Snowdon 1085
Ben Nevis 1343
C. Finisterre
C. St. Vincent
C. Trafalgar
C. Spartel
C. da Roca
C. Matapan
C. Bon
C. Blanco
Land's End
Lindesnes
Heligoland
Netherlands
German Bight
NORTH UTSIRE
SOUTH UTSIRE
FISHER
VIKING
FORTIES
DOGGER
HUMBER
THAMES
DOVER
WIGHT
PORTLAND
PLYMOUTH
LUNDY
FASTNET
SOLE
SHANNON
ROCKALL
BAILEY
HEBRIDES
FAIR ISLE
FAEROES
SOUTH EAST ICELAND
CROMARTY
FORTH
TYNE
IRISH SEA
MALIN
BISCAY
FINISTERRE
COPYRIGHT, GEORGE PHILIP & SON, LTD.
Projection: Bonne West from Greenwich 0 East from Greenwich
Sea areas named in weather forecasts
m 4000 2000 1000 400 200 0
0 200 2000 4000 m

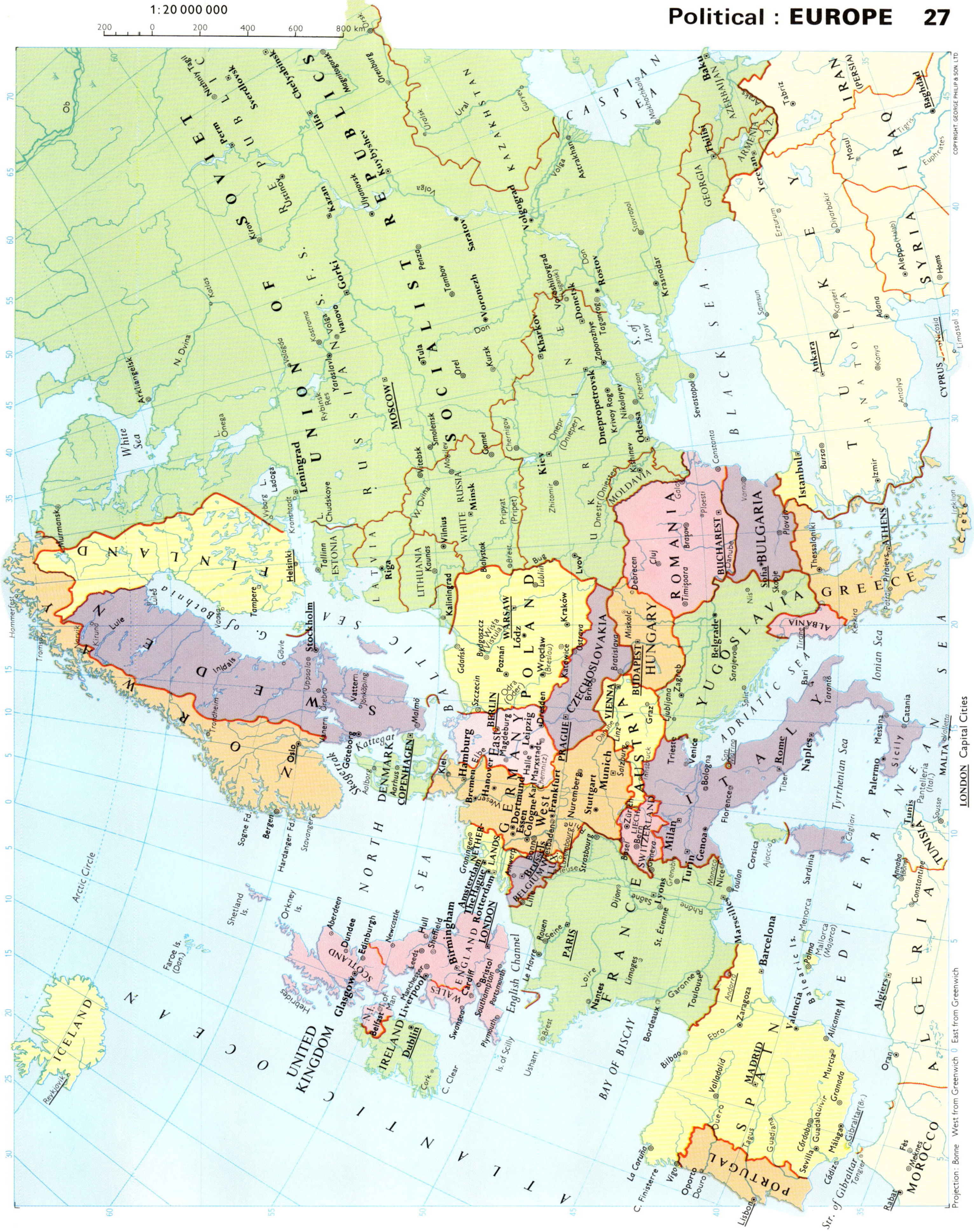
1:20 000 000
200 0 200 400 600 800 km
UNION OF SOVIET SOCIALIST REPUBLICS
R. S. F. S. R.
KAZAKHSTAN
GEORGIA
ARMENIA
AZERBAIJAN
UKRAINE
MOLDAVIA
WHITE RUSSIA
LITHUANIA
LATVIA
ESTONIA
FINLAND
SWEDEN
NORWAY
DENMARK
POLAND
EAST GERMANY
WEST GERMANY
NETHERLANDS
BELGIUM
LUX.
FRANCE
SWITZERLAND
LIECH.
AUSTRIA
CZECHOSLOVAKIA
HUNGARY
ROMANIA
BULGARIA
YUGOSLAVIA
ALBANIA
GREECE
TURKEY
IRAN (PERSIA)
IRAQ
SYRIA
CYPRUS
ITALY
SAN MARINO
MALTA
TUNISIA
ALGERIA
MOROCCO
SPAIN
PORTUGAL
ANDORRA
UNITED KINGDOM
SCOTLAND
ENGLAND
WALES
N.I.
IRELAND
ICELAND
ATLANTIC OCEAN
NORTH SEA
BALTIC SEA
MEDITERRANEAN SEA
BLACK SEA
CASPIAN SEA
ADRIATIC SEA
BAY OF BISCAY
English Channel
Tyrrhenian Sea
Ionian Sea
White Sea
Gulf of Bothnia
Kattegat
Skagerrak
Str. of Gibraltar
Arctic Circle
MOSCOW
LONDON
PARIS
BERLIN
WARSAW
PRAGUE
VIENNA
BUDAPEST
BUCHAREST
Sofia
Belgrade
Tirane
ATHENS
Rome
MADRID
Lisbon
Dublin
COPENHAGEN
Oslo
Stockholm
Helsinki
Reykjavik
Brussels
The Hague
Amsterdam
Bonn
Ankara
Nicosia
Valletta
Tunis
Algiers
Rabat
Baghdad
LONDON Capital Cities
Projection: Bonne
West from Greenwich 0 East from Greenwich
COPYRIGHT, GEORGE PHILIP & SON, LTD

EUROPE : Climate and Natural Vegetation

1:40 000 000

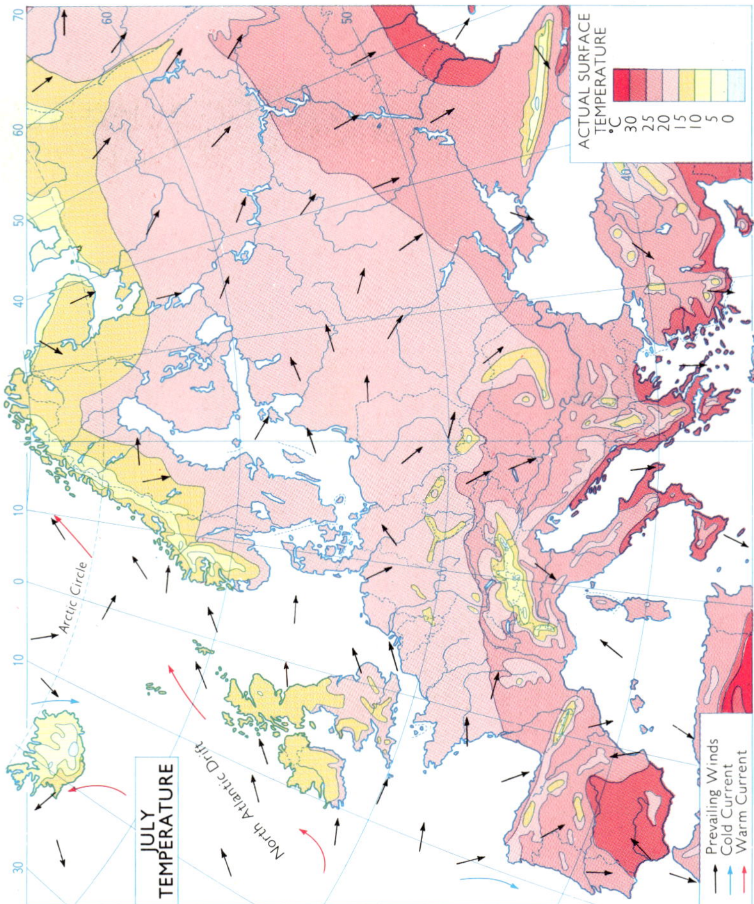

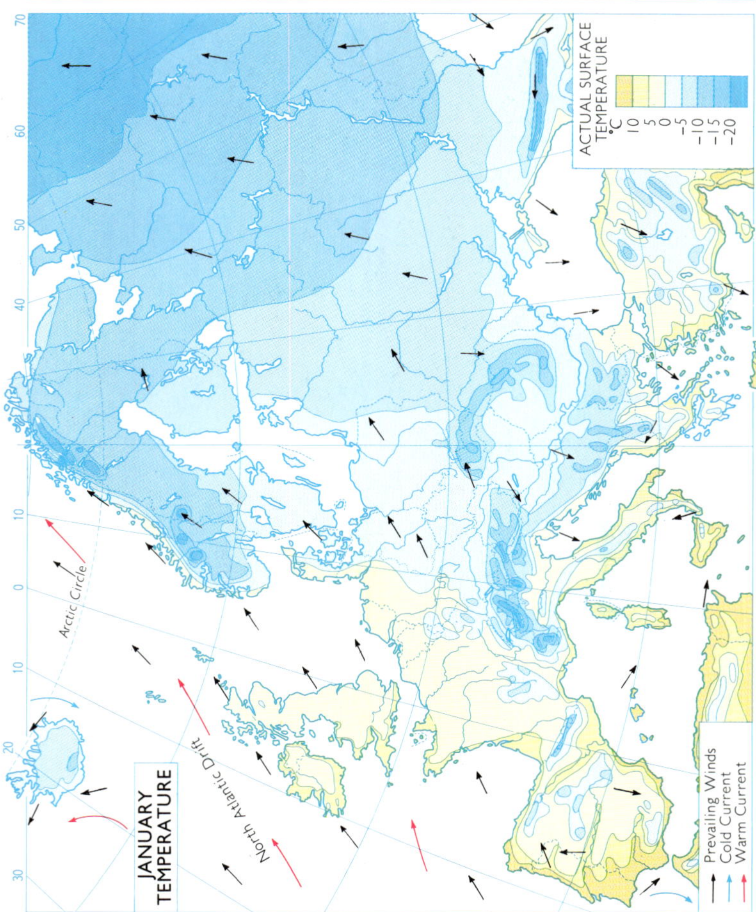

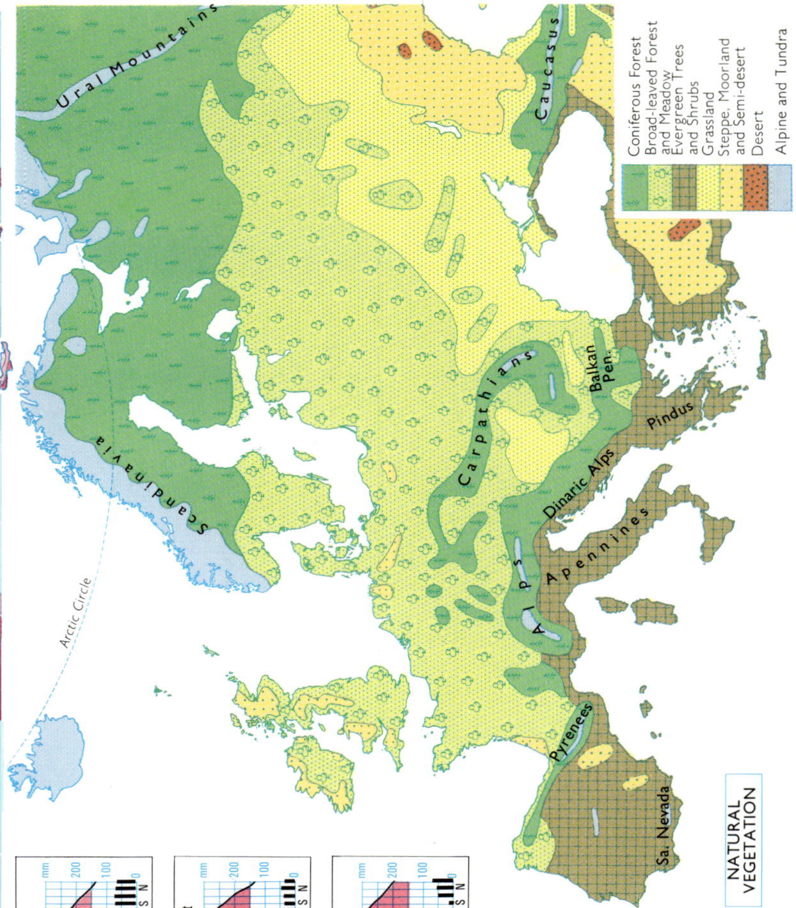

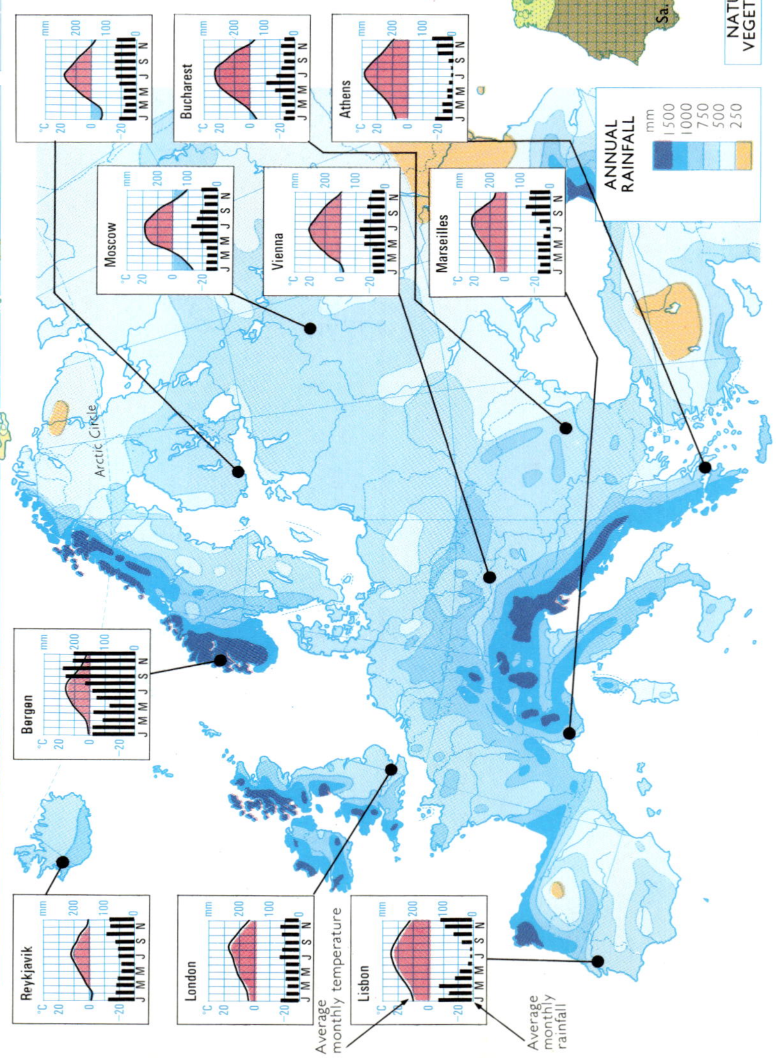

Projection: Bonne

1:20 000 000

200 0 200 400 600 800 km

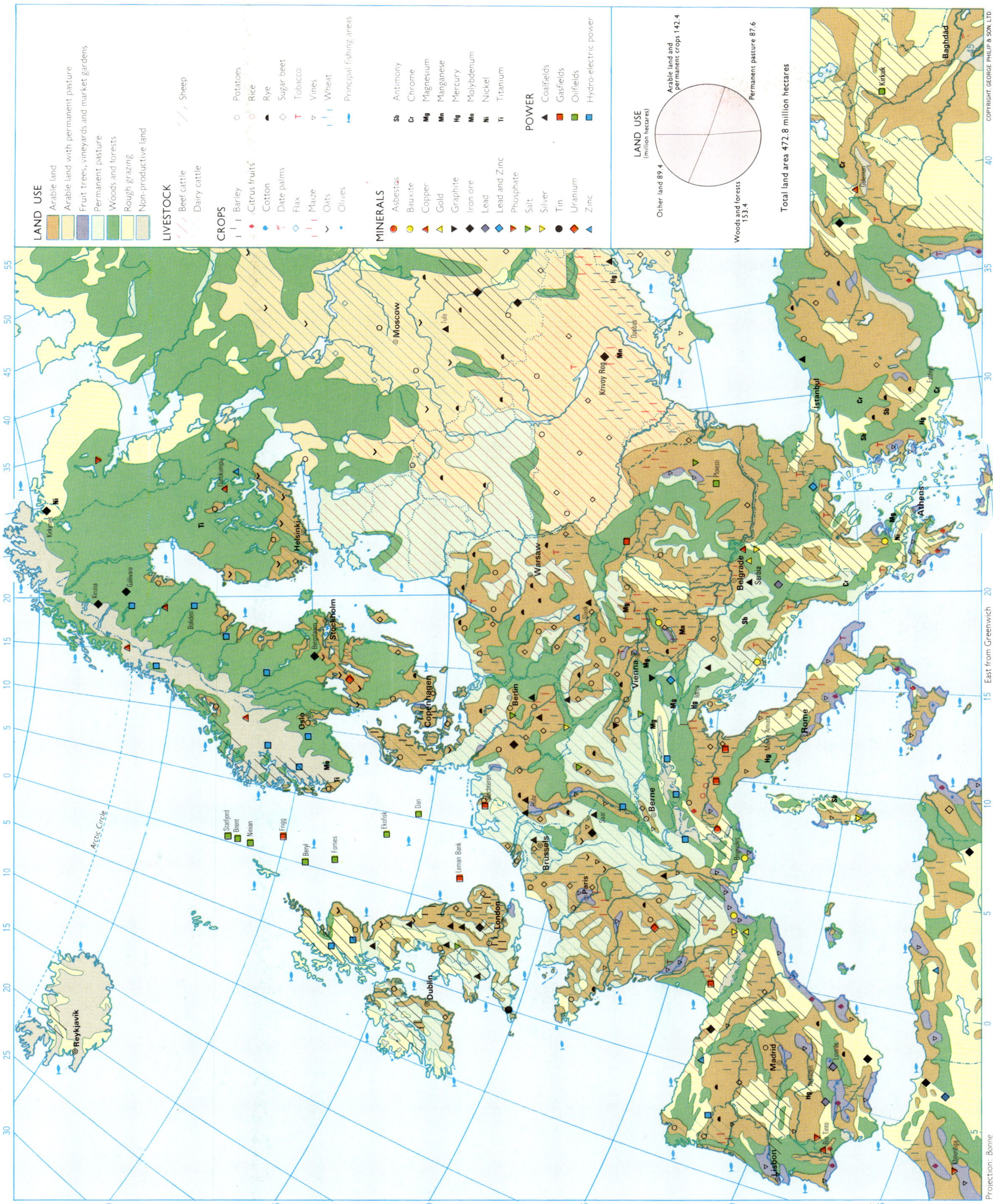

DENSITY OF POPULATION

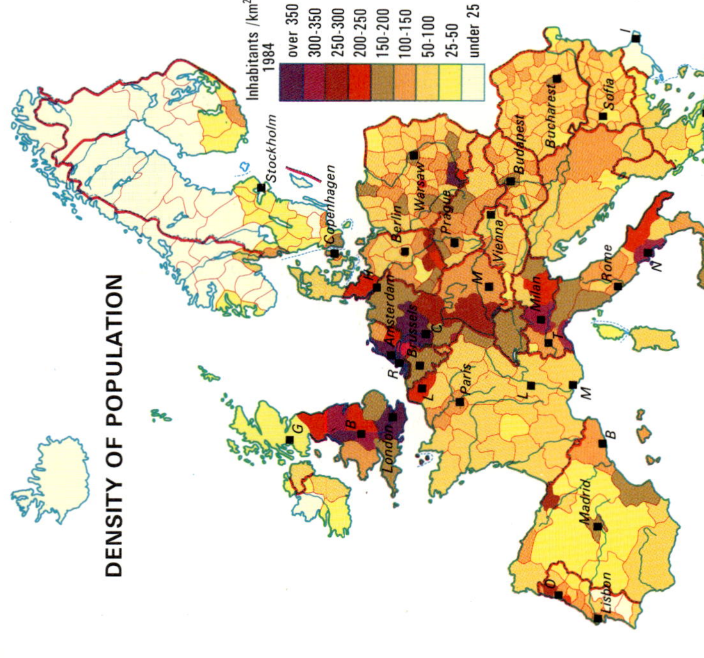

■ Urban areas with over 1 000 000 inhabitants

POPULATION CHANGE

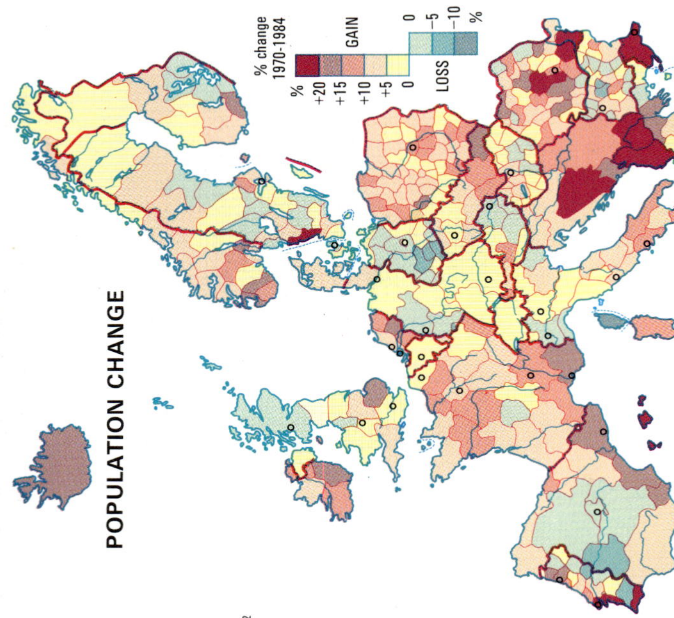

The population of Europe increased by 7.7% between 1970 and 1984

HEALTH

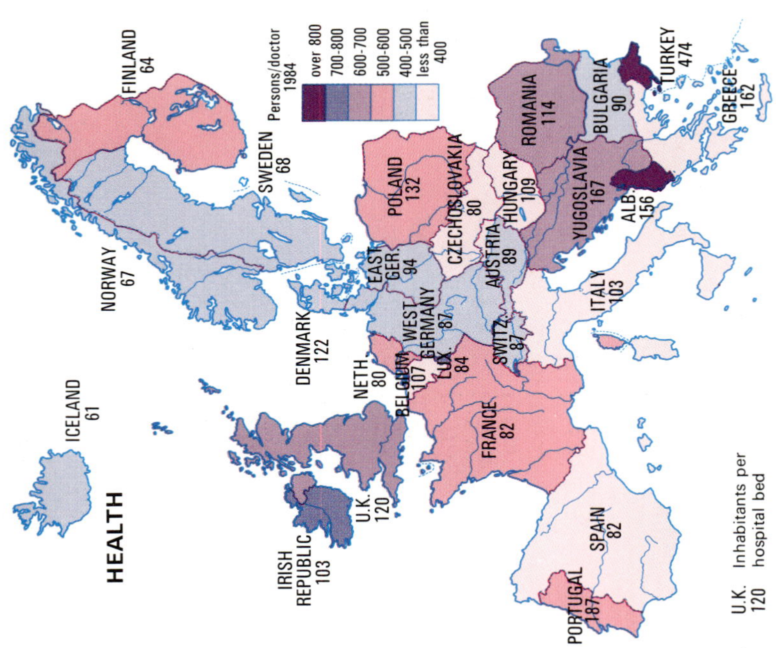

U.K. 120 Inhabitants per hospital bed

UNEMPLOYMENT

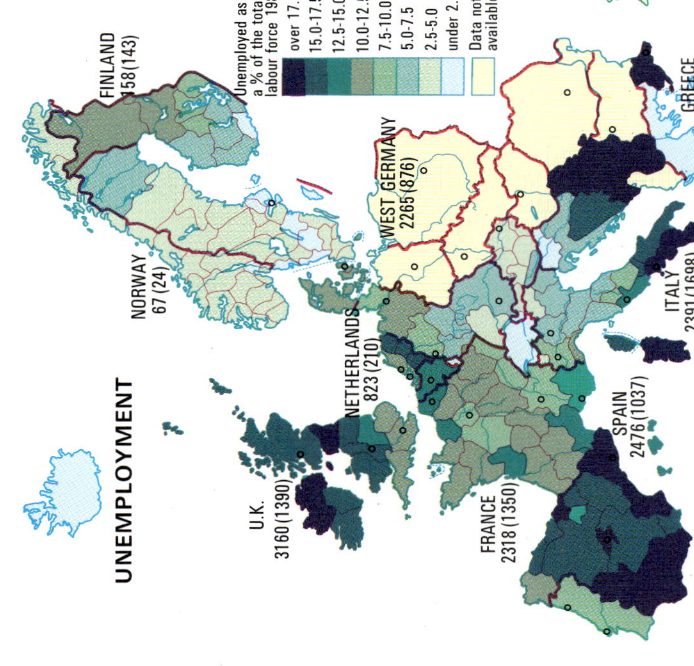

Unemployment figures in thousands for selected countries 1984. (1979 figures are given in brackets)

EMPLOYMENT BY ECONOMIC ACTIVITY

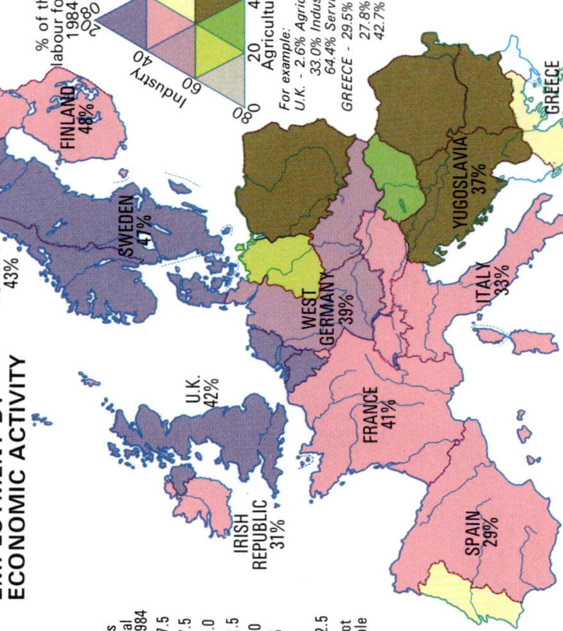

U.K. 42% % of labour force who are female for selected countries

IMPORTANCE OF AGRICULTURE

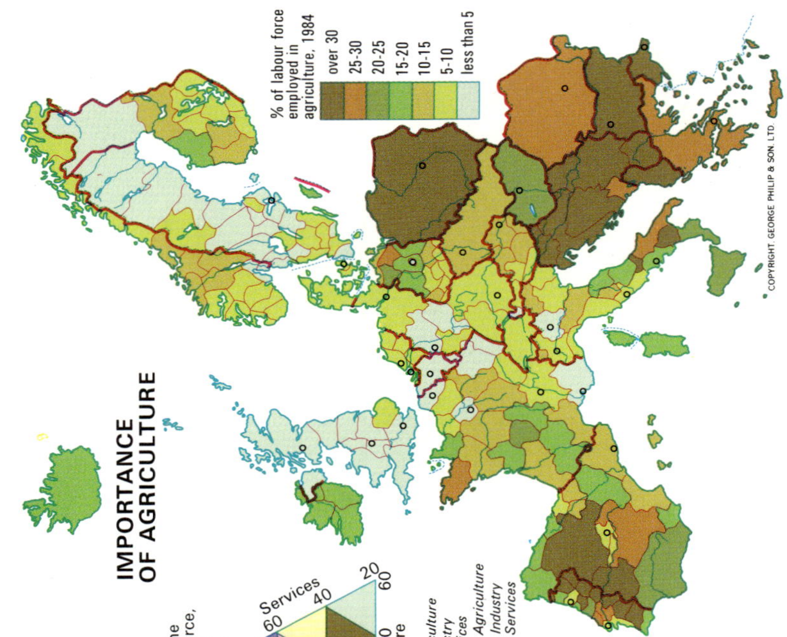

STANDARDS OF LIVING

Gross Domestic Product (GDP) is a measure of a country's total production of goods and services

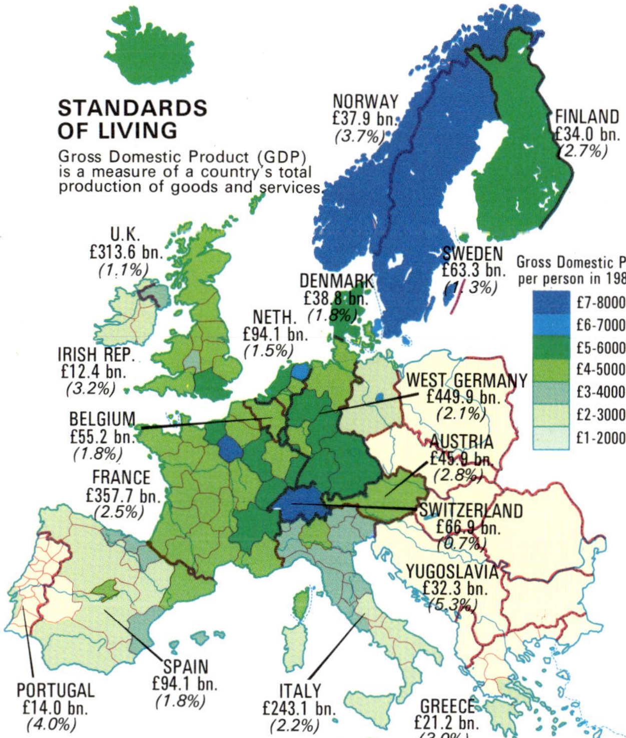

Gross Domestic Product in 1983 in £ billions
(% annual average growth 1973-83 is given in brackets)

INFLATION

The rate of inflation shows the increase in the price of a broad selection of household goods and services in each country.

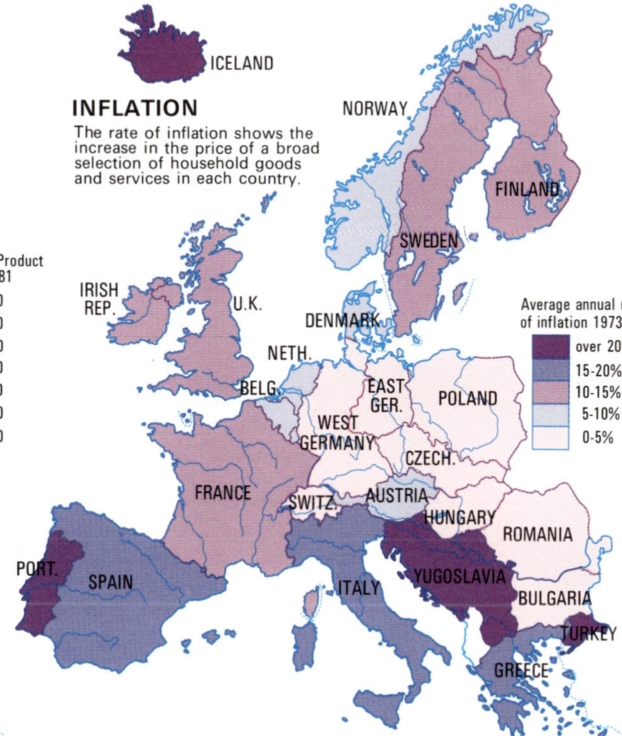

ENERGY CONSUMPTION

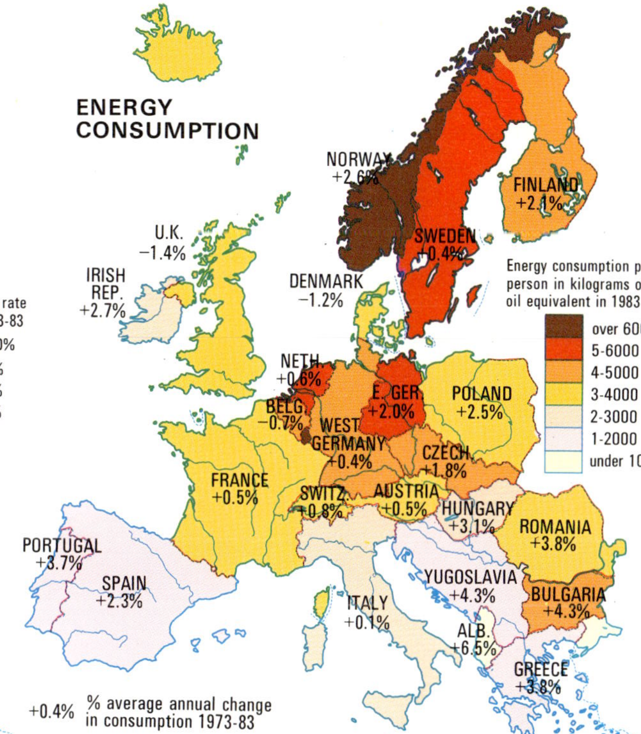

+0.4% % average annual change in consumption 1973-83

TRADE ORGANISATIONS

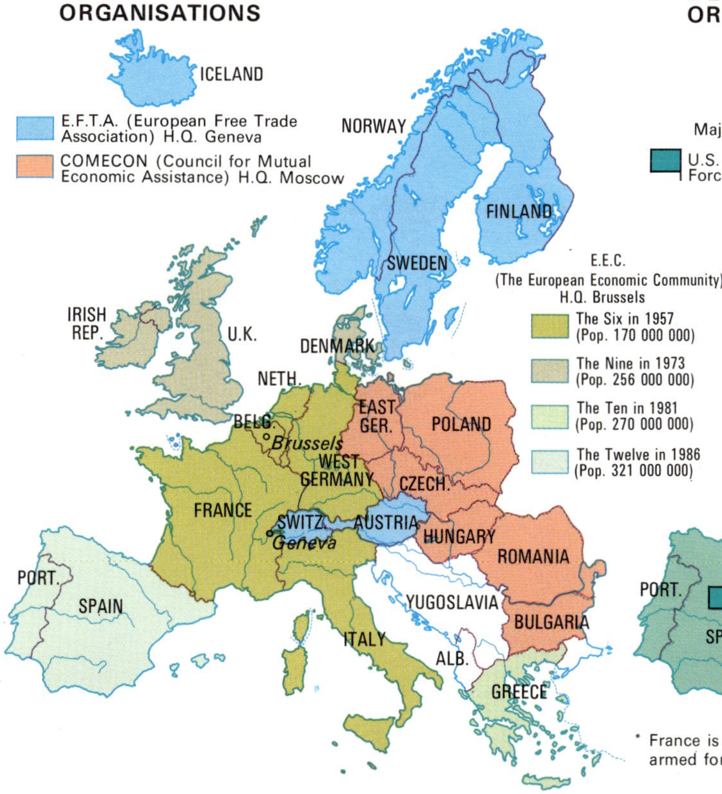

DEFENCE ORGANISATIONS

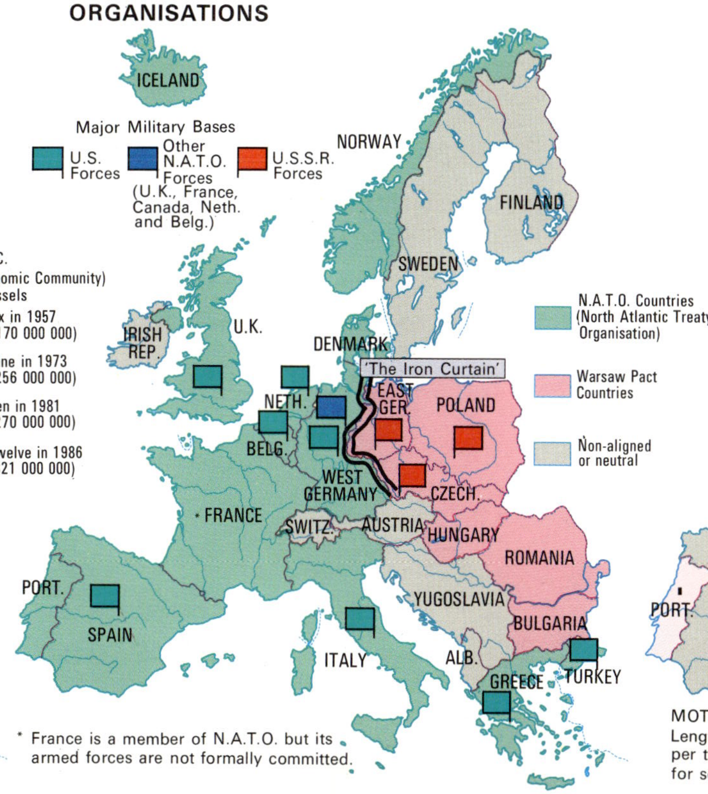

* France is a member of N.A.T.O. but its armed forces are not formally committed.

TRANSPORT

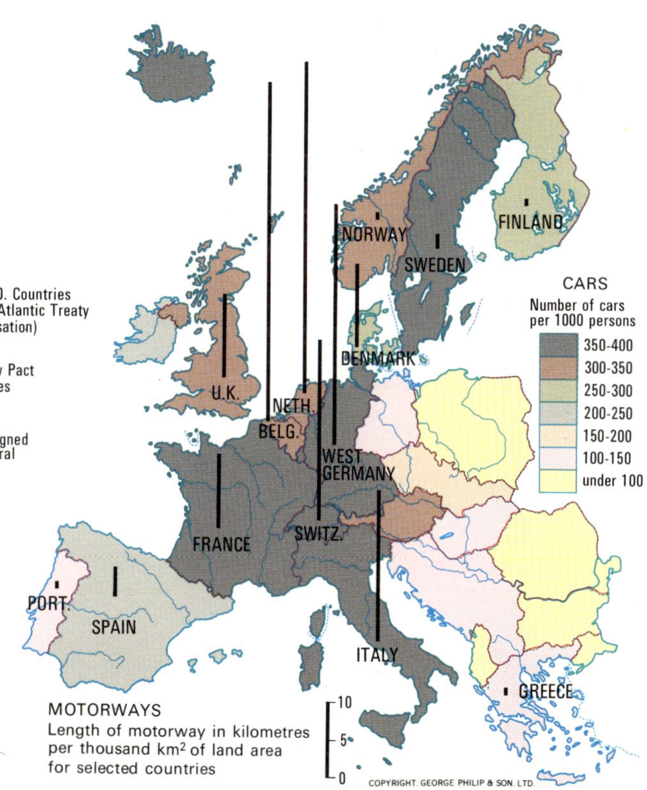

MOTORWAYS
Length of motorway in kilometres per thousand km² of land area for selected countries

	Population								Land			Agriculture		
	Total	Density	Birth Rate	Death Rate	Life Expectancy	Growth 1965-80	Growth 1980-88	Urban	Area	Arable	Forest	Agricultural Population	Index of Production	Food Intake
	th.	persons per km²	per th. popn.	per th. popn.	yrs.	av. % per annum	av. % per annum	%	th. km²	th. km²	th. km²	% of total popn.	1979-81 = 100	calories per day
Albania	3145	117	26	6	72	2.5	2.1	35	27	7	11	51	111	2726
Austria	7563	91	12	11	74	0.3	0	57	83	15	32	7	105	3428
Belgium *	9867	329	12	11	75	0.3	0	97	30	8	7	2	116	3679
Bulgaria	8995	81	13	12	72	0.5	0.2	70	111	41	39	13	103	3663
Czechoslovakia	15610	125	14	11	71	0.5	0.3	68	125	51	46	10	125	3465
Denmark	5133	122	12	12	76	0.5	0	86	42	26	5	5	120	3633
Finland	4944	16	12	10	76	0.3	0.4	60	305	24	232	9	103	3122
France	55873	102	14	9	77	0.7	0.5	74	546	195	147	6	104	3336
Germany, East	16665	157	13	13	73	–0.2	–0.1	78	106	49	30	9	116	3791
Germany,West	61049	250	11	11	75	0.3	–0.1	86	244	75	73	4	112	3528
Greece	10030	77	11	10	76	0.7	0.5	61	131	39	26	26	104	3688
Hungary	10604	115	12	13	70	0.4	–0.1	59	92	53	17	13	105	3569
Iceland	249	3	17	7	77	0.8	1.1	90	100	0.1	1	8	106	3142
Ireland	3574	52	17	9	74	1	0.6	58	69	10	3	15	105	3632
Italy	57470	196	10	9	77	0.6	0.2	68	294	122	67	8	100	3523
Luxembourg *	371	143	12	10	74	0.9	0.2	83	3	0.6				
Malta	345	1150	15	8	73	0.2	–0.9	87	0.3	0.1	0	4	111	2682
Netherlands	14760	434	13	8	77	0.9	0.5	88	34	9	3	4	115	3326
Norway	4205	14	14	11	77	0.6	0.3	74	308	9	83	6	112	3223
Poland	37873	124	16	10	72	0.8	0.8	61	305	147	87	23	109	3336
Portugal	10162	111	12	9	74	0.6	0.3	32	92	28	36	19	107	3151
Romania	23052	100	16	11	70	1	0.4	49	230	107	63	23	114	3373
Spain	38997	78	11	8	77	1	0.5	77	499	204	157	12	114	3359
Sweden	8357	20	13	12	77	0.5	0.1	84	412	30	280	4	93	3064
Switzerland	6545	164	12	9	77	0.5	0.3	61	40	4	11	5	111	3437
United Kingdom	57019	236	14	11	75	0.2	0.2	92	242	70	23	2	106	3256
Yugoslavia	23552	92	15	9	72	0.9	0.7	48	255	78	93	25	103	3563
U.S.S.R.	285659	13	20	10	69	0.9	0.9	68	22272	2325	9440	15	118	3440

* Many figures for Luxembourg included in Belgium.

Population. This is the United Nation's estimate for the mid-year 1988 (thousands)

Population Density. This is the quoted population total divided by the quoted land area (persons per square kilometre).

Birth Rates and Death Rates. These are the registered or United Nation's estimated rates per thousand population.

Life Expectancy. This figure indicates the number of years that a child born today can expect to live if the levels of death of today last throughout its life. The figure is the average of that for men and women. The figure for women is usually higher than that for men (U.K. Male 75, female 78 years).

Population Growth. This shows the average annual percentage change in population for two periods, 1965–1980 and 1980–1988.

Urbanization. This is the percentage of the total population living in urban areas. The definition of urban is that of the individual nation and usually includes quite small towns.

Land Area. This is the total area of the country minus the area covered by major lakes and rivers (thousand square kilometres).

Arable Land and Permanent Crops. This excludes fallow land but includes temporary pasture (thousand square kilometres).

Forest and Woodland. This includes natural and planted woodland and land recently cleared of timber which will be replanted (thousand square kilometres).

Agricultural Population. This is the percentage of the economically active population working in agriculture. It also includes those people working in forestry, hunting and fishing.

Index of Agricultural Production. The base period for this index is 1979–1981 and it shows the level of production in each country in 1988 in comparison with that of the earlier period. Only edible crops and meat are included.

Food Intake. The figures are the average intake per person in calories per day for the year 1986.

	Trade		Education		Health	Energy	Consumer Price Index	G.N.P.		G.D.P.		Loans & Debt		
	Imports	Exports	Primary	Secondary					Growth per capita	Part formed by Agric.	Part formed by Indust.			
	US$ per capita	US$ per capita	% of age group	% of age group	Popn. per doctor	Consumption in kg of oil equiv. per capita	1980 = 100	US$ per capita	% per year 1965-88	%	%	end 1987 US$ millions	as % of G.N.P.	
		159	96	70		1178		900						Albania
	4315	3592	100	79	388	3465	133	11980	3.1	3	37	302	0.2	Austria
	8371	8407	96	96	331	4844	146	11480	2.6	2	31	592	0.4	* Belgium
	1843	1915	100	100	277	4705		6295	3.1	15	62			Bulgaria
	1554	1477	97	37	277	4954	111	8280	2.3	7	61			Czechoslovakia
	4936	4811	98	100	399	3887	165	14930	1.9	5	29	922	0.9	Denmark
	4017	4053	100	100	443	5581	170	14470	3.2	7	35	610	0.6	Finland
	2819	2561	100	95	320	3729	172	12790	2.7	4	31	6959	0.7	France
	1727	1792	100	78	439	6031		9800	3	13	66			Germany, East
	3724	4812	97	72	377	4531	122	14400	2.5	2	38	4700	0.4	Germany,West
	1347	649	100	88	351	1971	416	4020	3.1	16	29	23120	0.1	Greece
	929	903	98	70	307	3062	184	2240	3.8	15	40	18957	79	Hungary
	6321	5719	99	95	435	6884	1050	20160	2.4	10	16			Iceland
	3809	4468	100	96	676	2503	195	6120	2	10	37	57	0.2	Ireland
	2127	2029	97	76	234	2676	222	10350	2.7	4	34	2615	0.4	Italy
			100	74	552	11330	142	22600	1.7	3	29			* Luxembourg
	3299	1751	97	75	879	1501	103	5050	2.7	4	29			Malta
	6187	9293	100	100	450	5198	135	11860	2.1	4	30	2231	1	Netherlands
	5369	5101	98	97	451	8932	192	17190	3.5	4	35	988	1	Norway
	286	322	100	80	487	3336	928	1930	3.4	13	49	42135	58	Poland
	1322	902	100	52	412	1322	381	2830	3.2	9	40	18245	63	Portugal
	496	544	97	79	567	3464		5200	4.3	15		6662	5	Romania
	1257	874	100	98	317	1939	214	6010	2.3	6	37			Spain
	4861	5303	99	83	387	6453	177	15500	1.8	3	35	1534	0.9	Sweden
	7725	6930	100		696	4105	128	21330	1.4	2	21	615	0.3	Switzerland
	2708	2300	100	85	611	3805	160	10420	1.7	2	38	2615	0.3	United Kingdom
	533	494	95	82	549	2115	2891	2480	3.7	11	43	23518	41	Yugoslavia
	336	378	100	99	270	5006	108	7120	2.5	20	45			U.S.S.R.

Andorra, Land 0.5/Popn. 51; Faeroe Is. 1.4/46; Gibraltar 0.01/30; Liechtenstein 0.2/28; Monaco 0.0015/27; San Marino 0.06/23; Svalbard 62/4.

Trade. The trade figures are for the year 1988. The total trade figures have been divided by the population and are a measure of the country's external trade (U.S. $ per capita).

Education. The ages of primary school are taken to be 6–11 years and secondary school 12–17 years. The percentage of total school age group in this type of education is shown.

Energy. All forms of energy have been converted to their equivalent in oil. Firewood and other traditional forms used in developing countries are not included and so the energy consumption in those countries is understated (kilograms of oil equivalent per capita).

Consumer Price Index. The base year is 1980 which is 100 and the level of consumer prices in 1987 or 1988 are shown in relation to the base year. It is a measure of inflation.

G.N.P. (Gross National Product) This figure is an estimate of the average production per person measured in U.S. dollars and for 1988. The G.N.P. measures the value of goods and services produced in a country, plus the balance, positive or negative, of income from abroad, for example investments, interest on capital, money returned from foreign labour, etc. The rate of change is the average annual percentage change during the period 1965–1988 in the G.N.P. The G.D.P. (Gross Domestic Product) is the G.N.P. minus the foreign balances. The adjoining two columns show the percentage contribution to the G.D.P. made by the agricultural and mining and manufacturing sectors.

Loans and Debts. This figure in millions of U.S. dollars shows the external public debt ar the end of 1988. This is then shown as a percentage of the annual G.N.P. The figures in red show official development assistance made by the developed countries and also as a percentage of the donor country's G.N.P.

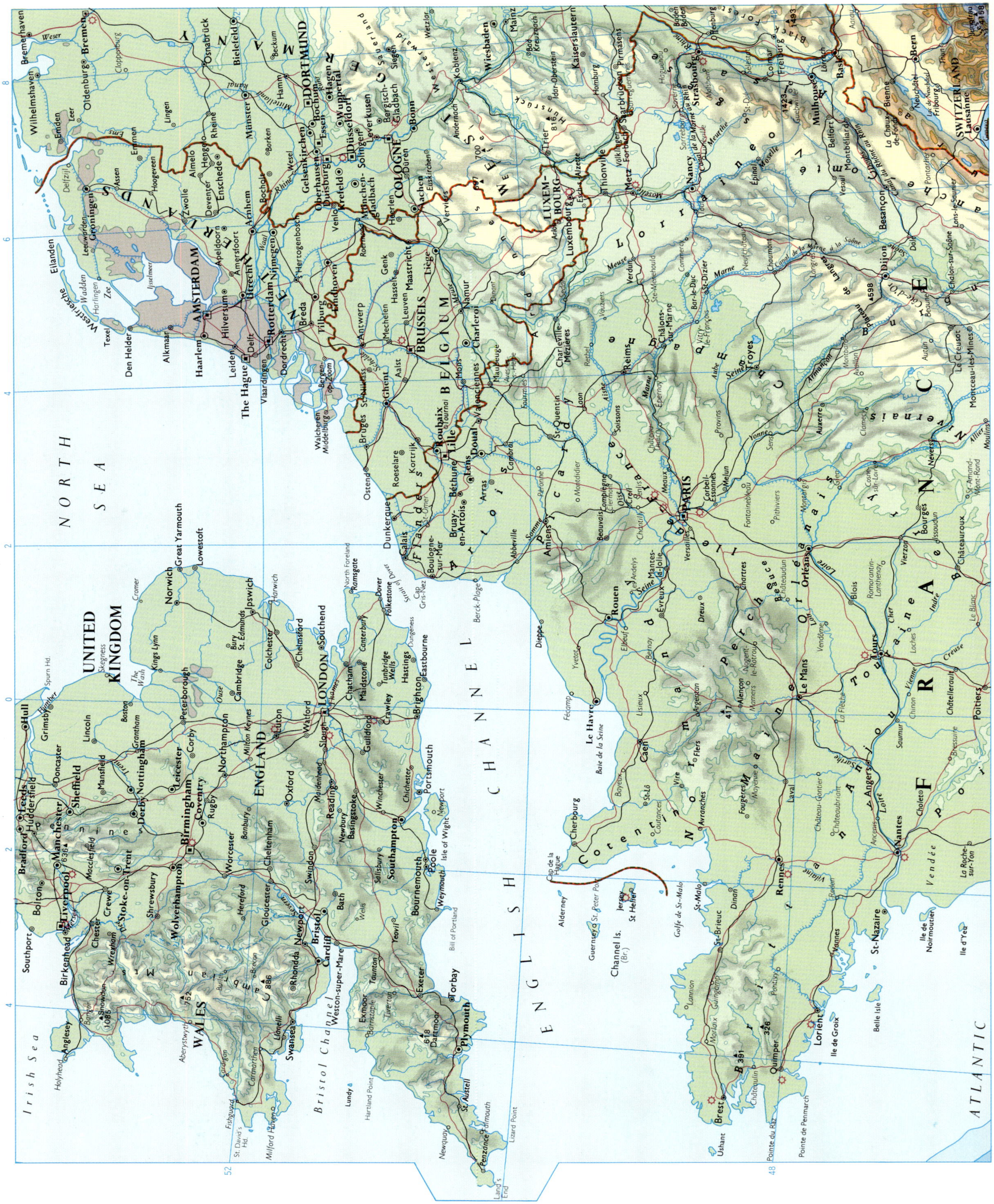
NORTH SEA
ENGLISH CHANNEL
ATLANTIC
Irish Sea
Bristol Channel
UNITED KINGDOM
ENGLAND
WALES
NETHERLANDS
BELGIUM
LUXEMBOURG
GERMANY
SWITZERLAND
FRANCE
LONDON
PARIS
BRUSSELS
AMSTERDAM
COLOGNE
DORTMUND
Luxembourg
Rotterdam
The Hague
Antwerp
Birmingham
Manchester
Liverpool
Leeds
Sheffield
Bristol
Cardiff
Southampton
Plymouth
Norwich
Hull
Rouen
Le Havre
Caen
Cherbourg
Rennes
Nantes
Brest
Le Mans
Orléans
Tours
Lille
Reims
Metz
Nancy
Strasbourg
Dijon
Besançon
Bern
Lausanne
Channel Is. (Br.)
Jersey
Guernsey
Alderney

1: 4 000 000

20 0 20 40 60 80 100 120 km

LOW COUNTRIES AND LOWER RHINE

1:2 000 000

Projection: Conical with two standard parallels

East from Greenwich

1: 5 000 000

50 0 50 100 150 200 km

Projection: Conical with two standard parallels.

1:10 000 000

100 0 100 200 300 400 km

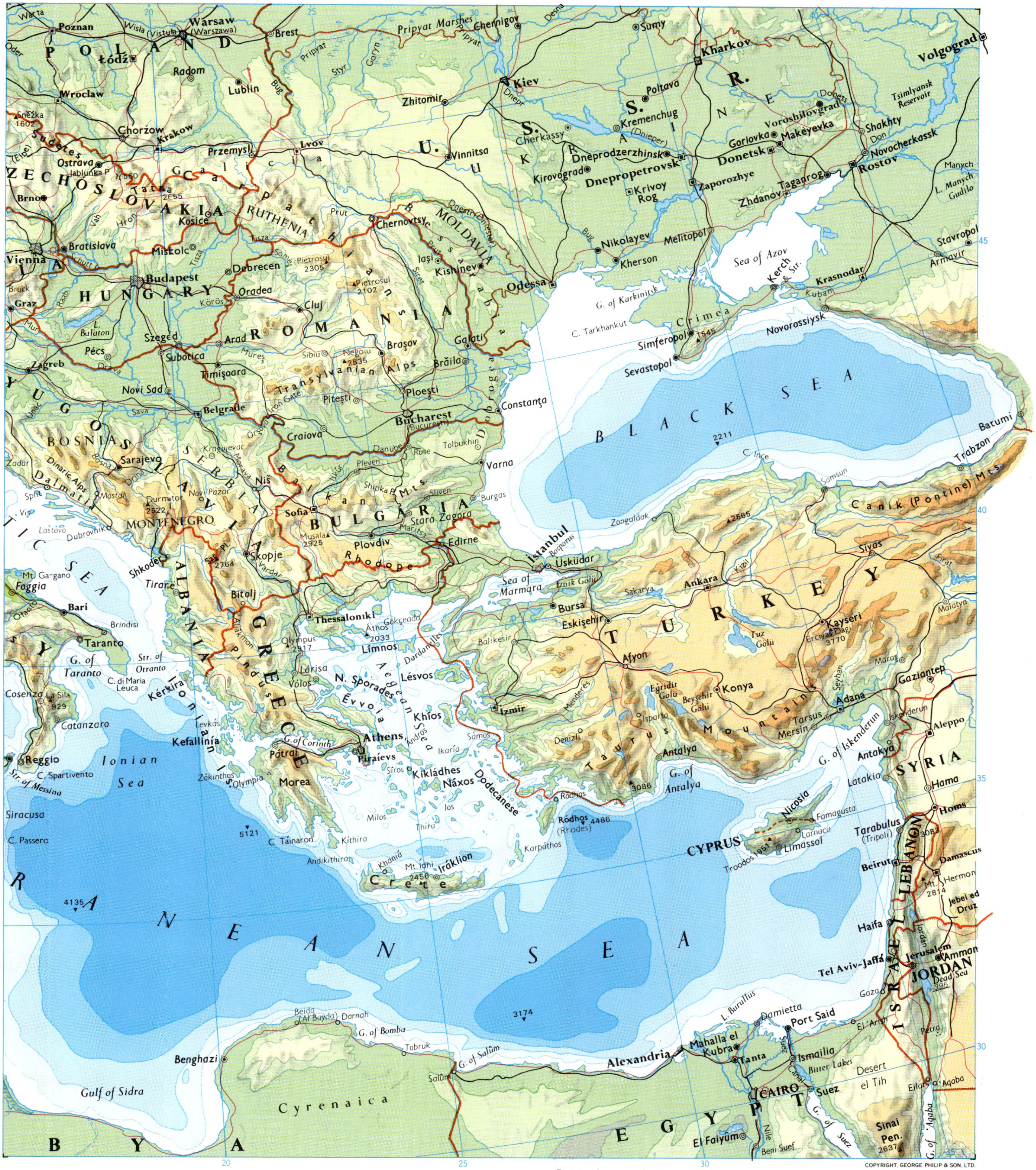

Division between Greeks and Turks in Cyprus; Turks to the North.

SWITZERLAND
Lyons
Geneva
Grenoble
DAUPHINE
Turin (Torino)
PIEDMONT
Milan (Milano)
LOMBARDY
Como
Bergamo
Brescia
Novara
Vercelli
Pavia
Piacenza
Cremona
Alessandria
Asti
Cuneo
Avignon
PROVENCE
Aix
Marseilles
Toulon
Nice
Cannes
Iles d'Hyères
Genoa (Genova)
G. of Genoa
La Spezia
Parma
Reggio
Modena
Bologna
Ferrara
Ravenna
Forli
Rimini
San Marino
Pesaro
Ancona
Mantua (Mantova)
Verona
Vicenza
Padua (Padova)
Venice (Venezia)
Gulf of Venice
Treviso
Trento
Bolzano
Udine
Trieste
Pordenone
Rovigo
Brenner P.
Klagenfurt
Maribor
Ljubljana
Zagreb
Rijeka
Pula (Pola)
Cres
Lošinj
Krk
Pag
Dugi Otok
Split
Brač
Hvar
Korčula
Lastovo
Vis
Palagruža (Yugoslavia)
BOSNIA AND HERCE
YU
LIGURIAN SEA
Leghorn (Livorno)
Pisa
Lucca
Pistoia
Prato
Florence (Firenze)
TUSCANY
Siena
Arezzo
Perugia
UMBRIA
L. Trasimeno
Grosseto
Viterbo
Terni
Macerata
Ascoli Piceno
Teramo
Gran Sasso 2914
L'Aquila
Pescara
Chieti
ABRUZZI
MARCHE
ROME (Roma)
Latina
MOLISE
Campobasso
Foggia
Mt. Gargano
G. of Manfredonia
Cerignola
Barletta
Andria
Bari
Benevento
Caserta
Avellino
Naples (Napoli)
Capri
Salerno
Potenza
BASILICATA
Matera
Taranto
G. of Taranto
Cosenza
Catanzaro
C. Rizzuto
Reggio
CALABRIA
Str. of Messina
Messina
Palermo
Trapani
Egadi Is.
Marsala
Agrigento
Caltanissetta
Catánia
Siracusa (Syracuse)
Ragusa
C. Passero
Lipari Is.
Stromboli
Ustica (It.)
Pantelleria (Ital.)
Lampedusa (Ital.)
Gozo
Valletta
MALTA
CORSICA
Bastia
Ajaccio
Bonifacio Str.
Elba
SARDINIA
Sassari
Olbia
Cagliari
G. of Cagliari
C. Carbonara
C. Spartivento
G. of Oristano
Oristano
Asinara
C. Falcone
TYRRHENIAN SEA
ADRIATIC SEA
MEDITE
AFRICA
C. Bon
MALTA 1:1 000 000
Gozo
Comino
Victoria (Rabat)
St. Pauls Bay
Mosta
Mdina
Rabat
Valletta
Marsaxlokk
S.E. EUROPE POLITICAL 1:25 000 000
FRANCE
SWITZ.
Liechtenstein
AUSTRIA
Vienna
HUNGARY
Budapest
ROMANIA
Bucharest
U.S.S.R.
YUGOSLAVIA
Belgrade
Sofia
BULGARIA
Istanbul
TURKEY
ALBANIA
Tirana
GREECE
Thessaloniki
Athens
AEGEAN SEA
Crete
ITALY
Rome
Naples
Venice
Trieste
San Marino
MONACO
Corsica (Fr.)
Sardinia
Sicily
MALTA
MEDITERRANEAN SEA
Projection: Conical with two standard parallels

1:5 000 000

50 0 50 100 150 200 km

NORTH SEA
BALTIC
Frisian Islands
NETHERLANDS
BELGIUM
LUX.
WEST GERMANY
EAST GERMANY
CZECHOSLOVAKIA
AUSTRIA
SWITZERLAND
FRANCE
ITALY
LIECHTENSTEIN
Flensburg
SCHLESWIG
HOLSTEIN
Kiel
Kiel Bay
Lolland
Falster
Fehmarn
Fehmarn Belt
Lübeck Bay
Rügen
Stralsund
Rostock
Lübeck
Hamburg
Altona
Bremerhaven
Wilhelmshaven
Heligoland
Heligoland Bay
Cuxhaven
Emden
Groningen
Leeuwarden
Den Helder
Alkmaar
IJsselmeer
Zaandam
Haarlem
North Sea Canal
Amsterdam
The Hague
Leiden
Hook of Holland
Utrecht
Apeldoorn
Arnhem
Nijmegen
Rotterdam
Dordrecht
's Hertogenbosch
Tilburg
Eindhoven
Flushing
Zeebrugge
Ostend
Bruges
Ghent
Antwerp
FLANDERS
Kortrijk
Mechelen
Brussels
Leuven
Tourcoing
Roubaix
Lille
Maastricht
Liège
Namur
Mons
Charleroi
Meuse
Ardennes
Luxembourg
Oldenburg
Bremen
LOWER SAXONY
Lüneburg
Heath
Schwerin
Neu Brandenburg
Haff
Szczecin (Stettin)
Stargard Szczeciński
Koszalin
Słupsk
Piła
Gorzów Wielkopolski
Poznań
Noteć (Netze)
Warta (Warthe)
Zielona Góra
Głogów
Lubin
Legnica
Wałbrzych
Jelenia Góra
Osnabrück
Münster
Enschede
Teutoburger Wald
Herford
Bielefeld
NORTH RHINE-WESTPHALIA
Hanover (Hannover)
Hildesheim
Hameln
Brunswick
Wolfsburg
Salzgitter
Magdeburg
Halberstadt
Brocken
1142
Harz Mts.
Spandau
Charlottenburg
BERLIN
Brandenburg
Potsdam
Frankfurt
Dessau
Halle
Cottbus
Gelsenkirchen
Oberhausen
Duisburg
Essen
Bochum
Dortmund
Hamm
Hagen
Wuppertal
Remscheid
Krefeld
M. Gladbach
Düsseldorf
Cologne (Köln)
Aachen
Bonn
RHINE-LAND
Paderborn
Göttingen
Kassel
Rothaar G.
840
Siegen
Westerwald
Koblenz
Eifel
Leipzig
Erfurt
Gotha
Jena
Gera
Dresden
Görlitz
Karl Marx Stadt (Chemnitz)
Zwickau
Plauen
Reichenbach
Erz Gebirge
Usti nad Labem
Liberec
Riesen G. (Giant Mts.)
Sudeten Highlands
Thuringian Forest
Rhön
Vogels Berg
772
Fulda
950
Taunus
Wiesbaden
Frankfurt
Offenbach
Mainz
Hunsrück
PALATINATE
Worms
Trier
Kaiserslautern
SAAR
Ludwigshafen
Mannheim
Heidelberg
Darmstadt
Würzburg
Bamberg
Erlangen
Fichtel Geb.
1051
Fürth
Nuremberg (Nürnberg)
Saarbrücken
Karlsruhe
Heilbronn
BADEN
Pforzheim
Stuttgart
WURTTEMBERG
Regensburg
BAVARIA
Ingolstadt
Cheb
Plzeň (Pilsen)
Prague (Praha)
Kladno
BOHEMIA
Bohemian Forest
1457
1373
České Budějovice
Hradec Králové
Pardubice
Labe (Elbe)
Moravian Hts.
Brno (Brünn)
Olomouc
1492
Passau
Isar
Danube
Ulm
Augsburg
Munich (München)
Rosenheim
Salzburg
Linz
UPPER AUSTRIA
LOWER AUSTRIA
Steyr
Enns
St. Pölten
Krems
Vienna (Wien)
Wiener Neustadt
Semmering
985
Neusiedler
Reims
Épernay
Châlons sur Marne
CHAMPAGNE
Metz
Thionville
LORRAINE
Nancy
St. Dizier
Bar-le-Duc
Troyes
Aube
Seine
Marne
Chaumont
Épinal
Vosges
1424
Colmar
Strasbourg
ALSACE
Black Forest
Swabian Jura
Freiburg
Mulhouse
Basle
Schaffhausen
Winterthur
Zürich
Lake Constance
St. Gallen
Bregenz
VORARLBERG
Plateau de Langres
FRANCHE COMTÉ
Montbéliard
Belfort
Dijon
Côte d'Or
Besançon
BURGUNDY
Doubs
Saône
Chalon sur Saône
Mâcon
1012
Biel
Neuchâtel
Aarau
Solothurn
Luzern
Zug
Schwyz
Bern
Fribourg
Jura
Lausanne
Montreux
Interlaken
Geneva
L. Geneva
St. Gotthard P.
Simplon P.
Matterhorn
4478
4634
Maggiore
Lugano
Bellinzona
Chur
Rhine
Engadine
Bernina
4049
Innsbruck
Arlberg P.
TYROL
Brenner P.
1372
Gr. Glockner
3797
SALZBURG
Hohe Tauern
Carinthia
Drave
Villach
Klagenfurt
STYRIA
Graz
Mur
BURGENLAND
Szombathely
Zalaegerszeg
Maribor
Varaždin
Celje
Ljubljana
Zagreb
CROATIA
Karlovac
Sisak
Lyons
Rhône
Vienne
St. Étienne
Annecy
SAVOIE
Chambéry
Mt. Blanc
4807
Gt. St. Bernard P.
AOSTA
Little St. Bernard P.
2188
Gran Paradiso
4061
Graian Alps
Mt. Cenis P.
2083
Isère
Grenoble
Turin (Torino)
PIEDMONT
DAUPHINÉ
Mt. Pelvoux
4103
Valence
Montélimar
Mt. Viso
3841
Gap
Cuneo
Maritime Alps
3052
Col di Tenda
Digne
Durance
Nîmes
Avignon
Arles
PROVENCE
Verdon
Grasse
Aix
Marseilles
Nice
Cannes
Monaco & Monte Carlo
Riviera
Novara
Milan (Milano)
Como
L. Como
Bergamo
LOMBARDY
Brescia
Garda
Pavia
Ticino
Adda
Po
Piacenza
Cremona
Mantua (Mantova)
Alessandria
Asti
Tanaro
P. dei Giovi
472
Savona
Genoa (Genova)
Gulf of Genoa
Liguria
Apennines
EMILIA
ROMAGNA
Parma
Reggio
Modena
Bologna
Mte. Cimone
2165
Trebbia
Reno
Spezia
Pistoia
Prato
Florence (Firenze)
Lucca
Pisa
Ferrara
Ravenna
Forlì
Rubicone
Rimini
San Marino
Pesaro
Stelvio P.
Ortles
3899
Bolzano
TRENTINO
ALTO ADIGE
Adamello
3554
Trento
Dolomites
Marmolada
3342
Carnic Alps
FRIULI-VENEZIA GIULIA
Udine
Triglav
2863
Karawanken
Sava
Julian Alps
Karst
Vicenza
Verona
Padua (Padova)
Treviso
VENETO
Adige
Piave
Venice (Venezia)
Gulf of Venice
Trieste
Istria
Pula
Rijeka
SLOVENIA
Kapela
Krk
Cres
Lošinj
Velebit Planina
Pag
Dugi Otok
Zadar
ADRIATIC SEA
Una
Banja Luka
Dinara Pl.
1913
Troglav
Sana
BOSNIA AND HERCEGOVINA
Projection: Conical with two standard parallels
East from Greenwich
m
4000
3000
2000
1500
1000
400
200
0
200
m

1: 5 000 000

CENTRAL EUROPE POLITICAL
1: 25 000 000
DENMARK
Copenhagen
Hamburg
Amsterdam
Berlin
WEST GERMANY
EAST GERMANY
Bonn
Brussels
BELGIUM
LUX.
POLAND
Warsaw
U. S. S. R.
Kiev
Lvov
Prague
CZECHOSLOVAKIA
FRANCE
Bern
SWITZ.
Liechtenstein
AUSTRIA
Vienna
Budapest
HUNGARY
ROMANIA
Bucharest
Trieste
ITALY
Monaco
San Marino
Belgrade
YUGOSLAVIA
BULGARIA
Sofia
Rome
Gdansk Bay
Kaliningrad
Chernyakhovsk
LITHUANIA S.S.R.
Vilnius
Gdynia
Sopot
Gdańsk
Elbląg
Tczew
Olsztyn
Suwałki
Grodno
WHITE RUSSIA S.S.R.
Masurian Lakes Plateau
Grudziądz
Bydgoszcz
Toruń
Lomza
Ostrołęka
Białystok
Volkovysk
Slonim
Narew
Ciechanów
Inowrocław
Włocławek
Płock
Gniezno
Warsaw (Warszawa)
Siedlce
Biała Podlaska
Brest
Pripyat
POLAND
Konin
Kalisz
Łódź
Ostrów Wielkopolski
Sieradz
Pabianice
Tomaszów Mazowiecki
Piotrków
Pilica
Radom
Lublin
Chełm
Kovel
Pripyat Marshes
Uzh
Korosten
Desna
Kiev
Wrocław (Breslau)
Opole
Częstochowa
Kielce
Ostrowiec Świętokrzyski
Zamość
Vladimir Volynski
Lutsk
Rovno
Zhitomir
Shepetovka
Fastov
Belaya Tserkov
Zabrze
Bytom
Gliwice
Sosnowiec
Chorzów
Katowice
Tychy
Kraków
Tarnów
Rzeszów
Tarnobrzeg
Stalowa Wola
Berdichev
Kazatin
Starokonstantinov
Przemyśl
Lvov
Zolochev
Ternopol
Khmelnitskiy
Opava
Ostrava
Bielsko
Nowy Sącz
Krosno
Dukla P.
Drogobych
Dnestr
U. S. S. R.
UKRAINE S. S. R.
Vinnitsa
Zhmerinka
Uman
West Beskids
High Tatra
Carpathians
East Beskids
Žilina
Gottwaldov
White Mts.
Low Tatra
Prešov
Košice
Ivano-Frankovsk
Kamenets Podolski
Bug
Pervomaisk
SLOVAKIA
Banská Bystrica
Slovakian Ore Mts.
Uzhgorod
Mukachevo
Ruthenia
Pass of the Tartars
Chernovtsy
Khotin
Nitra
Trnava
Bratislava
Miskolc
Eger
Nyíregyháza
Satu Mare
Baia Mare
Pietrosu
Botoşani
Beltsy
MOLDAVIA S.S.R.
Kishinev
Bendery
Tiraspol
Kotovsk
Győr
Tatabánya
Bakony Forest
Székesfehérvár
Veszprém
L. Balaton
BUDAPEST
Újpest
Szolnok
Debrecen
Cegléd
HUNGARY
Kecskemét
Békéscsaba
Hódmezővásárhely
Oradea
Cluj
Bistrita
Suceava
Iaşi
Piatra Neamţ
Bacau
Odessa
Belgorod Dnestrovski
Tîrgu Mureş
Mt. Bihor
Transylvania
Miercurea Ciuc
Kaposvár
Szekszárd
Pécs
Subotica
Szeged
Arad
Alba-Iulia
Sfîntu Gheorghe
Focşani
Galaţi
Izmail
Sasyk
Drava
Senta
Sombor
Kikinda
Timişoara
Sibiu
Braşov
Transylvanian Alps
Mt. Negoiu
Omul
Brăila
Tulcea
Osijek
Novi Sad
Zrenjanin (Petrovgrad)
Hunedoara
Deva
Reşiţa
Banat
Retezat
Parîngu Mare
Rîmnicu Vîlcea
Ploieşti
Buzău
Danube
Dobrogea
Sremska Mitrovica
Vršac
Porta Orientalis
Tîrgu-Jiu
Tîrgovişte
Piteşti
Slobozia
Ialomita
Belgrade (Beograd)
Smederevo
Bela Crkva
Iron Gate
Turnu-Severin
Walachia
Bucharest (Bucureşti)
BLACK SEA
Constanta
Trajan's Wall
Tuzla
Craiova
Slatina
Arges
Calarasi
YUGOSLAVIA
Kragujevac
Sarajevo
Morava
Timok
Alexandria
Giurgiu
Ruse (Ruschuk)
Tolbukhin
BULGARIA
ROMANIA
1848
2305
2102
2518
2509
2535
2507
2655
1725
1881
2061
931
1346

BARENTS SEA
U.S.S.R.
Murmansk
Kandalaksha
Kandalaksha Gulf
Monchegorsk
Imandra Lake
Nikel
Kirkenes
Vadsø
Varanger Fjord
Tana Fjord
Lakse Fjord
Porsangen
North Cape
Hammerfest
Sørøya
Lopphavet
Kvænangen
Tromsø
Senja
Andfjord
Narvik
Ofotfjord
Vesterålen
Lofoten
Vestfjorden
Bodø
Fauske
Mo i Rana
Mosjøen
Vega
Namsos
Steinkjer
Levanger
Trondheim
N. TRØNDELAG
SØR-TRØNDELAG
Frohavet
Hitra
Kristiansund
Molde
Ålesund
Stadlandet
MØRE OG ROMSDAL
SOGN OG FJORDANE
Florø
Arctic Circle
NORWEGIAN SEA
FINNMARK
TROMS
NORDLAND
Inari
Inari L.
Ivalo
Sodankylä
Kemijoki
Kemijärvi
Rovaniemi
LAPPI
Kemi
Tornio
Haparanda
Oulu
Oulujärvi
Kajaani
OULU
Kokkola (Gamlakarleby)
Pietarsaari
Vaasa
VAASA
KESKI-SUOMI
Jyväskylä
KUOPIO
Kuopio
Iisalmi
Varkaus
MIKKELI
Mikkeli
Savonlinna
Joensuu
POHJOIS-KARJALA
Nurmes
Kuusamo
Kristinankaupunki
Kaskinen
GULF OF BOTHNIA
Kvarken
Torneälv
Torneträsk
Kiruna
Gällivare
Malmberget
Luleå
Boden
Piteå
Skellefteå
Umeå
Lycksele
Örnsköldsvik
Härnösand
Sundsvall
Hudiksvall
Kramfors
NORRBOTTEN
VÄSTERBOTTEN
VÄSTERNORRLAND
JÄMTLAND
Östersund
Storsjön
Storuman
Vilhelmina
Arvidsjaur
Jokkmokk
Stora Lulevatten
Kebnekaise
2122
Sarektjåkkå
2090
Uddjaur
Hornavan
Överkalix
Ångermanälven
Indalsälven
Ljusnan
Ljungan
Trondheimsfjorden
Orkla
Gaula
Røros
Femund
Dovrefjell
2286
Jotunheimen
ICELAND
At the same scale as main map
West from Greenwich
Arctic Circle
Grímsey
Siglufjörður
Eyjafjörður
Akureyri
Húsavík
Skjálfandafljót
Mývatn
Raufarhöfn
Vopnafjörður
Seyðisfjörður
Egilsstaðir
Stokksnes
Vatnajökull
Öræfajökull
2119
Hofsjökull
Langjökull
Mýrdalsjökull
Hekla
1491
Vestmannaeyjar
Surtsey
Reykjavík
Keflavík
Hafnarfjörður
Akranes
Borgarnes
Faxaflói
Snæfellsjökull
1446
Breiðafjörður
Ísafjörður
Ísafjarðardjúp
Bolungarvík
Drangajökull
Horn
Húnaflói
Skagafjörður
Sauðárkrókur
Blönduós
Selfoss
Reykjanes

1:6 000 000

50 0 50 100 150 200 250 km

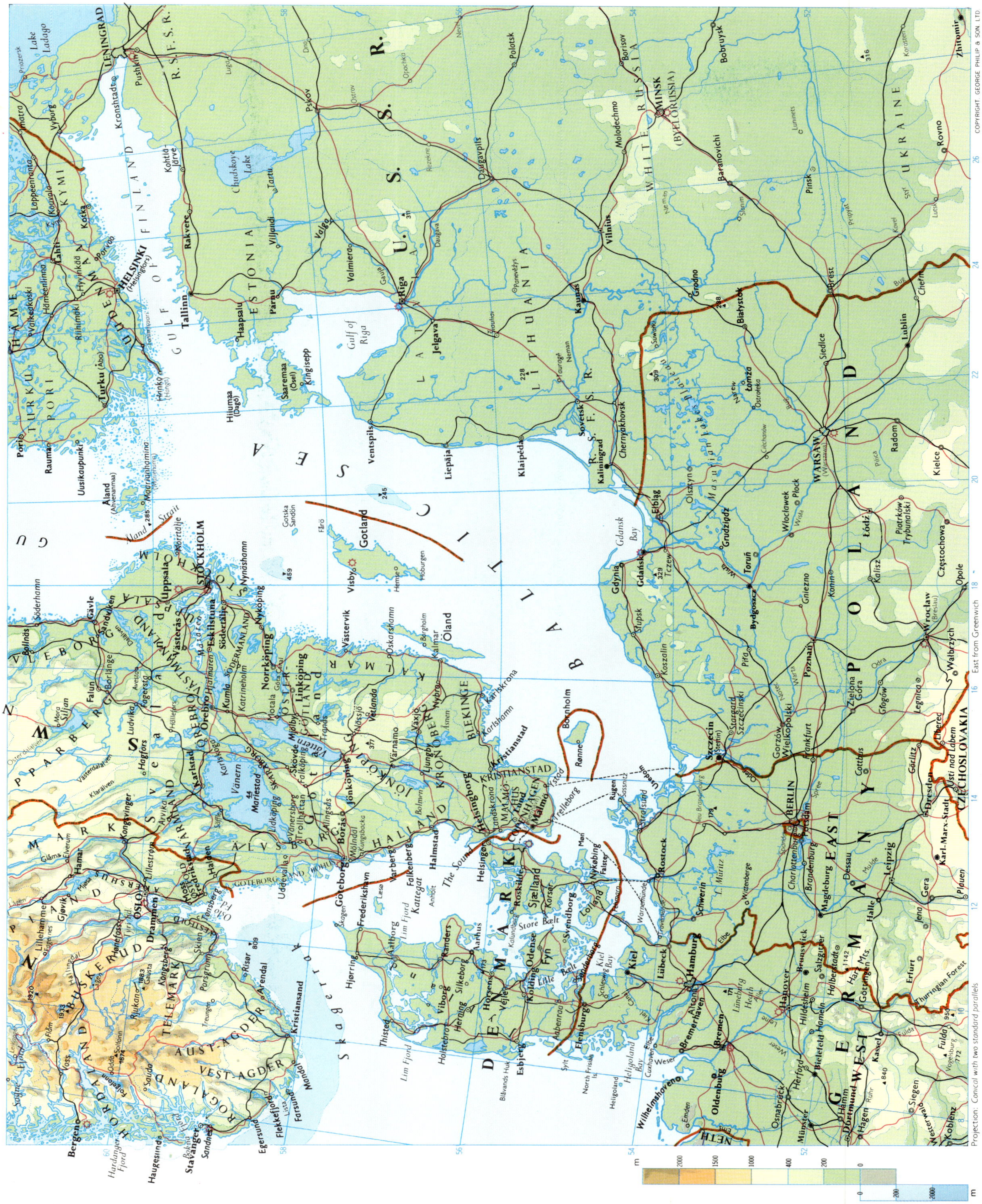

Vorkuta
Salekhard
Labytnangi
Berezovo
Ivdel
Krasnoturinsk
Serov
Sosva
Nizhniy Tagil
SVERDLOVSK
Pervouralsk
Zlatoust
Miass
Beloretsk
Magnitogorsk
Novotroitsk
Orsk
UFA
Sterlitamak
Salavat
Kumertau
Orenburg
Uralsk
Solikamsk
Berezniki
Kizel
Chusovoy
Lysva
PERM
Kungur
Votkinsk
Sarapul
Ustinov (Izhevsk)
Glazov
Kama
Chernikovsk
Birsk
Belaya
BASHKIR A.S.S.R.
Naberezhnyye
Brezhnev
Bugulma
Buguruslan
Buzuluk
Sorochinsk
KUYBYSHEV
Novokuybyshevsk
Tolyatti
Syzran
Kuybyshev Reservoir
TATAR A.S.S.R.
KAZAN
Zelenodolsk
Cheboksary
CHUVASH A.S.S.R.
Yoshkar Ola
MARI A.S.S.R.
UDMURT A.S.S.R.
Kirov
Slobodskoy
Vyatka
Nolinsk
Kotelnich
Sharya
Shakhunya
Vetluga
GORKI
Gorki Reservoir
Dzerzhinsk
Arzamas
Alatyr
Ulyanovsk
MORDOVIAN A.S.S.R.
Saransk
Penza
Serdobsk
Kuznetsk
Volsk
Balakovo
Engels
Saratov
Balashov
Tambov
Morshansk
Michurinsk
Lipetsk
Yelets
Voronezh
Kursk
Orel
Bryansk
Tula
Kaluga
Novomoskovsk
Ryazan
Kolomna
Serpukhov
Podolsk
MOSCOW
Zagorsk
Orekhovo-Zuyevo
Vladimir
Murom
Kovrov
Ivanovo
Kineshma
Kostroma
Yaroslavl
Rostov
Andropov (Rybinsk)
Rybinsk Reservoir
Cherepovets
Vologda
Bui
Neya
Kalinin
Kimry
Rzhev
Vyshniy Volochek
Valdai Hills
Novgorod
L. Ilmen
Staraya Russa
Velikiye Luki
Pskov
Luga
Smolensk
Vitebsk
Roslavl
Mogilev
Gomel
Chernigov
Bobruysk
MINSK
Baranovichi
Pinsk
Pripyat Marshes
Brest
Lutsk
Grodno
Vilnius
Kaunas
Siauliai (Shyaulyay)
Daugavpils
Polotsk
Orsha
Berezina
Dnepr
Desna
Sozh
WHITE RUSSIA (BYELORUSSIA)
LITHUANIA
LATVIA
ESTONIA
Riga
G. of Riga
Jelgava
Liepaja
Ventspils
Klaipeda (Memel)
Sovetsk
Kaliningrad (Königsberg)
R.S.F.S.R.
Neman
Bialystok
WARSAW (Warszawa)
POLAND
Lublin
Lomza
Bug
Tallinn
Tartu
Narva
Pärnu
Chudskoye L.
Hiiumaa
Saaremaa
Gulf of Finland
LENINGRAD
L. Ladoga
Novaya Ladoga
Volkhov
Lodeynoye Pole
Podporozhye
Vytegra
Beloye L.
Belozersk
Onega L.
Kondopoga
Petrozavodsk
Olonets
Svir
Sortavala
Priozersk
Medvezhyegorsk
Segozero
Povenets
KARELIAN A.S.S.R.
Belomorsk
Kem
Kuito L.
Top L.
Pya L.
Kandalaksha
Kandalaksha G.
White Sea
G. of Onega
Onega
Severodvinsk (Molotovsk)
Dvina B.
Arkhangelsk (Archangel)
N. Dvina
Plesetsk
Nyandoma
Konosha
Kotlas
Velikiy Ustyug
Velsk
Totma
Kharovsk
Sukhona
Koslan
Mikun
Syktyvkar
Vychegda
Zheleznodorozhny
Ukhta
Sosnogorsk
Troitsko-Pechorsk
Pechora
Ust Tsilma
Ust Usa
Inta
Usa
Arctic Circle
Naryan-Mar
Bolshezemelskaya Tundra
Malozemelskaya Tundra
Timan Ridge
G. of Pechora
Kolguyev
Cheshskaya B.
Kanin Pen.
Mezen
Karpogory
Pinega
C. Kanin Nos
Gremikha
Ponoi
Kola Pen.
Kirovsk
Monchegorsk
Imandra L.
Murmansk
Kola B.
Rybachi Pen.
Pechenga
Ural Mts.
Uvaly
RUSSIAN SOVIET FEDERATIVE SOCIALIST REPUBLIC
Narodnaya 1894
Telpos Iz 1617
1569
FINLAND
Inari L.
Kemijärvi
Kemi
Tornio
Oulu
Oulu L.
Kajaani
Kuopio
Pielinen L.
Joensuu
Savonlinna
Saimaa
Vyborg
Kotka
Lahti
Päijänne
Tampere
Pori
Turku
Helsinki
Hanko
Vaasa
Aland Is. (Ahvenanmaa)
Gulf of Bothnia
Stockholm
Söderhamn
Sundsvall
Umeå
Luleå
Kalix
Torne
Gällivare
Kiruna
Kebnekaise 2123
Narvik
Bodø
SWEDEN
NORWAY
LAPLAND
Angerman
Ume
Lule
Pite
Torne L.

1:10 000 000

100 0 100 200 300 400 km

Projection: Conical with two standard parallels

Division between Greeks and Turks in Cyprus, Turks to the North

Projection: Conical Orthomorphic with two standard parallels

1:20 000 000
200 0 200 400 600 800 km
C. Dezhneva (East C.)
Chukchi Sea
Wrangel I.
St. Lawrence I. (U.S.A.)
Gulf of Anadyr
East Siberian Sea
De Long Is.
New Siberian Is.
Faddeyev I.
New Siberia
Kotelny I.
Lyakhov Is.
Bolshoi I.
Dimitri Laptev Str.
Medvezhi Is.
Komsomolets I.
October Revolution I.
Bolshevik I.
Severnaya Zemlya
Boris Vilkitski Str.
OCEAN
Laptev Sea
Byrranga Mts.
Taimyr Pena.
L. Taimyr
Begichev I.
Nordvik
Tiksi
Chukot Range
Koryak Range
Kolyma Ra.
Cherskiy Ra.
Verkhoyansk Range
Verkhoyansk
Sredne Kolymsk
Magadan
Shelekhov Gulf
Penzhina G.
Gizhiga G.
Kamchatka Pena.
Bering Sea
Komandorskiye Is.
Petropavlovsk-Kamchatskiy
Sea of Okhotsk
Okhotsk
Dzhugdzhur Ra.
Central Siberian Plateau
Norilsk
Igarka
Arctic Circle
Yakutsk
Vilyuysk
Olekminsk
Lena
YAKUT A.S.S.R.
SOCIALIST REPUBLIC
Stanovoy Ra.
Sakhalin
Okha
Nikolayevsk
Yuzhno-Sakhalinsk
Kuril Islands
Sikhote Alin Ra.
Khabarovsk
Komsomolsk
Birobidzhan
Blagoveshchensk
Vladivostok
Nakhodka
Hokkaidō
Sapporo
Hakodate
Aomori
Honshū
Niigata
Kanazawa
Sea of JAPAN
Krasnoyarsk
Achinsk
Kansk
Bratsk
Kirensk
Eastern Sayan
Western Sayan
TUVA A.S.S.R.
Irkutsk
Angarsk
Ulan Ude
Chita
BURYAT A.S.S.R.
Yablonovyy Ra.
L. Baykal
Kyzyl
Ulan Bator (Ulaanbaatar)
MONGOLIA
GOBI
Hentiyn Nuruu
Manzhouli
Hulun Nur
Great Khingan
Qiqihar
Harbin
Manchuria
Jilin
Changchun
Shenyang (Mukden)
Fushun
Anshan
Dalian
Peking
Baotou
Inner Mongolia
PEOPLE'S REPUBLIC
North KOREA
Pyongyang
Wŏnsan
Chongjin
Seoul
South KOREA
Pusan
Boundaries of U.S.S.R.
Boundaries of S.S.R.
Boundaries of A.S.S.R.
COPYRIGHT. GEORGE PHILIP & SON. LTD.

1:50 000 000

500 0 500 1000 1500 2000 km

1:50 000 000

500 0 500 1000 1500 2000 km

ASIA : Climate and Natural Vegetation

1:100 000 000

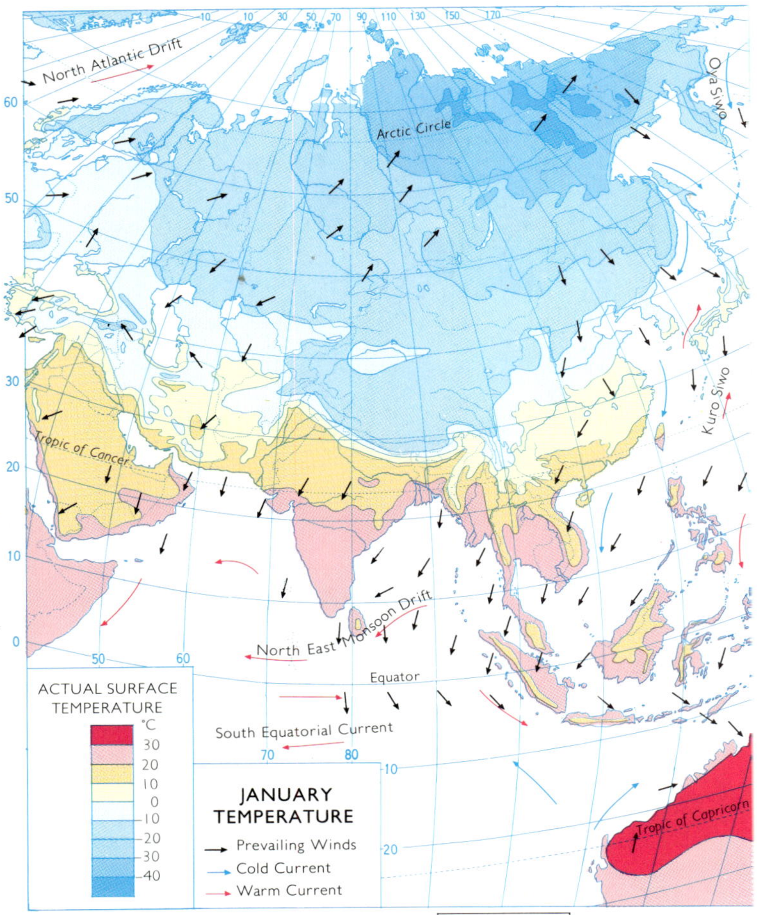

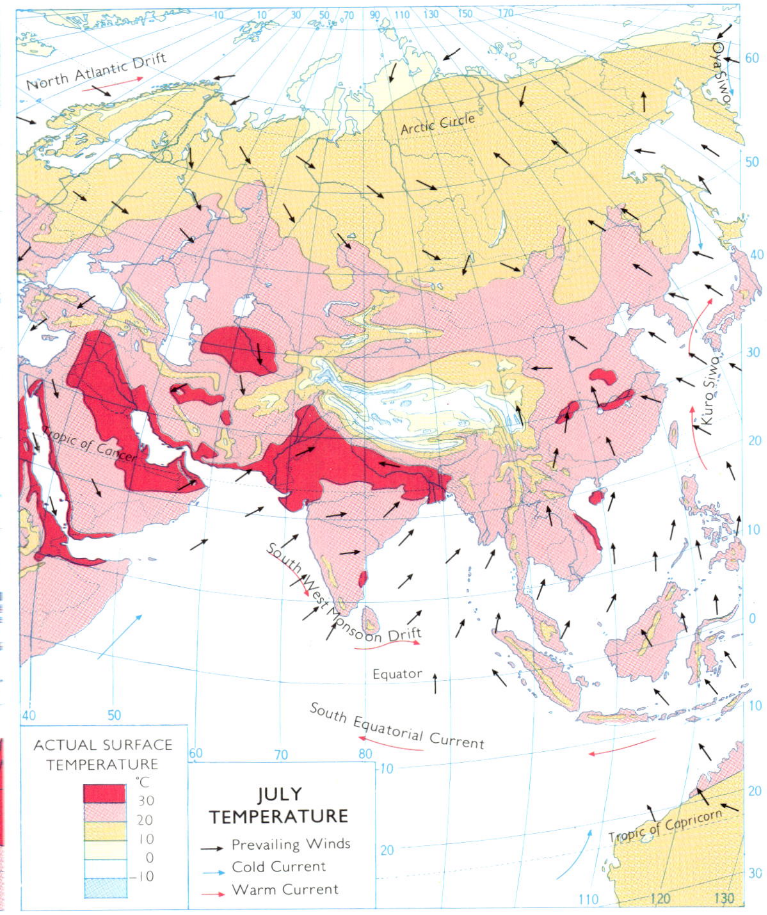

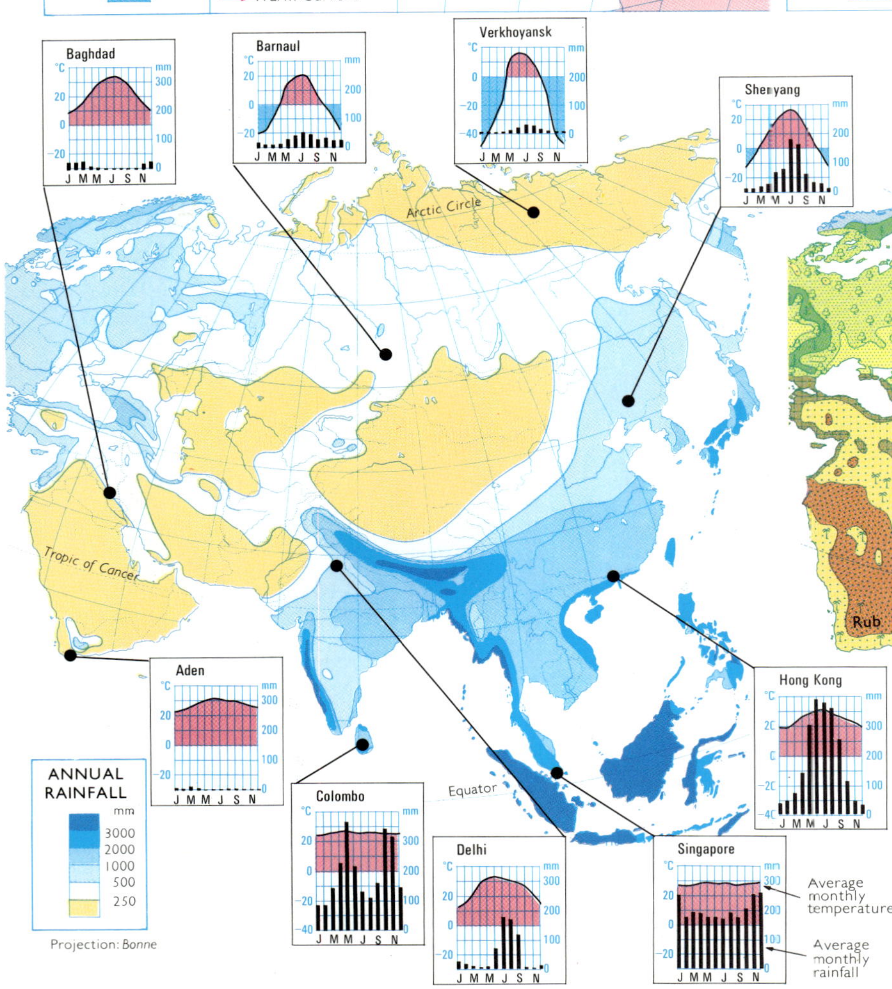

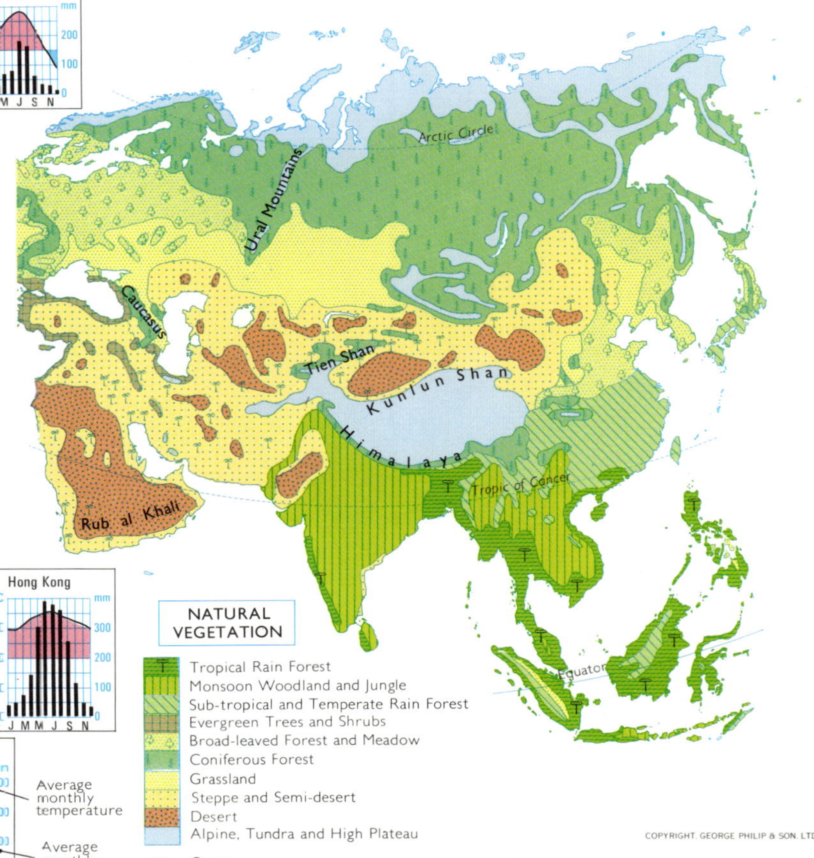

1:50 000 000

500 0 500 1000 1500 2000 km

	Population								Land			Agriculture		
	Total	Density	Birth Rate	Death Rate	Life Expectancy	Growth 1965-80	Growth 1980-88	Urban	Area	Arable	Forest	Agricultural Population	Index of Production	Food Intake
	th.	persons per km²	per th. popn.	per th. popn.	yrs.	av. % per annum	av. % per annum	%	th. km²	th. km²	th. km²	% of total popn.	1979-81 = 100	calories per day
Afghanistan	15513	24	48	22	37	2.4	2.6	22	648	81	19	57	99	2055
Bangladesh	115244	130	42	12	51	2.7	2.8	13	134	92	21	71	109	1927
Burma (Myanmar)	40162	61	31	10	60	2.3	2.2	24	658	101	324	49	146	2609
Cambodia	7869	45	41	17	48	0.3	2.9	12	177	31	134	71	173	2276
China	1083889	116	21	7	70	2.2	1.2	38	9326	970	1166	70	140	2630
Cyprus	686	76	19	8	76		1.1	53	9	2	1	22	96	3378
Hong Kong	5674	5674	13	5	76	2.1	1.5	93	1	0.1	0.1	1	60	2859
India	813990	274	32	11	58	2.3	2.1	27	2973	1689	671	68	133	2238
Indonesia	174832	97	27	11	61	2.3	2.1	27	1812	212	1215	51	138	2579
Iran	48555	30	43	12	63	3.2	3	53	1636	148	180	30	121	3313
Iraq	17657	41	43	8	64	3.4	3.6	72	434	55	19	23	136	2932
Israel	4444	222	23	7	76	2.8	1.7	91	20	4	1	5	115	3061
Japan	122433	330	11	6	78	1.2	0.6	77	371	47	251	8	102	2864
Jordan	3937	41	46	7	66	2.6	3.7	66	97	4	0.7	7	158	2991
Korea, North	21877	182	29	5	69	2.7	2.5	67	120	24	90	36	132	3151
Korea, South	42593	435	16	6	70	1.9	1.4	69	98	21	65	28	112	2907
Laos	3879	17	41	16	49	1.4	2.4	17	231	9	130	73	132	2391
Lebanon	2827	283	29	8	67	1.6	−0.01	83	10	3	0.8	11	129	2995
Malaysia	16921	51	29	6	70	2.5	2.6	40	329	44	196	35	165	2730
Mongolia	2086	1	39	8	64	3	2.9	51	1565	13	152	33	119	2807
Nepal	18053	132	40	15	51	2.4	2.7	9	137	23	23	92	125	2052
Pakistan	105677	136	33	8	55	3.1	3.1	31	779	208	31	51	140	2315
Philippines	59686	200	33	8	64	2.9	2.4	41	298	79	110	48	109	2372
Saudi Arabia	14016	7	42	8	64	4.6	3.7	75	2150	12	12	42	332	3004
Singapore	2639	4398	20	5	73	1.6	1.1	100	0.6	0.03	0.03	1	91	2840
Sri Lanka	16565	255	21	6	71	1.8	1.5	21	65	19	18	52	100	2401
Syria	11667	63	44	7	65	3.4	3.6	51	184	56	5	26	126	3260
Taiwan	19673	547	16	5	73		1.5	72	36	9	2	26	104	
Thailand	54469	106	22	7	65	2.7	1.9	21	512	201	144	66	120	2331
Turkey	53772	70	28	8	64	2.4	2.3	47	771	279	202	51	119	3229
Vietnam	66682	205	32	10	66	3.1	2.6	21	325	65	130	63	136	2297
Yemen, North	8742	45	48	16	46	2.8	2.7	23	195	14	16	65	132	2318
Yemen, South	2339	7	47	16	51	2	2.9	42	333	1	15	34	108	2299
U.S.S.R. †														
Oceania														
Australia	16506	2	15	7	76	1.8	1.4	86	7618	471	1060	6	114	3326
New Zealand	3623	14	17	8	75	1.3	1	84	269	5	73	10	93	3463
Papua New Guinea	3804	8	35	12	54	2.3	2.7	15	452	4	383	70	121	2205

† See statistics table for Europe.

Population. This is the United Nation's estimate for the mid-year 1988 (thousands)

Population Density. This is the quoted population total divided by the quoted land area (persons per square kilometre).

Birth Rates and Death Rates. These are the registered or United Nation's estimated rates per thousand population.

Life Expectancy. This figure indicates the number of years that a child born today can expect to live if the levels of death of today last throughout its life. The figure is the average of that for men and women. The figure for women is usually higher than that for men (U.K. Male 75, female 78 years).

Population Growth. This shows the average annual percentage change in population for two periods, 1965–1980 and 1980–1988.

Urbanization. This is the percentage of the total population living in urban areas. The definition of urban is that of the individual nation and usually includes quite small towns.

Land Area. This is the total area of the country minus the area covered by major lakes and rivers (thousand square kilometres).

Arable Land and Permanent Crops. This excludes fallow land but includes temporary pasture (thousand square kilometres).

Forest and Woodland. This includes natural and planted woodland and land recently cleared of timber which will be replanted (thousand square kilometres).

Agricultural Population. This is the percentage of the economically active population working in agriculture. It also includes those people working in forestry, hunting and fishing.

Index of Agricultural Production. The base period for this index is 1979–1981 and it shows the level of production in each country in 1988 in comparison with that of the earlier period. Only edible crops and meat are included.

Food Intake. The figures are the average intake per person in calories per day for the year 1986.

Trade		Education		Health	Energy	Consumer Price Index	G.N.P.		G.D.P.		Loans & Debt		
Imports	Exports	Primary	Secondary					Growth per capita	Part formed by Agric.	Part formed by Indust.			
US$ per capita	US$ per capita	% of age group	% of age group	Popn. per doctor	Consumption in kg of oil equiv. per capita	1980 = 100	US$ per capita	% per year 1965-88	%	%	end 1987 US$ millions	as % of G.N.P.	
91	36	18	6	6419	71				69	14			Afghanistan
150	62	60	18	6731	47	199	160	0.3	47	13	9432	49	Bangladesh
16	5	100	24	3743	73	190	200	2.3	51	10	4386	46	Burma (Myanmar)
					59				41	17			Cambodia
40	36	100	42	1000	525		290	5.2	31	49	27919	7	China
		99	90	746	1599	148	6260		7	16	1439	35	Cyprus
8541	8543	100	69	1075	1525	180	8070	6.2	0	29			Hong Kong
23	15	92	35	2521	208	201	300	1.8	30	30	41694	16	India
83	98	100	41	9464	216	199	450	4.5	26	33	47562	59	Indonesia
377	417	100	18	2780	955				26	36			Iran
420	511	99	52	1806	732				18	46			Iraq
3217	1907	99	79	345	1965	46447	6800	2.5	5	21	26332	87	Israel
1192	1870	100	96	663	3232	116	15760	4.2	3	41			Japan
684	236	99	79	1139	750	134	1560		9	28	3585	67	Jordan
				420	2165								Korea, North
961	1107	94	95	1166	1475	160	2690	6.4	11	43	23907	14	Korea, South
18	8	94	19	1362	37		170				833	165	Laos
665	209	100	56	667	871				9	12	496		Lebanon
739	1055	100	54	1935	771	130	1810	4.1	20	31	19377	56	Malaysia
		100	92	104	1181								Mongolia
32	8	79	25	30230	23	204	160	0.5	57	14	1060	34	Nepal
55	39	52	24	2941	207	129	350	2.5	23	28	13072	37	Pakistan
120	35	100	68	6700	241	289	590	1.7	24	33	23710	60	Philippines
1460	1650	71	44	688	3292	95	6200	4	4	50			Saudi Arabia
12308	10834	100	71	1309	4436	118	7940	7.2	1	38			Singapore
126	84	100	66	5516	160	234	400	3	27	27	3956	56	Sri Lanka
218	116	100	60	1309	900	538	1640	3.3	27	19	4678	24	Syria
1754	2721	100	95	1016	73	174			6	40			Taiwan
238	214	99	29	6294	330	139	850	3.9	17	23	17685	31	Thailand
263	190	100	44	1381	763	528	1210	2.6	17	36	30697	42	Turkey
28	16	100	43	995	88		300		29	17			Vietnam
150	2	79	15	6268	100		590		28	17	2166	39	Yemen, North
620	175	66	19	4344	707		420		16	23	1689	171	Yemen, South
													† U.S.S.R.
													Oceania
1776	1532	100	96	436	4821	176	11100	1.8	4	33	501	0.3	Australia
2002	1982	100	84	576	4211	245	7750	0.9	8	31	84	0.5	New Zealand
321	308	60	11	6160	229	158	700	0.8	34	26	2218	64	Papua New Guinea

Bahrain, Land 0.6/Popn. 445; Bhutan 47/1370; Brunei 5.3/235; Kuwait 17.8/1919; Macau 0.02/429; Maldives 0.3/200; Oman 212.5/1402; Qatar 11/332; U.A.E. 83.6/1500.
American Samoa 0.2/36; Cocos Is. 0.01/0.6; Cook Is. 0.2/20; Fed. States of Micronesia 0.7/90; Fiji 18.3/722; Fr. Polynesia 3.7/179; Guam 0.6/128; Kiribati 0.7/66; Nauru 0.02/8; New Caledonia 18.8/158; Niue I. 0.26/2; Norfolk I. 0.036/2; Northern Marianas 0.5/17; Palau 0.5/12; Samoa 2.9/163; Solomon Is. 27.5/293; Tokelau 0.01/2; Tonga 0.7/100; Tuvalu 0.2/8; Vanuatu 14.8/150; Wallis & Futuna 0.2/14.

Trade. The trade figures are for the year 1988. The total trade figures have been divided by the population and are a measure of the country's external trade (U.S. $ per capita).

Education. The ages of primary school are taken to be 6–11 years and secondary school 12–17 years. The percentage of total school age group in this type of education is shown.

Energy. All forms of energy have been converted to their equivalent in oil. Firewood and other traditional forms used in developing countries are not included and so the energy consumption in those countries is understated (kilograms of oil equivalent per capita).

Consumer Price Index. The base year is 1980 which is 100 and the level of consumer prices in 1987 or 1988 are shown in relation to the base year. It is a measure of inflation.

G.N.P. (Gross National Product) This figure is an estimate of the average production per person measured in U.S. dollars and for 1988. The G.N.P. measures the value of goods and services produced in a country, plus the balance, positive or negative, of income from abroad, for example investments, interest on capital, money returned from foreign labour, etc. The rate of change is the average annual percentage change during the period 1965–1988 in the G.N.P. The G.D.P. (Gross Domestic Product) is the G.N.P. minus the foreign balances. The adjoining two columns show the percentage contribution to the G.D.P. made by the agricultural and mining and manufacturing sectors.

Loans and Debts. This figure in millions of U.S. dollars shows the external public debt ar the end of 1988. This is then shown as a percentage of the annual G.N.P. The figures in red show official development assistance made by the developed countries and also as a percentage of the donor country's G.N.P.

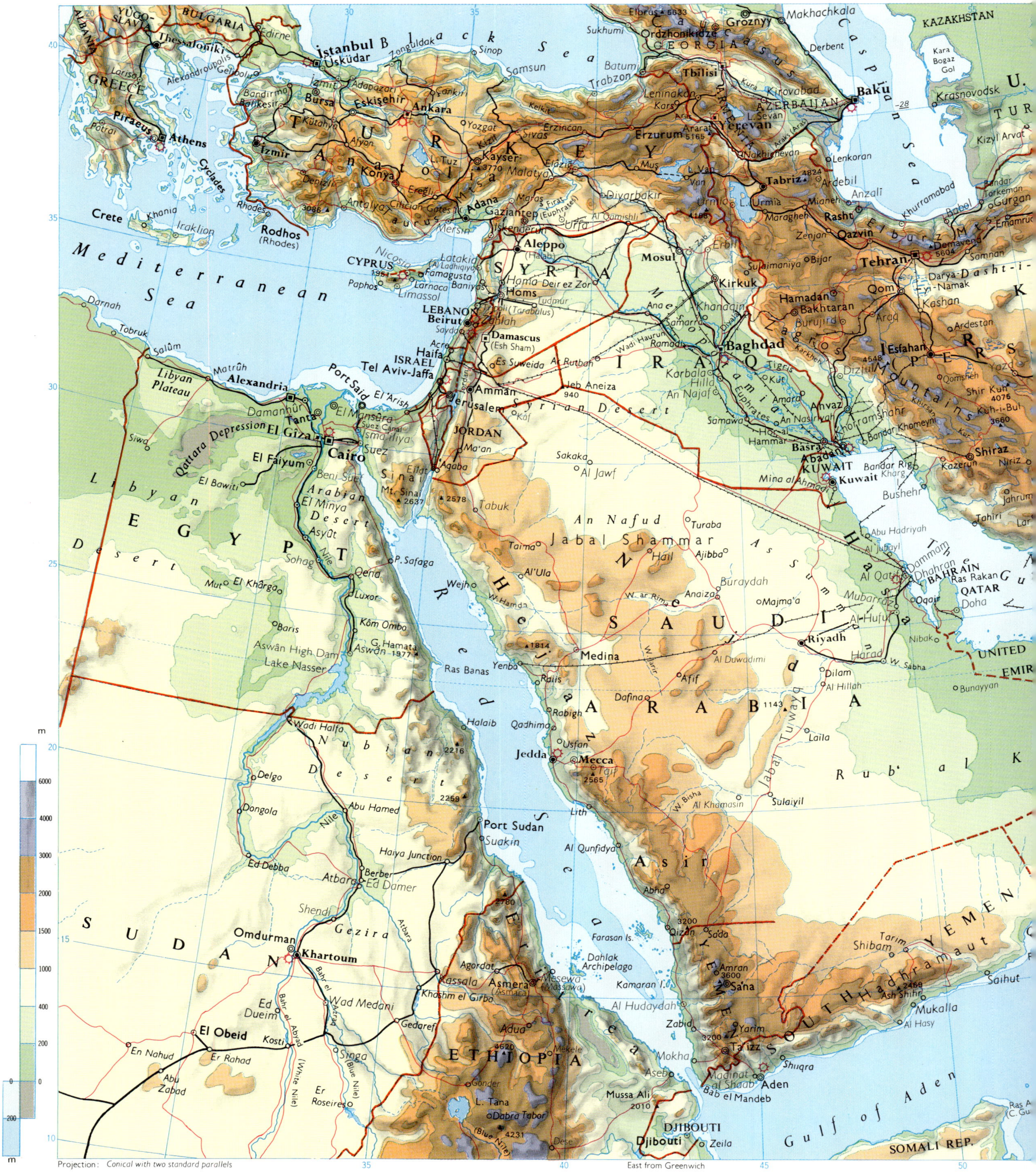

Projection: Conical with two standard parallels East from Greenwich

1:15 000 000

100 0 100 200 300 400 500 600 km

THE HOLY LAND

Armistice boundaries between Arab States and Israel, 1949–1974

1:1 500 000

10 0 10 20 30 40 50 km

Projection: *Conical with two standard parallels*

1:10 000 000

100 0 100 200 300 400 km

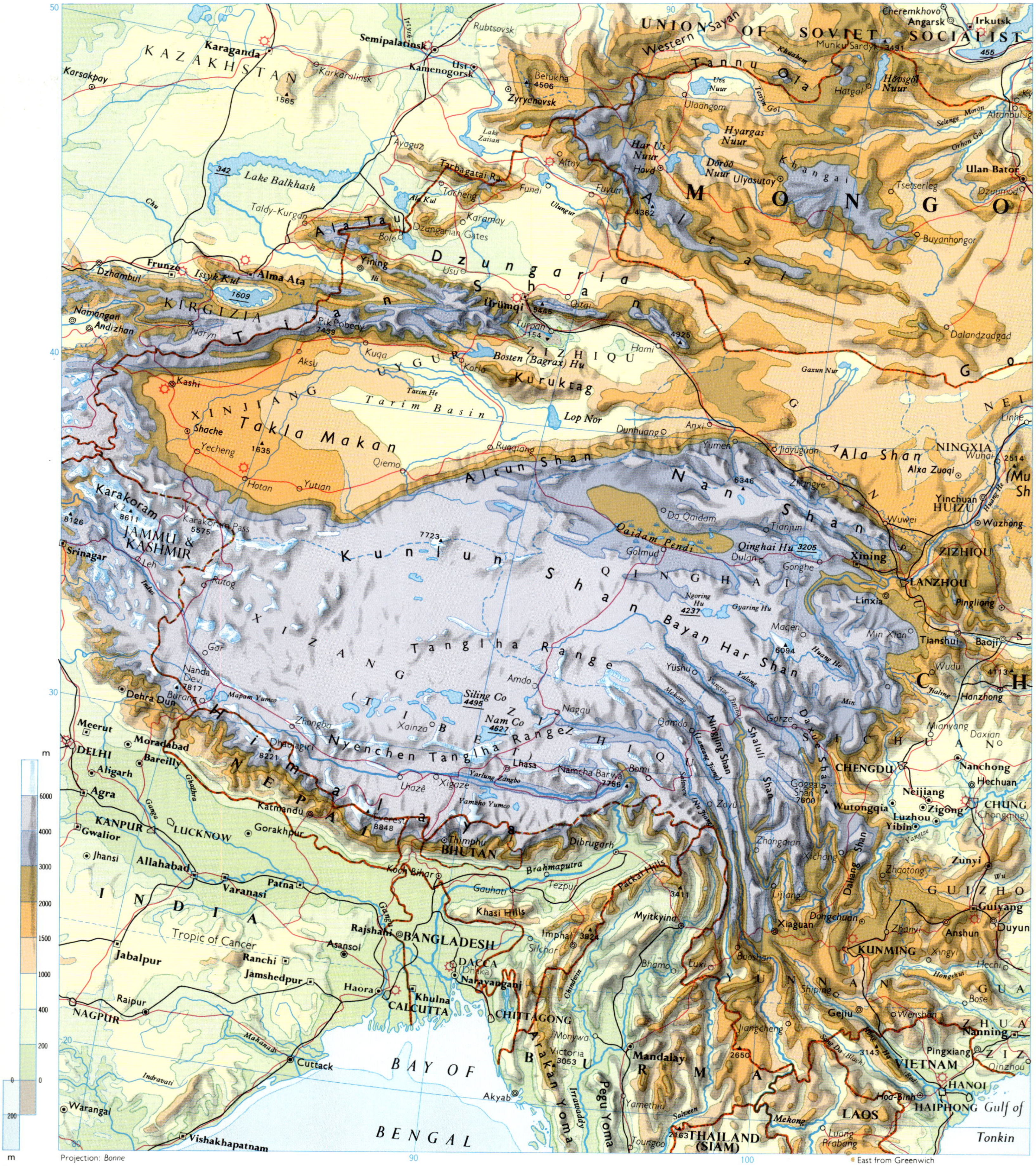

Projection: Bonne

East from Greenwich

1:15 000 000

100 0 100 200 300 400 500 600 km
Lake Baykal
REPUBLICS
Chita
Ulan Ude
Yablonovyy Range
Nerchinsk
Borzya
Argun
Manzhouli
Hulun Nur
Hailar
Buir Nur
Choybalsan
Kerulen
Hentiyn Nuruu
L I A
Sayshand
Dzamin Üüd
Erenhot
Abagnar Qi
INNER MONGOLIA
b i
Great Khingan Mts.
Oroqen Zizhiqi
Nenjiang
Butha Qi
Horqin Youyi Qianqi
HEILONGJIANG
Amur
Svobodny
Blagoveshchensk
Aihui
Little Khingan Mts.
Bei'an
Qiqihar
Anda
Suihua
Yichun
Hegang
Jiamusi
Shuangyashan
Tao'an
HARBIN
Manchuria
Mudanjiang
Jixi
Mishan
Lake Khanka
JILIN
Jilin
CHANGCHUN
Shuangliao
Tongliao
Siping
Liaoyuan
Songhua Lake
Yanji
1949
Chifeng
Fuxin
Chaoyang
Liaoyang
FUSHUN
SHENYANG
Mukden
Benxi
ANSHAN
Jinzhou
Yingkou
Dandong
Tonghua
2744
Chengde
Zhangjiakou
Jining
Hohhot
Baotou
Datong
Xuanhua
Qinghuangdao
Tangshan
G. of Liaodong
Liaodong Pen.
Korea Bay
PYONGYANG
DALIAN (Lüda)
PEKING (Beijing)
Baoding
TIENTSIN (Tianjin)
Cangzhou
G. of Chihli (Bo Hai)
HEBEI
Shijiazhuang
Yangquan
3053
TAIYUAN
Ordos
Us
GREAT WALL
SHANXI
Yuci
Fenyang
Yan'an
Changzhi
Handan
Anyang
Dezhou
Huang He
JINAN
Tai'an
Zibo
Weifang
Ye Xian
Yantai
Weihai
SHANDONG
QINGDAO
Jining
Xinxiang
Tongchuan
Kaifeng
Luoyang
Sanmenxia
Xianyang
XIAN (Xi'an)
ZHENGZHOU
Pingdingshan
Nanyang
HENAN
Shangqiu
Shangshui
Xuzhou
Lianyungang
Qingjiang
Grand Canal
JIANGSU
Bengbu
Huainan
Hongze Hu
Ankang
Han Shui
Zhumadian
Daba Shan
Xiangfan
Dabie Shan
Hefei
ANHUI
NANKING (Nanjing)
Zhenjiang
Changzhou
Nantong
Wuxi
Suzhou
SHANGHAI
Wuhu
Tongling
Anqing
HUBEI
Wanxian
Yichang
Shashi
WUHAN
Huangshi
Hangzhou
Hangzhou Wan
Shaoxing
Ningbo
ZHEJIANG
Jinhua
Tunxi
Jiujiang
Jingdezhen
Poyang L.
Dongting L.
Changde
Nanchang
Shangrao
Yiyang
Changsha
HUNAN
Xiangtan
Zhuzhou
JIANGXI
Wuyi Shan
2120
Wenzhou
2683
Shaoyang
Hengyang
Jian
Nanping
Sanming
Fuzhou
Ganzhou
FUJIAN
Quanzhou
Nan Ling
Guilin
Shaoguan
Zhangzhou
Xiamen (Amoy)
Liuzhou
Wuzhou
GUANGDONG
Mei Xian
Chao'an
Shantou
CANTON (Guangzhou)
Foshan
Jiangmen
HONG KONG (Br.)
Macau (Port.)
Beihai
Maoming
Zhanjiang
Leizhou Penin.
Hainan Str.
Haikou
Hainan
1879
Formosa Strait
Chilung
TAIPEI
Taichung
Yu Shan
3997
Chiai
TAIWAN
Tainan
KAOHSIUNG
Batan Is.
Babuyan Is.
SOUTH CHINA SEA
Chegdomyn
Komsomolsk
Aleksandrovsk
Amur
L. Bolon
Birobidzhan
Khabarovsk
Sikhote Alin Ra.
Bikin
Ussuriysk
Vladivostok
Nakhodka
Chongjin
NORTH KOREA
Yalu
Hungnam
Wŏnsan
Haeju
Kaesong
SEOUL
INCHON
SOUTH
Taejon
TAEGU
PUSAN
Kwangju
Masan
1915
Cheju Do
1950
Korea Str.
YELLOW SEA
SEA OF JAPAN
Sakhalin
Poronaysk
C. Terpeniya
Yuzhno-Sakhalinsk
La Perouse Str.
Wakkanai
Asahigawa
2290
Hokkaido
Otaru
SAPPORO
Kushiro
C. Erimo
Hakodate
Tsugaru Strait
Aomori
Hachinohe
Morioka
Akita
Honshu
Sado
Niigata
Sendai
Koriyama
Utsunomiya
Kanazawa
Toyama
TOKYO
KAWASAKI
YOKOHAMA
NAGOYA
Fuji-san
3776
Yokosuka
Shizuoka
Hamamatsu
KYOTO
OSAKA
KOBE
Sakai
Wakayama
Okayama
Hiroshima
Shimonoseki
KITAKYUSHU
FUKUOKA
Sasebo
Nagasaki
Kumamoto
Kyushu
Kagoshima
Tanega
Shikoku
Kochi
Matsuyama
JAPAN
Amami-ō-Shima
Ryukyu Islands
Okinawa
Naha
Sakashima Gunto
EAST CHINA SEA
PACIFIC OCEAN
Tropic of Cancer
110
120
130
140
50
40
30
20

1:7 500 000

50 0 50 100 150 200 250 300 km
Sea of Okhotsk
HOKKAIDO
Wakkanai
Rebun
Rishiri
Teshio
Otoineppu
Monbetsu
Shibetsu
Kitami
Abashiri
Rumoi
Asahigawa
Daisetsu 2290
Nemuro Str.
Nemuro
Kushiro
Obihiro
Tokachi 2052
Iwamisawa
Otaru Bay
Otaru
Sapporo
Tomakomai
Mombetsu
Urakawa
C. Erimo
C. Kamui
Setana
Okushiri
Uchiura Bay
Muroran
Esashi
Hakodate
C. Yesan
Tsugaru Strait
C. Shiriya
Matsumae
Mutsu
Aomori
Hirosaki
Hachinohe
Odate
Noshiro
C. Oga
Akita
Morioka
Miyako
Hanamaki
Kitakami
Ichinoseki
Sakata
Tsuruoka
Mogami
Ishinomaki
Yamagata
Sendai
Sado
Niigata
Shibata
Yonezawa
Fukushima
Agano
Bandai 1819
C. Suzu
Nagaoka
Aizuwakamatsu
Koriyama
Tajima
Iwaki
Nanao
Toyama Bay
Takada
Nikko
Hitachi
Takaoka
Kanazawa
Toyama
Nagano
Maebashi
Kiryu
Utsunomiya
Tochigi
Mito
Tsuchiura
Oki Is.
Fukui
Matsumoto
Ueda
Takasaki
Takayama
Ontake 3063
Kawagoe
Omiya
Tone
Choshi
C. Kyo
Wakasa Bay
Tsuruga
Kofu
Kawaguchi
Ichikawa
TOKYO
Chiba
Kawasaki
Yokohama
Yokosuka
Fuji-San 3776
Fujisawa
C. Hino
Matsue
Tottori
Izumo
Yonago
Maizuru
Biwa
Gifu
Ichinomiya
Nagoya
Numazu
Shimizu
Shizuoka
Ito
Tateyama
O-Shima
Hamada
Masuda
Tsuyama
Okayama
Kurashiki
Fukuyama
Himeji
Amagasaki
Kobe
Kyoto
Otsu
Yokkaichi
Okazaki
Tsu
Toyohashi
Hamamatsu
Ise-Wan
Akashi
Osaka
Sakai
Nara
Hiroshima
Hagi
Kure
Tokuyama
Takamatsu
Tokushima
Kishiwada
Wakayama
Shimonoseki
Ube
Suo Bay
Inland Sea
Niihama
Matsuyama
SHIKOKU
Kii Channel
Shingu
C. Shio
Kochi
C. Muroto
Uwajima
Yawatahama
C. Ashizuri
Bungo Channel
Kitakyushu
Fukuoka
Iki
Tsushima
Tsushima Strait
KOREA STRAIT
Sasebo
Kurume
Beppu
Oita
Aso
Kuju 1787
Nagasaki
Fukue
Kumamoto
Yatsushiro
KYUSHU
Nobeoka
Amakusa
Sendai
Miyazaki
Kagoshima
Miyakonojo
Kanoya
Osumi Channel
Osumi Islands
Tanega
Yaku
Kuchinoerabu-Jima
Tokara Channel
Nakano
Suwanose
Hachijo
Aoga
SEA OF JAPAN
PACIFIC OCEAN
CHINA
U. S. S. R.
NORTH KOREA
SOUTH KOREA
Lake Khanka
Mudanjiang
Spassk-Dalni
Dalnegorsk
Sikhote Alin
Ussuriysk
Yanji
Vladivostok
Nakhodka
Petra Velikogo Bay
Chongjin
Tanchon
Samchok
Ullung Do
Pusan
RYUKYU ISLANDS
Continuation southwards in same scale
Tokara Ch.
Yaku
Nakano
Suwanose
Amami
Tokuno
Okinoerabu
Okinawa-Shoto
Okinawa
Kerama
Naha
Miyako
Yaeyama
Ishigaki
Iriomote
7507
PACIFIC OCEAN
m
1500
1000
400
200
0
200
m
Projection: Bonne
East from Greenwich
130
135
140
145
125
45
40
35
30
25

1:15 000 000

100 0 100 200 300 400 500 600 km

EUROPE
Leningrad
Moskva
Volga
Sverdlovsk
U. S. S. R.
Tomsk
Novosibirsk
Irkutsk
Ozero Baykal
Chita
Lena
Okhotsk
Sea of Okhotsk
Kamchatka
Komandorskie Is. (U.S.S.R.)
Petropavlovsk
Bering Sea
Andreanov Is.
Aleutian Is
Aleutian Trench
7822
Semipalatinsk
Blagoveshchensk
Amur
G. of Sakhalin
Sakhalin
Khabarovsk
L. Balkhash
Ulan Bator
MONGOLIA
Altai
Manchuria
Harbin
Changchun
Shenyang
Vladivostok
Hakodate
La Perouse Strait
Kuril Is.
10,542
Kuril Trench
Emperor Seamount Chain
7168
Aral Sea
Alma Ata
Urumqi
ASIA
Tashkent
Peking
Tientsin
Taiyuan
Dalian
KOREA
Seoul
Sea of Japan
JAPAN
Sendai
TOKYO
Yokohama
8412
Fuji-san 3776
Kyoto
Nagoya
Osaka
Shikoku
Kyushu
Japan Trench
10,554
AFGHANISTAN
Kabul
Srinagar
Kunlun
Lanzhou
Huang
Xian
CHINA
Nanking
Wuhan
Yellow Sea
SHANGHAI
Qingdao
Kitakyushu
Lahore
PAKISTAN
TIBET
Mt. Everest 8848
Lhasa
Himalaya
NEPAL
Chungking
Changsha
Yangtze
Delhi
Kanpur
Brahmaputra
Fuzhou
East China Sea
Taipei
Ryukyu Is.
South Honshu Ridge
Bonin Is.
Volcano Is.
Minami-Tori-Shima (Marcus I.)
6603
Midway Is.
Hawaii
Lisianski I.
Ganges
Calcutta
BANGLADESH
Dacca
Kunming
Canton
MACAU (Port.)
HONG KONG
Taiwan (Formosa)
INDIA
BURMA
Mandalay
Irrawaddy
Salween
Hanoi
Chiengmai
Hyderabad
Bay of Bengal
Rangoon
THAILAND
VIETNAM
Hainan
C. Engano
Marcus Necker Ridge
Wake I. (U.S.)
NORTHERN MARIANAS (U.S.)
Saipan
GUAM (U.S.)
Mariana Trench
11,022
PACIFIC
Bangkok
CAMBODIA
Manila
PHILIPPINES
Madras
Andaman Is.
Mindoro
Samar
10,497
Bikini Atoll
MARSHALL IS.
Enewetak Atoll
International Date Line
Gulf of Thailand
Phnom Penh
Ho Chi Minh City
South China Sea
Palawan
Sulu Sea
Mindanao
Mindanao Trench
Yap
Micronesia
FEDERATED STATES OF MICRONESIA
Truk
Pohnpei
SRI LANKA
Colombo
Nicobar Is.
BELAU (U.S.)
Caroline Islands
Jaluit
Butaritari
Gilbert Is.
Baker I. (U.S.)
4101
SABAH
BRUNEI
Kuala Lumpur
PEN. MALAYSIA
MALAYSIA
SARAWAK
SINGAPORE
Celebes Sea
Moluccas
Halmahera
Melanesia
NAURU
Banaba
Sumatra
Borneo
Celebes
INDONESIA
Buru
Ceram
Irian Jaya
PAPUA NEW GUINEA
Bismarck Arch.
New Ireland
Admiralty Is.
Abariringa
KIRIBATI
Palembang
Java Sea
Jakarta
Ujung Pandang
Flores Sea
Banda Sea
5029
7440
Rabaul
New Britain
9103
SOLOMON IS.
Honiara
Guadalcanal
TUVALU (Ellice Is.)
Tokelau Is.
Sunda Strait
Surabaya
Java
Bali
Sumbawa
Flores
Sumba
Timor
Arafura Sea
Torres Strait
Port Moresby
Lae
Sta. Cruz I.
9165
Christmas I. (Austral.)
Java Trench
7450
Sunda Islands
C. Arnhem
C. York
Darwin
G. of Carpentaria
Louisiade Arch. (Austral.)
Rotuma
Wallis & Futuna (Fr.)
WESTERN SAMOA
Apia
Cocos (Keeling) Is. (Austral.)
INDIAN OCEAN
Cairns
Coral Sea
VANUATU
FIJI
Vanua Levu
Viti Levu
Suva
Tonga Trench
NORTHERN TERRITORY
Mt. Isa
Townsville
Chesterfield Is.
7570
N.W. Cape
AUSTRALIA
Great Divide
Rockhampton
New Caledonia (Fr.)
Nouméa
Loyalty Is.
TONGA
Friendly Is.
10,882
Alice Springs
WESTERN AUSTRALIA
QUEENSLAND
Brisbane
Lord Howe Rise
Norfolk I. (Aust.)
Kermadec Is. (N.Z.)
Kermadec Trench
10,047
L. Eyre
SOUTH AUSTRALIA
Darling
Perth
NEW SOUTH WALES
Sydney
Lord Howe I. (Aust.)
Great Australian Bight
Adelaide
Murray
Canberra
Mt. Kosciusko 2230
VICTORIA
Melbourne
Tasman Sea
Auckland
NEW ZEALAND
Cook Strait
Wellington
Mid-Indian Ridge
Amsterdam I. (Fr.)
St. Paul I. (Fr.)
Bass Strait
TASMANIA
Hobart
Mt. Cook 3764
Christchurch
Chatham Is. (N.Z.)
Dunedin
Invercargill
Crozet Is. (Fr.)
Kerguelen (Fr.)
Bounty Is. (N.Z.)
Antipodes Is. (N.Z.)
Auckland Is. (N.Z.)
Campbell I. (N.Z.)
Macquarie Is. (Austral.)
Heard Is. (Aust.)
Projection: Mollweide's Homolographic
East from Greenwich
m
6000
4000
2000
1000
200
0
200
2000
4000
6000
8000

ALASKA
6050
Bristol Bay
Gulf of Alaska
Juneau
Prince of Wales I.
Prince Rupert
Kitimat
Queen Charlotte Is.
Rocky Mountains
CANADA
Edmonton
Hudson Bay
L. Winnipeg
NORTH AMERICA
Labrador
Vancouver
Vancouver I.
Victoria
Calgary
Regina
Winnipeg
St. Lawrence
NORTH
Newfoundland
Seattle
Missouri
L. Superior
Montréal
Quebec
Pr. Edward I.
Portland
Boise
Snake
Minneapolis
L. Huron
Ottawa
L. Michigan
Toronto
L. Ontario
Saint John
Boston
C. Sable
CHICAGO
L. Erie
Buffalo
Detroit
Pittsburgh
NEW YORK
Philadelphia
C. Mendocino
Salt Lake City
Denver
Kansas
St. Louis
Cincinnati
Appalachian Mts.
Baltimore
Washington
ATLANTIC
Colorado
San Francisco
4418
UNITED STATES
Memphis
Mississippi
Oklahoma
Atlanta
C. Hatteras
6741
Los Angeles
San Diego
Dallas
Ciudad Juarez
Jacksonville
Bermuda (U.K.)
Houston
New Orleans
San Antonio
6225
MEXICO
Sierra Madre
Gulf of California
Gulf of Mexico
Miami
Florida Strait
OCEAN
BAHAMAS
Laysan I.
Hawaiian Ridge
Hawaiian Is. (U.S.)
Tropic of Cancer
Monterrey
Havana
Oahu
Honolulu
Hawaii
Yucatan Channel
CUBA
West Indies
Hispaniola
9200
Revilla Gigedo Is. (Mexico)
Guadalajara
México
Mérida
7680
JAMAICA
HAITI
DOM. REP.
Puebla
5700
Kingston
PUERTO RICO
Leeward Is.
Johnston I. (U.S.)
PACIFIC
Acapulco
BELIZE
HONDURAS
Caribbean Sea
N.W. Christmas Island Ridge
GUATEMALA
Guatemala
6662
Salvador
EL SALVADOR
NICARAGUA
Managua
BARBADOS
Windward Is.
TRINIDAD & TOBAGO
CENTRAL AMERICA
Barranquilla
Maracaibo
Clipperton I. (Fr.)
San José
COSTA RICA
Colón
Panama
PANAMA
Canal
Caracas
Orinoco
VENEZUELA
Palmyra Is. (U.S.)
Teraina
Tabuaeran
Kiritimati
Cocos I.
Medellín
Bogota
Cali
COLOMBIA
OCEAN
Line Islands
Jarvis I. (U.S.)
Equator
Galápagos (Ecuador)
Quito
ECUADOR
Guayaquil
Manaus
Amazon
Enderbury I.
Phoenix Is.
KIRIBATI
Malden I.
Starbuck I.
Iquitos
C. Pariñas
BRAZIL
East Pacific Ridge
Marquesas Is.
(N.Z.)
Tongareva
Penrhyn Is.
Caroline I.
Trujillo
SOUTH
Manihiki
Vostok I.
Flint I.
6369
PERU
Lima
Pukapuka
Suwarrow Is.
AMERICA
Leeward Is.
Cuzco
Tutuila
AMER. SAMOA (U.S.)
Cook Islands (N.Z.)
Society Is.
Tuamotu Archipelago
L. Titicaca
Illampu & Ancohuma
6550
Arequipa
La Paz
Windward Is.
Tahiti
6866
BOLIVIA
Niue (N.Z.)
Austral
Manuae
FRENCH POLYNESIA
Tuamotu Ridge
Peru-Chile Trench
ANDES
Iquique
Rarotonga
Austral Seamount Chain
Pitcairn I. (U.K.)
Tropic of Capricorn
PARAGUAY
8050
Antofagasta
Tubuai Is. (Austral Is.)
Ducie I (U.K.)
Sala-y-Gomez (Chile)
San Félix (Chile)
Asunción
Easter Is. (Chile)
San Ambrosio (Chile)
Tucumán
Rapa Iti
Pto. Alegre
Pacific-Antarctic Ridge
Arch. de Juan Fernández (Chile)
6960
Córdoba
Rosario
URUGUAY
Valparaiso
Santiago
Buenos Aires
Montevideo
Río de la Plata
Chile Rise
Concepción
ARGENTINA
Patagonia
SOUTH ATLANTIC OCEAN
Chonos Arch.
G. of Penas
6212
Falkland Is. (U.K.)
Punta Arenas
Str. of Magellan
Tierra del Fuego
South Georgia
C. Horn
C. Farewell
GREENLAND
160
140
120
100
West from Greenwich
80
60
40
20
60
50
40
30
20
10
0
10
20
30
40
50
COPYRIGHT, GEORGE PHILIP & SON, LTD.

Java Trench
6389
TIMOR SEA
Ashmore Reef
Scott Reef
Bonaparte Archipelago
C. Londonderry
C. Bougainville
Admiralty G.
Cambridge G.
Joseph Bonaparte Gulf
Croker I.
Cobourg Pen.
Melville I.
Bathurst I.
Van Diemen Gulf
Clarence Str.
P. Darwin
Darwin
Crocodile Is.
Arnhem B.
Arnhem Land
Rum Jungle
Anson B.
Batchelor
Daly
Katherine
Roper
Mataranka
Limmen
Birdum
Daly
McArthur
Drysdale
Mt. Hann
776
Wyndham
Kununurra
Victoria
Collier B.
King Sd.
C. Levêque
Lacepede Is.
Kimberley
L. Argyle
Ord
Mt. Ord
1007
King Leopold Ras.
Durack Range
Derby
Fitzroy
Fitzroy Crossing
Hall's Creek
Wave Hill
Newcastle Waters
L. Woods
Barkly
Rowley Shoals
Broome
Roebuck B.
Gordon Downs
Sturt
Tanami Desert
Tennant Creek
NORTHERN TERRITORY
Murchison Ra.
Davenport Ra.
Eighty Mile Beach
Gregory Lake
Hordern Hills
INDIAN OCEAN
Dampier Archipelago
P. Hedland
Mount Goldsworthy
De Grey
Great Sandy Desert
Mt. Singleton
808
Sandover
Barrow I.
C. Dampier
Karratha
Roebourne
Pilbara
Marble Bar
Throssell Ra.
L. Dora
L. Mackay
Reynolds Ra.
998
Fortescue
Nullagine
Mt. Ziel
1510
Macdonnell Ras.
Alice Springs
N.W. Cape
Exmouth
Learmonth
Exmouth G.
Onslow
Hamersley Ra.
Mt. Bruce
1235
Tom Price
Ophthalmia Ra.
Robertson Ra.
L. Macdonald
L. Disappointment
James Ra.
Hugh
Finke
Palmer
Paraburdoo
Ashburton
Mount Whaleback
Newman
Gibson Desert
Rawlinson Ra.
L. Amadeus
Mt. Olga
1069
Ayers Rock
868
Simpson Desert
WESTERN AUSTRALIA
L. McLeod
Lyons
Mt. Augustus
1105
Blackstone Ra.
Musgrave Ranges
1549
Mt. Woodroffe
Hamilton
Alberga
Geographe Chan.
Carnarvon
Gascoyne
Robinson Ra.
Peak Hill
L. Carnegie
L. Wells
661
Everard Ras.
Oodnadatta
Wooramel
Shark B.
Dirk Hartog I.
Denham
Meekatharra
Wiluna
Murchison
L. Yeo
Warrina
L. Austin
Great Victoria Desert
Tallering Peak
453
Mt. Magnet
Sandstone
Laverton
Coober Pedy
Stuart Ra.
Houtman Abrolhos
Northampton
Mullewa
Geraldton
L. Monger
L. Barlee
Leonora
L. Carey
L. Minigwal
SOUTH AUSTRALIA
L. Ballard
Menzies
Ooldea
Tarcoola
Dongara
L. Moore
Deakin
Kanowna
Kalgoorlie-Boulder
Rawlinna
Nullarbor Plain
Bonnie Rock
Bencubbin
Coolgardie
L. Lefroy
Hampton Tableland
Head of Bight
L. Everard
L. Gairdner
Nukey Bluff
472
Penong
Ceduna
C. Adieu
Southern Cross
L. Cowan
Eyre
Darling Range
Swan
Northam
Kellerberrin
The Johnston Lakes
Norseman
L. Dundas
Nuyts Archipelago
Streaky B.
Kimba
Perth
Fremantle
Kwinana
York
Great Australian Bight
Anxious B.
Eyre Penin.
Pinjarra
Narrogin
Esperance
Coffin B. Penin.
Bunbury
Geographe B.
Collie
Wagin
C. Pasley
Archipelago of the Recherche
Port Lincoln
Katanning
Stirling Ra.
Busselton
Bridgetown
Manjimup
Mt Barker
Albany
C. Knob
Investigator
Augusta
C. Leeuwin
Flinders B.
m
2000
1500
1000
400
200
0
200
2000
4000
6000
m
115
120
125
130
135
15
20
25
30
35
Projection: Bonne
East from Greenwich

1:12 000 000

100 0 100 200 300 400 500 km
AUSTRALASIA
POLITICAL
1:80 000 000
200 0 400 800 1200 1600 km
INDONESIA
PAPUA NEW GUINEA
IRIAN JAYA
Bismarck Arch.
New Ireland
New Britain
SOLOMON ISLANDS
Sulawesi
Banda Sea
Timor
Arafura Sea
Timor Sea
Darwin
Gulf of Carpentaria
Louisiade Arch. (Austral.)
Coral Sea
Santa Cruz Is.
Vanuatu
INDIAN OCEAN
NORTHERN TERRITORY
QUEENSLAND
Cairns
Townsville
Îles Chesterfield (Fr.)
Nouvelle Calédonie (Fr.)
Nouméa
Îles Loyauté (Fr.)
FIJI
Suva
TONGA (Friendly)
SAMOA
AMER. SAMOA
WESTERN AUSTRALIA
AUSTRALIA
Alice Springs
Mt. Isa
Rockhampton
Brisbane
Tropic of Capricorn
PACIFIC OCEAN
SOUTH AUSTRALIA
NEW SOUTH WALES
Norfolk I. (Austral.)
Lord Howe I. (Austral.)
Kermadec Is. (N.Z.)
International Date Line
Geraldton
Perth
Great Australian Bight
Broken Hill
Adelaide
Newcastle
Sydney
Canberra
VICTORIA
Melbourne
Bass Strait
Tasman Sea
Auckland
Wellington
Christchurch
Dunedin
NEW ZEALAND
Chatham Is.
Hobart
TASMANIA
Banks I.
C. York
Prince of Wales I.
Endeavour Str.
Wessel Is.
C. Wilberforce
C. Arnhem
Nhulunbuy
C. Grey
Gulf of Carpentaria
Alyangula
Groote Eylandt
Bight
Sir Edward Pellew Group
Borroloola
Mornington I.
Wellesley Is.
Bentinck I.
Shelburne B.
C. Grenville
Albatross B.
Weipa
Cape York Peninsula
Wenlock
McIlwraith Ra.
Coen
Princess Charlotte B.
C. Melville
Osprey Rf.
Great Barrier Reef
Coleman
Normanby
C. Flattery
Laura
Cooktown
Mitchell
Mossman
Gilbert
Chillagoe
Mareeba
Cairns
Atherton
Bartle Frere
Innisfail
Normanton
Burketown
Croydon
Hinchinbrook I.
Ingham
Palm Is.
Halifax B.
C. Cleveland
Townsville
Seaview Ra.
Forsayth
Gregory Ra.
Norman
Leichhardt
Flinders
Tableland
Camooweal
Kajabbi
Mount Isa
Mary Kathleen
Cloncurry
Richmond
Hughenden
Charters Towers
Home Hill
Bowen
Whitsunday I.
Proserpine
Collinsville
Selwyn Range
Georgina
Dajarra
Mackay
Sarina
Broad Sd.
Denham Ra.
Isaac
Belyando
Winton
QUEENSLAND
Great Dividing Range
Blair Athol
Peak Ra.
Clermont
Drummond Ra.
Emerald
Mackenzie
Hay
Diamantina
Longreach
Thomson
Barcaldine
Alpha
Townshend I.
Rockhampton
Yeppoon
Keppel B.
Curtis I.
Gladstone
Biloela
Bedourie
Eyre Cr.
Barcoo
Blackall
Warrego Ra.
Yaraka
Mt. Morgan
Dawson
Expedition Ra.
Windorah
Birdsville
Grey Range
Bulloo
Quilpie
Charleville
Mitchell
Maranoa
Roma
Miles
Balonne
Bundaberg
Hervey Bay
Sandy C.
Fraser I.
Gayndah
Maryborough
Gympie
Nambour
Kingaroy
Dalby
Toowoomba
Moonie
Ipswich
BRISBANE
Gold Coast
L. Yamma Yamma
Cooper Creek
Macumba
Warburton
L. Eyre (North)
L. Gregory
L. Eyre (South)
L. Elanche
Strzelecki Cr.
Thargomindah
Cunnamulla
St. George
Goondiwindi
Dirranbandi
Warwick
Murwillumbah
Tibooburra
Paroo
Macintyre
Gwydir
Moree
Lismore
Casino
Tenterfield
Clarence
Grafton
Inverell
Glen Innes
New England Range
Ben Lomond
Armidale
Coffs Harbour
Macleay
Marree
Leigh Creek
Flinders Ranges
L. Frome
Woomera
L. Torrens
St. Mary Pk.
Barrier Ra.
Broken Hill
Bourke
Barwon
Walgett
Narrabri
Bogan
Macquarie
Coonamble
Liverpool Plains
Gunnedah
Tamworth
NEW SOUTH WALES
Cobar
Nyngan
Wilcannia
Darling
Menindee
Liverpool Ra.
Quorn
Port Augusta
Iron Knob
Whyalla
Peterborough
Jamestown
Burra
Port Pirie
Narromine
Dubbo
Condobolin
Parkes
Mudgee
Singleton
Muswellbrook
Barrington Tops
Taree
Port Macquarie
Maitland
Newcastle
Hillston
Lachlan
Forbes
Orange
Bathurst
Cessnock
Lithgow
Blue Mts.
Penrith
Hawkesbury R.
SYDNEY
Port Jackson
Wollongong
Shellharbour
Wallaroo
Kadina
Spencer Gulf
Yorke Penin.
G. St. Vincent
Renmark
Murray
Wentworth
Mildura
Balranald
Murrumbidgee
Hay
Griffith
Leeton
Cootamundra
Young
Cowra
Junee
Goulburn
Bowral
Elizabeth
Adelaide
Loxton
Ouyen
Swan Hill
Kerang
Deniliquin
Riverina
Wagga Wagga
Tumut
Canberra
CAPITAL TERR.
Queanbeyan
Jervis B.
Batemans B.
Murray Bridge
Mt. Lofty Ra.
Encounter B.
Victor Harbor
Spencer
Gulf Str.
Kangaroo I.
Wimmera
Bordertown
Albury
L. Hume
Wangaratta
Benalla
Mt. Bogong
Mt. Kosciusko
Cooma
Bega
Kingston S.E.
Naracoorte
Horsham
Stawell
Shepparton
Bendigo
VICTORIA
Australian Alps
Bombala
Millicent
Mt. Gambier
Hamilton
Ararat
Maryborough
Castlemaine
Ballarat
MELBOURNE
Gippsland
Geelong
Moe
Sale
Bairnsdale
Discovery B.
C. Bridgewater
Portland
Warrnambool
Colac
Port Phillip B.
C. Otway
Morwell
Ninety Mile Beach
Snowy
Pt. Hicks
C. Howe
Tasman Sea
Lihou Reef & Cays
CORAL SEA ISLANDS TERRITORY
PACIFIC OCEAN
Îles Chesterfield
Kenn Reef
Bellona Rfs.
Swain Rfs.
Saumarez Rf.
Bird I.
Cato I.
Tropic of Capricorn
Bass Strait
King I.
Flinders I.
Furneaux Group
C. Grim
Devonport
Burnie
Ulverstone
Scottsdale
Launceston
Ben Lomond
Mt. Ossa
Macquarie Harb.
Queenstown
TASMANIA
New Norfolk
Hobart
Glenorchy
Tasman Penin.
Storm B.
Bruny I.
S.E. Cape
on same scale
COPYRIGHT, GEORGE PHILIP & SON, LTD

1:60 000 000

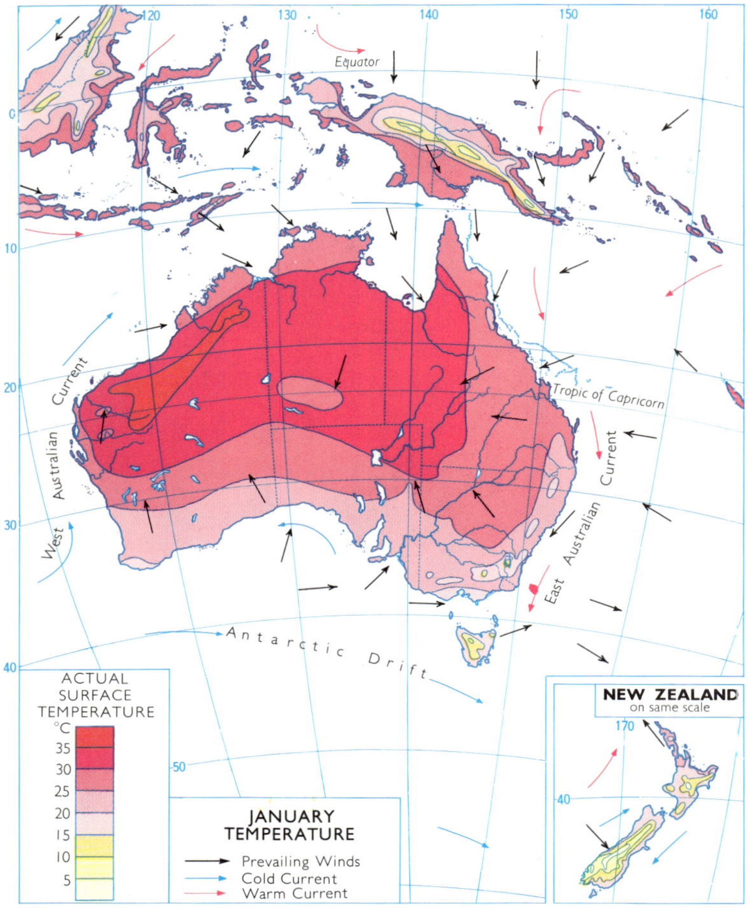
Equator
Tropic of Capricorn
West Australian Current
East Australian Current
Antarctic Drift
ACTUAL SURFACE TEMPERATURE
°C
35
30
25
20
15
10
5
JANUARY TEMPERATURE
Prevailing Winds
Cold Current
Warm Current
NEW ZEALAND
on same scale

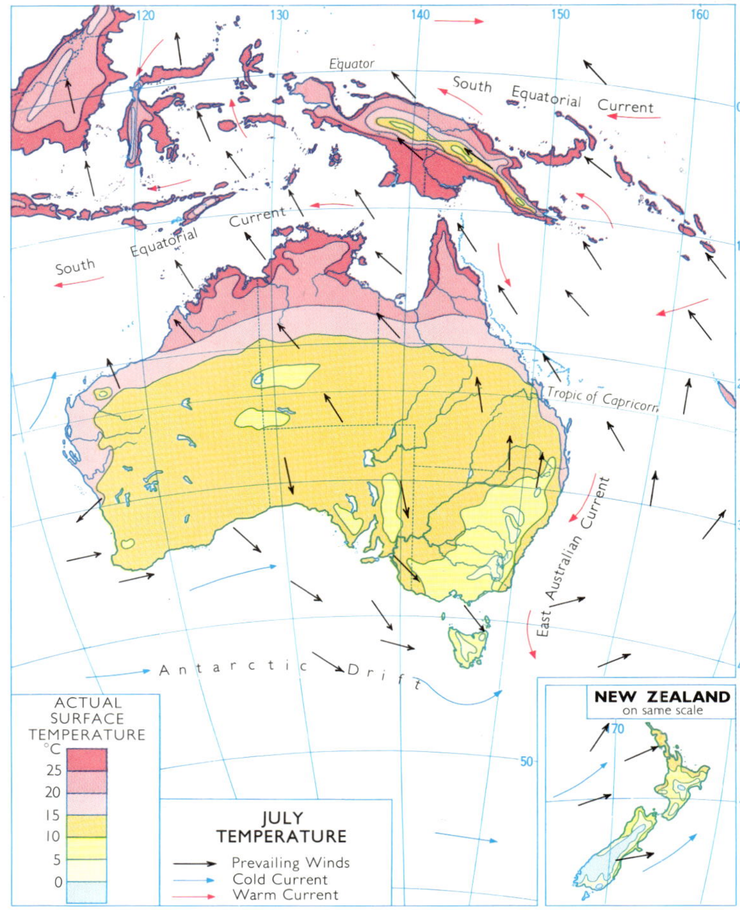
Equator
South Equatorial Current
Tropic of Capricorn
East Australian Current
Antarctic Drift
ACTUAL SURFACE TEMPERATURE
°C
25
20
15
10
5
0
JULY TEMPERATURE
Prevailing Winds
Cold Current
Warm Current
NEW ZEALAND
on same scale

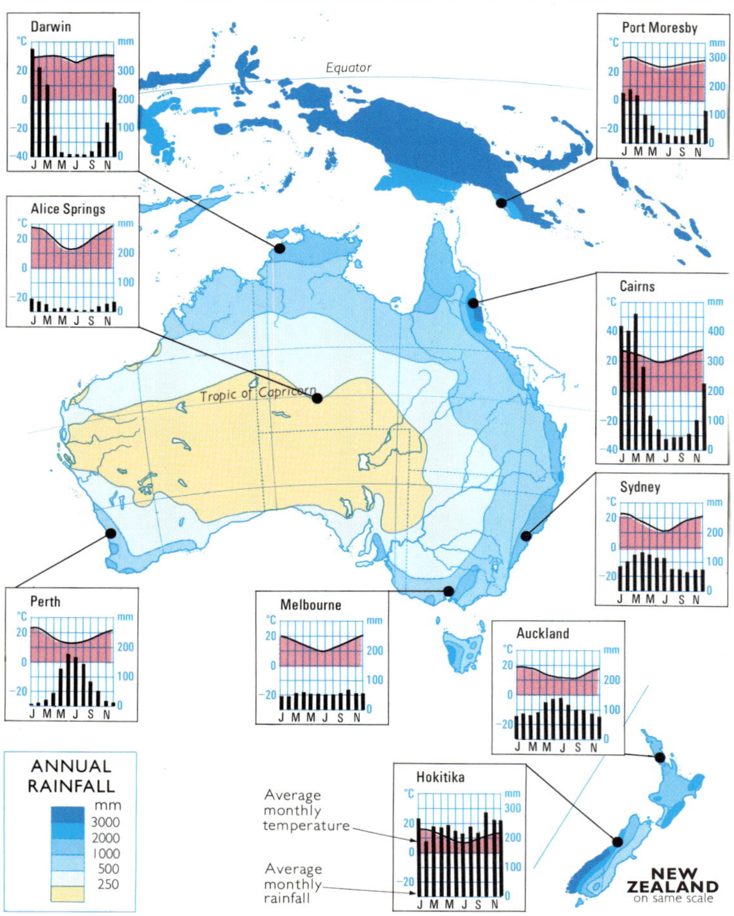
Equator
Tropic of Capricorn
Darwin
Port Moresby
Alice Springs
Cairns
Sydney
Perth
Melbourne
Auckland
Hokitika
Average monthly temperature
Average monthly rainfall
ANNUAL RAINFALL
mm
3000
2000
1000
500
250
NEW ZEALAND
on same scale

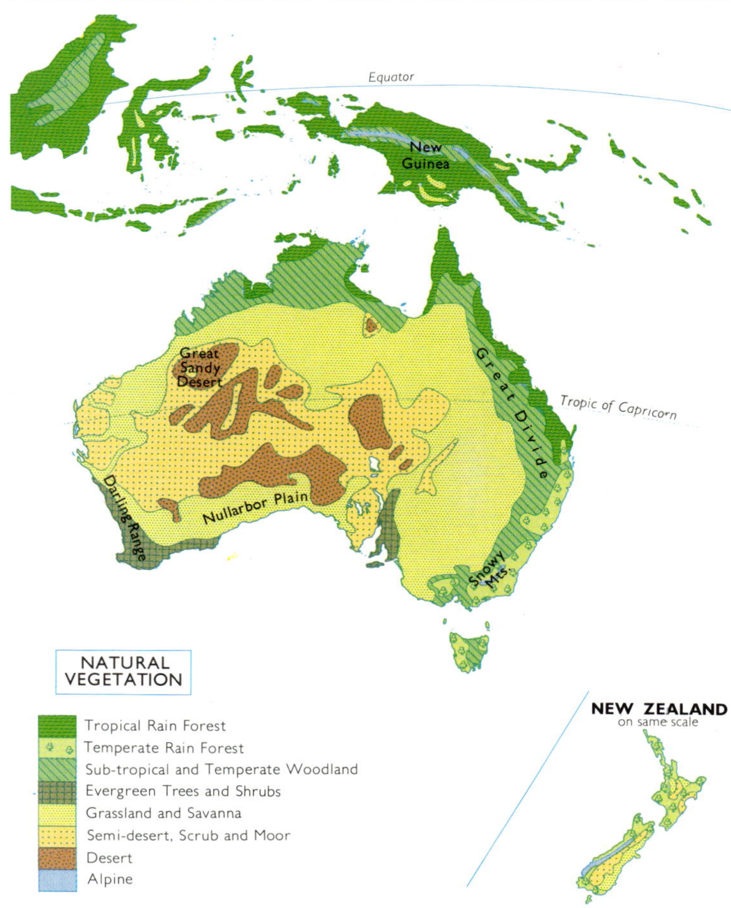
Equator
New Guinea
Great Sandy Desert
Great Divide
Tropic of Capricorn
Darling Range
Nullarbor Plain
Snowy Mts.
NATURAL VEGETATION
Tropical Rain Forest
Temperate Rain Forest
Sub-tropical and Temperate Woodland
Evergreen Trees and Shrubs
Grassland and Savanna
Semi-desert, Scrub and Moor
Desert
Alpine
NEW ZEALAND
on same scale

1:20 000 000

200 0 200 400 600 800 km

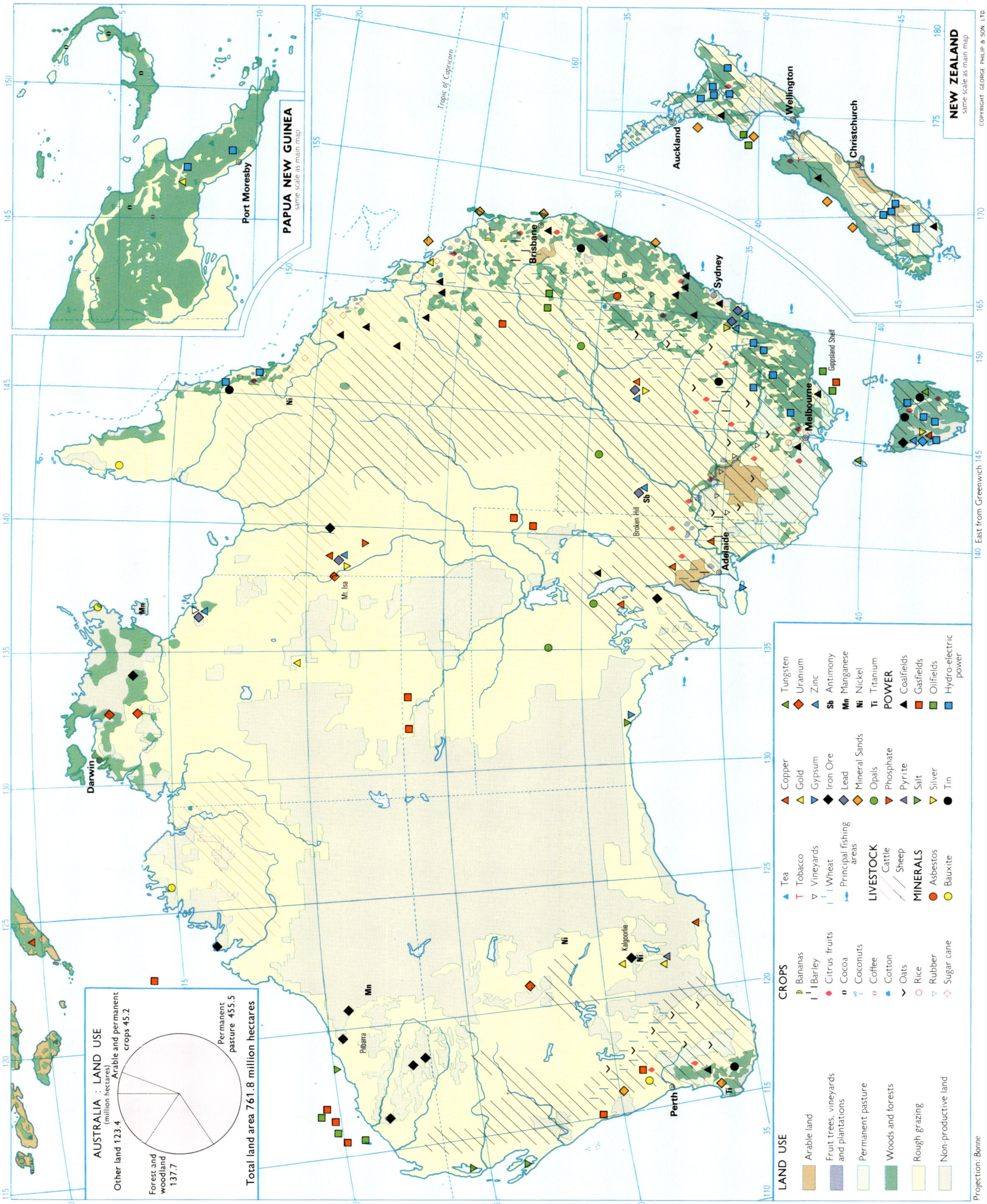

1:4 500 000

25 0 25 50 75 100 125 150 175 200 km

m: 2000, 1500, 1000, 400, 200, 0

m: 0, 200, 2000, 4000

1: 6 000 000

NEW ZEALAND & DEPENDENCIES
1: 60 000 000
New Zealand Territory
Self-governing Territory
Tokelau or Union Group
WESTERN SAMOA
AMERICAN SAMOA
Savaii
Upolu
Pukapuka (Danger)
Rakahanga
Manihiki
Nassau
Suwarrow
Northern Group
Tongareva (Penrhyn) I.
Cook Is.
Îles de la Société
Rotuma (Fiji)
Vanua Levu
FIJI
Viti Levu
Fiji Is.
Lau or Eastern Group
TONGA (Friendly Is.)
Niue
Palmerston Atoll
Aitutaki
Lower Group
Rarotonga
Mitiaro
Mauke
Atiu
Mangaia
Tropic of Capricorn
PACIFIC OCEAN
Raoul (Sunday) I.
Macauley
Curtis
Kermadec Is.
Three Kings Is.
Auckland
NORTH I.
Cook Strait
Wellington
NEW ZEALAND
SOUTH I.
Christchurch
Chatham Is.
Dunedin
Bounty Is.
Tasman Sea
Stewart I.
Snares
Antipodes Is.
Campbell I.
Auckland Is.
Macquarie I. (Austr.)
SOUTHERN OCEAN
NORTH ISLAND
NORTHLAND
Whangarei
Dargaville
Kaitaia
Houhora
North C.
C. Maria van Diemen
C. Brett
Gt. Barrier I.
Hauraki Gulf
C. Colville
Coromandel
Takapuna
Devonport
CENTRAL AUCKLAND
AUCKLAND
Manukau
Thames
Waihi
Hamilton
Tauranga
Mt. Maunganui
Bay of Plenty
Whakatane
Opotiki
C. Runaway
East C.
Hikurangi 1754
SOUTH AUCKLAND BAY OF PLENTY
Rotorua
Tokoroa
Te Kuiti
Te Awamutu
Raukumara Ra.
EAST COAST
Gisborne
L. Taupo
Taupo
Taumarunui
North Taranaki Bight
Waitara
New Plymouth
Inglewood
Mt. Egmont 2518
C. Egmont
Opunake
Stratford
Eltham
Hawera
Patea
South Taranaki Bight
TARANAKI
Ruapehu 2797
Raetihi
Ohakune
Waiouru
Taihape
Kaimanawa Mts.
Wanganui
Marton
Feilding
Palmerston N.
Foxton
Levin
Otaki
Napier
Hastings
C. Kidnappers
Hawke Bay
Mahia Peninsula
Wairoa
HAWKE'S BAY
Ruahine Ra.
Waipawa
Waipukurau
Dannevirke
Woodville
Pahiatua
WELLINGTON
Tararua Ra.
Masterton
Carterton
Martinborough
Up. Hutt
Porirua
Lr. Hutt
Eastbourne
WELLINGTON
Cook Strait
PACIFIC OCEAN
TASMAN SEA
SOUTH ISLAND
C. Farewell
Golden Bay
Collingwood
Takaka
Tasman Mts.
D'Urville I.
Tasman Bay
Motueka
Nelson
Richmond
Picton
Blenheim
MARLBOROUGH
Karamea Bight
Westport
Lyell Ra.
Reefton
Mt. Travers 2338
Tapuaenuku 2885
Kaikoura Ra.
Kaikoura
Spenser Mts.
Runanga
Greymouth
Hokitika
L. Brunner
Arthur's Pass
Waiau
Hurunui
Waipara
Rangiora
Pegasus Bay
Oxford
Coleridge
Christchurch
New Brighton
Riccarton
Lyttelton
Banks Peninsula
Akaroa
L. Ellesmere
CANTERBURY
Canterbury Plains
Ashburton
Canterbury Bight
Temuka
Timaru
Westland Bight
Mt. Cook 3764
Southern Alps
WESTLAND
Methven
L. Tekapo
L. Pukaki
Fairlie
Mt. Aspiring 3027
Mt. Earnslaw 2819
L. Wanaka
L. Hawea
L. Ohau
Wanaka
Milford Sd.
Queenstown
Cromwell
Dunstan Mts.
Kurow
Waimate
Oamaru
Kakanui Mts.
Alexandra
OTAGO
Wakatipu
Kingston
Secretary I.
Doubtful Sd.
L. Te Anau
L. Manapouri
Eyre Mts.
Garvie Mts.
Roxburgh
Palmerston
Port Chalmers
Dunedin
Mosgiel
C. Saunders
St. Kilda
Resolution I.
Mossburn
SOUTHLAND
Kelso
Winton
Gore
Mataura
Milton
Balclutha
Nugget Pt.
Tuatapere
Riverton
Invercargill
Bluff
Foveaux Str.
Ruapuke I.
Oban
Stewart I.
Port Pegasus
S.W. Cape
SAMOA ISLANDS
1:12 000 000
WESTERN SAMOA
Savai'i
Apia
Upolu
AMERICAN SAMOA
Pago Pago
Tutuila
Manua Is.
Rose I.
Futuna (Fr.)
Niuafo'ou (Tonga)
Thikombia
Lambasa
Vanua Levu
FIJI
Yasawa Group
Taveuni
Koro
Vanua Balavu
Lau or Eastern Group
Lautoka
Nadi
Viti Levu
1323
Levuka
Ovalau
Suva
Gau
Koro Sea
Lakemba
Moala
Kandavu
Vatoa
Vava'u
TONGA
Tonga (Friendly) Is.
Tofua I.
Ha'apai Group
Tongatapu
Nuku'alofa
FIJI AND TONGA ISLANDS
1:12 000 000
Projection: Conical with two standard parallels
COPYRIGHT, GEORGE PHILIP & SON, LTD.

1: 40 000 000

Projection: *Zenithal Equidistant*. West from Greenwich 0 East from Greenwich

1:40 000 000

400 0 400 800 1200 1600 km

Projection: Zenithal Equidistant. West from Greenwich 0 East from Greenwich

AFRICA : Climate and Natural Vegetation

1:80 000 000

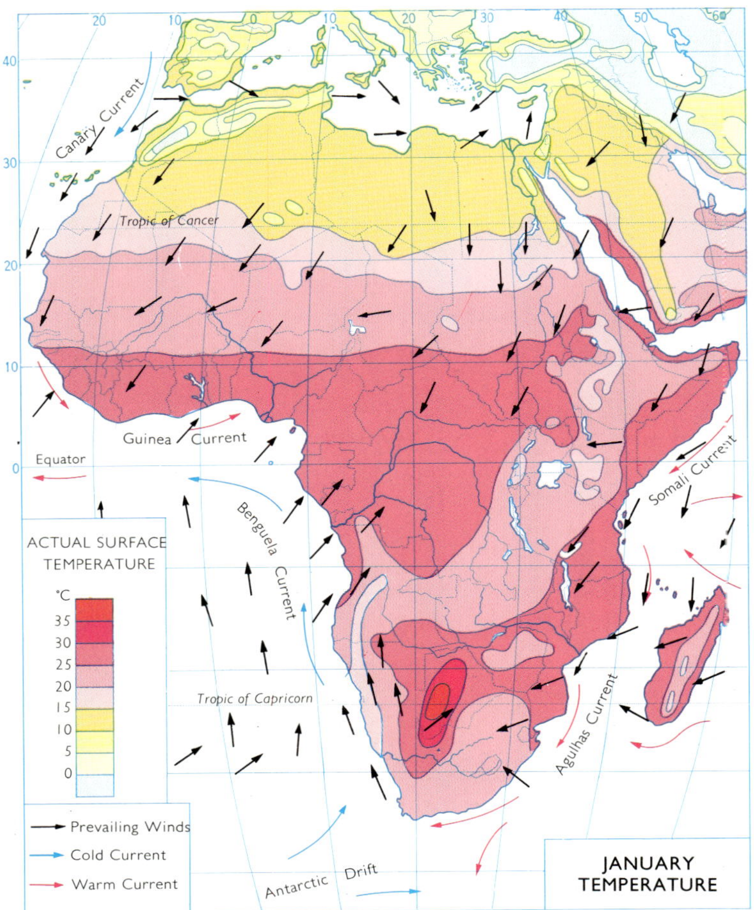

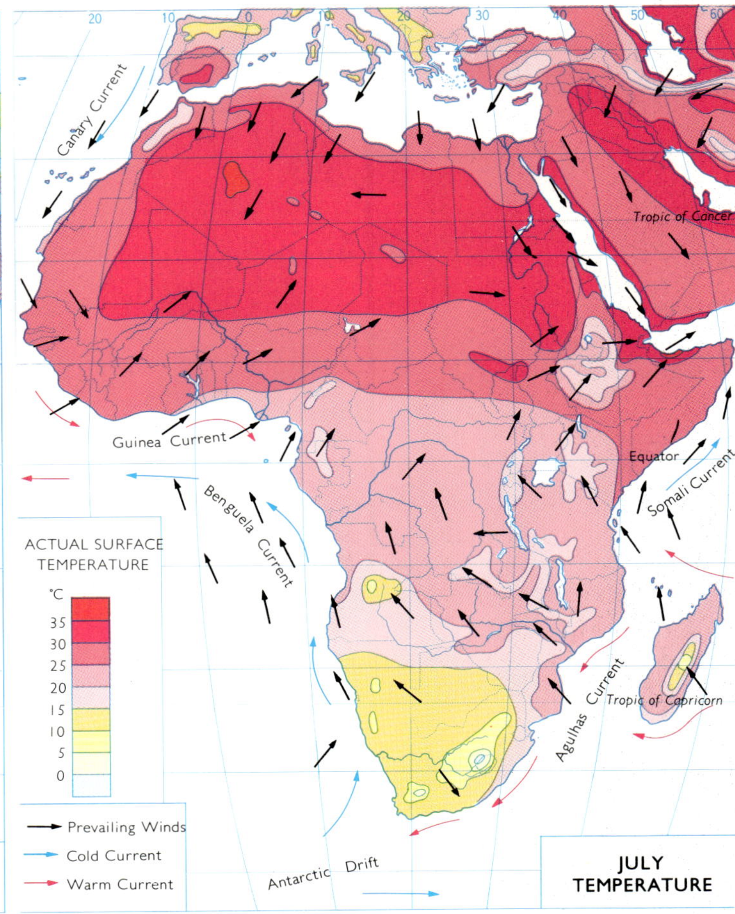

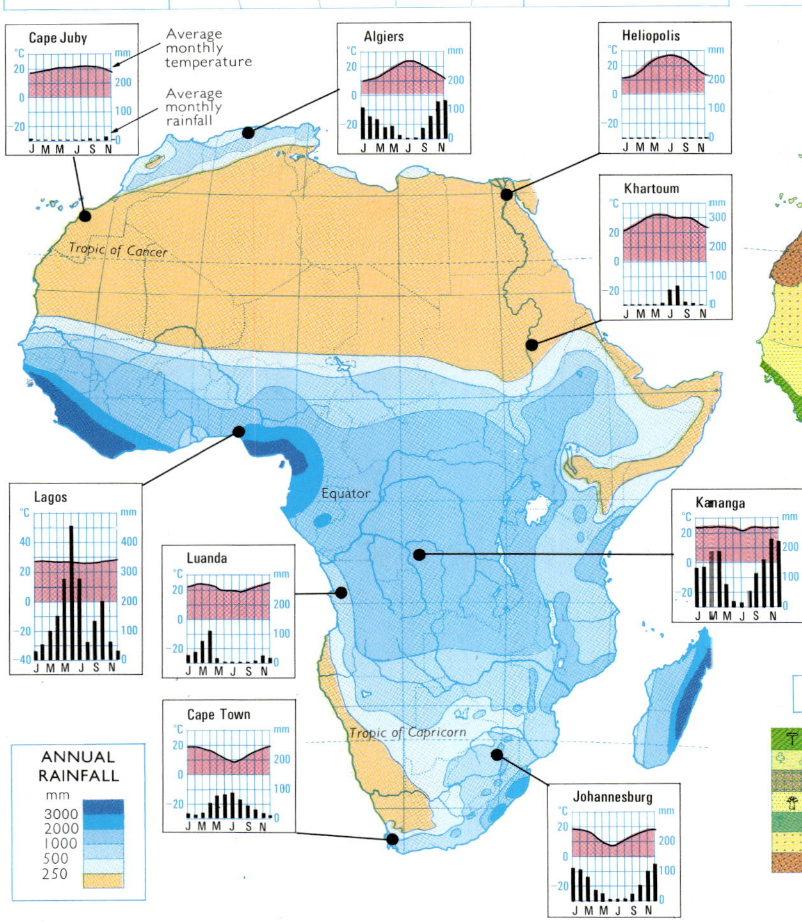

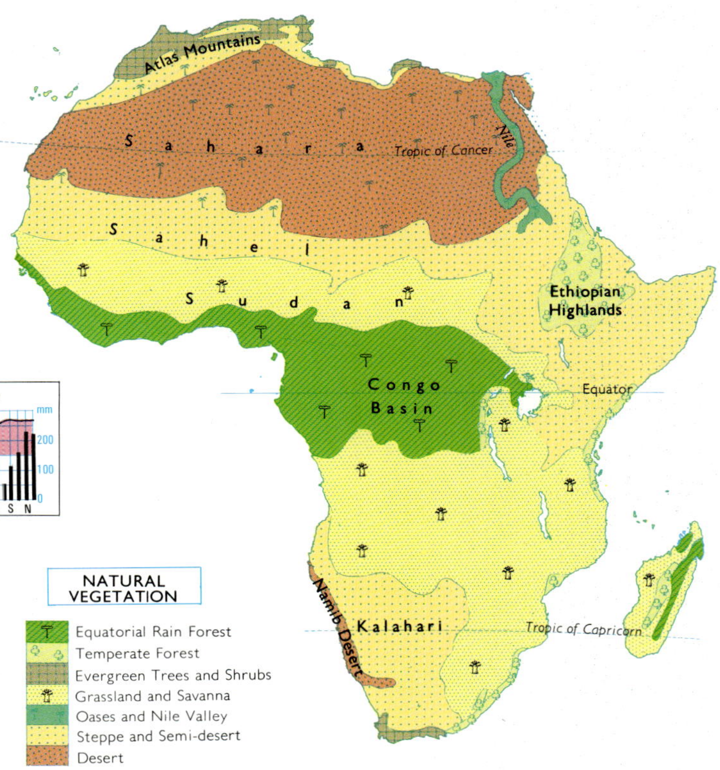

Projection: *Sanson-Flamsteed's Sinusoidal*

1:40 000 000

0 400 800 1200 1600 km

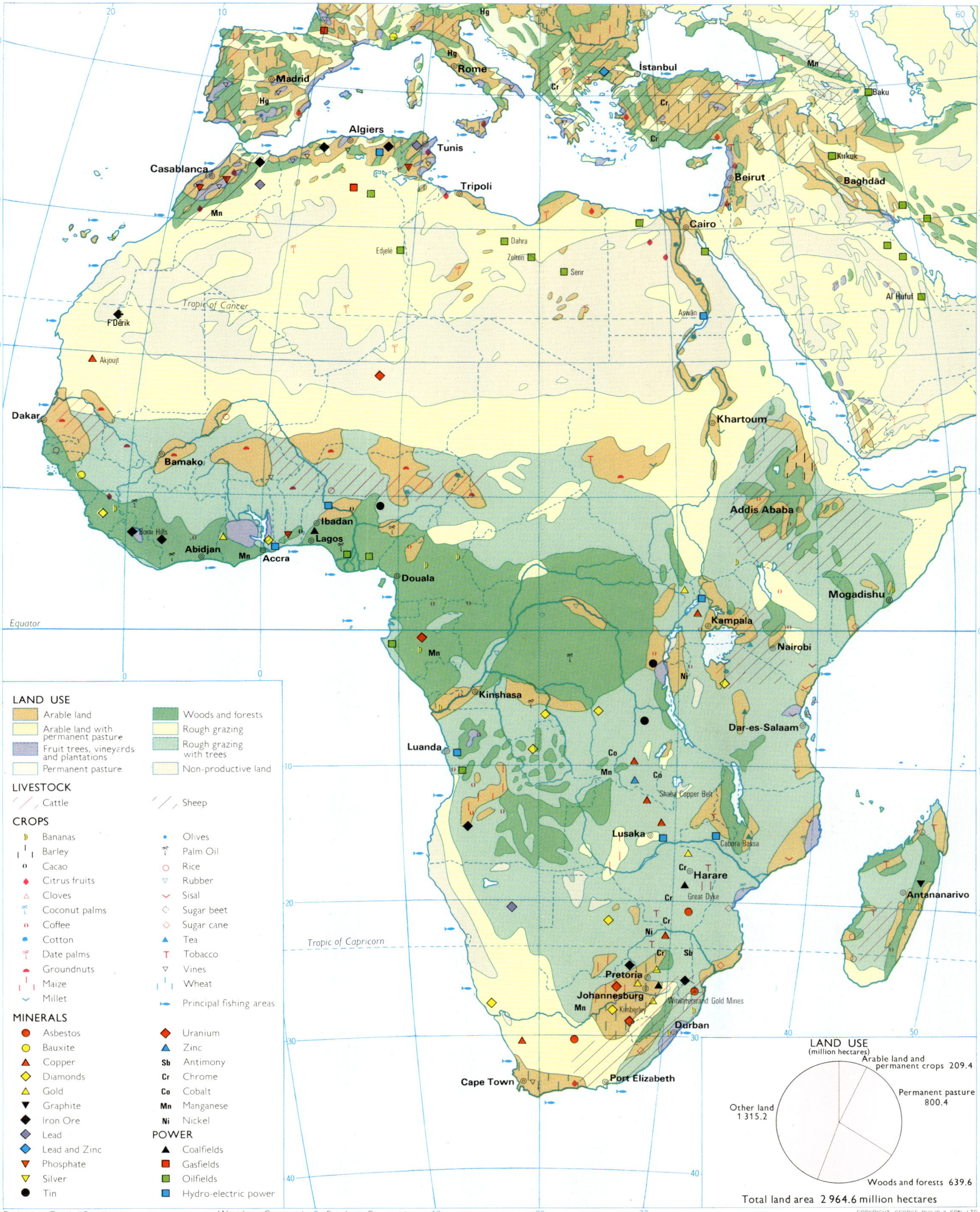

Projection: Zenithal Equidistant West from Greenwich 0 East from Greenwich

	Population								Land			Agriculture		
	Total	Density	Birth Rate	Death Rate	Life Expectancy	Growth 1965-80	Growth 1980-88	Urban	Area	Arable	Forest	Agricultural Population	Index of Production	Food Intake
	th.	persons per km²	per th. popn.	per th. popn.	yrs.	av. % per annum	av. % per annum	%	th. km²	th. km²	th. km²	% of total popn.	1979-81 = 100	calories per day
Algeria	23805	10	40	9	63	3.1	3.1	44	2382	75	47	25	121	2715
Angola	9421	8	47	20	45	2.8	2.5	25	1247	36	531	71	104	1969
Benin	4454	40	51	19	51	2.7	3.2	39	111	18	36	64	143	2184
Botswana	1164	2	47	12	68	3.5	3.3	21	585	14	10	65	100	2201
Burkina Faso	8546	31	47	19	47	2	2.6	8	274	31	68	85	148	2139
Burundi	5149	198	46	17	49	1.9	2.9	7	26	13	0.7	92	128	2343
Cameroon	11213	24	42	16	57	2.7	3.2	46	469	70	249	64	118	2028
Central Africa	2794	4	44	20	48	1.8	2.5	45	623	20	358	66	101	1949
Chad	5399	4	44	20	46	2	2.4	30	1259	32	130	77	127	1717
Congo	2100	6	44	17	59	2.7	3.4	41	342	7	212	60	116	2619
Egypt	51447	52	41	9	61	2.4	2.7	48	995	26	0.03	42	148	3342
Ethiopia	46144	42	44	24	48	2.7	2.5	12	1101	139	451	76	108	1749
Gabon	1077	4	39	16	53	3.5	3.9	43	258	5	200	70	112	2521
Gambia	822	82	47	21	44	2.6	3.3	21	10	2	2	82	131	2251
Ghana	14040	61	44	13	54	2.2	3.5	32	230	29	83	52	142	1759
Guinea	6641	27	47	22	42	1.9	2.4	24	246	16	100	76	109	1777
Guinea-Bissau	940	34	41	20	40	1.4	1.9	27	28	3	11	80	155	2505
Ivory Coast	11587	36	51	14	53	4.2	4.2	44	318	36	64	59	131	2562
Kenya	23021	40	54	12	56	3.6	4.2	22	569	24	37	78	125	2060
Lesotho	1673	56	41	12	56	2.3	2.7	19	30	3	0	82	108	2303
Liberia	2401	25	45	13	55	3	3.3	42	96	4	21	71	120	2381
Libya	4249	2	38	9	61	4.6	4.3	67	1760	22	7	13	126	3601
Madagascar	11259	19	46	14	54	2.5	3.3	23	582	31	147	78	117	2440
Malawi	8155	87	49	25	46	2.9	3.8	13	94	24	43	78	108	2310
Mali	7989	7	47	20	47	2.1	2.4	19	1220		85	82	135	2074
Mauritania	1907	2	46	19	46	2.3	2.6	38	1030	2	150	66	112	2322
Morocco	23920	54	35	10	61	2.5	2.7	47	446	85	52	39	150	2915
Mozambique	14967	19	45	19	48	2.5	2.7	23	784	31	149	83	103	1595
Namibia	1262	2	44	12	57		3.2	51	823	7	184	37	126	2197
Niger	6998	6	51	21	45	2.7	3	18	1267	35	25	89	124	2432
Nigeria	110131	121	50	16	52	2.5	3.4	33	911	313	143	66	126	2146
Rwanda	6657	266	51	17	49	3.3	3.3	7	25	11	5	92	97	1830
Senegal	7154	37	46	19	48	2.5	2.9	37	192	52	59	79	127	2350
Sierra Leone	3938	55	48	23	42	2	2.4	26	72	18	21	65	108	1855
Somalia	5882	9	51	20	47	2.7	2.9	36	627	9	88	72	131	2135
South Africa	33938	28	32	10	61	2.4	2.3	57	1221	132	45	15	104	2924
Sudan	23776	10	45	16	50	3	3.1	21	2376	125	468	64	128	2208
Swaziland	737	43	47	13	56		3.4	26	17	2	1	69	127	2553
Tanzania	24739	28	51	14	53	3.3	3.5	29	886	52	424	82	116	2192
Togo	3362	62	45	14	53	3	3.4	24	54	14	14	71	111	2207
Tunisia	7796	50	28	7	66	2.1	2.5	54	155	47	6	27	110	2994
Uganda	16195	81	50	15	51	2.9	3.2	10	200	67	57	82	108	2344
Zaire	33615	15	46	14	53	2.8	3.1	38	2268	67	1753	68	120	2164
Zambia	7486	10	51	14	54	3.1	3.6	53	741	52	292	70	126	2137
Zimbabwe	9257	24	42	10	63	3.1	3.6	26	387	28	199	70	123	2132

For explanations see pages 54–55 or 86–87.

Trade		Education		Health	Energy	Consumer Price Index	G.N.P.		G.D.P.		Loans & Debt		
Imports	Exports	Primary	Secondary					Growth per capita	Part formed by Agric.	Part formed by Indust.			
US$ per capita	US$ per capita	% of age group	% of age group	Popn. per doctor	Consumption in kg of oil equiv. per capita	1980 = 100	US$ per capita	% per year 1965-88	%	%	end 1987 US$ millions	as % of G.N.P.	
295	343	95	54	2327	1003	153	2680	3.2	12	42	18574	34	Algeria
72	195	93	13	17784	203			–4.8	10	39			Angola
94	38	65	16	15937	46		310	0.2	46	14	907	51	Benin
		100	31	6910	429	189	1050	8.9	3	57	518		Botswana
63	24	35	6	57183	18	139	190	1.6	38	25	825	44	Burkina Faso
40	16	59	4	21120	20	166	250	1.6	59	14	745	68	Burundi
193	153	100	23	13990	144	203	970	3.8	24	31	3002	23	Cameroon
67	47	66	13	23067	30	140	330	–0.3	41	13	573	51	Central Africa
30	26	43	6	38358	18	160	150	–2	43	18	280	35	Chad
271	421	100	52	8138	223	178	870	4.2	12	33	694	171	Congo
164	78	87	66	786	588	118	680	3.5	21	25	39338	104	Egypt
25	9	36	12	77356	21	127	130	0.1	42	18	2526	46	Ethiopia
776	1193	100	27	2793	1121	168	2700	1.1	11	14	1893	55	Gabon
168	140	75	20	11688	68	331			28	7	283	99	Gambia
60	75	63	35	14894	129	1583	390	–1.6	51	16	2390	46	Ghana
56	70	29	9	57390	59		350		40	22	1678	75	Guinea
78	26	60	11	7262	37						351	271	Guinea-Bissau
187	257	78	20	15234	172	154	740	1	36	25	12632	127	Ivory Coast
76	42	94	20	10101	99	233	330	1.9	31	19	5178	61	Kenya
		100	22	18614	10	287	370	4.7	21	28	373	101	Lesotho
87	160	66	20	9240	169	129	450	–1.6	37	28	1618		Liberia
1148	2524	100	87	694	2674		5460	–2.3	2	65			Libya
34	28	100	36	10002	39	416	210	–1.8	43	16	3235	172	Madagascar
34	32	64	4	11564	40	337	160	1.4	37	18	1228	85	Malawi
56	27	22	7	23487	24	230	210	1.6	54	12	1924	99	Mali
249	224	46	15	12113	113	480	440	–0.4	37	22	1931	193	Mauritania
177	117	79	34	4749	242	179	610	1.8	19	31	19500	103	Morocco
32	6	82	7	37949	86		170		50	12			Mozambique
		100	45										Namibia
60	52	29	6	38775	42	130	260	–2.2	34	24	1561	65	Niger
71	67	92	29	7978	133	274	370	1.1	30	43	29721	98	Nigeria
53	18	67	3	34681	42	145	300	1.6	37	23	565	26	Rwanda
164	90	55	13	13445	155	178	520	–0.6	22	27	3290	66	Senegal
34	30	58	17	13626	77	3952	300	0.2	45	19	659		Sierra Leone
77	16	20	12	16089	81	1113	290	0.3	65	9	1733	173	Somalia
431	591	100	39	1906	2465	299	1890	0.6	6	44			South Africa
29	20	50	20	10108	58	598	330	–0.5	37	15	8468	96	Sudan
		100	43	18848	291	253	790		21	20			Swaziland
47	14	69	3	26552	35	643	180	–0.4	61	8	4316	151	Tanzania
124	88	100	21	8724	52	144	290	0	29	18	1042	85	Togo
388	276	100	39	2154	496	191	1180	3.6	18	32	6012	60	Tunisia
29	20	58	8	21903	26	11644	260	–2.7	76	5	1256	23	Uganda
34	47	76	22	13041	73	1714	150	–2.4	32	33	7211	111	Zaire
100	116	100	19	7102	380	846	250	–2.1	12	36	4330	144	Zambia
114	147	100	46	7188	512	255	580	0.9	11	43	2537	40	Zimbabwe

Cape Verde, Land 4.0/Popn. 359; Comoros 2.2/434; Djibouti 22/484; Eq. Guinea 28/300; Mauritius 1.9/1056; Reunion 2.5/575; St. Helena 0.3/6; Sao Tome 0.9/115; Seychelles 0.3/67; Western Sahara 266/180.

Projection: Sanson Flamsteed's Sinusoidal

1:15 000 000

100 0 100 200 300 400 500 600 km

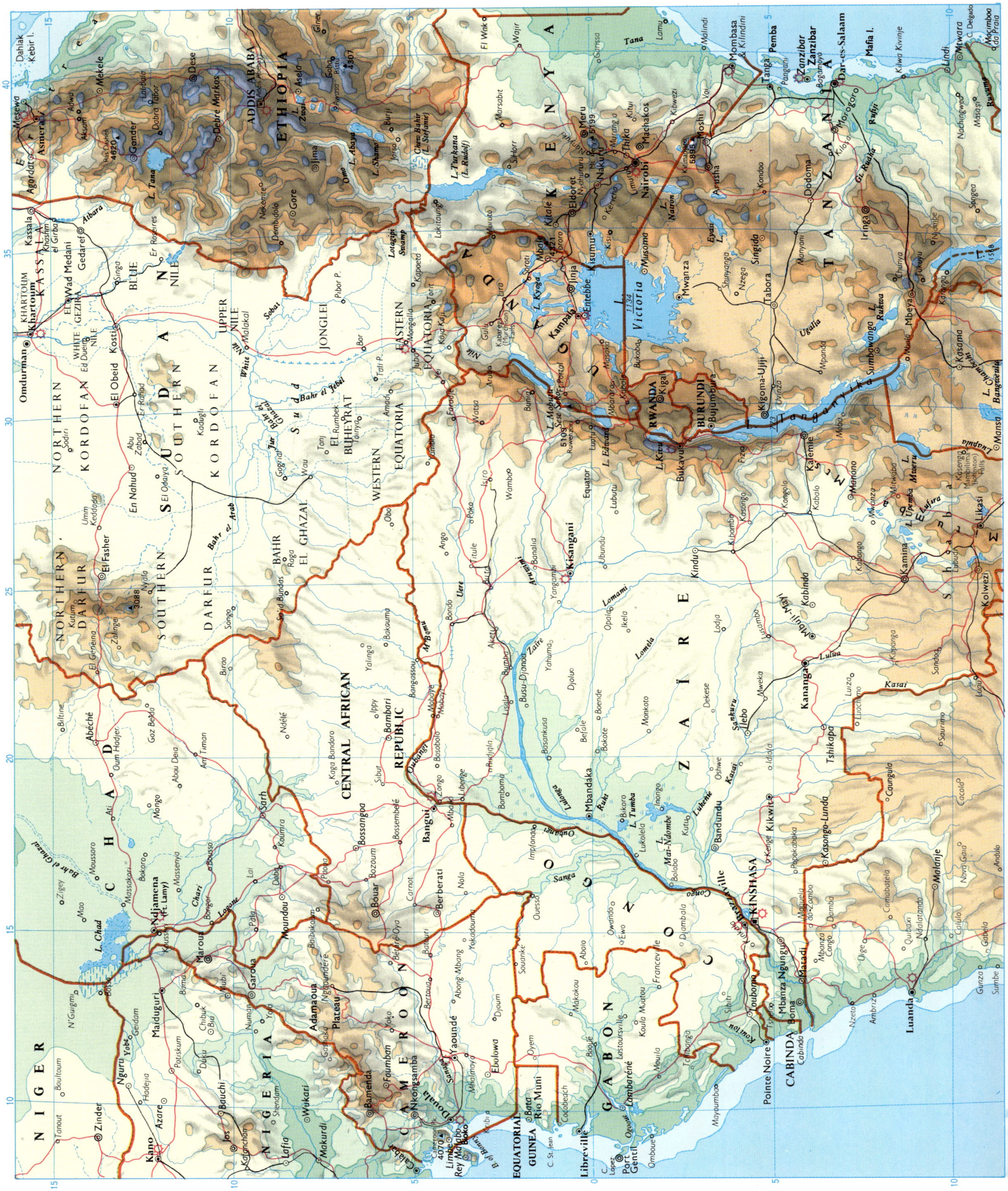
ETHIOPIA
ADDIS ABABA
KENYA
UGANDA
TANZANIA
RWANDA
BURUNDI
ZAÏRE
CONGO
GABON
CAMEROON
CENTRAL AFRICAN REPUBLIC
CHAD
NIGER
NIGERIA
SUDAN
EQUATORIAL GUINEA
Rio Muni
CABINDA
KINSHASA
Brazzaville
Libreville
Bangui
Ndjamena
Yaoundé
Luanda
Nairobi
Kampala
Kigali
Bujumbura
Dar-es-Salaam
Zanzibar
Mombasa
Kisangani
Lubumbashi
Kolwezi
Khartoum
Omdurman
Asmera
L. Victoria
L. Tanganyika
L. Chad
L. Turkana (L. Rudolf)
L. Tana
L. Albert
L. Edward
L. Kivu
L. Mweru
L. Kyoga
Kasai
Sanga
Ubangi
Zaïre
NORTHERN KORDOFAN
SOUTHERN KORDOFAN
NORTHERN DARFUR
SOUTHERN DARFUR
BAHR EL GHAZAL
UPPER NILE
BLUE NILE
JONGLEI
EASTERN EQUATORIA
WESTERN EQUATORIA
KASSALA
WHITE NILE
Sudd

1:15 000 000

100 0 100 200 300 400 500 600 km

1:35 000 000

400 0 400 800 1200 km

Projection: Bonne

West from Greenwich

1:35 000 000

400 0 400 800 1200 km

Projection: Bonne

NORTH AMERICA : Climate and Natural Vegetation

1:70 000 000

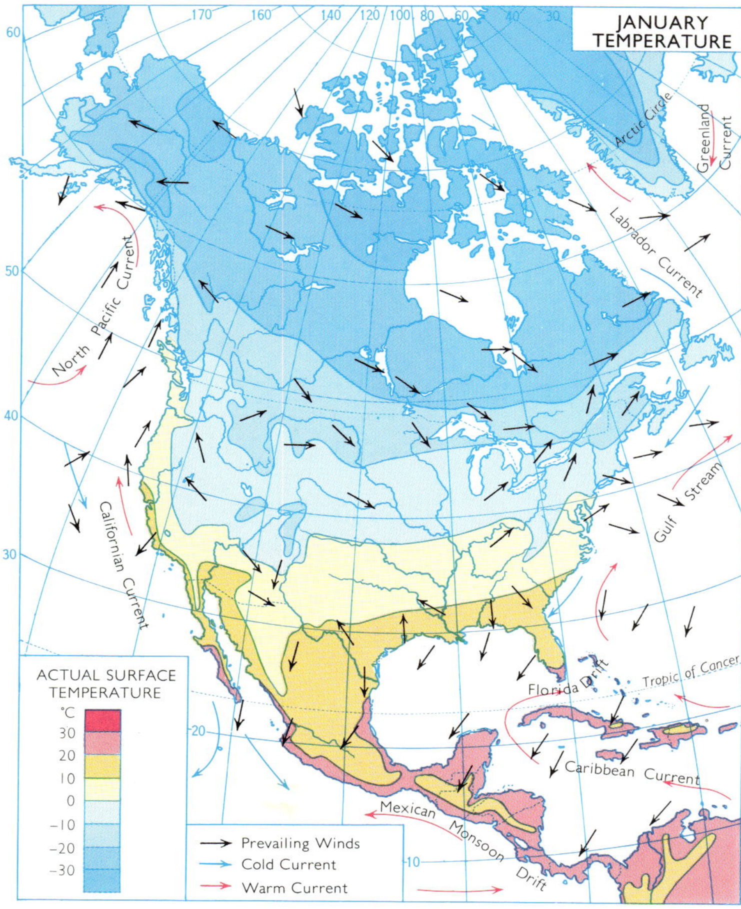

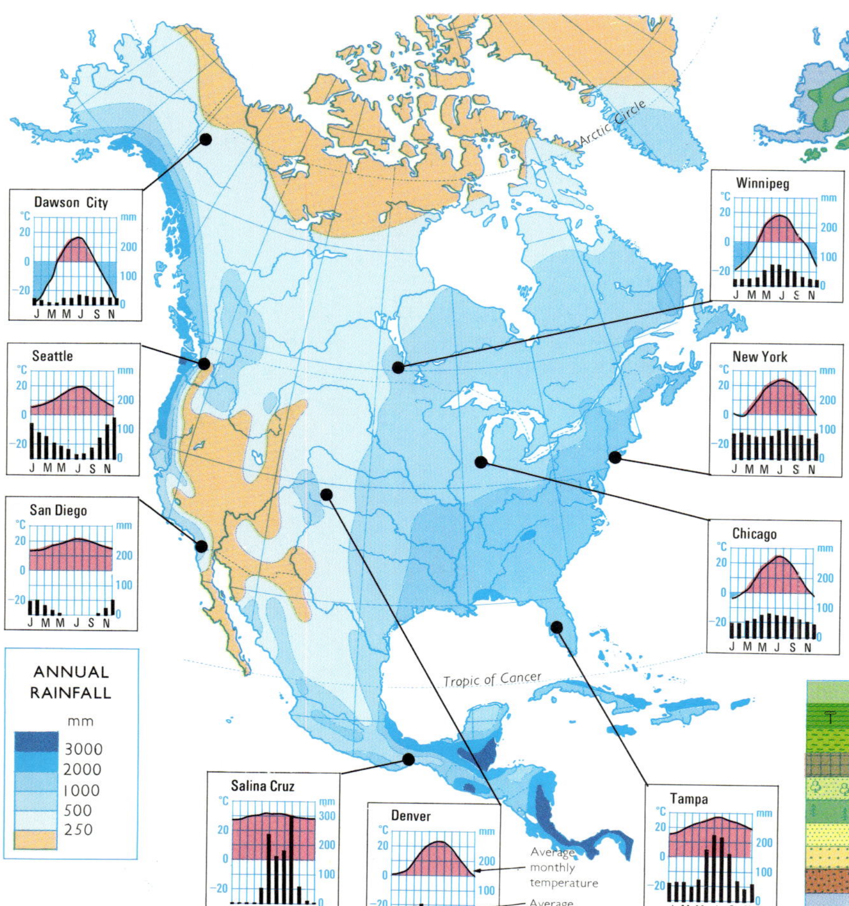

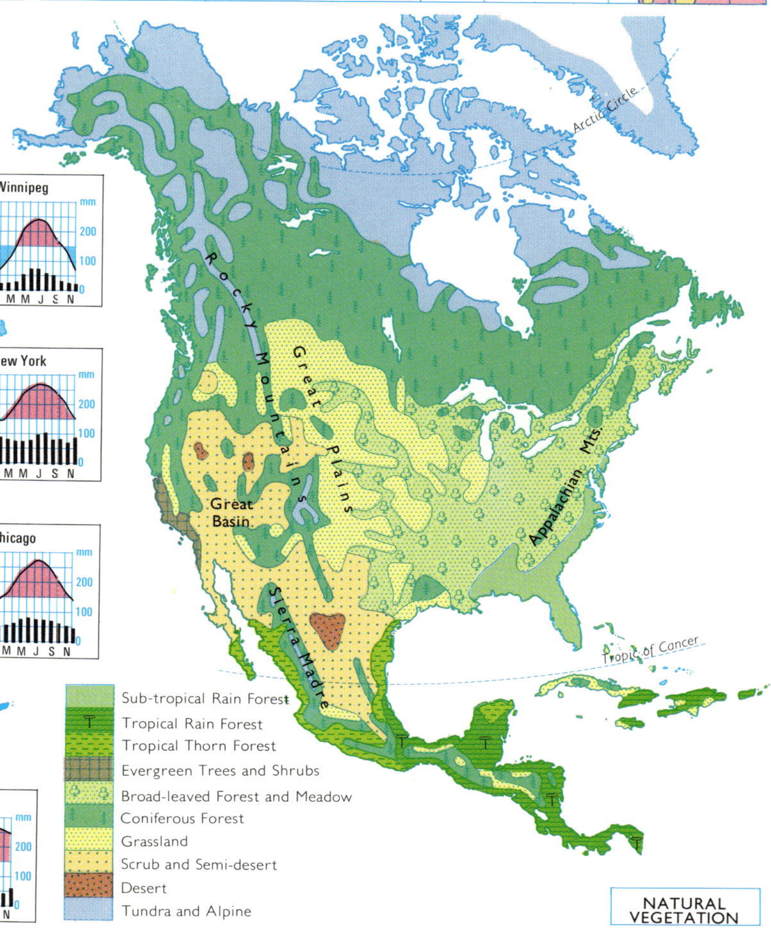

Projection: *Lambert's Equivalent Azimuthal*

1:32 000 000

400 0 400 800 1200 km

Projection: Polyconic

	Population								Land			Agriculture		
	Total	Density	Birth Rate	Death Rate	Life Expectancy	Growth 1965-80	Growth 1980-88	Urban	Area	Arable	Forest	Agricultural Population	Index of Production	Food Intake
	th.	persons per km²	per th. popn.	per th. popn.	yrs.	av. % per annum	av. % per annum	%	th. km²	th. km²	th. km²	% of total popn.	1979-81 = 100	calories per day
Bahamas	242	24	18	6	70		2	75	10	0.1	3	7		2699
Barbados	254	633	15	9	75		0.3	44	0.4	0.3	0	8	75	3020
Canada	26104	3	14	7	77	1	1	76	9221	460	3540	4	100	3462
Costa Rica	2670	52	29	4	74	2.6	2.3	45	51	5	16	26	108	2803
Cuba	10394	92	18	7	75	1.5	0.9	75	111	33	33	21	110	3122
Dominican Rep.	6859	134	31	7	66	2.9	2.4	58	48	15	6	39	110	2477
El Salvador	5056	234	36	9	63	2.7	1.4	44	21	7	1	39	98	2160
Guadaloupe	338	185	19	7	74		0.5	48	2	0.4	0.7	11	120	2512
Guatemala	8688	76	39	6	62	2.8	2.9	33	108	19	40	53	120	2307
Haiti	6254	191	34	13	55	2	1.8	29	28	9	0.5	66	103	1902
Honduras	4837	40	40	8	64	3.2	3.6	42	112	18	18	57	114	2068
Jamaica	2429	216	22	5	74	1.5	1.4	51	11	3	2	28	110	2590
Martinique	330	298	19	6	74		0.2	75	1	0.2	0.3	9	127	2673
Mexico	83593	41	29	5	69	3.1	2.2	71	1923	247	441	32	112	3132
Nicaragua	3623	28	42	10	64	3.1	3.4	58	119	13	37	41	86	2495
Panama	2315	29	25	4	72	2.6	2.1	54	76	6	40	27	111	2446
Puerto Rico	3376	393	19	7	75		0.6	74	9	1	2	3	98	
Trinidad and Tobago	1241	236	27	7	70	1.3	1.6	67	5	1	2	8	81	3082
U.S.A.	245871	26	16	9	75	1	1	74	9167	1899	2652	3	92	3645
Argentina	31506	11	21	8	71	1.6	1.4	85	2737	358	595	11	108	3210
Bolivia	6917	6	47	5	53	2.5	2.7	50	1084	34	558	43	117	2143
Brazil	144369	16	29	6	65	2.4	2.2	75	8457	775	5579	26	132	2656
Chile	12760	16	22	6	72	1.8	1.7	85	749	56	87	14	124	2579
Colombia	30007	28	29	5	66	2.2	1.9	69	1039	53	512	30	120	2543
Ecuador	10154	35	35	5	65	3.1	2.8	55	277	27	118	33	116	2058
Guyana	1006	5	28	7	70			35	197	5	164	24	80	2359
Paraguay	4042	10	35	3	67	2.8	3.2	46	397	22	156	47	150	2853
Peru	20681	16	35	9	62	2.8	2.2	69	1280	37	692	36	126	2246
Surinam	429	2	28	7	67		2.6	48	161	0.7	149	17	112	2524
Uruguay	3004	17	18	10	71	0.4	0.5	85	174	14	7	14	108	2648
Venezuela	18759	20	28	4	70	3.5	2.8	83	882	39	311	12	114	2494

Population. This is the United Nation's estimate for the mid-year 1988 (thousands)

Population Density. This is the quoted population total divided by the quoted land area (persons per square kilometre).

Birth Rates and Death Rates. These are the registered or United Nation's estimated rates per thousand population.

Life Expectancy. This figure indicates the number of years that a child born today can expect to live if the levels of death of today last throughout its life. The figure is the average of that for men and women. The figure for women is usually higher than that for men (U.K. Male 75, female 78 years).

Population Growth. This shows the average annual percentage change in population for two periods, 1965–1980 and 1980–1988.

Urbanization. This is the percentage of the total population living in urban areas. The definition of urban is that of the individual nation and usually includes quite small towns.

Land Area. This is the total area of the country minus the area covered by major lakes and rivers (thousand square kilometres).

Arable Land and Permanent Crops. This excludes fallow land but includes temporary pasture (thousand square kilometres).

Forest and Woodland. This includes natural and planted woodland and land recently cleared of timber which will be replanted (thousand square kilometres).

Agricultural Population. This is the percentage of the economically active population working in agriculture. It also includes those people working in forestry, hunting and fishing.

Index of Agricultural Production. The base period for this index is 1979–1981 and it shows the level of production in each country in 1988 in comparison with that of the earlier period. Only edible crops and meat are included.

Food Intake. The figures are the average intake per person in calories per day for the year 1986.

Trade: Imports	Trade: Exports	Education: Primary	Education: Secondary	Health	Energy	Consumer Price Index	G.N.P.	G.N.P.: Growth per capita	G.D.P.: Part formed by Agric.	G.D.P.: Part formed by Indust.	Loans & Debt	Loans & Debt	
US$ per capita	US$ per capita	% of age group	% of age group	Popn. per doctor	Consumption in kg of oil equiv. per capita	1980 = 100	US$ per capita	% per year 1965-88	%	%	end 1987 US$ millions	as % of G.N.P.	
6673	68[illegible]4	99	99	1050	2390	148	10570	–0.5	4	12	189	7	Bahamas
2752	2657	100	94	1300	1410	159	5990	2.3	6	13			Barbados
3547	3558	100	100	510	9690	162	15160	2.7	3	35	2340	0.5	Canada
516	433	100	42	960	470	703	1610	1.5	18	29	4100	67	Costa Rica
732	520	100	89	720	1420		1400		4	43			Cuba
260	104	100	47	1760	450	269	730	2.3	17	30	2609	53	Dominican Rep.
193	125	70	24	2830	170	391	860	–0.4	14	22	1762	39	El Salvador
4902	781	100	34	1020	930	174	4330	4.7	7	7			Guadaloupe
170	125	76	20	2180	190	202	950	1.2	25	16	2187	30	Guatemala
60	42	78	18	7180	50	141	360	0.5	32	17	713	29	Haiti
185	171	100	36	1510	200	148	810	0.7	22	24	2410	53	Honduras
497	267	100	58	2060	1090	284	940	–1.5	6	41	3322	99	Jamaica
6455	1130	100	47	900	950	183	4270	3.3	6	5			Martinique
152	250	100	55	1240	1600	9907	1830	2.5	9	34	90938	49	Mexico
255	83	98	42	1500	310		830	–2.5	21	34	5343	198	Nicaragua
539	154	100	59	980	640	119	2240	2.4	9	18	3722	68	Panama
		100	78	800	2210	124	5540	0.8	2	41			Puerto Rico
982	1178	95	76	960	7590	233	4210	1.3	4	39	1154	24	Trinidad and Tobago
1718	1027	100	100	470	9490	144	18350	1.5	2	30	12170	0.25	U.S.A.
185	202	100	74	370	1740	2.6 mill	2390	0.1	13	43	55709	63	Argentina
112	82	87	37	1540	340	9.1 mill	580	–0.5	24	24	4769	107	Bolivia
115	182	100	36	1080	760	53000	2020	4.1	11	38	100781	26	Brazil
315	399	100	70	1230	920	431	1310	0.2	6	31	15448	70	Chile
141	167	100	56	1190	780	526	1240	2.7	19	35	15851	41	Colombia
222	199	100	55	830	660	731	1040	3.2	16	31	9438	85	Ecuador
219	209	90	55	9600	650	209	410	–0.2	20	15			Guyana
297	236	99	30	1460	250	334	990	3.4	27	26	2246	50	Paraguay
146	126	100	65	1040	520	85519	1470	0.2	11	33	11049	45	Peru
1879	1935	100	51	1725	1370	255	2450	3.4	9	21			Surinam
379	396	100	71	510	610	2978	2190	1.4	15	40	3090	41	Uruguay
465	563	100	46	700	3380	159	3230	–0.9	6	38	31326	53	Venezuela

Antigua & Barbuda, Land 0.4/Popn. 82; Belize 23/145; Bermuda 0.05/55; Br. Virgin Is. 0.2/13; Cayman Is. 0.3/24; Dominica 0.8/94; Greenland 342/54; Grenada 0.3/92; Montserrat 0.1/12; Netherlands Antilles 1/189; St. Christopher-Nevis 0.4/44; St. Lucia 0.6/147; St. Pierre & M. 0.2/6; St. Vincent 0.3/113; Turks & Caicos Is. 0.4/11; U.S. Virgin Is. 0.3/110.
Falkland Is. 12/2; Fr. Guiana 89/91.

Trade. The trade figures are for the year 1988. The total trade figures have been divided by the population and are a measure of the country's external trade (U.S. $ per capita).

Education. The ages of primary school are taken to be 6–11 years and secondary school 12–17 years. The percentage of total school age group in this type of education is shown.

Energy. All forms of energy have been converted to their equivalent in oil. Firewood and other traditional forms used in developing countries are not included and so the energy consumption in those countries is understated (kilograms of oil equivalent per capita).

Consumer Price Index. The base year is 1980 which is 100 and the level of consumer prices in 1987 or 1988 are shown in relation to the base year. It is a measure of inflation.

G.N.P. (Gross National Product) This figure is an estimate of the average production per person measured in U.S. dollars and for 1988. The G.N.P. measures the value of goods and services produced in a country, plus the balance, positive or negative, of income from abroad, for example investments, interest on capital, money returned from foreign labour, etc. The rate of change is the average annual percentage change during the period 1965–1988 in the G.N.P. The G.D.P. (Gross Domestic Product) is the G.N.P. minus the foreign balances. The adjoining two columns show the percentage contribution to the G.D.P. made by the agricultural and mining and manufacturing sectors.

Loans and Debts. This figure in millions of U.S. dollars shows the external public debt ar the end of 1988. This is then shown as a percentage of the annual G.N.P. The figures in red show official development assistance made by the developed countries and also as a percentage of the donor country's G.N.P.

PACIFIC OCEAN
YUKON TERRITORY
NORTHWEST TERRITORIES
BRITISH COLUMBIA
ALBERTA
SASKATCHEWAN
MANITOBA
WASHINGTON
MONTANA
NORTH DAKOTA
SOUTH DAKOTA
MINNESOTA
NEBRASKA
WYOMING
UNITED STATES
Victoria Island
Banks Island
Prince of Wales Island
Somerset Island
Boothia Peninsula
Amundsen Gulf
Coronation Gulf
Queen Maud Gulf
M'Clintock Channel
Viscount Melville Sound
Great Bear Lake
Great Slave L.
Lake Athabasca
Reindeer Lake
Lake Winnipeg
L. Manitoba
Mackenzie Mountains
Rocky Mountains
Coast Mts.
Cassiar Mountains
Queen Charlotte Is.
Vancouver I.
Juneau
Whitehorse
Dawson
Yellowknife
Edmonton
Calgary
Vancouver
Victoria
Seattle
Tacoma
Spokane
Kamloops
Kelowna
Prince George
Lethbridge
Medicine Hat
Red Deer
Saskatoon
Regina
Moose Jaw
Prince Albert
Brandon
Winnipeg
Grand Forks
Fargo
Bismarck
Minneapolis
St. Paul
Duluth
Pierre
Rapid City
Sioux Falls
Sioux City
Omaha
Des Moines
Anchorage
Fairbanks
Projection: Bonne
ALASKA
1:30 000 000
0 200 400 600 km
BERING SEA
GULF OF ALASKA
PACIFIC OCEAN
Aleutian Is.
Alaska Peninsula
Brooks Range
Kodiak I.
West from Greenwich
m
3000
2000
1500
1000
400
200
0
200
2000
m

Devon Island
Lancaster Sound
Bylot I.
Pond Inlet
Baffin Bay
Svartenhuk Peninsula
Disko I.
GREENLAND
Søndre Strømfjord
Angmagssalik
King Frederick VI Coast
Godthaab
Frederikshaab
Julianehaab
Sydproven
C. Farewell
Brodeur Peninsula
Gulf of Boothia
Baffin Island
C. Hewett
Home B.
Davis Strait
C. Dyer
Cumberland Peninsula
C. Mercy
Cumberland Sd.
Fury & Hecla Str.
Melville Peninsula
Committee B.
Prince Charles I.
Foxe Basin
Nettilling L.
Amadjuak L.
Foxe Penin.
Frobisher Bay
Resolution I.
Circle
Wager B.
Roes Welcome Sd.
C. Dorchester
Foxe Channel
Southampton I.
Hudson Strait
Chesterfield Inlet
Coats I.
Mansel I.
Ivujivik
Maricourt (Wakeham Bay)
Koartac
Akpatok I.
C. Chidley
Payne (Bellin)
Ungava Bay
Port Nouveau-Quebec
George
Ungava Peninsula
Payne L.
Leaf
Koksoak
Kaniapiskau
Hudson Bay
Ottawa Is.
Kuujjuaq
L. Minto
King George Is.
Belcher Is.
Clearwater L.
Lac Bienville
Schefferville
Petitsikapau L.
Nain
Hopedale
C. Harrison
Indian Harbour
Rigolet
LABRADOR
L. Melville
Cartwright
Michikamau L.
Happy Valley Goose Bay
Churchill
Battle Harb.
Str. of Belle Isle
NEWFOUNDLAND
Poste de la Baleine (Great Whale River)
Kaniapiskau L.
Labrador City
C. Henrietta Maria
Severn
Winisk
Big Trout L.
Ft. George
James Bay
Akimiski I.
Attawapiskat
Gagnon
Manicouagan
QUEBEC
Natashquan
Mingan
Anticosti I.
Sept Iles
Port Cartier
Gander
Bonavista
Grand Falls
Carbonear
St. John's
Corner Brook
C. Race
Channel-Port aux Basques
C. Ray
Cabot Str.
Gulf of St. Lawrence
C. Gaspé
Gaspé Pen.
Eastmain
Fort Rupert (Rupert House)
Rupert
Mistassini L.
Albany
Moosonee
ONTARIO
Harricanaw
Baie Comeau
R. St. Lawrence
Matane
Rimouski
Campbellton
Bathurst
Chatham
PR. EDWARD I.
Summerside
Charlottetown
Cape Breton I.
Glace Bay
Sydney
ST. PIERRE & MIQUELON (Fr.)
L. St. Joseph
Missinaibi
Chibougamau
St. John
Saguenay
Jonquière
Chicoutimi
Riviere du Loup
NEW BRUNSWICK
Moncton
Northumberland Str.
Amherst
NOVA SCOTIA
New Glasgow
Truro
Nipigon
Geraldton
Hearst
Mattagami
L. Abitibi
Gouin Reservoir
Edmundston
Sable I. (Nova Scotia)
Thunder Bay
Oba
Timmins
Rouyn
Val d'Or
Kirkland Lake
La Tuque
Quebec
Fredericton
Saint John
Kentville
Dartmouth
Halifax
Bridgewater
Lake Superior
Cabonga Reservoir
Shawinigan
Trois Rivieres
Thetford Mines
MAINE
Bangor
B. of Fundy
Yarmouth
C. Sable
Sault Ste. Marie
Sudbury
North Bay
MONTREAL
St. Hyacinthe
Sherbrooke
Marquette
MICHIGAN
Escanaba
Georgian Bay
Ottawa
Hull
Cornwall
Burlington
L. Champlain
Lewiston
Portland
Lake Huron
Orillia
Peterborough
Kingston
VERMONT
NEW HAMPSHIRE
Manchester
Concord
Wausau
Green Bay
Appleton
WISCONSIN
Traverse City
Owen Sound
TORONTO
Oshawa
L. Ontario
Rochester
Syracuse
MASS.
BOSTON
C. Cod
Providence
Saginaw
Kitchener
Niagara Falls
Albany
NEW YORK
Springfield
CONN.
RHODE I.
MILWAUKEE
L. Michigan
Grand Rapids
London
Sarnia
Hamilton
St. Catharines
BUFFALO
Binghamton
Scranton
New Haven
Madison
DETROIT
Windsor
Lake Erie
Erie
NEW YORK
Rockford
CHICAGO
ILLINOIS
Gary
INDIANA
Toledo
OHIO
Akron
CLEVELAND
PENNSYLVANIA
Newark
NEW JERSEY
Allentown
ATLANTIC OCEAN
West from Greenwich

Projection: Albers' Equal Area with two standard parallels.

West from Greenwich

1:12 000 000

100 0 100 200 300 400 500 km

Projection: Albers' Equal Area with two standard parallels

GULF OF
ST. LAWRENCE
ATLANTIC
OCEAN
Anticosti I.
Jupiter
West Pt.
Heath Pt.
Port Cartier
Cap Chat
Gaspé
C. Gaspé
Shickshock Mts.
Gaspé Peninsula
Matane
1310
572
Magdalen
Is.
(Quebec)
C. North
Cape Breton
Island
Glace Bay
Sydney
832
Bras d'Or L.
PRINCE EDWARD
ISLAND
North Pt.
Tignish
Summerside
Charlottetown
East Pt.
Northumberland Str.
Chaleur Bay
Dalhousie
Campbellton
Bathurst
Miramichi B.
Newcastle
Chatham
NEW
BRUNSWICK
Edmundston
819
Grand Falls
Rimouski
Rivière du Loup
St. Lawrence
Pipmuacan L.
Chibougamau
Chibougamau L.
556
Gouin
Res.
St. Félicien
Roberval
Dolbeau
Peribonca
Lac
St. Jean
Jonquière
Chicoutimi
Saguenay
La Tuque
Baie St. Paul
Gatineau
bonga
Res.
QUEBEC
Montmagny
Quebec
Levis
St. John
Presque Isle
Houlton
Grand Mère
Shawinigan
960
Trois Rivieres
Joliette
ont Laurier
Sorel
Victoriaville
Thetford Mines
Drummondville
St. Jérôme
St. Hyacinthe
MONTREAL
Buckingham
Hull
Ottawa
Ottawa
St. Jean
Valleyfield
Cornwall
Sherbrooke
Magog
Megantic
Moosehead
L.
Mt. Katahdin
1606
Fredericton
Grand L.
Chipman
Moncton
Sussex
Saint
John
St. Stephen
Bay of Fundy
Springhill
New Glasgow
Stellarton
Truro
Chedabucto B.
Canso
NOVA SCOTIA
Kentville
Dartmouth
Halifax
Digby
Bridgewater
L. Rossignol
Yarmouth
Shelburne
C. Sable
Grand
Manan I.
MAINE
Penobscot
Kennebec
Bangor
Waterville
Augusta
Mt. Desert
I.
Lewiston
Auburn
Rockland
Portland
Biddeford
Newport
Plattsburg
L.
Champlain
Burlington
Ogdensburg
ckville
Montpelier
Barre
Berlin
1917
VERMONT
NEW HAMPSHIRE
Connecticut
Adirondack Mts.
1629
Watertown
L.
George
Rutland
Laconia
Concord
Rochester
Dover
Portsmouth
Glen Falls
Oneida L.
Rome
Utica
Syracuse
Schenectady
Keene
Manchester
Fitchburg
Nashua
Bennington
Troy
Albany
Lawrence
Lowell
Salem
Massachusetts
Bay
NEW YORK
Cortland
Pittsfield
MASS.
Worcester
Newton
BOSTON
Quincy
C. Cod
Holyoke
Cambridge
Brockton
Cape
Cod B.
Catskill
Mts.
1281
Binghamton
Delaware
Springfield
Hartford
Woonsocket
Pawtucket
Providence
Fall River
New Bedford
Poughkeepsie
Hudson
New Britain
CONN.
R.I.
Newburgh
Waterbury
Meriden
Newport
Nantucket
Sd.
ranton
Middletown
New
Haven
Nantucket I.
Martha's Vineyard
Block I.
New London
Wilkes Barre
Bridgeport
Stamford
Long Island
Hazleton
Paterson
Yonkers
Bethlehem
Newark
NEW YORK
Jersey City
Allentown
Elizabeth
Edison
Reading
Trenton
ADELPHIA
Camden
NEW
JERSEY
Newark
Wilmington
Vineland
DELAWARE
Atlantic City
ND
Dover
Cape May
Salisbury
Bay
Cape Charles
76
74
72
70
68
66
64
62
60
48
44
42
40
38
West from Greenwich

San Diego
Yuma
Phoenix
Tijuana
Mexicali
Ensenada
Tucson
Nogales
Agua Prieta
Ciudad Juárez
El Paso
Carlsbad
Wichita Falls
Fort Worth
Dallas
Abilene
Pecos
Birmingham
Shreveport
Monroe
Tyler
Jackson
Montgomery
UNITED STATES
Pt. Baja
Sebastian Vizcaino Bay
Pt. Sta. Eugenia
Lower California
Gulf of California
Sonora
Tiburón I.
Hermosillo
Empalme
Guaymas
Sta. Rosalía
Ciudad Obregon
Navojoa
Yaqui
Villa Ahumada
Sta. María
Río Grande
San Angelo
Waco
Brazos
Trinity
Sabine
Red
Mississippi
Alexandria
Baton Rouge
Mobile
Alabama
Pensacola
Beaumont
Lake Charles
Lafayette
New Orleans
Austin
San Antonio
Houston
Port Arthur
Galveston
C. San Blas
Mississippi Delta
Chihuahua
Conchos
Piedras Negras
Eagle Pass
Nueva Rosita
Sabinas
Delicias
Laredo
Nuevo Laredo
Matagorda I.
Corpus Christi
Padre I.
Brownsville
Matamoros
Rio Grande del Norte
Laguna de la Madre
GULF OF MEXICO
Fuerte
Los Machis
Guamúchil
Culiacán
Hidalgo del Parral
Monclova
Falcon Res.
Sabinas Hidalgo
Reynosa
S. Pedro
Gómez Palacio
Torreón
Saltillo
Monterrey
Nazas
Montemorelos
Concepción del Oro
Sierra Madre
MEXICO
Elota
Durango
Mazatlán
Rosario
C. San Lucas
Matehuala
Ciudad Victoria
Fresnillo
Zacatecas
San Luis Potosí
Ciudad Mante
Ciudad Madero
Tampico
Tropic of Cancer
Yucatan Strait
Pinar del Río
PACIFIC OCEAN
Las Tres Marías
Tepic
Aguascalientes
C. Rojo
Tuxpan
Guadalajara
León
Irapuato
Querétaro
Pachuca
Pánuco
C. Corrientes
Ameca
Celaya
Colima Vol.
Zamora
Morelia
Colima
Manzanillo
MEXICO
Toluca
Cuernavaca
Iguala
Popocatépetl
Puebla
Citlaltépetl
Jalapa Enríquez
Veracruz
Orizaba
Gulf of Campeche
Progreso
Mérida
Valladolid
I. de Cozumel
Peto
Campeche
Ciudad del Carmen
Laguna de Términos
Yucatan
Chetumal
Balsas
Chilpancingo
Acapulco
Mexcala
Minatitlán
Coatzacoalcos
Villahermosa
Isthmus of Tehuantepec
Usumacinta
Belmopan
Belize
BELIZE
Turneffe Is.
Gulf of Honduras
Ometepec
Oaxaca
Verde
Salina Cruz
Juchitán
Tuxtla Gutiérrez
San Cristóbal
Tonalá
Chiapa
Pto. Barrios
Pto. Cortés
Tela
La Ceiba
GUATEMALA
S. Pedro Sula
HONDURAS
G. of Tehuantepec
Tapachula
Guatemala
Quezaltenango
Sta. Ana
Comayagua
Tegucigalpa
San Salvador
EL SALVADOR
S. Miguel
G. of Fonseca
Choluteca
NICARAGUA
Leon
Managua
Granada
L. Nicaragua
Nicoya Pen.
Puntarenas
Colón
Coco Solo
Fort Randolph
Cristóbal
Sherman
Margarita
Puerto Pilón
Chagres
Gatun
Gatun Locks
Gatun Dam
Zorra I.
El Limón
Madden L.
Juan Gallegos
Madden Dam
Gatun Lake
Frijoles
Buenos Aires
Escobal
Colorado I.
Darien
Chagres
Gamboa
The Gaillard Cut
Balboa Hill
350
Las Cascadas
Culebra
Paraíso
Pedro Miguel
Pedro Miguel Locks
Miraflores Locks
Corozal
Fort Clayton
Curundu
Albrook
Balboa
Fort Amador
Arraiján
La Chorrera
PANAMA
Panama Bay
PANAMA CANAL
1:1 000 000
Montego Bay
Falmouth
St. Ann's Bay
Galina Point
Annotto Bay
Port Antonio
Savanna la Mar
Mandeville
KINGSTON
May Pen
Spanish Town
2256
Morant Point
Morant Bay
Portland Point
JAMAICA
1:5 000 000
TRINIDAD AND TOBAGO
1:5 000 000
Charlotteville
Tobago
Scarborough
Port of Spain
940
Arima
Sangre Grande
Gulf of Paria
TRINIDAD
San Fernando
Rio Claro
Point Fortin
Princes Town
Siparia
Serpent's Mouth
The Valley
Anguilla (Br.)
Marigot
St. Martin (Fr.)
St. Maarten (Neth.)
St. Barthélemy (Fr.)
Saba (Neth.)
St. Eustatius (Neth.)
Codrington
Barbuda
St. Christopher (St. Kitts)
Basseterre
ST. CHRISTOPHER-NEVIS
ANTIGUA & BARBUDA
Charlestown
Nevis
St. John's
Antigua
Redonda
Montserrat
Plymouth
Guadeloupe Passage
GUADELOUPE (Fr.)
Grande Terre
Ste Rose
Moule
Désirade (Fr.)
Basse Terre
Pointe-à-Pitre
Marie-Galante (Fr.)
Basse Terre
I. des Saintes (Fr.)
Dominica Passage
Grand Bourg
Portsmouth
Morne Diablotin
1490
Roseau
DOMINICA (Windward Is.)
LEEWARD ISLANDS
1:5 000 000
Martinique Passage
Mt. Pelée
1397
Ste. Marie
St. Pierre
Fort de France
Le François
Lamentin
MARTINIQUE (Fr.)
Ste. Anne
St. Lucia Channel
Castries
Soufrière
ST. LUCIA
Vieux Fort
St. Vincent Passage
Soufrière
1178
Georgetown
Kingstown
ST. VINCENT & Bequia
BARBADOS
Speightstown
Bridgetown
THE GRENADINES
Mustique
Canouan
Union
Carriacou
Hillsborough
The Grenadines
Ronde
St. George's
840
Grenville
GRENADA
WINDWARD ISLANDS
1:5 000 000
Projection: Bonne

ATLANTIC OCEAN
CARIBBEAN SEA
Bermuda
Hamilton
Atlanta
Augusta
Macon
Colombus
Savannah
Charleston
C. Fear
Albany
Jacksonville
Tallahassee
Daytona Beach
C. Canaveral
Orlando
St. Petersburg
Tampa
West Palm Beach
L. Okeechobee
Fort Lauderdale
Miami
C. Sable
Key West
Florida
Florida Str.
Grand Bahama I.
Freeport
Gt. Abaco I.
New Providence I.
Eleuthera I.
Nassau
Cat I.
Andros I.
BAHAMAS
S. Salvador
Long I.
Tropic of Cancer
Havana
Matanzas
Cárdenas
Sagua la Grande
Sta. Clara
Morón
Camagüey
Cienfuegos
Sancti Spíritus
Ciego de Avila
Holguín
I. de Juventud
Manzanillo
Bayamo
Santiago de Cuba
Guantánamo
Mayaguana
Acklins I.
Caicos I. (Br.)
Turks Is.(Br.)
Gt. Inagua I.
Windward Passage
Cap Haïtien
Santiago
San Francisco de Macorís
Gonaïves
DOMINICAN REP.
La Romana
Santo Domingo
Baní
Barahona
Port au Prince
Hispaniola
Les Cayes
Mona Passage
PUERTO RICO (U.S.A.)
San Juan
Mayagüez
Ponce
Caguas
St. Thomas (U.S.A.)
Charlotte Amalie
Virgin Is.(Br.)
St. Croix (U.S.A.)
Anguilla
St. Martin (Fr. & Neth.)
ST. CHRISTOPHER-NEVIS (St. Kitts)
ANTIGUA & BARBUDA
St. John's
Montserrat
Guadeloupe (Fr.)
Pointe à Pitre
DOMINICA
Leeward Islands
LESSER ANTILLES
Fort de France
Martinique (Fr.)
ST. LUCIA
BARBADOS
Bridgetown
Windward Islands
ST. VINCENT & THE GRENADINES
GRENADA
GREATER ANTILLES
Grand Cayman (Br.)
Montego Bay
JAMAICA
Kingston
Caratasca Lagoon
C. Gracias á Dios
Mosquito Coast
Providencia (Col.)
San Andrés (Col.)
Bluefields
Limón
San José
Vol. Barú
Colón
Panama
PANAMA
David
Coiba
Azuero Pen.
G. of Panama
G. of Darién
Pta. Gallinas
Pen. de la Guajira
Gulf of Venezuela
Aruba (Neth.)
Netherlands Antilles
Curaçao (Neth.)
Willemstad
Bonaire (Neth.)
Pen. de Paraguaná
Punta Fijo
Coro
Santa Marta
Barranquilla
Sierra Nevada de Santa Marta
Cartagena
Sincelejo
Maracaibo
Cabimas
L. de Maracaibo
Valera
Barquisimeto
Maracay
Valencia
Caracas
Barcelona
La Blanquilla (Ven.)
Margarita
La Tortuga (Ven.)
Cumaná
Carúpano
G. of Paria
Port of Spain
TRINIDAD & TOBAGO
Tobago
San Fernando
Delta of the Orinoco
Maturín
El Tigre
Orinoco
Ciudad Guayana
Ciudad Bolívar
El Callao
San Fernando de Apure
Apure
Arauca
Cord. de Mérida
Cúcuta
San Cristóbal
Bucaramanga
Barrancabermeja
Tunja
Medellín
Atrato
Cauca
Quibdó
Manizales
Pereira
Armenia
Ibagué
Tolima
Girardot
Bogotá
Buenaventura
Cali
Popayán
Magdalena
Guaviare
Meta
Pto. Ayacucho
COLOMBIA
VENEZUELA
Caura
Paragua
Roraima
Sierra Pacaraima
Cuyuni
Essequibo
GUYANA
Georgetown
New Amsterdam
Corentyne
SURINAM
Casiquiare
BRAZIL

1:30 000 000

Projection: *Lambert's Equivalent Azimuthal*

1:30 000 000

200 0 200 400 600 800 1000 km

Projection: Lambert's Equivalent Azimuthal

West from Greenwich

BUENOS AIRES Capital Cities

1:70 000 000

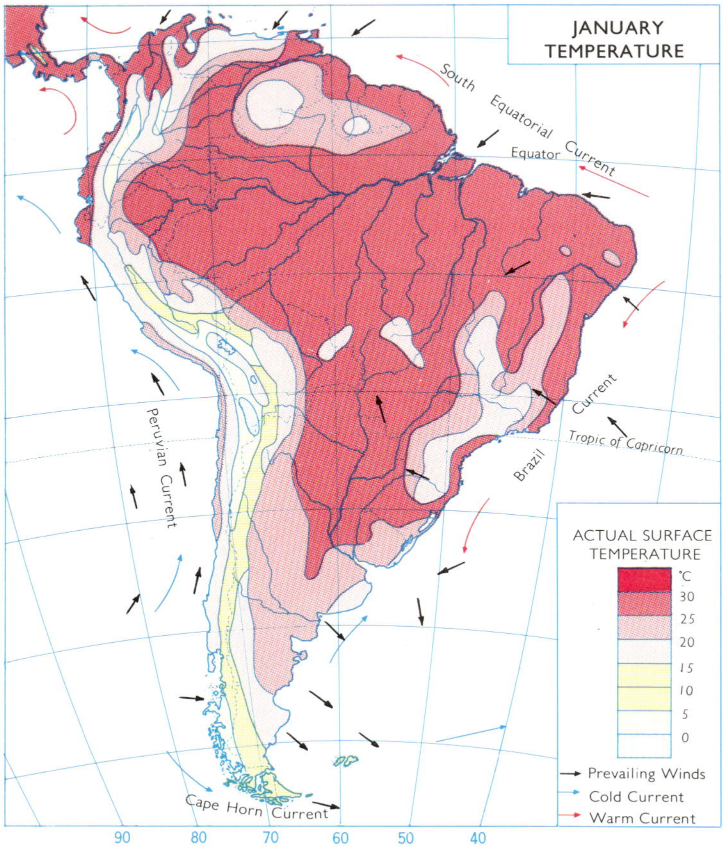

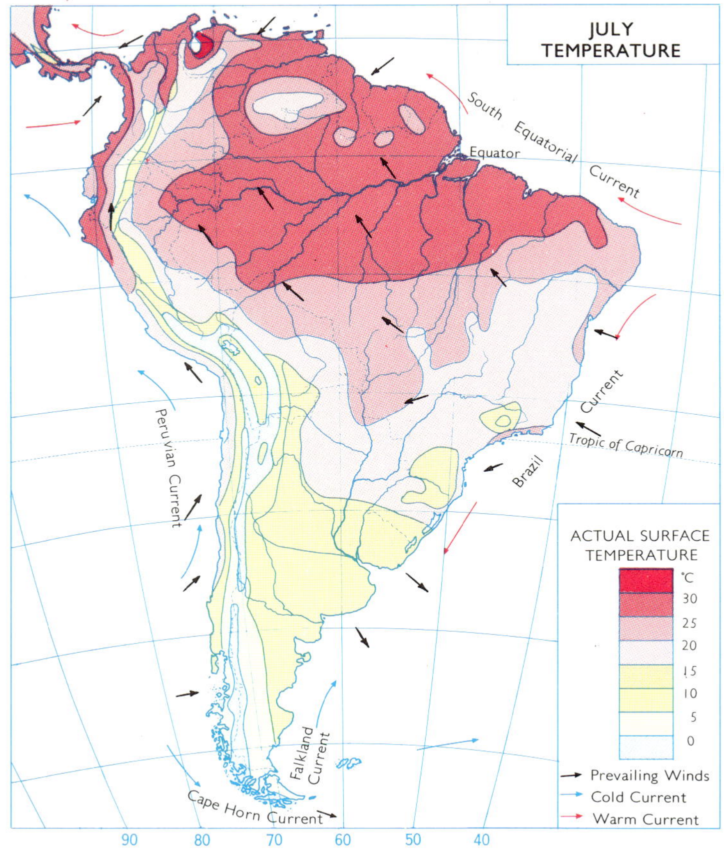

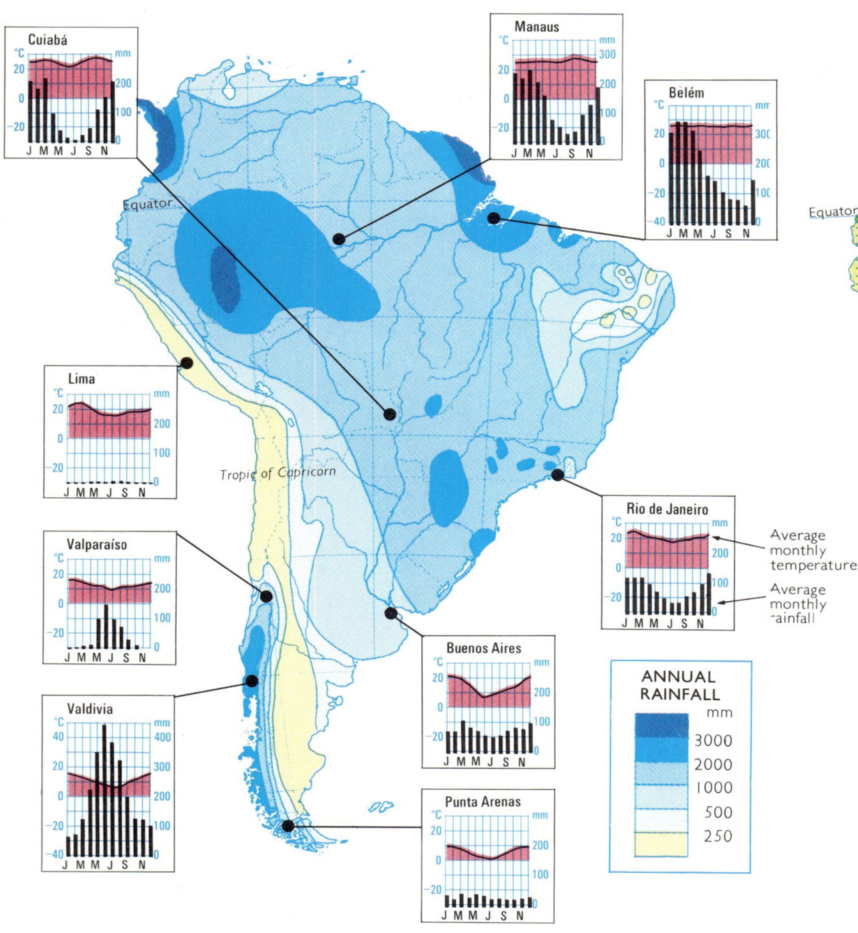

Projection: *Lambert's Equivalent Azimuthal*

1:30 000 000

200 0 200 400 600 800 1000 km

Projection: *Lambert's Equivalent Azimuthal*

Projection: Sanson-Flamsteed's Sinusoidal

1:16 000 000

200 100 0 200 400 600 km

1:16 000 000

200 100 0 200 400 600 km

Projection: Sanson-Flamsteed's Sinusoidal

West from Greenwich

1:50 000 000

500 0 500 1000 1500 2000 km

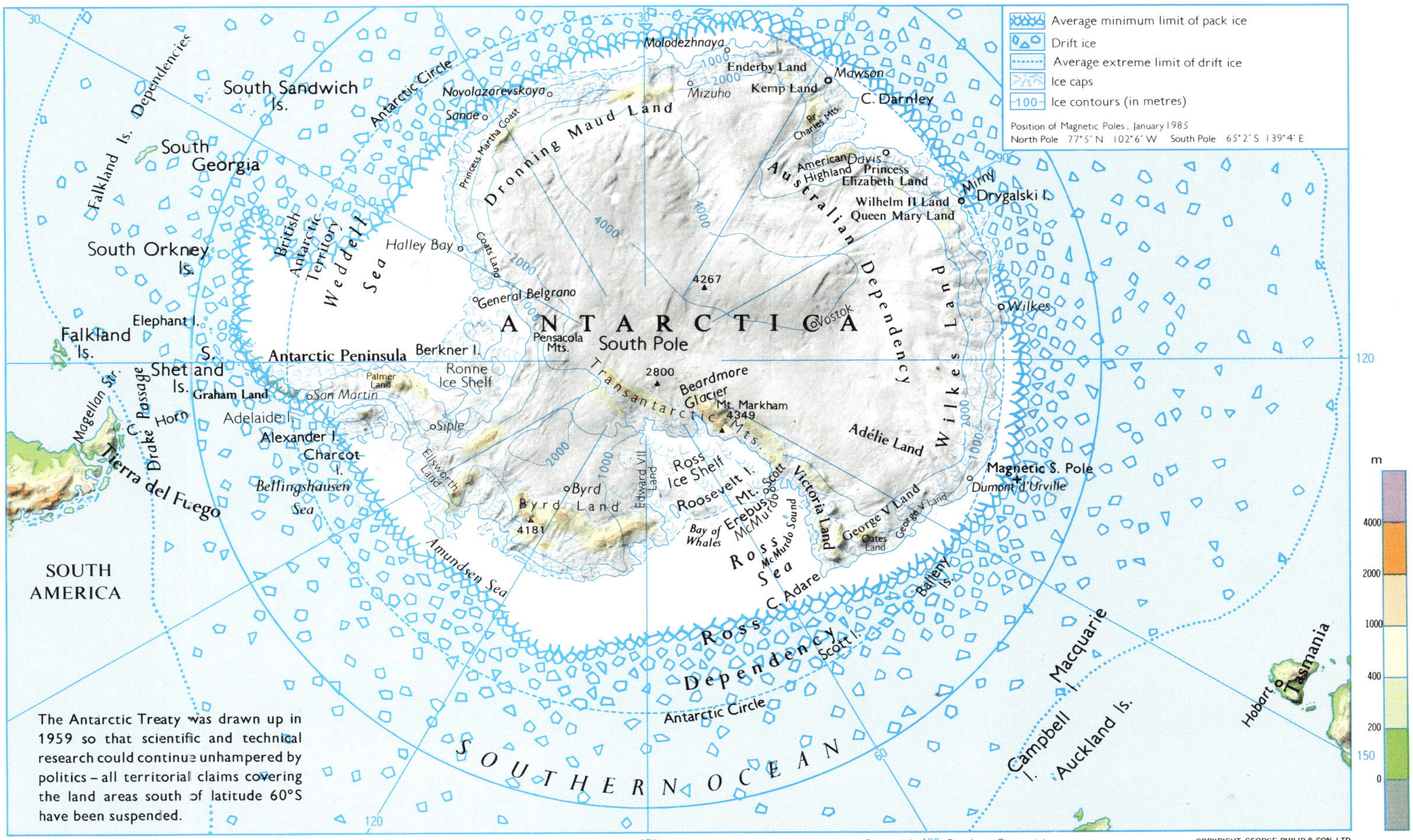

The Antarctic Treaty was drawn up in 1959 so that scientific and technical research could continue unhampered by politics – all territorial claims covering the land areas south of latitude 60°S have been suspended.

Projection: *Zenithal Equidistant*

West from Greenwich 180 East from Greenwich

Projection: Hammer Equal Area

HEIGHT OF LAND
in metres

- Above 6 000
- 4 000–6 000
- 2 000–4 000
- 1000–2 000
- 200–1000
- 0–200
- Below Sea-Level

DEPTH OF SEA
in metres

- 0–200
- 200–4000
- 4000–8000
- Below 8000

STRUCTURE

1: 95 000 000

Structural Regions of the Land

- Pre-Cambrian shields
- Sedimentary cover on Pre-Cambrian shields
- Palæozoic (Caledonian and Hercynian) folding
- Sedimentary cover on Palæozoic folding
- Mesozoic folding
- Sedimentary cover on Mesozoic folding
- Cainozoic folding
- Sedimentary cover on Cainozoic folding
- Intensive Mesozoic and Cainozoic vulcanism
- Oceanic-type crust raised above sea level

Structural Regions of the Oceans

- Regions of continental-type crust
- Limit of continental shelf
- Oceanic marginal troughs
- Mid-oceanic volcanic ridges
- Rift valleys in mid-oceanic ridges

- Principal faults
- Frontal line of overthrust folds

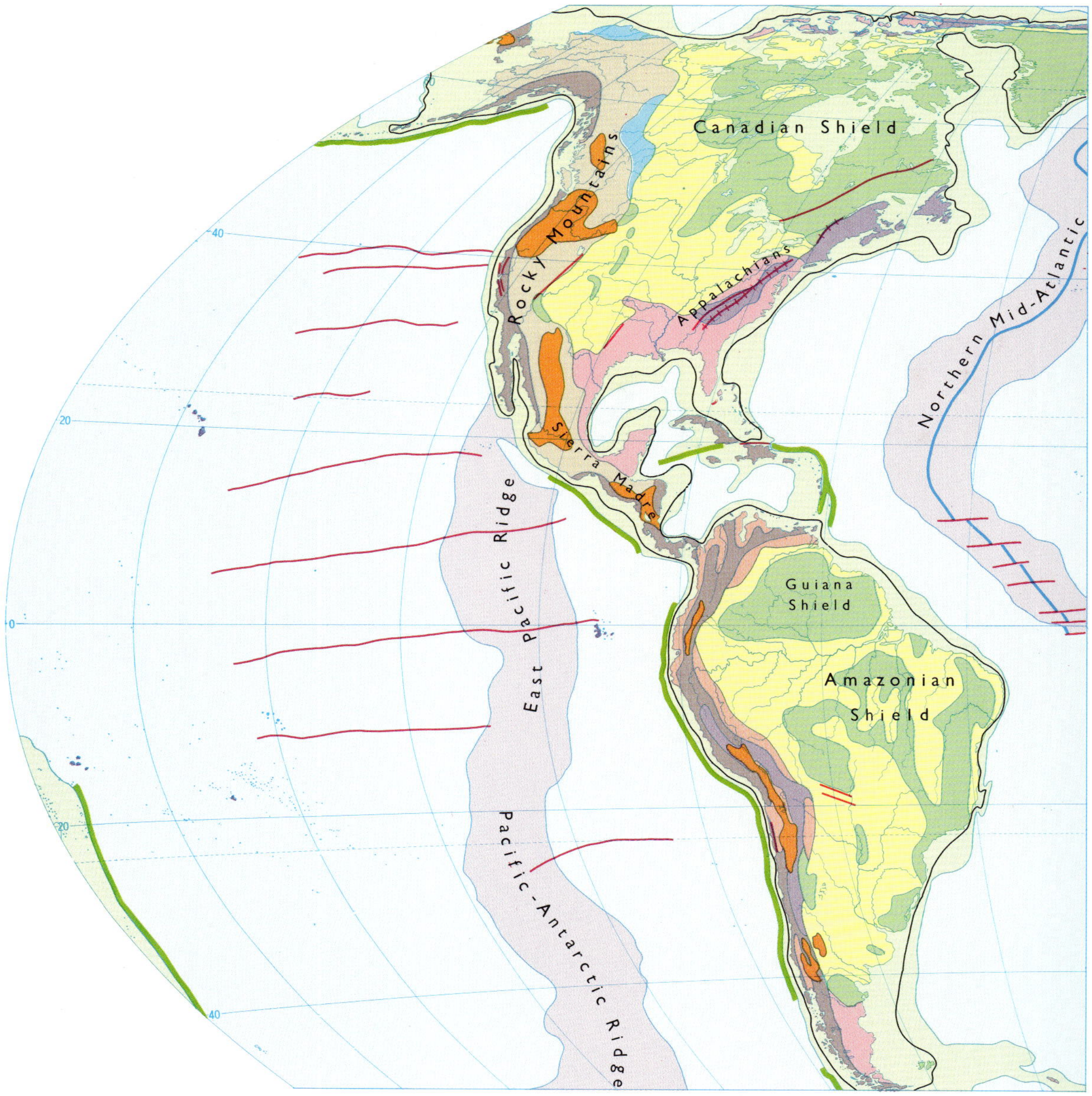

GEOLOGICAL TIME SCALE

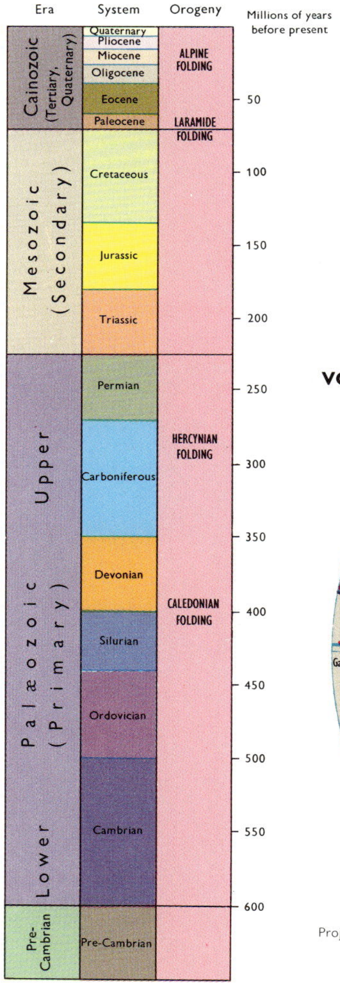

VOLCANOES

Equatorial Scale 1: 280 000 000

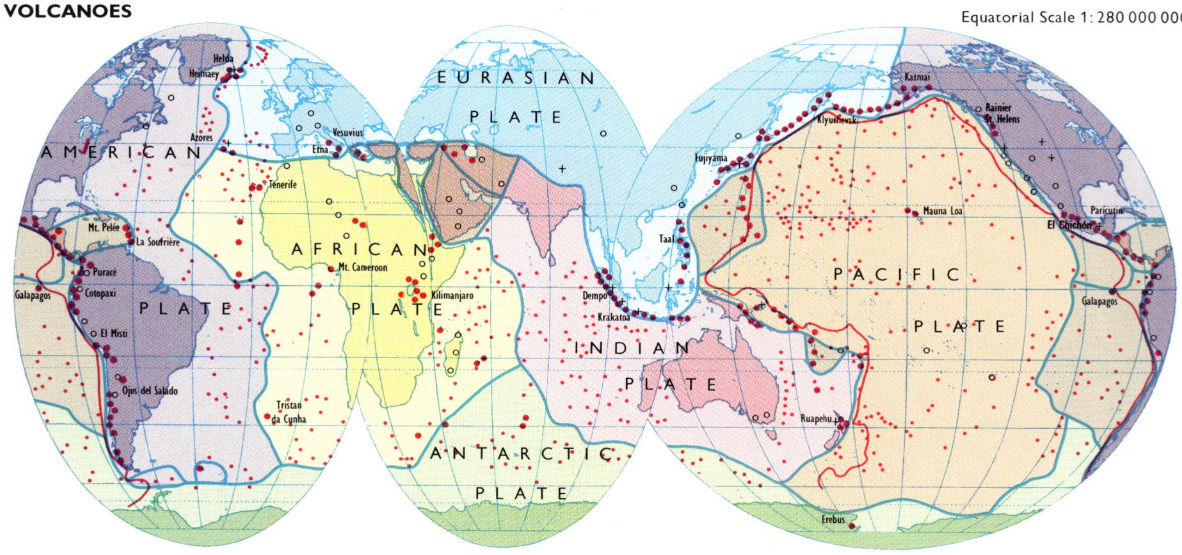

Projection: *Interrupted Mollweide's Homolographic*

- Land volcanoes active since 1700
- Land volcanoes inactive since 1700
- Submarine volcanoes
- Geysers
- Plate boundaries
- Andesite line (boundary between sial continental crust and sima oceanic crust in the Pacific)

1: 95 000 000

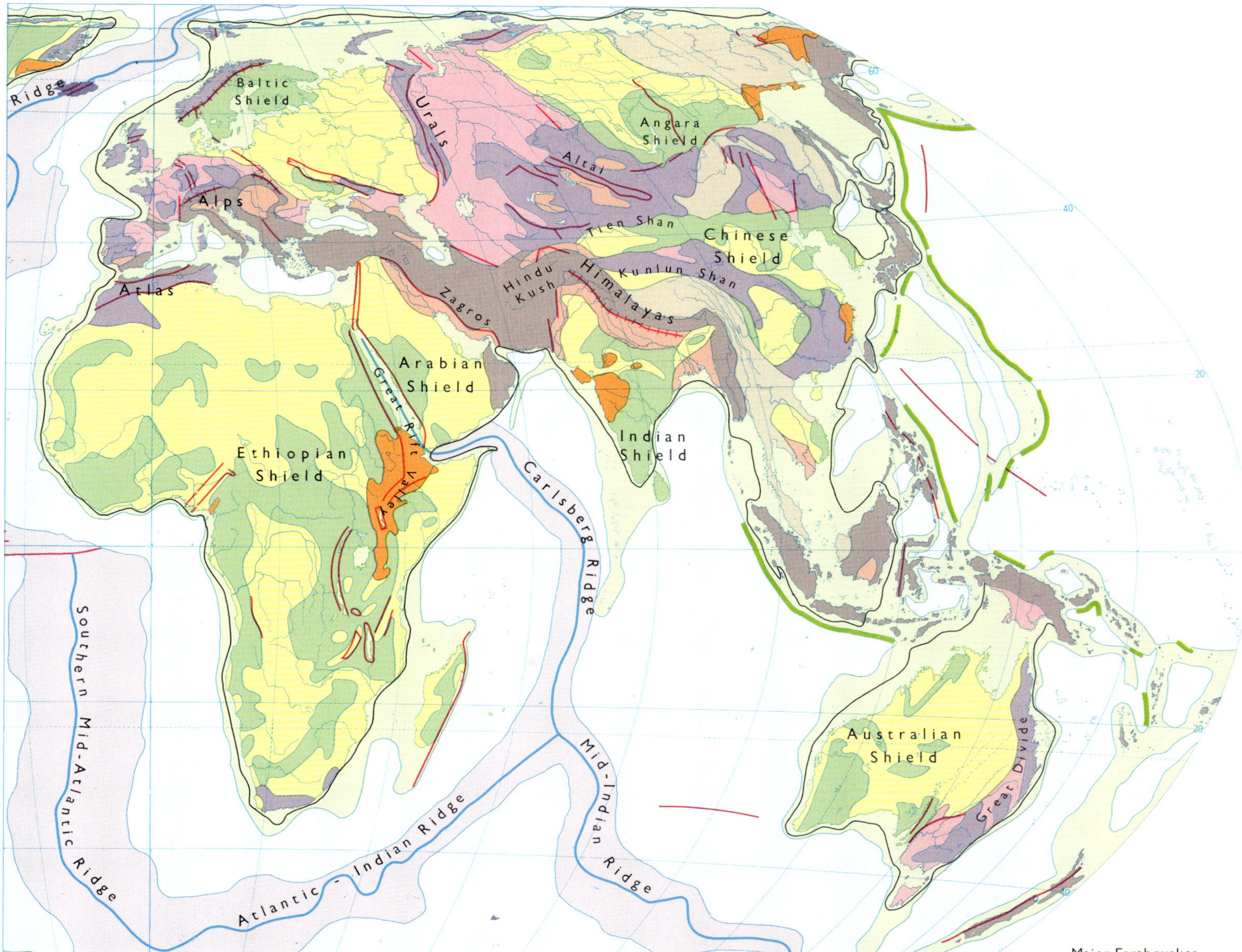

Projection: *Hammer Equal Area*

EARTHQUAKES

Equatorial Scale 1: 280 000 000

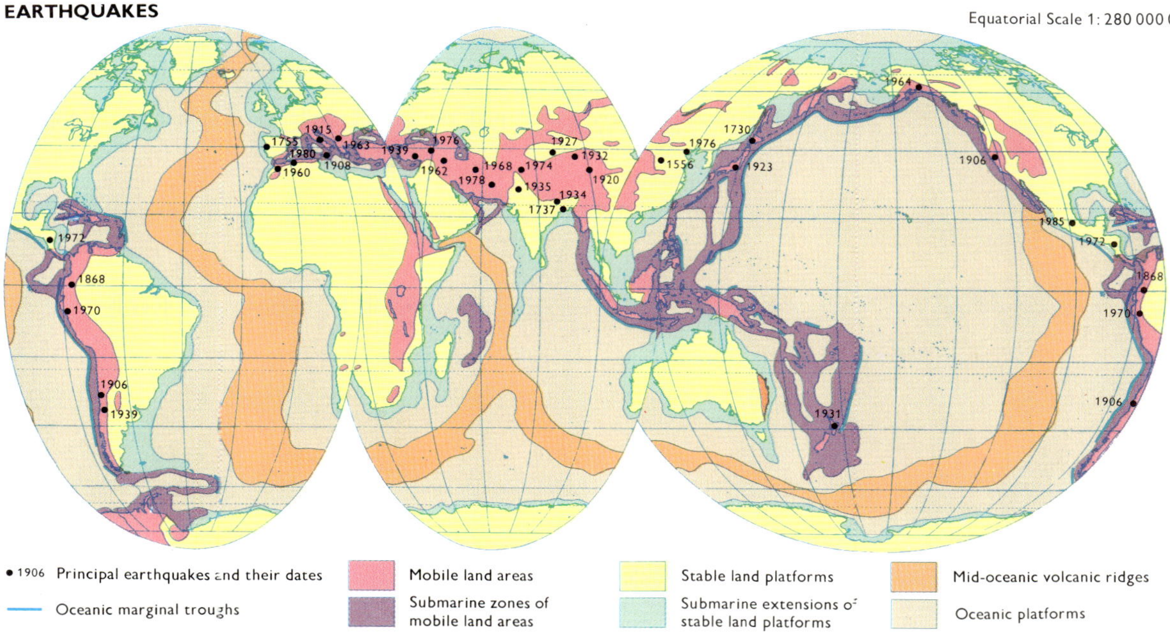

Major Earthquakes

		Nos. killed
1556	Shaanxi, China	830 000
1730	Hokkaido, Japan	137 000
1737	Calcutta, India	300 000
1755	Lisbon, Portugal	60 000
1868	Ecuador and N. Peru	40 000
1906	Valparaiso, Chile	22 000
1906	San Francisco, U.S.A.	450
1908	Messina, Italy	77 000
1915	Avezzano, Italy	30 000
1920	Gansu, China	180 000
1923	Yokohama, Japan	143 000
1927	Nan Shan, China	200 000
1931	Napier, N. Zealand	250
1932	Gansu, China	70 000
1934	Nepal	11 700
1935	Quetta, Pakistan	30 000
1939	Erzincan, Turkey	30 000
1960	Agadir, Morocco	12 000
1962	Khorasan, Iran	10 000
1963	Skopje, Yugoslavia	1000
1964	Anchorage, Alaska	100
1968	N.E. Iran	12 000
1970	N. Peru	67 000
1972	Managua, Nicaragua	7 000
1974	N. Pakistan	10 000
1976	Tangshan, China	650 000
1978	Tabas, Iran	11 000
1980	El Asnam, Algeria	20 000
1985	Mexico	20 000
1988	Armenia	55 000

108 THE WORLD : Climatic Regions, Soils and Vegetation

CLIMATES

after Köppen

Climatic group	Climate		Temperature		Rainfall
TROPICAL RAINY CLIMATES **A**	**Af**	RAIN-FOREST CLIMATE	All mean monthly temperatures above 18°C		(chart)
	Am	MONSOON CLIMATE			
	Aw	SAVANNA CLIMATE			
DRY CLIMATES **B**	**BS**	STEPPE CLIMATE	Mean annual temperature **h** = above 18°C **k** = below 18°C		(chart) – – – – summer rainfall ——— winter rainfall –·–·– rainfall evenly distributed
	BW	DESERT CLIMATE			
WARM TEMPERATE RAINY CLIMATES **C**	**Cw**	DRY WINTER CLIMATE	Mean temperature of the coldest month between −3°C to 18°C	**a** Mean temperature of hottest month above 22°C, and with more than 4 months of over 10°C	**w** dry winter Rainfall of the driest month of the cold season is one-tenth or less of the rainfall of the wettest month of the hot season
	Cs	DRY SUMMER CLIMATE (Mediterranean)		**b** Mean temperature of hottest month below 22°C and with more than 4 months of over 10°C	**s** dry summer Rainfall of the driest month of the hot season is less than one-third of the rainfall of the wettest month of the cold season and less than 40mm.
	Cf	CLIMATE WITH NO DRY SEASON			
COLD TEMPERATE RAINY CLIMATES **D**	**Dw**	DRY WINTER CLIMATE	Mean temperature of the coldest month below −3°C	**c** Mean temperature of hottest month below 22°C, but with less than 4 months of over 10°C	**f** with no dry season Rainfall does not correspond to w or s climates
	Df	CLIMATE WITH NO DRY SEASON		**d** Mean temperature of hottest month below 22°C, and of the coldest month below −38°C	
POLAR CLIMATES **E**	**ET**	TUNDRA CLIMATE	Mean temperature of the hottest month below 10°C	Mean temperature of the hottest month between 0°C and 10°C	**H** More than 1500m above sea level
	EF	PERPETUAL FROST		Mean temperature of the hottest month between 0°C and 10°C	

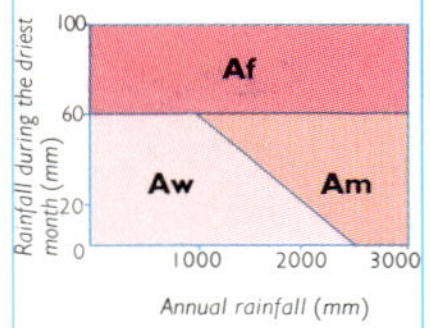

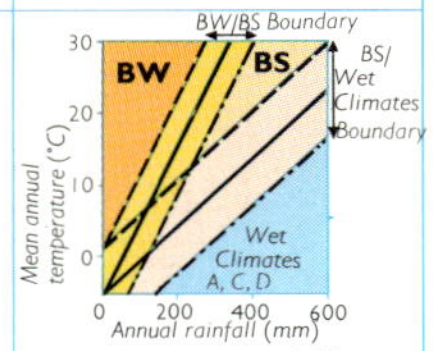

SOIL REGIONS

1:240 000 000

after Glinka, Stremme, Marbut, and others

- Tundra Soil
- Podzols
- Brown Forest Soil
- Lightly leached Dry Forest Soil
- Red and yellow Sub-tropical Forest Soil
- Reddish Savanna Soil and Tropical Red Earths
- Laterites
- Chernozem
- Degraded Chernozem
- Black Savanna Soil
- Chestnut Steppe Soil
- Grey, light brown and red brown Desert Steppe Soils
- Alluvium
- Mountain and High Plateau Soils
- Oases Soil
- Tropical and Mangrove Swamp

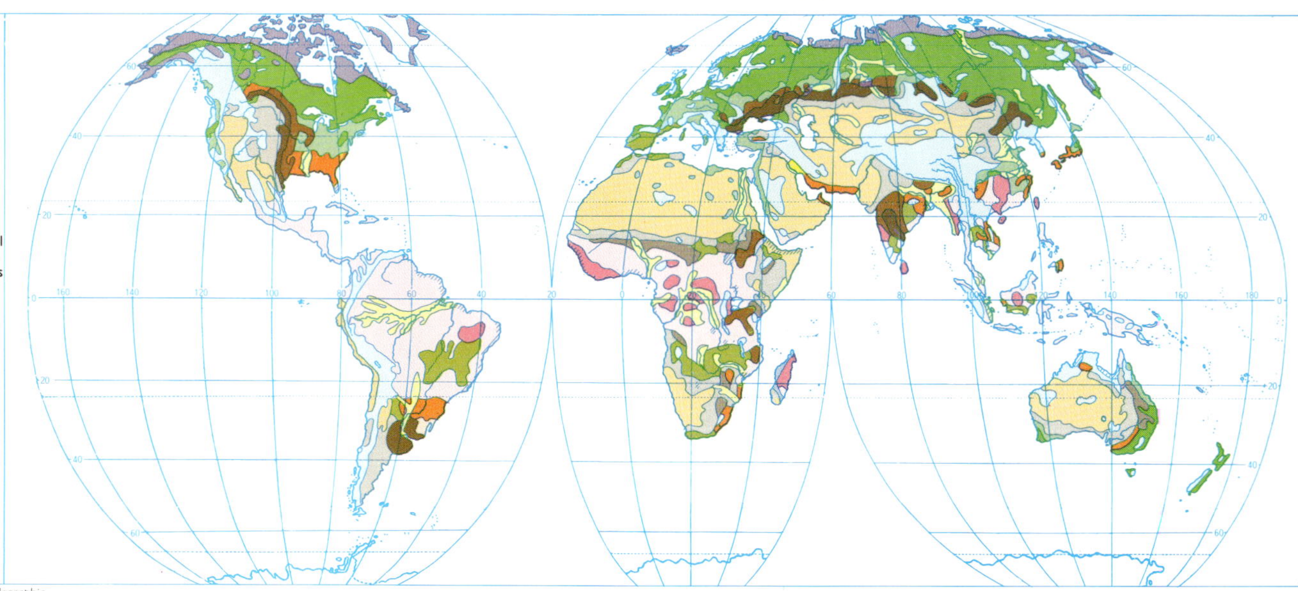

Projection: *Interrupted Mollweide's Homolographic*

1:120 000 000

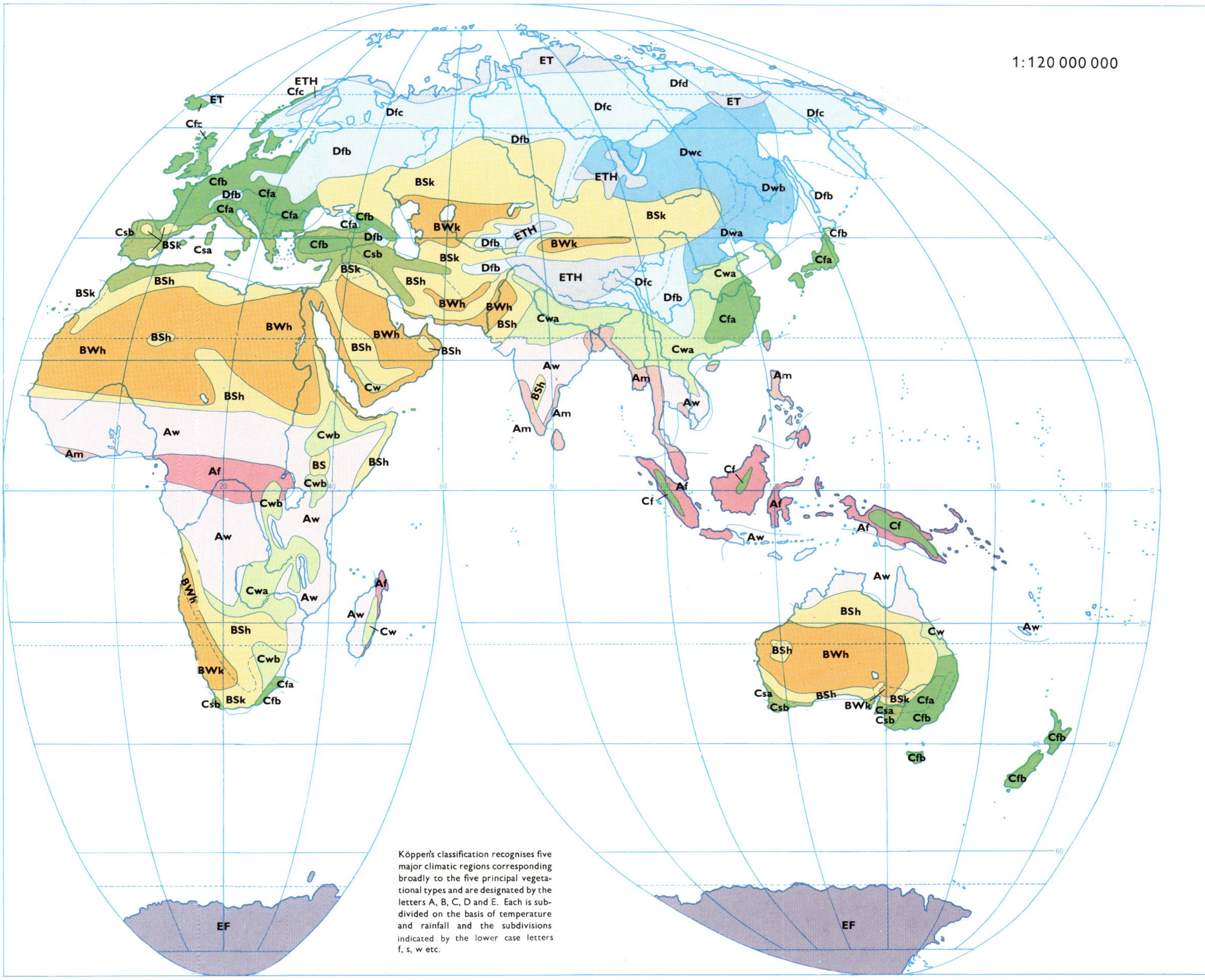

Köppen's classification recognises five major climatic regions corresponding broadly to the five principal vegetational types and are designated by the letters A, B, C, D and E. Each is subdivided on the basis of temperature and rainfall and the subdivisions indicated by the lower case letters f, s, w etc.

NATURAL VEGETATION

1:240 000 000

- Coniferous Forest
- Broad-leaved Forest and Meadow
- Evergreen Trees and Shrubs
- Temperate Rain Forest
- Monsoon Forest
- Tropical Rain Forest
- Thorn Forest
- Grassland
- Scrub, Steppe and Semi-desert
- Desert
- Alpine Tundra and Ice Desert

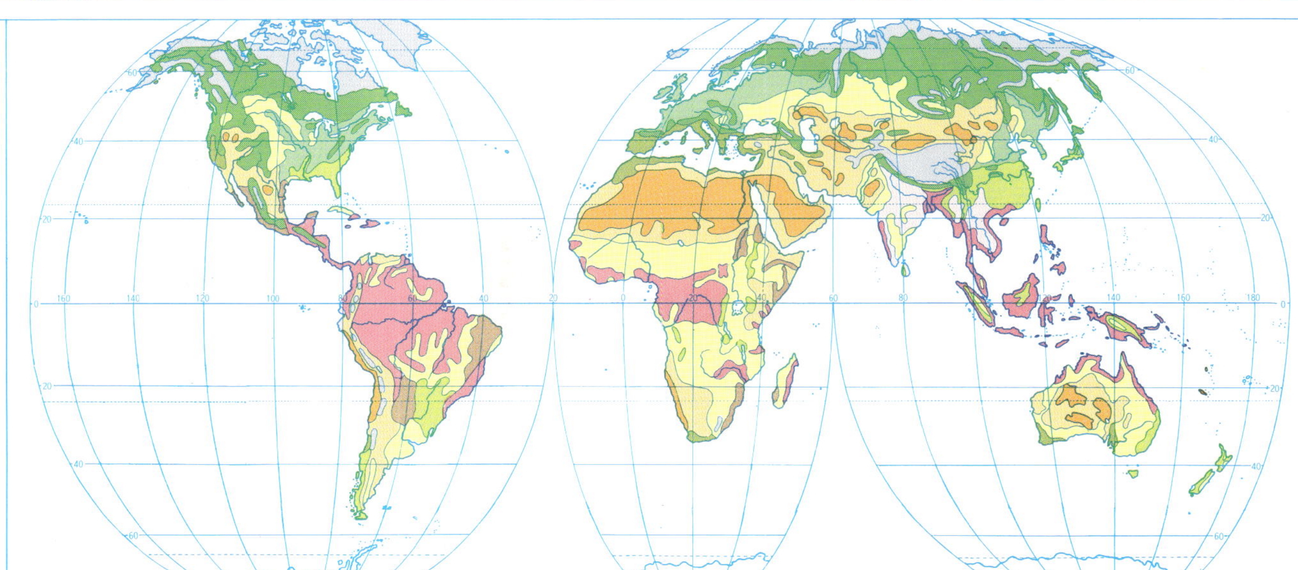

These four pages give temperature and precipitation statistics for over 80 stations, which are arranged by listing the continents and the places within each continent in alphabetical order. The elevation of each station, in metres above mean sea level, is stated beneath its name. The average monthly temperature, in degrees Celsius, and the average monthly precipitation, in millimetres, are given. To the right, the average yearly rainfall, the average yearly temperature, and the annual range of temperature (the difference between the warmest and the coldest months) are also stated.

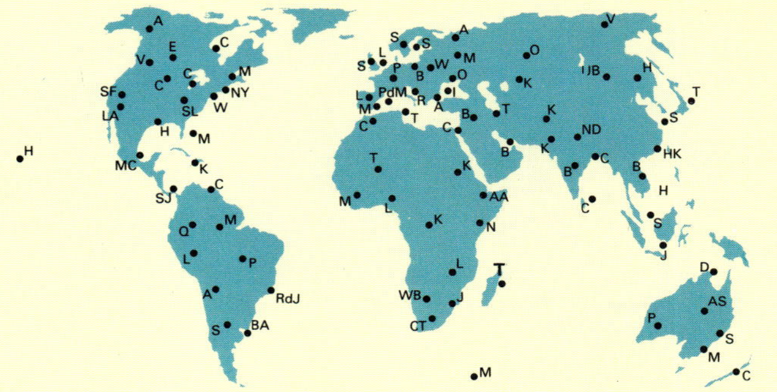

AFRICA

		Jan.	Feb.	Mar.	Apr.	May	June	July	Aug.	Sept.	Oct.	Nov.	Dec.	Year	Annual Range
Addis Ababa, Ethiopia															
	Precipitation	<3	3	25	135	213	201	206	239	102	28	<3	0	1 151	
2 450 m	*Temperature*	19	20	20	20	19	18	18	19	21	22	21	20	20	4
Cairo, Egypt															
	Precipitation	5	5	5	3	3	<3	0	0	<3	<3	3	5	28	
116 m	*Temperature*	13	15	18	21	25	28	28	28	26	24	20	15	22	15
Cape Town, South Africa															
	Precipitation	15	8	18	48	79	84	89	66	43	31	18	10	508	
17 m	*Temperature*	21	21	20	17	14	13	12	13	14	16	18	19	17	9
Casablanca, Morocco															
	Precipitation	53	48	56	36	23	5	0	<3	8	38	66	71	404	
50 m	*Temperature*	13	13	14	16	18	20	22	23	22	19	16	13	18	10
Johannesburg, South Africa															
	Precipitation	114	109	89	38	25	8	8	8	23	56	107	125	709	
1 665 m	*Temperature*	20	20	18	16	13	10	11	13	16	18	19	20	16	10
Khartoum, Sudan															
	Precipitation	<3	<3	<3	<3	3	8	53	71	18	5	<3	0	158	
390 m	*Temperature*	24	25	28	31	33	34	32	31	32	32	28	25	29	9
Kinshasa, Zaïre															
	Precipitation	135	145	196	196	158	8	3	3	31	119	221	142	1 354	
325 m	*Temperature*	26	26	27	27	26	24	23	24	25	26	26	26	25	4
Lagos, Nigeria															
	Precipitation	28	46	102	150	269	460	279	64	140	206	69	25	1 836	
3 m	*Temperature*	27	28	29	28	28	26	26	25	26	26	28	28	27	4
Lusaka, Zambia															
	Precipitation	231	191	142	18	3	<3	<3	0	<3	10	91	150	836	
1 277 m	*Temperature*	21	22	21	21	19	16	16	18	22	24	23	22	21	8
Monrovia, Liberia															
	Precipitation	31	56	97	216	516	973	996	373	744	772	236	130	5 138	
23 m	*Temperature*	26	26	27	27	26	25	24	25	25	25	26	26	26	3
Nairobi, Kenya															
	Precipitation	38	64	125	211	158	46	15	23	31	53	109	86	958	
1 820 m	*Temperature*	19	19	19	19	18	16	16	16	18	19	18	18	18	3
Tananarive, Madagascar															
	Precipitation	300	279	178	53	18	8	8	10	18	61	135	287	1 356	
1 372 m	*Temperature*	21	21	21	19	18	15	14	15	17	19	21	21	19	7
Timbuktu, Mali															
	Precipitation	<3	<3	3	<3	5	23	79	81	38	3	<3	<3	231	
301 m	*Temperature*	22	24	28	32	34	35	32	30	32	31	28	23	29	13
Tunis, Tunisia															
	Precipitation	64	51	41	36	18	8	3	8	33	51	48	61	419	
66 m	*Temperature*	10	11	13	16	19	23	26	27	25	20	16	11	18	17
Walvis Bay, South Africa															
	Precipitation	<3	5	8	3	3	<3	<3	3	<3	<3	<3	<3	23	
7 m	*Temperature*	19	19	19	18	17	16	15	14	14	15	17	18	18	5

AMERICA, NORTH

		Jan.	Feb.	Mar.	Apr.	May	June	July	Aug.	Sept.	Oct.	Nov.	Dec.	Year	Annual Range
Anchorage, Alaska, U.S.A.															
	Precipitation	20	18	15	10	13	18	41	66	66	56	25	23	371	
40 m	*Temperature*	–11	–8	–5	2	7	12	14	13	9	2	–5	–11	2	25
Cheyenne, Wyo., U.S.A.															
	Precipitation	10	15	25	48	61	41	53	41	31	25	13	13	376	
1 871 m	*Temperature*	–4	–3	1	5	10	16	19	19	14	7	1	–2	7	23
Chicago, Ill., U.S.A.															
	Precipitation	51	51	66	71	86	89	84	81	79	66	61	51	836	
251 m	*Temperature*	–4	–3	2	9	14	20	23	22	19	12	5	–1	10	27
Churchill, Man., Canada															
	Precipitation	15	13	18	23	32	44	46	58	51	43	39	21	402	
13 m	*Temperature*	–28	–26	–20	–10	–2	6	12	11	5	–2	–12	–22	–7	40

		Jan.	*Feb.*	*Mar.*	*Apr.*	*May*	*June*	*July*	*Aug.*	*Sept.*	*Oct.*	*Nov.*	*Dec.*	*Year*	*Annual range*
Edmonton, Alta., Canada															
	Precipitation	25	19	19	22	43	77	89	78	39	17	16	25	466	
676 m	*Temperature*	−15	−10	−5	4	11	15	17	16	11	6	−4	−10	3	32
Honolulu, Hawaii, U.S.A.															
	Precipitation	104	66	79	48	25	18	23	28	36	48	64	104	643	
12 m	*Temperature*	23	18	19	20	22	24	25	26	26	24	22	19	22	8
Houston, Tex., U.S.A.															
	Precipitation	89	76	84	91	119	117	99	99	104	94	89	109	1 171	
12 m	*Temperature*	12	13	17	21	24	27	28	29	26	22	16	12	21	17
Kingston, Jamaica															
	Precipitation	23	15	23	31	102	89	38	91	99	180	74	36	800	
34 m	*Temperature*	25	25	25	26	26	28	28	28	27	27	26	26	26	3
Los Angeles, Calif., U.S.A.															
	Precipitation	79	76	71	25	10	3	< 3	< 3	5	15	31	66	381	
95 m	*Temperature*	13	14	14	16	17	19	21	22	21	18	16	14	17	9
Mexico City, Mexico															
	Precipitation	13	5	10	20	53	119	170	152	130	51	18	8	747	
2 309 m	*Temperature*	12	13	16	18	19	19	17	18	18	16	14	13	16	7
Miami, Fla., U.S.A.															
	Precipitation	71	53	64	81	173	178	155	160	203	234	71	51	1 516	
8 m	*Temperature*	20	20	22	23	25	27	28	28	27	25	22	21	24	8
Montreal, Que., Canada															
	Precipitation	72	65	74	74	66	82	90	92	88	76	81	87	946	
57 m	*Temperature*	−10	−9	−3	−6	13	18	21	20	15	9	2	−7	6	31
New York, N.Y., U.S.A.															
	Precipitation	94	97	91	81	81	84	107	109	86	89	76	91	1 092	
96 m	*Temperature*	−1	−1	3	10	16	20	23	23	21	15	7	2	8	24
St. Louis, Mo., U.S.A.															
	Precipitation	58	64	89	97	114	114	89	86	81	74	71	64	1 001	
173 m	*Temperature*	0	1	7	13	19	24	26	26	22	15	8	2	14	26
San Francisco, Calif., U.S.A.															
	Precipitation	119	97	79	38	18	3	< 3	< 3	8	25	64	112	561	
16 m	*Temperature*	10	12	13	13	14	15	15	15	17	16	14	11	14	7
San José, Costa Rica															
	Precipitation	15	5	20	46	229	241	211	241	305	300	145	41	1 798	
1 146 m	*Temperature*	19	19	21	21	22	21	21	21	21	20	20	19	20	2
Vancouver, B.C., Canada															
	Precipitation	154	115	101	60	52	45	32	41	67	114	150	182	1113	
14 m	*Temperature*	3	5	6	9	12	15	17	17	14	10	6	4	10	14
Washington, D.C , U.S.A.															
	Precipitation	86	76	91	84	94	99	112	109	94	74	66	79	1 064	
22 m	*Temperature*	1	2	7	12	18	23	25	24	20	14	8	3	13	24

AMERICA, SOUTH

		Jan.	*Feb.*	*Mar.*	*Apr.*	*May*	*June*	*July*	*Aug.*	*Sept.*	*Oct.*	*Nov.*	*Dec.*	*Year*	*Annual range*
Antofagasta, Chile															
	Precipitation	0	0	0	< 3	< 3	3	5	3	< 3	3	< 3	0	13	
94 m	*Temperature*	21	21	20	18	16	15	14	14	15	16	18	19	17	7
Buenos Aires, Argentina															
	Precipitation	79	71	109	89	76	61	56	61	79	86	84	99	950	
27 m	*Temperature*	23	23	21	17	13	9	10	11	13	15	19	22	16	14
Caracas, Venezuela															
	Precipitation	23	10	15	33	79	102	109	109	107	109	94	46	836	
1 042 m	*Temperature*	19	19	20	21	22	21	21	21	21	21	20	20	21	3
Lima, Peru															
	Precipitation	3	< 3	< 3	< 3	5	5	8	8	8	3	3	< 3	41	
120 m	*Temperature*	23	24	24	22	19	17	17	16	17	18	19	21	20	8
Manaus, Brazil															
	Precipitation	249	231	262	221	170	84	58	38	46	107	142	203	1 811	
44 m	*Temperature*	28	28	28	27	28	28	28	28	29	29	29	28	28	2
Paraná, Brazil															
	Precipitation	287	236	239	102	13	< 3	3	5	28	127	231	310	1 582	
260 m	*Temperature*	23	23	23	23	23	21	21	22	24	24	24	23	23	3
Quito, Ecuador															
	Precipitation	99	112	142	175	137	43	20	31	69	112	97	79	1 115	
2 879 m	*Temperature*	15	15	15	15	15	14	14	15	15	15	15	15	15	1
Rio de Janeiro, Brazil															
	Precipitation	125	122	130	107	79	53	41	43	66	79	104	137	1 082	
61 m	*Temperature*	26	26	25	24	22	21	21	21	21	22	23	25	23	5
Santiago, Chile															
	Precipitation	3	3	5	13	64	84	76	56	31	15	8	5	358	
520 m	*Temperature*	21	20	18	15	12	9	9	10	12	15	17	19	15	12

ASIA

		Jan.	Feb.	Mar.	Apr.	May	June	July	Aug.	Sept.	Oct.	Nov.	Dec.	Year	Annual range
Bahrain															
	Precipitation	8	18	13	8	< 3	0	0	0	0	0	18	18	81	
5 m	*Temperature*	17	18	21	25	29	32	33	34	31	28	24	19	26	16
Bangkok, Thailand															
	Precipitation	8	20	36	58	198	160	160	175	305	206	66	5	1 397	
2 m	*Temperature*	26	28	29	30	29	29	28	28	28	28	26	25	28	5
Beirut, Lebanon															
	Precipitation	191	158	94	53	18	3	< 3	< 3	5	51	132	185	892	
34 m	*Temperature*	14	14	16	18	22	24	27	28	26	24	19	16	21	14
Bombay, India															
	Precipitation	3	3	3	< 3	18	485	617	340	264	64	13	3	1 809	
11 m	*Temperature*	24	24	26	28	30	29	27	27	27	28	27	26	27	6
Calcutta, India															
	Precipitation	10	31	36	43	140	297	325	328	252	114	20	5	1 600	
6 m	*Temperature*	20	22	27	30	30	30	29	29	29	28	23	19	26	11
Colombo, Sri Lanka															
	Precipitation	89	69	147	231	371	224	135	109	160	348	315	147	2 365	
7 m	*Temperature*	26	26	27	28	23	27	27	27	27	27	26	26	27	2
Harbin, China															
	Precipitation	5	5	10	23	43	94	112	104	46	33	8	5	488	
160 m	*Temperature*	–18	–15	–5	6	13	19	22	21	14	4	–6	–16	3	40
Ho Chi Minh City, Vietnam															
	Precipitation	15	3	13	43	221	330	315	269	335	269	114	56	1 984	
9 m	*Temperature*	26	27	29	30	29	28	28	28	27	27	27	26	28	4
Jakarta, Indonesia															
	Precipitation	300	300	211	147	114	97	64	43	66	112	142	203	1 798	
8 m	*Temperature*	26	26	27	27	27	27	27	27	27	27	27	26	27	1
Hong Kong															
	Precipitation	33	46	74	137	292	394	381	361	257	114	43	31	2 162	
33 m	*Temperature*	16	15	18	22	26	28	28	28	27	25	21	18	23	13
Kabul, Afghanistan															
	Precipitation	31	36	94	102	20	5	3	3	< 3	15	20	10	338	
1 815 m	*Temperature*	–3	–1	6	13	18	22	25	24	20	14	7	3	12	28
Karachi, Pakistan															
	Precipitation	13	10	8	3	3	18	81	41	13	< 3	3	5	196	
4 m	*Temperature*	19	20	24	28	30	31	30	29	28	28	24	20	26	12
New Delhi, India															
	Precipitation	23	18	13	8	13	74	180	172	117	10	3	10	640	
218 m	*Temperature*	14	17	23	28	33	34	31	30	29	26	20	15	25	20
Shanghai, China															
	Precipitation	48	58	84	94	94	180	147	142	130	71	51	36	1 135	
7 m	*Temperature*	4	5	9	14	20	24	28	28	23	19	12	7	16	24
Singapore															
	Precipitation	252	173	193	188	173	173	170	196	178	208	254	257	2 413	
10 m	*Temperature*	26	27	28	28	28	28	28	27	27	27	27	27	27	2
Tehran, Iran															
	Precipitation	46	38	46	36	13	3	3	3	3	8	20	31	246	
1 220 m	*Temperature*	2	5	9	16	21	26	30	29	25	18	12	6	17	28
Tokyo, Japan															
	Precipitation	48	74	107	135	147	165	142	152	234	208	97	56	1 565	
6 m	*Temperature*	3	4	7	13	17	21	25	26	23	17	11	6	14	23
Ulan Bator, Mongolia															
	Precipitation	< 3	< 3	3	5	10	28	76	51	23	5	5	3	208	
1 325 m	*Temperature*	–26	–21	–13	–1	6	14	16	14	8	–1	–13	–22	–3	42

AUSTRALIA, NEW ZEALAND and ANTARCTICA

		Jan.	Feb.	Mar.	Apr.	May	June	July	Aug.	Sept.	Oct.	Nov.	Dec.	Year	Annual range
Alice Springs, Australia															
	Precipitation	43	33	28	10	15	13	8	8	8	18	31	38	252	
579 m	*Temperature*	29	28	25	20	15	12	12	14	18	23	26	28	21	17
Christchurch, New Zealand															
	Precipitation	56	43	48	48	66	66	69	48	46	43	48	56	638	
10 m	*Temperature*	16	16	14	12	9	6	6	7	9	12	14	16	11	10
Darwin, Australia															
	Precipitation	386	312	254	97	15	3	< 3	3	13	51	119	239	1 491	
30 m	*Temperature*	29	29	29	29	28	26	25	26	28	29	30	29	28	5
Mawson, Antarctica															
	Precipitation	11	30	20	10	44	180	4	40	3	20	0	0	362	
14 m	*Temperature*	0	–5	–10	–14	–15	–16	–18	–18	–19	–13	–5	–1	–11	18

		Jan.	Feb.	Mar.	Apr.	May	June	July	Aug.	Sept.	Oct.	Nov.	Dec.	Year	Annual Range
Melbourne, Australia															
	Precipitation	48	46	56	58	53	53	48	48	58	66	58	58	653	
35 m	*Temperature*	20	20	18	15	13	10	9	11	13	14	16	18	15	11
Perth, Australia															
	Precipitation	8	10	20	43	130	180	170	149	86	56	20	13	881	
60 m	*Temperature*	23	23	22	19	16	14	13	13	15	16	19	22	18	10
Sydney, Australia															
	Precipitation	89	102	127	135	127	117	117	76	73	71	73	73	1 181	
42 m	*Temperature*	22	22	21	18	15	13	12	13	15	18	19	21	17	10

EUROPE and U.S.S.R.

		Jan.	Feb.	Mar.	Apr.	May	June	July	Aug.	Sept.	Oct.	Nov.	Dec.	Year	Annual Range
Archangel, U.S.S.R.															
	Precipitation	31	19	25	29	42	52	62	56	63	63	47	41	530	
13 m	*Temperature*	–16	–14	–9	0	7	12	15	14	8	2	–4	–11	0	31
Athens, Greece															
	Precipitation	62	37	37	23	23	14	6	7	15	51	56	71	402	
107 m	*Temperature*	10	10	12	16	20	25	28	28	24	20	15	11	18	18
Berlin, Germany															
	Precipitation	46	40	33	42	49	65	73	69	48	49	46	43	603	
55 m	*Temperature*	–1	0	4	9	14	17	19	18	15	9	5	1	9	20
Istanbul, Turkey															
	Precipitation	109	92	72	46	38	34	34	30	58	81	103	119	816	
114 m	*Temperature*	5	6	7	11	16	20	23	23	20	16	12	8	14	18
Kazalinsk, U.S.S.R.															
	Precipitation	10	10	13	13	15	5	5	8	8	10	13	15	125	
63 m	*Temperature*	–12	–11	–3	6	18	23	25	23	16	8	–1	–7	7	37
Lisbon, Portugal															
	Precipitation	111	76	109	54	44	16	3	4	33	62	93	103	708	
77 m	*Temperature*	11	12	14	16	17	20	22	23	21	18	14	12	17	12
London, U.K.															
	Precipitation	54	40	37	37	46	45	57	59	49	57	64	48	593	
5 m	*Temperature*	4	5	7	9	12	16	18	17	15	11	8	5	11	14
Málaga, Spain															
	Precipitation	61	51	62	46	26	5	1	3	29	64	64	62	474	
33 m	*Temperature*	12	13	15	17	19	29	25	26	23	20	16	13	18	17
Moscow, U.S.S.R.															
	Precipitation	39	38	36	37	53	58	88	71	58	45	47	54	624	
156 m	*Temperature*	–13	–10	–4	6	13	16	18	17	12	6	–1	–7	4	31
Odessa, U.S.S.R.															
	Precipitation	57	62	30	21	34	34	42	37	37	13	35	71	473	
64 m	*Temperature*	–3	–1	2	9	15	20	22	22	18	12	9	1	10	25
Omsk, U.S.S.R.															
	Precipitation	15	8	8	13	31	51	51	51	28	25	18	20	318	
85 m	*Temperature*	–22	–19	–12	–1	10	16	18	16	10	1	–11	–18	–1	40
Palma de Mallorca, Spain															
	Precipitation	39	34	51	32	29	17	3	25	55	77	47	40	449	
10 m	*Temperature*	10	11	12	15	17	21	24	25	23	18	14	11	17	15
Paris, France															
	Precipitation	56	46	35	42	57	54	59	64	55	50	51	50	619	
75 m	*Temperature*	3	4	8	11	15	18	20	19	17	12	7	4	12	17
Rome, Italy															
	Precipitation	71	62	57	51	46	37	15	21	63	99	129	93	744	
17 m	*Temperature*	8	9	11	14	18	22	25	25	22	17	13	10	16	17
Shannon, Irish Republic															
	Precipitation	94	67	56	53	61	57	77	79	86	86	96	117	929	
2 m	*Temperature*	5	5	7	9	12	14	16	16	14	11	8	6	10	11
Stavanger, Norway															
	Precipitation	93	56	45	70	49	84	93	118	142	129	125	126	1 130	
85 m	*Temperature*	1	1	3	6	10	13	15	15	13	9	6	3	8	14
Stockholm, Sweden															
	Precipitation	43	30	25	31	34	45	61	76	60	48	53	48	554	
44 m	*Temperature*	–3	–3	–1	5	10	15	18	17	12	7	3	0	7	21
Verkhoyansk, U.S.S.R.															
	Precipitation	5	5	3	5	8	23	28	25	13	8	8	5	134	
100 m	*Temperature*	–50	–45	–32	–15	0	12	14	9	2	–15	–38	–48	–17	64
Warsaw, Poland															
	Precipitation	27	32	27	37	46	69	96	65	43	38	31	44	555	
110 m	*Temperature*	–3	–3	2	7	14	17	19	18	14	9	3	0	8	22

1:190 000 000

January Temperature and Ocean Currents
(Northern Hemisphere—Winter)

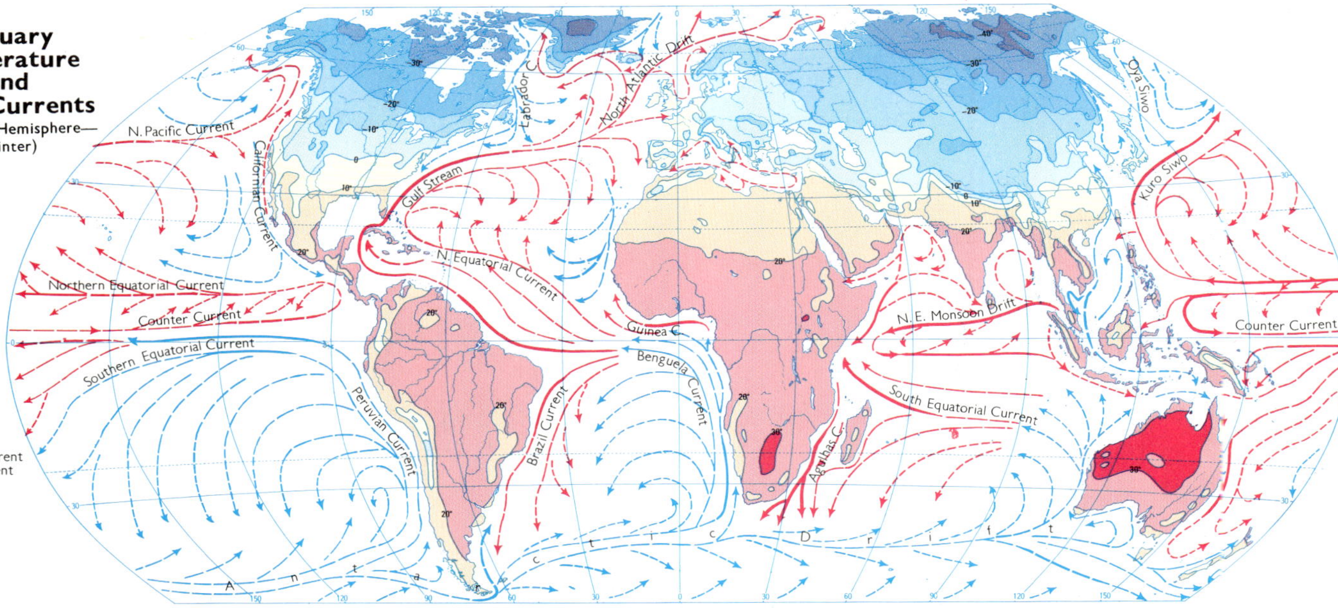

ACTUAL SURFACE TEMPERATURE
°C
30
20
10
0
−10
−20
−30
−40

Warm Current
Cold Current

July Temperature and Ocean Currents
(Northern Hemisphere—Summer)

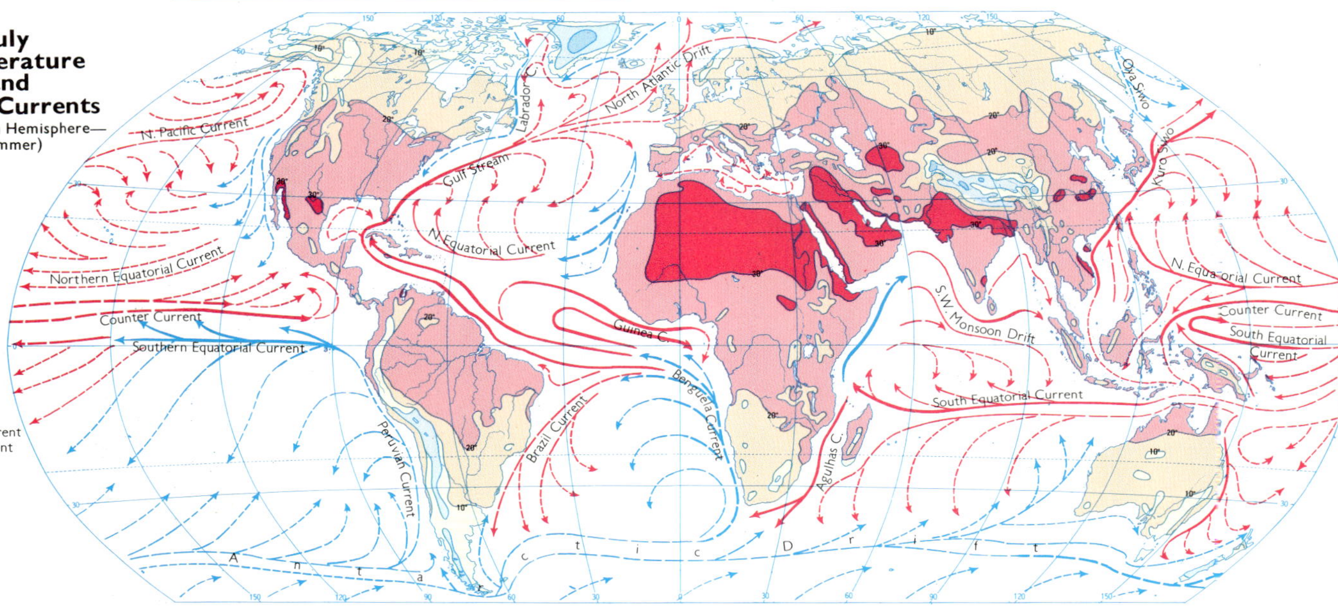

ACTUAL SURFACE TEMPERATURE
°C
30
20
10
0
−10

Warm Current
Cold Current

Annual Range of Temperature

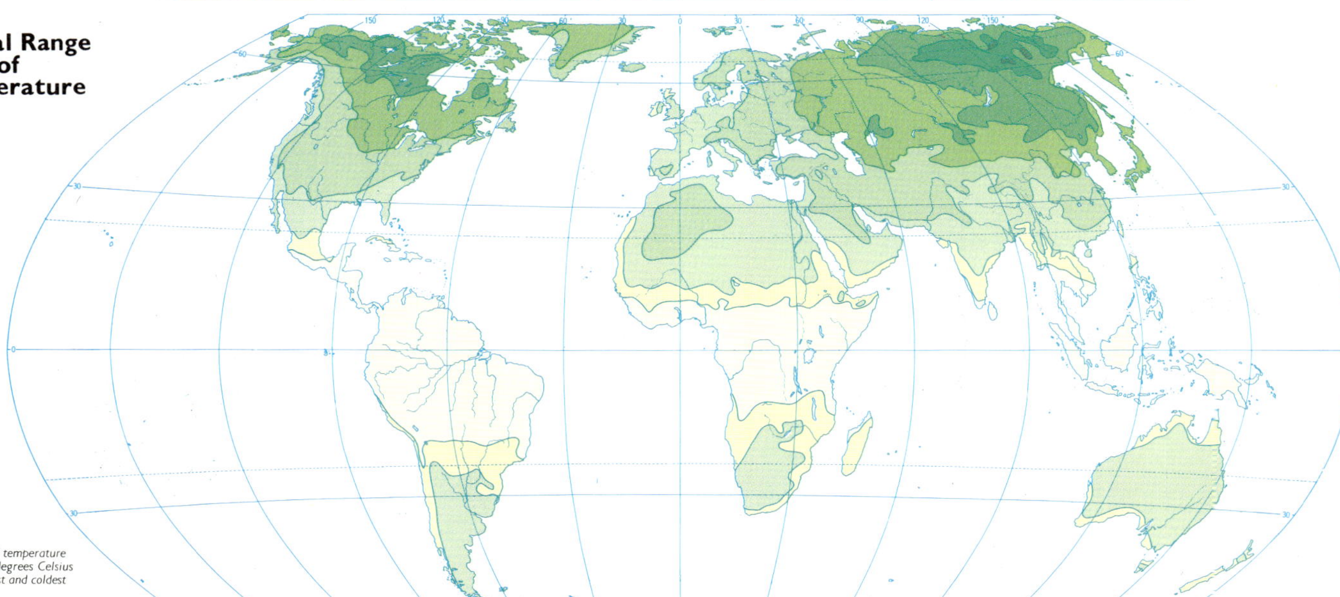

°C
60
50
40
30
20
10
5
0

The annual range of temperature is the difference in degrees Celsius between the warmest and coldest months of the year.

Projection: *Hammer Equal Area*

January Pressure and Winds

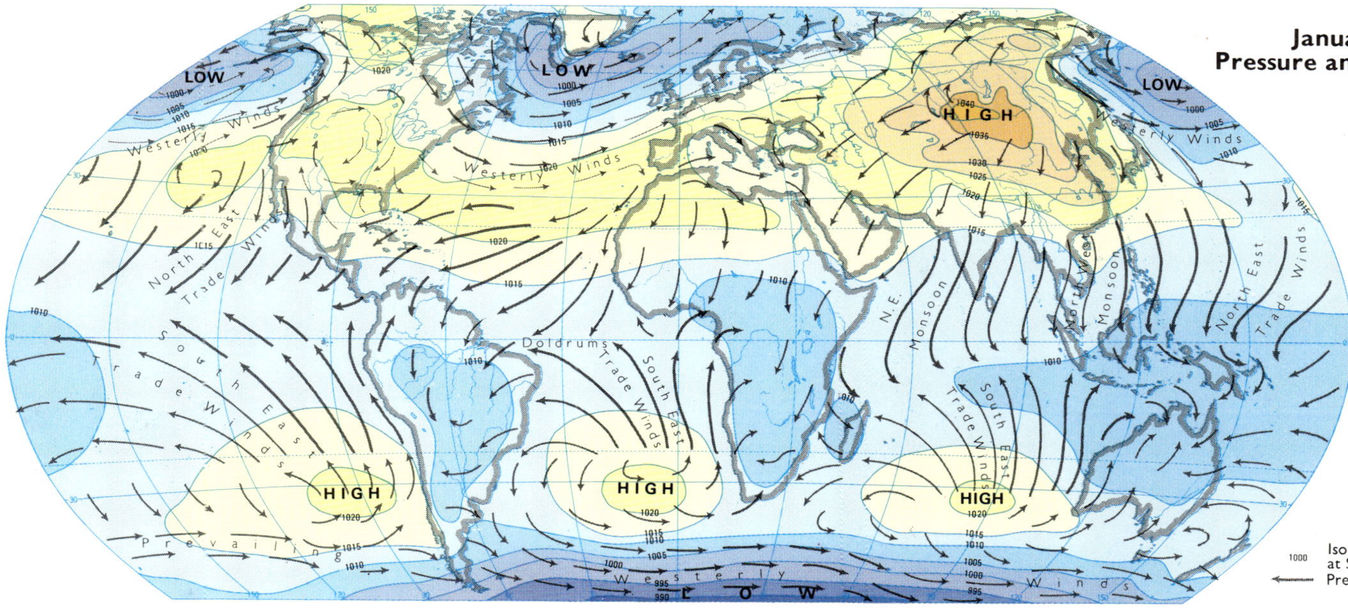

mb: 1040, 1035, 1030, 1025, 1020, 1015, 1010, 1005, 1000, 995, 990

1000 Isobars in millibars at Sea Level
Prevailing Winds

July Pressure and Winds

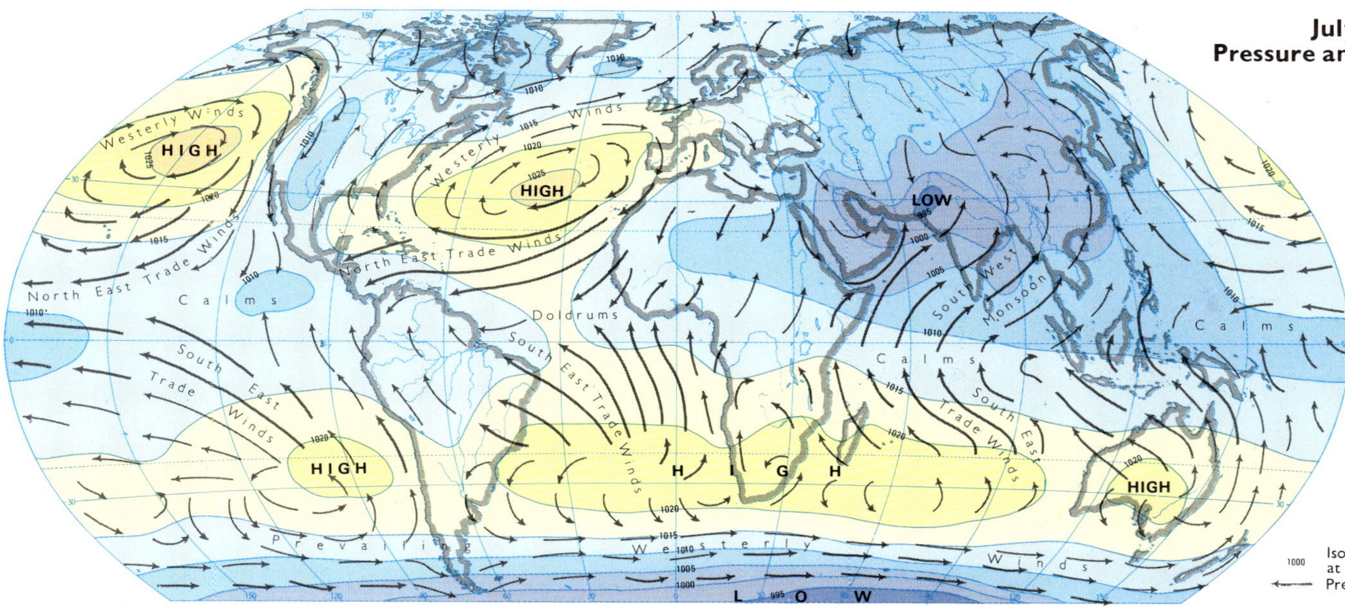

mb: 1025, 1020, 1015, 1010, 1005, 1000, 995

1000 Isobars in millibars at Sea Level
Prevailing Winds

Annual Precipitation

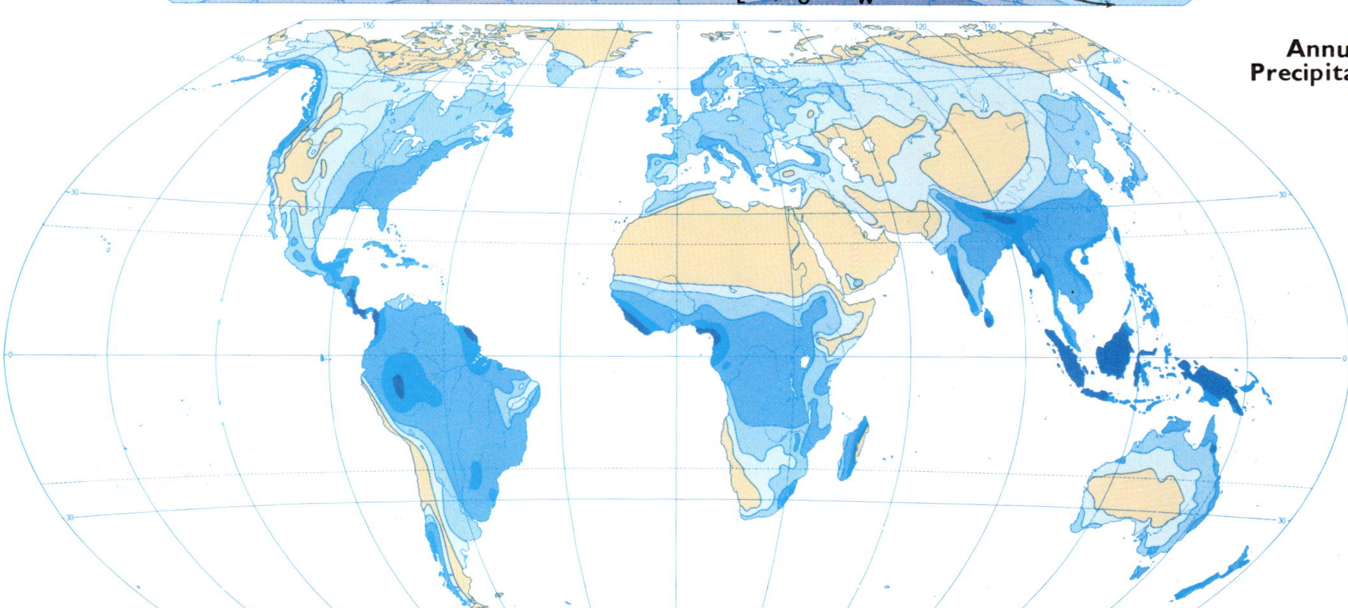

mm: 3000, 2000, 1000, 500, 250

Projection: *Hammer Equal Area*

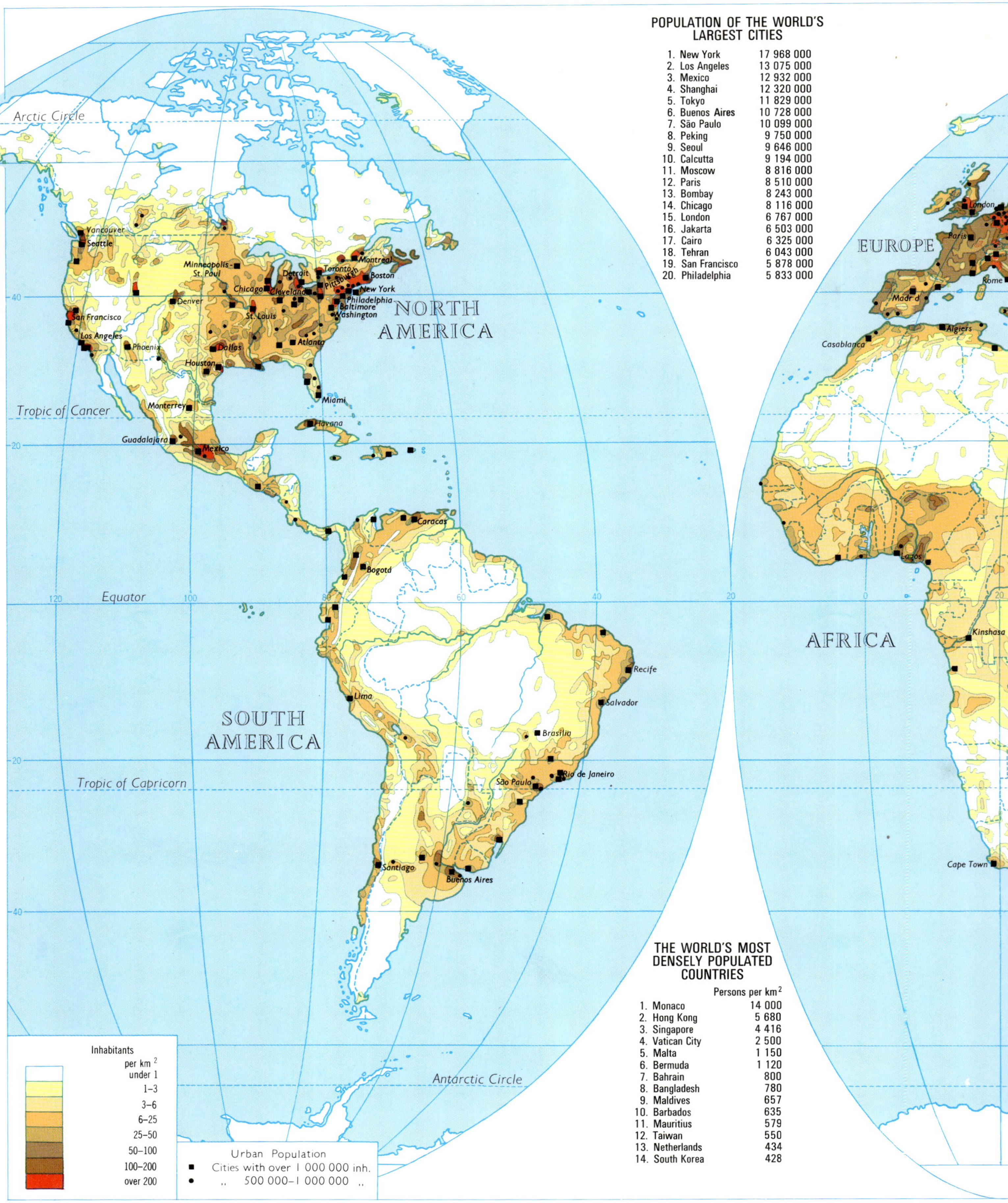

Projection: Mollweide's interrupted Homolographic

POPULATION OF THE WORLD'S LARGEST CITIES

1.	New York	17 968 000
2.	Los Angeles	13 075 000
3.	Mexico	12 932 000
4.	Shanghai	12 320 000
5.	Tokyo	11 829 000
6.	Buenos Aires	10 728 000
7.	São Paulo	10 099 000
8.	Peking	9 750 000
9.	Seoul	9 646 000
10.	Calcutta	9 194 000
11.	Moscow	8 816 000
12.	Paris	8 510 000
13.	Bombay	8 243 000
14.	Chicago	8 116 000
15.	London	6 767 000
16.	Jakarta	6 503 000
17.	Cairo	6 325 000
18.	Tehran	6 043 000
19.	San Francisco	5 878 000
20.	Philadelphia	5 833 000

THE WORLD'S MOST DENSELY POPULATED COUNTRIES

		Persons per km²
1.	Monaco	14 000
2.	Hong Kong	5 680
3.	Singapore	4 416
4.	Vatican City	2 500
5.	Malta	1 150
6.	Bermuda	1 120
7.	Bahrain	800
8.	Bangladesh	780
9.	Maldives	657
10.	Barbados	635
11.	Mauritius	579
12.	Taiwan	550
13.	Netherlands	434
14.	South Korea	428

THE WORLD'S MOST DENSELY POPULATED COUNTRIES

Continuation

	Persons per km^2
15. San Marino	383
16. Puerto Rico	370
17. Saint Vincent	353
18. Japan	330
19. Grenada	327
20. Belgium	301
21. Lebanon	283
22. Rwanda	270
23. India	268
24. Sri Lanka	255
25. West Germany	251
26. El Salvador	243
27. Trinidad and Tobago	243
28. UK	236

Some of the lesser islands have high densities but have been omitted from this table.

For comparison the London urban area has a density of 4 270 persons per km^2.

The population figures used are from censuses or more recent estimates and are given in thousands for towns and cities over 250,000 (over 500,000 in India and U.S.S.R. and over 750,000 in China). Where possible the population of the metropolitan area is given e.g. Greater London etc.

AFRICA

ALGERIA (1983)
Algiers 1 722
Oran 664
Constantine 449
Annaba 348

ANGOLA (1988)
Luanda 1 200

BENIN (1982)
Cotonou 487

BURKINA FASO (1985)
Ouagadougou 375

BURUNDI (1986)
Bujumbura 273

CAMEROON (1986)
Douala 1 030
Yaoundé 654

CENTRAL AFRICAN REPUBLIC (1988)
Bangui 597

CHAD (1986)
Ndjamena 512

CONGO (1985)
Brazzaville 596
Pointe-Noire 298

DJIBOUTI (1988)
Djibouti 290

EGYPT (1986)
Cairo 6 325
Alexandria 2 893
El Giza 1 671
Shubra el Kheima 533
El Mahalla el Kubra 385
Port Said 382
Tanta 374
El Mansûra 358
Helwân 352
Asyût 292
Zagazig 274
Suez 265

ETHIOPIA (1985)
Addis Ababa 1 465
Asmera 285

GABON (1983)
Libreville 350

GHANA (1984)
Accra 965
Kumasi 489

GUINEA (1983)
Conakry 705

IVORY COAST (1982)
Abidjan 1 850
Bouaké 640
Man-Danane 450
Korhogo 280

KENYA (1986)
Nairobi 1 200
Mombasa 457

LIBERIA (1984)
Monrovia 425

LIBYA (1982)
Tripoli 980
Benghazi 650
Misrātah 285

MADAGASCAR (1986)
Antananarivo 703

MALAWI (1985)
Blantyre 355

MALI (1976)
Bamako 419

MAURITANIA (1985)
Nouakchott 500

MOROCCO (1982)
Casablanca 2 158
Rabat-Salé 893
Fès 548
Marrakesh 482
Oujda 479
Kénitra 450
Meknès 386
Tétouan 365
Tangier 312
Safi 256

MOZAMBIQUE (1986)
Maputo 883
Beira 270

NIGER (1983)
Niamey 399

NIGERIA (1983)
Lagos 1 097
Ibadan 1 060
Ogbomosho 527
Kano 487
Oshogbo 345
Ilorin 344
Abeokuta 309
Port Harcourt 296
Zaria 274
Ilesha 273
Onitsha 269
Ado-Ekiti 266
Iwo 262

SENEGAL (1979)
Dakar 979

SIERRA LEONE (1988)
Freetown 470

SOMALI REP. (1986)
Mogadishu 1 000
Hargeisa 400
Baidoa 300
Burao 300

SOUTH AFRICA (1980)
Johannesburg 1 726
Cape Town 1 491
Durban 961
Pretoria 739
Port Elizabeth 585
Vanderbijlpark-Vereeniging 448

SUDAN (1983)
Omdurman 526
Khartoum 476
Khartoum North 341

TANZANIA (1985)
Dar-es-Salaam 1 096
Mwanza 252

TOGO (1983)
Lomé 366

TUNISIA (1984)
Tunis 774

UGANDA (1980)
Kampala 458

ZAÏRE (1984)
Kinshasa 2 654
Lubumbashi 543
Mbuji Mayi 423
Kananga 291
Kisangani 283

ZAMBIA (1987)
Lusaka 819
Kitwe 449
Ndola 418

ZIMBABWE (1983)
Harare 681
Bulawayo 429

ASIA

AFGHANISTAN (1982)
Kābul 1 127

BANGLADESH (1982)
Dacca 3 459
Chittagong 1 388
Khulna 623
Narayanganj 298

BURMA (MYANMAR) (1983)
Rangoon 2 459
Mandalay 533
Kanbe 254

CAMBODIA (KAMPUCHEA) (1983)
Phnom Penh 500

CHINA (1986)
Shanghai 12 320
Peking 9 750
Tientsin 5 459
Shenyang 4 285
Wuhan 3 493
Canton 3 359
Chungking 2 832
Harbin 2 668
Chengtu 2 642
Sian 2 387
Zibo 2 329
Nanchang 2 289
Nanking 2 289
Lupanshui 2 247
Taiyuan 1 929
Changchun 1 908
Dalian 1 682
Zhaozhuang 1 612
Zhengzhou 1 610
Kunming 1 516
Jinan 1 464
Tangshan 1 410
Guiyang 1 403
Lanzhou 1 391
Linyi 1 385
Pingxiang 1 305
Qiqihar 1 301
Anshan 1 298
Qingdao 1 273
Xintao 1 272
Hangzhou 1 271
Fushun 1 270
Yancheng 1 265
Yulin 1 255
Dongguang 1 230
Chao'an 1 227
Xiaogan 1 219
Fuzhou, Fujian 1 205
Suining 1 195
Changsha 1 193
Shijiazhuang 1 187
Jilin 1 169
Xintai 1 167
Puyang 1 125
Baotou 1 119
Bozhou 1 112
Zhongshan 1 073
Luoyang 1 063
Laiwu 1 054
Leshan 1 039
Ürümqi 1 038
Ningbo 1 033
Datong 1 020
Huainan 1 019
Heze 1 017
Handan 1 014
Linhai 1 012
Macheng 1 010
Changshu 1 004
Haicheng 992
Rizhao 988
Fuling 986
Huzhou 974
Tianshui 965
Wafangdian 965
Nanning 963
Jingmen 957
Zhanjiang 947
Qinzhou 944
Dingzhou 938
Zigong 924
Ezhou 922
Gongzhuling 910
Hefei 902
Chifeng 896
Mianyang 859
Daqing 854
Pingdingshan 843
Xuzhou 841
Benxi 839
Yichun, Heilongjiang 830
Guangyuan 819
Jixi 816
Wuwei 814
Hohhot 810
Qingzhou 794
Jinzhou 789
Yichun, Jiangxi 785
Yuyao 778
Qujing 775
Shantou 774
Deyang 768
Zhaodong 754

HONG KONG (1986)
Kowloon 2 302
Hong Kong 1 176
Tsuen Wan 654

INDIA (1981)
Calcutta 9 194
Bombay 8 243
Delhi 5 729
Madras 4 289
Bangalore 2 922
Ahmadabad 2 548
Hyderabad 2 546
Pune 1 686
Kanpur 1 639
Nagpur 1 302
Jaipur 1 015
Lucknow 1 008
Coimbatore 920
Patna 919
Surat 914
Madurai 908
Indore 829
Varanasi 797
Jabalpur 757
Agra 747
Vadodara 744
Cochin 686
Dhanbad 678
Bhopal 671
Jamshedpur 670
Allahabad 650
Ulhasnagar 649
Tiruchchirappalli 610
Ludhiana 606
Srinagar 606
Vishakhapatnam 604
Amritsar 595
Gwalior 556
Calicut 546
Vijayawada 543
Meerut 537
Dharwad 527
Trivandrum 520
Salem 519
Solapur 515
Jodhpur 506
Ranchi 503

INDONESIA (1980)
Jakarta 6 503
Surabaya 2 028
Bandung 1 462
Medan 1 379
Semarang 1 026
Palembang 787
Ujung Pandang 709
Malang 512
Padang 481
Surakarta 470
Yogyakarta 399
Banjarmasin 381
Pontianak 305
Tanjung Karang 284
Balikpapan 281
Samarinda 265

IRAN (1986)
Tehrān 6 043
Mashhad 1 464
Esfahān 987
Tabrīz 971
Shīrāz 848
Ahvāz 580
Bākhtarān 561
Qom 543
Abadan 308
Orūmīyeh 301
Rasht 291
Ardabīl 282
Karaj 275
Hamadan 272
Arak 265
Kerman 257
Islam Shahr/Qasemabad 108

IRAQ (1985)
Baghdād 4 649
Basra 617
Mosul 571
Irbil 334
As Sulaymaniyah 279

ISRAEL (1987)
Jerusalem 483
Tel Aviv-Jaffa 320

JAPAN (1985)
Tōkyō 11 829
Yokohama 2 993
Ōsaka 2 636
Nagoya 2 116
Sapporo 1 543
Kyōto 1 479
Kobe 1 411
Fukuoka 1 160
Kawasaki 1 089
Kitakyūshū 1 056
Hiroshima 1 044
Sakai 818
Chiba 789
Sendai 700
Okayama 572
Kumamoto 556
Kagoshima 531
Higashiōsaka 523
Hamamatsu 514
Amagasaki 509
Funabashi 507
Sagamihara 483
Niigata 476
Shizuoka 468
Himeji 453
Nagasaki 449
Kanazawa 430
Hachiōji 427
Matsudo 427
Matsuyama 427
Yokosuka 427
Nishinomiya 421
Kurashiki 414
Toyonaka 413
Gifu 412
Utsunomiya 405
Kawaguchi 403
Wakayama 401
Ichikawa 398
Oita 390
Hirakata 382
Urawa 377
Omiya 373
Asahikawa 364
Fukuyama 360
Iwaki 351
Suita 349
Takatsuki 349
Nagano 337
Fujisawa 329
Nara 328
Takamatsu 327
Toyohashi 322
Machida 321
Hakodate 319
Toyama 314
Kōchi 312
Toyota 308
Naha 304
Kōriyama 302
Akita 296
Aomori 294
Kawagoe 285
Okazaki 285
Miyazaki 279
Maebashi 277
Yao 276
Tokorozawa 275
Kashiwa 273
Fukushima 271
Shimonoseki 269
Akashi 263
Yokkaichi 263
Neyagawa 258
Tokushima 258
Ichinomiya 257
Kasugai 257
Koshigaya 253
Sasebo 251
Fukui 250
Ibaraki 250

JORDAN (1986)
'Ammān 834
Az-Zarqā 285

KOREA, NORTH (1984)
Pyŏngyang 2 639
Hamhung 775
Chongjin 754
Chinnamp'o 691
Sinŭiju 500
Wŏnsan 350
Kaesŏng 346
Kimchaek 281

KOREA, SOUTH (1985)
Seoul 9 646
Pusan 3 517
Taegu 2 031
Inchŏn 1 387
Kwangju 906
Taejon 866
Ulsan 551
Punch'ŏn 456
Masan 449
Songnam 448
Suwŏn 431
Chonju 426
Anyang 362
Chŏngju 350
P'ohang 261

LAOS (1985)
Vientiane 377

LEBANON (1980)
Beirut 702

MACAU (1986)
Macau 395

MALAYSIA (1980)
Kuala Lumpur 938
Ipoh 301
George Town 251
Johor Baharu 250

MONGOLIA (1988)
Ulan Bator 500

PAKISTAN (1981)
Karachi 5 181
Lahore 2 953
Faisalabad 1 104
Rawalpindi 795
Hyderabad 752
Multan 722
Gujranwala 659
Peshawar 556
Sialkot 302
Sargodha 291
Quetta 286

PHILIPPINES (1984)
Manila 1 728
Quezon City 1 326
Cebu 552
Caloocan 524
Makati 409
Zamboanga 379
Pasay 321
Pasig 319
Bacolod 288
Cagayan de Oro 276
Valenzuela 276
Iloilo 263
Paranque 253

SAUDI ARABIA (1974)
Riyadh 667
Jedda 561
Mecca 367

SINGAPORE (1987)
Singapore 2 600

SRI LANKA (1985)
Colombo 1 412

SYRIA (1986)
Damascus 1 219
Aleppo 1 191
Homs 428

TAIWAN (1987)
Taipei 2 637
Kaohsiung 1 343
Taichung 715

- Tainan 657
- Panchiao 506
- Sanchung 362
- Keelung 349
- Chilung 348
- Chungho 343
- Hsinchu 310
- Fengshan 276
- Hainchung 259
- Chiai 255

THAILAND (1982)
- Bangkok 5 468

TURKEY (1985)
- İstanbul 5 495
- Ankara 2 252
- İzmir 1 490
- Adana 776
- Bursa 614
- Gaziantep 466
- Konya 439
- Kayseri 378
- Eskişehir 367
- Mersin 314
- Diyarbakir 305
- Samsun 280
- Antalya 258
- Erzurum 253
- Malatya 251

UNITED ARAB EMIRATES (1984)
- Dubai 266

VIETNAM (1979)
- Ho Chi Minh City 3 420
- Hanoi 2 571
- Haiphong 1 279
- Da-Nang (1973) 492

YEMEN, NORTH (1981)
- Sana' 278

YEMEN, SOUTH (1981)
- Aden 264

EUROPE

AUSTRIA (1984)
- Vienna 1 531

BELGIUM (1988)
- Brussels 970
- Antwerp 476

BULGARIA (1987)
- Sofia 1 129
- Plovdiv 357
- Varna 306

CZECHOSLOVAKIA (1987)
- Prague 1 206
- Bratislava 430
- Brno 388
- Ostrava 330

DENMARK (1988)
- Copenhagen 1 344
- Aarhus 258

FINLAND (1987)
- Helsinki 978
- Turku 262
- Tampere 258

FRANCE (1982)
- Paris 8 510
- Lyons 1 170
- Marseilles 1 080
- Lille 935
- Bordeaux 628
- Toulouse 523
- Nantes 465
- Nice 449
- Toulon 410
- Grenoble 392
- Rouen 380
- Strasbourg 373
- Valenciennes 337
- Lens 323
- St-Étienne 317
- Grasse-Cannes 296
- Nancy 278
- Clermont-Ferrand 256
- Le Havre 255
- Tours 255

GERMANY, EAST (1986)
- East Berlin 1 223
- Leipzig 552
- Dresden 520
- Karl-Marx-Stadt 314
- Magdeburg 289

GERMANY, WEST (1987)
- West Berlin 1 879
- Hamburg 1 571
- Munich 1 275
- Cologne 914
- Essen 615
- Frankfurt 592
- Dortmund 568
- Stuttgart 565
- Düsseldorf 561
- Bremen 522
- Duisburg 515
- Hanover 506
- Nuremberg 467
- Bochum 381
- Wuppertal 374
- Bielefeld 299
- Mannheim 295
- Bonn 291
- Gelsenkirchen 284
- Karlsruhe 268
- Münster 268
- Wiesbaden 267
- Mönchengladbach 255

GREECE (1981)
- Athens 3 027
- Thessaloníki 871

HUNGARY (1988)
- Budapest 2 105

IRISH REPUBLIC (1986)
- Dublin 921

ITALY (1987)
- Rome 2 817
- Milan 1 479
- Naples 1 201
- Turin 1 025
- Palermo 729
- Genoa 722
- Bologna 427
- Florence 421
- Catánia 372
- Bari 359
- Venice 328
- Messina 271
- Verona 259

NETHERLANDS (1988)
- Rotterdam 1 036
- Amsterdam 1 031
- The Hague 680
- Utrecht 521
- Eindhoven 381
- Arnhem 297
- Heerlen-Kerkrade 267
- Enschede-Hengelo 250

NORWAY (1988)
- Oslo 643

POLAND (1988)
- Warsaw 1 671
- Łodz 845
- Kraków 745
- Wrocław 640
- Poznań 586
- Gdansk 469
- Szczecin 397
- Bydgoszcz 373
- Katowice 369
- Lublin 333
- Białystok 260
- Sosnowiec 260
- Częstochowa 253
- Gdynia 250

PORTUGAL (1981)
- Lisbon 1 612
- Oporto 1 315

ROMANIA (1985)
- Bucharest 1 976
- Braşov 347
- Constanţa 323
- Timişoara 319
- Iaşi 314
- Cluj-Napoca 310
- Galaţi 293
- Craiova 275

SPAIN (1987)
- Madrid 3 101
- Barcelona 1 704
- Valencia 732
- Seville 655
- Zaragoza 575
- Málaga 566
- Bilbao 382
- Las Palmas 358
- Valladolid 329
- Palma de Mallorca 307
- Murcia 305
- Córdoba 298
- Hospitalet 278
- Vigo 263
- Gijón 259
- Alicante 258
- Granada 257

SWEDEN (1988)
- Stockholm 1 471
- Göteborg 720
- Malmö 466

SWITZERLAND (1986)
- Zürich 840
- Geneva 385
- Basle 363
- Bern 300
- Lausanne 262

U.S.S.R. (1987)
- Moscow 8 816
- Leningrad 4 948
- Kiev 2 544
- Tashkent 2 124
- Baku 1 741
- Kharkov 1 587
- Minsk 1 543
- Gorki 1 425
- Novosibirsk 1 423
- Sverdlovsk 1 331
- Kuybyshev 1 280
- Tbilisi 1 194
- Dnepropetrovsk 1 182
- Yerevan 1 168
- Odessa 1 141
- Omsk 1 134
- Chelyabinsk 1 119
- Alma-Ata 1 108
- Ufa 1 092
- Donetsk 1 090
- Perm 1 075
- Kazan 1 068
- Rostov 1 004
- Volgograd 988
- Saratov 918
- Riga 900
- Krasnoyarsk 899
- Zaporozhye 875
- Voronezh 827
- Lvov 767
- Krivoy Rog 698
- Kishinev 663
- Yaroslavl 634
- Karaganda 633
- Frunze 632
- Izhevsk (Ustinov) 631
- Togliatti 627
- Krasnodar 623
- Vladivostok 615
- Irkutsk 609
- Khabarovsk 591
- Novokuznetsk 589
- Ulyanovsk 589
- Dushanbe 582
- Barnaul 569
- Vilnius 566
- Penza 540
- Tula 538
- Orenburg 537
- Zhdanov 529
- Kemerovo 520
- Astrakhan 509
- Voroshilovgrad 509
- Ryazan 508
- Nikolayev 501

UNITED KINGDOM (1981)
- London (1985) 6 767
- Birmingham (1985) 1 007
- Glasgow (1985) 734
- Liverpool 510
- Leeds 449
- Manchester 449
- Sheffield 447
- Edinburgh (1985) 439
- Bristol 388
- Belfast 374
- Coventry 314
- Leicester 283
- Bradford 281
- Cardiff 274
- Nottingham 271
- Hull 268
- Stoke-on-Trent 252
- Wolverhampton 252

YUGOSLAVIA (1981)
- Belgrade 1 088
- Zagreb 650
- Skopje 408
- Sarajevo 319

NORTH AMERICA

CANADA (1986)
- Toronto 3 427
- Montréal 2 921
- Vancouver 1 381
- Ottawa 819
- Edmonton 785
- Calgary 671
- Winnipeg 625
- Québec 603
- Hamilton 557
- St. Catherines 343
- London 342
- Kitchener 311
- Halifax 296
- Victoria 256
- Windsor 254

CUBA (1987)
- Havana 2 059
- Santiago de Cuba 390
- Camagüey 275

DOMINICAN REP. (1981)
- Santo Domingo 1 313
- Santiago 279

EL SALVADOR (1983)
- San Salvador 884

GUATEMALA (1983)
- Guatemala 1 300

HAITI (1984)
- Port-au-Prince 738

HONDURAS (1986)
- Tegucigalpa 598
- San Pedro Sula 397

JAMAICA (1982)
- Kingston 525

MEXICO (1980)
- Mexico 12 932
- Guadalajara 2 245
- Monterrey 1 916
- Puebla 836
- León 656
- Ciudad Juárez 567
- Culiacán Rosales 560
- Mexicali 511
- Tijuana 461
- Mérida 425
- Acapulco 409
- Chihuahua 407
- San Luis Potosi 407
- Torreón 364
- Aguascalientes 359
- Toluca 357
- Morelia 353
- Hermosillo 341
- Saltillo 322
- Durango 321
- Veracruz 305
- Querétaro 294
- Tampico 268
- Villahermosa 251
- Mazatlán 250

NICARAGUA (1981)
- Managua 615

PANAMA (1984)
- Panama 625

PUERTO RICO (1984)
- San Juan 1 816
- Caguas 275

UNITED STATES (1986)
- New York 7 263
- Los Angeles 3 259
- Chicago 3 010
- Houston 1 729
- Philadelphia 1 643
- Detroit 1 086
- San Diego 1 015
- Dallas 1 004
- San Antonio 914
- Phoenix 894
- Baltimore 753
- San Francisco 749
- Indianapolis 720
- San Jose 712
- Memphis 653
- Washington 626
- Jacksonville (Fl.) 610
- Milwaukee 605
- Boston 574
- Columbus (Oh.) 566
- New Orleans 554
- Cleveland 536
- Denver 505
- El Paso 492
- Seattle 486
- Nashville-Davidson 474
- Austin 467
- Oklahoma 446
- Kansas City (Mo.) 441
- Fort Worth 430
- St. Louis 426
- Atlanta 422
- Long Beach 396
- Portland (Or.) 388
- Pittsburgh 387
- Miami 374
- Tulsa 374
- Honolulu 372
- Cincinnati 370
- Albuquerque 367
- Tucson 359
- Minneapolis 357
- Oakland 357
- Charlotte 352
- Omaha 349
- Toledo 341
- Virginia Beach 333
- Buffalo 325
- Sacramento 324
- Newark (N.J.) 316
- Wichita 289
- Louisville 286
- Fresno 285
- Birmingham 278
- Tampa 278
- Norfolk 275
- Colorado Springs 273
- Corpus Christi 264
- St. Paul 264
- Mesa 251
- Arlington 250

OCEANIA

AUSTRALIA (1986)
- Sydney 3 431
- Melbourne 2 942
- Brisbane 1 171
- Perth 1 025
- Adelaide 993
- Newcastle 429
- Canberra 286

NEW ZEALAND (1988)
- Auckland 842
- Wellington 325
- Christchurch 301

SOUTH AMERICA

ARGENTINA (1985)
- Buenos Aires 10 728
- Córdoba 1 055
- Rosario 1 016
- Mendoza 668
- La Plata 611
- San Miguel de Tucumán 571
- Mar del Plata 448
- San Juan 324
- Santa Fé 310
- Salta 302
- Resistencia 262

BOLIVIA (1985)
- La Paz 993
- Santa Cruz 442
- Cochabamba 317

BRAZIL (1985)
- São Paulo 10 099
- Rio de Janeiro 5 615
- Belo Horizonte 2 122
- Salvador 1 811
- Fortaleza 1 589
- Brasilia 1 577
- Nova Iguaçu 1 325
- Recife 1 290
- Curitiba 1 285
- Pôrto Alegre 1 275
- Belém 1 221
- Goiânia 928
- Campinas 845
- Manaus 834
- São Gonçalo 731
- Guarulhos 718
- Duque de Caxias 666
- Santo André 637
- Osasco 594
- São Bernardo do Campo 566
- São Luis 564
- Natal 512
- Maceió 484
- Teresina 476
- Santos 461
- São João de Meriti 459
- Niterói 443
- Jaboatao 411
- João Pessoa 398
- Campo Grande 386
- Contagem 386
- Ribeirão Preto 385
- São José dos Campos 375
- Campos 367
- Aracaju 362
- Feira de Santana 357
- Juiz de Fora 351
- Londrina 348
- Olinda 336
- Sorocaba 329
- Diadema 322
- Jundiaí 315
- Uberlândia 314
- Joinville 304
- Cuiabá 283
- Campina Grande 281
- Pelotas 278
- Petrópolis 275
- Mauá 271
- Carapicuiba 268
- Caxias do Sul 268
- Canoas 262
- Vitoria 254
- Piracicaba 253
- Vila Velha 253

CHILE (1985)
- Santiago 4 318
- Viña del Mar 316
- Valparaiso 267

COLOMBIA (1985)
- Bogotá 3 975
- Medellin 1 419
- Cali 1 324
- Barranquilla 897
- Cartagena 491
- Cucuta 357
- Bucaramanga 342
- Manizales 275
- Ibagué 270

ECUADOR (1982)
- Guayaquil 1 301
- Quito 1 110
- Cuenca 272

PARAGUAY (1983)
- Asunción 708

PERU (1988)
- Lima 4 605
- Arequipa 592
- Trujillo 491
- Chiclayo 395
- Callao 318
- Piura 297
- Chimbote 255
- Cuzco 255

URUGUAY (1985)
- Montevideo 1 248

VENEZUELA (1986)
- Caracas 3 185
- Maracaibo 1 261
- Valencia 1 089
- Maracay 826
- Barquisimento 696
- Ciudad Guayana 442
- San Cristóbal 331
- Ciudad Bolivar 250

1:105 000 000

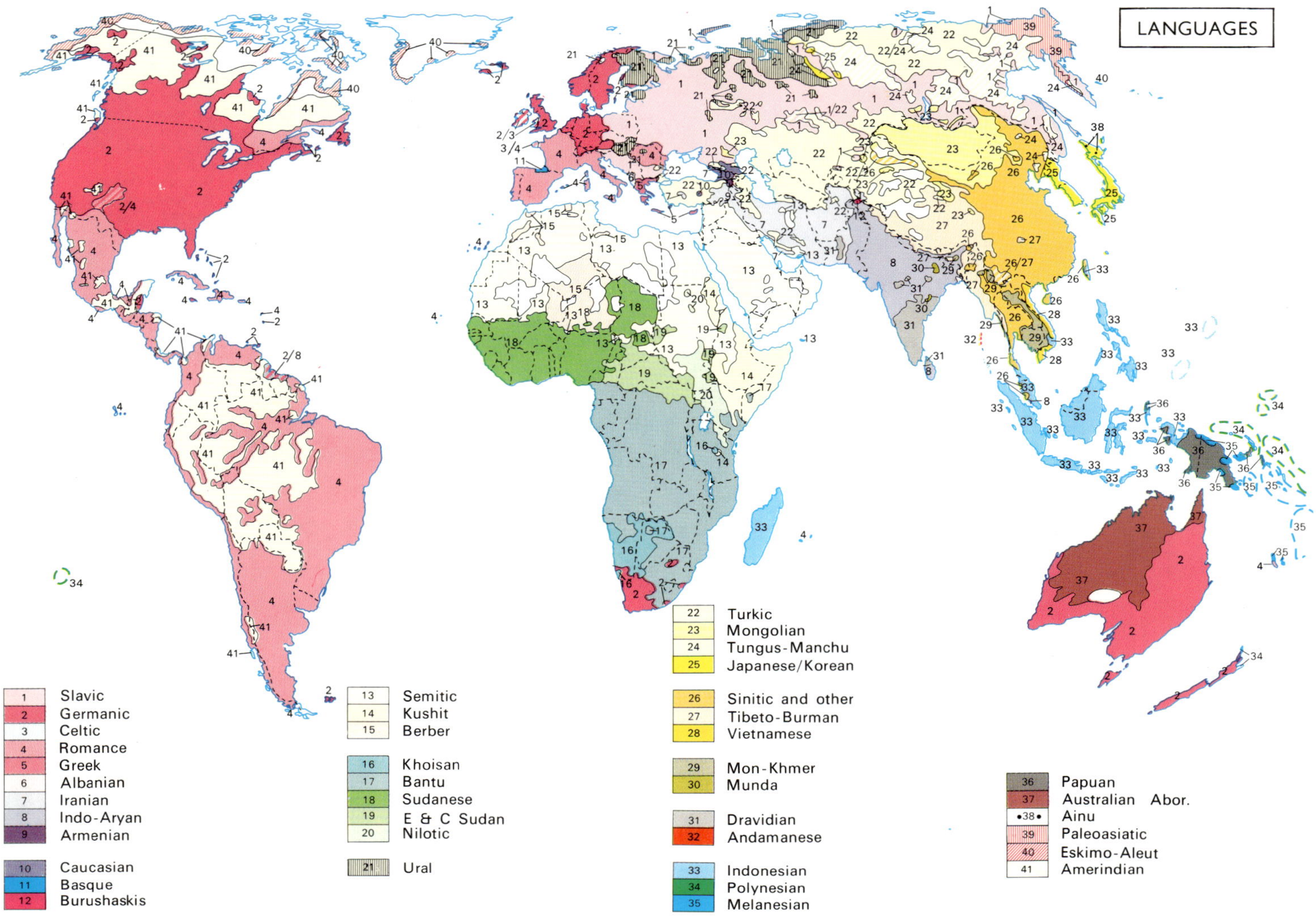
LANGUAGES
1 Slavic
2 Germanic
3 Celtic
4 Romance
5 Greek
6 Albanian
7 Iranian
8 Indo-Aryan
9 Armenian
10 Caucasian
11 Basque
12 Burushaskis
13 Semitic
14 Kushit
15 Berber
16 Khoisan
17 Bantu
18 Sudanese
19 E & C Sudan
20 Nilotic
21 Ural
22 Turkic
23 Mongolian
24 Tungus-Manchu
25 Japanese/Korean
26 Sinitic and other
27 Tibeto-Burman
28 Vietnamese
29 Mon-Khmer
30 Munda
31 Dravidian
32 Andamanese
33 Indonesian
34 Polynesian
35 Melanesian
36 Papuan
37 Australian Abor.
38 Ainu
39 Paleoasiatic
40 Eskimo-Aleut
41 Amerindian

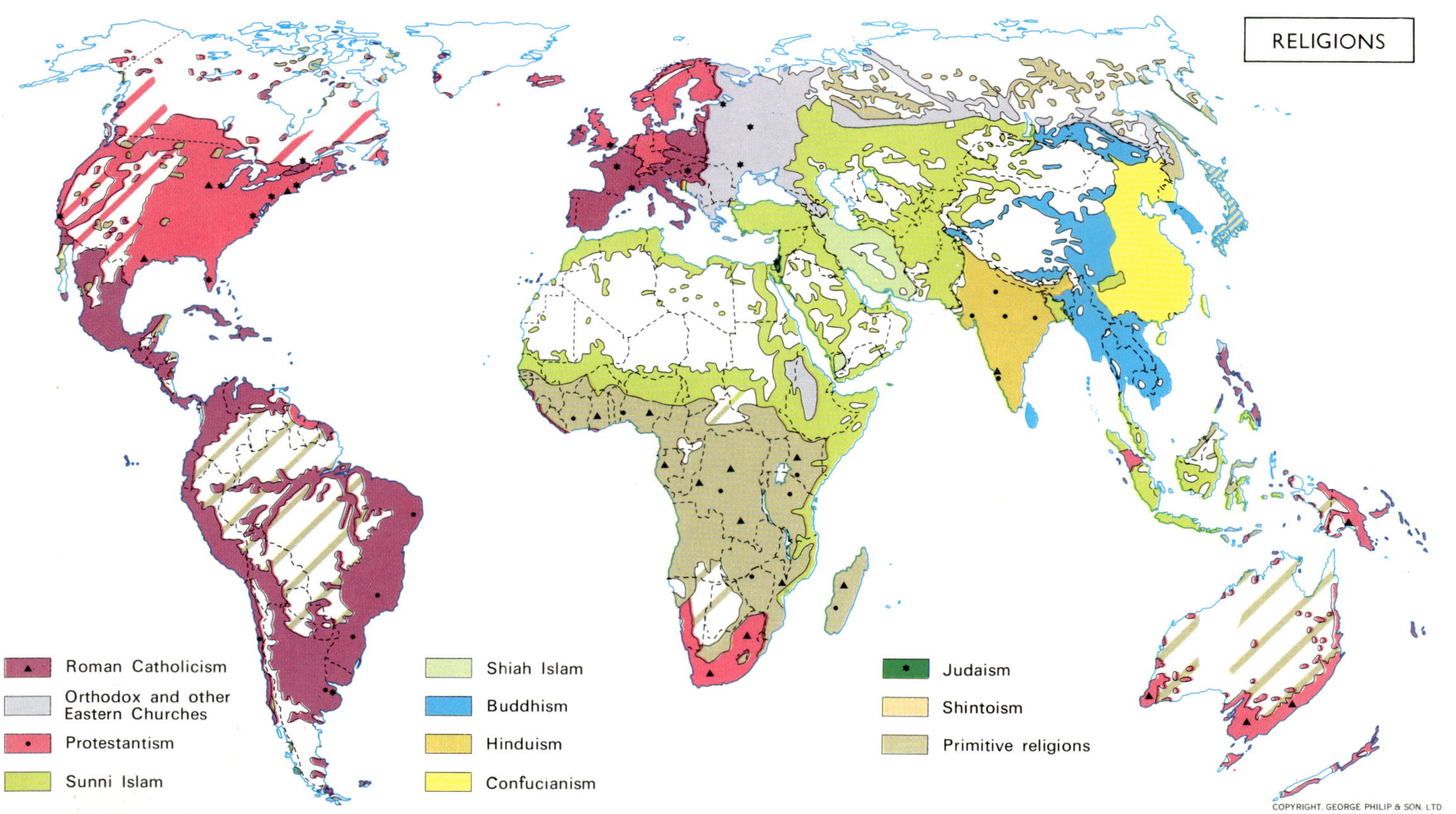
RELIGIONS
Roman Catholicism
Orthodox and other Eastern Churches
Protestantism
Sunni Islam
Shiah Islam
Buddhism
Hinduism
Confucianism
Judaism
Shintoism
Primitive religions

UNITED NATIONS

The United Nations was created in 1945 to promote world peace and co-operation between nations. It is the largest international organisation in the world. It has 160 members and a budget of over two billion U.S. dollars each year. Member countries meet each year to discuss their problems and disputes in the General Assembly. Each member has one vote. The Security Council consists of 15 members who are responsible for keeping the peace between nations. The Economic and Social Council consists of 54 members who are responsible for economic, social, cultural, educational, health and related matters. The Trusteeship Council is responsible for safeguarding the interests of the inhabitants of territories which are not yet fully self-governing. The Secretariat is the chief administrative officer of the organisation. The United Nations has a number of specialised agencies which help members in many fields such as economic development (UNDP), education (UNESCO), farming (FAO) and medicine (WHO). The United Nations is based in New York.

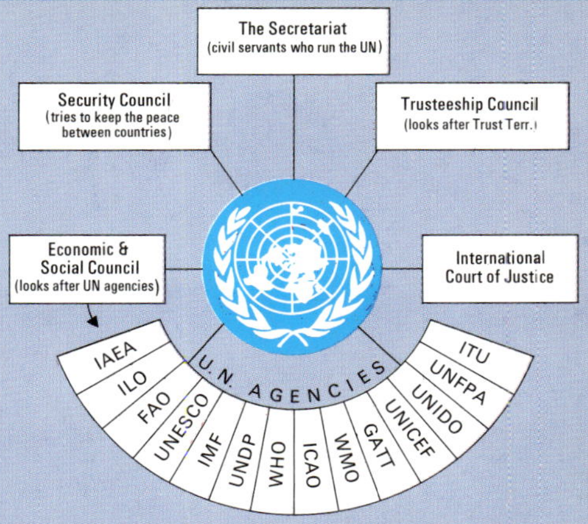

COMMONWEALTH

The Commonwealth maintains many of the ties that were formed in the days of the British Empire. The 50 members are all equal in status. There is no formal treaty or aim. The Commonwealth represents about one quarter of the world's population.

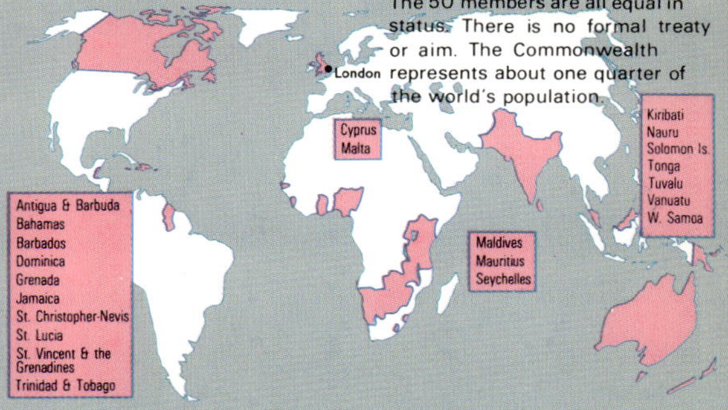

EFTA

The European Free Trade Association was founded in 1960. There are no customs duties between its members and the E.E.C. for industrial goods.

COMECON

The Council for Mutual Economic Assistance was formed to develop the trade and resources of the Soviet bloc countries.

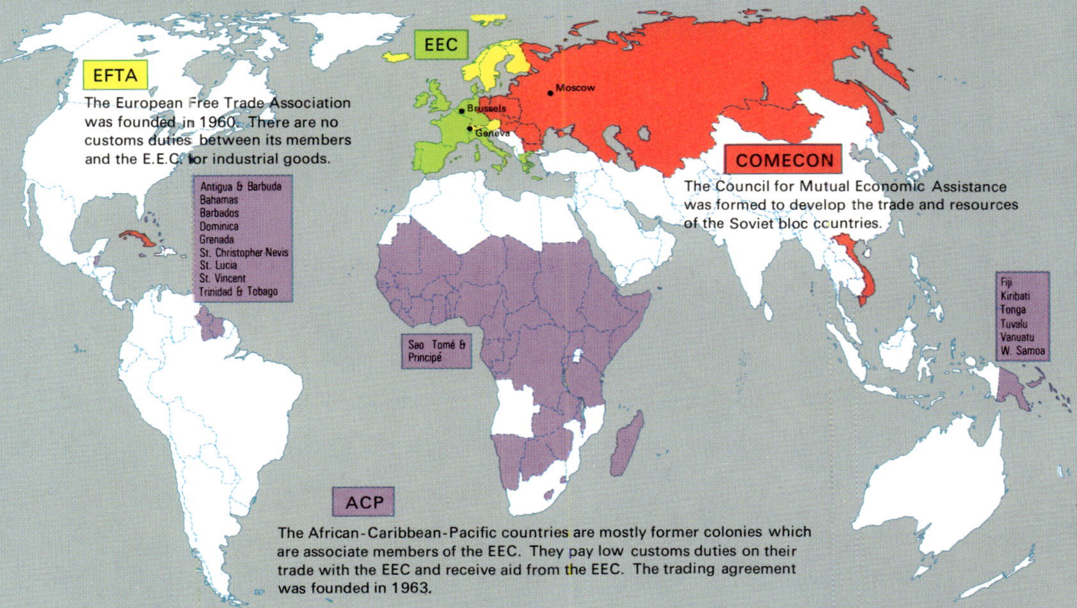

ACP

The African-Caribbean-Pacific countries are mostly former colonies which are associate members of the EEC. They pay low customs duties on their trade with the EEC and receive aid from the EEC. The trading agreement was founded in 1963.

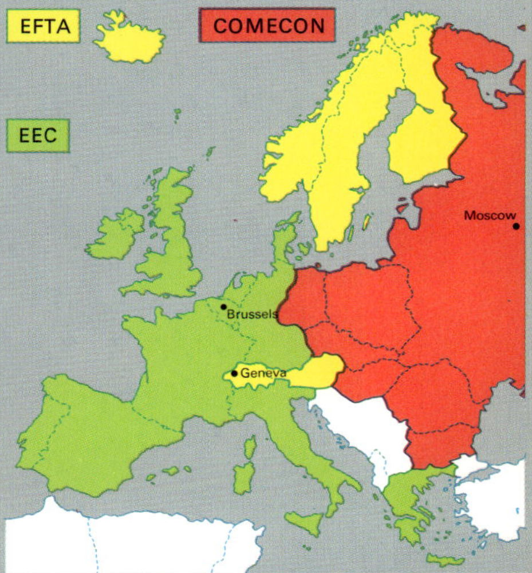

The European Economic Community or the Common Market was founded in 1957 by the Treaty of Rome. The EEC aims to integrate its members economies, coordinate social developments and to bring about political union of the democratic countries in Europe. Its members share common agricultural and industrial policies and tariffs on external trade. The EEC has over 320 million inhabitants and is one of the wealthiest markets in the world. Some 60 nations in Africa, the Caribbean and the Pacific (ACP) are affiliated with the EEC under the Lomé Convention.

NATO

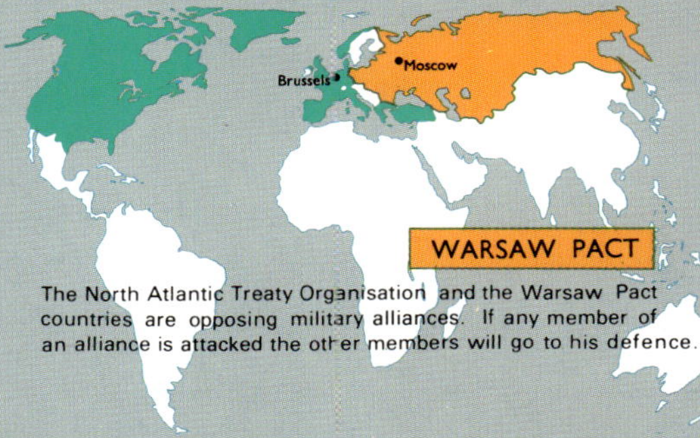

WARSAW PACT

The North Atlantic Treaty Organisation and the Warsaw Pact countries are opposing military alliances. If any member of an alliance is attacked the other members will go to his defence.

OAU

The Organisation of African Unity was formed in 1963 between 30 countries. It aims to end colonialism in Africa and to defend the independence of its members. There are now 52 members, representing over 90% of the people in Africa.

ASEAN

The Association of South East Asian Nations was formed to promote political and economic co-operation among the non-communist states of the region.

OAS

The Organisation of American States encourages the social and economic growth of the developing countries of Latin America with aid from the developed countries in North America.

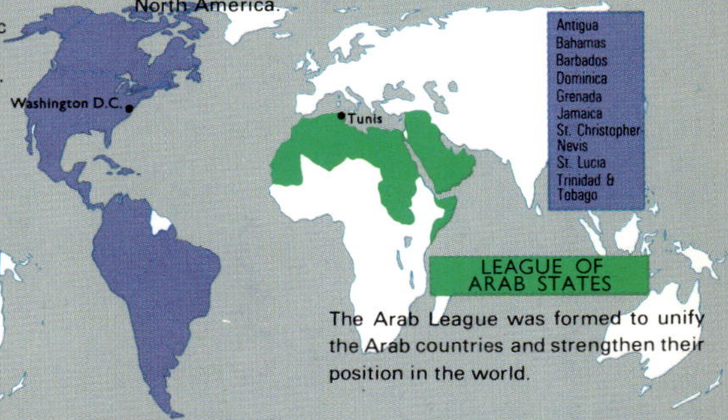

LEAGUE OF ARAB STATES

The Arab League was formed to unify the Arab countries and strengthen their position in the world.

LAIA

OECD

The Organisation for Economic Co-operation and Development encourages economic growth and trade between developed and developing countries.

LAIA stands for Latin American Integration Association. It was recently formed to replace the Latin American Free Trade Association. It encourages free trade between its members.

COLOMBO PLAN

The six developed countries in the plan (Australia, Canada, Japan, New Zealand, U.K. and U.S.A.) provide aid to the developing countries in the plan.

OPEC

The Organisation of Petroleum Exporting Countries was formed in 1960. It maintains the price of oil on the world market. It controls three quarters of the world's oil supply and it is therefore very powerful.

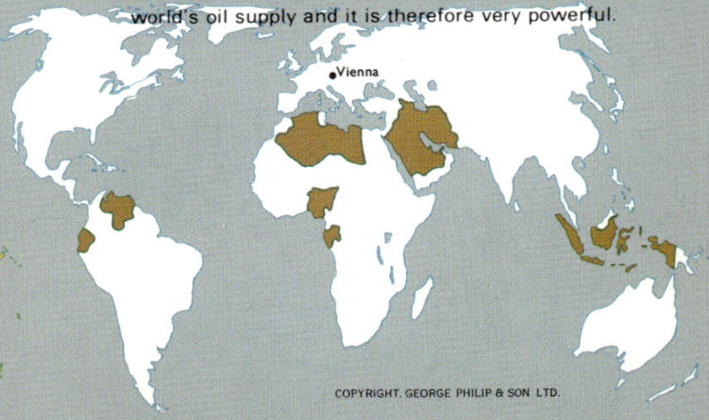

NATURAL INCREASE

The birth rates and death rates are the number of births and deaths per 1000 population each year.

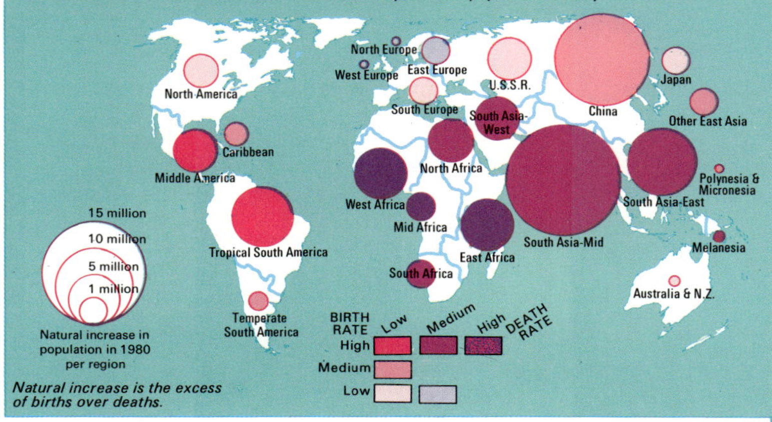

Natural increase is the excess of births over deaths.

FAMILY SIZE

Family size is the total number of children an average woman will bear in her lifetime, for each region. In 1980 the world average was 3.6 children; in 2000 it is expected to be 2.8 children.

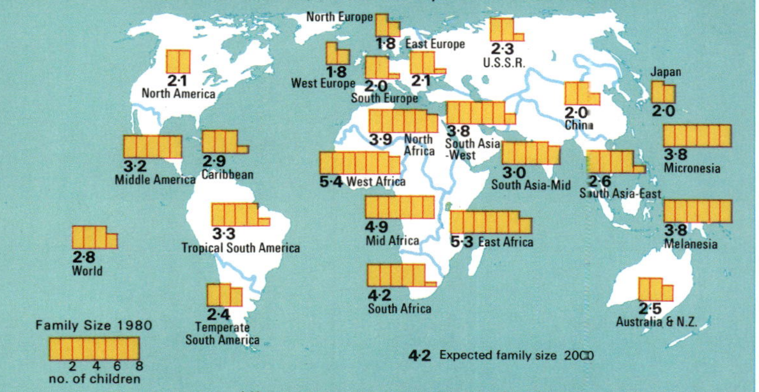

LIFE EXPECTANCY

Life expectancy is the average number of years a newly-born baby can expect to live. The world average has risen from 47 years in 1950 to 58 years in 1980, and is expected to be 64 years in 2000.

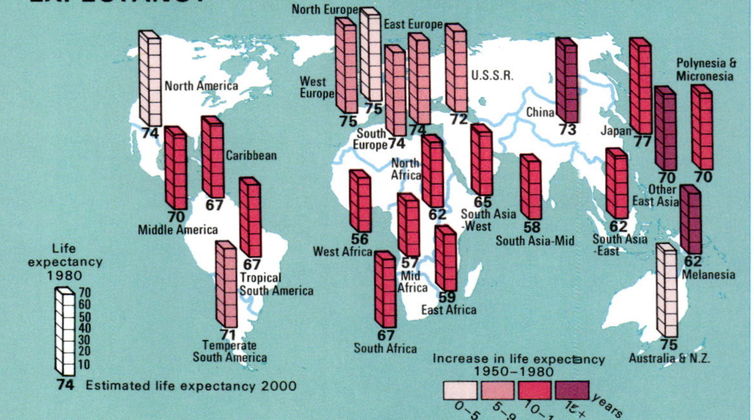

INFANT MORTALITY

The infant mortality rate for the world was 113 in 1960. It is now 81 and is expected to fall to 53 by 2000.

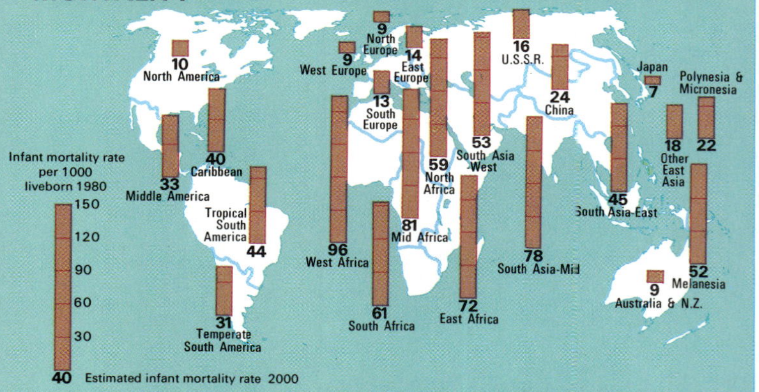

YOUNG AND OLD

Median Age is the age in years which divides the population into two equal parts, one young and the other old. The median age for the world is 23

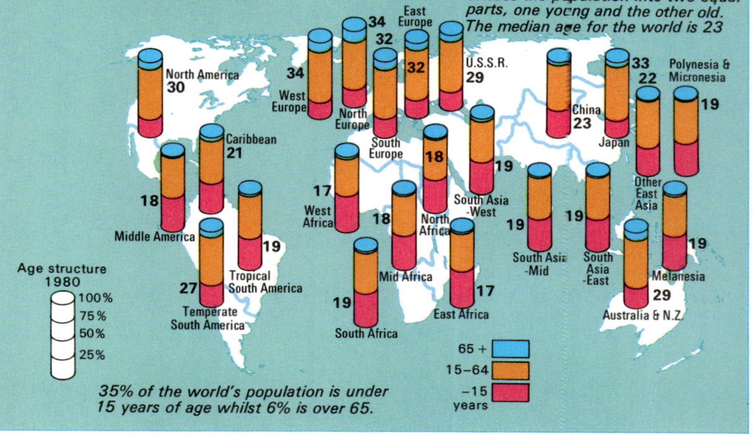

35% of the world's population is under 15 years of age whilst 6% is over 65.

The bars represent the percentage of the population in the age group shown. The blue bars represent the males, the red bars the females. The developing countries such as India tend to have a higher proportion of young people than the developed countries such as Canada.

AGE DISTRIBUTION PYRAMIDS

See page 8 for age distribution pyramid of the U.K.

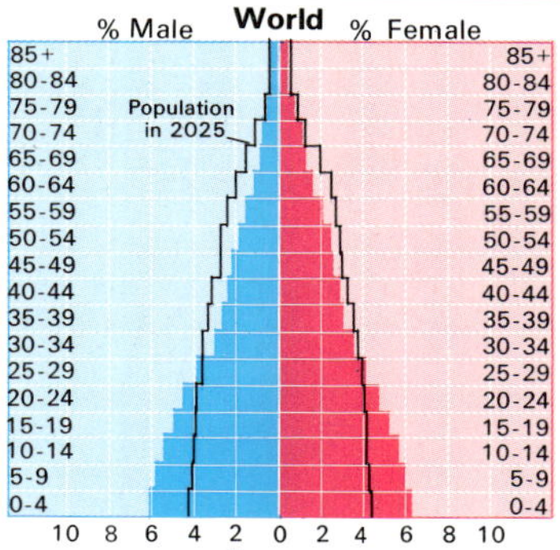

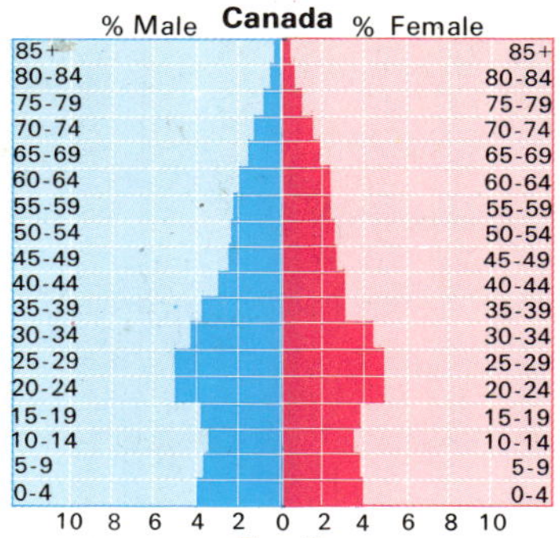

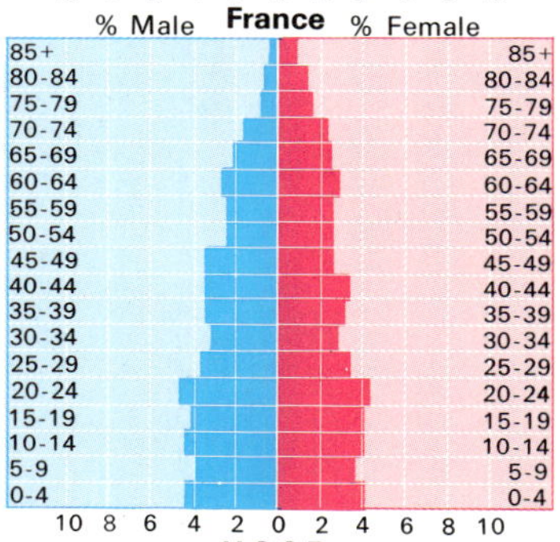

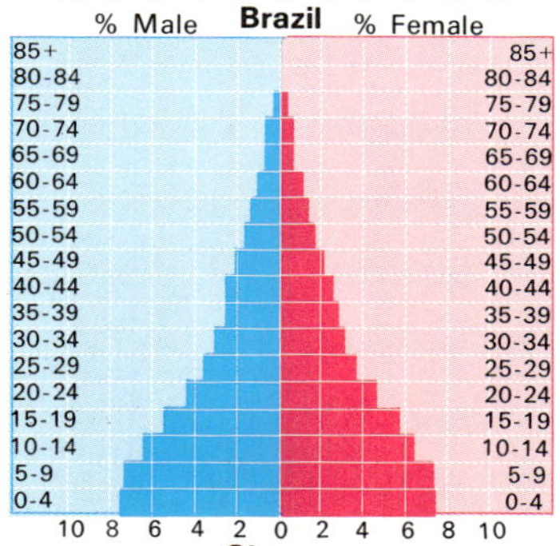

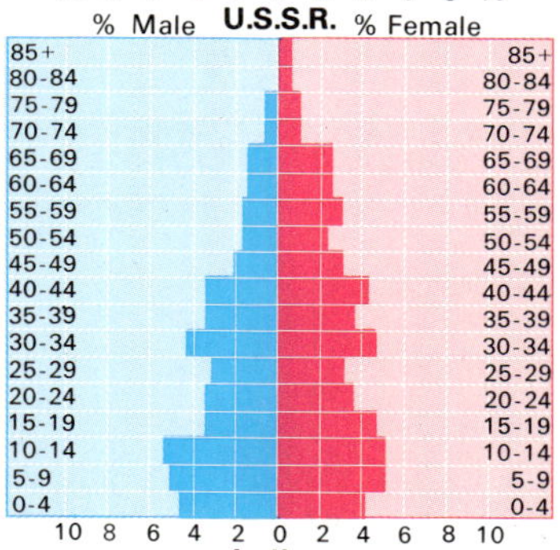

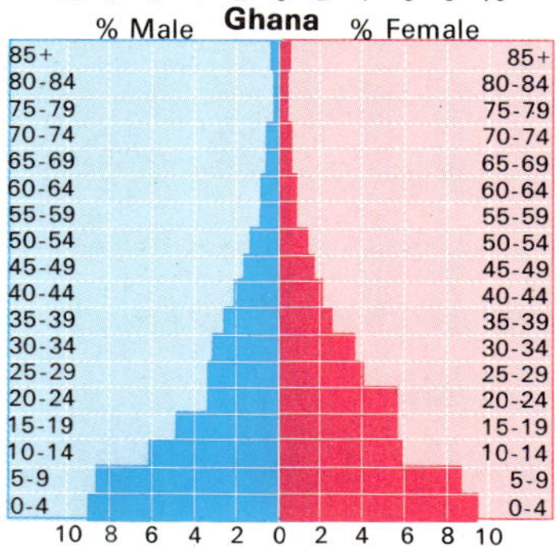

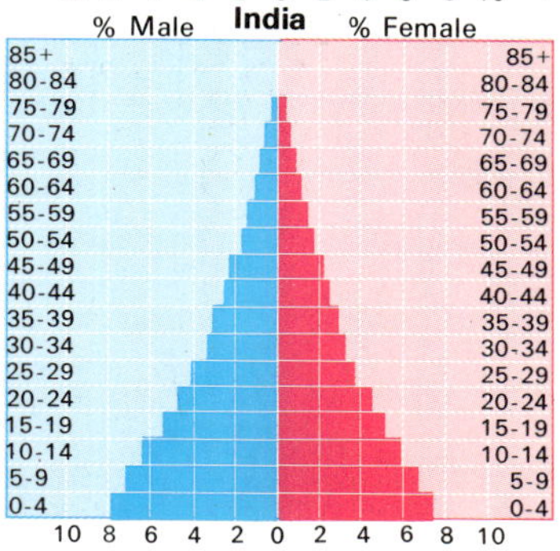

See page 125 for maps of Population Growth and Urbanisation

POPULATION BY COUNTRY

See map on pages 116-117 for greater detail.

The most populous country (China) contains a quarter of the world's population. The four most populous countries (China, India, U.S.S.R., and U.S.A.) contain half, and the first eighteen (all those countries named in larger type on the map) contain over three-quarters of the world's population. The remaining 150 countries contain only one quarter.

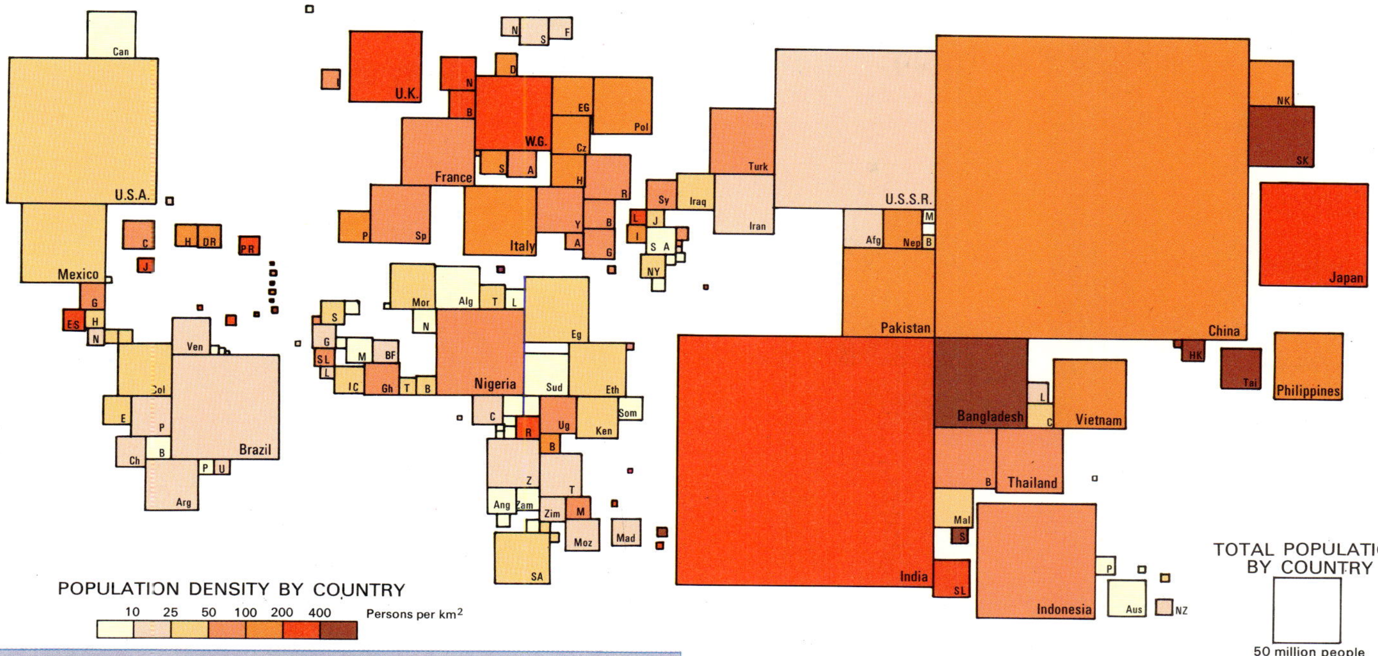

MIGRATIONS

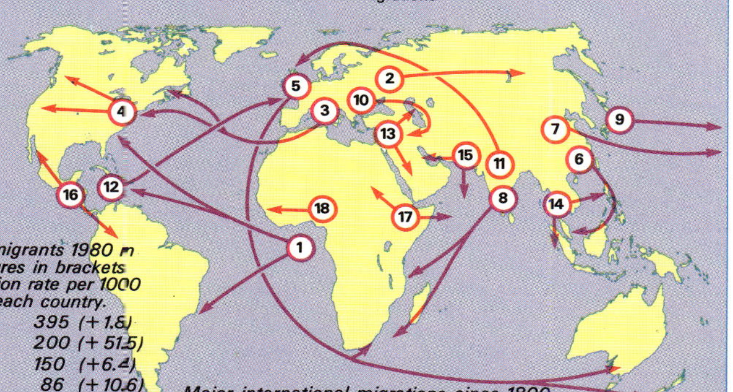

Number of immigrants 1980 in thousands. Figures in brackets show immigration rate per 1000 population for each country.

1. U.S.A. 395 (+1.8)
2. Somalia 200 (+51.5)
3. Canada 150 (+6.4)
4. S. Arabia 86 (+10.6)
5. Hong Kong 75 (+15.8)
6. Venezuela 60 (+4.2)
7. Puerto Rico 59 (+17.3)
8. Australia 50 (+3.6)
9. Ivory Coast 38 (+5.1)
10. U.A.E 30 (+45.7)

Number of emigrants 1980 in thousands. Figures in brackets show emigration rate per 1000 population for each country.

1. Ethiopia 200 (−6.6)
2. Vietnam 146 (−2.9)
3. Lebanon 80 (−29.5)
4. Cambodia 80 (−11.6)
5. Colombia 60 (−2.5)
6. Mexico 50 (−0.8)
7. Sri Lanka 43 (−3.0)
8. Philippines 40 (−0.9)
9. S. Yemen 36 (−5.4)
10. U.K. 30 (−0.5)

Major international migrations since 1800

1. Slave trade from Africa to the Americas (1500–1850)
2. Russian colonisation of Siberia (1850–1950)
3. European emigration to N. America (1850–1920)
4. Colonisation of the American West (1860–1960)
5. European emigration to Southern Africa and Oceania (1840-1960)
6. Chinese emigration to Indo-China (1860–1910)
7. Chinese emigration to the Americas (1900–1950)
8. Indian emigration to Africa (1860–1910)
9. Japanese emigration to N. America (1870–1910)
10. Jewish emigration to Israel (1949–)
11. Asian emigration to Europe (1950–1970)
12. W. Indian emigration to Europe (1950–1970)
13. Palestinian refugees to Middle East (1950–)
14. Indo-Chinese refugees to S.E. Asia, China, and North America (1970–80)
15. Afghan refugees to Pakistan and Iran (1970–)
16. Refugees in Central America (1979–)
17. Ethiopian refugees in Somalia and Sudan (1977–)
18. Immigrants evicted from Nigeria (1983)

ABORTION AND BIRTH CONTROL

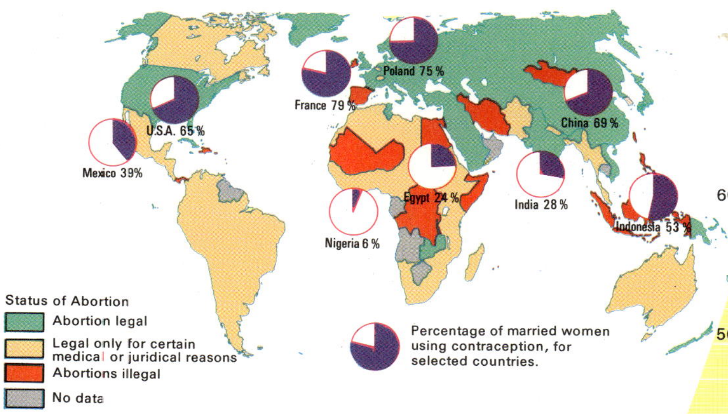

Legally induced abortions per 1000 live births. Total abortions in thousands are in brackets.

Bulgaria	1216 (152)	Canada	175 (66)
U.S.A.	347 (1 158)	New Zealand	133 (7)
France	207 (171)	Tunisia	77 (16)
Poland	192 (141)	India	27 (346)
Great Britain	189 (137)		

POPULATION IN 2000 A.D.

Percentage of world total is given in brackets.

World	6 119		
South Asia	2 075 (34%)	U.S.S.R.	310 (5%)
East Asia	1 475 (24%)	Europe	512 (8.5%)
Oceania	30 (0.5%)		
Africa	853 (14%)		
South America	566 (9%)		
N. America	299 (5%)		

Until comparatively recently there was little increase in the population of the world. It is thought there were about 200 million in 600 B.C., 300 million in 1000 A.D., and 500 million by 1600 A.D.. This diagram shows how the world's population has increased since then at an ever increasing rate. 90% of this increase has been in the less developed regions The world population of 1950 doubled by 1987 and if present trends continue it will have trebled by 2010

POPULATION INCREASE SINCE 1650

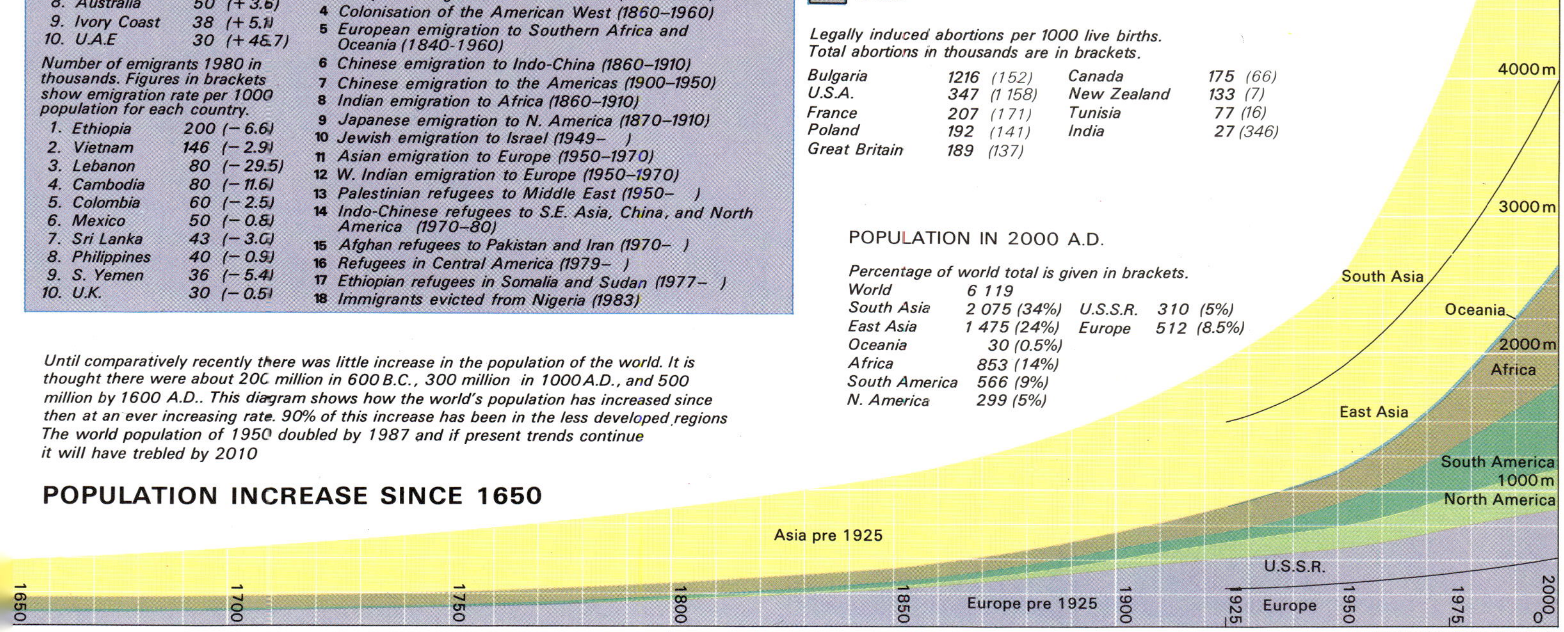

NATURAL DISASTERS

EARTHQUAKES AND VOLCANOES

- ○ Major earthquakes with dates
- ▲ Major volcanoes
- Earthquake zones (land and sea)

STORMS AND FLOODS

- * Major storms and floods with dates
- Paths of winter blizzards
- Paths of tropical storms
- Areas liable to flood

PESTS

- Locust invasion areas
- Main tsetse fly areas

MAJOR FAMINES

- ◉ Sahel 1973

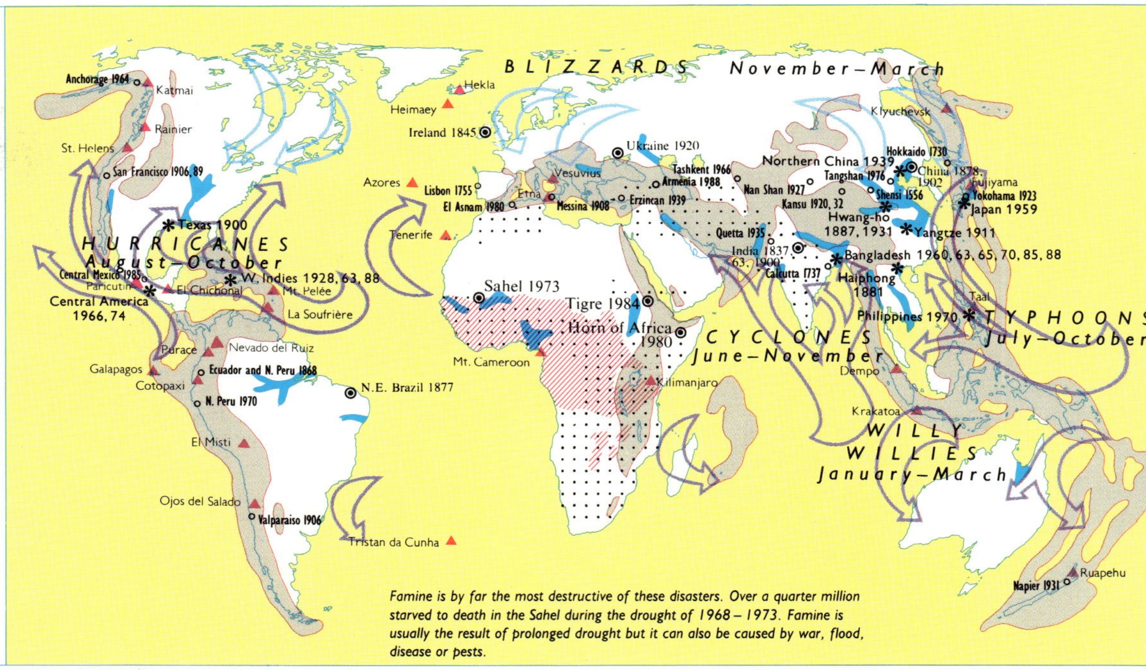

Famine is by far the most destructive of these disasters. Over a quarter million starved to death in the Sahel during the drought of 1968–1973. Famine is usually the result of prolonged drought but it can also be caused by war, flood, disease or pests.

MAN-MADE PROBLEMS

Since 1945 there have been over 300 wars. Few countries in the world have been unaffected by war, strife or terrorism.

- ★ Major wars since 1945
- ϟ Other recent conflicts
- Heavily polluted sea and lakes
- Other polluted sea and lakes
- Principal oil tanker routes
- Disastrous oil spills
- Main areas of industrial pollution
- Areas affected by acid rain
- Major deserts
- Areas threatened by desertification
- Areas of rapid deforestation
- ⊙ Other recent man-made disasters

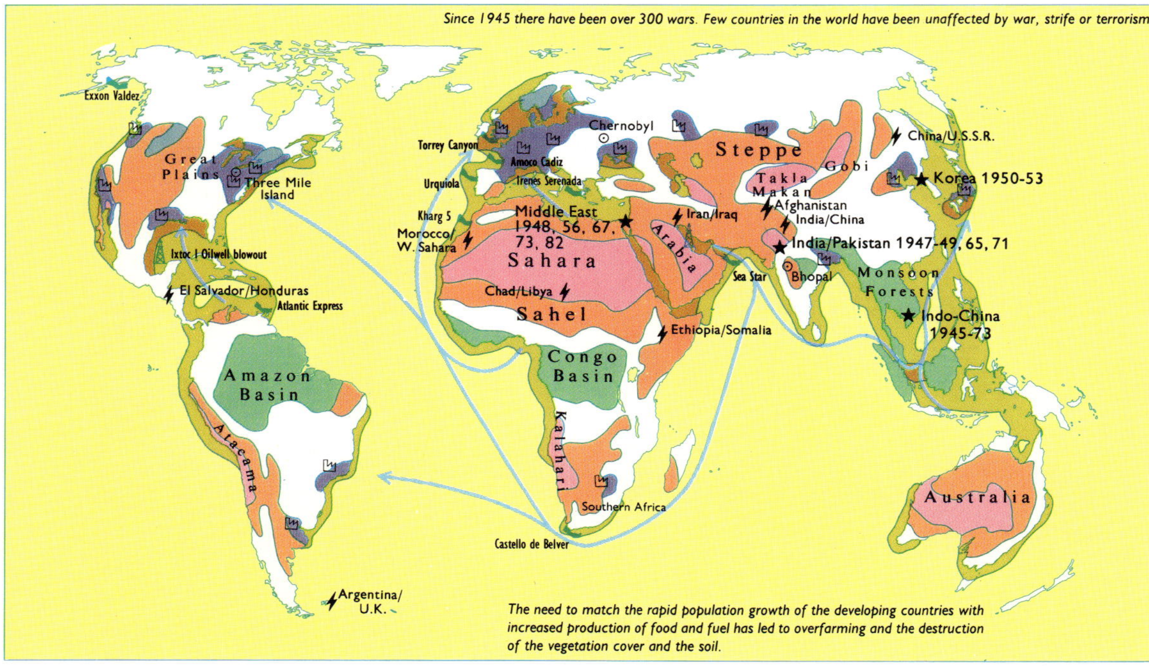

The need to match the rapid population growth of the developing countries with increased production of food and fuel has led to overfarming and the destruction of the vegetation cover and the soil.

Pollution tends to be a greater problem for the developed countries with their intensive industry and agriculture. Prevailing winds can carry air pollution a long way before it falls as acid rain, which is now a serious problem in Canada and Scandinavia. Traces of pollution have even been discovered in the ice of Antarctica.

MEDICAL CARE

Persons per doctor in each country

- over 25000
- 10000 – 25000
- 5000 – 10000
- 1000 – 5000
- less than 1000

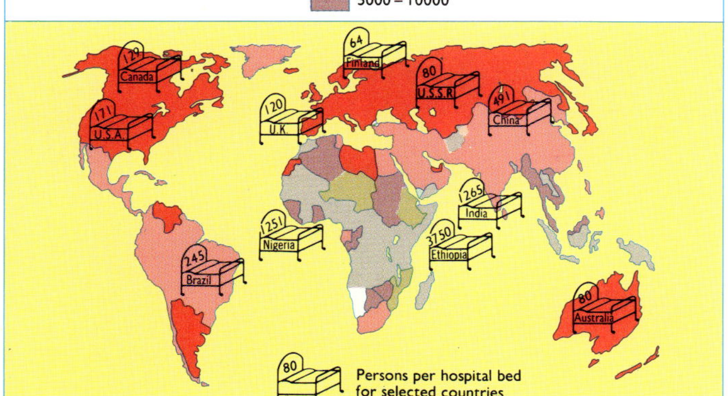

NUTRITION

Calorie intake as a percentage of needs per person

- less than 80%
- 80 – 90%
- 90 – 100%
- 100 – 110%
- 110 – 120%
- over 120%

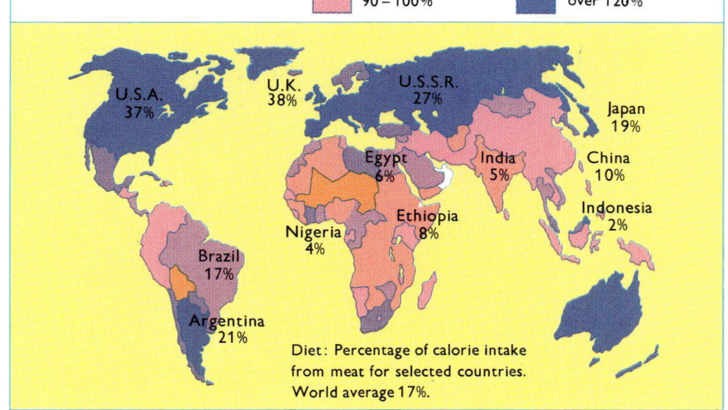

STANDARDS OF LIVING

THE RICH

Countries with more than four times the world's average income

Countries with more than twice the world's average income

Countries with incomes just above the world's average

THE POOR

Countries with incomes just below the world's average

Countries with less than half of the world's average income

Countries with less than one quarter of the world's average income

Data not available

The world's average income is just under 2200 US$ per annum. The richest country on a per capita basis is Kuwait with an income over 200 times that of the poorest country, Mali.

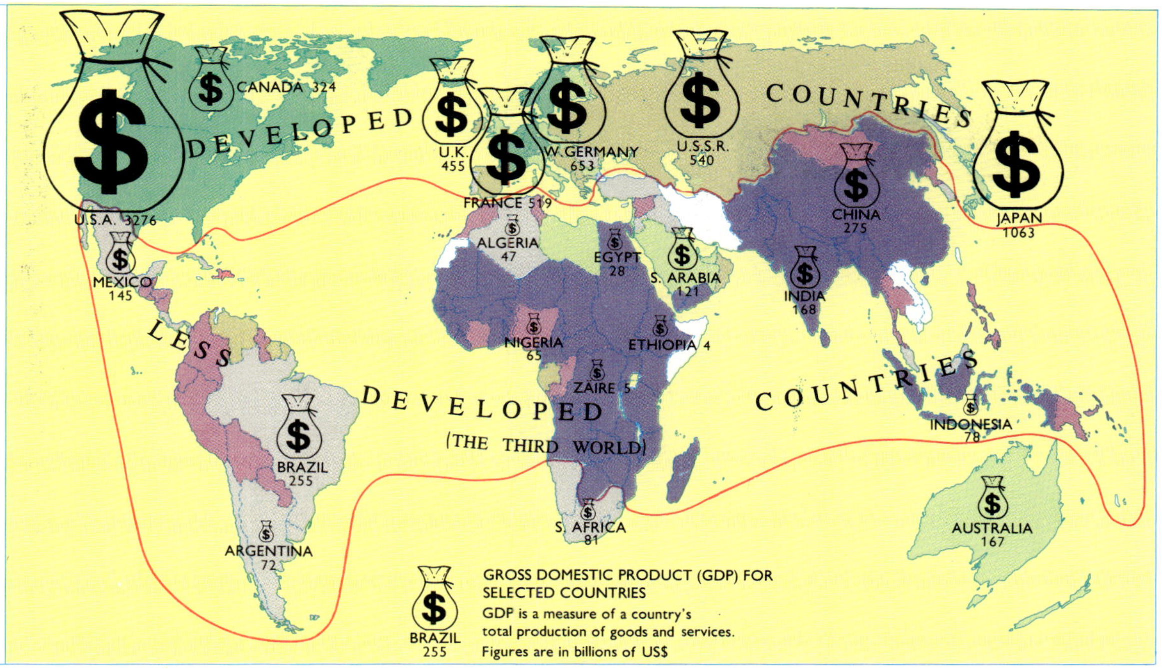

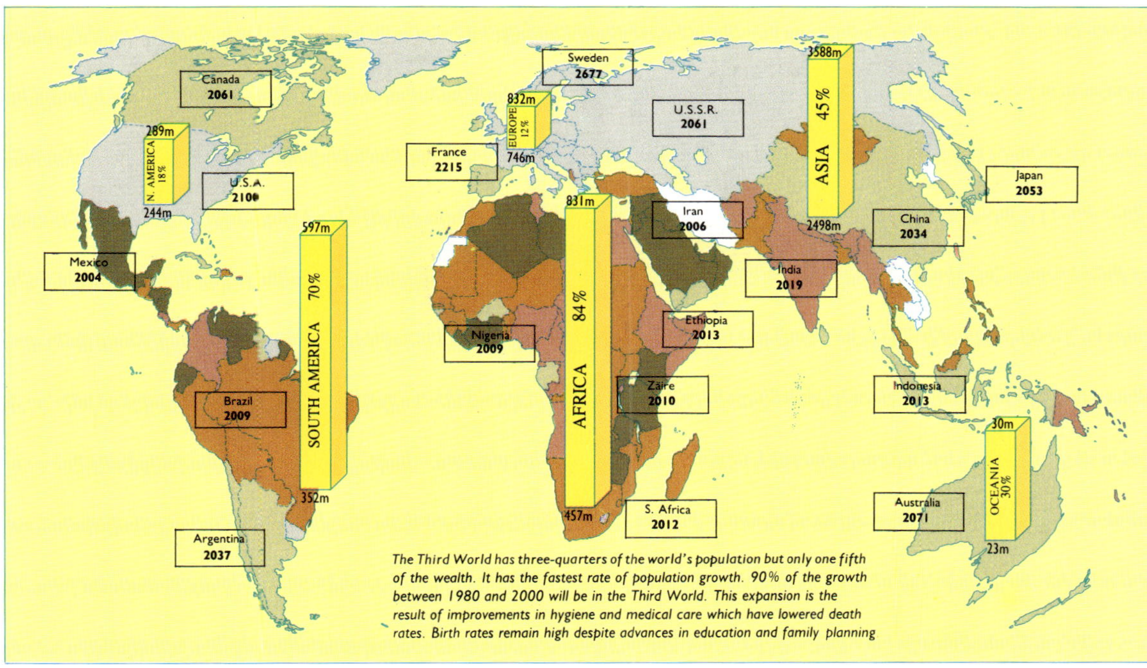

The Third World has three-quarters of the world's population but only one fifth of the wealth. It has the fastest rate of population growth. 90% of the growth between 1980 and 2000 will be in the Third World. This expansion is the result of improvements in hygiene and medical care which have lowered death rates. Birth rates remain high despite advances in education and family planning

POPULATION EXPLOSION IN THE THIRD WORLD

CURRENT RATE OF INCREASE

- less than 1%
- 1 – 2%
- 2 – 2½%
- 2½% – 3%
- over 3%

Annual rate of population growth in each country

EXPECTED RATE OF INCREASE

2034 — Date by which 1984 population of selected countries will double if present trends continue.

World = 2025

Population in 2000

Expected rate of population increase 1980 – 2000 for each continent (1mm = 2%)

Population in 1980

URBANISATION

- 75 – 100%
- 50 – 75%
- 25 – 50%
- 0 – 25%

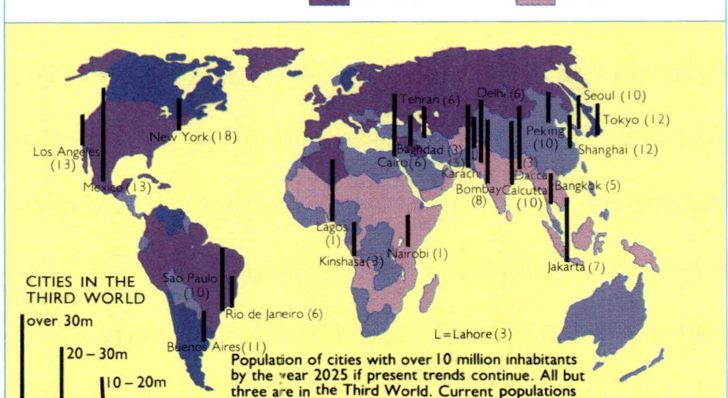

ILLITERACY

Percentage of population in each country who are illiterate

- 80 – 100%
- 60 – 80%
- 40 – 60%
- 20 – 40%
- 0 – 20%

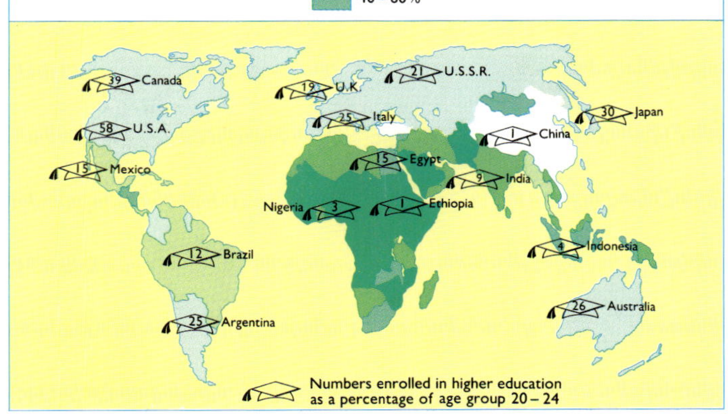

ENERGY CONSUMPTION

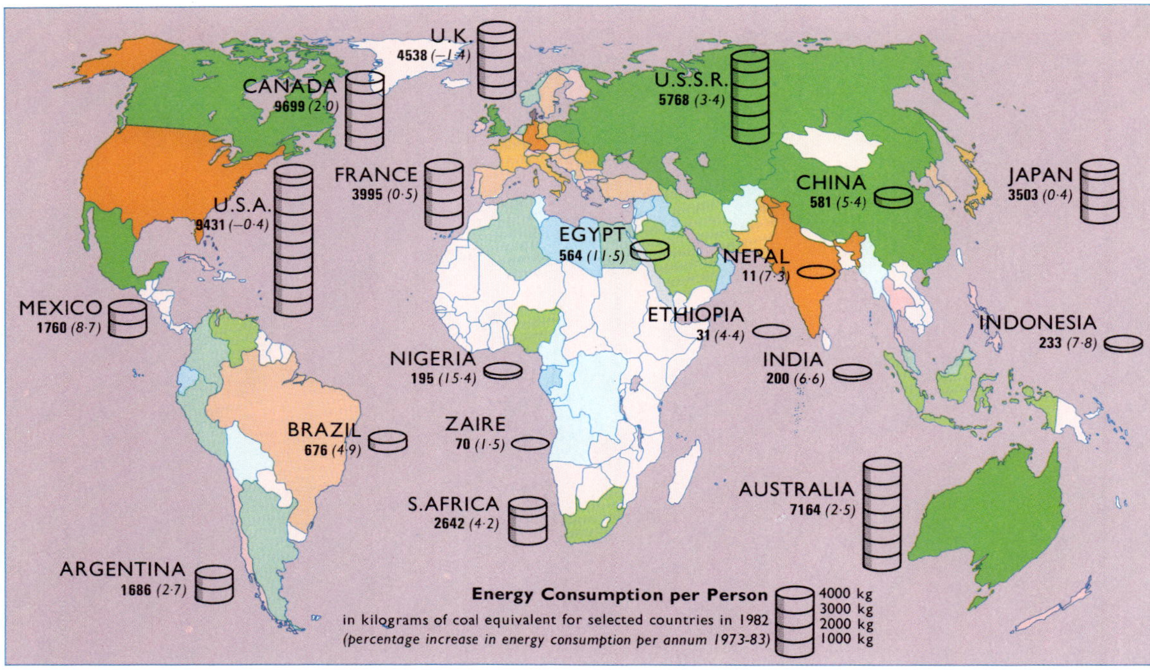

Total Energy Consumption and Production – Key to Map Colours

Figures are in million tonnes of coal equivalent for 1982

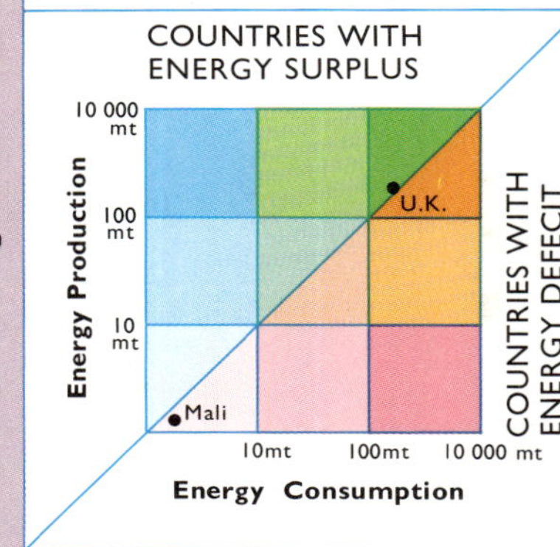

Examples :- U.K. produced 311 mt
consumed 233 mt
Mali produced 0.006 mt
consumed 0.203 mt

IMPORTANCE OF PRIMARY COMMODITIES

Primary commodities as a percentage of total exports. Primary commodities are raw materials such as minerals, fuel, food and timber.

0-25% | 25-50% | 50-75% | 75-100%

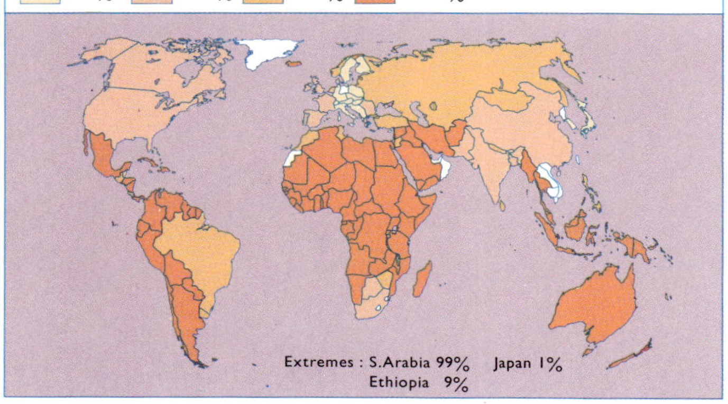

DEPENDENCE UPON AGRICULTURE

Value of agriculture as a percentage of G.D.P. (Gross Domestic Product)

0-10% | 10-20% | 20-30% | 30-40% | 40-50% | over 50%

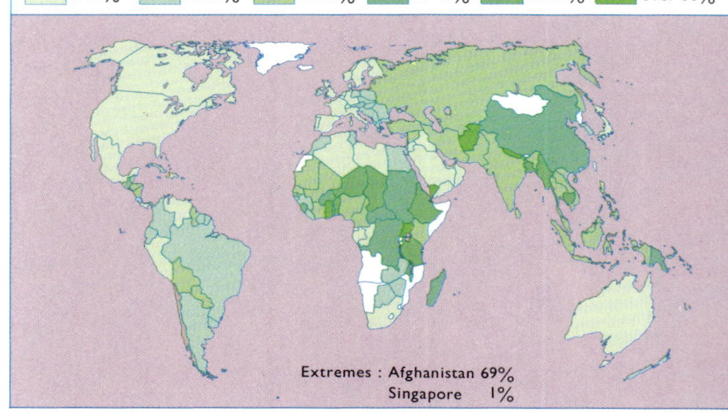

FOOD PRODUCTION

Food production per person

Percentage change from 1974-6 to 1981-3 for each country

INCREASE: over 20% | 15-20% | 10-15% | 5-10% | 0-5%

DECREASE: 0-5% | 5-10% | 10-15% | 15-20% | over 20%

TRADE IN FOOD

60.6 U.K. — Cereal imports per person for selected countries in 1983 (figures in kilograms)

Net exporters of food (value of food exports greater than food imports

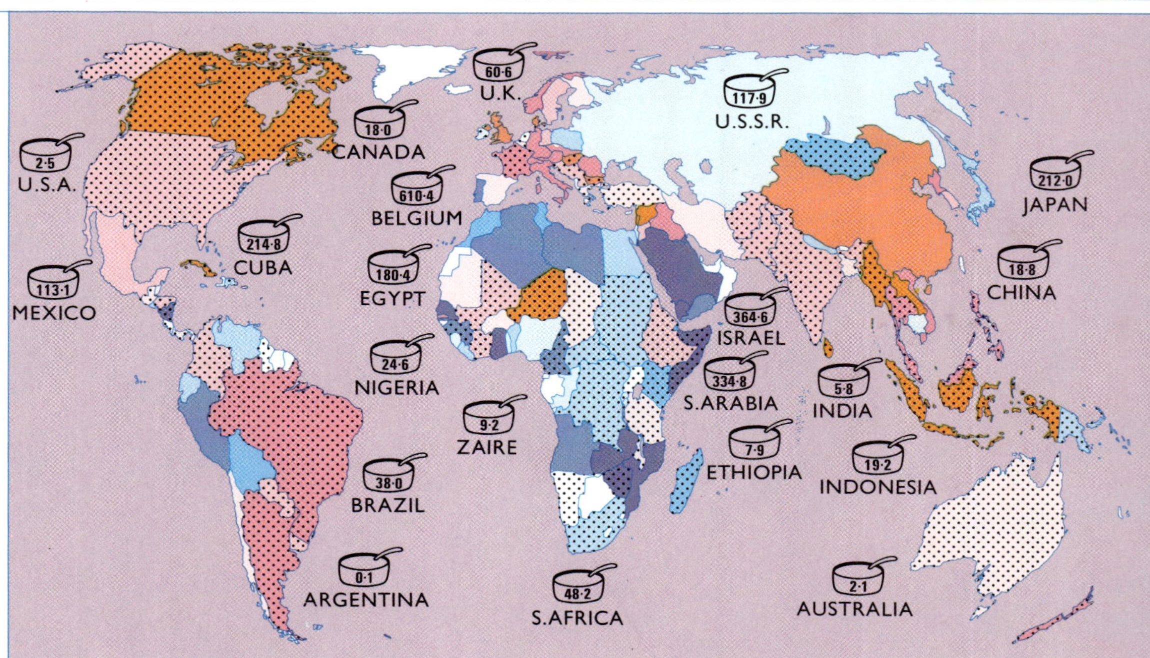

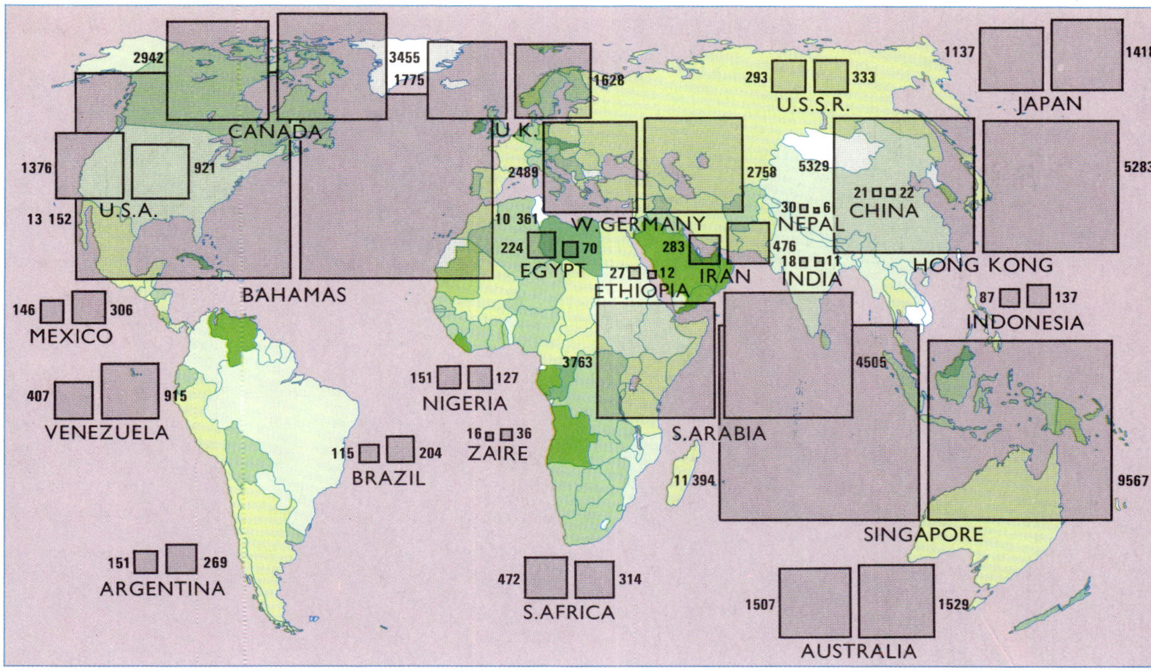

TRADE

Dependence upon Trade

Exports as a percentage of G.D.P. (Gross Domestic Product) for each country for 1982

- over 50%
- 40-50%
- 30-40%
- 20-30%
- 10-20%
- 0-10%

Value of Trade per person

Imports Exports

Figures are in U.S. $ for selected countries in 1983

DEVELOPMENT AID

Development aid received per person in U.S. $, 1979-81 average

0-10$ | 10-20$ | 20-50$ | 50-100$ | over 100$

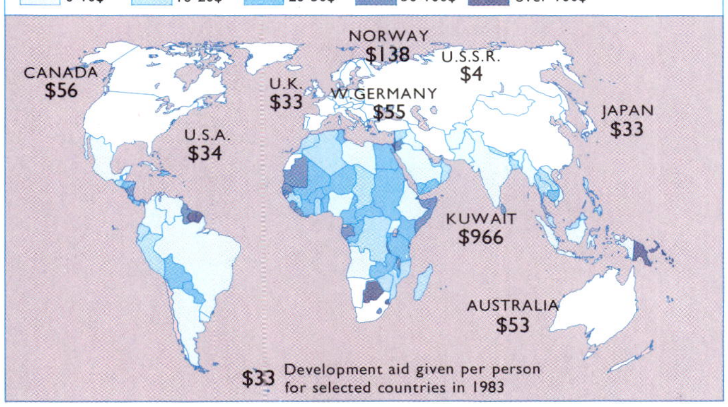

$33 Development aid given per person for selected countries in 1983

INFLATION

Annual average rate of increase 1973-83

0-5% | 5-10% | 10-15% | 15-20% | 20-50% | 50-100% | over 100%

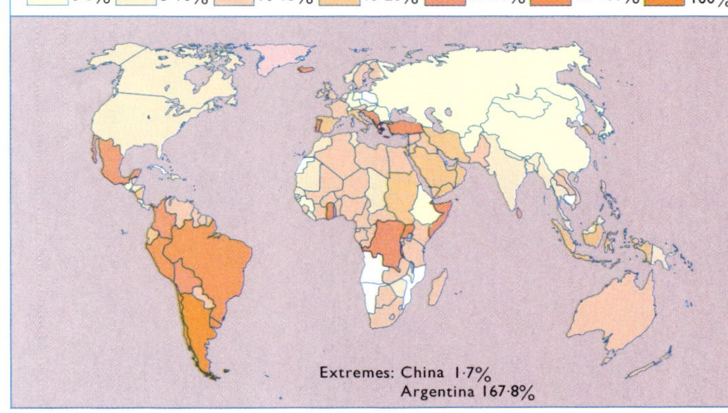

Extremes: China 1·7%
Argentina 167·8%

EMPLOYMENT

Employment by Sector in 1980
Key to Map Colours

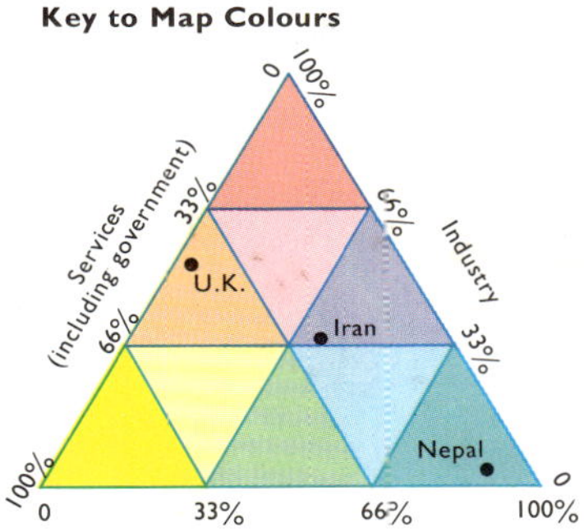

Examples: Nepal 93% in agriculture
2% in industry
5% in services

U.K. 2% in agriculture
42% in industry
56% in services

Iran 38% in agriculture
33% in industry
29% in services

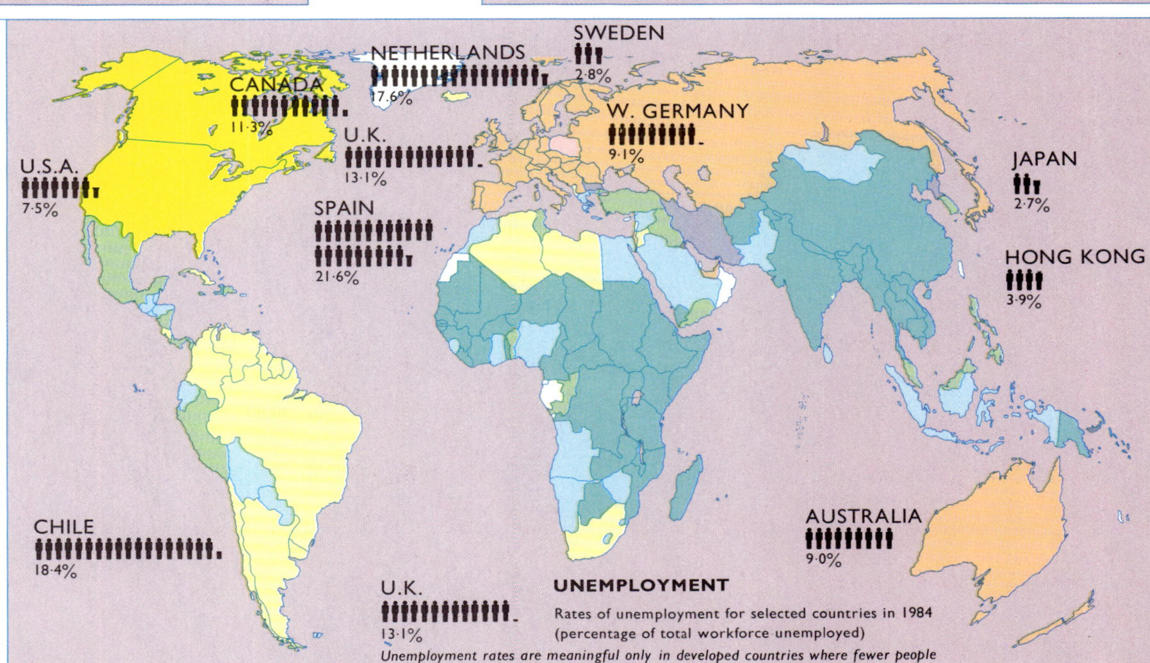

UNEMPLOYMENT

Rates of unemployment for selected countries in 1984 (percentage of total workforce unemployed)

Unemployment rates are meaningful only in developed countries where fewer people live on the land.

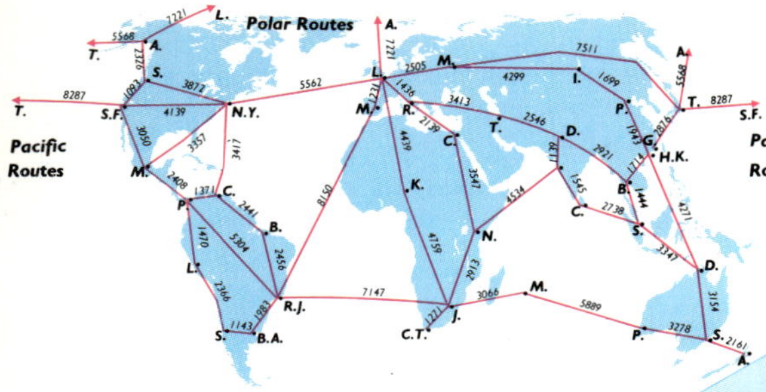

Principal Air Routes
Distances in km

Projection: Hammer Equal Area

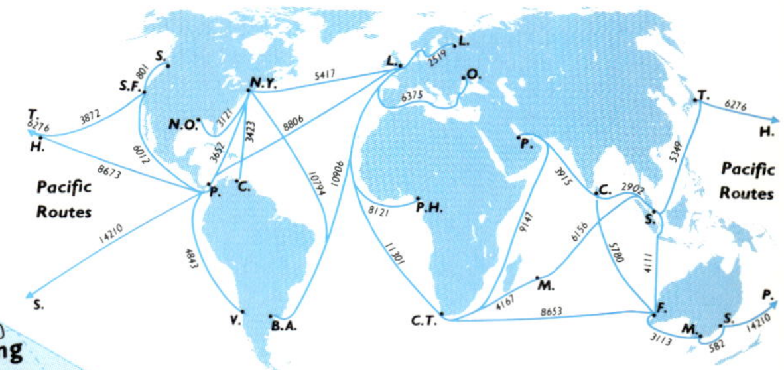

Principal Sea Routes
Distances in km

Theoretically a time zone extends for 15° of longitude (360° ÷ 24 hours = 15°) so that the sun is overhead at noon in each zone. Zone boundaries are rarely lines of longitude, but are adjusted to follow international boundaries or to avoid separating cities and towns from neighbours by a time difference. Countries such as U.S.A. and Canada, the U.S.S.R. and Australia which stretch through many degrees of longitude have a number of time zones. To relate work and leisure, normally planned with clock time, more closely to sun time or daylight, the standard zone time can be adjusted for part of the year; Summer Time is an example of this.

Projection: *Mercator*

Actual solar time when it is noon at Greenwich is shown along the top of the map

Mexico City
19 26N 99 4W

London
51 28N 0 27W

These circular maps are drawn on an Azimuthal Equidistant projection with its origin, its centre, at the city shown. The whole world is shown and so there are some strange distortions of the coastline at the edges, for example, in that of Singapore. The principal property of the projection is that all distances measured through the centre of the circle are true to scale, and so a straight line passing from the centre to any other point is a great circle and shows the shortest distance between the cities. Also that line is correct for direction/bearing and shows the great circle flight path.

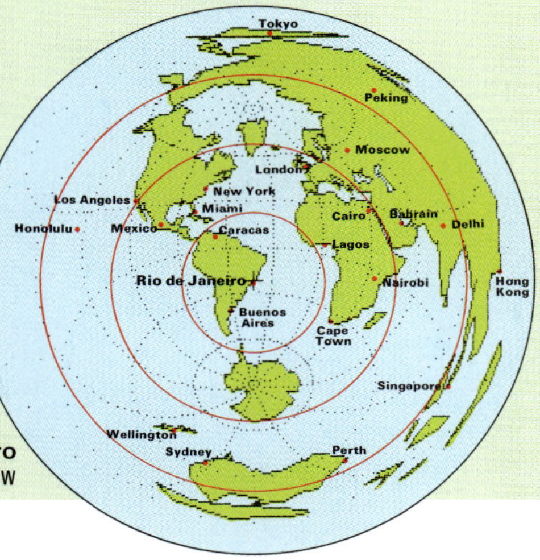

Rio de Janeiro
22 50S 43 15W

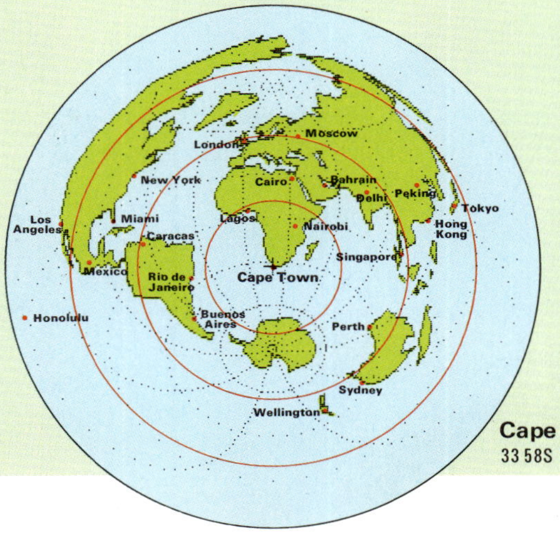

Cape Town
33 58S 18 36E

	Bahrain	Buenos Aires	Cairo	Cape Town	Caracas	Delhi	Hong Kong	Honolulu	Lagos	London	Los Angeles	Mexico	Miami	Moscow	Nairobi	New York	Peking	Perth	Rio de Janeiro	Singapore	Sydney	Tokyo
Buenos Aires	13 291																					
Cairo	1 927	11 845																				
Cape Town	7 496	6 880	7 246																			
Caracas	12 121	5 124	10 200	10 254																		
Delhi	2 618	15 784	4 400	9 278	14 186																	
Hong Kong	6 387	18 442	8 121	11 852	16 340	3 768																
Honolulu	13 882	12 158	14 195	18 555	9 671	11 984	8 911															
Lagos	5 454	7 932	3 926	4 783	7 722	8 071	11 832	16 286														
London	5 089	11 128	3 528	9 672	7 465	6 726	9 637	11 617	4 998													
Los Angeles	13 210	9 854	12 206	16 067	5 813	12 863	11 634	4 105	12 408	8 752												
Mexico	13 962	7 391	12 360	13 701	3 572	14 651	12 121	6 096	11 043	8 898	2 498											
Miami	12 182	7 113	10 441	12 334	2 190	13 495	14 430	7 806	9 045	7 102	3 759	2 050										
Moscow	3 466	13 488	2 909	10 150	9 900	4 359	7 148	11 289	6 250	2 505	9 748	10 682	9 191									
Nairobi	3 298	10 413	3 542	4 096	11 545	5 413	8 750	17 255	3 828	6 835	15 560	14 812	12 771	6 365								
New York	10 613	8 526	9 009	12 551	3 402	11 747	12 956	8 000	8 437	5 535	3 968	3 361	1 751	7 476	11 828							
Peking	6 180	19 273	7 526	12 956	14 356	3 804	1 985	8 124	11 452	8 146	10 030	12 426	12 475	5 789	9 217	10 971						
Perth	9 467	12 562	11 256	8 684	17 610	7 874	6 030	10 886	12 517	14 495	14 986	16 247	18 281	12 236	8 889	18 699	8 000					
Rio de Janeiro	11 462	1 990	9 897	6 080	4 522	14 054	17 688	13 330	6 022	9 248	10 132	7 659	6 713	11 528	8 937	7 724	17 306	13 527				
Singapore	6 319	15 860	8 246	9 650	18 332	4 148	2 581	10 789	11 149	10 867	14 099	16 593	16 951	8 437	7 446	15 330	4 489	3 909	15 729			
Sydney	12 502	11 760	14 391	10 982	15 341	10 424	7 370	8 163	15 514	17 005	12 052	12 973	15 012	14 501	12 125	16 001	8 956	3 274	13 512	6 294		
Tokyo	8 271	18 338	9 552	14 710	14 154	5 852	2 874	6 185	13 475	9 584	8 806	11 304	11 991	7 487	11 243	10 869	2 089	7 896	18 557	5 300	7 809	
Wellington	14 678	9 943	16 503	11 287	13 119	12 647	9 424	7 508	16 047	18 816	10 787	11 099	13 054	16 547	13 643	14 406	10 782	5 246	11 865	8 521	2 226	9 258

These distances are in kilometres and are the great circle distances between the cities (international airports). Great circle distances are the shortest distances between two points on the globe. They are the normal flight paths for aircraft where they are free from the restrictions of air corridors or national airspace.

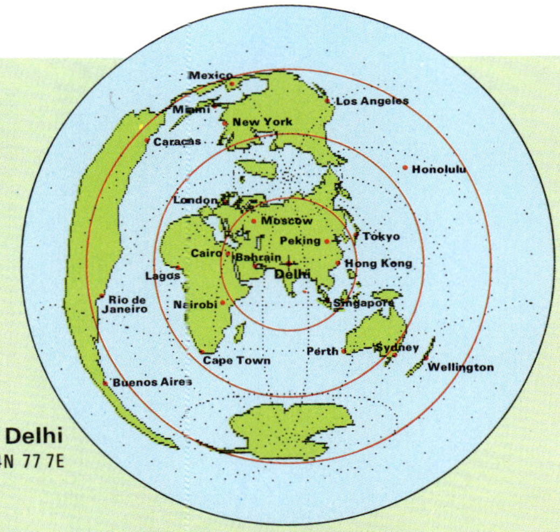

Delhi
28 34N 77 7E

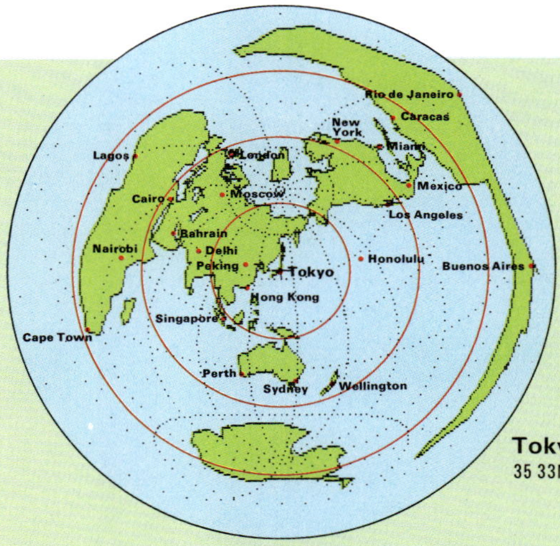

Tokyo
35 33N 139 46E

The three circles are drawn at radius 5 000, 10 000 and 15 000 km from the central city

• Cities shown on the distance table

The co-ordinates given are for the airport of each city

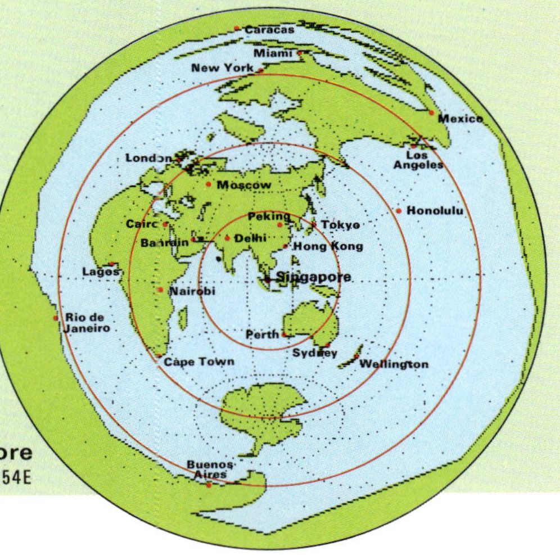

Singapore
1 21N 103 54E

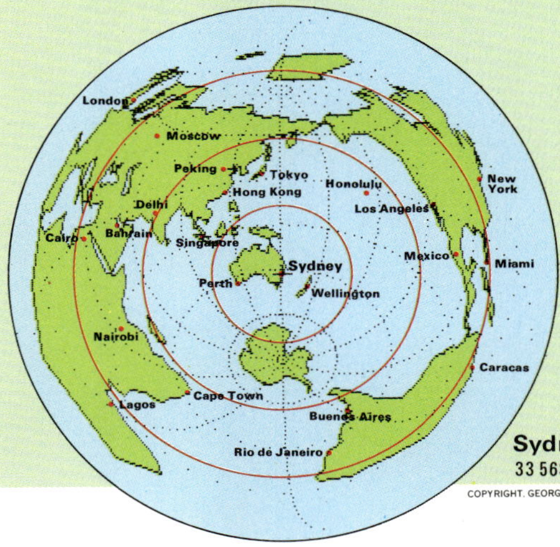

Sydney
33 56S 151 10E

INDEX

The number in bold type which follows each name in the index refers to the number of the page where that feature or place will be found.

The geographical co-ordinates which follow the place name are sometimes only approximate but are close enough for the place name to be located.

An open square □ signifies that the name refers to an administrative division of a country while a solid square ■ follows the name of a country.

Rivers have been indexed to their mouth or to their confluence.

The alphabetical order of names composed of two or more words is governed primarily by the first word and then by the second. This is an example of the rule:

West Wyalong
West Yorkshire
Westbourne
Westbury
Westbury-on-Severn
Western Australia

Names composed of a proper name (Gibraltar) and a description (Strait of) are positioned alphabetically by the proper name. All river names are followed by ↝. If the same word occurs in the name of a town and a geographical feature, the town name is listed first followed by the name or names of the geographical features.

Names beginning with M', Mc are all indexed as if they were spelled Mac.

If the same place name occurs twice or more in the index and the places are in different countries they will be followed by the country names and the latter in alphabetical order.

Sydney, Australia
Sydney, Canada

In the index each placename is followed by its geographical co-ordinates which allow the reader to find the place on the map. These co-ordinates give the latitude and longitude of a particular place.

The latitude (or parallel) is the distance of a point north or south of the Equator measured as an angle with the centre of the earth. The Equator is latitude 0°, the North Pole is 90°N and the South Pole 90°S. On a globe the lines could be drawn as concentric circles parallel to the Equator, decreasing in diameter from the Equator until they become a point at the Poles. On the maps these lines of latitude are usually represented as lines running across the map from East to West in smooth curves. They are numbered on the sides of the map; north of the Equator the numbers increase northwards, to the south they increase southwards. The degree interval between them depends on the scale of the map. On a large scale map (for example, 1:2 000 000) the interval is one degree, but on a small scale (for example 1:50 000 000) it will be ten degrees.

Lines of longitude (or meridians) cut the latitude lines at right angles on the globe and intersect with one another at the Poles. Longitude is measured by the angle at the centre of the earth between it and the meridian of origin which runs through Greenwich (0°). It may be a measurement East or West of this line and from 0° to 180° in each direction. The longitude line of 180° runs North – South through the Pacific Ocean. On a particular map the interval between the lines of longitude is always the same as that between the lines of latitude and normally they are drawn vertically. They are numbered in the top and bottom margins and a note states East or West from Greenwich.

The unit of measurement for latitude and longitude is the degree and it is subdivided into 60 minutes. An index entry states the position of a place in degrees and minutes, a space being left between the degrees and minutes. The latitude is followed by N(orth) or S(outh) and the longitude by E(ast) or W(est).

The diagram illustrates how the reader has to estimate the required distance from the nearest line of latitude or longitude. In the diagram there is one degree, or 60 minutes between the lines and so to find the position of Calais an estimate has to be made, 57 parts of 60 north of the 50 degree latitude line and 50 parts of 60, or 50 minutes east of the one degree longitude line.

Where the map is smaller in scale it is more difficult to calculate the position of a place because there are five or ten degree intervals between the lines.

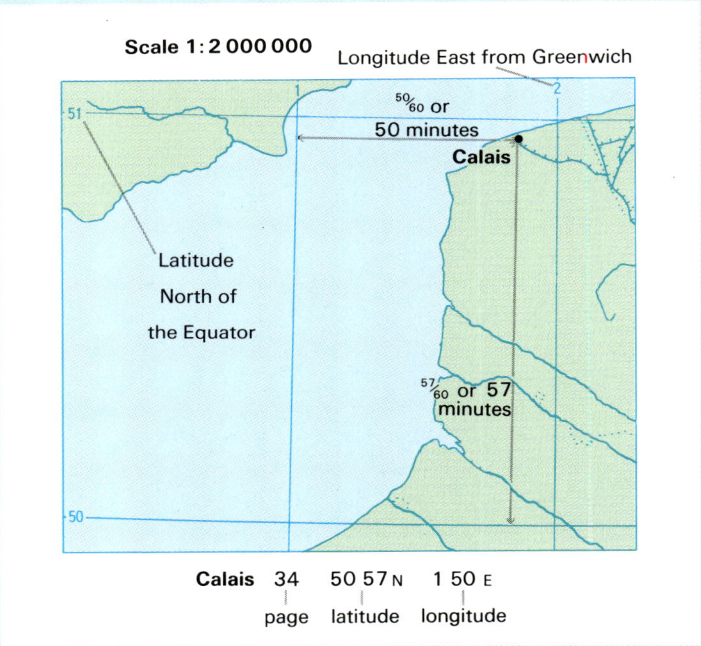

The following is a list of the principal abbreviations used in the Index.

A.S.S.R. – Autonomous Soviet Socialist Republic
Afg. – Afghanistan
Afr. – Africa
Alb. – Albania
Alg. – Algeria
Am. – America
Ant. – Antarctica
Arch. – Archipelago
Arg. – Argentina
Atl. Oc. – Atlantic Ocean
B. – Bay
B. Faso – Burkina Faso
Barb. – Barbados
Berm. – Bermuda
Bol. – Bolivia
Bots. – Botswana
Bulg. – Bulgaria
Bur. – Burma
C. – Cape (Cap, Cabo)
C.A.R. – Central African Republic
C.R. – Costa Rica
Cam. – Cameroon
Carib. – Caribbean Sea
Chan. – Channel
Col. – Colombia
Cont. – Continent
Cr. – Creek
Cur. – Curaçao
Dom. – Dominica
Dom. Rep. – Dominican Republic
E. – East
Eq. Guin. – Equatorial Guinea
Eth. – Ethiopia
Falk. – Falkland Is.
Fr. – France
Fr. G. – French Guiana
G. – Gulf (Golf, Golfo)
Ga. – Georgia
Ger. – Germany
Gr. – Great
Green. – Greenland
Gren. – Grenada
Guad. – Guadeloupe
Guat. – Guatemala
Guin. – Guinea
Guy. – Guyana
Hond. – Honduras
Hr. – Harbour
Hts. – Heights
I. – Island (Isle, Ile, Isla)
Ill. – Illinois
Ind. – Indies
Kor. – Korea
Kuw. – Kuwait
L. – Lake (Lac, Loch, Lough, Lago)
Leb. – Lebanon
Les. – Lesotho
Lib. – Liberia
Mart. – Martinique
Mass. – Massachusetts
Maurit. – Mauritania
Minn. – Minnesota
Miss. – Mississippi
Mong. – Mongolia
Mor. – Morocco
Mt. – Mountain (Mount, Mont, Monte, Monti, Montana)
N. – North
N. Cal. – New Caledonia
Nam. – Namibia
Nic. – Nicaragua
Nig. – Nigeria
Nor. – Norway
Oc. – Oceania
P.N.G. – Papua New Guinea
P.R. – Puerto Rico
Pac. Oc. – Pacific Ocean
Pan. – Panama
Par. – Paraguay
Pen. – Peninsula
Pk. – Peak
Pt. – Point (Pointe, Punta)
Ra. – Range
Rom. – Romania
S. – South
S. Oc. – Southern Ocean
Sd. – Sound
Sene. – Senegal
Si. Arab. – Saudi Arabia
Som. – Somalia
St. L. – St. Lucia
Str. – Strait
Swaz. – Swaziland
Tanz. – Tanzania
U.A.E. – United Arab Emirates
Ven. – Venezuela
W. – West
Yem. – Yemen
Zam. – Zambia
Zim. – Zimbabwe

A

Aachen, *W. Ger.* **36** 50 47N 6 4 E
Aalborg, *Den.* **45** 57 2N 9 54 E
Aalst, *Belg.* **36** 50 56N 4 2 E
Aarhus, *Den.* **45** 56 8N 10 11 E
Ābādān, *Iran* **56** 30 22N 48 20 E
Abbey Town, *U.K.* **18** 54 50N 3 18W
Abbots Bromley, *U.K.* **14** 52 50N 1 52W
Abbots Langley, *U.K.* **15** 51 43N 0 25W
Abbotsbury, *U.K.* **14** 50 40N 2 36W
Abéché, *Chad* **79** 13 50N 20 35 E
Aberaeron, *U.K.* **17** 52 15N 4 16W
Aberdare, *U.K.* **17** 51 43N 3 27W
Aberdeen, *U.K.* **23** 57 9N 2 6W
Aberdour, *U.K.* **21** 56 2N 3 18W
Aberdovey, *U.K.* **17** 52 33N 4 3W
Aberfeldy, *U.K.* **23** 56 37N 3 50W
Aberfoyle, *U.K.* **20** 56 10N 4 23W
Abergavenny, *U.K.* **17** 51 49N 3 1W
Abergele, *U.K.* **17** 53 17N 3 35W
Aberlady, *U.K.* **21** 56 0N 2 51W
Abernethy, *U.K.* **21** 56 19N 3 18W
Aberporth, *U.K.* **17** 52 8N 4 32W
Abersoch, *U.K.* **17** 52 50N 4 30W
Abersychan, *U.K.* **17** 51 44N 3 3W
Abertillery, *U.K.* **17** 51 44N 3 9W
Aberystwyth, *U.K.* **17** 52 25N 4 6W
Abidjan, *Ivory C.* **78** 5 26N 3 58W
Abingdon, *U.K.* **14** 51 40N 1 17W
Abington, *U.K.* **21** 55 30N 3 42W
Aboyne, *U.K.* **23** 57 4N 2 48W
Abū Dhabī, *U.A.E.* **57** 24 28N 54 36 E
Acapulco, *Mex.* **94** 16 51N 99 56W
Accra, *Ghana* **78** 5 35N 0 6W
Accrington, *U.K.* **18** 53 46N 2 22W
Achill Hd., *Ire.* **24** 53 59N 10 15W
Achill I., *Ire.* **24** 53 58N 10 5W
Achinsk, *U.S.S.R.* **49** 56 20N 90 20 E
Achnasheen, *U.K.* **22** 57 35N 5 5W
Acklins I., *Baham.* **95** 22 30N 74 0W
Acle, *U.K.* **15** 52 38N 1 32 E
Aconcagua, Cerro, *Arg.* **102** 32 39S 70 0W
Acre, *Isr.* **57** 32 55N 35 4 E
Acton Burnell, *U.K.* **14** 52 37N 2 41W
Adamaoua Plateau, *Cam.* **80** 7 20N 12 20 E
Adam's Bridge, *Sri L.* **58** 9 15N 79 40 E
Adana, *Turk.* **47** 37 0N 35 16 E
Adapazarı, *Turk.* **47** 40 48N 30 25 E
Addis Ababa, *Eth.* **79** 9 2N 38 42 E
Addlestone, *U.K.* **15** 51 22N 0 30W
Adelaide, *Austral.* **67** 34 52S 138 30 E
Adélie Land, *Ant.* **103** 68 0S 140 0 E
Aden, *S. Yem.* **56** 12 45N 45 0 E
Aden, G. of, *Asia* **56** 13 0N 50 0 E
Adirondack Mts., *U.S.A.* **93** 44 0N 74 15W
Admiralty Is., *P.N.G.* **64** 2 0S 147 0 E
Adrar, *Alg.* **78** 27 51N 0 11W
Adriatic Sea, *Europe* **40** 43 0N 16 0 E
Adwick le Street, *U.K.* **19** 53 35N 1 12W
Ægean Sea, *Europe* **41** 37 0N 25 0 E
Afghanistan ■, *Asia* **57** 33 0N 65 0 E
Agadès, *Niger* **78** 16 58N 7 59 E
Agadir, *Mor.* **78** 30 28N 9 35W
Agartala, *India* **59** 23 50N 91 23 E
Agra, *India* **58** 27 17N 77 58 E
Agrigento, *It.* **40** 37 19N 13 33 E
Aguascalientes, *Mex.* **94** 21 53N 102 12W
Ahmadabad, *India* **58** 23 0N 72 40 E
Ahvāz, *Iran* **56** 31 20N 48 40 E
Ahvenanmaa = Åland, *Fin.* **45** 60 15N 20 0 E
Ailsa Craig, *U.K.* **20** 55 15N 5 7W
Ainsdale, *U.K.* **18** 53 37N 3 2W
Airdrie, *U.K.* **21** 55 53N 3 57W
Aire →, *U.K.* **19** 53 42N 0 55W
Aisgill, *U.K.* **18** 54 23N 2 21W
Aix-en-Provence, *Fr.* **35** 43 32N 5 27 E
Ajaccio, *Fr.* **35** 41 55N 8 40 E
Akashi, *Jap.* **62** 34 45N 135 0 E
Akita, *Jap.* **62** 39 45N 140 7 E
Akranes, *Ice.* **44** 64 19N 21 58W
Akron, *U.S.A.* **92** 41 7N 81 31W
Aktyubinsk, *U.S.S.R.* **47** 50 17N 57 10 E
Akure, *Nig.* **78** 7 15N 5 5 E
Akureyri, *Ice.* **44** 65 40N 18 6W
Al Ḥudaydah, *Yem.* **56** 14 50N 43 0 E
Al Hūfuf, *Si. Arab.* **56** 25 25N 49 45 E
Al Jawf, *Si. Arab.* **56** 29 55N 39 40 E
Al Qaṭīf, *Si. Arab.* **56** 26 35N 50 0 E
Al Qunaytirah, *Syria* **57** 32 55N 35 45 E
Alabama □, *U.S.A.* **91** 33 0N 87 0W
Åland, *Fin.* **45** 60 15N 20 0 E
Alaska □, *U.S.A.* **88** 65 0N 150 0W
Alaska, G. of, *Pac. Oc.* **88** 58 0N 145 0W
Alaska Pen., *U.S.A.* **88** 56 0N 160 0W
Alaska Range, *U.S.A.* **88** 62 50N 151 0W
Alba Iulia, *Rom.* **43** 46 8N 23 39 E
Albacete, *Sp.* **37** 39 0N 1 50W
Albania ■, *Europe* **41** 41 0N 20 0 E
Albany, *Austral.* **66** 35 1S 117 58 E
Albany, *Ga., U.S.A.* **91** 31 40N 84 10W
Albany, *N.Y., U.S.A.* **93** 42 35N 73 47W
Albany →, *Canada* **89** 52 17N 81 31W
Alberta □, *Canada* **88** 54 40N 115 0W
Albrighton, *U.K.* **14** 52 38N 2 17W
Albuquerque, *U.S.A.* **90** 35 5N 106 47W
Albury, *Austral.* **70** 36 3S 146 56 E
Alcalá de Henares, *Sp.* **37** 40 28N 3 22W
Alcester, *U.K.* **14** 52 13N 1 52W
Aldan →, *U.S.S.R.* **49** 63 28N 129 35 E
Aldborough, *U.K.* **19** 54 6N 1 21W
Aldbourne, *U.K.* **14** 51 28N 1 38W
Aldbrough, *U.K.* **19** 53 50N 0 7W
Aldeburgh, *U.K.* **15** 52 9N 1 35 E
Alderbury, *U.K.* **14** 51 4N 1 45W
Alderley Edge, *U.K.* **18** 53 18N 2 15W
Alderney, *U.K.* **34** 49 42N 2 12W
Aldershot, *U.K.* **15** 51 15N 0 43W
Aldingham, *U.K.* **18** 54 8N 3 3W
Aleppo, *Syria* **56** 36 10N 37 15 E
Alessándria, *It.* **40** 44 54N 8 37 E
Ålesund, *Nor.* **44** 62 28N 6 12 E
Aleutian Is., *Pac. Oc.* **88** 52 0N 175 0W
Alexander Arch., *U.S.A.* **88** 57 0N 135 0W
Alexandria, *Egypt* **79** 31 0N 30 0 E
Alexandria, *U.K.* **20** 55 59N 4 40W
Alexandria, *U.S.A.* **91** 31 20N 92 30W
Alford, *Grampian, U.K.* **23** 57 13N 2 42W
Alford, *Lincs., U.K.* **19** 53 16N 0 10 E
Alfreton, *U.K.* **19** 53 6N 1 22W
Alfriston, *U.K.* **15** 50 48N 0 10 E
Algarve, *Port.* **37** 36 58N 8 20W
Algeciras, *Sp.* **37** 36 9N 5 28W
Algeria ■, *Africa* **78** 35 10N 3 11 E
Algiers, *Alg.* **78** 36 42N 3 8 E
Alicante, *Sp.* **37** 38 23N 0 30W
Alice Springs, *Austral.* **66** 23 40S 133 50 E
Aligarh, *India* **58** 27 55N 78 10 E
Alkmaar, *Neth.* **36** 52 37N 4 45 E
Allahabad, *India* **59** 25 25N 81 58 E
Allegheny Mts., *U.S.A.* **92** 38 0N 80 0W
Allen →, *U.K.* **21** 54 53N 2 13W
Allen, Bog of, *Ire.* **25** 53 15N 7 0W
Allen, L., *Ire.* **24** 54 12N 8 5W
Allendale, *U.K.* **21** 54 55N 2 15W
Allenheads, *U.K.* **21** 54 49N 2 12W
Allentown, *U.S.A.* **93** 40 36N 75 30W
Alloa, *U.K.* **21** 56 7N 3 49W
Allonby, *U.K.* **18** 54 45N 3 27W
Alma Ata, *U.S.S.R.* **48** 43 15N 76 57 E
Almelo, *Neth.* **36** 52 22N 6 42 E
Almería, *Sp.* **37** 36 52N 2 27W
Almond →, *U.K.* **21** 56 27N 3 27W
Almondsbury, *U.K.* **14** 51 33N 2 34W
Aln →, *U.K.* **21** 55 27N 1 32W
Alness, *U.K.* **23** 57 41N 4 15W
Alnmouth, *U.K.* **21** 55 24N 1 37W
Alnwick, *U.K.* **19** 55 25N 1 42W
Alphen, *Neth.* **36** 51 29N 4 58 E
Alphington, *U.K.* **16** 50 41N 3 32W
Alps, *Europe* **42** 47 0N 8 0 E
Alrewas, *U.K.* **14** 52 43N 1 44W
Alsager, *U.K.* **18** 53 7N 2 20W
Alston, *U.K.* **18** 54 48N 2 26W
Altai Mts., *Asia* **60** 46 40N 92 45 E
Altarnun, *U.K.* **16** 50 35N 4 30W
Altay, *China* **60** 47 48N 88 10 E
Alton, *U.K.* **15** 51 8N 0 59W
Altoona, *U.S.A.* **92** 40 32N 78 24W
Altrincham, *U.K.* **18** 53 25N 2 21W
Altun Shan, *China* **60** 38 30N 88 0 E
Alva, *U.K.* **21** 56 9N 3 49W
Alvechurch, *U.K.* **14** 52 22N 1 58W
Alwinton, *U.K.* **21** 55 20N 2 7W
Alyth, *U.K.* **23** 56 38N 3 15W
Amadjuak L., *Canada* **89** 65 0N 71 8W
Amagasaki, *Jap.* **62** 34 42N 135 20 E
Amarillo, *U.S.A.* **90** 35 14N 101 46W
Amazon →, *S. Am.* **100** 0 5S 50 0W
Amazonas □, *Brazil* **101** 4 0S 62 0W
Amble, *U.K.* **21** 55 20N 1 36W
Ambleside, *U.K.* **18** 54 26N 2 58W
Ambon, *Indon.* **63** 3 35S 128 20 E
American Samoa ■, *Pac. Oc.* **65** 14 20S 170 40W
Amersfoort, *Neth.* **36** 52 9N 5 23 E
Amersham, *U.K.* **15** 51 40N 0 38W
Amesbury, *U.K.* **14** 51 10N 1 46W
Amiens, *Fr.* **34** 49 54N 2 16 E
Amlwch, *U.K.* **17** 53 24N 4 21W
'Ammān, *Jord.* **57** 31 57N 35 52 E
Ammanford, *U.K.* **17** 51 48N 4 0W
Amoy = Xiamen, *China* **61** 24 25N 118 4 E
Ampleforth, *U.K.* **19** 54 13N 1 8W
Ampthill, *U.K.* **15** 52 3N 0 30W
Amravati, *India* **58** 20 55N 77 45 E
Amritsar, *India* **58** 31 35N 74 57 E
Amsterdam, *Neth.* **36** 52 23N 4 54 E
Amudarya →, *U.S.S.R.* **48** 43 40N 59 0 E
Amundsen Gulf, *Canada* **88** 71 0N 124 0W
Amundsen Sea, *Ant.* **103** 72 0S 115 0W
Amur →, *U.S.S.R.* **49** 52 56N 141 10 E
An Nafūd, *Si. Arab.* **56** 28 15N 41 0 E
An Najaf, *Iraq* **56** 32 3N 44 15 E
An Uaimh, *Ire.* **24** 53 39N 6 40W
Anadyr, G. of, *U.S.S.R.* **49** 64 0N 180 0 E
Anaheim, *U.S.A.* **90** 33 50N 118 0W
Anápolis, *Brazil* **101** 16 15S 48 50W
Anatolia, *Turk.* **47** 38 0N 30 0 E
Ancaster, *U.K.* **19** 52 59N 0 32W
Ancholme →, *U.K.* **19** 53 42N 0 32W
Anchorage, *U.S.A.* **88** 61 10N 149 50W
Ancona, *It.* **40** 43 37N 13 30 E
Ancrum, *U.K.* **21** 55 31N 2 35W
Anda, *China* **61** 46 24N 125 19 E
Andalusia, Reg., *Sp.* **37** 37 35N 5 0W
Andaman Is., *India* **51** 12 30N 92 30 E
Anderlecht, *Belg.* **36** 50 50N 4 19 E
Andes, *S. Am.* **96** 20 0S 68 0W
Andhra Pradesh □, *India* **58** 16 0N 79 0 E
Andizhan, *U.S.S.R.* **48** 41 10N 72 0 E
Andorra ■, *Europe* **35** 42 30N 1 30 E
Andover, *U.K.* **14** 51 13N 1 29W
Andreanof Is., *Pac. Oc.* **88** 52 0N 178 0W
Andreas, *U.K.* **18** 54 23N 4 25W
Ándria, *It.* **40** 41 13N 16 17 E
Andropov, *U.S.S.R.* **46** 58 5N 38 50 E
Andros I., *Baham.* **95** 24 30N 78 0W
Angara →, *U.S.S.R.* **49** 58 30N 97 0 E
Angarsk, *U.S.S.R.* **49** 52 30N 104 0 E
Angers, *Fr.* **34** 47 30N 0 35W
Anglesey, *U.K.* **17** 53 17N 4 20W
Angmagssalik, *Green.* **89** 65 40N 37 20W
Angmering, *U.K.* **15** 50 48N 0 28W
Angola ■, *Africa* **81** 12 0S 18 0 E
Angoulême, *Fr.* **35** 45 39N 0 10 E
Anguilla, *W. Ind.* **94** 18 14N 63 5W
Angus, Braes of, *U.K.* **23** 56 51N 3 10W
Anhui □, *China* **61** 32 0N 117 0 E
Anjou, *Fr.* **34** 47 20N 0 15W
Ankara, *Turk.* **47** 40 0N 32 54 E
Ann Arbor, *U.S.A.* **92** 42 17N 83 45W
Annaba, *Alg.* **78** 36 50N 7 46 E
Annalee →, *Ire.* **24** 54 3N 7 15W
Annan, *U.K.* **21** 55 0N 3 17W
Annan →, *U.K.* **21** 54 58N 3 18W
Annandale, *U.K.* **21** 55 10N 3 25W
Annecy, *Fr.* **35** 45 55N 6 8 E
Annfield Plain, *U.K.* **19** 54 52N 1 45W
Annobón, *Atl. Oc.* **73** 1 25S 5 36 E
Anshan, *China* **61** 41 5N 122 58 E
Anshun, *China* **60** 26 18N 105 57 E
Anstey, *U.K.* **14** 52 41N 1 14W
Anstruther, *U.K.* **21** 56 14N 2 40W
Antalya, *Turk.* **47** 36 52N 30 45 E
Antananarivo, *Madag.* **81** 18 55S 47 31 E
Antarctic Pen., *Ant.* **103** 67 0S 60 0W
Antarctica, *Cont.* **103** 90 0S 0 0 E
Anticosti, I. d', *Canada* **93** 49 30N 63 0W
Antigua & Barbuda ■, *W. Ind.* **94** 17 20N 61 48W
Antofagasta, *Chile* **102** 23 50S 70 30W
Antony, *U.K.* **16** 50 22N 4 13W
Antrim, *U.K.* **24** 54 43N 6 13W
Antrim □, *U.K.* **24** 54 55N 6 20W
Antrim, Mts. of, *U.K.* **24** 54 57N 6 8W
Antsiranana, *Madag.* **81** 12 25S 49 20 E
Antwerp, *Belg.* **36** 51 13N 4 25 E
Anyang, *China* **61** 36 5N 114 21 E
Anzhero-Sudzhensk, *U.S.S.R.* **48** 56 10N 86 0 E
Aomori, *Jap.* **62** 40 45N 140 45 E
Apeldoorn, *Neth.* **36** 52 13N 5 57 E
Apennines, *It.* **40** 44 20N 10 20 E
Appalachian Mts., *U.S.A.* **91** 38 0N 80 0W
Appleby, *U.K.* **18** 54 35N 2 29W
Appledore, *Devon, U.K.* **16** 51 3N 4 12W
Appledore, *Kent, U.K.* **15** 51 2N 0 47 E
Arabia, *Asia* **50** 25 0N 45 0 E
Arabian Desert, *Egypt* **79** 26 0N 33 30 E
Arabian Sea, *Ind. Oc.* **50** 16 0N 65 0 E
Aracaju, *Brazil* **101** 10 55S 37 4W
Araçatuba, *Brazil* **101** 21 10S 50 30W
Arad, *Rom.* **43** 46 10N 21 20 E
Arafura Sea, *E. Ind.* **64** 9 0S 135 0 E
Aragón □, *Sp.* **37** 41 25N 1 0W
Araguaia →, *Brazil* **101** 5 21S 48 41W
Arakan Yoma, *Burma* **59** 20 0N 94 40 E
Aral Sea, *U.S.S.R.* **48** 44 30N 60 0 E
Aralsk, *U.S.S.R.* **48** 46 50N 61 20 E
Aran I., *Ire.* **24** 55 0N 8 30W
Aran Is., *Ire.* **25** 53 5N 9 42W
Arapiraca, *Brazil* **101** 9 45S 36 39W
Ararat, *Austral.* **70** 37 16S 143 0 E
Arbroath, *U.K.* **23** 56 34N 2 35W
Arctic Ocean, *Arctic* **103** 78 0N 160 0W
Arctic Red River, *Canada* **88** 67 15N 134 0W
Ardbeg, *U.K.* **20** 55 38N 6 6W
Ardchyle, *U.K.* **20** 56 26N 4 24W
Ardee, *Ire.* **24** 53 51N 6 32W
Ardennes, *Belg.* **36** 50 0N 5 10 E
Ardentinny, *U.K.* **20** 56 3N 4 56W
Ardgour, *U.K.* **22** 56 45N 5 25W
Ardingly, *U.K.* **15** 51 3N 0 3W
Ardlui, *U.K.* **20** 56 19N 4 43W
Ardmore Pt., *U.K.* **20** 55 40N 6 0W
Ardnamurchan, Pt. of, *U.K.* **22** 56 44N 6 14W
Ardnave Pt., *U.K.* **20** 55 54N 6 20W
Ardrishaig, *U.K.* **20** 56 0N 5 27W
Ardrossan, *U.K.* **20** 55 39N 4 50W
Ards □, *U.K.* **24** 54 35N 5 30W
Ards Pen., *U.K.* **24** 54 30N 5 25W
Ardvasar, *U.K.* **22** 57 5N 5 52W
Arendal, *Nor.* **45** 58 28N 8 46 E
Arequipa, *Peru* **100** 16 20S 71 30W
Argentina ■, *S. Am.* **102** 35 0S 66 0W
Argyll, *U.K.* **20** 56 14N 5 10W
Arica, *Chile* **100** 18 32S 70 20W
Arima, *Trin. & Tob.* **94** 10 38N 61 17W
Arinagour, *U.K.* **20** 56 38N 6 31W
Arisaig, *U.K.* **22** 56 55N 5 50W
Arizona □, *U.S.A.* **90** 34 20N 111 30W
Arkaig, L., *U.K.* **22** 56 58N 5 10W
Arkansas □, *U.S.A.* **91** 35 0N 92 30W
Arkansas →, *U.S.A.* **91** 33 48N 91 4W
Arkhangelsk, *U.S.S.R.* **46** 64 40N 41 0 E
Arkle →, *U.K.* **18** 54 25N 1 55W
Arklow, *Ire.* **25** 52 48N 6 10W
Arles, *Fr.* **35** 43 41N 4 40 E
Arlon, *Belg.* **36** 49 42N 5 49 E
Armadale, *U.K.* **21** 55 54N 3 42W
Armagh, *U.K.* **24** 54 22N 6 40W
Armagh □, *U.K.* **24** 54 18N 6 37W
Armenia, *Col.* **100** 4 35N 75 45W
Armenia □, *U.S.S.R.* **47** 40 0N 41 0 E
Armidale, *Austral.* **67** 30 30S 151 40 E
Arnhem, *Neth.* **36** 51 58N 5 55 E
Arnhem Land, *Austral.* **66** 13 10S 134 30 E
Arnold, *U.K.* **19** 53 0N 1 8W
Arnside, *U.K.* **18** 54 12N 2 49W
Arran, *U.K.* **20** 55 34N 5 12W
Arras, *Fr.* **34** 50 17N 2 46 E
Arrochar, *U.K.* **20** 56 12N 4 45W
Arrow, L., *Ire.* **24** 54 3N 8 20W
Arun →, *U.K.* **15** 50 48N 0 33W
Arunachal Pradesh □, *India* **59** 28 0N 95 0 E
Arundel, *U.K.* **15** 50 52N 0 32W
Arusha, *Tanz.* **80** 3 20S 36 40 E
As Salt, *Jord.* **57** 32 2N 35 43 E
As Summān, *Si. Arab.* **56** 25 0N 47 0 E
Asahigawa, *Jap.* **62** 43 46N 142 22 E
Asansol, *India* **59** 23 40N 87 1 E
Ascension I., *Atl. Oc.* **128** 8 0S 14 15W
Ascot, *U.K.* **15** 51 24N 0 41W
Asfordby, *U.K.* **15** 52 45N 0 57W
Ash, *Kent, U.K.* **15** 51 17N 1 16 E
Ash, *Surrey, U.K.* **15** 51 14N 0 43W
Ashbourne, *U.K.* **19** 53 2N 1 44W
Ashburton, *N.Z.* **71** 43 53S 171 48 E
Ashburton, *U.K.* **16** 50 31N 3 45W
Ashburton →, *Austral.* **66** 21 40S 114 56 E
Ashby-de-la-Zouch, *U.K.* **14** 52 45N 1 29W
Ashchurch, *U.K.* **14** 52 0N 2 7W
Ashdown Forest, *U.K.* **15** 51 4N 0 2 E
Ashford, *Derby, U.K.* **19** 53 13N 1 43W
Ashford, *Kent, U.K.* **15** 51 8N 0 53 E
Ashington, *U.K.* **21** 55 12N 1 35W
Ashkhabad, *U.S.S.R.* **48** 38 0N 57 50 E
Ashq'elon, *Isr.* **57** 31 42N 34 35 E
Ashton-in-Makerfield, *U.K.* **18** 53 29N 2 39W
Ashton-under-Lyne, *U.K.* **18** 53 30N 2 8W
Ashurstwood, *U.K.* **15** 51 6N 0 2 E
Ashwater, *U.K.* **16** 50 43N 4 18W
Ashwick, *U.K.* **14** 51 13N 2 31W
'Asīr □, *Si. Arab.* **56** 18 40N 42 30 E
Asir, Ras, *Som.* **73** 11 55N 51 10 E
Askrigg, *U.K.* **18** 54 19N 2 6W
Aslackby, *U.K.* **19** 52 53N 0 23W
Asmera, *Eth.* **79** 15 19N 38 55 E
Aspatria, *U.K.* **18** 54 45N 3 20W
Assam □, *India* **59** 26 0N 93 0 E
Assen, *Neth.* **36** 53 0N 6 35 E
Assynt, L., *U.K.* **22** 58 25N 5 15W
Asti, *It.* **40** 44 54N 8 11 E
Aston Clinton, *U.K.* **15** 51 48N 0 44W
Astrakhan, *U.S.S.R.* **47** 46 25N 48 5 E
Astwood Bank, *U.K.* **14** 52 15N 1 55W
Asunción, *Par.* **102** 25 10S 57 30W
Aswân, *Egypt* **79** 24 4N 32 57 E
Atacama, Desierto de, *Chile* **102** 24 0S 69 20W
Atbara, *Sudan* **79** 17 42N 33 59 E
Athabasca, L., *Canada* **88** 59 15N 109 15W
Athboy, *Ire.* **24** 53 37N 6 55W
Athenry, *Ire.* **25** 53 18N 8 45W
Athens, *Greece* **41** 37 58N 23 46 E
Atherstone, *U.K.* **14** 52 35N 1 32W
Atherton, *U.K.* **18** 53 32N 2 30W
Athínai = Athens, *Greece* **41** 37 58N 23 46 E
Athlone, *Ire.* **24** 53 26N 7 57W
Atholl, Forest of, *U.K.* **23** 56 51N 3 50W
Athy, *Ire.* **25** 53 0N 7 0W
Atlanta, *U.S.A.* **91** 33 50N 84 24W
Atlantic City, *U.S.A.* **93** 39 25N 74 25W
Atlantic Ocean **128** 0 0 20 0W
Atlas Mts., *Mor.* **72** 32 30N 5 0W
Attleborough, *U.K.* **15** 52 32N 1 1 E
Auchencairn, *U.K.* **21** 54 51N 3 52W
Auchinleck, *U.K.* **20** 55 28N 4 18W
Auchterarder, *U.K.* **21** 56 18N 3 43W
Auchterderran, *U.K.* **21** 56 8N 3 16W
Auchtermuchty, *U.K.* **21** 56 18N 3 15W
Auchtertyre, *U.K.* **22** 57 17N 5 35W
Auckland, *N.Z.* **71** 36 52S 174 46 E
Audlem, *U.K.* **18** 52 59N 2 31W
Aughnacloy, *U.K.* **24** 54 25N 6 58W
Augsburg, *W. Ger.* **42** 48 22N 10 54 E
Augusta, *U.S.A.* **91** 33 29N 81 59W
Aurangabad, *India* **58** 19 50N 75 23 E
Aurora, *U.S.A.* **92** 41 42N 88 12W
Austin, *U.S.A.* **90** 30 20N 97 45W
Australia ■, *Oc.* **66** 23 0S 135 0 E
Australian Alps, *Austral.* **70** 36 30S 148 30 E
Australian Cap. Terr. □, *Austral.* **70** 35 30S 149 0 E
Austria ■, *Europe* **42** 47 0N 14 0 E
Auxerre, *Fr.* **34** 47 48N 3 32 E

Avebury, U.K. 14 51 25N 1 52W
Avellino, It. 40 40 54N 14 46 E
Aveton Gifford, U.K. 16 50 17N 3 51W
Avich, L., U.K. 20 56 17N 5 25W
Aviemore, U.K. 23 57 11N 3 50W
Avignon, Fr. 35 43 57N 4 50 E
Ávila, Sp. 37 40 39N 4 43W
Avoca, Ire. 25 52 52N 6 13W
Avon □, U.K. 14 51 30N 2 40W
Avon →, Avon, U.K. 14 51 30N 2 43W
Avon →, Hants., U.K. 14 50 44N 1 45W
Avon →, Warwick, U.K. 14 52 0N 2 9W
Avonmouth, U.K. 14 51 30N 2 42W
Awe, L., U.K. 20 56 15N 5 15W
Axbridge, U.K. 14 51 17N 2 50W
Axe →, U.K. 14 51 17N 2 52W
Axe Edge, U.K. 18 53 14N 1 59W
Axholme, Isle of, U.K. 19 53 30N 0 55W
Axminster, U.K. 16 50 47N 3 1W
Axmouth, U.K. 16 50 43N 3 2W
Ayers Rock, Austral. 66 25 23S 131 5 E
Aylesbury, U.K. 15 51 48N 0 49W
Aylesford, U.K. 15 51 18N 0 29 E
Aylsham, U.K. 15 52 48N 1 16 E
Aynho, U.K. 14 51 59N 1 15W
Ayr, U.K. 20 55 28N 4 37W
Ayr →, U.K. 20 55 29N 4 40W
Ayr, Heads of, U.K. 20 55 25N 4 43W
Ayre, Pt. of, U.K. 18 54 27N 4 21W
Aysgarth, U.K. 18 54 18N 2 0W
Ayton, Borders, U.K. 21 55 51N 2 6W
Ayton, N. Yorks., U.K. 19 54 15N 0 29W
Az Zarqā, Jord. 57 32 5N 36 4 E
Azores, Atl. Oc. 128 38 44N 29 0W
Azov Sea, U.S.S.R. 47 46 0N 36 30 E
Azuero, Pen. de, Pan. 95 7 30N 80 30W

B

Bābol, Iran 56 36 40N 52 50 E
Bacabal, Brazil 101 4 15S 44 45W
Bacău, Rom. 43 46 35N 26 55 E
Back, U.K. 22 58 17N 6 20W
Bacolod, Phil. 63 10 40N 122 57 E
Bacton, U.K. 15 52 50N 1 29 E
Bacup, U.K. 18 53 42N 2 12W
Badajoz, Sp. 37 38 50N 6 59W
Badalona, Sp. 37 41 26N 2 15 E
Baffin B., Canada 89 72 0N 64 0W
Baffin I., Canada 89 68 0N 75 0W
Bagenalstown = Muine Bheag, Ire. 25 52 42N 6 57W
Baggy Pt., U.K. 16 51 11N 4 12W
Baghdād, Iraq 56 33 20N 44 30 E
Bagshot, U.K. 15 51 22N 0 41W
Bahamas ■, Atl. Oc. 95 24 0N 75 0W
Bahawalpur, Pak. 58 29 24N 71 40 E
Bahía = Salvador, Brazil 101 13 0S 38 30W
Bahía Blanca, Arg. 102 38 35S 62 13W
Bahrain ■, Asia 56 26 0N 50 35 E
Baia Mare, Rom. 43 47 40N 23 35 E
Baildon, U.K. 19 53 52N 1 46W
Baile Atha Cliath = Dublin, Ire. 24 53 20N 6 18W
Bain →, U.K. 19 53 10N 0 15W
Bainbridge, U.K. 18 54 18N 2 7W
Bakersfield, U.S.A. 90 35 25N 119 0W
Bakewell, U.K. 19 53 13N 1 40W
Bākhtarān, Iran 56 34 23N 47 0 E
Baku, U.S.S.R. 47 40 25N 49 45 E
Bala, U.K. 17 52 54N 3 36W
Bala, L. = Tegid, L., U.K. 17 52 53N 3 38W
Balallan, U.K. 22 58 5N 6 35W
Balaton, Hung. 43 46 50N 17 40 E
Balbeggie, U.K. 21 56 26N 3 19W
Balboa, Pan. 94 9 0N 79 30W
Balbriggan, Ire. 24 53 35N 6 10W
Balderton, U.K. 19 53 3N 0 46W
Baldock, U.K. 15 51 59N 0 11W
Balearic Is., Sp. 37 39 30N 3 0 E
Balfron, U.K. 20 56 4N 4 20W
Bali □, Indon. 63 8 20S 115 0 E
Balikesir, Turk. 47 39 35N 27 58 E
Balikpapan, Indon. 63 1 10S 116 55 E
Balkan Mts., Bulg. 41 43 15N 23 0 E
Balkan Pen., Europe 26 42 0N 22 0 E
Balkhash, L., U.S.S.R. 48 46 0N 74 50 E
Ballachulish, U.K. 22 56 40N 5 10W
Ballantrae, U.K. 20 55 6N 5 0W
Ballarat, Austral. 70 37 33S 143 50 E
Ballasalla, U.K. 18 54 7N 4 36W
Ballater, U.K. 23 57 2N 3 2W
Ballaugh, U.K. 18 54 20N 4 32W
Ballina, Mayo, Ire. 24 54 7N 9 10W
Ballina, Tipp., Ire. 25 52 49N 8 27W
Ballinasloe, Ire. 25 53 20N 8 12W
Ballinrobe, Ire. 24 53 36N 9 13W
Ballinskelligs B., Ire. 25 51 46N 10 11W
Balloch, U.K. 20 56 0N 4 35W
Ballycastle, U.K. 24 55 12N 6 15W
Ballyclare, U.K. 24 54 46N 6 0W
Ballymena, U.K. 24 54 53N 6 18W
Ballymena □, U.K. 24 54 53N 6 18W
Ballymoney, U.K. 24 55 5N 6 30W
Ballymoney □, U.K. 24 55 5N 6 23W
Ballynahinch, U.K. 24 54 24N 5 55W
Ballyshannon, Ire. 24 54 30N 8 10W
Balmaclellan, U.K. 21 55 6N 4 5W
Balmoral, U.K. 23 57 3N 3 13W
Balquhidder, U.K. 20 56 22N 4 22W
Balsas →, Mex. 94 17 55N 102 10W
Baltic Sea, Europe 45 56 0N 20 0 E
Baltimore, Ire. 25 51 29N 9 22W
Baltimore, U.S.A. 92 39 18N 76 37W
Baluchistan □, Pak. 58 27 30N 65 0 E
Balurghat, India 59 25 15N 88 44 E
Balvicar, U.K. 20 56 17N 5 38W
Bamako, Mali 78 12 34N 7 55W
Bamberg, W. Ger. 42 49 54N 10 53 E
Bamburgh, U.K. 21 55 36N 1 42W
Bamenda, Cam. 80 5 57N 10 11 E
Bamford, U.K. 19 53 21N 1 41W
Bampton, Devon, U.K. 16 50 59N 3 29W
Bampton, Oxon., U.K. 14 51 44N 1 33W
Banaras = Varanasi, India 59 25 22N 83 0 E
Banbridge, U.K. 24 54 21N 6 17W
Banbridge □, U.K. 24 54 21N 6 16W
Banbury, U.K. 14 52 4N 1 21W
Banchory, U.K. 23 57 3N 2 30W
Banda Aceh, Indon. 63 5 35N 95 20 E
Banda Sea, Indon. 63 6 0S 130 0 E
Bandār 'Abbās, Iran 57 27 15N 56 15 E
Bandar Seri Begawan, Brunei 63 4 52N 115 0 E
Bandon, Ire. 25 51 44N 8 45W
Bandon →, Ire. 25 51 40N 8 41W
Bandundu, Zaïre 80 3 15S 17 22 E
Bandung, Indon. 63 6 54S 107 36 E
Banff, U.K. 23 57 40N 2 32W
Bangalore, India 58 12 59N 77 40 E
Bangka, Selat, Indon. 63 2 30S 105 30 E
Bangkok, Thai. 63 13 45N 100 35 E
Bangladesh ■, Asia 59 24 0N 90 0 E
Bangor, N. Ireland, U.K. 24 54 40N 5 40W
Bangor, Wales, U.K. 17 53 13N 4 9W
Bangor, U.S.A. 93 44 48N 68 42W
Bangui, C.A.R. 80 4 23N 18 35 E
Banham, U.K. 15 52 27N 1 3 E
Banjarmasin, Indon. 63 3 20S 114 35 E
Banjul, Gambia 78 13 28N 16 40W
Bankend, U.K. 21 55 2N 3 31W
Bankfoot, U.K. 21 56 30N 3 31W
Banks I., Canada 88 73 15N 121 30W
Banks Pen., N.Z. 71 43 45S 173 15 E
Bann →, Down, U.K. 24 54 30N 6 31W
Bann →, Londonderry, U.K. 24 55 10N 6 34W
Bannockburn, U.K. 21 56 5N 3 55W
Bantry, Ire. 25 51 40N 9 28W
Bantry, B., Ire. 25 51 35N 9 50W
Banwell, U.K. 14 51 19N 2 51W
Baoding, China 61 38 50N 115 28 E
Baoji, China 60 34 20N 107 5 E
Baotou, China 61 40 32N 110 2 E
Barbados ■, W. Ind. 94 13 0N 59 30W
Barcaldine, Austral. 67 23 43S 145 6 E
Barcelona, Sp. 37 41 21N 2 10 E
Bardney, U.K. 19 53 13N 0 19W
Bardsey I., U.K. 17 52 46N 4 47W
Bareilly, India 58 28 22N 79 27 E
Barents Sea, Arctic 48 73 0N 39 0 E
Barford, U.K. 14 52 15N 1 35W
Bargoed, U.K. 17 51 42N 3 22W
Barham, U.K. 15 51 12N 1 10 E
Bari, It. 40 41 6N 16 52 E
Bari Doab, Pak. 58 30 20N 73 0 E
Barisal, Bangla. 59 22 45N 90 20 E
Barisan Mts., Indon. 63 3 30S 102 15 E
Barking, U.K. 15 51 31N 0 10 E
Barkly Tableland, Austral. 67 17 50S 136 40 E
Barlborough, U.K. 19 53 17N 1 17W
Barlby, U.K. 19 53 48N 1 3W
Barletta, It. 40 41 20N 16 17 E
Barmby Moor, U.K. 19 53 55N 0 47W
Barmoor Castle, U.K. 21 55 38N 2 0W
Barmouth, U.K. 17 52 44N 4 3W
Barnard Castle, U.K. 18 54 33N 1 55W
Barnaul, U.S.S.R. 48 53 20N 83 40 E
Barnet, U.K. 15 51 37N 0 15W
Barnetby le Wold, U.K. 19 53 34N 0 24W
Barnoldswick, U.K. 18 53 55N 2 11W
Barnsley, U.K. 19 53 33N 1 29W
Barnstaple, U.K. 16 51 5N 4 3W
Barnstaple B., U.K. 16 51 5N 4 25W
Baroda = Vadodara, India 58 22 20N 73 10 E
Barquísimeto, Ven. 100 10 4N 69 19W
Barr, U.K. 20 55 13N 4 44W
Barra, U.K. 22 57 0N 7 30W
Barra, Sd. of, U.K. 22 57 4N 7 25W
Barra Hd., U.K. 22 56 47N 7 40W
Barrancabermeja, Col. 100 7 0N 73 50W
Barranquilla, Col. 100 11 0N 74 50W
Barrhead, U.K. 20 55 48N 4 23W
Barrhill, U.K. 20 55 7N 4 46W
Barrow →, Ire. 25 52 10N 6 57W
Barrow-in-Furness, U.K. 18 54 8N 3 15W
Barrow upon Humber, U.K. 19 53 41N 0 22W
Barrowford, U.K. 18 53 51N 2 14W
Barry, S. Glam., U.K. 17 51 23N 3 19W
Barry, Tayside, U.K. 21 56 29N 2 45W
Barton, U.K. 19 54 28N 1 38W
Barton-upon-Humber, U.K. 19 53 41N 0 27W
Barvas, U.K. 22 58 21N 6 31W
Barwell, U.K. 14 52 35N 1 22W
Basildon, U.K. 15 51 34N 0 29 E
Basingstoke, U.K. 14 51 15N 1 5W
Basle, Switz. 42 47 35N 7 35 E
Basra, Iraq 56 30 30N 47 50 E
Bass Rock, U.K. 21 56 5N 2 40W
Bass Str., Austral. 67 39 15S 146 30 E
Basse-Terre, Guad. 94 16 0N 61 40W
Bassein, Burma 59 16 45N 94 30 E
Bassenthwaite, L., U.K. 18 54 40N 3 14W
Basseterre, Guad. 94 17 17N 62 43W
Bastia, Fr. 35 42 40N 9 30 E
Baston, U.K. 15 52 43N 0 19W
Bata, Eq. Guin. 80 1 57N 9 50 E
Batangas, Phil. 63 13 35N 121 10 E
Bath, U.K. 14 51 22N 2 22W
Bathford, U.K. 14 51 23N 2 18W
Bathgate, U.K. 21 55 54N 3 38W
Bathurst, Austral. 70 33 25S 149 31 E
Bathurst, Canada 93 47 37N 65 43W
Batley, U.K. 19 53 43N 1 38W
Batna, Alg. 78 35 34N 6 15 E
Baton Rouge, U.S.A. 91 30 30N 91 5W
Battle, U.K. 15 50 55N 0 30 E
Batumi, U.S.S.R. 47 41 30N 41 30 E
Bauru, Brazil 101 22 10S 49 0W
Bavaria □, W. Ger. 42 49 7N 11 30 E
Bawdsey, U.K. 15 52 1N 1 27 E
Bawtry, U.K. 19 53 25N 1 1W
Bayamo, Cuba 95 20 20N 76 40W
Bayan Har Shan, China 60 34 0N 98 0 E
Bayeux, Fr. 34 49 17N 0 42W
Baykal, L., U.S.S.R. 49 53 0N 108 0 E
Bayonne, Fr. 35 43 30N 1 28W
Beachley, U.K. 14 51 37N 2 39W
Beachy Head, U.K. 15 50 44N 0 16 E
Beaconsfield, U.K. 15 51 36N 0 39W
Beadnell, U.K. 21 55 33N 1 38W
Beagle, Canal, S. Am. 102 55 0S 68 30W
Beaminster, U.K. 14 50 48N 2 44W
Bear I., Ire. 25 51 38N 9 50W
Beardmore Glacier, Ant. 103 84 30S 170 0 E
Bearsden, U.K. 20 55 55N 4 21W
Bearsted, U.K. 15 51 15N 0 35 E
Beattock, U.K. 21 55 19N 3 27W
Beaufort Sea, Arctic 103 72 0N 140 0W
Beaulieu, U.K. 14 50 49N 1 27W
Beauly, U.K. 23 57 29N 4 27W
Beauly →, U.K. 23 57 26N 4 28W
Beaumaris, U.K. 17 53 16N 4 7W
Beaumont, U.S.A. 91 30 5N 94 8W
Beauvais, Fr. 34 49 25N 2 8 E
Bebington, U.K. 18 53 23N 3 1W
Beccles, U.K. 15 52 27N 1 33 E
Béchar, Alg. 78 31 38N 2 18W
Beckermet, U.K. 18 54 26N 3 31W
Beckfoot, U.K. 18 54 50N 3 25W
Beckingham, U.K. 19 53 24N 0 49W
Bedale, U.K. 19 54 18N 1 35W
Beddgelert, U.K. 17 53 2N 4 8W
Bedford, U.K. 15 52 8N 0 29W
Bedford □, U.K. 15 52 4N 0 28W
Bedford Level, U.K. 15 52 25N 0 5 E
Bedlington, U.K. 21 55 8N 1 35W
Bedworth, U.K. 14 52 28N 1 29W
Beeford, U.K. 19 53 58N 0 18W
Beer, U.K. 16 50 41N 3 5W
Beersheba, Isr. 57 31 15N 34 48 E
Beeston, U.K. 19 52 55N 1 11W
Bei'an, China 61 48 10N 126 20 E
Beighton, U.K. 19 53 21N 1 21W
Beijing = Peking, China 61 39 55N 116 20 E
Beira, Mozam. 81 19 50S 34 52 E
Beira-Baixa, Port. 37 40 2N 7 30W
Beirut, Leb. 57 33 53N 35 31 E
Beith, U.K. 20 55 45N 4 38W
Bejaïa, Golfe de, Alg. 78 36 42N 5 13 E
Belbroughton, U.K. 14 52 23N 2 5W
Belcher Is., Canada 89 56 15N 78 45W
Belém, Brazil 101 1 20S 48 30W
Belfast, U.K. 24 54 35N 5 56W
Belfast □, U.K. 24 54 35N 5 56W
Belfast L., U.K. 24 54 40N 5 50W
Belford, U.K. 21 55 36N 1 50W
Belfort, Fr. 34 47 38N 6 50 E
Belgium ■, Europe 36 50 30N 5 0 E
Belgorod, U.S.S.R. 47 50 35N 36 35 E
Belgrade, Yug. 41 44 50N 20 37 E
Beliton, Is., Indon. 63 3 10S 107 50 E
Belize ■, Cent. Am. 94 17 0N 88 30W
Belize City, Belize 94 17 25N 88 0W
Bell Rock = Inchcape Rock, U.K. 21 56 26N 2 24W
Bellary, India 58 15 10N 76 56 E
Belle-Ile, Fr. 34 47 20N 3 10W
Belle Isle, Str. of, Canada 89 51 30N 56 30W
Belleville, Canada 92 44 10N 77 23W
Bellingham, U.K. 21 55 9N 2 16W
Belmopan, Belize 94 17 18N 88 30W
Belmullet, Ire. 24 54 13N 9 58W
Belo Horizonte, Brazil 101 19 55S 43 56W
Beloye More, U.S.S.R. 46 66 30N 38 0 E
Belper, U.K. 19 53 2N 1 29W
Belsay, U.K. 21 55 6N 1 53W
Belton, Humberside, U.K. 19 53 33N 0 49W
Belton, Norfolk, U.K. 15 52 35N 1 39 E
Belturbet, Ire. 24 54 6N 7 28W
Bembridge, U.K. 14 50 41N 1 4W
Ben Bheigeir, U.K. 20 55 43N 6 6W
Ben Chonzie, U.K. 21 56 27N 4 0W
Ben Cruachan, U.K. 20 56 26N 5 8W
Ben Dearg, U.K. 23 57 47N 4 58W
Ben Dorain, U.K. 20 56 30N 4 42W
Ben Hope, U.K. 23 58 24N 4 36W
Ben Lawers, U.K. 23 56 33N 4 13W
Ben Lomond, U.K. 20 56 12N 4 39W
Ben Lui, U.K. 20 56 24N 4 50W
Ben Macdhui, U.K. 23 57 4N 3 40W
Ben Mhor, U.K. 22 57 16N 7 21W
Ben More, Central, U.K. 20 56 23N 4 31W
Ben More, Strathclyde, U.K. 20 56 26N 6 2W
Ben More Assynt, U.K. 23 58 7N 4 51W
Ben Nevis, U.K. 22 56 48N 5 0W
Ben Venue, U.K. 20 56 13N 4 28W
Ben Vorlich, U.K. 20 56 22N 4 15W
Ben Wyvis, U.K. 23 57 40N 4 35W
Benalla, Austral. 70 36 30S 146 0 E
Benares = Varanasi, India 59 25 22N 83 0 E
Benbecula, U.K. 22 57 26N 7 21W
Bendigo, Austral. 70 36 40S 144 15 E
Beneraird, U.K. 20 55 4N 4 57W
Benevento, It. 40 41 7N 14 45 E
Bengal, Bay of, Ind. Oc. 59 18 0N 90 0 E
Bengbu, China 61 32 58N 117 20 E
Benghazi, Libya 79 32 11N 20 3 E
Beni Suef, Egypt 79 29 5N 31 6 E
Benin ■, Africa 78 10 0N 2 0 E
Benin, Bight of, W. Afr. 78 5 0N 3 0 E
Benin City, Nig. 78 6 20N 5 31 E
Benington, U.K. 19 52 59N 0 5 E
Bennane Hd., U.K. 20 55 9N 5 2W
Benoni, S. Afr. 81 26 11S 28 18 E
Benson, U.K. 14 51 37N 1 6W
Bentley, Hants., U.K. 15 51 12N 0 52W
Bentley, S. Yorks., U.K. 19 53 33N 1 9W
Benue →, Nig. 78 7 48N 6 46 E
Benxi, China 61 41 20N 123 48 E
Berbera, Som. 73 10 30N 45 2 E
Berbérati, C.A.R. 80 4 15N 15 40 E
Bere Alston, U.K. 16 50 29N 4 11W
Bere Regis, U.K. 14 50 45N 2 13W
Berezniki, U.S.S.R. 46 59 24N 56 46 E
Bérgamo, It. 40 45 42N 9 40 E
Bergen, Nor. 45 60 23N 5 20 E
Bergen-op-Zoom, Neth. 36 51 30N 4 18 E
Bergerac, Fr. 35 44 51N 0 30 E
Bergisch-Gladbach, W. Ger. 36 50 59N 7 9 E
Berhampore, India 59 24 2N 88 27 E
Berhampur, India 59 19 15N 84 54 E
Bering Sea, Pac. Oc. 88 58 0N 167 0 E
Bering Str., N. Am. 103 66 0N 170 0W
Berkeley, U.K. 14 51 41N 2 28W
Berkhamsted, U.K. 15 51 45N 0 33W
Berkshire □, U.K. 14 51 30N 1 20W
Berkshire Downs, U.K. 15 51 30N 1 30W
Berlin, Ger. 42 52 32N 13 24 E
Bermuda ■, Atl. Oc. 95 32 45N 65 0W
Bern, Switz. 42 46 57N 7 28 E
Berry Hd., U.K. 16 50 24N 3 29W
Berwick-upon-Tweed, U.K. 19 55 47N 2 0W
Berwyn Mts., U.K. 17 52 54N 3 26W
Besançon, Fr. 34 47 15N 6 0 E
Bethesda, U.K. 17 53 11N 4 3W
Bethlehem, Jord. 57 31 43N 35 12 E
Bethlehem, U.S.A. 93 40 39N 75 24W
Béthune, Fr. 34 50 30N 2 38 E
Betws-y-Coed, U.K. 17 53 4N 3 49W
Beverley, U.K. 19 53 52N 0 26W
Beverwijk, Neth. 36 52 28N 4 38 E
Bewdley, U.K. 14 52 23N 2 19W
Bexhill, U.K. 15 50 51N 0 29 E
Bexley, U.K. 15 51 26N 0 10 E
Béziers, Fr. 35 43 20N 3 12 E
Bhagalpur, India 59 25 10N 87 0 E
Bhatinda, India 58 30 15N 74 57 E
Bhatpara, India 59 22 50N 88 25 E
Bhavnagar, India 58 21 45N 72 10 E
Bhimavaram, India 59 16 30N 81 30 E
Bhopal, India 58 23 20N 77 30 E
Bhubaneshwar, India 59 20 15N 85 50 E
Bhutan ■, Asia 59 27 25N 90 30 E
Białystok, Pol. 43 53 10N 23 10 E
Biarritz, Fr. 35 43 29N 1 33W
Bibury, U.K. 14 51 46N 1 50W
Bicester, U.K. 14 51 53N 1 9W
Bicton, U.K. 14 52 43N 2 47W
Biddenden, U.K. 15 51 7N 0 40 E
Biddulph, U.K. 18 53 8N 2 11W
Bideford, U.K. 16 51 1N 4 13W
Bideford Bay, U.K. 16 51 5N 4 20W
Bidford on Avon, U.K. 14 52 9N 1 53W
Bié Plateau, Angola 81 12 0S 16 0 E
Biel, Switz. 42 47 8N 7 14 E
Bielefeld, W. Ger. 42 52 2N 8 31 E
Bigbury, U.K. 16 50 17N 3 52W
Bigbury B., U.K. 16 50 18N 3 58W
Biggar, U.K. 21 55 38N 3 31W
Biggleswade, U.K. 15 52 6N 0 16W
Bighorn Mts., U.S.A. 90 44 30N 107 30W
Bihar □, India 59 25 0N 86 0 E
Bikaner, India 58 28 2N 73 18 E

Bikini Atoll, *Pac. Oc.* .. **64** 12 0N 167 30 E
Bilbao, *Sp.* **37** 43 16N 2 56W
Billericay, *U.K.* .... **15** 51 38N 0 25 E
Billesdon, *U.K.* **15** 52 38N 0 56W
Billingham, *U.K.* **19** 54 36N 1 18W
Billinghay, *U.K.* **19** 53 5N 0 17W
Billings, *U.S.A.* **90** 45 43N 108 29W
Billingshurst, *U.K.* **15** 51 2N 0 28W
Bilston, *U.K.* **14** 52 34N 2 5W
Binbrook, *U.K.* **19** 53 26N 0 9W
Bingham, *U.K.* **19** 52 57N 0 55W
Binghamton, *U.S.A.* .. **93** 42 9N 75 54W
Bingley, *U.K.* **18** 53 51N 1 50W
Bioko, *Eq. Guin.* ...... **80** 3 30N 8 40 E
Birch, *U.K.* .... **15** 51 50N 0 54 E
Birchington, *U.K.* ...... **15** 51 22N 1 18 E
Birdlip, *U.K.* **14** 51 50N 2 7W
Birkdale, *U.K.* **18** 53 38N 3 2W
Birkenhead, *U.K.* **18** 53 24N 3 1W
Birmingham, *U.K.* **14** 52 30N 1 55W
Birmingham, *U.S.A.* ... **91** 33 31N 86 50W
Birr, *Ire.* **25** 53 7N 7 55W
Birtley,
Northumberland, U.K. **21** 55 5N 2 12W
Birtley, *Tyne & Wear,*
U.K. **21** 54 53N 1 34W
Biscay, B. of, *Atl. Oc.* . **35** 45 0N 2 0W
Bishop Auckland, *U.K.* **19** 54 40N 1 40W
Bishop's Castle, *U.K.* . **14** 52 29N 3 0W
Bishop's Cleeve, *U.K.* . **14** 51 56N 2 3W
Bishop's Frome, *U.K.* . **14** 52 8N 2 29W
Bishops Lydeard, *U.K.* **14** 51 4N 3 12W
Bishop's Nympton, *U.K.* **16** 50 58N 3 44W
Bishop's Stortford, *U.K.* **15** 51 52N 0 11 E
Bishop's Waltham, *U.K.* **15** 50 57N 1 13W
Bishopsteignton, *U.K.* . **16** 50 32N 3 32W
Bishopstoke, *U.K.* **14** 50 58N 1 19W
Biskra, *Alg.* .... **78** 34 50N 5 44 E
Bismarck Arch., *P.N.G.* **64** 2 30S 150 0 E
Bissau, *Guin.-Biss.* ... **78** 11 45N 15 45W
Bitola, *Yug.* .... **41** 41 5N 21 10 E
Bitton, *U.K.* **14** 51 25N 2 27W
Biwa-Ko, *Jap.* .... **62** 35 15N 136 10 E
Biysk, *U.S.S.R.* .... **48** 52 40N 85 0 E
Blaby, *U.K.* **14** 52 34N 1 10W
Black Combe, *U.K.* **18** 54 16N 3 20W
Black Esk ⟶, *U.K.* .. **21** 55 14N 3 13W
Black Forest, Mts.,
W. Ger. .... **42** 48 0N 8 0 E
Black Hd., *U.K.* **16** 50 1N 5 6W
Black Mt. = Mynydd
Du, *U.K.* **17** 51 45N 3 45W
Black Mts., *U.K.* **17** 51 52N 3 5W
Black Sea, *Europe* .... **47** 43 30N 35 0 E
Black Volta ⟶, *Africa* **78** 8 41N 1 33W
Blackall, *Austral.* ..... **67** 24 25S 145 45 E
Blackburn, *U.K.* **18** 53 44N 2 30W
Blackdown Hills, *U.K.* . **14** 50 57N 3 15W
Blackford, *U.K.* **21** 56 15N 3 48W
Blackmoor Gate, *U.K.* . **16** 51 9N 3 55W
Blackmoor Vale, *U.K.* . **14** 50 54N 2 28W
Blackpool, *U.K.* **18** 53 48N 3 3W
Blacksod B., *Ire.* **24** 54 6N 10 0W
Blacktown, *Austral.* ... **70** 33 48S 150 55 E
Blackwater ⟶, *Ire.* .. **25** 51 55N 7 50W
Blackwater ⟶, *Essex,*
U.K. .... **15** 51 44N 0 53 E
Blackwater ⟶,
N. Ireland, U.K. **24** 54 31N 6 35W
Blackwood, *U.K.* **21** 55 40N 3 56W
Blaenau Ffestiniog, *U.K.* **17** 53 0N 3 57W
Blaenavon, *U.K.* **17** 51 46N 3 5W
Blagdon, *U.K.* **14** 51 19N 2 42W
Blagoveshchensk,
U.S.S.R. .... **49** 50 20N 127 30 E
Blair Athol, *Austral.* ... **67** 22 42S 147 31 E
Blair Atholl, *U.K.* **23** 56 46N 3 50W
Blairgowrie, *U.K.* **23** 56 36N 3 20W
Blakeney, *Gloucs., U.K.* **14** 51 45N 2 29W
Blakeney, *Norfolk, U.K.* **15** 52 57N 1 1 E
Blanc, Mont, *Europe* .. **35** 45 48N 6 50 E
Blandford Forum, *U.K.* **14** 50 52N 2 10W
Blantyre, *Malawi* ..... **81** 15 45S 35 0 E
Blarney, *Ire.* **25** 51 57N 8 35W
Blaydon, *U.K.* **19** 54 56N 1 47W
Bleadon, *U.K.* **14** 51 18N 2 57W
Blean, *U.K.* .... **15** 51 18N 1 3 E
Bleasdale Moors, *U.K.* **18** 53 57N 2 40W
Blenheim, *N.Z.* .... **71** 41 38S 173 57 E
Bletchingdon, *U.K.* ... **14** 51 51N 1 16W
Bletchley, *U.K.* **15** 51 59N 0 44W
Blisworth, *U.K.* **15** 52 11N 0 56W
Blockley, *U.K.* **14** 52 1N 1 45W
Bloemfontein, *S. Afr.* .. **81** 29 6S 26 14 E
Blofield, *U.K.* .... **15** 52 38N 1 25 E
Blois, *Fr.* .... **34** 47 35N 1 20 E
Bloody Foreland, *Ire.* . **24** 55 10N 8 18W
Bloxham, *U.K.* **14** 52 1N 1 22W
Blue Mts., *Austral.* ... **70** 33 40S 150 0 E
Blue Mts., *U.S.A.* **90** 45 15N 119 0W
Blue Nile ⟶, *Sudan* .. **79** 12 30N 34 30 E
Blue Ridge Mts., *U.S.A.* **91** 36 30N 80 15W
Blue Stack Mts., *Ire.* . **24** 54 46N 8 5W
Blumenau, *Brazil* **102** 27 0S 49 0W
Blundeston, *U.K.* ..... **15** 52 33N 1 42 E
Blyth, *Northumberland,*
U.K. **19** 55 8N 1 32W
Blyth, *Notts., U.K.* ... **19** 53 22N 1 2W
Blyth ⟶, *U.K.* **21** 55 8N 1 30W
Blyth Bridge, *U.K.* **21** 55 41N 3 22W
Blyton, *U.K.* **19** 53 25N 0 42W
Bobo-Dioulasso,
B. Faso **78** 11 8N 4 13W
Bocholt, *W. Ger.* ..... **36** 51 50N 6 35 E
Bochum, *W. Ger.* ..... **36** 51 28N 7 12 E
Bodenham, *U.K.* **14** 52 9N 2 41W
Bodensee, *W. Ger.* ... **42** 47 35N 9 25 E
Bodiam, *U.K.* .... **15** 51 1N 0 33 E
Bodinnick, *U.K.* **16** 50 20N 4 37W
Bodmin, *U.K.* **16** 50 28N 4 44W
Bodmin Moor, *U.K.* ... **16** 50 33N 4 36W
Bodø, *Nor.* .... **44** 67 17N 14 24 E
Bogan ⟶, *Austral.* .. **67** 29 59S 146 17 E
Boggeragh Mts., *Ire.* .. **25** 52 2N 8 55W
Bognor Regis, *U.K.* ... **15** 50 47N 0 40W
Bogor, *Indon.* .... **63** 6 36S 106 48 E
Bogota, *Col.* **100** 4 34N 74 0W
Bohemian Forest,
Czech. .... **42** 49 20N 13 0 E
Boise, *U.S.A.* **90** 43 43N 116 9W
Bolgatanga, *Ghana* ... **78** 10 44N 0 53W
Bolivia ■, *S. Am.* **100** 17 6S 64 0W
Bolivian Plateau, *S. Am.* **96** 20 0S 67 30W
Bollington, *U.K.* **18** 53 18N 2 8W
Bolney, *U.K.* **15** 50 59N 0 11W
Bologna, *It.* .... **40** 44 30N 11 20 E
Bolshevik, I., *U.S.S.R.* . **49** 78 30N 102 0 E
Bolshezemelsk
Tundra, *U.S.S.R.* ... **46** 67 0N 56 0 E
Bolsover, *U.K.* **19** 53 14N 1 18W
Bolt Head, *U.K.* **16** 50 13N 3 48W
Bolt Tail, *U.K.* **16** 50 13N 3 55W
Bolton, *U.K.* **18** 53 35N 2 26W
Bolton Abbey, *U.K.* ... **18** 53 59N 1 53W
Bolton by Bowland,
U.K. **18** 53 56N 2 21W
Bolton le Sands, *U.K.* . **18** 54 7N 2 49W
Bolungavík, *Ice.* **44** 66 9N 23 15W
Bolzano, *It.* .... **40** 46 30N 11 20 E
Boma, *Zaïre* .... **80** 5 50S 13 4 E
Bombay, *India* .... **58** 18 55N 72 50 E
Bonaparte Archipelago,
Austral. .... **66** 14 0S 124 30 E
Bonarbridge, *U.K.* **23** 57 53N 4 20W
Bonchester Bridge, *U.K.* **21** 55 23N 2 36W
Bonchurch, *U.K.* **14** 50 36N 1 11W
Bo'ness, *U.K.* **21** 56 0N 3 38W
Bonifacio, Str. of, *Fr.* . **40** 41 12N 9 15 E
Bonn, *W. Ger.* .... **36** 50 43N 7 6 E
Bonnyrigg, *U.K.* **21** 55 52N 3 8W
Boot, *U.K.* **18** 54 24N 3 18W
Boothia, Gulf of,
Canada **89** 71 0N 90 0W
Boothia Pen., *Canada* . **88** 71 0N 94 0W
Bootle, *Cumbria, U.K.* . **18** 54 17N 3 24W
Bootle, *Merseyside,*
U.K. **18** 53 28N 3 1W
Borås, *Swed.* .... **45** 57 43N 12 56 E
Bordeaux, *Fr.* **35** 44 50N 0 36W
Borders □, *U.K.* **21** 55 35N 2 50W
Bordon, *U.K.* **15** 51 6N 0 52W
Borehamwood, *U.K.* .. **15** 51 40N 0 15W
Boreland, *U.K.* **21** 55 12N 3 16W
Borgarnes, *Ice.* **44** 64 32N 21 55W
Borneo, *E. Ind.* ...... **63** 1 0N 115 0 E
Bornholm, *Den.* ...... **45** 55 10N 15 0 E
Boroughbridge, *U.K.* .. **19** 54 6N 1 23W
Borrowdale, *U.K.* **18** 54 31N 3 10W
Borth, *U.K.* **17** 52 29N 4 3W
Bosbury, *U.K.* **14** 52 5N 2 27W
Boscastle, *U.K.* **16** 50 42N 4 42W
Bosham, *U.K.* **15** 50 50N 0 51W
Bosporus, *Turk.* ...... **47** 41 10N 29 10 E
Boston, *U.K.* **19** 52 59N 0 2W
Boston, *U.S.A.* **93** 42 20N 71 0W
Botany Bay, *Austral.* .. **70** 34 0S 151 14 E
Bothel, *U.K.* **18** 54 43N 3 16W
Bothnia, G. of, *Europe* **44** 63 0N 20 0 E
Botswana ■, *Africa* ... **81** 22 0S 24 0 E
Bottesford, *U.K.* **19** 52 57N 0 48W
Bottrop, *W. Ger.* ..... **36** 51 34N 6 59 E
Bouaké, *Ivory C.* **78** 7 40N 5 2W
Bouar, *C.A.R.* .... **80** 6 0N 15 40 E
Boulogne-sur-Mer, *Fr.* **34** 50 42N 1 36 E
Bourges, *Fr.* .... **34** 47 9N 2 25 E
Bourgogne, *Fr.* .... **34** 47 0N 4 50 E
Bourke, *Austral.* ...... **67** 30 8S 145 55 E
Bourne, *U.K.* **15** 52 46N 0 22W
Bournemouth, *U.K.* ... **14** 50 43N 1 53W
Bourton-on-the-Water,
U.K. **14** 51 53N 1 45W
Bovey Tracey, *U.K.* ... **16** 50 36N 3 40W
Bowen, *Austral.* ...... **67** 20 0S 148 16 E
Bowes, *U.K.* **18** 54 31N 1 59W
Bowland, Forest of,
U.K. **18** 54 0N 2 30W
Bowmore, *U.K.* **20** 55 45N 6 18W
Bowness, *Solway, U.K.* **18** 54 57N 3 13W
Bowness, *Windermere,*
U.K. **18** 54 22N 2 56W
Box, *U.K.* **14** 51 24N 2 16W
Box Hill, *U.K.* **15** 51 16N 0 16W
Boxley, *U.K.* .... **15** 51 17N 0 34 E
Boyle, *Ire.* **24** 53 58N 8 19W
Boyne ⟶, *Ire.* **24** 53 43N 6 15W
Bozeat, *U.K.* **15** 52 14N 0 41W
Bracadale, L., *U.K.* ... **22** 57 20N 6 30W
Bracebridge Heath,
U.K. **19** 53 13N 0 32W
Brackley, *U.K.* **14** 52 3N 1 9W
Bracknell, *U.K.* **15** 51 24N 0 45W
Braco, *U.K.* **21** 56 16N 3 55W
Bradda Hd., *U.K.* **18** 54 6N 4 46W
Bradford, *U.K.* **19** 53 47N 1 45W
Bradford-on-Avon, *U.K.* **14** 51 20N 2 15W
Brading, *U.K.* **14** 50 41N 1 9W
Bradwell-on-Sea, *U.K.* **15** 51 44N 0 55 E
Bradworthy, *U.K.* **16** 50 54N 4 22W
Braemar, *U.K.* **23** 57 2N 3 20W
Braga, *Port.* **37** 41 35N 8 25W
Brahmaputra ⟶, *India* **59** 24 2N 90 59 E
Braich-y-pwll, *U.K.* ... **17** 52 47N 4 46W
Brăila, *Rom.* .... **43** 45 19N 27 59 E
Brailsford, *U.K.* **19** 52 58N 1 35W
Braintree, *U.K.* .... **15** 51 53N 0 34 E
Bramford, *U.K.* .... **15** 52 5N 1 6 E
Brampton, *Canada* ... **92** 43 45N 79 45W
Brampton, *Cambs.,*
U.K. **15** 52 19N 0 13W
Brampton, *Cumbria,*
U.K. **18** 54 56N 2 43W
Bramshott, *U.K.* **15** 51 5N 0 47W
Brancaster, *U.K.* ..... **15** 52 58N 0 40 E
Branco ⟶, *Brazil* **100** 1 20S 61 50W
Brander, Pass of, *U.K.* **20** 56 25N 5 10W
Brandon, *Canada* **88** 49 50N 99 57W
Brandon, *Durham, U.K.* **19** 54 46N 1 37W
Brandon, *Suffolk, U.K.* **15** 52 27N 0 37 E
Brandon, Mt., *Ire.* **25** 52 15N 10 15W
Brandon B., *Ire.* **25** 52 17N 10 8W
Branston, *U.K.* **19** 53 13N 0 28W
Brantford, *Canada* **92** 43 10N 80 15W
Brasília, *Brazil* .... **101** 15 47S 47 55 E
Braşov, *Rom.* .... **43** 45 38N 25 35 E
Brasted, *U.K.* .... **15** 51 16N 0 8 E
Bratislava, *Czech.* .... **43** 48 10N 17 7 E
Bratsk, *U.S.S.R.* ..... **49** 56 10N 101 30 E
Braunton, *U.K.* **16** 51 6N 4 9W
Bray, *Ire.* **25** 53 12N 6 6W
Bray, *U.K.* **15** 51 30N 0 42W
Brazil ■, *S. Am.* **101** 10 0S 50 0W
Brazilian Highlands,
Brazil **101** 18 0S 46 30W
Brazzaville, *Congo* ... **80** 4 9S 15 12 E
Breadalbane, *U.K.* **20** 56 30N 4 15W
Breage, *U.K.* **16** 50 6N 5 17W
Breamish ⟶, *U.K.* ... **21** 55 30N 1 55W
Brechin, *U.K.* **23** 56 44N 2 40W
Breckland, *U.K.* ...... **15** 52 30N 0 40 E
Brecon, *U.K.* **17** 51 57N 3 23W
Brecon Beacons, *U.K.* **17** 51 53N 3 27W
Brede, *U.K.* .... **15** 50 56N 0 37 E
Bredon Hill, *U.K.* **14** 52 3N 2 2W
Breiðafjörður, *Ice.* **44** 65 15N 23 15W
Bremen, *W. Ger.* ..... **42** 53 4N 8 47 E
Bremerhaven, *W. Ger.* **42** 53 34N 8 35 E
Brendon Hills, *U.K.* ... **14** 51 6N 3 25W
Brenner Pass, *Alps* ... **42** 47 0N 11 30 E
Brent, *U.K.* **15** 51 33N 0 18W
Brentwood, *U.K.* ...... **15** 51 37N 0 19 E
Bréscia, *It.* .... **40** 45 33N 10 13 E
Breslau = Wrocław,
Pol. .... **43** 51 5N 17 5 E
Bressay I., *U.K.* **22** 60 10N 1 5W
Brest, *Fr.* **34** 48 24N 4 31W
Brest, *U.S.S.R.* ...... **46** 52 10N 23 40 E
Bretagne, *Fr.* **34** 48 0N 3 0W
Brewood, *U.K.* **14** 52 41N 2 10W
Brezhnev, *U.S.S.R.* ... **46** 55 42N 52 19 E
Bride, *U.K.* **18** 54 24N 4 23W
Bridestowe, *U.K.* **16** 50 41N 4 7W
Bridge, *U.K.* .... **15** 51 14N 1 8 E
Bridge of Allan, *U.K.* .. **21** 56 9N 3 57W
Bridge of Earn, *U.K.* .. **21** 56 20N 3 25W
Bridge of Orchy, *U.K.* . **20** 56 29N 4 48W
Bridge of Weir, *U.K.* .. **20** 55 51N 4 35W
Bridgend, *Islay, U.K.* .. **20** 55 46N 6 15W
Bridgend, *Mid Glam.,*
U.K. **17** 51 30N 3 35W
Bridgeport, *U.S.A.* ... **93** 41 12N 73 12W
Bridgetown, *Barb.* **94** 13 0N 59 30W
Bridgnorth, *U.K.* **14** 52 33N 2 25W
Bridgwater, *U.K.* **14** 51 7N 3 0W
Bridgwater B., *U.K.* ... **14** 51 15N 3 15W
Bridlington, *U.K.* **19** 54 6N 0 11W
Bridlington B., *U.K.* .. **19** 54 4N 0 10W
Bridport, *U.K.* **14** 50 43N 2 45W
Brierfield, *U.K.* **18** 53 49N 2 15W
Brierley Hill, *U.K.* **14** 52 29N 2 7W
Brigg, *U.K.* **19** 53 33N 0 30W
Brighouse, *U.K.* **19** 53 42N 1 47W
Brighstone, *U.K.* **15** 50 38N 1 23W
Brightlingsea, *U.K.* ... **15** 51 49N 1 1 E
Brighton, *U.K.* **15** 50 50N 0 9W
Brigstock, *U.K.* **15** 52 27N 0 38W
Brill, *U.K.* **14** 51 49N 1 3W
Brimfield, *U.K.* **14** 52 18N 2 42W
Bríndisi, *It.* .... **41** 40 39N 17 55 E
Brinklow, *U.K.* **14** 52 25N 1 22W
Brinkworth, *U.K.* **14** 51 33N 1 59W
Brisbane, *Austral.* .... **67** 27 25S 153 2 E
Bristol, *U.K.* **14** 51 26N 2 35W
Bristol Channel, *U.K.* . **16** 51 18N 4 30W
Briston, *U.K.* .... **15** 52 52N 1 4 E
British Columbia □,
Canada **88** 55 0N 125 15W
British Guiana =
Guyana ■, *S. Am.* .. **100** 5 0N 59 0W
British Isles, *Europe* .. **4** 55 0N 4 0W
Briton Ferry, *U.K.* **17** 51 37N 3 50W
Brittany = Bretagne, *Fr.* **34** 48 0N 3 0W
Brixham, *U.K.* **16** 50 24N 3 31W
Brixworth, *U.K.* **15** 52 20N 0 54W
Brize Norton, *U.K.* **14** 51 46N 1 35W
Brno, *Czech.* .... **42** 49 10N 16 35 E
Broad B., *U.K.* **22** 58 14N 6 16W
Broad Chalke, *U.K.* ... **14** 51 2N 1 54W
Broad Haven, *Ire.* **24** 54 20N 9 55W
Broad Law, *U.K.* **21** 55 30N 3 22W
Broad Sd., *U.K.* **16** 49 56N 6 19W
Broadclyst , *U.K.* **16** 50 46N 3 27W
Broadford, *U.K.* **22** 57 14N 5 55W
Broadhembury, *U.K.* .. **16** 50 49N 3 16W
Broads, The, *U.K.* .... **15** 52 45N 1 30 E
Broadstairs, *U.K.* ..... **15** 51 21N 1 28 E
Broadway, *U.K.* **14** 52 2N 1 51W
Broadwindsor, *U.K.* ... **14** 50 49N 2 49W
Brockenhurst, *U.K.* ... **14** 50 49N 1 34W
Brockton, *U.S.A.* **93** 42 25N 79 26W
Brockworth, *U.K.* **14** 51 51N 2 9W
Brodick, *U.K.* **20** 55 34N 5 9W
Broken Hill, *Austral.* .. **70** 31 58S 141 29 E
Bromborough, *U.K.* ... **18** 53 20N 3 0W
Bromfield, *U.K.* **14** 52 25N 2 45W
Bromham, *U.K.* **14** 51 23N 2 3W
Bromley, *U.K.* .... **15** 51 20N 0 5 E
Brompton, *U.K.* **19** 54 22N 1 25W
Bromsgrove, *U.K.* **14** 52 20N 2 3W
Bromyard, *U.K.* **14** 52 12N 2 30W
Brooks, *Canada* **88** 50 35N 111 55W
Brooks Ra., *U.S.A.* ... **88** 68 40N 147 0W
Broom, L., *U.K.* **22** 57 55N 5 15W
Broomfield, *U.K.* ..... **14** 51 46N 0 28 E
Broomhill, *U.K.* **21** 55 19N 1 36W
Brora, *U.K.* **23** 58 0N 3 50W
Brora ⟶, *U.K.* **23** 58 4N 3 52W
Broseley, *U.K.* **14** 52 36N 2 30W
Brosna ⟶, *Ire.* **25** 53 8N 8 0W
Brothertoft, *U.K.* **19** 53 0N 0 5W
Brotton, *U.K.* **19** 54 34N 0 55W
Brough, *Cumbria, U.K.* **18** 54 32N 2 19W
Brough, *Humberside,*
U.K. **19** 53 44N 0 35W
Broughton, *Borders,*
U.K. **21** 55 37N 3 25W
Broughton,
Humberside, U.K. .. **19** 53 33N 0 36W
Broughton, *N. Yorks.,*
U.K. **19** 54 26N 1 8W
Broughton, *Northants.,*
U.K. **15** 52 22N 0 45W
Broughton-in-Furness,
U.K. **18** 54 17N 3 12W
Broughty Ferry, *U.K.* .. **21** 56 29N 2 50W
Brown Willy, *U.K.* **16** 50 35N 4 34W
Brownhills, *U.K.* **14** 52 38N 1 57W
Broxburn, *U.K.* **21** 55 56N 3 23W
Bruay-en-Artois, *Fr.* .. **34** 50 29N 2 33 E
Bruce, Mt., *Austral.* .. **66** 22 37S 118 8 E
Brue ⟶, *U.K.* **14** 51 10N 2 59W
Bruges, *Belg.* .... **36** 51 13N 3 13 E
Brunei ■, *E. Ind.* .... **63** 4 50N 115 0 E
Brunswick, *W. Ger.* ... **42** 52 17N 10 28 E
Brunton, *U.K.* **21** 55 2N 2 6W
Brussels, *Belg.* ...... **36** 50 51N 4 21 E
Bruton, *U.K.* **14** 51 6N 2 28W
Bryansk, *U.S.S.R.* .... **46** 53 13N 34 25 E
Bryher I., *U.K.* **16** 49 57N 6 21W
Brynamman, *U.K.* **17** 51 49N 3 52W
Brynmawr, *U.K.* **17** 51 48N 3 11W
Bucaramanga, *Col.* ... **100** 7 0N 73 0W
Buchan, *U.K.* **23** 57 32N 2 8W
Buchan Ness, *U.K.* ... **23** 57 29N 1 48W
Bucharest, *Rom.* ..... **43** 44 27N 26 10 E
Buchlyvie, *U.K.* **20** 56 7N 4 20W
Buckden, *U.K.* **15** 52 17N 0 16W
Buckfastleigh, *U.K.* .. **16** 50 28N 3 47W
Buckhaven, *U.K.* **21** 56 10N 3 2W
Buckie, *U.K.* **23** 57 40N 2 58W
Buckingham, *U.K.* **15** 52 0N 0 59W
Buckingham □, *U.K.* .. **15** 51 50N 0 55W
Buckland Brewer, *U.K.* **16** 50 56N 4 14W
Buckland Newton, *U.K.* **14** 50 45N 2 25W
Buckley, *U.K.* **17** 53 10N 3 5W
Budapest, *Hung.* ..... **43** 47 29N 19 5 E
Buddon Ness, *U.K.* ... **21** 56 29N 2 42W
Bude, *U.K.* **16** 50 49N 4 33W
Bude Bay, *U.K.* **16** 50 50N 4 40W
Budle B., *U.K.* **21** 55 37N 1 45W
Budleigh Salterton, *U.K.* **16** 50 37N 3 19W
Buenaventura, *Col.* ... **100** 3 53N 77 4W
Buenos Aires, *Arg.* ... **102** 34 30S 58 20W
Buffalo, *U.S.A.* **92** 42 55N 78 50W
Bug ⟶, *Pol.* .... **43** 52 31N 21 5 E
Bug ⟶, *U.S.S.R.* .... **47** 46 59N 31 58 E
Buglawton, *U.K.* **18** 53 12N 2 11W
Bugle, *U.K.* **16** 50 23N 4 46W
Buie L., *U.K.* **20** 56 20N 5 55W
Builth Wells, *U.K.* ... **17** 52 10N 3 26W
Bujumbura, *Bur.* ..... **80** 3 16S 29 18 E
Bukavu, *Zaïre* .... **80** 2 20S 28 52 E
Bukhara, *U.S.S.R.* ... **48** 39 48N 64 25 E
Bulawayo, *Zimb.* ..... **81** 20 7S 28 32 E
Bulford, *U.K.* **14** 51 11N 1 45W
Bulgaria ■, *Europe* ... **41** 42 35N 25 30 E
Bulwell, *U.K.* **19** 53 1N 1 12W
Bunbury, *Austral.* .... **66** 33 20S 115 35 E
Buncrana, *Ire.* **24** 55 8N 7 28W
Bundaberg, *Austral.* .. **67** 24 54S 152 22 E
Bundoran, *Ire.* **24** 54 24N 8 17W

Bunessan, U.K. 20 56 18N 6 15W
Bungay, U.K. 15 52 27N 1 26 E
Buntingford, U.K. 15 51 57N 0 1W
Bunwell, U.K. 15 52 30N 1 9 E
Buraydah, Si. Arab. 56 26 20N 44 8 E
Burbage, Derby, U.K. 18 53 15N 1 55W
Burbage, Leics., U.K. 14 52 31N 1 20W
Burbage, Wilts., U.K. 14 51 21N 1 40W
Burdwan, India 59 23 14N 87 39 E
Bure →, U.K. 15 52 38N 1 45 E
Burford, U.K. 14 51 48N 1 38W
Burgas, Bulg. 41 42 33N 27 29 E
Burgess Hill, U.K. 15 50 57N 0 7W
Burgh-le-Marsh, U.K. 19 53 10N 0 15 E
Burgos, Sp. 37 42 21N 3 41W
Burgundy = Bourgogne, Fr. 34 47 0N 4 50 E
Burkina Faso ■, Africa 78 12 0N 1 0W
Burley, Hants., U.K. 14 50 49N 1 41W
Burley, N. Yorks., U.K. 19 53 55N 1 46W
Burlington, U.S.A. 93 44 27N 73 14W
Burma ■, Asia 59 21 0N 96 30 E
Burnham, Essex, U.K. 15 51 37N 0 50 E
Burnham, Somerset, U.K. 14 51 14N 3 0W
Burnham Market, U.K. 15 52 57N 0 43 E
Burnie, Austral. 67 41 4S 145 56 E
Burnley, U.K. 18 53 47N 2 15W
Burnmouth, U.K. 21 55 50N 2 4W
Burntisland, U.K. 21 56 4N 3 14W
Burrelton, U.K. 21 56 30N 3 16W
Burrow Hd., U.K. 20 54 40N 4 23W
Burry Port, U.K. 17 51 41N 4 17W
Bursa, Turk. 47 40 15N 29 5 E
Burstwick, U.K. 19 53 43N 0 6W
Burton, U.K. 18 54 10N 2 43W
Burton Agnes, U.K. 19 54 4N 0 18W
Burton Bradstock, U.K. 14 50 41N 2 43W
Burton Fleming, U.K. 19 54 8N 0 20W
Burton Latimer, U.K. 15 52 23N 0 41W
Burton upon Stather, U.K. 19 53 39N 0 41W
Burton-upon-Trent, U.K. 14 52 48N 1 39W
Burundi ■, Africa 80 3 15S 30 0 E
Burwash, U.K. 15 50 59N 0 24 E
Burwell, U.K. 15 52 17N 0 20 E
Bury, U.K. 18 53 36N 2 19W
Bury St. Edmunds, U.K. 15 52 15N 0 42 E
Buryat A.S.S.R. □, U.S.S.R. 49 53 0N 110 0 E
Būshehr, Iran 56 28 20N 51 45 E
Bushey, U.K. 15 51 38N 0 20W
Bushmills, U.K. 24 55 14N 6 32W
Bute, U.K. 20 55 48N 5 2W
Bute, Kyles of, U.K. 20 55 55N 5 10W
Bute, Sd. of, U.K. 20 55 43N 5 8W
Buttermere, U.K. 18 54 32N 3 17W
Butuan, Phil. 63 8 57N 125 33 E
Buxton, U.K. 18 53 16N 1 54W
Buzău, Rom. 43 45 10N 26 50 E
Bydgoszcz, Pol. 43 53 10N 18 0 E
Byfield, U.K. 14 52 10N 1 15W
Byrd Land, Ant. 103 79 30S 125 0W
Byrranga Mts., U.S.S.R. 49 75 0N 100 0 E
Bytom, Pol. 43 50 25N 18 54 E

C

Cabimas, Ven. 100 10 23N 71 25W
Cabinda □, Angola 80 5 0S 12 30 E
Čačak, Yug. 41 43 54N 20 20 E
Cáceres, Sp. 37 39 26N 6 23W
Cachoeira do Sul, Brazil 102 30 3S 52 53W
Cader Idris, U.K. 17 52 43N 3 56W
Cádiz, Sp. 37 36 30N 6 20W
Caen, Fr. 34 49 10N 0 22W
Caenby Corner, U.K. 19 53 23N 0 32W
Caernarfon, U.K. 17 53 8N 4 17W
Caernarfon B., U.K. 17 53 4N 4 40W
Caerphilly, U.K. 17 51 34N 3 13W
Caersws, U.K. 17 52 32N 3 27W
Cagayan de Oro, Phil. 63 8 30N 124 40 E
Cágliari, It. 40 39 15N 9 6 E
Caha Mts., Ire. 25 51 45N 9 40W
Caher, Ire. 25 52 23N 7 56W
Cahersiveen, Ire. 25 51 57N 10 13W
Cahore Pt., Ire. 25 52 34N 6 11W
Caicos Is., W. Ind. 95 21 40N 71 40W
Cairn Gorm, U.K. 23 57 7N 3 40W
Cairn Table, U.K. 21 55 30N 4 0W
Cairn Toul, U.K. 23 57 3N 3 44W
Cairngorm Mts., U.K. 23 57 6N 3 42W
Cairnryan, U.K. 20 54 59N 5 0W
Cairns, Austral. 67 16 57S 145 45 E
Cairo, Egypt 79 30 1N 31 14 E
Caister-on-Sea, U.K. 15 52 38N 1 43 E
Caistor, U.K. 19 53 29N 0 20W
Caithness, Ord of, U.K. 23 58 9N 3 37W
Cajamarca, Peru 100 7 5S 78 28W
Calabar, Nig. 78 4 57N 8 20 E
Calábria □, It. 40 39 24N 16 30 E
Calais, Fr. 34 50 57N 1 50 E
Calbayog, Phil. 63 12 4N 124 38 E
Calcutta, India 59 22 36N 88 24 E
Caldbeck, U.K. 18 54 45N 3 3W
Calder →, U.K. 19 53 44N 1 21W
Calder Bridge, U.K. 18 54 27N 3 31W
Caldew →, U.K. 18 54 54N 2 59W
Caledonian Canal, U.K. 23 56 50N 5 6W
Calf of Man, U.K. 18 54 4N 4 48W
Calgary, Canada 88 51 0N 114 10W
Calgary, U.K. 20 56 34N 6 17W
Cali, Col. 100 3 25N 76 35W
Caliach Pt., U.K. 20 56 37N 6 20W
Calicut, India 58 11 15N 75 43 E
California □, U.S.A. 90 37 25N 120 0W
California, G. of, N. Am. 94 27 0N 111 0W
Callan, Ire. 25 52 33N 7 25W
Callander, U.K. 20 56 15N 4 14W
Callao, Peru 100 12 0S 77 0W
Calne, U.K. 14 51 26N 2 0W
Calshot, U.K. 14 50 49N 1 18W
Calstock, U.K. 16 50 30N 4 13W
Caltanissetta, It. 40 37 30N 14 3 E
Cam →, U.K. 15 52 21N 0 16 E
Camagüey, Cuba 95 21 20N 78 0W
Camargue, Fr. 35 43 34N 4 34 E
Cambay, G. of, India 58 20 45N 72 30 E
Camberley, U.K. 15 51 20N 0 44W
Cambo, U.K. 21 55 9N 1 57W
Cambodia ■, Asia 63 12 15N 105 0 E
Camborne, U.K. 16 50 13N 5 18W
Cambrian Mts., U.K. 17 52 25N 3 52W
Cambridge, U.K. 15 52 13N 0 8 E
Cambridge, U.S.A. 93 42 20N 71 8W
Cambridge Bay, Canada 88 69 10N 105 0W
Cambridgeshire □, U.K. 15 52 12N 0 7 E
Camden, U.K. 15 51 33N 0 10W
Camden, U.S.A. 93 39 57N 75 7W
Camel →, U.K. 16 50 28N 4 49W
Camelford, U.K. 16 50 37N 4 41W
Cameroon ■, Africa 80 6 0N 12 30 E
Campbellton, Canada 93 49 17N 54 56W
Campbelltown, Austral. 70 34 53S 138 40 E
Campbeltown, U.K. 20 55 25N 5 36W
Campeche, Mex. 94 19 50N 90 32W
Campeche, G. of, Mex. 94 19 30N 93 0W
Campina Grande, Brazil 101 7 20S 35 47W
Campinas, Brazil 102 22 50S 47 0W
Campo Grande, Brazil 101 20 25S 54 40W
Campos, Brazil 101 21 50S 41 20W
Campsie Fells, U.K. 20 56 2N 4 20W
Camrose, Canada 88 53 0N 112 50W
Can Tho, Viet. 63 10 2N 105 46 E
Canada ■, N. Am. 88 60 0N 100 0W
Canary Is., Atl. Oc. 78 29 30N 17 0W
Canaveral, C., U.S.A. 91 28 28N 80 31W
Canberra, Austral. 70 35 15S 149 8 E
Canik Mts., Turk. 47 40 30N 38 0 E
Canna, U.K. 22 57 3N 6 33W
Cannes, Fr. 35 43 32N 7 0 E
Cannington, U.K. 14 51 8N 3 4W
Cannock, U.K. 14 52 42N 2 2W
Cannock Chase, U.K. 14 52 43N 2 0W
Canonbie, U.K. 21 55 4N 2 58W
Cantabrian Mts., Sp. 37 43 0N 5 10W
Canterbury, U.K. 15 51 17N 1 5 E
Canterbury Plains, N.Z. 71 43 55S 171 22 E
Canton = Guangzhou, China 61 23 5N 113 10 E
Canton, U.S.A. 92 40 47N 81 22W
Canvey, U.K. 15 51 32N 0 35 E
Caoles, U.K. 20 56 32N 6 43W
Caolisport, Loch, U.K. 20 55 54N 5 40W
Cape Breton I., Canada 93 46 0N 60 30W
Cape Coast, Ghana 78 5 5N 1 15W
Cape Province □, S. Afr. 81 32 0S 23 0 E
Cape Town, S. Afr. 81 33 55S 18 22 E
Cape Verde Is. ■, Atl. Oc. 128 17 10N 25 20W
Cape York Peninsula, Austral. 67 12 0S 142 30 E
Capel, U.K. 15 51 8N 0 18W
Caracas, Ven. 100 10 30N 66 55W
Caratinga, Brazil 101 19 50S 42 10W
Carbost, U.K. 22 57 19N 6 21W
Cardiff, U.K. 17 51 28N 3 11W
Cardigan, U.K. 17 52 6N 4 41W
Cardigan B., U.K. 17 52 30N 4 30W
Cardington, U.K. 15 52 7N 0 23W
Carey, L., Austral. 66 29 0S 122 15 E
Caribbean Sea 95 15 0N 75 0W
Carisbrooke, U.K. 14 50 42N 1 19W
Cark, U.K. 18 54 11N 2 59W
Carleton Rode, U.K. 15 52 30N 1 6 E
Carlingford, L., Ire. 24 54 0N 6 5W
Carlisle, U.K. 18 54 54N 2 55W
Carlops, U.K. 21 55 47N 3 20W
Carlow, Ire. 25 52 50N 6 58W
Carlow □, Ire. 25 52 43N 6 50W
Carloway, U.K. 22 58 17N 6 48W
Carlton, U.K. 19 52 58N 1 6W
Carlton Colville, U.K. 15 52 27N 1 41 E
Carlton Miniott, U.K. 19 54 13N 1 22W
Carluke, U.K. 21 55 44N 3 50W
Carmarthen, U.K. 17 51 52N 4 20W
Carmarthen B., U.K. 17 51 40N 4 30W
Carnarvon, Austral. 66 24 51S 113 42 E
Carndonagh, Ire. 24 55 15N 7 16W
Carnegie, L., Austral. 66 26 5S 122 30 E
Carnforth, U.K. 18 54 8N 2 47W
Carno, U.K. 17 52 34N 3 31W
Carnoustie, U.K. 21 56 30N 2 41W
Carnsore Pt., Ire. 25 52 10N 6 20W
Carnwath, U.K. 21 55 42N 3 38W
Caroline Is., Pac. Oc. 64 8 0N 150 0 E
Carpathians, Mts., Europe 43 49 50N 21 0 E
Carpentaria, G. of, Austral. 67 14 0S 139 0 E
Carradale, U.K. 20 55 35N 5 30W
Carrauntoohill, Mt., Ire. 25 52 0N 9 49W
Carrick, U.K. 20 55 12N 4 38W
Carrick-on-Shannon, Ire. 24 53 57N 8 7W
Carrick-on-Suir, Ire. 25 52 22N 7 30W
Carrickfergus, U.K. 24 54 43N 5 50W
Carrickfergus □, U.K. 24 54 43N 5 49W
Carrickmacross, Ire. 24 54 0N 6 43W
Carron →, U.K. 22 57 30N 5 30W
Carron, L., U.K. 22 57 22N 5 35W
Carronbridge, U.K. 21 55 16N 3 46W
Carse of Gowrie, U.K. 21 56 30N 3 10W
Carsphairn, U.K. 20 55 13N 4 15W
Carstairs, U.K. 21 55 42N 3 41W
Cartagena, Col. 100 10 25N 75 33W
Cartagena, Sp. 37 37 38N 0 59W
Cartmel, U.K. 18 54 13N 2 57W
Caruaru, Brazil 101 8 15S 35 55W
Carúpano, Ven. 100 10 39N 63 15W
Casablanca, Mor. 78 33 36N 7 36W
Cascade Ra., U.S.A. 90 47 0N 121 30W
Cashel, Ire. 25 52 31N 7 53W
Casper, U.S.A. 90 42 52N 106 20W
Caspian Sea, U.S.S.R. 47 43 0N 50 0 E
Castellón □, Sp. 37 40 15N 0 5W
Castle Acre, U.K. 15 52 42N 0 42 E
Castle Cary, U.K. 14 51 5N 2 32W
Castle Donington, U.K. 14 52 50N 1 20W
Castle Douglas, U.K. 21 54 57N 3 57W
Castle Eden, U.K. 19 54 45N 1 20W
Castlebar, Ire. 24 53 52N 9 17W
Castlebay, U.K. 22 56 57N 7 30W
Castleblaney, Ire. 24 54 7N 6 44W
Castleford, U.K. 19 53 43N 1 21W
Castlereagh, Ire. 24 53 47N 8 30W
Castlereagh □, U.K. 24 54 33N 5 53W
Castlereagh →, Austral. 70 30 12S 147 32 E
Castleside, U.K. 18 54 50N 1 52W
Castleton, Derby, U.K. 19 53 20N 1 47W
Castleton, N. Yorks., U.K. 19 54 27N 0 57W
Castletown, U.K. 18 54 4N 4 40W
Castletown Bearhaven, Ire. 25 51 40N 9 54W
Castries, St. Lucia 94 14 0N 60 50W
Catánia, It. 40 37 31N 15 4 E
Catanzaro, It. 40 38 54N 16 38 E
Catcleugh, U.K. 21 55 19N 2 22W
Caterham, U.K. 15 51 16N 0 4W
Caton, U.K. 18 54 5N 2 41W
Catrine, U.K. 20 55 30N 4 20W
Catsfield, U.K. 15 50 53N 0 28 E
Catterick, U.K. 19 54 23N 1 38W
Catterick Camp, U.K. 19 54 22N 1 43W
Catton, U.K. 21 54 56N 2 16W
Caucasus, U.S.S.R. 47 43 0N 44 0 E
Caulkerbush, U.K. 21 54 54N 3 40W
Cavan, Ire. 24 54 0N 7 22W
Cavan □, Ire. 24 53 58N 7 10W
Cawood, U.K. 19 53 50N 1 7W
Cawston, U.K. 15 52 47N 1 10 E
Caxias, Brazil 101 4 55S 43 20W
Caxias do Sul, Brazil 102 29 10S 51 10W
Cayenne, Fr. G. 101 5 0N 52 18W
Ceanannus Mor, Ire. 24 53 42N 6 53W
Cebu, Phil. 63 10 18N 123 54 E
Cedar Rapids, U.S.A. 91 42 0N 91 38W
Celbridge, Ire. 25 53 20N 6 33W
Celebes = Sulawesi □, Indon. 63 2 0S 120 0 E
Celebes Sea, E. Ind. 63 3 0N 123 0 E
Cemaes Bay, U.K. 17 53 24N 4 27W
Central □, U.K. 20 56 10N 4 30W
Central African Republic ■, Africa 80 7 0N 20 0 E
Central Russian Uplands, U.S.S.R. 26 54 0N 36 0 E
Central Siberian Plateau, U.S.S.R. 49 65 0N 105 0 E
Cephalonia = Kefallinía, Greece 41 38 20N 20 30 E
Ceram, Indon. 63 3 10S 129 0 E
Ceres, U.K. 21 56 18N 2 57W
Cerignola, It. 40 41 17N 15 53 E
Cerne Abbas, U.K. 14 50 49N 2 29W
Cerrig-y-drudion, U.K. 17 53 2N 3 34W
Cessnock, Austral. 70 32 50S 151 21 E
Ceuta, Mor. 78 35 52N 5 18W
Cévennes, Fr. 35 44 10N 3 50 E
Ceylon = Sri Lanka ■, Asia 58 7 30N 80 50 E
Chacewater, U.K. 16 50 15N 5 8W
Chad ■, Africa 78 15 0N 17 15 E
Chad, L., Chad 79 13 30N 14 30 E
Chagford, U.K. 16 50 40N 3 50W
Chale, U.K. 14 50 35N 1 19W
Chalfont St. Peter, U.K. 15 51 36N 0 33W
Châlons-sur-Marne, Fr. 34 48 58N 4 20 E
Chambéry, Fr. 35 45 34N 5 55 E
Champagne, Fr. 34 48 40N 4 20 E
Champlain, L., U.S.A. 93 44 30N 73 20W
Chandigarh, India 58 30 43N 76 47 E
Chandler's Ford, U.K. 14 50 59N 1 23W
Changchun, China 61 43 58N 125 19 E
Changde, China 61 29 4N 111 35 E
Changsha, China 61 28 5N 113 1 E
Changzhou, China 61 31 47N 119 58 E
Channel Is., U.K. 34 49 30N 2 40W
Chao Phraya →, Thai. 63 13 32N 100 36 E
Chapel-en-le-Frith, U.K. 18 53 19N 1 54W
Chapel St. Leonards, U.K. 19 53 13N 0 19 E
Chard, U.K. 14 50 52N 2 59W
Chardzhou, U.S.S.R. 48 39 6N 63 34 E
Charing, U.K. 15 51 12N 0 49 E
Charlbury, U.K. 14 51 52N 1 29W
Charleroi, Belg. 36 50 24N 4 27 E
Charleston, U.S.A. 91 32 47N 79 56W
Charleville = Rath Luirc, Ire. 25 52 21N 8 40W
Charleville, Austral. 67 26 24S 146 15 E
Charleville-Mézières, Fr. 34 49 44N 4 40 E
Charlotte, U.S.A. 91 35 16N 80 46W
Charlottenburg, W. Ger. 42 52 31N 13 15 E
Charlottetown, Canada 93 46 14N 63 8W
Charlton Kings, U.K. 14 51 52N 2 3W
Charlwood, U.K. 15 51 8N 0 12W
Charminster, U.K. 14 50 43N 2 28W
Charmouth, U.K. 14 50 45N 2 54W
Charnwood Forest, U.K. 14 52 43N 1 18W
Charters Towers, Austral. 67 20 5S 146 13 E
Chartham, U.K. 15 51 14N 1 1 E
Chartres, Fr. 34 48 29N 1 30 E
Châteauroux, Fr. 34 46 50N 1 40 E
Chatham, U.K. 15 51 22N 0 32 E
Chattanooga, U.S.A. 91 35 2N 85 17W
Chatteris, U.K. 15 52 27N 0 3 E
Chatton, U.K. 21 55 34N 1 55W
Cheadle, Gr. Manchester, U.K. 18 53 23N 2 14W
Cheadle, Staffs., U.K. 18 52 59N 1 59W
Cheadle Hulme, U.K. 18 53 22N 2 12W
Cheboksary, U.S.S.R. 46 56 8N 47 12 E
Cheddar, U.K. 14 51 16N 2 47W
Cheddleton, U.K. 18 53 5N 2 2W
Chelmarsh, U.K. 14 52 29N 2 25W
Chelmer →, U.K. 15 51 45N 0 42 E
Chelmsford, U.K. 15 51 44N 0 29 E
Cheltenham, U.K. 14 51 55N 2 5W
Chelyabinsk, U.S.S.R. 48 55 10N 61 24 E
Chenab →, Pak. 58 30 23N 71 2 E
Chengdu, China 60 30 38N 104 2 E
Chepstow, U.K. 17 51 38N 2 40W
Cherbourg, Fr. 34 49 39N 1 40W
Cheremkhovo, U.S.S.R. 49 53 8N 103 1 E
Cherepovets, U.S.S.R. 46 59 5N 37 55 E
Cheriton, U.K. 14 51 3N 1 9W
Cheriton Fitzpaine, U.K. 16 50 51N 3 38W
Cherkassy, U.S.S.R. 47 49 27N 32 4 E
Chernigov, U.S.S.R. 46 51 28N 31 20 E
Chernovtsy, U.S.S.R. 47 48 15N 25 52 E
Chertsey, U.K. 15 51 23N 0 30W
Cherwell →, U.K. 14 51 46N 1 18W
Chesapeake Bay, U.S.A. 92 38 0N 76 12W
Chesham, U.K. 15 51 42N 0 36W
Cheshire □, U.K. 18 53 14N 2 30W
Cheshunt, U.K. 15 51 42N 0 1W
Chesil Beach, U.K. 14 50 37N 2 33W
Chester, U.K. 18 53 12N 2 53W
Chester-le-Street, U.K. 19 54 53N 1 34W
Chesterfield, U.K. 19 53 14N 1 26W
Chesterfield Inlet, Canada 88 63 30N 90 45W
Cheviot, The, U.K. 19 55 29N 2 8W
Cheviot Hills, U.K. 19 55 20N 2 30W
Chew Magna, U.K. 14 51 21N 2 37W
Chiai, China 61 23 29N 120 25 E
Chiba, Jap. 62 35 30N 140 7 E
Chicago, U.S.A. 92 41 53N 87 40W
Chichester, U.K. 15 50 50N 0 47W
Chiclayo, Peru 100 6 42S 79 50W
Chicoutimi, Canada 93 48 28N 71 5W
Chiddingfold, U.K. 15 51 6N 0 37W
Chidley, C., Canada 89 60 23N 64 26W
Chieti, It. 40 42 22N 14 10 E
Chihli, G. of, China 61 38 30N 119 0 E
Chihuahua, Mex. 94 28 40N 106 3W
Chile ■, S. Am. 102 35 0S 72 0W
Chilham, U.K. 15 51 15N 0 59 E
Chillán, Chile 102 36 40S 72 10W
Chilpancingo, Mex. 94 17 30N 99 30W
Chiltern Hills, U.K. 15 51 44N 0 42W
Chilung, Taiwan 61 25 3N 121 45 E
Chimborazo, Ecuad. 100 1 29S 78 55W
Chimbote, Peru 100 9 0S 78 35W
Chimkent, U.S.S.R. 48 42 18N 69 36 E
China ■, Asia 60 30 0N 110 0 E
Chincha Alta, Peru 100 13 25S 76 7W
Chingola, Zam. 81 12 31S 27 53 E
Chipata, Zam. 81 13 38S 32 28 E
Chippenham, U.K. 14 51 27N 2 7W
Chipping Campden, U.K. 14 52 4N 1 48W
Chipping Norton, U.K. 14 51 56N 1 32W
Chipping Ongar, U.K. 15 51 43N 0 15 E
Chipping Sodbury, U.K. 14 51 31N 2 23W
Chirbury, U.K. 14 52 35N 3 6W
Chirnside, U.K. 21 55 47N 2 11W
Chiseldon, U.K. 14 51 30N 1 44W
Chita, U.S.S.R. 49 52 0N 113 35 E
Chittagong, Bangla. 59 22 19N 91 48 E

Chollerton, *U.K.* 21 55 4N 2 7W
Cholsey, *U.K.* 14 51 34N 1 10W
Chongjin, *N. Kor.* 61 41 47N 129 50 E
Chongqing = Chungking, *China* 60 29 35N 106 25 E
Chorley, *U.K.* 18 53 39N 2 39W
Chorrera, La, *Pan.* 94 8 50N 79 50W
Chorzów, *Pol.* 43 50 18N 18 57 E
Choybalsan, *Mong.* 61 48 4N 114 30 E
Christchurch, *N.Z.* 71 43 33S 172 47 E
Christchurch, *U.K.* 14 50 44N 1 33W
Chudleigh, *U.K.* 16 50 35N 3 36W
Chulmleigh, *U.K.* 16 50 55N 3 52W
Chungking, *China* 60 29 35N 106 25 E
Chur, *Switz.* 42 46 52N 9 32 E
Church Stretton, *U.K.* 14 52 32N 2 49W
Churchdown, *U.K.* 14 51 53N 2 9W
Churchill →, *Canada* 88 58 47N 94 12W
Ciénaga, *Col.* 100 11 1N 74 15W
Cienfuegos, *Cuba* 95 22 10N 80 30W
Cincinnati, *U.S.A.* 92 39 10N 84 26W
Cinderford, *U.K.* 14 51 49N 2 30W
Cirencester, *U.K.* 14 51 43N 1 59W
Citlaltépetl, *Mex.* 94 19 0N 97 20W
Ciudad Bolívar, *Ven.* 100 8 5N 63 36W
Ciudad Guayana, *Ven.* 100 8 0N 62 30W
Ciudad Juárez, *Mex.* 94 31 40N 106 28W
Ciudad Madero, *Mex.* 94 22 19N 97 50W
Ciudad Obregón, *Mex.* 94 27 28N 109 59W
Ciudad Real, *Sp.* 37 38 59N 3 55W
Ciudad Victoria, *Mex.* 94 23 41N 99 9W
Clabhach, *U.K.* 20 56 38N 6 36W
Clach Leathad, *U.K.* 20 56 36N 7 52W
Clachan, *U.K.* 20 55 45N 5 35W
Clackmannan, *U.K.* 21 56 10N 3 50W
Clacton-on-Sea, *U.K.* 15 51 47N 1 10 E
Cladich, *U.K.* 20 56 21N 5 5W
Clara, *Ire.* 25 53 20N 7 38W
Clare, *U.K.* 15 52 5N 0 36 E
Clare □, *Ire.* 25 52 20N 9 0W
Clare →, *Ire.* 24 53 22N 9 5W
Clare I., *Ire.* 24 53 48N 10 0W
Claremorris, *Ire.* 24 53 45N 9 0W
Clarksville, *U.S.A.* 91 36 32N 87 20W
Clatteringshaws L., *U.K.* 20 55 3N 4 17W
Claverley, *U.K.* 14 52 32N 2 19W
Clay Cross, *U.K.* 19 53 11N 1 26W
Clay Hd., *U.K.* 18 54 13N 4 23W
Claydon, *U.K.* 15 52 6N 1 7 E
Clear, C., *Ire.* 25 51 26N 9 30W
Clear I., *Ire.* 25 51 26N 9 30W
Cleator Moor, *U.K.* 18 54 30N 3 32W
Clee Hills, *U.K.* 14 52 26N 2 35W
Cleethorpes, *U.K.* 19 53 33N 0 2W
Cleeve Cloud, *U.K.* 14 51 56N 2 0W
Clent, *U.K.* 14 52 25N 2 6W
Cleobury Mortimer, *U.K.* 14 52 23N 2 28W
Clermont-Ferrand, *Fr.* 35 45 46N 3 4 E
Clevedon, *U.K.* 14 51 26N 2 52W
Cleveland, *U.S.A.* 92 41 28N 81 43W
Cleveland □, *U.K.* 19 54 35N 1 8 E
Cleveland Hills, *U.K.* 19 54 25N 1 11W
Clew B., *Ire.* 24 53 54N 9 50W
Cley, *U.K.* 15 52 57N 1 3 E
Clifden, *Ire.* 24 53 30N 10 2W
Cliffe, *U.K.* 15 51 27N 0 31 E
Clifford, *U.K.* 14 52 6N 3 6W
Clipston, *U.K.* 15 52 26N 0 58W
Clitheroe, *U.K.* 18 53 52N 2 23W
Clonakilty, *Ire.* 25 51 37N 8 53W
Clonakilty B., *Ire.* 25 51 33N 8 50W
Cloncurry, *Austral.* 67 20 40S 140 28 E
Clones, *Ire.* 24 54 10N 7 13W
Clonmel, *Ire.* 25 52 22N 7 42W
Closeburn, *U.K.* 21 55 13N 3 45W
Cloughton, *U.K.* 19 54 20N 0 27W
Clovelly, *U.K.* 16 51 0N 4 25W
Clowne, *U.K.* 19 53 18N 1 16W
Cluj-Napoca, *Rom.* 43 46 47N 23 38 E
Clun, *U.K.* 14 52 26N 3 2W
Clun Forest, *U.K.* 14 52 27N 3 7W
Clunbury, *U.K.* 14 52 25N 2 55W
Clwyd □, *U.K.* 17 53 5N 3 20W
Clwyd →, *U.K.* 17 53 20N 3 30W
Clyde →, *U.K.* 20 55 56N 4 29W
Clyde, Firth of, *U.K.* 20 55 20N 5 0W
Clydebank, *U.K.* 20 55 54N 4 25W
Clydesdale, *U.K.* 21 55 42N 3 50W
Coalbrookdale, *U.K.* 14 52 38N 2 30W
Coalburn, *U.K.* 21 55 35N 3 55W
Coalville, *U.K.* 14 52 43N 1 21W
Coast Mts., *Canada* 88 55 0N 129 0W
Coast Ranges, *U.S.A.* 90 41 0N 123 0W
Coatbridge, *U.K.* 21 55 52N 4 2W
Coatzacoalcos, *Mex.* 94 18 7N 94 25W
Cóbh, *Ire.* 25 51 50N 8 18W
Cobourg Pen., *Austral.* 66 11 20S 132 15 E
Cochabamba, *Bol.* 100 17 26S 66 10W
Cochin, *India* 58 9 59N 76 22 E
Cockburnspath, *U.K.* 21 55 56N 2 23W
Cockenzie, *U.K.* 21 55 58N 2 59W
Cockerham, *U.K.* 18 53 58N 2 49W
Cockermouth, *U.K.* 18 54 40N 3 22W
Cockfield, *U.K.* 15 52 8N 0 47 E
Cod, C., *U.S.A.* 93 42 8N 70 10W
Coddenham, *U.K.* 15 52 8N 1 8 E
Coffs Harbour, *Austral.* 67 30 16S 153 5 E
Coggeshall, *U.K.* 15 51 53N 0 41 E
Coimbatore, *India* 58 11 2N 76 59 E
Coimbra, *Port.* 37 40 15N 8 27W
Colac, *Austral.* 70 38 21S 143 35 E
Colby, *U.K.* 18 54 6N 4 42W
Colchester, *U.K.* 15 51 54N 0 55 E
Cold Fell, *U.K.* 18 54 54N 2 40W
Coldingham, *U.K.* 21 55 53N 2 10W
Coldstream, *U.K.* 21 55 39N 2 14W
Colebrooke, *U.K.* 16 50 45N 3 44W
Coleford, *U.K.* 14 51 46N 2 38W
Coleraine, *U.K.* 24 55 8N 6 40W
Coleraine □, *U.K.* 24 55 8N 6 40 E
Coleshill, *U.K.* 14 52 30N 1 42W
Colima, *Mex.* 94 19 14N 103 43W
Colinton, *U.K.* 21 55 54N 3 17W
Coll, *U.K.* 20 56 40N 6 35W
Collie, *Austral.* 66 33 22S 116 8 E
Collier Law Pk., *U.K.* 18 54 47N 1 59W
Collin, *U.K.* 21 55 4N 3 30W
Collingbourne, *U.K.* 14 51 16N 1 39W
Collooney, *Ire.* 24 54 11N 8 28W
Colmar, *Fr.* 34 48 5N 7 20 E
Colmonel, *U.K.* 20 55 8N 4 55W
Colne, *U.K.* 18 53 51N 2 11W
Colne →, *Essex, U.K.* 15 51 55N 0 50 E
Colne →, *Herts., U.K.* 15 51 36N 0 30W
Cologne, *W. Ger.* 36 50 56N 6 58 E
Colombia ■, *S. Am.* 100 3 45N 73 0W
Colombo, *Sri L.* 58 6 56N 79 58 E
Colón, *Mex.* 94 20 48N 100 3W
Colonsay, *U.K.* 20 56 4N 6 12W
Colorado □, *U.S.A.* 90 37 40N 106 0W
Colorado →, *Calif., U.S.A.* 90 34 45N 114 40W
Colorado →, *Tex., U.S.A.* 90 28 36N 95 58W
Colorado Plateau, *U.S.A.* 90 36 40N 110 30W
Colorado Springs, *U.S.A.* 90 38 55N 104 50W
Colstorworth, *U.K.* 15 52 48N 0 37W
Coltishall, *U.K.* 15 52 44N 1 21 E
Columbia, *Miss., U.S.A.* 90 31 16N 89 50W
Columbia, *S.C., U.S.A.* 91 34 0N 81 0W
Columbia →, *N. Am.* 90 46 15N 124 5W
Columbus, *Ga., U.S.A.* 91 32 30N 84 58W
Columbus, *Ohio, U.S.A.* 92 39 57N 83 1W
Colwell, *U.K.* 21 55 4N 2 4W
Colwich, *U.K.* 14 52 48N 1 58W
Colwyn Bay, *U.K.* 17 53 17N 3 44W
Colyton, *U.K.* 16 50 44N 3 4W
Combe Martin, *U.K.* 16 51 12N 4 2W
Comber, *U.K.* 24 54 33N 5 45W
Comeragh Mts., *Ire.* 25 52 17N 7 35W
Comilla, *Bangla.* 59 23 28N 91 10 E
Comino, *Malta* 40 36 0N 14 20 E
Communism Pk., *U.S.S.R.* 48 38 40N 72 20 E
Como, *It.* 40 45 48N 9 5 E
Como, L., *It.* 40 46 5N 9 17 E
Comodoro Rivadavia, *Arg.* 102 45 50S 67 40W
Comorin, C., *India* 58 8 3N 77 40 E
Comoro Is. ■, *Ind. Oc.* 73 12 10S 44 15 E
Compiègne, *Fr.* 34 49 24N 2 50 E
Comrie, *U.K.* 21 56 22N 4 0W
Conakry, *Guin.* 78 9 29N 13 49W
Concepción, *Chile* 102 36 50S 73 0W
Conchos →, *Mex.* 94 29 32N 104 25W
Concordia, *Arg.* 102 31 20S 58 2W
Condover, *U.K.* 14 52 39N 2 46W
Congleton, *U.K.* 18 53 10N 2 12W
Congo = Zaïre →, *Africa* 80 6 4S 12 24 E
Congo ■, *Africa* 80 1 0S 16 0 E
Congo Basin, *Africa* 72 0 10S 24 30 E
Congresbury, *U.K.* 14 51 20N 2 49W
Coningsby, *U.K.* 19 53 7N 0 9W
Conisbrough, *U.K.* 19 53 29N 1 12W
Coniston, *U.K.* 18 54 22N 3 6W
Coniston Water, *U.K.* 18 54 20N 3 5W
Conn, L., *Ire.* 24 54 3N 9 15W
Connacht, *Ire.* 24 53 23N 8 40W
Connah's Quay, *U.K.* 17 53 13N 3 6W
Connecticut □, *U.S.A.* 93 41 40N 72 40W
Connecticut →, *U.S.A.* 93 41 17N 72 21W
Connel, *U.K.* 20 56 27N 5 24W
Connel Park, *U.K.* 20 55 22N 4 15W
Connemara, *Ire.* 24 53 29N 9 45W
Conon →, *U.K.* 23 57 33N 4 28W
Cononbridge, *U.K.* 23 57 32N 4 30W
Consett, *U.K.* 18 54 52N 1 50W
Constance, L. = Bodensee, *W. Ger.* 42 47 35N 9 25 E
Constanța, *Rom.* 43 44 14N 28 38 E
Constantine, *Alg.* 78 36 25N 6 42 E
Conwy, *U.K.* 17 53 17N 3 50W
Conwy →, *U.K.* 17 53 18N 3 50W
Cook, Mt., *N.Z.* 71 43 36S 170 9 E
Cook Is., *Pac. Oc.* 65 17 0S 160 0W
Cook Strait, *N.Z.* 71 41 15S 174 29 E
Cookham, *U.K.* 15 51 33N 0 42W
Cookstown, *U.K.* 24 54 40N 6 43W
Cookstown □, *U.K.* 24 54 40N 6 43W
Coolgardie, *Austral.* 66 30 55S 121 8 E
Cootamundra, *Austral.* 70 34 36S 148 1 E
Cootehill, *Ire.* 24 54 5N 7 5W
Copenhagen, *Den.* 45 55 41N 12 34 E
Coppermine, *Canada* 88 67 50N 115 5W
Coppermine →, *Canada* 88 67 49N 116 4W
Copythorne, *U.K.* 14 50 56N 1 34W
Coquet →, *U.K.* 19 55 18N 1 45W
Coquet, I., *U.K.* 21 55 21N 1 30W
Coral Sea, *Pac. Oc.* 64 15 0S 150 0 E
Coral Sea Islands Terr., *Austral.* 67 20 0S 155 0 E
Corbridge, *U.K.* 21 54 58N 2 0W
Corby, *U.K.* 15 52 29N 0 41W
Corby Glen, *U.K.* 15 49N 0 31W
Córdoba, *Arg.* 102 31 20S 64 10W
Córdoba, *Sp.* 37 37 50N 4 50W
Cordova, *U.S.A.* 88 60 36N 145 45W
Corfe Castle, *U.K.* 14 50 37N 2 3W
Corfe Mullen, *U.K.* 14 50 45N 2 0W
Corfu = Kérkira, *Greece* 41 39 38N 19 50 E
Corinth, G. of, *Greece* 41 38 16N 22 30 E
Cork, *Ire.* 25 51 54N 8 30W
Cork □, *Ire.* 25 51 50N 8 50W
Cork Harbour, *Ire.* 25 51 46N 8 16W
Corner Brook, *Canada* 89 48 57N 57 58W
Cornforth, *U.K.* 19 54 42N 1 28W
Cornwall □, *U.K.* 16 50 26N 4 40W
Cornwall, C., *U.K.* 16 50 8N 5 42W
Coro, *Ven.* 100 11 25N 69 41W
Coromandel Coast, *India* 58 12 30N 81 0 E
Coronation Gulf, *Canada* 88 68 25N 110 0W
Corpus Christi, *U.S.A.* 90 27 50N 97 28W
Corrib, L., *Ire.* 24 53 5N 9 10W
Corrie, *U.K.* 20 55 39N 5 10W
Corrientes, *Arg.* 102 27 30S 58 45W
Corringham, *U.K.* 19 53 25N 0 42W
Corryvreckan, G. of, *U.K.* 20 56 10N 5 44W
Corsewall Pt., *U.K.* 20 55 0N 5 10W
Corsham, *U.K.* 14 51 25N 2 11W
Corsica, I., *Medit. S.* 35 42 0N 9 0 E
Corsley, *U.K.* 14 51 12N 2 14W
Corsock, *U.K.* 21 55 54N 3 56W
Corton, *U.K.* 15 52 31N 1 46 E
Corumbá, *Brazil* 100 19 0S 57 30W
Coruña, La, *Sp.* 37 43 20N 8 25W
Corve →, *U.K.* 14 52 22N 2 43W
Coseley, *U.K.* 14 52 33N 2 6W
Cosenza, *It.* 40 39 17N 16 14 E
Cosham, *U.K.* 14 50 51N 1 3W
Costa Rica ■, *Cent. Am.* 95 10 0N 84 0W
Costessey, *U.K.* 15 52 40N 1 11 E
Côte d'Or, *Fr.* 34 47 10N 4 50 E
Cotherstone, *U.K.* 18 54 34N 1 59W
Cotonou, *Benin* 78 6 20N 2 25 E
Cotopaxi, Vol., *Ecuad.* 100 0 40S 78 30W
Cotswold Hills, *U.K.* 14 51 42N 2 10W
Cottbus, *E. Ger.* 42 51 44N 14 20 E
Cottenham, *U.K.* 15 52 18N 0 8 E
Cottingham, *U.K.* 19 53 47N 0 29W
Coulport, *U.K.* 20 56 3N 4 53W
Council Bluffs, *U.S.A.* 90 41 20N 95 50W
Coupar Angus, *U.K.* 21 56 33N 3 17W
Coventry, *U.K.* 14 52 25N 1 31W
Cover →, *U.K.* 18 54 14N 1 45W
Coverack, *U.K.* 16 50 2N 5 6W
Covington, *U.S.A.* 92 39 5N 84 30W
Cowal, *U.K.* 20 56 5N 5 8W
Cowan, L., *Austral.* 66 31 45S 121 45 E
Cowbridge, *U.K.* 17 51 28N 3 28W
Cowdenbeath, *U.K.* 21 56 7N 3 20W
Cowes, *U.K.* 14 50 45N 1 18W
Cowfold, *U.K.* 15 50 58N 0 16W
Cowley, *U.K.* 14 51 43N 1 12W
Cowpen, *U.K.* 21 55 8N 1 34W
Cowra, *Austral.* 70 33 49S 148 42 E
Craigavon □, *U.K.* 24 54 30N 6 25W
Craighouse, *U.K.* 20 55 50N 5 58W
Craignish, L., *U.K.* 20 56 11N 5 32W
Crail, *U.K.* 21 56 16N 2 38W
Craiova, *Rom.* 43 44 21N 23 48 E
Cramlington, *U.K.* 21 55 5N 1 36W
Cranborne, *U.K.* 14 50 55N 1 55W
Cranborne Chase, *U.K.* 14 50 56N 2 6W
Cranbrook, *Canada* 88 49 30N 115 46W
Cranbrook, *U.K.* 15 51 6N 0 33 E
Cranleigh, *U.K.* 15 51 8N 0 29W
Cranshaws, *U.K.* 21 55 51N 2 30W
Cranwell, *U.K.* 19 53 4N 0 29W
Craven Arms, *U.K.* 14 52 27N 2 49W
Crawford, *U.K.* 21 55 28N 3 40W
Crawley, *U.K.* 15 51 7N 0 10W
Credenhill, *U.K.* 14 52 6N 2 49W
Crediton, *U.K.* 16 50 47N 3 39W
Cree →, *U.K.* 20 54 51N 4 24W
Creeside, *U.K.* 20 55 4N 4 41W
Creetown, *U.K.* 20 54 54N 4 23W
Cremona, *It.* 40 45 8N 10 2 E
Crete, I., *Greece* 41 35 15N 25 0 E
Creusot, Le, *Fr.* 34 46 48N 4 24 E
Crewe, *U.K.* 18 53 6N 2 28W
Crewkerne, *U.K.* 14 50 53N 2 48W
Crianlarich, *U.K.* 20 56 24N 4 37W
Criccieth, *U.K.* 17 52 55N 4 15W
Crick, *U.K.* 14 52 22N 1 9W
Crickhowell, *U.K.* 17 51 52N 3 8W
Cricklade, *U.K.* 14 51 38N 1 50W
Crieff, *U.K.* 21 56 22N 3 50W
Criffell, *U.K.* 21 54 56N 3 38W
Crimea, *U.S.S.R.* 47 45 0N 34 0 E
Crinan, *U.K.* 20 56 6N 5 34W
Crinan Canal, *U.K.* 20 56 4N 5 30W
Croaghpatrick, *Ire.* 24 53 46N 9 40W
Crocketford, *U.K.* 21 55 3N 3 49W
Croglin, *U.K.* 18 54 50N 2 37W
Cromarty, *U.K.* 23 57 40N 4 2W
Cromarty Firth, *U.K.* 23 57 40N 4 15W
Cromer, *U.K.* 15 52 56N 1 18 E
Crondall, *U.K.* 15 51 13N 0 51W
Crook, *U.K.* 19 54 43N 1 45W
Crooklands, *U.K.* 18 54 16N 2 43W
Crosby, *Cumbria, U.K.* 18 54 45N 3 25W
Crosby, *Merseyside, U.K.* 18 53 30N 3 2W
Crosby Ravensworth, *U.K.* 18 54 34N 2 35W
Cross Fell, *U.K.* 18 54 44N 2 29W
Crosshaven, *Ire.* 25 51 48N 8 19W
Crosshill, *U.K.* 20 55 19N 4 39W
Crouch →, *U.K.* 15 51 37N 0 53 E
Crow Hd., *Ire.* 25 51 34N 10 9W
Crow Sound, *U.K.* 16 49 56N 6 16W
Crowborough, *U.K.* 15 51 3N 0 9 E
Crowland, *U.K.* 15 52 41N 0 10W
Crowle, *U.K.* 19 53 36N 0 49W
Croyde, *U.K.* 16 51 7N 4 13W
Croydon, *U.K.* 15 51 18N 0 5W
Crudgington, *U.K.* 14 52 46N 2 33W
Crummock Water, *U.K.* 18 54 33N 3 18W
Cruzeiro do Sul, *Brazil* 100 7 35S 72 35W
Cuba ■, *W. Ind.* 95 22 0N 79 0W
Cuckfield, *U.K.* 15 51 0N 0 8W
Cúcuta, *Col.* 100 7 54N 72 31W
Cudworth, *U.K.* 19 53 35N 1 25W
Cuenca, *Ecuad.* 100 2 50S 79 9W
Cuenca, *Sp.* 37 40 5N 2 10W
Cuernavaca, *Mex.* 94 18 55N 99 15W
Cuiabá, *Brazil* 101 15 30S 56 0W
Cuillin Hills, *U.K.* 22 57 14N 6 15W
Cuillin Sd., *U.K.* 22 57 4N 6 20W
Culiacán, *Mex.* 94 24 50N 107 23W
Cullen, *U.K.* 23 57 45N 2 50W
Culloden Moor, *U.K.* 23 57 29N 4 7W
Cullompton, *U.K.* 16 50 52N 3 23W
Culm →, *U.K.* 16 50 46N 3 31W
Culrain, *U.K.* 23 57 55N 4 25W
Culross, *U.K.* 21 56 4N 3 38W
Cumaná, *Ven.* 100 10 30N 64 5W
Cumberland Plateau, *U.S.A.* 91 36 0N 84 30W
Cumbrae Is., *U.K.* 20 55 46N 4 54W
Cumbria □, *U.K.* 18 54 35N 2 55W
Cumbrian Mts., *U.K.* 18 54 30N 3 0W
Cummertrees, *U.K.* 21 55 0N 3 20W
Cumnock, *U.K.* 20 55 27N 4 18W
Cumnor, *U.K.* 14 51 44N 1 20W
Cumwhinton, *U.K.* 18 54 51N 2 49W
Cúneo, *It.* 40 44 23N 7 31 E
Cunninghame, *U.K.* 20 55 38N 4 35W
Cupar, *U.K.* 21 56 20N 3 0W
Curitiba, *Brazil* 102 25 20S 49 10W
Currie, *U.K.* 21 55 53N 3 17W
Curry Rivel, *U.K.* 14 51 2N 2 52W
Cuttack, *India* 59 20 25N 85 57 E
Cuzco, *Peru* 100 13 32S 72 0W
Cwmbran, *U.K.* 17 51 39N 3 0W
Cyclades = Kikládhes, *Greece* 41 37 20N 24 30 E
Cyprus ■, *Medit. S.* 47 35 0N 33 0 E
Czechoslovakia ■, *Europe* 42 49 0N 17 0 E
Częstochowa, *Pol.* 43 50 49N 19 7 E

D

Da Lat, *Viet.* 63 11 56N 108 25 E
Da Nang, *Viet.* 63 16 4N 108 13 E
Dacca, *Bangla.* 59 23 43N 90 26 E
Daer →, *U.K.* 21 55 23N 3 39W
Dailly, *U.K.* 20 55 16N 4 44W
Daingean, *Ire.* 25 53 18N 7 15W
Dakar, *Sene.* 78 14 34N 17 29W
Dakhla, *W. Sah.* 78 23 50N 15 53W
Dalbeattie, *U.K.* 21 54 55N 3 50W
Dalian, *China* 61 38 50N 121 40 E
Dalkeith, *U.K.* 21 55 54N 3 5W
Dallas, *U.S.A.* 91 32 50N 96 50W
Dalmally, *U.K.* 20 56 25N 5 0W
Dalmatia, *Yug.* 40 43 20N 17 0 E
Dalmellington, *U.K.* 20 55 20N 4 25W
Daloa, *Ivory C.* 78 7 0N 6 30W
Dalry, *U.K.* 20 55 44N 4 42W
Dalrymple, *U.K.* 20 55 24N 4 36W
Dalton, *Cumbria, U.K.* 18 54 9N 3 11W
Dalton, *Dumf. & Gall., U.K.* 21 55 3N 3 22W
Dalton, *N. Yorks., U.K.* 19 54 28N 1 32W
Dalwhinnie, *U.K.* 23 56 56N 4 14W
Damascus, *Syria* 57 33 30N 36 18 E
Damerham, *U.K.* 14 50 57N 1 52W
Dampier, *Austral.* 66 20 41S 116 42 E
Dandenong, *Austral.* 70 38 0S 145 15 E
Dandong, *China* 61 40 10N 124 20 E
Dannevirke, *N.Z.* 71 40 12S 176 8 E
Danube →, *Europe* 43 45 20N 29 40 E
Dar-es-Salaam, *Tanz.* 80 6 50S 39 12 E
Dar'ā, *Syria* 57 32 36N 36 7 E
Dardanelles, *Turk.* 47 40 0N 26 0 E
Darent →, *U.K.* 15 51 22N 0 12 E

Dargaville, N.Z. 71 35 57S 173 52 E
Darién, G. del, Col. 95 9 0N 77 0W
Darlaston, U.K. 14 52 35N 2 1W
Darling →, Austral. 70 34 4S 141 54 E
Darling Ra., Austral. 66 32 30S 116 0 E
Darlington, U.K. 19 54 33N 1 33W
Darmstadt, W. Ger. 42 49 51N 8 40 E
Dart →, U.K. 16 50 24N 3 36W
Dartford, U.K. 15 51 26N 0 15 E
Dartington, U.K. 16 50 26N 3 42W
Dartmoor, U.K. 16 50 36N 4 0W
Dartmouth, Canada 93 44 40N 63 30W
Dartmouth, U.K. 16 50 21N 3 35W
Darton, U.K. 19 53 36N 1 32W
Darvel, U.K. 20 55 37N 4 20W
Darwen, U.K. 18 53 42N 2 29W
Darwin, Austral. 66 12 25S 130 51 E
Dasht-e Kavīr, Iran 57 34 30N 55 0 E
Dasht-e Lūt, Iran 57 31 30N 58 0 E
Datong, China 61 40 6N 113 18 E
Dauphin, Canada 88 51 9N 100 5W
Dauphiné, Fr. 35 45 15N 5 25 E
Davao, Phil. 63 7 0N 125 40 E
Davenport, U.S.A. 92 41 30N 90 40W
Daventry, U.K. 14 52 16N 1 10W
David, Pan. 95 8 30N 82 30W
Davis Str., N. Am. 89 65 0N 58 0W
Dawley, U.K. 14 52 40N 2 29W
Dawlish, U.K. 16 50 34N 3 28W
Dawson, Canada 88 64 10N 139 30W
Dawson Creek, Canada 88 55 45N 120 15W
Dayton, U.S.A. 92 39 45N 84 10W
De Aar, S. Afr. 81 30 39S 24 0 E
De Grey →, Austral. 66 20 12S 119 13 E
Dead Sea, Asia 57 31 30N 35 30 E
Deal, U.K. 15 51 13N 1 25 E
Dean, Forest of, U.K. 14 51 50N 2 35W
Dearham, U.K. 18 54 43N 3 28W
Dease Lake, Canada 88 58 25N 130 6W
Death Valley, U.S.A. 90 36 19N 116 52W
Deben →, U.K. 15 52 4N 1 19 E
Debenham, U.K. 15 52 14N 1 10 E
Debrecen, Hung. 43 47 33N 21 42 E
Deccan, India 58 18 0N 79 0 E
Deddington, U.K. 14 51 58N 1 19W
Dee →, Scotland, U.K. 23 57 4N 2 7W
Dee →, Wales, U.K. 17 53 15N 3 7W
Deeping St. Nicholas, U.K. 15 52 44N 0 11W
Deeping Fen, U.K. 15 52 45N 0 15W
Dehra Dun, India 58 30 20N 78 4 E
Delabole, U.K. 16 50 37N 4 45W
Delaware □, U.S.A. 93 39 0N 75 40W
Delaware →, U.S.A. 93 39 20N 75 25W
Delft, Neth. 36 52 1N 4 22 E
Delhi, India 58 28 38N 77 17 E
Den Helder, Neth. 36 52 57N 4 45 E
Denbigh, U.K. 17 53 12N 3 26W
Denby Dale, U.K. 19 53 35N 1 40W
Deniliquin, Austral. 70 35 30S 144 58 E
Denizli, Turk. 47 37 42N 29 2 E
Denmark ■, Europe 45 55 30N 9 0 E
Denmark Str., Atl. Oc. 103 66 0N 30 0W
Denny, U.K. 21 56 1N 3 55W
Dent, U.K. 18 54 17N 2 28W
Denton, E. Sussex, U.K. 15 50 48N 0 5 E
Denton, Gr. Manchester, U.K. 18 53 26N 2 10W
Denton, Lincs., U.K. 19 52 52N 0 42W
Denver, U.S.A. 90 39 45N 105 0W
Derby, U.K. 19 52 55N 1 28W
Derby □, U.K. 19 52 55N 1 28W
Derg →, U.K. 24 54 42N 7 26W
Derg, L., Ire. 25 53 0N 8 20W
Derry = Londonderry, U.K. 24 55 0N 7 20W
Derryveagh Mts., Ire. 24 55 0N 8 40W
Dervaig, U.K. 20 56 35N 6 13W
Derwent →, Derby, U.K. 19 52 53N 1 17W
Derwent →, N. Yorks., U.K. 19 53 45N 0 57W
Derwent →, Tyne & Wear, U.K. 21 54 58N 1 40W
Derwent Water, L., U.K. 18 54 35N 3 9W
Des Moines, U.S.A. 91 41 35N 93 37W
Des Moines →, U.S.A. 91 40 23N 91 25W
Desborough, U.K. 15 52 27N 0 50W
Desford, U.K. 14 52 38N 1 19W
Dessau, E. Ger. 42 51 49N 12 15 E
Detroit, U.S.A. 92 42 23N 83 5W
Deurne, Belg. 36 51 12N 4 24 E
Deventer, Neth. 36 52 15N 6 10 E
Deveron →, U.K. 23 57 40N 2 31W
Devizes, U.K. 14 51 21N 2 0W
Devonport, N.Z. 71 36 49S 174 49 E
Devonport, U.K. 16 50 23N 4 11W
Devonshire □, U.K. 16 50 50N 3 40W
Dewsbury, U.K. 19 53 42N 1 38W
Dhanbad, India 59 23 50N 86 30 E
Dharwad, India 58 15 22N 75 15 E
Dhule, India 58 20 58N 74 50 E
Diamantina →, Austral. 67 26 45S 139 10 E
Dibden, U.K. 14 50 53N 1 24W
Didcot, U.K. 14 51 36N 1 14W
Dieppe, Fr. 34 49 54N 1 4 E
Dijon, Fr. 34 47 20N 5 0 E
Dillingham, U.S.A. 88 59 5N 158 30W
Dinaric Alps, Yug. 40 44 0N 16 30 E
Dingle, Ire. 25 52 9N 10 17W
Dingle B., Ire. 25 52 3N 10 20W
Dingwall, U.K. 23 57 36N 4 26W
Diss, U.K. 15 52 23N 1 6 E
Distington, U.K. 18 54 35N 3 33W
Ditchingham, U.K. 15 52 28N 1 26 E
Ditchling Beacon, U.K. 15 50 49N 0 7W
Dittisham, U.K. 16 50 22N 3 36W
Ditton Priors, U.K. 14 52 30N 2 33W
Diyarbakir, Turk. 47 37 55N 40 18 E
Dizzard Pt., U.K. 16 50 46N 4 38W
Djibouti ■, Africa 56 12 0N 43 0 E
Dnepr →, U.S.S.R. 46 46 30N 32 18 E
Dneprodzerzhinsk, U.S.S.R. 47 48 32N 34 37 E
Dnepropetrovsk, U.S.S.R. 47 48 30N 35 0 E
Dnestr →, U.S.S.R. 47 46 18N 30 17 E
Docking, U.K. 15 52 55N 0 39 E
Doddington, Cambs., U.K. 15 52 29N 0 3 E
Doddington, Northumberland, U.K. 21 55 33N 2 0W
Dodecanese, Greece 41 36 35N 27 0 E
Dodman Pt., U.K. 16 50 13N 4 49W
Dodoma, Tanz. 80 6 8S 35 45 E
Dogger Bank, N. Sea 26 54 50N 2 0 E
Dolgarrog, U.K. 17 53 11N 3 50W
Dolgellau, U.K. 17 52 44N 3 53W
Dollar, U.K. 21 56 9N 3 41W
Dolomites, It. 40 46 30N 11 40 E
Dolphinton, U.K. 21 55 42N 3 28W
Dolton, U.K. 16 50 53N 4 2W
Dominica ■, W. Ind. 94 15 20N 61 20W
Dominican Rep. ■, W. Ind. 95 19 0N 70 30W
Don →, Humberside, U.K. 19 53 41N 0 51W
Don →, Grampian, U.K. 23 57 14N 2 5W
Don →, U.S.S.R. 47 47 4N 39 18 E
Donaghadee, U.K. 24 54 38N 5 32W
Doncaster, U.K. 19 53 31N 1 9W
Dondra Head, Sri L. 58 5 55N 80 40 E
Donegal, Ire. 24 54 39N 8 8W
Donegal □, Ire. 24 54 53N 8 0W
Donegal B., Ire. 24 54 30N 8 35W
Donetsk, U.S.S.R. 47 48 0N 37 45 E
Dongting Hu, China 61 29 18N 112 45 E
Donhead, U.K. 14 51 1N 2 8W
Donington, U.K. 19 52 54N 0 12W
Donna Nook, Pt., U.K. 19 53 29N 0 9 E
Doon →, U.K. 20 55 26N 4 41W
Doon, L., U.K. 20 55 15N 4 22W
Dorchester, Dorset, U.K. 14 50 42N 2 28W
Dorchester, Oxon., U.K. 14 51 38N 1 10W
Dordrecht, Neth. 36 51 48N 4 39 E
Dorking, U.K. 15 51 14N 0 20W
Dornoch, U.K. 23 57 52N 4 0W
Dornoch Firth, U.K. 23 57 52N 4 0W
Dorset □, U.K. 14 50 48N 2 25W
Dorstone, U.K. 14 52 4N 3 0W
Dortmund, W. Ger. 36 51 32N 7 28 E
Douai, Fr. 34 50 21N 3 4 E
Douala, Cam. 80 4 0N 9 45 E
Douglas, I. of M., U.K. 18 54 9N 4 29W
Douglas, Strathclyde, U.K. 21 55 33N 3 50W
Douglas Hd., U.K. 18 54 9N 4 28W
Doune, U.K. 21 56 12N 4 3W
Dounreay, U.K. 23 58 34N 3 44W
Douro →, Port. 37 41 8N 8 40W
Dove →, N. Yorks., U.K. 19 54 20N 0 55W
Dove →, Staffs., U.K. 18 52 51N 1 36W
Dove Dale, U.K. 19 53 10N 1 47W
Dover, U.K. 15 51 7N 1 19 E
Dover, Str. of, Europe 34 51 0N 1 30 E
Doveridge, U.K. 18 52 54N 1 49 E
Dovey →, U.K. 17 52 32N 4 0W
Down □, U.K. 24 54 20N 6 0W
Downham, U.K. 15 52 26N 0 15 E
Downham Market, U.K. 15 52 36N 0 22 E
Downpatrick, U.K. 24 54 20N 5 43W
Downpatrick Hd., Ire. 24 54 20N 9 21W
Downton, U.K. 14 51 0N 1 44W
Drake Passage, S. Oc. 103 58 0S 68 0W
Drakensberg, S. Afr. 81 31 0S 28 0 E
Drammen, Nor. 45 59 42N 10 12 E
Drava →, Yug. 43 45 33N 18 55 E
Dreghorn, U.K. 20 55 36N 4 30W
Drenthe □, Neth. 36 52 52N 6 40 E
Dresden, E. Ger. 42 51 2N 13 45 E
Driffield, U.K. 19 54 0N 0 25W
Drina →, Yug. 41 44 53N 19 21 E
Drogheda, Ire. 24 53 45N 6 20W
Droichead Nua, Ire. 25 53 11N 6 50W
Droitwich, U.K. 14 52 16N 2 10W
Dronfield, U.K. 19 53 18N 1 29W
Dronning Maud Land, Ant. 103 72 30S 12 0 E
Drumheller, Canada 88 51 25N 112 40W
Drumjohn, U.K. 20 55 14N 4 15W
Drummondville, Canada 93 45 55N 72 25W
Drummore, U.K. 20 54 41N 4 53W
Druridge B., U.K. 21 55 16N 1 32W
Drymen, U.K. 20 56 4N 4 28W
Dubai, U.A.E. 57 25 18N 55 20 E
Dubbo, Austral. 70 32 11S 148 35 E
Dubh Artach, U.K. 20 56 8N 6 40W
Dublin, Ire. 24 53 20N 6 18W
Dublin □, Ire. 24 53 24N 6 20W
Dublin B., Ire. 25 53 18N 6 5W
Dubrovnik, Yug. 41 42 39N 18 6 E
Duddington, U.K. 15 52 36N 0 32W
Duddon →, U.K. 18 54 12N 3 15W
Dudley, U.K. 14 52 30N 2 5W
Duero →, Sp. 37 41 8N 8 40W
Duffield, U.K. 19 52 59N 1 30W
Dufftown, U.K. 23 57 26N 3 9W
Duisburg, W. Ger. 36 51 27N 6 42 E
Dukinfield, U.K. 18 53 29N 2 7W
Duluth, U.S.A. 92 46 48N 92 10W
Dulverton, U.K. 14 51 2N 3 33W
Dumbarton, U.K. 20 55 58N 4 35W
Dumfries, U.K. 21 55 4N 3 37W
Dumfries & Galloway □, U.K. 21 55 0N 4 0W
Dun Laoghaire, Ire. 25 53 17N 6 9W
Dunans, U.K. 20 56 4N 5 9W
Dunbar, U.K. 21 56 0N 2 32W
Dunblane, U.K. 21 56 10N 3 58W
Duncansby Head, U.K. 23 58 39N 3 0W
Dunchurch, U.K. 14 52 21N 1 19W
Dundalk, Ire. 24 54 1N 6 25W
Dundalk Bay, Ire. 24 53 55N 6 15W
Dundee, U.K. 21 56 29N 3 0W
Dundrennan, U.K. 21 54 49N 3 56W
Dundrum, U.K. 24 54 17N 5 50W
Dundrum B., U.K. 24 54 12N 5 40W
Dunedin, N.Z. 71 45 50S 170 33 E
Dunfermline, U.K. 21 56 5N 3 28W
Dungannon, U.K. 24 54 30N 6 47W
Dungannon □, U.K. 24 54 30N 6 55W
Dungarvan, Ire. 25 52 6N 7 40W
Dungarvan Bay, Ire. 25 52 5N 7 35W
Dungavel, U.K. 21 55 37N 4 7W
Dungeness, U.K. 15 50 54N 0 59 E
Dunkeld, U.K. 23 56 34N 3 36W
Dunkerque, Fr. 34 51 2N 2 20 E
Dunkery Beacon, U.K. 14 51 15N 3 37W
Dunkirk = Dunkerque, Fr. 34 51 2N 2 20 E
Dúnleary = Dun Laoghaire, Ire. 25 53 17N 6 9W
Dunlop, U.K. 20 55 43N 4 32W
Dunmanus B., Ire. 25 51 31N 9 50W
Dunmore Hd., Ire. 25 52 10N 10 35W
Dunnet Hd., U.K. 23 58 38N 3 22W
Dunning, U.K. 21 56 18N 3 37W
Dunoon, U.K. 20 55 57N 4 56W
Duns, U.K. 21 55 47N 2 20W
Dunscore, U.K. 21 55 8N 3 48W
Dunsford, U.K. 16 50 41N 3 40W
Dunstable, U.K. 15 51 53N 0 31W
Dunster, U.K. 14 51 11N 3 28W
Dunston, U.K. 14 52 46N 2 7W
Dunvegan, U.K. 22 57 26N 6 35W
Durango, Mex. 94 24 3N 104 39W
Durban, S. Afr. 81 29 49S 31 1 E
Düren, W. Ger. 36 50 48N 6 30 E
Durg, India 59 21 15N 81 22 E
Durgapur, India 59 23 30N 87 20 E
Durham, U.K. 19 54 47N 1 34W
Durham, U.S.A. 91 36 0N 78 55W
Durham □, U.K. 18 54 42N 1 45W
Durlston Hd., U.K. 14 50 35N 1 58W
Durness, U.K. 23 58 34N 4 45W
Durrësi, Alb. 41 41 19N 19 28 E
Durrington, U.K. 14 51 12N 1 47W
Dursley, U.K. 14 51 41N 2 21W
Dushanbe, U.S.S.R. 48 38 33N 68 48 E
Düsseldorf, W. Ger. 36 51 15N 6 46 E
Duyun, China 60 26 18N 107 29 E
Dvina, N. →, U.S.S.R. 46 61 40N 45 30 E
Dyfed □, U.K. 17 52 0N 4 30W
Dymchurch, U.K. 15 51 2N 1 0 E
Dymock, U.K. 14 51 58N 2 27W
Dysart, U.K. 21 56 8N 3 8W
Dzerzhinsk, U.S.S.R. 46 56 14N 43 30 E
Dzhambul, U.S.S.R. 48 42 54N 71 22 E
Dzungaria, China 60 44 10N 88 0 E

E

Eaglesfield, U.K. 21 55 3N 3 12W
Eagleshan, U.K. 20 55 44N 4 18W
Eakring, U.K. 19 53 9N 0 59W
Ealing, U.K. 15 51 30N 0 19W
Earby, U.K. 18 53 55N 2 8W
Eardisland, U.K. 14 52 14N 2 50W
Eardisley, U.K. 14 52 8N 3 0W
Earith, U.K. 15 52 21N 0 1 E
Earl Shilton, U.K. 14 52 35N 1 20W
Earl Soham, U.K. 15 52 14N 1 15 E
Earls Barton, U.K. 15 52 16N 0 44W
Earl's Colne, U.K. 15 51 56N 0 43 E
Earlsferry, U.K. 21 56 11N 2 50W
Earlston, U.K. 21 55 39N 2 40W
Earn →, U.K. 21 56 20N 3 19W
Earn, L., U.K. 20 56 23N 4 14W
Earsdon, U.K. 21 55 4N 1 30W
Easebourne, U.K. 15 51 0N 0 42W
Easington, Durham, U.K. 19 54 50N 1 24W
Easington, Humberside, U.K. 19 53 40N 0 7 E
Easington Colliery, U.K. 19 54 49N 1 19W
Easingwold, U.K. 19 54 8N 1 11W
East Anglian Hts., U.K. 15 52 10N 0 17 E
East Bergholt, U.K. 15 51 58N 1 2 E
East Brent, U.K. 14 51 14N 2 55W
East China Sea, Asia 61 30 5N 126 0 E
East Cowes, U.K. 14 50 45N 1 17W
East Dereham, U.K. 15 52 40N 0 57 E
East Fen, U.K. 19 53 4N 0 5 E
East Germany ■, Europe 42 52 0N 12 0 E
East Grinstead, U.K. 15 51 8N 0 1W
East Harling, U.K. 15 52 26N 0 55 E
East Ilsley, U.K. 14 51 33N 1 15W
East Indies, Asia 50 0 0 120 0 E
East Kilbride, U.K. 20 55 46N 4 10W
East Kirkby, U.K. 19 53 5N 1 15W
East Linton, U.K. 21 56 0N 2 40W
East London, S. Afr. 81 33 0S 27 55 E
East Markham, U.K. 19 53 15N 0 53W
East Moor, U.K. 19 53 15N 1 30W
East Retford, U.K. 19 53 19N 0 55W
East Siberian Sea, U.S.S.R. 49 73 0N 160 0 E
East Sussex □, U.K. 15 51 0N 0 20 E
East Wemyss, U.K. 21 56 8N 3 5W
East Wittering, U.K. 15 50 46N 0 53W
East Woodhay, U.K. 14 51 21N 1 26W
Eastbourne, U.K. 15 50 46N 0 18 E
Eastchurch, U.K. 15 51 23N 0 53 E
Easter Islands, Pac. Oc. 65 27 0S 109 0W
Eastern Ghats, India 58 14 0N 78 50 E
Eastleigh, U.K. 14 50 58N 1 21W
Eastnor, U.K. 14 52 2N 2 22W
Easton, Avon, U.K. 14 51 28N 2 42W
Easton, Dorset, U.K. 14 50 32N 2 27W
Easton, Northants., U.K. 15 52 37N 0 31W
Eastry, U.K. 15 51 15N 1 19 E
Eastwood, U.K. 19 53 2N 1 17W
Eaton, U.K. 15 52 52N 0 46W
Eaton Socon, U.K. 15 52 13N 0 18W
Eau Claire, U.S.A. 92 44 46N 91 30W
Ebberston, U.K. 19 54 14N 0 35W
Ebbw Vale, U.K. 17 51 47N 3 12W
Ebro →, Sp. 37 40 43N 0 54 E
Ecclefechan, U.K. 21 55 3N 3 18W
Eccleshall, U.K. 14 52 52N 2 14W
Ech Cheliff, Alg. 78 36 10N 1 20 E
Echo Bay, Canada 88 66 5N 117 55W
Echuca, Austral. 70 36 10S 144 20 E
Eck, L., U.K. 20 56 5N 5 0W
Eckington, U.K. 19 53 19N 1 21W
Ecuador ■, S. Am. 100 2 0S 78 0W
Edam, Neth. 36 52 31N 5 3 E
Eday, U.K. 23 59 11N 2 47W
Eddrachillis B., U.K. 22 58 16N 5 10W
Eddystone, U.K. 16 50 11N 4 16W
Ede, Neth. 36 52 4N 5 40 E
Eden →, U.K. 18 54 57N 3 2W
Edenbridge, U.K. 15 51 12N 0 4 E
Edenderry, Ire. 25 53 21N 7 3W
Edge Hill, U.K. 14 52 7N 1 28W
Edinburgh, U.K. 21 55 57N 3 12W
Edington, U.K. 14 51 17N 2 6W
Edmondbyers, U.K. 18 54 50N 1 59W
Edmonton, Canada 88 53 30N 113 30W
Edmundston, Canada 93 47 23N 68 20W
Edward, L., Africa 80 0 25S 29 40 E
Egersund, Nor. 45 58 26N 6 1 E
Egham, U.K. 15 51 25N 0 33W
Egmont, Mt., N.Z. 71 39 17S 174 5 E
Egremont, U.K. 18 54 28N 3 33W
Egton, U.K. 19 54 27N 0 45W
Egypt ■, Africa 79 28 0N 31 0 E
Eifel, W. Ger. 36 50 10N 6 45 E
Eigg, U.K. 22 56 54N 6 10W
Eighty Mile Beach, Austral. 66 19 30S 120 40 E
Eil, L., U.K. 22 56 50N 5 15W
Eildon, L., Austral. 70 37 10S 146 0 E
Eindhoven, Neth. 36 51 26N 5 30 E
Eire ■, Europe 25 53 0N 8 0W
El Aaiún, W. Sah. 78 27 9N 13 12W
El Asnam = Ech Cheliff, Alg. 78 36 10N 1 20 E
El Faiyûm, Egypt 79 29 19N 30 50 E
El Fâsher, Sudan 79 13 33N 25 26 E
El Gîza, Egypt 79 30 0N 31 10 E
El Jadida, Mor. 78 33 11N 8 17W
El Mahalla el Kubra, Egypt 79 31 0N 31 0 E
El Mansûra, Egypt 79 31 0N 31 19 E
El Minyâ, Egypt 79 28 7N 30 33 E
El Obeid, Sudan 79 13 8N 30 10 E
El Paso, U.S.A. 90 31 50N 106 30W
El Qâhira = Cairo, Egypt 79 30 1N 31 14 E
El Salvador ■, Cent. Am. 94 13 50N 89 0W
Elba, It. 40 42 48N 10 15 E
Elbasani, Alb. 41 41 9N 20 9 E
Elbe →, W. Ger. 42 53 50N 9 0 E
Elbląg, Pol. 43 54 10N 19 25 E
Elburz Mts., Iran 56 36 0N 52 0 E
Elche, Sp. 37 38 15N 0 42W
Eldoret, Kenya 80 0 30N 35 17 E
Eleuthera, Baham. 95 25 0N 76 20W
Elgin, U.K. 23 57 39N 3 20W
Elham, U.K. 15 51 9N 1 7 E
Elie, U.K. 21 56 11N 2 50W

Elishaw, *U.K.* **21** 55 16N 2 14W
Elizabeth, *Austral.* **67** 34 42S 138 41 E
Elizabeth, *U.S.A.* **93** 40 37N 74 12W
Elland, *U.K.* **19** 53 41N 1 49W
Ellen →, *U.K.* **18** 54 44N 3 30W
Eller Beck Bridge, *U.K.* **19** 54 23N 0 40W
Ellesmere, *U.K.* **18** 52 55N 2 53W
Ellesmere I., *Canada* **103** 79 30N 80 0W
Ellesmere Port, *U.K.* **18** 53 17N 2 55W
Ellice Is. = Tuvalu ■, *Pac. Oc.* **64** 8 0S 178 0 E
Ellington, *U.K.* **21** 55 14N 1 34W
Ellon, *U.K.* **23** 57 21N 2 5W
Elmira, *U.S.A.* **92** 42 8N 76 49W
Elmswell, *U.K.* **15** 52 14N 0 53 E
Eluru, *India* **59** 16 48N 81 8 E
Ely, *U.K.* **15** 52 24N 0 16 E
Emāmrūd, *Iran* **56** 36 30N 55 0 E
Embleton, *U.K.* **21** 55 30N 1 38W
Emden, *W. Ger.* **36** 53 22N 7 12 E
Emerald, *Austral.* **67** 23 32S 148 10 E
Emmeloord, *Neth.* **36** 52 44N 5 46 E
Emmen, *Neth.* **36** 52 48N 6 57 E
Ems →, *W. Ger.* **36** 52 37N 9 26 E
Enard B., *U.K.* **22** 58 5N 5 20W
Enderbury I., *Pac. Oc.* **64** 3 8S 171 5W
Enderby, *U.K.* **14** 52 35N 1 15W
Enderby Land, *Ant.* **103** 66 0S 53 0 E
Enfield, *U.K.* **15** 51 39N 0 4W
England □, *U.K.* **5** 53 0N 2 0W
English Channel, *Europe* **15** 50 0N 2 0W
Ennerdale Water, *U.K.* **18** 54 32N 3 24W
Ennis, *Ire.* **25** 52 51N 8 59W
Enniscorthy, *Ire.* **25** 52 30N 6 35W
Enniskillen, *U.K.* **24** 54 20N 7 40W
Ennistimon, *Ire.* **25** 52 56N 9 18W
Enschede, *Neth.* **36** 52 13N 6 53 E
Ensenada, *Mex.* **94** 31 50N 116 50W
Enstone, *U.K.* **14** 51 55N 1 25W
Entebbe, *Uganda* **80** 0 4N 32 28 E
Enugu, *Nig.* **78** 6 20N 7 30 E
Epping, *U.K.* **15** 51 42N 0 8 E
Epping Forest, *U.K.* **15** 51 40N 0 5 E
Epsom, *U.K.* **15** 51 19N 0 16W
Epworth, *U.K.* **19** 53 30N 0 50W
Equatorial Guinea ■, *Africa* **80** 2 0S 8 0 E
Erebus, Mt., *Ant.* **103** 77 35S 167 0 E
Erfurt, *E. Ger.* **42** 50 58N 11 2 E
Eriboll, L., *U.K.* **23** 58 28N 4 41W
Erie, *U.S.A.* **92** 42 10N 80 7W
Erie, L., *N. Am.* **92** 42 15N 81 0W
Eritrea □, *Eth.* **79** 14 0N 41 0 E
Erlangen, *W. Ger.* **42** 49 35N 11 0 E
Erne →, *U.K.* **24** 54 30N 8 16W
Erne, Lough, *U.K.* **24** 54 26N 7 46W
Erode, *India* **58** 11 24N 77 45 E
Errigal, Mt., *Ire.* **24** 55 2N 8 8W
Erris Hd., *Ire.* **24** 54 19N 10 0W
Errol, *U.K.* **21** 56 24N 3 13W
Erzurum, *Turk.* **47** 39 57N 41 15 E
Esbjerg, *Den.* **45** 55 29N 8 29 E
Esch, *Neth.* **36** 51 37N 5 17 E
Eschweiler, *W. Ger.* **36** 50 49N 6 14 E
Escrick, *U.K.* **19** 53 53N 1 3W
Eşfahān, *Iran* **56** 33 0N 53 0 E
Esk →, *Cumbria, U.K.* **18** 54 23N 3 21W
Esk →, *Dumf. & Gall., U.K.* **21** 54 58N 3 4W
Esk →, *N. Yorks., U.K.* **19** 54 27N 0 36W
Eskdale, *U.K.* **21** 55 12N 3 4W
Eskifjörður, *Ice.* **44** 65 3N 13 55W
Eskilstuna, *Swed.* **45** 59 22N 16 32 E
Eskimo Pt., *Canada* **88** 61 10N 94 15W
Eskişehir, *Turk.* **47** 39 50N 30 35 E
Esmeraldas, *Ecuad.* **100** 1 0N 79 40W
Esperance, *Austral.* **66** 33 45S 121 55 E
Espinhaço, Serra do, *Brazil* **101** 17 30S 43 30W
Essen, *W. Ger.* **36** 51 28N 6 59 E
Essex □, *U.K.* **15** 51 48N 0 30 E
Eston, *U.K.* **19** 54 33N 1 6W
Estonian S.S.R. □, *U.S.S.R.* **46** 58 30N 25 30 E
Etchingham, *U.K.* **15** 51 0N 0 27 E
Ethiopia ■, *Africa* **78** 8 0N 40 0 E
Ethiopian Highlands, *Eth.* **72** 10 0N 37 0 E
Etive, L., *U.K.* **20** 56 30N 5 12W
Etna, *It.* **40** 37 45N 15 0 E
Eton, *U.K.* **15** 51 29N 0 37W
Ettington, *U.K.* **14** 52 8N 1 38W
Ettrick Forest, *U.K.* **21** 55 30N 3 0W
Ettrick Water →, *U.K.* **21** 55 31N 2 55W
Eugene, *U.S.A.* **90** 44 0N 123 8W
Euphrates →, *Asia* **56** 31 0N 47 25 E
Euston, *Austral.* **70** 34 30S 142 46 E
Euxton, *U.K.* **18** 53 41N 2 42W
Evansville, *U.S.A.* **92** 38 0N 87 35W
Evercreech, *U.K.* **14** 51 8N 2 30W
Everest, Mt., *Nepal* **60** 28 5N 86 58 E
Evesham, *U.K.* **14** 52 6N 1 57W
Évora, *Port.* **37** 38 33N 7 57W
Évreux, *Fr.* **34** 49 0N 1 8 E
Évvoia, *Greece* **41** 38 30N 24 0 E
Ewe, L., *U.K.* **22** 57 49N 5 38W
Ewell, *U.K.* **15** 51 20N 0 15W
Ewhurst, *U.K.* **15** 51 9N 0 25W
Exe →, *U.K.* **16** 50 38N 3 27W
Exeter, *U.K.* **16** 50 43N 3 31W
Exford, *U.K.* **14** 51 8N 3 39W
Exminster, *U.K.* **16** 50 40N 3 29W
Exmoor, *U.K.* **16** 51 10N 3 59W
Exmouth, *Austral.* **66** 21 54S 114 10 E
Exmouth, *U.K.* **16** 50 37N 3 26W
Exmouth G., *Austral.* **66** 22 15S 114 15 E
Exton, *U.K.* **15** 52 42N 0 38W
Eyam, *U.K.* **19** 53 17N 1 40W
Eye, *Cambs., U.K.* **15** 52 36N 0 11W
Eye, *Suffolk, U.K.* **15** 52 19N 1 9 E
Eye Pen., *U.K.* **22** 58 13N 6 10W
Eyemouth, *U.K.* **21** 55 53N 2 5W
Eynsham, *U.K.* **14** 51 47N 1 21W
Eyre, L., *Austral.* **67** 29 30S 137 26 E
Eyre Cr. →, *Austral.* **67** 26 40S 139 0 E
Eyre Pen., *Austral.* **66** 33 30S 137 17 E

F

Fair Hd., *U.K.* **24** 55 14N 6 10W
Fairbanks, *U.S.A.* **88** 64 50N 147 50W
Fairfield, *Austral.* **70** 33 53S 150 57 E
Fairford, *U.K.* **14** 51 42N 1 48W
Fairlie, *N.Z.* **71** 44 5S 170 49 E
Fairlie, *U.K.* **20** 55 44N 4 52W
Fairlight, *U.K.* **15** 50 53N 0 40 E
Faisalabad, *Pak.* **58** 31 30N 73 5 E
Faizabad, *India* **59** 26 45N 82 10 E
Fakenham, *U.K.* **15** 52 50N 0 51 E
Faldingworth, *U.K.* **19** 53 21N 0 22W
Falkenberg, *Swed.* **45** 56 54N 12 30 E
Falkirk, *U.K.* **21** 56 0N 3 47W
Falkland, *U.K.* **21** 56 15N 3 13W
Falkland Is., *Atl. Oc.* **102** 51 30S 59 0W
Fall River, *U.S.A.* **93** 41 45N 71 5W
Falmouth, *U.K.* **16** 50 9N 5 5W
Falmouth B., *U.K.* **16** 50 7N 5 3W
Falstone, *U.K.* **21** 55 10N 2 26W
Falun, *Swed.* **45** 60 37N 15 37 E
Famagusta, *Cyprus* **47** 35 8N 33 55 E
Fannich, L., *U.K.* **22** 57 40N 5 0W
Fareham, *U.K.* **14** 50 52N 1 11W
Faringdon, *U.K.* **14** 51 39N 1 34W
Farnborough, *U.K.* **15** 51 17N 0 46W
Farne Is., *U.K.* **19** 55 38N 1 37W
Farnham, *U.K.* **15** 51 13N 0 49W
Farnworth, *U.K.* **18** 53 33N 2 24W
Faroe Is., *Atl. Oc.* **26** 62 0N 7 0W
Farrar →, *U.K.* **23** 57 30N 4 30W
Faslane, *U.K.* **20** 56 3N 4 49W
Fastnet Rock, *Ire.* **25** 51 22N 9 37W
Fauldhouse, *U.K.* **21** 55 50N 3 44W
Faversham, *U.K.* **15** 51 18N 0 54 E
Fawley, *U.K.* **14** 50 49N 1 20W
Faya-Largeau, *Chad* **79** 17 58N 19 6 E
Fayetteville, *U.S.A.* **91** 35 0N 78 58W
Fazeley, *U.K.* **14** 52 36N 1 42W
Fdérik, *Maurit.* **78** 22 40N 12 45W
Feale →, *Ire.* **25** 52 26N 9 40W
Feilding, *N.Z.* **71** 40 13S 175 35 E
Feira de Santana, *Brazil* **101** 12 15S 38 57W
Felixstowe, *U.K.* **15** 51 58N 1 22 E
Felpham, *U.K.* **15** 50 47N 0 38W
Felton, *U.K.* **21** 55 18N 1 42W
Feltwell, *U.K.* **15** 52 29N 0 32 E
Fenit, *Ire.* **25** 52 17N 9 51W
Fenny Bentley, *U.K.* **19** 53 4N 1 43W
Fenny Compton, *U.K.* **14** 52 9N 1 20W
Fenny Stratford, *U.K.* **15** 51 59N 0 42W
Fens, The, *U.K.* **15** 52 45N 0 2 E
Fenwick, *U.K.* **20** 55 38N 4 25W
Fergana, *U.S.S.R.* **48** 40 23N 71 19 E
Fermanagh □, *U.K.* **24** 54 21N 7 40W
Fermoy, *Ire.* **25** 52 4N 8 18W
Fernhurst, *U.K.* **15** 51 3N 0 43W
Ferrara, *It.* **40** 44 50N 11 36 E
Ferryhill, *U.K.* **19** 54 42N 1 32W
Fès, *Mor.* **78** 34 0N 5 0W
Fetlar, *U.K.* **22** 60 36N 0 52W
Ffestiniog, *U.K.* **17** 52 58N 3 56W
Fianarantsoa, *Madag.* **81** 21 26S 47 5 E
Fife □, *U.K.* **21** 56 13N 3 2W
Fife Ness, *U.K.* **21** 56 17N 2 35W
Fiji ■, *Pac. Oc.* **64** 17 20S 179 0 E
Filby, *U.K.* **15** 52 40N 1 39 E
Filey, *U.K.* **19** 54 13N 0 18W
Filey B., *U.K.* **19** 54 12N 0 15W
Filton, *U.K.* **14** 51 29N 2 34W
Fincham, *U.K.* **15** 52 38N 0 30 E
Findhorn →, *U.K.* **23** 57 38N 3 38W
Findon, *U.K.* **15** 50 53N 0 24W
Finedon, *U.K.* **15** 52 20N 0 40W
Fingest, *U.K.* **15** 51 35N 0 52W
Finisterre, C., *Sp.* **37** 42 50N 9 19W
Finland ■, *Europe* **44** 63 0N 27 0 E
Finland, G. of, *Europe* **45** 60 0N 26 0 E
Finn →, *Ire.* **24** 54 50N 7 55W
Finnart, *U.K.* **20** 56 7N 4 48W
Finnmark fylke □, *Nor.* **44** 69 30N 25 0 E
Finstown, *U.K.* **23** 59 0N 3 8W
Fionnphort, *U.K.* **20** 56 19N 6 23W
Firozabad, *India* **58** 27 10N 78 25 E
Fishguard, *U.K.* **17** 51 59N 4 59W
Fishtoft, *U.K.* **19** 52 27N 0 2 E
Fitzroy →, *Austral.* **66** 17 31S 123 35 E
Flamborough, *U.K.* **19** 54 7N 0 7W
Flamborough Hd., *U.K.* **19** 54 8N 0 4W
Flanders, *Belg.* **34** 51 10N 3 15 E
Flatey, *Ice.* **44** 65 22N 22 56W
Fleet, *U.K.* **15** 51 16N 0 50W
Fleetwood, *U.K.* **18** 53 55N 3 1W
Flensburg, *W. Ger.* **42** 54 46N 9 28 E
Fletton, *U.K.* **15** 52 34N 0 13W
Flimby, *U.K.* **18** 54 42N 3 31W
Flinders →, *Austral.* **67** 17 36S 140 36 E
Flinders Ranges, *Austral.* **67** 31 30S 138 30 E
Flint, *U.K.* **17** 53 15N 3 7W
Flint, *U.S.A.* **92** 43 5N 83 40W
Flint →, *U.S.A.* **91** 30 52N 84 38W
Flitwick, *U.K.* **15** 51 59N 0 30W
Flodden, *U.K.* **19** 55 37N 2 8W
Florence, *It.* **40** 43 47N 11 15 E
Flores, *Indon.* **63** 8 35S 121 0 E
Flores Sea, *Indon.* **63** 6 30S 124 0 E
Florianópolis, *Brazil* **102** 27 30S 48 30W
Florida □, *U.S.A.* **91** 28 30N 82 0W
Florida, Straits of, *U.S.A.* **95** 25 0N 80 0W
Florida Keys, *U.S.A.* **91** 25 0N 80 40W
Florissant, *U.S.A.* **91** 38 48N 90 20W
Flushing = Vlissingen, *Neth.* **36** 51 26N 3 34 E
Fóggia, *It.* **40** 41 28N 15 31 E
Folkestone, *U.K.* **15** 51 5N 1 11 E
Fontainebleau, *Fr.* **34** 48 24N 2 40 E
Forbach, *Fr.* **34** 49 10N 6 52 E
Ford, *U.K.* **20** 56 10N 5 27W
Fordham, *U.K.* **15** 52 19N 0 23 E
Fordingbridge, *U.K.* **14** 50 56N 1 48W
Forest Row, *U.K.* **15** 51 6N 0 3 E
Forfar, *U.K.* **23** 56 40N 2 53W
Formby, *U.K.* **18** 53 34N 3 4W
Formby Pt., *U.K.* **18** 53 33N 3 7W
Formosa = Taiwan ■, *Asia* **61** 23 30N 121 0 E
Formosa Strait, *Asia* **61** 24 40N 120 0 E
Forres, *U.K.* **23** 57 37N 3 38W
Fort Augustus, *U.K.* **23** 57 9N 4 40W
Fort Collins, *U.S.A.* **90** 40 30N 105 4W
Fort-de-France, *Mart.* **94** 14 36N 61 2W
Fort George, *Canada* **89** 53 50N 79 0W
Fort Lauderdale, *U.S.A.* **91** 26 10N 80 5W
Fort McMurray, *Canada* **88** 56 44N 111 7W
Fort Smith, *U.S.A.* **91** 35 25N 94 25W
Fort Wayne, *U.S.A.* **92** 41 5N 85 10W
Fort William, *U.K.* **22** 56 48N 5 8W
Fort Worth, *U.S.A.* **90** 32 45N 97 25W
Fortaleza, *Brazil* **101** 3 45S 38 35W
Forth, *U.K.* **21** 55 45N 3 42W
Forth, Firth of, *U.K.* **21** 56 5N 2 55W
Forth Bridge, *U.K.* **21** 56 0N 3 24W
Fortrose, *U.K.* **23** 57 35N 4 10W
Foshan, *China* **61** 23 4N 113 5 E
Fothergill, *U.K.* **18** 54 43N 3 30W
Fotheringhay, *U.K.* **15** 52 32N 0 28W
Foulness I., *U.K.* **15** 51 36N 0 55 E
Foulness Pt., *U.K.* **15** 51 36N 0 59 E
Foulsham, *U.K.* **15** 52 48N 1 1 E
Fountainhall, *U.K.* **21** 55 45N 2 55W
Fountains Abbey, *U.K.* **19** 54 8N 1 35W
Fovant, *U.K.* **14** 51 4N 2 0W
Foveaux Str., *N.Z.* **71** 46 42S 168 10 E
Fowey, *U.K.* **16** 50 20N 4 39W
Fowey →, *U.K.* **16** 50 20N 4 39W
Fownhope, *U.K.* **14** 52 0N 2 37W
Foxdale, *U.K.* **18** 54 12N 4 38W
Foxe Chan., *Canada* **89** 65 0N 80 0W
Foyle, Lough, *U.K.* **24** 55 6N 7 8W
Foynes, *Ire.* **25** 52 37N 9 5W
Fraddon, *U.K.* **16** 50 22N 4 55W
Framlingham, *U.K.* **15** 52 14N 1 20 E
France ■, *Europe* **34** 47 0N 3 0 E
Frankfurt am Main, *W. Ger.* **42** 50 7N 8 40 E
Frankston, *Austral.* **70** 38 8S 145 8 E
Frant, *U.K.* **15** 51 5N 0 17 E
Franz Josef Land, *U.S.S.R.* **48** 82 0N 55 0 E
Fraser →, *Canada* **88** 49 7N 123 11W
Fraser I., *Austral.* **67** 25 15S 153 10 E
Fraserburgh, *U.K.* **23** 57 41N 2 0W
Fredericton, *Canada* **93** 45 57N 66 40W
Frederikshavn, *Den.* **45** 57 28N 10 31 E
Fredrikstad, *Nor.* **45** 59 13N 10 57 E
Freetown, *Sa. Leone* **78** 8 30N 13 17W
Freiburg, *W. Ger.* **42** 48 0N 7 52 E
Fremantle, *Austral.* **66** 32 7S 115 47 E
French Guiana ■, *S. Am.* **101** 4 0N 53 0W
French Polynesia □, *Pac. Oc.* **65** 20 0S 145 0 E
Freshwater, *U.K.* **14** 50 42N 1 31W
Fresnillo, *Mex.* **94** 23 10N 103 0W
Fresno, *U.S.A.* **90** 36 47N 119 50W
Freuchie, *U.K.* **21** 56 14N 3 8W
Fridaythorpe, *U.K.* **19** 54 2N 0 40W
Friesland □, *Neth.* **36** 53 5N 5 50 E
Frimley, *U.K.* **15** 51 18N 0 43W
Frinton-on-Sea, *U.K.* **15** 51 50N 1 16 E
Frisa, Loch, *U.K.* **20** 56 34N 6 5W
Frisian Is., *Europe* **36** 53 30N 6 0 E
Frizington, *U.K.* **18** 54 33N 3 30W
Frobisher B., *Canada* **89** 62 30N 66 0W
Frodsham, *U.K.* **18** 53 17N 2 45W
Frome, *U.K.* **14** 51 16N 2 17W
Frome →, *U.K.* **14** 50 44N 2 5W
Frome, L., *Austral.* **67** 30 45S 139 45 E
Frunze, *U.S.S.R.* **48** 42 54N 74 46 E
Fuji-San, *Jap.* **62** 35 22N 138 44 E
Fujian □, *China* **61** 26 0N 118 0 E
Fukui, *Jap.* **62** 36 0N 136 10 E
Fukuoka, *Jap.* **62** 33 39N 130 21 E
Fukushima, *Jap.* **62** 37 44N 140 28 E
Fukuyama, *Jap.* **62** 34 35N 133 20 E
Fulwood, *U.K.* **18** 53 47N 2 41W
Fundy, B. of, *Canada* **93** 45 0N 66 0W
Furneaux Group, *Austral.* **67** 40 10S 147 50 E
Furness, Pen., *U.K.* **18** 54 12N 3 10W
Fürth, *W. Ger.* **42** 49 29N 11 0 E
Fury and Hecla Str., *Canada* **89** 69 56N 84 0W
Fushun, *China* **61** 41 50N 123 56 E
Fuxin, *China* **61** 42 5N 121 48 E
Fuzhou, *China* **61** 26 5N 119 16 E
Fylde, *U.K.* **18** 53 50N 2 58W
Fylingdales Moor, *U.K.* **19** 54 22N 0 32W
Fyn, *Den.* **45** 55 20N 10 30 E
Fyne, L., *U.K.* **20** 56 0N 5 20W
Fyvie, *U.K.* **23** 57 26N 2 24W

G

Gabès, *Tunisia* **78** 33 53N 10 2 E
Gabon ■, *Africa* **80** 0 10S 10 0 E
Gaborone, *Bots.* **81** 24 45S 25 57 E
Gabrovo, *Bulg.* **41** 42 52N 25 19 E
Gainesville, *U.S.A.* **91** 29 38N 82 20W
Gainford, *U.K.* **19** 54 34N 1 44W
Gainsborough, *U.K.* **19** 53 23N 0 46W
Gairdner L., *Austral.* **66** 31 30S 136 0 E
Gairloch, *U.K.* **22** 57 42N 5 40W
Gairloch, L., *U.K.* **22** 57 43N 5 45W
Galápagos, *Pac. Oc.* **65** 0 0 89 0W
Galashiels, *U.K.* **21** 55 37N 2 50W
Galaţi, *Rom.* **43** 45 27N 28 2 E
Galgate, *U.K.* **18** 53 59N 2 47W
Galilee, Sea of = Kinneret, Lake, *Isr.* **57** 32 45N 35 35 E
Galle, *Sri L.* **58** 6 5N 80 10 E
Galley Hd., *Ire.* **25** 51 32N 8 56W
Gällivare, *Swed.* **44** 67 9N 20 40 E
Galloway, *U.K.* **20** 55 0N 4 25W
Galloway, Mull of, *U.K.* **20** 54 38N 4 50W
Galmpton, *U.K.* **16** 50 23N 3 32W
Galston, *U.K.* **20** 55 36N 4 22W
Galty Mts., *Ire.* **25** 52 22N 8 10W
Galtymore, *Ire.* **25** 52 22N 8 12W
Galveston, *U.S.A.* **91** 29 15N 94 48W
Galway, *Ire.* **25** 53 16N 9 4W
Galway □, *Ire.* **24** 53 16N 9 3W
Galway B., *Ire.* **25** 53 10N 9 20W
Gambia ■, *W. Afr.* **78** 13 25N 16 0W
Gamboa, *Pan.* **94** 9 8N 79 42W
Gamlingay, *U.K.* **15** 52 9N 0 11W
Gan Jiang →, *China* **61** 29 15N 116 0 E
Ganga →, *India* **59** 23 20N 90 30 E
Ganganagar, *India* **58** 29 56N 73 56 E
Ganges = Ganga →, *India* **59** 23 20N 90 30 E
Gansu □, *China* **60** 36 0N 104 0 E
Gao, *Mali* **78** 16 15N 0 5W
Gap, *Fr.* **35** 44 33N 6 5 E
Garboldisham, *U.K.* **15** 52 24N 0 57 E
Garda, L. di, *It.* **40** 45 40N 10 40 E
Gare, L., *U.K.* **20** 56 1N 4 50W
Garelochhead, *U.K.* **20** 56 7N 4 50W
Garforth, *U.K.* **19** 53 48N 1 22W
Gargrave, *U.K.* **18** 53 58N 2 7W
Garlieston, *U.K.* **20** 54 47N 4 22W
Garonne →, *Fr.* **35** 45 2N 0 36W
Garoua, *Cam.* **80** 9 19N 13 21 E
Garry →, *U.K.* **23** 56 47N 3 47W
Garsdale Head, *U.K.* **18** 54 19N 2 19W
Garstang, *U.K.* **18** 53 53N 2 47W
Garston, *U.K.* **18** 53 21N 2 55W
Garvald, *U.K.* **21** 55 55N 2 39W
Garvellachs, Is., *U.K.* **20** 56 14N 5 48W
Gary, *U.S.A.* **92** 41 35N 87 20W
Garzê, *China* **60** 31 39N 99 58 E
Gascony, *Fr.* **35** 43 45N 0 20 E
Gascoyne →, *Austral.* **66** 24 52S 113 37 E
Gaspé, Pén. de, *Canada* **93** 48 45N 65 40W
Gatehouse of Fleet, *U.K.* **20** 54 53N 4 10W
Gateshead, *U.K.* **19** 54 57N 1 37W
Gatley, *U.K.* **18** 53 25N 2 15W
Gatun, *Pan.* **94** 9 16N 79 55W
Gatun, L., *Pan.* **94** 9 7N 79 56W
Gävle, *Swed.* **45** 60 40N 17 9 E
Gawthwaite, *U.K.* **18** 54 16N 3 6W
Gaya, *India* **59** 24 47N 85 4 E
Gayton, *U.K.* **15** 52 45N 0 35 E
Gaywood, *U.K.* **15** 52 46N 0 26 E
Gaza, *Egypt* **57** 31 30N 34 28 E
Gaziantep, *Turk.* **47** 37 6N 37 23 E
Gdańsk, *Pol.* **43** 54 22N 18 40 E
Gdańsk Bay, *Pol.* **43** 54 30N 19 20 E
Gdynia, *Pol.* **43** 54 35N 18 33 E
Gedney, *U.K.* **15** 52 48N 0 5 E
Geelong, *Austral.* **70** 38 10S 144 22 E
Gejiu, *China* **60** 23 20N 103 10 E
Gelderland □, *Neth.* **36** 52 5N 6 10 E

Gelsenkirchen, W. Ger. 36 51 30N 7 5 E
Geneva, Switz. 42 46 12N 6 9 E
Geneva, L., Switz. 42 46 26N 6 30 E
Genk, Belg. 36 50 58N 5 32 E
Gennargentu, Mti. del, It. 40 40 0N 9 10 E
Genoa, It. 40 44 24N 8 56 E
Geographe Chan., Austral. 66 24 30S 113 0 E
George, S. Afr. 81 33 58S 22 29 E
George Town, Malay. 63 5 25N 100 15 E
Georgetown, Guy. 100 6 50N 58 12W
Georgia □, U.S.A. 91 32 0N 82 0W
Georgia □, U.S.S.R. 47 42 0N 43 0 E
Georgian B., Canada 92 45 15N 81 0W
Gera, E. Ger. 42 50 53N 12 11 E
Geraldton, Austral. 66 28 48S 114 32 E
Germiston, S. Afr. 81 26 15S 28 10 E
Gerona, Sp. 37 41 58N 2 46 E
Gerrans B., U.K. 16 50 12N 4 57W
Gerrards Cross, U.K. 15 51 35N 0 32W
Ghaghara →, India 59 25 45N 84 40 E
Ghana ■, W. Afr. 78 6 0N 1 0W
Ghaziabad, India 58 28 42N 77 26 E
Ghent, Belg. 36 51 2N 3 42 E
Giant's Causeway, U.K. 24 55 15N 6 30W
Gibraltar, Europe 37 36 7N 5 22W
Gibraltar, Str. of, Medit. S. 37 35 55N 5 40W
Gibraltar Pt., U.K. 19 53 6N 0 20 E
Gibson Desert, Austral. 66 24 0S 126 0 E
Gifford, U.K. 21 55 54N 2 45W
Gifu, Jap. 62 35 30N 136 45 E
Giggleswick, U.K. 18 54 5N 2 19W
Gigha, U.K. 20 55 42N 5 45W
Gijón, Sp. 37 43 32N 5 42W
Gilbert Is. = Kiribati ■, Pac. Oc. 65 1 0N 176 0 E
Gillingham, Dorset, U.K. 14 51 2N 2 15W
Gillingham, Kent, U.K. 15 51 23N 0 34 E
Gilsland, U.K. 18 55 0N 2 34W
Girdle Ness, U.K. 23 57 9N 2 2W
Gironde →, Fr. 35 45 32N 1 7W
Girvan, U.K. 20 55 15N 4 50W
Girvan →, U.K. 20 55 18N 4 51W
Gisborne, N.Z. 71 38 39S 178 5 E
Gisburn, U.K. 18 53 56N 2 16W
Gizhiga, U.S.S.R. 49 62 3N 160 30 E
Gizhiga, G., U.S.S.R. 49 61 0N 158 0 E
Gladstone, Austral. 67 25 57S 114 17 E
Glanton, U.K. 21 55 25N 1 54W
Glasgow, U.K. 20 55 52N 4 14W
Glastonbury, U.K. 14 51 9N 2 42W
Glemsford, U.K. 15 52 6N 0 41 E
Glen →, U.K. 15 52 50N 0 7W
Glen Affric, U.K. 22 57 15N 5 0W
Glen Almond, U.K. 21 56 28N 3 50W
Glen Coe, U.K. 19 56 40N 5 0W
Glen Etive, U.K. 20 56 37N 5 0W
Glen Garry, U.K. 22 57 3N 5 7W
Glen Helen, U.K. 18 54 14N 4 35W
Glen Mor, U.K. 23 57 12N 4 37 E
Glen Moriston, U.K. 22 57 10N 4 58W
Glen Orchy, U.K. 20 56 27N 4 52W
Glen Spean, U.K. 23 56 53N 4 40W
Glenbarr, U.K. 20 55 34N 5 40W
Glendale, U.S.A. 90 34 7N 118 18W
Gleneagles, U.K. 21 56 16N 3 44W
Glengarriff, Ire. 25 51 45N 9 33W
Glenkens, The, U.K. 20 55 10N 4 15W
Glenluce, U.K. 20 54 53N 4 50W
Glenmaye, U.K. 18 54 11N 4 42W
Glenorchy, Austral. 67 31 55S 139 46 E
Glenrothes, U.K. 20 56 12N 3 11W
Glenties, Ire. 24 54 48N 8 18W
Glentrool Village, U.K. 20 55 5N 4 30W
Gliwice, Pol. 43 50 22N 18 41 E
Glossop, U.K. 18 53 27N 1 56W
Gloucester, U.K. 14 51 52N 2 15W
Gloucestershire □, U.K. 14 51 44N 2 10W
Gnosall, U.K. 14 52 48N 2 15W
Goa □, India 58 15 33N 73 59 E
Goat Fell, U.K. 20 55 37N 5 11W
Gobi, Asia 60 44 0N 111 0 E
Godalming, U.K. 15 51 12N 0 37W
Godavari →, India 59 16 25N 82 18 E
Godmanchester, U.K. 15 52 19N 0 11W
Godshill, U.K. 14 50 38N 1 13W
Godstone, U.K. 15 51 15N 0 -3W
Goiânia, Brazil 101 16 43S 49 20W
Goil, L., U.K. 20 56 8N 4 52W
Gold Coast, Austral. 67 28 0S 153 25 E
Golden Vale, Ire. 25 52 33N 8 17W
Golspie, U.K. 23 57 58N 3 58W
Gomel, U.S.S.R. 46 52 28N 31 0 E
Gometra I., U.K. 20 56 30N 6 18W
Gómez Palacio, Mex. 94 25 40N 104 0W
Gonder, Eth. 79 12 39N 37 30 E
Good Hope, C. of, S. Afr. 81 34 24S 18 30 E
Goodrich, U.K. 14 51 52N 2 38W
Goodwood, U.K. 15 50 53N 0 44W
Goole, U.K. 19 53 42N 0 52W
Goondiwindi, Austral. 67 28 30S 150 21 E
Gorakhpur, India 59 26 47N 83 23 E
Gordon, U.K. 21 55 41N 2 32W
Gorebridge, U.K. 21 55 51N 3 2W
Gorey, Ire. 25 52 41N 6 18W
Goring, Oxon., U.K. 14 51 31N 1 8W
Goring, W. Sussex, U.K. 15 50 49N 0 26W
Gorki, U.S.S.R. 46 56 20N 44 0 E
Gorleston, U.K. 15 52 35N 1 44 E
Görlitz, E. Ger. 42 51 10N 14 59 E
Gort, Ire. 25 53 4N 8 50W
Gorzów Wielkopolski, Pol. 42 52 43N 15 15 E
Gosberton, U.K. 19 52 52N 0 10W
Gosford, Austral. 70 33 23S 151 18 E
Gosforth, U.K. 18 54 24N 3 27W
Gosport, U.K. 14 50 48N 1 8W
Göteborg, Swed. 45 57 43N 11 59 E
Gotha, E. Ger. 42 50 56N 10 42 E
Gotland, Swed. 45 57 30N 18 33 E
Gouda, Neth. 36 52 1N 4 42 E
Goudhurst, U.K. 15 51 7N 0 28 E
Gouin, Rés., Canada 93 48 35N 74 40W
Goulburn, Austral. 70 34 44S 149 44 E
Gourock, U.K. 20 55 58N 4 49W
Governador Valadares, Brazil 101 18 15S 41 57W
Gower, The, U.K. 17 51 35N 4 10W
Gowna, L., Ire. 24 53 52N 7 35W
Gowrie, Carse of, U.K. 21 56 30N 3 10W
Goya, Arg. 102 29 10S 59 10W
Gozo, Malta 40 36 0N 14 13 E
Grafham Water, U.K. 15 52 18N 0 17W
Grafton, Austral. 67 29 38S 152 58 E
Graham Bell, I., U.S.S.R. 48 80 5N 70 0 E
Graham Land, Ant. 103 65 0S 64 0W
Grainthorpe, U.K. 19 53 27N 0 5 E
Grampian □, U.K. 23 57 0N 3 0W
Grampian Mts., U.K. 23 56 50N 4 0W
Gran Canaria, Can. Is. 78 27 55N 15 35W
Gran Chaco, S. Am. 96 25 0S 61 0W
Granada, Sp. 37 37 10N 3 35W
Granard, Ire. 24 53 47N 7 30W
Grand Bahama, Baham. 95 26 40N 78 30W
Grand Canyon National Park, U.S.A. 90 36 15N 112 20W
Grand Cayman, W. Ind. 95 19 20N 81 20W
Grand Rapids, U.S.A. 92 42 57N 86 40W
Grande de Santiago →, Mex. 94 21 36N 105 26W
Grande Prairie, Canada 88 55 10N 118 50W
Grange-over-Sands, U.K. 18 54 12N 2 55W
Grangemouth, U.K. 21 56 1N 3 43W
Grangetown, U.K. 19 54 36N 1 7W
Grantham, U.K. 19 52 55N 0 39W
Grantown-on-Spey, U.K. 23 57 19N 3 36W
Grantshouse, U.K. 21 55 53N 2 17W
Grasmere, U.K. 18 54 28N 3 2W
Grassington, U.K. 18 54 5N 2 0W
Gravesend, U.K. 15 51 25N 0 22 E
Grayrigg, U.K. 18 54 22N 2 40W
Grays, U.K. 15 51 28N 0 23 E
Graz, Austria 42 47 4N 15 27 E
Great Abaco I., Baham. 95 26 25N 77 10W
Great Australian Bight, Austral. 66 33 30S 130 0 E
Great Ayton, U.K. 19 54 29N 1 8W
Great Baddow, U.K. 15 51 43N 0 31 E
Great Barrier Reef, Austral. 67 18 0S 146 50 E
Great Basin, U.S.A. 90 40 0N 116 30W
Great Bear L., Canada 88 65 30N 120 0W
Great Bentley, U.K. 15 51 51N 1 5 E
Great Blasket I., Ire. 25 52 5N 10 30W
Great Britain, Europe 5 54 0N 2 15W
Great Chesterford, U.K. 15 52 4N 0 11 E
Great Clifton, U.K. 18 54 39N 3 29W
Great Divide, The, Austral. 70 35 0S 149 17 E
Great Dividing Ra., Austral. 67 23 0S 146 0 E
Great Dunmow, U.K. 15 51 52N 0 22 E
Great Falls, U.S.A. 90 47 27N 111 12W
Great Harwood, U.K. 18 53 43N 2 30W
Great Inagua I., Baham. 95 21 0N 73 20W
Great Indian Desert = Thar Desert, India 58 28 0N 72 0 E
Great Malvern, U.K. 14 52 7N 2 19W
Great Massingham, U.K. 15 52 47N 0 41 E
Great Missenden, U.K. 15 51 42N 0 42W
Great Orme's Head, U.K. 17 53 20N 3 52W
Great Ouse →, U.K. 15 52 47N 0 22 E
Great Plains, N. Am. 82 47 0N 105 0W
Great Salt Lake, U.S.A. 90 41 0N 112 30W
Great Sandy Desert, Austral. 66 21 0S 124 0 E
Great Shefford, U.K. 14 51 29N 1 27W
Great Shelford, U.K. 15 52 9N 0 9 E
Great Shunner Fell, U.K. 18 54 22N 2 16W
Great Slave L., Canada 88 61 23N 115 38W
Great Stour = Stour →, U.K. 15 51 15N 1 20 E
Great Torrington, U.K. 16 50 57N 4 9W
Great Victoria Desert, Austral. 66 29 30S 126 30 E
Great Waltham, U.K. 15 51 47N 0 29 E
Great Whernside, U.K. 18 54 9N 1 59W
Great Wyrley, U.K. 14 52 40N 2 1W
Great Yarmouth, U.K. 15 52 40N 1 45 E
Great Yeldham, U.K. 15 52 1N 0 33 E
Greater Antilles, W. Ind. 95 17 40N 74 0W
Greater London □, U.K. 15 51 30N 0 5W
Greater Manchester □, U.K. 18 53 30N 2 15W
Greater Sunda Is., Indon. 63 7 0S 112 0 E
Greatham, U.K. 19 54 38N 1 14W
Greece ■, Europe 41 40 0N 23 0 E
Greeley, U.S.A. 90 40 30N 104 40W
Green B., U.S.A. 92 45 0N 87 30W
Green Bay, U.S.A. 92 44 30N 88 0W
Green Hammerton, U.K. 19 54 2N 1 17W
Green Lowther, U.K. 21 55 22N 3 44W
Greenhead, U.K. 21 54 58N 2 31W
Greenland ■, N. Am. 89 66 0N 45 0W
Greenland Sea, Arctic 103 73 0N 10 0W
Greenlaw, U.K. 21 55 42N 2 28W
Greenock, U.K. 20 55 57N 4 46W
Greenodd, U.K. 18 54 14N 3 3W
Greenore, Ire. 24 54 2N 6 8W
Greenore Pt., Ire. 25 52 15N 6 20W
Greensboro, U.S.A. 91 36 7N 79 46W
Greenwich, U.K. 15 51 28N 0 0 E
Grenada ■, W. Ind. 94 12 10N 61 40W
Grenoble, Fr. 35 45 12N 5 42 E
Greta →, U.K. 18 54 9N 2 36W
Gretna, U.K. 21 54 59N 3 4W
Gretna Green, U.K. 21 55 0N 3 3W
Gretton, U.K. 15 52 33N 0 40W
Grey Range, Austral. 67 27 0S 143 30 E
Greymouth, N.Z. 71 42 29S 171 13 E
Greystoke, U.K. 18 54 39N 2 52W
Gribbin Head, U.K. 16 50 18N 4 41W
Griffith, Austral. 70 34 18S 146 2 E
Grimsby, U.K. 19 53 35N 0 5W
Gris-Nez, C., Fr. 34 50 52N 1 35 E
Grizebeck, U.K. 18 54 16N 3 10W
Grodno, U.S.S.R. 46 53 42N 23 52 E
Groningen, Neth. 36 53 15N 6 35 E
Groote Eylandt, Austral. 67 14 0S 136 40 E
Groznyy, U.S.S.R. 47 43 20N 45 45 E
Gruinard B., U.K. 22 57 56N 5 35W
Guadalajara, Mex. 94 20 40N 103 20W
Guadalajara, Sp. 37 40 37N 3 12W
Guadalete →, Sp. 37 36 35N 6 13W
Guadeloupe ■, W. Ind. 94 16 20N 61 40W
Guadiana →, Port. 37 37 14N 7 22W
Guadix, Sp. 37 37 18N 3 11W
Gualeguay, Arg. 102 33 10S 59 14W
Guam, Pac. Oc. 64 13 27N 144 45 E
Guangdong □, China 61 23 0N 113 0 E
Guangxi Zhuangzu Zizhiqu □, China 61 24 0N 109 0 E
Guangzhou, China 61 23 5N 113 10 E
Guantánamo, Cuba 95 20 10N 75 14W
Guaporé →, Brazil 100 11 55S 65 4W
Guard Bridge, U.K. 21 56 21N 2 52W
Guardafui, C. = Asir, Ras, Som. 73 11 55N 51 10 E
Guatemala, Guat. 94 14 40N 90 22W
Guatemala ■, Cent. Am. 94 15 40N 90 30W
Guaviare →, Col. 100 4 3N 67 44W
Guayaquil, Ecuad. 100 2 15S 79 52W
Guaymas, Mex. 94 27 59N 110 54W
Guelph, Canada 92 43 35N 80 20W
Guernsey, U.K. 34 49 30N 2 35W
Guestling Green, U.K. 15 50 53N 0 40 E
Guildford, U.K. 15 51 14N 0 34W
Guilin, China 61 25 18N 110 15 E
Guinea ■, W. Afr. 78 10 20N 10 0W
Guinea, Gulf of, Atl. Oc. 72 3 0N 2 30 E
Guinea-Bissau ■, Africa 78 12 0N 15 0W
Guisborough, U.K. 19 54 32N 1 2W
Guiyang, China 60 26 32N 106 40 E
Guizhou □, China 60 27 0N 107 0 E
Gujarat □, India 58 23 20N 71 0 E
Gujranwala, Pak. 58 32 10N 74 12 E
Gujrat, Pak. 58 32 40N 74 2 E
Gulbarga, India 58 17 20N 76 50 E
Gulf, The, Asia 56 27 0N 50 0 E
Gullane, U.K. 21 56 2N 2 50W
Guntur, India 59 16 23N 80 30 E
Gurnard's Head, U.K. 16 50 12N 5 37W
Guyana ■, S. Am. 100 5 0N 59 0W
Gwalchmai, U.K. 17 53 16N 4 23W
Gwalior, India 58 26 12N 78 10 E
Gweebarra B., Ire. 24 54 52N 8 21W
Gweedore, Ire. 24 55 4N 8 15W
Gweek, U.K. 16 50 6N 5 12W
Gwennap, U.K. 16 50 12N 5 9W
Gwent □, U.K. 17 51 45N 2 55W
Gweru, Zimb. 81 19 28S 29 45 E
Gwynedd □, U.K. 17 53 0N 4 0W
Gympie, Austral. 67 26 11S 152 38 E
Györ, Hung. 43 47 41N 17 40 E

H

Haarlem, Neth. 36 52 23N 4 39 E
Hachinohe, Jap. 62 40 30N 141 29 E
Hackney, U.K. 15 51 33N 0 2W
Hackthorpe, U.K. 18 54 37N 2 42W
Haddenham, U.K. 15 51 46N 0 56W
Haddington, U.K. 21 55 57N 2 48W
Hadleigh, U.K. 15 52 3N 0 58 E
Hadley, U.K. 14 52 42N 2 28W
Hadlow, U.K. 15 51 12N 0 20 E
Hadrians Wall, U.K. 19 55 0N 2 30W
Haeju, N. Kor. 61 38 3N 125 45 E
Hafnarfjörður, Ice. 44 64 4N 21 57W
Hagen, W. Ger. 36 51 21N 7 29 E
Hags Hd., Ire. 25 52 57N 9 30W
Haifa, Isr. 57 32 46N 35 0 E
Haikou, China 61 20 1N 110 16 E
Ḥā'il, Si. Arab. 56 27 28N 41 45 E
Hailar, China 61 49 12N 119 37 E
Hailsham, U.K. 15 50 52N 0 17 E
Hainan, China 61 19 0N 109 30 E
Hainton, U.K. 19 53 21N 0 13W
Haiphong, Viet. 60 20 47N 106 41 E
Haiti ■, W. Ind. 95 19 0N 72 30W
Hakodate, Jap. 62 41 45N 140 44 E
Halberton, U.K. 16 50 55N 3 24W
Hale, U.K. 18 53 24N 2 21W
Halesowen, U.K. 14 52 27N 2 2W
Halesworth, U.K. 15 52 21N 1 30 E
Halifax, Canada 93 44 38N 63 35W
Halifax, U.K. 18 53 43N 1 51W
Halifax B., Austral. 67 18 50S 147 0 E
Halkirk, U.K. 23 58 30N 3 30W
Halle, Ger. 42 51 29N 12 0 E
Hallow, U.K. 14 52 14N 2 15W
Hallworthy, U.K. 16 50 38N 4 34W
Halmahera, Indon. 63 0 40N 128 0 E
Halmstad, Swed. 45 56 41N 12 52 E
Halstead, U.K. 15 51 59N 0 39 E
Haltwhistle, U.K. 21 54 58N 2 27W
Hamadān, Iran 56 34 52N 48 32 E
Hamāh, Syria 56 35 5N 36 40 E
Hamamatsu, Jap. 62 34 45N 137 45 E
Hambledon, U.K. 14 50 56N 1 6W
Hambleton Hills, U.K. 19 54 17N 1 12W
Hamburg, W. Ger. 42 53 32N 9 59 E
Hämeenlinna, Fin. 45 61 0N 24 28 E
Hamersley Ra., Austral. 66 22 0S 117 45 E
Hamilton, Berm. 95 32 15N 64 45W
Hamilton, Canada 92 43 15N 79 50W
Hamilton, N.Z. 71 37 47S 175 19 E
Hamilton, U.K. 21 55 47N 4 2W
Hamm, W. Ger. 36 51 40N 7 49 E
Hammerfest, Nor. 44 70 39N 23 41 E
Hammersmith, U.K. 15 51 30N 0 15W
Hammond, U.S.A. 92 41 40N 87 30W
Hampshire □, U.K. 14 51 3N 1 20W
Hampshire Downs, U.K. 14 51 10N 1 10W
Hampton in Arden, U.K. 14 52 26N 1 42W
Hangzhou, China 61 30 18N 120 11 E
Hanko, Fin. 45 59 59N 22 57 E
Hanningfield Water, U.K. 15 51 40N 0 30 E
Hanoi, Viet. 60 21 5N 105 55 E
Hanover, W. Ger. 42 52 23N 9 43 E
Haora, India 59 22 37N 88 20 E
Happy Valley, Canada 89 53 15N 60 20W
Harare, Zimb. 81 17 43S 31 2 E
Harbin, China 61 45 46N 126 51 E
Hardangerfjorden, Nor. 45 60 15N 6 0 E
Harewood, U.K. 19 53 54N 1 30W
Haringey, U.K. 15 51 35N 0 7W
Harlech, U.K. 17 52 52N 4 7W
Harleston, U.K. 15 52 25N 1 18 E
Harlingen, Neth. 36 53 11N 5 25 E
Harlow, U.K. 15 51 47N 0 9 E
Harpenden, U.K. 15 51 48N 0 20W
Harrietsham, U.K. 15 51 15N 0 41 E
Harrington, U.K. 18 54 37N 3 55W
Harris, U.K. 22 57 50N 6 55W
Harris, Sd. of, U.K. 22 57 44N 7 6W
Harrisburg, U.S.A. 93 40 18N 76 52W
Harrogate, U.K. 19 53 59N 1 32W
Harrow, U.K. 15 51 35N 0 15W
Hartest, U.K. 15 52 7N 0 41 E
Hartford, U.S.A. 93 41 47N 72 41W
Harthill, U.K. 21 55 52N 3 45W
Hartland, U.K. 16 50 59N 4 29W
Hartland Pt., U.K. 16 51 2N 4 32W
Hartlebury, U.K. 14 52 20N 2 13W
Hartlepool, U.K. 19 54 42N 1 11W
Hartley, U.K. 21 55 5N 1 27W
Hartpury, U.K. 14 51 55N 2 18W
Harwell, U.K. 14 51 40N 1 17W
Harwich, U.K. 15 51 56N 1 18 E
Harz, Europe 26 51 40N 10 40 E
Hasa, Si. Arab. 56 26 0N 49 0 E
Haslemere, U.K. 15 51 5N 0 41W
Haslingden, U.K. 18 53 43N 2 20W
Hasselt, Belg. 36 50 56N 5 21 E
Hastings, N.Z. 71 39 39S 176 52 E
Hastings, U.K. 15 50 51N 0 36 E
Hatfield, U.K. 15 51 46N 0 11W
Hatfield Broad Oak, U.K. 15 51 48N 0 16 E
Hatherleigh, U.K. 16 50 49N 4 4W
Hathersage, U.K. 19 53 20N 1 39W
Hatteras, C., U.S.A. 91 35 10N 75 30W
Haugh of Urr, U.K. 21 55 0N 3 51W
Haughley, U.K. 15 52 13N 0 59 E
Hauraki Gulf, N.Z. 71 36 35S 175 5 E
Hauxley, U.K. 21 55 21N 1 35W
Havana, Cuba 95 23 8N 82 22W
Havant, U.K. 15 50 51N 0 59W
Haverfordwest, U.K. 17 51 48N 4 59W
Haverhill, U.K. 15 52 6N 0 27 E
Haverigg, U.K. 18 54 12N 3 16W
Havering, U.K. 15 51 33N 0 20 E
Havre, Le, Fr. 34 49 30N 0 5 E
Hawaiian Is., Pac. Oc. 90 20 30N 156 0W
Hawera, N.Z. 71 39 35S 174 19 E
Hawes, U.K. 18 54 18N 2 12W
Haweswater, U.K. 18 54 32N 2 48W
Hawick, U.K. 21 55 25N 2 48W
Hawkchurch, U.K. 16 50 47N 2 56W

Hawke B., N.Z. 71 39 25S 177 20 E
Hawkesbury Upton, U.K. 14 51 34N 2 19W
Hawkhurst, U.K. 15 51 2N 0 31 E
Hawkshead, U.K. 18 54 23N 3 0W
Haworth, U.K. 18 53 50N 1 57W
Hawsker, U.K. 19 54 27N 0 34W
Haxby, U.K. 19 54 1N 1 4W
Hay-on-Wye, U.K. 17 52 4N 3 9W
Hay River, Canada 88 60 51N 115 44W
Hayburn Wyke, U.K. 19 54 22N 0 28W
Haydon Bridge, U.K. 21 54 58N 2 15W
Hayle, U.K. 16 50 12N 5 25W
Hayton, U.K. 18 54 55N 2 45W
Haywards Heath, U.K. 15 51 0N 0 5W
Heacham, U.K. 15 52 55N 0 30 E
Headcorn, U.K. 15 51 10N 0 39 E
Heanor, U.K. 19 53 1N 1 20W
Heathfield, U.K. 15 50 58N 0 18 E
Hebburn, U.K. 21 54 59N 1 30W
Hebden Bridge, U.K. 18 53 45N 2 0W
Hebei □, China 61 39 0N 116 0 E
Hebrides, U.K. 22 57 30N 7 0W
Hechuan, China 60 30 2N 106 12 E
Heckington, U.K. 19 52 59N 0 17W
Hedmark fylke □, Nor. 44 61 17N 11 40 E
Hednesford, U.K. 14 52 43N 2 0W
Hedon, U.K. 19 53 44N 0 11W
Heerlen, Neth. 36 50 55N 6 0 E
Hefei, China 61 31 52N 117 18 E
Hegang, China 61 47 20N 130 19 E
Heidelberg, W. Ger. 42 49 23N 8 41 E
Heilbronn, W. Ger. 42 49 8N 9 13 E
Heilongjiang □, China 61 48 0N 126 0 E
Hekla, Ice. 44 63 56N 19 35W
Helensburgh, U.K. 20 56 0N 4 44W
Heligoland, W. Ger. 42 54 10N 7 51 E
Hellifield, U.K. 18 54 0N 2 13W
Helmond, Neth. 36 51 29N 5 41 E
Helmsdale, U.K. 23 58 7N 3 40W
Helmsley, U.K. 19 54 15N 1 2W
Helperby, U.K. 19 54 8N 1 20W
Helsby, U.K. 18 53 16N 2 47W
Helsingborg, Swed. 45 56 3N 12 42 E
Helsingør, Den. 45 56 2N 12 35 E
Helsinki, Fin. 45 60 15N 25 3 E
Helston, U.K. 16 50 7N 5 17W
Helvellyn, U.K. 18 54 31N 3 1W
Hemel Hempstead, U.K. 15 51 45N 0 28W
Hempton, U.K. 15 52 50N 0 49 E
Hemsworth, U.K. 19 53 37N 1 21W
Hemyock, U.K. 16 50 50N 3 15W
Henan □, China 61 34 0N 114 0 E
Henfield, U.K. 15 50 56N 0 17W
Hengelo, Neth. 36 52 16N 6 48 E
Hengyang, China 61 26 51N 112 30 E
Henley-in-Arden, U.K. 14 52 18N 1 47W
Henley-on-Thames, U.K. 15 51 32N 0 53W
Henlow, U.K. 15 52 2N 0 18W
Henstridge, U.K. 14 50 59N 2 24W
Henzada, Burma 59 17 38N 95 26 E
Herāt, Afg. 57 34 20N 62 7 E
Hereford, U.K. 14 52 4N 2 42W
Hereford and Worcester □, U.K. 14 52 10N 2 30W
Hermosillo, Mex. 94 29 4N 110 58W
Herne, W. Ger. 36 51 33N 7 12 E
Herne Bay, U.K. 15 51 22N 1 8 E
Herning, Den. 45 56 8N 8 58 E
Herstmonceux, U.K. 15 50 53N 0 21 E
Hertford, U.K. 15 51 47N 0 4W
Hertford □, U.K. 15 51 51N 0 5W
's-Hertogenbosch, Neth. 36 51 42N 5 17 E
Hesse □, W. Ger. 42 50 40N 9 20 E
Hessle, U.K. 19 53 44N 0 28 E
Hethersett, U.K. 15 52 35N 1 10 E
Hetton-le-Hole, U.K. 21 54 49N 1 26W
Hexham, U.K. 19 54 58N 2 7W
Heybridge, U.K. 15 51 44N 0 42 E
Heysham, U.K. 18 54 5N 2 53W
Heytesbury, U.K. 14 51 11N 2 7W
Heywood, U.K. 18 53 36N 2 13W
High Atlas, Mor. 72 32 30N 5 0W
High Bentham, U.K. 18 54 8N 2 31W
High Borrow Bridge, U.K. 18 54 26N 2 43W
High Ercall, U.K. 14 52 46N 2 37W
High Hesket, U.K. 18 54 47N 2 49W
High Pike, U.K. 18 54 43N 3 4W
High Willhays, U.K. 16 50 41N 3 59W
High Wycombe, U.K. 15 51 37N 0 45W
Higham Ferrers, U.K. 15 52 18N 0 36W
Highbridge, U.K. 14 51 13N 2 59W
Highclere, U.K. 14 51 20N 1 22W
Highland □, U.K. 22 57 30N 5 0W
Highley, U.K. 14 52 25N 2 23W
Hightae, U.K. 21 55 5N 3 27W
Highworth, U.K. 14 51 38N 1 42W
Hilgay, U.K. 15 52 34N 0 23 E
Hillingdon, U.K. 15 51 33N 0 29W
Hillsborough, U.K. 24 54 28N 6 6W
Hilo, U.S.A. 90 19 44N 155 5W
Hilpsford Pt., U.K. 18 54 4N 3 12W
Hilversum, Neth. 36 52 14N 5 10 E
Himachal Pradesh □, India 58 31 30N 77 0 E
Himalaya, Mts., Asia 60 29 0N 84 0 E
Himeji, Jap. 62 34 50N 134 40 E
Hinckley, U.K. 14 52 33N 1 21W
Hinderwell, U.K. 19 54 32N 0 45W
Hindhead, U.K. 15 51 6N 0 42W
Hindley, U.K. 18 53 32N 2 35W
Hindu Kush, Asia 57 36 0N 71 0 E
Hingham, U.K. 15 52 35N 0 59 E
Hinkley Pt., U.K. 14 50 59N 3 32W
Hinstock, U.K. 14 52 50N 2 28W
Hiroshima, Jap. 62 34 24N 132 30 E
Hispaniola, W. Ind. 95 19 0N 71 0W
Histon, U.K. 15 52 15N 0 6 E
Hitchin, U.K. 15 51 57N 0 16W
Ho Chi Minh City, Viet. 63 10 58N 106 40 E
Hobart, Austral. 67 42 50S 147 21 E
Hodder →, U.K. 18 53 57N 2 27W
Hoddesdon, U.K. 15 51 45N 0 1W
Hodge →, U.K. 19 54 14N 0 55W
Hoff, U.K. 18 54 34N 2 31W
Hoggar, Mts., Alg. 78 23 0N 6 30 E
Hog's Back, U.K. 15 51 13N 0 40W
Hohhot, China 61 40 52N 111 40 E
Hokitika, N.Z. 71 42 42S 171 0 E
Hokkaidō □, Jap. 62 43 30N 143 0 E
Holbeach, U.K. 15 52 48N 0 1 E
Holbeach Marsh, U.K. 15 52 52N 0 5 E
Holderness, U.K. 19 53 45N 0 5W
Holguín, Cuba 95 20 50N 76 20W
Holkham, U.K. 15 52 57N 0 48 E
Holland Fen, U.K. 19 53 0N 0 8W
Holland-on-Sea, U.K. 15 51 48N 1 12 E
Holme, Humberside, U.K. 19 53 50N 0 48W
Holme, N. Yorks., U.K. 18 53 34N 1 50W
Holmes Chapel, U.K. 18 53 13N 2 21W
Holmfirth, U.K. 19 53 34N 1 48W
Holmwood, U.K. 15 51 12N 0 19W
Holsworthy, U.K. 16 50 48N 4 21W
Holt, U.K. 15 52 55N 1 4 E
Holy I., England, U.K. 19 55 42N 1 48W
Holy I., Scotland, U.K. 20 55 31N 5 4W
Holy I., Wales, U.K. 17 53 17N 4 37W
Holyhead, U.K. 17 53 18N 4 38W
Holywell, U.K. 17 53 16N 3 14W
Holywood, U.K. 24 54 38N 5 50W
Homs, Syria 56 34 40N 36 45 E
Honduras ■, Cent. Am. 94 14 40N 86 30W
Honduras, G. de, Cent. Am. 94 16 50N 87 0W
Hong →, Viet. 60 20 17N 106 34 E
Hong Kong ■, Asia 61 22 11N 114 14 E
Honington, U.K. 19 52 58N 0 35W
Honiton, U.K. 16 50 48N 3 11W
Honolulu, U.S.A. 90 21 19N 157 52W
Honshū, Jap. 62 36 0N 138 0 E
Hoo, U.K. 15 51 25N 0 33 E
Hook, U.K. 15 51 17N 0 55W
Hook Hd., Ire. 25 52 8N 6 57W
Hoorn, Neth. 36 52 38N 5 4 E
Horden, U.K. 19 54 45N 1 17W
Horley, U.K. 15 51 10N 0 10W
Horn, C., Chile 102 55 50S 67 30W
Horn Head, Ire. 24 55 13N 8 0W
Horncastle, U.K. 19 53 13N 0 8W
Horndean, U.K. 15 50 50N 0 59W
Horningsham, U.K. 14 51 11N 2 16W
Hornsby, Austral. 70 33 42S 151 2 E
Hornsea, U.K. 19 53 55N 0 10W
Horsens, Den. 45 55 52N 9 51 E
Horsforth, U.K. 19 53 50N 1 39W
Horsham, Austral. 70 36 44S 142 13 E
Horsham, U.K. 15 51 4N 0 20W
Horsham St. Faith, U.K. 15 52 41N 1 15 E
Horsted Keynes, U.K. 15 51 2N 0 1W
Horton-in-Ribblesdale, U.K. 18 54 9N 2 19W
Horwich, U.K. 18 53 37N 2 33W
Hospitalet de Llobregat, Sp. 37 41 21N 2 6 E
Hotan, China 60 37 25N 79 55 E
Houghton-le-Spring, U.K. 19 54 51N 1 28W
Houghton Regis, U.K. 15 51 54N 0 32W
Hounslow, U.K. 15 51 29N 0 20W
Houston, U.S.A. 91 29 50N 95 20W
Hovd, Mong. 60 48 2N 91 37 E
Hove, U.K. 15 50 50N 0 10W
Hoveton, U.K. 15 52 45N 1 23 E
Hovingham, U.K. 19 54 10N 0 59W
Hövsgöl Nuur, Mong. 60 51 0N 100 30 E
Howden, U.K. 19 53 45N 0 52W
Howth Hd., Ire. 24 53 21N 6 0W
Hoxne, U.K. 15 52 22N 1 11 E
Hoy I., U.K. 23 58 50N 3 15W
Hoylake, U.K. 18 53 24N 3 11W
Hrádec Králové, Czech. 42 50 15N 15 50 E
Hron →, Czech. 43 47 49N 18 45 E
Huainan, China 61 32 39N 117 2 E
Huambo, Angola 81 12 42S 15 54 E
Huancayo, Peru 100 12 5S 75 12W
Huang He →, China 61 37 55N 118 50 E
Huangshi, China 61 30 10N 115 3 E
Huánuco, Peru 100 9 55S 76 15W
Hubei □, China 61 31 0N 112 0 E
Hucknall, U.K. 19 53 3N 1 12W
Huddersfield, U.K. 19 53 38N 1 49W
Hudson →, U.S.A. 93 40 42N 74 2W
Hudson Bay, Canada 89 52 51N 102 23W
Hudson Str., Canada 89 62 0N 70 0W
Hue, Viet. 63 16 30N 107 35 E
Huelva, Sp. 37 37 18N 6 57W
Huesca, Sp. 37 42 8N 0 25W
Hugh Town, U.K. 16 49 55N 6 19W
Hughenden, Austral. 67 20 52S 144 10 E
Hughes, U.S.A. 88 66 0N 154 20W
Hull, Canada 93 45 25N 75 44W
Hull = Kingston-upon-Hull, U.K. 19 53 45N 0 20W
Hull →, U.K. 19 53 43N 0 25W
Hullavington, U.K. 14 51 31N 2 9W
Hulme End, U.K. 18 53 8N 1 51W
Humber →, U.K. 19 53 40N 0 10W
Humber, Mouth of the, U.K. 19 53 32N 0 28W
Humberside □, U.K. 19 53 50N 0 30W
Humboldt →, U.S.A. 90 40 2N 118 31W
Hume, L., Austral. 70 36 0S 147 0 E
Humshaugh, U.K. 21 55 3N 2 8W
Húnaflói, Ice. 44 65 50N 20 50W
Hunan □, China 61 27 30N 111 30 E
Hungary ■, Europe 43 47 20N 19 20 E
Hungary, Plain of, Europe 26 47 0N 20 0 E
Hungerford, U.K. 14 51 25N 1 30W
Hŭngnam, N. Kor. 61 39 49N 127 45 E
Hunmanby, U.K. 19 54 12N 0 19W
Hunstanton, U.K. 15 52 57N 0 30 E
Hunter →, Austral. 70 32 52S 151 46 E
Hunterston, U.K. 20 55 43N 4 55W
Huntingdon, U.K. 15 52 20N 0 11W
Huntington, U.S.A. 92 38 20N 82 30W
Huntly, U.K. 23 57 27N 2 48W
Huntsville, U.S.A. 91 34 45N 86 35W
Hurlford, U.K. 20 55 35N 4 29W
Huron, L., N. Am. 92 45 0N 83 0W
Hursley, U.K. 14 51 1N 1 23W
Hurstbourne Tarrant, U.K. 14 51 17N 1 27W
Hurstpierpoint, U.K. 15 50 56N 0 11W
Húsavík, Ice. 44 66 3N 17 21W
Husband's Bosworth, U.K. 14 52 27N 1 3W
Huyton, U.K. 18 53 25N 2 52W
Hyde, U.K. 18 53 26N 2 6W
Hyderabad, India 58 17 22N 78 29 E
Hyderabad, Pak. 58 25 23N 68 24 E
Hynish, U.K. 20 56 27N 6 54W
Hynish B., U.K. 20 56 29N 6 40W
Hythe, U.K. 15 51 4N 1 5 E

I

Iaşi, Rom. 43 47 10N 27 40 E
Ibadan, Nig. 78 7 22N 3 58 E
Ibagué, Col. 100 4 20N 75 20W
Iberian Peninsula, Europe 26 40 0N 5 0W
Ibiza, Sp. 37 38 54N 1 26 E
Ibstock, U.K. 14 52 42N 1 23W
Icá, Peru 100 14 0S 75 48W
Iceland ■, Atl. Oc. 44 65 0N 19 0W
Ichinomiya, Jap. 62 35 18N 136 48 E
Idaho □, U.S.A. 90 44 10N 114 0W
Idar-Oberstein, W. Ger. 36 49 43N 7 19 E
Idle →, U.K. 19 53 27N 0 49W
Idmiston, U.K. 14 51 8N 1 43W
Idsworth, U.K. 15 50 56N 0 56W
Igarka, U.S.S.R. 49 67 30N 86 33 E
Iglésias, It. 40 39 19N 8 27 E
Iguaçu Falls, Brazil 102 25 41S 54 26W
IJsselmeer, Neth. 36 52 45N 5 20 E
Ilchester, U.K. 14 51 0N 2 41W
Île-de-France, Fr. 34 49 0N 2 20 E
Ilfracombe, U.K. 16 51 13N 4 8W
Ilhéus, Brazil 101 14 49S 39 2W
Ilkeston, U.K. 19 52 59N 1 19W
Ilkley, U.K. 18 53 56N 1 49W
Illinois □, U.S.A. 91 40 15N 89 30W
Ilminster, U.K. 14 50 55N 2 56W
Iloilo, Phil. 63 10 45N 122 33 E
Immingham, U.K. 19 53 37N 0 12W
Imphal, India 59 24 48N 93 56 E
Inari, Fin. 44 68 54N 27 5 E
Ince, U.K. 18 53 32N 2 38W
Inchcape Rock, U.K. 21 56 26N 2 24W
Inchkeith, I., U.K. 21 56 2N 3 8W
Inchon, S. Kor. 61 37 27N 126 40 E
Inchture, U.K. 21 56 26N 3 8W
Indaal, L., U.K. 20 55 44N 6 20W
India ■, Asia 58 20 0N 78 0 E
Indian Ocean 129 5 0S 75 0 E
Indiana □, U.S.A. 92 40 0N 86 0W
Indianapolis, U.S.A. 92 39 42N 86 10W
Indonesia ■, Asia 63 5 0S 115 0 E
Indore, India 58 22 42N 75 53 E
Indus →, Pak. 58 24 20N 67 47 E
Ingatestone, U.K. 15 51 40N 0 23 E
Ingleborough, U.K. 18 54 11N 2 23W
Ingleton, U.K. 18 54 9N 2 29W
Ingoldmells, Pt., U.K. 19 53 11N 0 21 E
Inishbofin, Ire. 24 53 35N 10 12W
Inishmore, Ire. 25 53 8N 9 45W
Inishowen, Ire. 24 55 14N 7 15W
Inkberrow, U.K. 14 52 13N 1 59W
Inkpen Beacon, U.K. 14 51 22N 1 28W
Inn →, Austria 40 48 35N 13 28 E
Innellan, U.K. 20 55 54N 4 58W
Inner Hebrides, U.K. 22 57 0N 6 30W
Inner Mongolia □, China 61 42 0N 112 0 E
Inner Sound, U.K. 22 57 30N 5 55W
Innerleithen, U.K. 21 55 37N 3 4W
Innsbruck, Austria 42 47 16N 11 23 E
Inny →, Ire. 25 53 30N 7 50W
Interlaken, Switz. 42 46 41N 7 50 E
Inuvik, Canada 88 68 16N 133 40W
Inveraray, U.K. 20 56 13N 5 5W
Inverbervie, U.K. 23 56 50N 2 17W
Invercargill, N.Z. 71 46 24S 168 24 E
Inverell, Austral. 67 29 45S 151 8 E
Invergarry, U.K. 23 57 5N 4 48W
Invergordon, U.K. 23 57 41N 4 10W
Invergowrie, U.K. 21 56 29N 3 5W
Inverkeithing, U.K. 21 56 2N 3 24W
Invermoriston, U.K. 23 57 13N 4 38W
Inverness, U.K. 23 57 29N 4 12W
Inverurie, U.K. 23 57 15N 2 21W
Iona, U.K. 20 56 20N 6 25W
Ionian Is., Greece 41 38 40N 20 0 E
Ionian Sea, Greece 41 37 30N 17 30 E
Iowa □, U.S.A. 91 42 18N 93 30W
Iowa City, U.S.A. 91 41 40N 91 35W
Ipoh, Malay. 63 4 35N 101 5 E
Ipswich, U.K. 15 52 4N 1 9 E
Iquique, Chile 100 20 19S 70 5W
Iquitos, Peru 100 3 45S 73 10W
Iráklion, Greece 41 35 20N 25 12 E
Iran ■, Asia 57 33 0N 53 0 E
Irapuato, Mex. 94 20 40N 101 30W
Iraq ■, Asia 56 33 0N 44 0 E
Irchester, U.K. 15 52 17N 0 40W
Ireland ■, Europe 24 53 0N 8 0W
Ireland's Eye, Ire. 24 53 25N 6 4W
Irian Jaya □, Indon. 64 4 0S 137 0 E
Iringa, Tanz. 80 7 48S 35 43 E
Irish Republic ■, Europe 25 53 0N 8 0W
Irish Sea, Europe 18 54 0N 5 0W
Irkutsk, U.S.S.R. 49 52 18N 104 20 E
Irlam, U.K. 18 53 26N 2 27W
Ironbridge, U.K. 14 52 38N 2 29W
Irrawaddy →, Burma 59 15 50N 95 6 E
Irt →, U.K. 18 54 24N 3 25W
Irthing →, U.K. 21 54 55N 2 55W
Irthlingborough, U.K. 15 52 20N 0 37W
Irtysh →, U.S.S.R. 48 61 4N 68 52 E
Irvine, U.K. 20 55 37N 4 40W
Irvine →, U.K. 20 55 35N 4 40W
Irvinestown, U.K. 24 54 28N 7 38W
Isabela, Phil. 63 10 12N 122 59 E
Ísafjörður, Ice. 44 66 5N 23 9W
Ishim →, U.S.S.R. 48 57 45N 71 10 E
İskenderun, Turk. 47 36 32N 36 10 E
Isla →, U.K. 23 56 32N 3 20W
Islamabad, Pak. 58 33 40N 73 10 E
Islay, U.K. 20 55 46N 6 10W
Islay Sound, U.K. 20 55 45N 6 5W
Isle of Whithorn, U.K. 20 54 42N 4 22W
Isle of Wight □, U.K. 14 50 40N 1 20W
Isleham, U.K. 15 52 21N 0 24 E
Islip, U.K. 14 51 49N 1 12W
Ismâ'ilîya, Egypt 79 30 37N 32 18 E
Israel ■, Asia 57 32 0N 34 50 E
İstanbul, Turk. 47 41 0N 29 0 E
Itabuna, Brazil 101 14 48S 39 16W
Italy ■, Europe 40 42 0N 13 0 E
Itchen →, U.K. 14 50 57N 1 20W
Ivanovo, U.S.S.R. 46 52 7N 25 29 E
Ivinghoe, U.K. 15 51 50N 0 38W
Ivory Coast ■, Africa 78 7 30N 5 0W
Ivugivik, Canada 89 62 24N 77 55W
Ivybridge, U.K. 16 50 24N 3 56W
Iwaki, Jap. 62 37 3N 140 55 E
Ixworth, U.K. 15 52 18N 0 50 E
Izhevsk = Ustinov, U.S.S.R. 46 56 51N 53 14 E
İzmir, Turk. 47 38 25N 27 8 E

J

Jabalpur, India 58 23 9N 79 58 E
Jackson, U.S.A. 91 32 20N 90 10W
Jacksonville, U.S.A. 91 30 15N 81 38W
Jaén, Sp. 37 37 44N 3 43W
Jaffna, Sri L. 58 9 45N 80 2 E
Jaipur, India 58 27 0N 75 50 E
Jakarta, Indon. 63 6 9S 106 49 E
Jamaica ■, W. Ind. 94 18 10N 77 30W
Jambi, Indon. 63 1 38S 103 30 E
James B., Canada 89 51 30N 80 0W
Jammu, India 58 32 43N 74 54 E
Jammu & Kashmir □, India 58 34 25N 77 0 E
Jamnagar, India 58 22 30N 70 6 E
Jamshedpur, India 59 22 44N 86 12 E
Japan ■, Asia 62 36 0N 136 0 E
Japan, Sea of, Asia 62 40 0N 135 0 E
Japurá →, Brazil 100 3 8S 64 46W
Jarrow, U.K. 21 54 58N 1 28W
Java, I., Indon. 63 7 0S 110 0 E
Java Sea, E. Ind. 63 4 35S 107 15 E
Jedburgh, U.K. 21 55 28N 2 33W
Jedda, Si. Arab. 56 21 29N 39 10 E
Jena, E. Ger. 42 50 56N 11 33 E
Jequié, Brazil 101 13 51S 40 5W
Jerez de la Frontera, Sp. 37 36 41N 6 7W
Jericho, Jord. 57 31 52N 35 27 E
Jersey, I., U.K. 34 49 13N 2 7W

Jersey City, *U.S.A.* . . . **93** 40 41N 74 8W
Jerusalem, *Asia* . . . . . . **57** 31 47N 35 10 E
Jervaulx, *U.K.* **19** 54 19N 1 41W
Jervis Bay, *Austral.* . . . **70** 35 8S 150 43 E
Jhansi, *India* . . . . **58** 25 30N 78 36 E
Jhelum →, *Pak.* . . . . . . **58** 31 20N 72 10 E
Jiamusi, *China* . . . . **61** 46 40N 130 26 E
Ji'an, *China* . . . . **61** 27 6N 114 59 E
Jiangsu □, *China* . . . . **61** 33 0N 120 0 E
Jiangxi □, *China* . . . . . **61** 27 30N 116 0 E
Jilin, *China* . . . . **61** 43 44N 126 30 E
Jilin □, *China* . . . . **61** 44 0N 124 0 E
Jima, *Eth.* . . . . **79** 7 40N 36 47 E
Jinan, *China* . . . . **61** 36 38N 117 1 E
Jinja, *Uganda* . . . . **80** 0 25N 33 12 E
Jinzhou, *China* . . . . . . **61** 41 5N 121 3 E
Jixi, *China* . . . . **61** 45 20N 130 50 E
João Pessoa, *Brazil* . . **101** 7 10S 34 52W
Johannesburg, *S. Afr.* . **81** 26 10S 28 2 E
John o' Groats, *U.K.* . . **23** 58 39N 3 3W
Johnstone, *U.K.* **20** 55 50N 4 31W
Johnstown, *U.S.A.* **92** 40 19N 78 53W
Johor Baharu, *Malay.* . **63** 1 28N 103 46 E
Jönköping, *Swed.* . . . . **45** 57 45N 14 10 E
Jonquière, *Canada* . . . **93** 48 27N 71 14W
Jordan ■, *Asia* . . . . . . **57** 31 0N 36 0 E
Jordan →, *Asia* . . . . . **57** 31 48N 35 32 E
Jos, *Nig.* . . . . **78** 9 53N 8 51 E
Joseph Bonaparte G.,
Austral. . . . . **66** 14 35S 128 50 E
Jotunheimen, *Nor.* . . . **44** 61 35N 8 25 E
Juan de Fuca Str.,
Canada **90** 48 15N 124 0W
Juàzeiro do Norte,
Brazil **101** 7 10S 39 18W
Juiz de Fora, *Brazil* . . . **101** 21 43S 43 19W
Juliaca, *Peru* **100** 15 25S 70 10W
Julianehåb, *Green.* . . . **89** 60 43N 46 0W
Jullundur, *India* . . . . . . **58** 31 20N 75 40 E
Jundiaí, *Brazil* **102** 24 30S 47 0W
Juneau, *U.S.A.* **88** 58 20N 134 20W
Jura, *U.K.* **20** 56 0N 5 50W
Jura, Mts., *Europe* . . . **42** 46 40N 6 5 E
Jura, Paps of, *U.K.* . . . **20** 55 55N 6 0W
Jura, Sd. of, *U.K.* **20** 55 57N 5 45W
Jurby Hd., *U.K.* **18** 54 23N 4 31W
Juruá →, *Brazil* **100** 2 37S 65 44W
Jutland = Jylland, *Den.* **45** 56 25N 9 30 E
Jylland, *Den.* . . . . **45** 56 25N 9 30 E
Jyväskylä, *Fin.* . . . . **44** 62 14N 25 50 E

K

Kābul, *Afg.* . . . . **57** 34 28N 69 11 E
Kabwe, *Zam.* . . . . **81** 14 30S 28 29 E
Kaduna, *Nig.* . . . . **78** 10 30N 7 21 E
Kaesŏng, *N. Kor.* . . . . . **61** 37 58N 126 35 E
Kagoshima, *Jap.* . . . . . **62** 31 35N 130 33 E
Kaifeng, *China* . . . . **61** 34 49N 114 30 E
Kaiserslautern, *W. Ger.* **36** 49 30N 7 43 E
Kaitaia, *N.Z.* . . . . **71** 35 8S 173 17 E
Kajaani, *Fin.* . . . . **44** 64 17N 27 46 E
Kakinada, *India* . . . . **59** 16 57N 82 11 E
Kalahari, *Africa* . . . . . . **81** 24 0S 21 30 E
Kalamazoo, *U.S.A.* **92** 42 20N 85 35W
Kalemie, *Zaïre* . . . . **80** 5 55S 29 9 E
Kalgoorlie-Boulder,
Austral. . . . . **66** 30 40S 121 22 E
Kalimantan, *Indon.* . . . **63** 0 0 114 0 E
Kalinin, *U.S.S.R.* . . . . . **46** 56 55N 35 55 E
Kaliningrad, *U.S.S.R.* . **46** 54 42N 20 32 E
Kaluga, *U.S.S.R.* . . . . . **46** 54 35N 36 10 E
Kamchatka Pen.,
U.S.S.R. . . . . **49** 57 0N 160 0 E
Kamensk Uralskiy,
U.S.S.R. . . . . **48** 56 25N 62 2 E
Kames, *U.K.* **20** 55 53N 5 15W
Kamina, *Zaïre* . . . . **80** 8 45S 25 0 E
Kamloops, *Canada* **88** 50 40N 120 20W
Kampala, *Uganda* . . . . **80** 0 20N 32 30 E
Kampuchea =
Cambodia ■, *Asia* . . **63** 12 15N 105 0 E
Kananga, *Zaïre* . . . . . . **80** 5 55S 22 18 E
Kanazawa, *Jap.* . . . . . . **62** 36 30N 136 38 E
Kanchenjunga, *Nepal* . **59** 27 50N 88 10 E
Kandy, *Sri L.* . . . . **58** 7 18N 80 43 E
Kangaroo I., *Austral.* . . **67** 35 45S 137 0 E
Kanin, Pen., *U.S.S.R.* . **46** 68 0N 45 0 E
Kankan, *Guin.* **78** 10 23N 9 15W
Kano, *Nig.* . . . . **78** 12 2N 8 30 E
Kanpur, *India* . . . . **58** 26 28N 80 20 E
Kansas □, *U.S.A.* **90** 38 40N 98 0W
Kansas City, *Kans.*,
U.S.A. **91** 39 0N 94 40W
Kansas City, *Mo.*,
U.S.A. **91** 39 3N 94 30W
Kansk, *U.S.S.R.* . . . . . . **49** 56 20N 95 37 E
Kanturk, *Ire.* **25** 52 10N 8 55W
Kaohsiung, *Taiwan* . . . **61** 22 35N 120 16 E
Kaolack, *Sene.* **78** 14 5N 16 8W
Kara Bogaz Gol, Zaliv,
U.S.S.R. . . . . **47** 41 0N 53 30 E
Kara Kalpak A.S.S.R. □,
U.S.S.R. . . . . **48** 43 0N 60 0 E
Kara Kum, *U.S.S.R.* . . . **48** 39 30N 60 0 E
Kara Sea, *U.S.S.R.* . . . **48** 75 0N 70 0 E
Karachi, *Pak.* . . . . **58** 24 53N 67 0 E
Karaganda, *U.S.S.R.* . . **48** 49 50N 73 10 E
Karakoram Ra., *Asia* . . **58** 35 30N 77 0 E
Karbalā, *Iraq* . . . . **56** 32 36N 44 3 E
Karl-Marx-Stadt, *E. Ger.* **42** 50 50N 12 55 E
Karlskrona, *Swed.* . . . . **45** 56 10N 15 35 E
Karlsruhe, *W. Ger.* . . . . **42** 49 3N 8 23 E
Karlstad, *Swed.* . . . . . . **45** 59 23N 13 30 E
Karratha, *Austral.* . . . . **66** 20 53S 116 40 E
Karsakpay, *U.S.S.R.* . . **48** 47 55N 66 40 E
Karshi, *U.S.S.R.* . . . . . **48** 38 53N 65 48 E
Kāshān, *Iran* . . . . **56** 34 5N 51 30 E
Kashi, *China* . . . . **60** 39 30N 76 2 E
Kassala, *Sudan* . . . . . . **79** 16 0N 36 0 E
Kassel, *W. Ger.* . . . . . . **42** 51 19N 9 32 E
Katmandu, *Nepal* . . . . **59** 27 45N 85 20 E
Katoomba, *Austral.* . . . **70** 33 41S 150 19 E
Katowice, *Pol.* . . . . **43** 50 17N 19 5 E
Katrine, L., *U.K.* **20** 56 15N 4 30W
Katsina, *Nig.* . . . . **78** 13 0N 7 32 E
Kattegatt, *Den.* . . . . . . **45** 57 0N 11 20 E
Kauai, *U.S.A.* **90** 22 0N 159 30W
Kaunas, *U.S.S.R.* . . . . . **46** 54 54N 23 54 E
Kavála, *Greece* . . . . . . **41** 40 57N 24 28 E
Kawagoe, *Jap.* . . . . . . **62** 35 55N 139 29 E
Kawasaki, *Jap.* . . . . . . **62** 35 35N 139 42 E
Kawthoolei □, *Burma* . **59** 18 0N 97 30 E
Kayes, *Mali* **78** 14 25N 11 30W
Kayseri, *Turk.* . . . . **47** 38 45N 35 30 E
Kazakhstan □, *U.S.S.R.* **48** 50 0N 70 0 E
Kazan, *U.S.S.R.* . . . . . . **46** 55 48N 49 3 E
Kea, *U.K.* **16** 50 13N 5 4W
Keady, *U.K.* **24** 54 15N 6 42W
Keal, Loch na, *U.K.* . . . **20** 56 30N 6 5W
Kecskemét, *Hung.* . . . . **43** 46 57N 19 42 E
Kediri, *Indon.* . . . . **63** 7 51S 112 1 E
Keelby, *U.K.* **19** 53 34N 0 15W
Keele, *U.K.* **18** 53 0N 2 17W
Keeper Hill, *Ire.* **25** 52 46N 8 17W
Keewatin, *Canada* **88** 49 46N 94 34W
Kefallinía, *Greece* . . . . **41** 38 20N 20 30 E
Keflavík, *Ice.* **44** 64 2N 22 35W
Kegworth, *U.K.* **14** 52 50N 1 17W
Keighley, *U.K.* **18** 53 52N 1 54W
Keith, *U.K.* **23** 57 33N 2 58W
Keld, *U.K.* **18** 54 24N 2 11W
Kellerberrin, *Austral.* . . **66** 31 36S 117 38 E
Kells = Ceanannus
Mor, *Ire.* **24** 53 42N 6 53W
Kells, Rhinns of, *U.K.* . **20** 55 9N 4 22W
Kelowna, *Canada* **88** 49 50N 119 25W
Kelsale, *U.K.* . . . . **15** 52 15N 1 30 E
Kelsall, *U.K.* **18** 53 14N 2 44W
Kelso, *U.K.* **21** 55 36N 2 27W
Kelvedon, *U.K.* . . . . **15** 51 50N 0 43 E
Kemble, *U.K.* **14** 51 40N 2 1W
Kemerovo, *U.S.S.R.* . . . **48** 55 20N 86 5 E
Kemi, *Fin.* . . . . **44** 65 44N 24 34 E
Kempsey, *U.K.* **14** 52 8N 2 11W
Kempston, *U.K.* **15** 52 7N 0 30W
Ken, L., *U.K.* **21** 55 0N 4 8W
Kendal, *U.K.* **18** 54 19N 2 44W
Kenilworth, *U.K.* **14** 52 22N 1 35W
Kenitra, *Mor.* **78** 34 15N 6 40W
Kenmare, *Ire.* **25** 51 52N 9 35W
Kenmare →, *Ire.* **25** 51 40N 10 0W
Kennet →, *U.K.* **14** 51 24N 0 58W
Kenninghall, *U.K.* . . . . **15** 52 26N 1 0 E
Kenora, *Canada* **88** 49 47N 94 29W
Kent □, *U.K.* . . . . **15** 51 12N 0 40 E
Kentisbeare, *U.K.* **16** 50 51N 3 18W
Kenton, *U.K.* **16** 50 37N 3 28W
Kentucky □, *U.S.A.* . . . **91** 37 20N 85 0W
Kenya ■, *Africa* . . . . . . **80** 1 0N 38 0 E
Kerala □, *India* . . . . . . **58** 11 0N 76 15 E
Kerch, *U.S.S.R.* . . . . . . **47** 45 20N 36 20 E
Kérkira, *Greece* . . . . . . **41** 39 38N 19 50 E
Kermān, *Iran* . . . . **57** 30 15N 57 1 E
Kerrera I., *U.K.* **20** 56 24N 5 32W
Kerry □, *Ire.* **25** 52 7N 9 35W
Kerry Hd., *Ire.* **25** 52 26N 9 56W
Kessingland, *U.K.* . . . . **15** 52 25N 1 41 E
Keswick, *U.K.* **18** 54 35N 3 9W
Ketchikan, *U.S.A.* **88** 55 25N 131 40W
Kettering, *U.K.* **15** 52 24N 0 44W
Kettle Ness, *U.K.* **19** 54 32N 0 41W
Kettlewell, *U.K.* **18** 54 8N 2 2W
Keweenaw Pen., *U.S.A.* **92** 47 30N 88 0W
Kexby, *U.K.* **19** 53 21N 0 41W
Key West, *U.S.A.* **91** 24 33N 82 0W
Keyingham, *U.K.* **19** 53 42N 0 7W
Keymer, *U.K.* **15** 50 55N 0 5W
Keynsham, *U.K.* **14** 51 25N 2 30W
Keyworth, *U.K.* **14** 52 52N 1 8W
Khabarovsk, *U.S.S.R.* . **49** 48 30N 135 5 E
Khaniá, *Greece* . . . . . . **41** 35 30N 24 4 E
Kharagpur, *India* . . . . . **59** 22 20N 87 25 E
Kharkov, *U.S.S.R.* . . . . **47** 49 58N 36 20 E
Khartoum, *Sudan* . . . . . **79** 15 31N 32 35 E
Khaskovo, *Bulg.* . . . . . . **41** 41 56N 25 30 E
Kherson, *U.S.S.R.* . . . . **47** 46 35N 32 35 E
Khíos, I., *Greece* . . . . . **41** 38 20N 26 0 E
Khorrāmshahr, *Iran* . . . **56** 30 29N 48 15 E
Khouribga, *Mor.* **78** 32 58N 6 57W
Khulna, *Bangla.* . . . . . **59** 22 45N 89 34 E
Khulna □, *Bangla.* . . . **59** 22 25N 89 35 E
Khurasan, *Iran* . . . . **57** 34 0N 57 0 E
Kibworth Beauchamp,
U.K. **15** 52 33N 0 59W
Kicking Horse Pass,
Canada **88** 51 28N 116 16W
Kidderminster, *U.K.* . . . **14** 52 24N 2 13W
Kidlington, *U.K.* **14** 51 49N 1 18W
Kidsgrove, *U.K.* **18** 53 6N 2 15W
Kidstones, *U.K.* **18** 54 15N 2 2W
Kidwelly, *U.K.* **17** 51 44N 4 20W
Kiel, *W. Ger.* . . . . **42** 54 16N 10 8 E
Kielce, *Pol.* . . . . **43** 50 52N 20 42 E
Kielder, *U.K.* **21** 55 14N 2 35W
Kiev, *U.S.S.R.* . . . . **47** 50 30N 30 28 E
Kigali, *Rwanda* . . . . . . **80** 1 59S 30 4 E
Kigoma-Ujiji, *Tanz.* . . . **80** 4 55S 29 36 E
Kikládhes, *Greece* . . . . **41** 37 20N 24 30 E
Kikwit, *Zaïre* . . . . **80** 5 5S 18 45 E
Kilbirnie, *U.K.* **20** 55 46N 4 42W
Kilbrannan Sd., *U.K.* . . **20** 55 40N 5 23W
Kilcreggan, *U.K.* **20** 55 59N 4 50W
Kildare, *Ire.* **25** 53 10N 6 50W
Kildare □, *Ire.* **25** 53 10N 6 50W
Kildonan, *U.K.* **23** 58 10N 3 50W
Kilfinan, *U.K.* **20** 55 57N 5 19W
Kilham, *U.K.* **19** 54 4N 0 22W
Kilimanjaro, *Tanz.* . . . . **80** 3 7S 37 20 E
Kilkee, *Ire.* **25** 52 41N 9 40W
Kilkeel, *U.K.* **24** 54 4N 6 0W
Kilkenny, *Ire.* **25** 52 40N 7 17W
Kilkenny □, *Ire.* **25** 52 35N 7 15W
Kilkhampton, *U.K.* **16** 50 53N 4 30W
Kilkieran B., *Ire.* **25** 53 18N 9 45W
Killala, *Ire.* **24** 54 13N 9 12W
Killala B., *Ire.* **24** 54 20N 9 12W
Killaloe, *Ire.* **25** 52 48N 8 28W
Killarney, *Ire.* **25** 52 2N 9 30W
Killarney, Lakes of, *Ire.* **25** 52 0N 9 30W
Killary Harbour, *Ire.* . . . **24** 53 38N 9 52W
Killchianaig, *U.K.* **20** 56 2N 5 48W
Killean, *U.K.* **20** 55 38N 5 40W
Killiecrankie, Pass of,
U.K. **23** 56 44N 3 46W
Killin, *U.K.* **20** 56 28N 4 20W
Killinghall, *U.K.* **19** 54 1N 1 33W
Killybegs, *Ire.* **24** 54 38N 8 26W
Kilmacolm, *U.K.* **20** 55 54N 4 39W
Kilmarnock, *U.K.* **20** 55 36N 4 30W
Kilmartin, *U.K.* **20** 56 8N 5 29W
Kilmaurs, *U.K.* **20** 55 37N 4 33W
Kilmelford, *U.K.* **20** 56 16N 5 30W
Kilninver, *U.K.* **20** 56 20N 5 30W
Kilrenny, *U.K.* **21** 56 15N 2 40W
Kilrush, *Ire.* **25** 52 39N 9 30W
Kilsby, *U.K.* **14** 52 20N 1 11W
Kilsyth, *U.K.* **21** 55 58N 4 3W
Kilwinning, *U.K.* **20** 55 40N 4 41W
Kimberley, *Austral.* . . . **66** 16 20S 127 0 E
Kimberley, *S. Afr.* . . . . **81** 28 43S 24 46 E
Kimbolton, *U.K.* **15** 52 17N 0 23W
Kincardine, *U.K.* **21** 56 4N 3 43W
Kindu, *Zaïre* . . . . **80** 2 55S 25 50 E
Kineton, *U.K.* **14** 52 10N 1 30W
King Frederick VI
Coast, *Green.* **89** 63 0N 43 0W
King Sd., *Austral.* . . . . **66** 16 50S 123 20 E
Kingarth, *U.K.* **20** 55 45N 5 2W
Kinghorn, *U.K.* **21** 56 4N 3 10W
King's Lynn, *U.K.* . . . . . **15** 52 45N 0 25 E
King's Sutton, *U.K.* . . . **14** 52 1N 1 16W
King's Worthy, *U.K.* . . . **14** 51 6N 1 18W
Kingsbarns, *U.K.* **21** 56 18N 2 40W
Kingsbridge, *U.K.* **16** 50 17N 3 46W
Kingsbury, *U.K.* **14** 52 33N 1 41W
Kingscourt, *Ire.* **24** 53 55N 6 48W
Kingskerswell, *U.K.* . . . **16** 50 30N 3 34W
Kingsland, *U.K.* **14** 52 15N 2 49W
Kingsteignton, *U.K.* . . . **16** 50 32N 3 35W
Kingston, *Canada* **92** 44 14N 76 30W
Kingston, *Jam.* **94** 18 0N 76 50W
Kingston, *U.K.* **14** 51 18N 1 40W
Kingston-upon-Hull,
U.K. **19** 53 45N 0 20W
Kingston-upon-Thames,
U.K. **15** 51 23N 0 20W
Kingstown, *St. Vinc.* . . **94** 13 10N 61 10W
Kingswear, *U.K.* **16** 50 21N 3 33W
Kingswood, *U.K.* **14** 51 26N 2 31W
Kington, *U.K.* **14** 52 12N 3 2W
Kingussie, *U.K.* **23** 57 5N 4 2W
Kinlochewe, *U.K.* **22** 57 37N 5 20W
Kinlochleven, *U.K.* . . . **22** 56 42N 4 59W
Kinnairds Hd., *U.K.* . . . **23** 57 40N 2 0W
Kinneret, Lake, *Isr.* . . . **57** 32 45N 35 35 E
Kinross, *U.K.* **21** 56 13N 3 25W
Kinsale, *Ire.* **25** 51 42N 8 31W
Kinsale, Old Hd. of, *Ire.* **25** 51 37N 8 32W
Kinshasa, *Zaïre* . . . . . . **80** 4 20S 15 15 E
Kintyre, *U.K.* **20** 55 30N 5 35W
Kintyre, Mull of, *U.K.* . . **20** 55 17N 5 55W
Kippen, *U.K.* **20** 56 8N 4 12W
Kippure, *Ire.* **25** 53 11N 6 23W
Kirensk, *U.S.S.R.* . . . . . **49** 57 50N 107 55 E
Kirgizia □, *U.S.S.R.* . . . **48** 42 0N 75 0 E
Kirgiziya Steppe,
U.S.S.R. . . . . **47** 50 0N 55 0 E
Kiribati ■, *Pac. Oc.* . . . **65** 1 0N 176 0 E
Kirk Michael, *U.K.* **18** 54 17N 4 35W
Kirkbean, *U.K.* **21** 54 56N 3 35W
Kirkbride, *U.K.* **18** 54 54N 3 13W
Kirkburton, *U.K.* **19** 53 36N 1 42W
Kirkby, *U.K.* **18** 53 29N 2 54W
Kirkby-in-Ashfield, *U.K.* **19** 53 6N 1 15W
Kirkby Lonsdale, *U.K.* . **18** 54 13N 2 36W
Kirkby Malzeard, *U.K.* . **19** 54 10N 1 38W
Kirkby Stephen, *U.K.* . . **18** 54 27N 2 23W
Kirkby Thore, *U.K.* **18** 54 38N 2 34W
Kirkbymoorside, *U.K.* . . **19** 54 16N 0 56W
Kirkcaldy, *U.K.* **21** 56 7N 3 10W
Kirkcolm, *U.K.* **20** 54 59N 5 4W
Kirkconnel, *U.K.* **21** 55 23N 4 0W
Kirkcowan, *U.K.* **20** 54 53N 4 38W
Kirkcudbright, *U.K.* . . . **21** 54 50N 4 3W
Kirkcudbright B., *U.K.* . **21** 54 46N 4 0W
Kirkham, *U.K.* **18** 53 47N 2 52W
Kirkinner, *U.K.* **20** 54 49N 4 28W
Kirkintilloch, *U.K.* **21** 55 57N 4 10W
Kirkland Lake, *Canada* **92** 48 9N 80 2W
Kirkliston, *U.K.* **21** 55 55N 3 27W
Kirkoswald, *U.K.* **18** 54 46N 2 41W
Kirkoswold, *U.K.* **20** 55 19N 4 48W
Kirkstone P., *U.K.* **18** 54 29N 2 55W
Kirkūk, *Iraq* . . . . **56** 35 30N 44 21 E
Kirkwall, *U.K.* **23** 58 59N 2 59W
Kirkwhelpington, *U.K.* . **21** 55 9N 2 0W
Kirov, *U.S.S.R.* . . . . **46** 58 35N 49 40 E
Kirovabad, *U.S.S.R.* . . **47** 40 45N 46 20 E
Kirovograd, *U.S.S.R.* . . **47** 48 35N 32 20 E
Kirovsk, *U.S.S.R.* . . . . . **46** 48 35N 38 30 E
Kirriemuir, *U.K.* **23** 56 41N 3 0W
Kirtling, *U.K.* . . . . **15** 52 11N 0 27 E
Kirtlington, *U.K.* **14** 51 54N 1 9W
Kirton, *U.K.* **19** 52 56N 0 3W
Kirton-in-Lindsey, *U.K.* **19** 53 29N 0 35W
Kiruna, *Swed.* . . . . **44** 67 52N 20 15 E
Kisangani, *Zaïre* . . . . . **80** 0 35N 25 15 E
Kishinev, *U.S.S.R.* . . . . **47** 47 0N 28 50 E
Kismayu, *Som.* . . . . **73** 0 22S 42 32 E
Kisumu, *Kenya* . . . . **80** 0 3S 34 45 E
Kitakyūshū, *Jap.* . . . . . **62** 33 50N 130 50 E
Kitchener, *Canada* . . . **92** 43 27N 80 29W
Kíthira, *Greece* . . . . . . **41** 36 9N 23 0 E
Kitikmeot □, *Canada* . **88** 70 0N 110 0W
Kitimat, *Canada* **88** 54 3N 128 38W
Kitwe, *Zam.* . . . . **81** 12 54S 28 13 E
Klagenfurt, *Austria* . . . **42** 46 38N 14 20 E
Klerksdorp, *S. Afr.* . . . **81** 26 51S 26 38 E
Klondike, *Canada* **88** 64 0N 139 26W
Knapdale, *U.K.* **20** 55 55N 5 30W
Knaresborough, *U.K.* . . **19** 54 1N 1 29W
Knebworth, *U.K.* **15** 51 52N 0 11W
Knighton, *U.K.* **17** 52 21N 3 2W
Knockmealdown Mts.,
Ire. **25** 52 16N 8 0W
Knossos, *Greece* . . . . . **41** 35 16N 25 10 E
Knott End, *U.K.* **18** 53 55N 3 0W
Knottingley, *U.K.* **19** 53 42N 1 15W
Knowle, *U.K.* **14** 52 23N 1 43W
Knoxville, *U.S.A.* **91** 35 58N 83 57W
Knutsford, *U.K.* **18** 53 18N 2 22W
Kōbe, *Jap.* . . . . **62** 34 45N 135 10 E
København =
Copenhagen, *Den.* . . **45** 55 41N 12 34 E
Koblenz, *W. Ger.* . . . . . **36** 50 21N 7 36 E
Kodiak I., *U.S.A.* **88** 57 30N 152 45W
Koforidua, *Ghana* **78** 6 3N 0 17W
Kokand, *U.S.S.R.* . . . . . **48** 40 30N 70 57 E
Kokchetav, *U.S.S.R.* . . **48** 53 20N 69 25 E
Kokkola, *Fin.* . . . . **44** 63 50N 23 8 E
Kola Pen., *U.S.S.R.* . . . **46** 67 30N 38 0 E
Kolding, *Den.* . . . . **45** 55 30N 9 29 E
Kolguyev, I., *U.S.S.R.* . **46** 69 20N 48 30 E
Kolomna, *U.S.S.R.* . . . . **46** 55 8N 38 45 E
Kolwezi, *Zaïre* . . . . **80** 10 40S 25 25 E
Kolyma →, *U.S.S.R.* . . **49** 69 30N 161 0 E
Kolyma Ra., *U.S.S.R.* . **49** 63 0N 157 0 E
Komandorskiye, Is.,
U.S.S.R. . . . . **49** 55 0N 167 0 E
Komsomolets I.,
U.S.S.R. . . . . **49** 80 30N 95 0 E
Komsomolsk, *U.S.S.R.* **49** 50 30N 137 0 E
Konya, *Turk.* . . . . **47** 37 52N 32 35 E
Kópavogur, *Ice.* **44** 64 6N 21 55W
Korce, *Alb.* . . . . **41** 40 37N 20 50 E
Korea, North ■, *Asia* . **61** 40 0N 127 0 E
Korea, South ■, *Asia* . **61** 36 0N 128 0 E
Korea Strait, *Asia* . . . . **61** 34 0N 129 30 E
Kōriyama, *Jap.* . . . . . . **62** 37 24N 140 23 E
Korla, *China* . . . . **60** 41 45N 86 4 E
Kortrijk, *Belg.* . . . . **36** 50 50N 3 17 E
Koryak Range, *U.S.S.R.* **49** 61 0N 171 0 E
Kos, *Greece* . . . . **41** 36 50N 27 15 E
Košice, *Czech.* . . . . **43** 48 42N 21 15 E
Kôstî, *Sudan* . . . . **79** 13 8N 32 43 E
Kostroma, *U.S.S.R.* . . . **46** 57 50N 40 58 E
Kota, *India* . . . . **58** 25 14N 75 49 E
Kota Baharu, *Malay.* . . **63** 6 7N 102 14 E
Kota Kinabalu, *Malay.* . **63** 6 0N 116 4 E
Kotka, *Fin.* . . . . **45** 60 28N 26 58 E
Kra, Isthmus of, *Thai.* . **63** 10 15N 99 30 E
Kragujevac, *Yug.* . . . . . **41** 44 2N 20 56 E
Krakatau, *Indon.* . . . . . **63** 6 10S 105 20 E
Kraków, *Pol.* . . . . **43** 50 4N 19 57 E
Krasnodar, *U.S.S.R.* . . . **47** 45 5N 39 0 E
Krasnoturinsk, *U.S.S.R.* **46** 59 46N 60 12 E
Krasnovodsk, *U.S.S.R.* **48** 40 0N 52 52 E
Krasnoyarsk, *U.S.S.R.* **49** 56 8N 93 0 E
Krefeld, *W. Ger.* . . . . . . **36** 51 20N 6 32 E
Kremenchug, *U.S.S.R.* . **47** 49 5N 33 25 E
Krishna →, *India* . . . . **59** 15 57N 80 59 E
Kristiansand, *Nor.* . . . . **45** 58 9N 8 1 E
Kristianstad, *Swed.* . . . **45** 56 2N 14 9 E
Kristiansund, *Nor.* . . . . **44** 63 7N 7 45 E
Krivoy Rog, *U.S.S.R.* . . **47** 47 51N 33 20 E
Kroonstad, *S. Afr.* . . . . **81** 27 43S 27 19 E
Krung Thep =
Bangkok, *Thai.* . . . . . **63** 13 45N 100 35 E
Kruševac, *Yug.* . . . . **41** 43 35N 21 28 E
Kuala Lumpur, *Malay.* . **63** 3 9N 101 41 E

Kuala Trengganu, *Malay.* 63 5 20N 103 8 E
Kuangchou = Guangzhou, *China* 61 23 5N 113 10 E
Kuantan, *Malay.* 63 3 49N 103 20 E
Kucing, *Malay.* 63 1 33N 110 25 E
Kueiyang = Guiyang, *China* 60 26 32N 106 40 E
Kumanovo, *Yug.* 41 42 9N 21 42 E
Kumasi, *Ghana* 78 6 41N 1 38W
Kunlun Shan, *Asia* 60 36 0N 86 30 E
Kunming, *China* 60 25 1N 102 41 E
Kuopio, *Fin.* 44 62 53N 27 35 E
Kura →, *U.S.S.R.* 47 39 50N 49 20 E
Kurashiki, *Jap.* 62 34 40N 133 50 E
Kure, *Jap.* 62 34 14N 132 32 E
Kurgan, *U.S.S.R.* 48 55 26N 65 18 E
Kuria Maria Is., *Ind. Oc.* 57 17 30N 55 58 E
Kuril Is., *U.S.S.R.* 49 45 0N 150 0 E
Kurnool, *India* 58 15 45N 78 0 E
Kurri Kurri, *Austral.* 70 32 50S 151 28 E
Kursk, *U.S.S.R.* 46 51 42N 36 11 E
Kurume, *Jap.* 62 33 15N 130 30 E
Kushiro, *Jap.* 62 43 0N 144 25 E
Kustanay, *U.S.S.R.* 48 53 10N 63 35 E
Kütahya, *Turk.* 47 39 30N 30 2 E
Kutaisi, *U.S.S.R.* 47 42 19N 42 40 E
Kutch, Gulf of, *India* 58 22 50N 69 15 E
Kutch, Rann of, *India* 58 24 0N 70 0 E
Kuwait, *Kuw.* 56 29 30N 47 30 E
Kuwait ■, *Asia* 56 29 30N 47 30 E
Kuybyshev, *U.S.S.R.* 46 53 8N 50 6 E
Kwangju, *S. Kor.* 61 35 9N 126 54 E
Kyle, *U.K.* 20 55 32N 4 25W
Kyle of Lochalsh, *U.K.* 22 57 17N 5 43W
Kyōto, *Jap.* 62 35 0N 135 45 E
Kyūshū, *Jap.* 62 33 0N 131 0 E
Kzyl-Orda, *U.S.S.R.* 48 44 48N 65 28 E

L

Labe = Elbe →, *Ger.* 42 53 50N 9 0 E
Labé, *Guin.* 78 11 24N 12 16W
Labrador, Coast of □, *Canada* 89 53 20N 61 0W
Labrador City, *Canada* 89 52 57N 66 55W
Laccadive Is. = Lakshadweep Is., *Ind. Oc.* 51 10 0N 72 30 E
Laceby, *U.K.* 19 53 32N 0 10W
Lachlan →, *Austral.* 70 34 22S 143 55 E
Lacock, *U.K.* 14 51 24N 2 8W
Ladock, *U.K.* 16 50 19N 4 58W
Ladoga, L., *U.S.S.R.* 46 61 15N 30 30 E
Ladybank, *U.K.* 21 56 16N 3 8W
Lafayette, *U.S.A.* 91 30 18N 92 0W
Lagan →, *U.K.* 24 54 35N 5 55W
Lagg, *U.K.* 20 55 51N 5 50W
Laggan B., *U.K.* 20 55 40N 6 20W
Lagos, *Nig.* 78 6 25N 3 27 E
Lagos, *Port.* 37 37 5N 8 41W
Lahore, *Pak.* 58 31 32N 74 22 E
Lahti, *Fin.* 45 60 58N 25 40 E
Lairg, *U.K.* 23 58 1N 4 24W
Lake Charles, *U.S.A.* 91 30 15N 93 10W
Lake District, *U.K.* 18 54 30N 3 10W
Lakenheath, *U.K.* 15 52 25N 0 30 E
Lakewood, *U.S.A.* 92 41 28N 81 50W
Lakshadweep Is., *Ind. Oc.* 51 10 0N 72 30 E
Lambay I., *Ire.* 24 53 30N 6 0W
Lamberhurst, *U.K.* 15 51 5N 0 21 E
Lambeth, *U.K.* 15 51 27N 0 7W
Lambley, *U.K.* 21 54 56N 2 30W
Lambourn, *U.K.* 14 51 31N 1 31W
Lamlash, *U.K.* 20 55 32N 5 8W
Lammermuir, *U.K.* 21 55 50N 2 25W
Lammermuir Hills, *U.K.* 21 55 50N 2 40W
Lampeter, *U.K.* 17 52 6N 4 6W
Lanark, *U.K.* 21 55 40N 3 48W
Lancashire □, *U.K.* 18 53 40N 2 30W
Lancaster, *U.K.* 18 54 3N 2 48W
Lancaster Sd., *Canada* 89 74 13N 84 0W
Lanchester, *U.K.* 19 54 50N 1 44W
Lancing, *U.K.* 15 50 49N 0 19W
Landkey, *U.K.* 16 51 2N 4 0W
Land's End, *U.K.* 16 50 4N 5 43W
Langholm, *U.K.* 21 55 9N 2 59W
Langness, *U.K.* 18 54 3N 4 37W
Langport, *U.K.* 14 51 2N 2 51W
Langstrothdale Chase, *U.K.* 18 54 14N 2 13W
Langtoft, *U.K.* 15 52 42N 0 19W
Langtree, *U.K.* 16 50 55N 4 11W
Lansing, *U.S.A.* 92 42 47N 84 40W
Lanzhou, *China* 60 36 1N 103 52 E
Laoag, *Phil.* 63 18 7N 120 34 E
Laois □, *Ire.* 25 53 0N 7 20W
Laos ■, *Asia* 63 17 45N 105 0 E
Lapford, *U.K.* 16 50 52N 3 49W
Lapland, *Europe* 44 68 7N 24 0 E
Laptev Sea, *U.S.S.R.* 49 76 0N 125 0 E
Larbert, *U.K.* 21 56 2N 3 50W
Laredo, *U.S.A.* 90 27 34N 99 29W
Largs, *U.K.* 20 55 48N 4 51W
Lárisa, *Greece* 41 39 49N 22 28 E
Larkhall, *U.K.* 21 55 44N 4 0W
Larne, *U.K.* 24 54 52N 5 50W
Las Palmas, *Can. Is.* 78 28 7N 15 26W
Las Vegas, *U.S.A.* 90 36 10N 115 5W
Laskill, *U.K.* 19 54 19N 1 6W
Lasswade, *U.K.* 21 55 53N 3 8W
Latakia, *Syria* 56 35 30N 35 45 E
Latina, *It.* 40 41 26N 12 53 E
Latvia □, *U.S.S.R.* 46 56 50N 24 0 E
Lauder, *U.K.* 21 55 43N 2 45W
Lauderdale, *U.K.* 21 55 43N 2 44W
Launceston, *Austral.* 67 41 24S 147 8 E
Launceston, *U.K.* 16 50 38N 4 21W
Laune →, *Ire.* 25 52 5N 9 40W
Laurencekirk, *U.K.* 23 56 50N 2 30W
Laurentian Plateau, *Canada* 82 52 0N 70 0W
Laurieston, *U.K.* 21 54 57N 4 2W
Lausanne, *Switz.* 42 46 32N 6 38 E
Laval, *Fr.* 34 48 4N 0 48W
Lavendon, *U.K.* 15 52 11N 0 39W
Lavenham, *U.K.* 15 52 7N 0 48 E
Lawers, *U.K.* 21 56 31N 4 9W
Lawrence, *U.S.A.* 93 42 40N 71 9W
Laxey, *U.K.* 18 54 15N 4 23W
Laxfield, *U.K.* 15 52 18N 1 23 E
Laxford, L., *U.K.* 22 58 25N 5 10W
Lazonby, *U.K.* 18 54 45N 2 42W
Lea, *U.K.* 19 53 22N 0 45W
Lea →, *U.K.* 15 51 30N 0 10W
Leadenham, *U.K.* 19 53 5N 0 33W
Leadhills, *U.K.* 21 55 25N 3 47W
Leamington, *U.K.* 14 52 18N 1 32W
Leatherhead, *U.K.* 15 51 18N 0 20W
Lebanon ■, *Asia* 56 34 0N 36 0 E
Lecce, *It.* 41 40 20N 18 10 E
Lechlade, *U.K.* 14 51 42N 1 40W
Ledbury, *U.K.* 14 52 3N 2 25W
Leduc, *Canada* 88 53 15N 113 30W
Lee, *U.K.* 14 50 47N 1 11W
Lee →, *Ire.* 25 51 50N 8 30W
Leeds, *U.K.* 19 53 48N 1 34W
Leek, *U.K.* 18 53 7N 2 2W
Leer, *W. Ger.* 36 53 13N 7 29 E
Leeton, *Austral.* 70 34 33S 146 23 E
Leeuwarden, *Neth.* 36 53 15N 5 48 E
Leeuwin, C., *Austral.* 66 34 20S 115 9 E
Leghorn, *It.* 40 43 32N 10 18 E
Legnica, *Pol.* 42 51 12N 16 10 E
Leicester, *U.K.* 14 52 39N 1 9W
Leicester □, *U.K.* 14 52 40N 1 10W
Leiden, *Neth.* 36 52 9N 4 30 E
Leigh, *Gr. Manchester, U.K.* 18 53 29N 2 31W
Leigh, *Hereford & Worcs., U.K.* 14 52 10N 2 21W
Leighton Buzzard, *U.K.* 15 51 55N 0 39W
Leinster □, *Ire.* 25 53 0N 7 10W
Leinster, Mt., *Ire.* 25 52 38N 6 47W
Leintwardine, *U.K.* 14 52 22N 2 51W
Leipzig, *E. Ger.* 42 51 20N 12 23 E
Leiston, *U.K.* 15 52 13N 1 35 E
Leith, *U.K.* 21 55 59N 3 10W
Leith Hill, *U.K.* 15 51 10N 0 23W
Leitholm, *U.K.* 21 55 42N 2 16W
Leitrim, *Ire.* 24 54 0N 8 5W
Leitrim □, *Ire.* 24 54 8N 8 0W
Lek →, *Neth.* 36 51 54N 4 35 E
Lelant, *U.K.* 16 50 11N 5 26W
Lelystad, *Neth.* 36 52 30N 5 25 E
Lena →, *U.S.S.R.* 49 72 52N 126 40 E
Lendalfoot, *U.K.* 20 55 12N 4 55W
Lenham, *U.K.* 15 51 14N 0 44 E
Leninakan, *U.S.S.R.* 47 40 47N 43 50 E
Leningrad, *U.S.S.R.* 46 59 55N 30 20 E
Leninsk-Kuznetskiy, *U.S.S.R.* 48 54 44N 86 10 E
Lennox Hills, *U.K.* 20 56 3N 4 12W
Lennoxtown, *U.K.* 20 55 58N 4 14W
Lens, *Fr.* 34 50 26N 2 50 E
Leominster, *U.K.* 14 52 15N 2 43W
León, *Mex.* 94 21 7N 101 40W
León, *Sp.* 37 42 38N 5 34W
Lérida, *Sp.* 37 41 37N 0 39 E
Lerwick, *U.K.* 22 60 10N 1 10W
Lesbos, I. = Lésvos, *Greece* 41 39 10N 26 20 E
Lesbury, *U.K.* 21 55 25N 1 37W
Leskovac, *Yug.* 41 43 0N 21 58 E
Leslie, *U.K.* 21 56 12N 3 12W
Lesmahagow, *U.K.* 21 55 38N 3 55W
Lesotho ■, *Africa* 81 29 40S 28 0 E
Lésvos, *Greece* 41 39 10N 26 20 E
Leswalt, *U.K.* 20 54 56N 5 6W
Letchworth, *U.K.* 15 51 58N 0 13W
Lethbridge, *Canada* 88 49 45N 112 45W
Letterkenny, *Ire.* 24 54 57N 7 42W
Leuchars, *U.K.* 21 56 23N 2 53W
Leven, *Fife, U.K.* 21 56 12N 3 0W
Leven, *Humberside, U.K.* 19 53 54N 0 18W
Leven →, *U.K.* 19 54 27N 1 15W
Leven, L., *U.K.* 21 56 12N 3 22W
Leverburgh, *U.K.* 22 57 46N 7 0W
Leverkusen, *W. Ger.* 36 51 2N 6 59 E
Lewes, *U.K.* 15 50 53N 0 2 E
Lewis, *U.K.* 22 58 10N 6 40W
Lewis, Butt of, *U.K.* 22 58 30N 6 12W
Lewisham, *U.K.* 15 51 27N 0 1W
Lexington, *U.S.A.* 92 38 6N 84 30W
Leyburn, *U.K.* 19 54 19N 1 50W
Leyland, *U.K.* 18 53 41N 2 42W
Leysdown on Sea, *U.K.* 15 51 23N 0 57 E
Lhasa, *China* 60 29 50N 91 3 E
Liaodong, Gulf of, *China* 61 40 20N 121 10 E
Liaoning □, *China* 61 41 40N 122 30 E
Liaoyang, *China* 61 41 15N 123 10 E
Liaoyüan, *China* 61 42 55N 125 10 E
Liberia ■, *W. Afr.* 78 6 30N 9 30W
Libreville, *Gabon* 80 0 25N 9 26 E
Libya ■, *N. Afr.* 79 27 0N 17 0 E
Libyan Desert, *Africa* 79 25 0N 25 0 E
Lichfield, *U.K.* 14 52 40N 1 50W
Lichinga, *Mozam.* 81 13 13S 35 11 E
Liechtenstein ■, *Europe* 42 47 8N 9 35 E
Liège, *Belg.* 36 50 38N 5 35 E
Liepaja, *U.S.S.R.* 46 56 30N 21 0 E
Liffey →, *Ire.* 25 53 21N 6 20W
Lifford, *Ire.* 24 54 50N 7 30W
Ligurian Sea, *It.* 40 43 20N 9 0 E
Likasi, *Zaïre* 80 10 55S 26 48 E
Lille, *Fr.* 34 50 38N 3 3 E
Lille Bælt, *Den.* 45 55 20N 9 45 E
Lillehammer, *Nor.* 45 61 8N 10 30 E
Lilleshall, *U.K.* 14 52 45N 2 22W
Lilongwe, *Malawi* 81 14 0S 33 48 E
Lima, *Peru* 100 12 0S 77 0W
Limassol, *Cyprus* 47 34 42N 33 1 E
Limavady, *U.K.* 24 55 3N 6 58W
Limavady □, *U.K.* 24 55 0N 6 55W
Limburg □, *Neth.* 36 51 20N 5 55 E
Limerick, *Ire.* 25 52 40N 8 38W
Limerick □, *Ire.* 25 52 30N 8 50W
Límnos, *Greece* 41 39 50N 25 5 E
Limoges, *Fr.* 35 45 50N 1 15 E
Limpopo →, *Mozam.* 81 25 15S 33 30 E
Limpsfield, *U.K.* 15 51 15N 0 1 E
Linares, *Sp.* 37 38 10N 3 40W
Lincluden, *U.K.* 21 55 5N 3 40W
Lincoln, *U.K.* 19 53 14N 0 32W
Lincoln, *U.S.A.* 90 40 50N 96 42W
Lincoln □, *U.K.* 19 53 14N 0 32W
Lincoln Wolds, *U.K.* 19 53 20N 0 5W
Lindale, *U.K.* 18 54 14N 2 54W
Lingfield, *U.K.* 15 51 11N 0 1W
Linkinhorne, *U.K.* 16 50 31N 4 22W
Linköping, *Swed.* 45 58 28N 15 36 E
Linlithgow, *U.K.* 21 55 58N 3 38W
Linnhe, L., *U.K.* 20 56 36N 5 25W
Linslade, *U.K.* 15 51 55N 0 40W
Linton, *U.K.* 15 52 6N 0 19 E
Linxia, *China* 60 35 36N 103 10 E
Linz, *Austria* 42 48 18N 14 18 E
Lion, G. du, *Fr.* 35 43 0N 4 0 E
Lípari, Is., *It.* 40 38 30N 14 50 E
Lipetsk, *U.S.S.R.* 46 52 37N 39 35 E
Lisbon, *Port.* 37 38 42N 9 10W
Lisburn, *U.K.* 24 54 30N 6 9W
Liscannor, B., *Ire.* 25 52 57N 9 24W
Liskeard, *U.K.* 16 50 27N 4 29W
Lismore, *Austral.* 67 28 44S 153 21 E
Lismore, *Ire.* 25 52 8N 7 58W
Lismore I., *U.K.* 20 56 30N 5 30W
Liss, *U.K.* 15 51 3N 0 53W
Listowel, *Ire.* 25 52 27N 9 30W
Litcham, *U.K.* 15 52 43N 0 49 E
Litherland, *U.K.* 18 53 29N 3 0W
Lithgow, *Austral.* 70 33 25S 150 8 E
Lithuania □, *U.S.S.R.* 46 55 30N 24 0 E
Little Minch, *U.K.* 22 57 35N 6 45W
Little Ouse →, *U.K.* 15 52 25N 0 50 E
Little Rock, *U.S.A.* 91 34 41N 92 10W
Little Walsingham, *U.K.* 15 52 53N 0 51 E
Littleborough, *U.K.* 18 53 38N 2 8W
Littlehampton, *U.K.* 15 50 48N 0 32W
Littleport, *U.K.* 15 52 27N 0 18 E
Littlestone-on-Sea, *U.K.* 15 50 59N 0 59 E
Liuzhou, *China* 61 24 22N 109 22 E
Liverpool, *Austral.* 70 33 54S 150 58 E
Liverpool, *U.K.* 18 53 25N 3 0W
Liverpool Plains, *Austral.* 70 31 15S 150 15 E
Livingston, *U.K.* 21 55 52N 3 33W
Livingstone, *Zam.* 81 17 46S 25 52 E
Lizard, *U.K.* 16 49 58N 5 10W
Lizard Pt., *U.K.* 16 49 57N 5 11W
Ljubljana, *Yug.* 40 46 4N 14 33 E
Llandeilo, *U.K.* 17 51 53N 4 0W
Llandovery, *U.K.* 17 51 59N 3 49W
Llandrindod Wells, *U.K.* 17 52 15N 3 23W
Llandudno, *U.K.* 17 53 19N 3 51W
Llanelli, *U.K.* 17 51 41N 4 11W
Llanerchymedd, *U.K.* 17 53 20N 4 22W
Llanfair Caereinion, *U.K.* 17 52 39N 3 20W
Llanfair Talhaiarn, *U.K.* 17 53 13N 3 37W
Llanfairfechan, *U.K.* 17 53 15N 3 58W
Llangefni, *U.K.* 17 53 15N 4 20W
Llangollen, *U.K.* 17 52 58N 3 10W
Llanidloes, *U.K.* 17 52 28N 3 31W
Llanllyfni, *U.K.* 17 53 2N 4 18W
Llanos, *S. Am.* 100 5 0N 71 35W
Llanrhystyd, *U.K.* 17 52 19N 4 9W
Llantrisant, *U.K.* 17 51 33N 3 22W
Llantwit-Major, *U.K.* 17 51 24N 3 29W
Llanwrtyd Wells, *U.K.* 17 52 6N 3 39W
Llanybldowel, *U.K.* 14 52 47N 3 8W
Llanymynech, *U.K.* 14 52 48N 3 6W
Lleyn Peninsula, *U.K.* 17 52 55N 4 35W
Loanhead, *U.K.* 21 55 53N 3 10W
Lobito, *Angola* 81 12 18S 13 35 E
Lochaber, *U.K.* 22 56 55N 5 0W
Lochans, *U.K.* 20 54 52N 5 1W
Lochboisdale, *U.K.* 22 57 10N 7 20W
Lochbuie, *U.K.* 20 56 21N 5 52W
Lochcarron, *U.K.* 22 57 25N 5 30W
Lochdonhead, *U.K.* 20 56 27N 5 40W
Lochearnhead, *U.K.* 20 56 24N 4 19W
Lochgelly, *U.K.* 21 56 7N 3 18W
Lochgilphead, *U.K.* 20 56 2N 5 37W
Lochgoilhead, *U.K.* 20 56 10N 4 54W
Lochinver, *U.K.* 22 58 9N 5 15W
Lochmaben, *U.K.* 21 55 8N 3 27W
Lochmaddy, *U.K.* 22 57 36N 7 10W
Lochnagar, *U.K.* 23 56 57N 3 14W
Lochranza, *U.K.* 20 55 42N 5 18W
Lochwinnoch, *U.K.* 20 55 47N 4 39W
Lochy →, *U.K.* 22 56 52N 5 3W
Lockerbie, *U.K.* 21 55 7N 3 21W
Lod, *Isr.* 57 31 57N 34 54 E
Loddon, *U.K.* 15 52 32N 1 29 E
Łódź, *Pol.* 43 51 45N 19 27 E
Lofoten, *Nor.* 44 68 30N 15 0 E
Loftus, *U.K.* 19 54 33N 0 52W
Logan, Mt., *Canada* 88 60 31N 140 22W
Logroño, *Sp.* 37 42 28N 2 27W
Loire →, *Fr.* 34 47 16N 2 10W
Lolland, *Den.* 45 54 45N 11 30 E
Lombardy □, *It.* 40 45 35N 9 45 E
Lomé, *Togo* 78 6 9N 1 20 E
Lomond, L., *U.K.* 20 56 8N 4 38W
Lomza, *Pol.* 43 53 10N 22 2 E
London, *Canada* 92 42 59N 81 15W
London, *U.K.* 15 51 30N 0 5W
London, Greater □, *U.K.* 15 51 30N 0 5W
Londonderry, *U.K.* 24 55 0N 7 20W
Londonderry □, *U.K.* 24 55 0N 7 20W
Londrina, *Brazil* 102 23 18S 51 10W
Long, L., *U.K.* 20 56 4N 4 50W
Long Beach, *U.S.A.* 90 33 46N 118 12W
Long Bennington, *U.K.* 19 52 59N 0 45W
Long Clawson, *U.K.* 15 52 51N 0 56W
Long Crendon, *U.K.* 15 51 47N 1 0W
Long Eaton, *U.K.* 19 52 54N 1 16W
Long I., *Baham.* 95 23 20N 75 10W
Long I., *U.S.A.* 93 40 50N 73 20W
Long Itchington, *U.K.* 14 52 16N 1 24W
Long Melford, *U.K.* 15 52 5N 0 44 E
Long Mynd, *U.K.* 14 52 35N 2 50W
Long Preston, *U.K.* 18 54 0N 2 16W
Long Sutton, *U.K.* 15 52 47N 0 9 E
Longford, *Ire.* 24 53 43N 7 50W
Longford, *U.K.* 14 51 53N 2 14W
Longford □, *Ire.* 24 53 42N 7 45W
Longforgan, *U.K.* 21 56 28N 3 8W
Longframlington, *U.K.* 21 55 18N 1 47W
Longhorsley, *U.K.* 21 55 15N 1 46W
Longhoughton, *U.K.* 21 55 26N 1 38W
Longridge, *U.K.* 18 53 50N 2 37W
Longton, *U.K.* 18 53 43N 2 48W
Longtown, *Cumbria, U.K.* 18 55 1N 2 59W
Longtown, *Hereford & Worcs., U.K.* 14 51 58N 2 59W
Löningen, *W. Ger.* 36 52 43N 7 44 E
Looe, *U.K.* 16 50 24N 4 25W
Loop Hd., *Ire.* 25 52 34N 9 55W
Lop Nor, *China* 60 40 20N 90 10 E
Lorca, *Sp.* 37 37 41N 1 42W
Lorient, *Fr.* 34 47 45N 3 23W
Lorn, *U.K.* 20 56 26N 5 10W
Lorn, Firth of, *U.K.* 20 56 20N 5 40W
Los Angeles, *Chile* 102 37 28S 72 23W
Los Angeles, *U.S.A.* 90 34 0N 118 10W
Los Mochis, *Mex.* 94 25 45N 108 57W
Lossiemouth, *U.K.* 23 57 43N 3 17W
Lostwithiel, *U.K.* 16 50 24N 4 41W
Lothian □, *U.K.* 21 55 50N 3 0W
Loughborough, *U.K.* 14 52 46N 1 11W
Loughrea, *Ire.* 25 53 11N 8 33W
Loughros More B., *Ire.* 24 54 48N 8 30W
Louisiana □, *U.S.A.* 91 30 50N 92 0W
Louisville, *U.S.A.* 92 38 15N 85 45W
Lourdes, *Fr.* 35 43 6N 0 3W
Louth, *Ire.* 24 53 47N 6 33W
Louth, *U.K.* 19 53 23N 0 0 E
Louth □, *Ire.* 24 53 55N 6 30W
Louvière, La, *Belg.* 36 50 27N 4 10 E
Lowell, *U.S.A.* 93 42 38N 71 19W
Lower Beeding, *U.K.* 15 51 2N 0 15W
Lower California, *Mex.* 94 31 10N 115 12W
Lower Hutt, *N.Z.* 71 41 10S 174 55 E
Lower Tunguska →, *U.S.S.R.* 49 64 20N 93 0 E
Lowes Water L., *U.K.* 18 54 35N 3 23W
Lowestoft, *U.K.* 15 52 29N 1 44 E
Lowick, *U.K.* 21 55 38N 1 57W
Lowther Hills, *U.K.* 21 55 20N 3 40W
Luanda, *Angola* 80 8 50S 13 15 E
Luanshya, *Zam.* 81 13 3S 28 28 E
Lubbock, *U.S.A.* 90 33 40N 101 53W
Lübeck, *W. Ger.* 42 53 52N 10 41 E
Lublin, *Pol.* 43 51 12N 22 38 E
Lubumbashi, *Zaïre* 81 11 40S 27 28 E
Luce Bay, *U.K.* 20 54 45N 4 48W
Lucknow, *India* 59 26 50N 81 0 E
Lüda = Dalian, *China* 61 38 50N 121 40 E
Ludgershall, *U.K.* 14 51 15N 1 38W
Ludgvan, *U.K.* 16 50 9N 5 30W
Ludhiana, *India* 58 30 57N 75 56 E
Ludlow, *U.K.* 14 52 23N 2 42W
Ludwigshafen, *W. Ger.* 42 49 27N 8 27 E

Lugano, *Switz.* **42** 46 0N 8 57 E
Lugnaquilla, *Ire.* **25** 52 58N 6 28W
Lugo, *Sp.* **37** 43 2N 7 35W
Lugwardine, *U.K.* **14** 52 4N 2 38W
Luing I., *U.K.* **20** 56 15N 5 40W
Luleå, *Swed.* **44** 65 35N 22 10 E
Lundy, *U.K.* **16** 51 10N 4 41W
Lune →, *U.K.* **18** 54 0N 2 51W
Lünen, *W. Ger.* **36** 51 36N 7 31 E
Luoyang, *China* **61** 34 40N 112 26 E
Lurgan, *U.K.* **24** 54 28N 6 20W
Lusaka, *Zam.* **81** 15 28S 28 16 E
Luss, *U.K.* **20** 56 6N 4 40W
Luton, *U.K.* **15** 51 53N 0 24W
Lutterworth, *U.K.* **14** 52 28N 1 12W
Luxembourg, *Lux.* **36** 49 37N 6 9 E
Luxembourg ■, *Europe* **36** 50 0N 6 0 E
Luzern, *Switz.* **42** 47 3N 8 18 E
Luzhou, *China* **60** 28 52N 105 20 E
Luzon, *Phil.* **63** 16 0N 121 0 E
Lvov, *U.S.S.R.* **47** 49 50N 24 0 E
Lyakhov Is., *U.S.S.R.* **49** 73 40N 141 0 E
Lybster, *U.K.* **23** 58 18N 3 16W
Lydd, *U.K.* **15** 50 57N 0 56 E
Lydford, *U.K.* **16** 50 38N 4 7W
Lydham, *U.K.* **14** 52 31N 2 59W
Lyell Range, *N.Z.* **71** 41 38S 172 20 E
Lyme Bay, *U.K.* **16** 50 36N 2 55W
Lyme Regis, *U.K.* **16** 50 44N 2 57W
Lyminge, *U.K.* **15** 51 7N 1 6 E
Lymington, *U.K.* **14** 50 46N 1 32W
Lymm, *U.K.* **18** 53 23N 2 30W
Lympne, *U.K.* **15** 51 4N 1 2 E
Lynchburg, *U.S.A.* **92** 37 23N 79 10W
Lyndhurst, *U.K.* **14** 50 53N 1 33W
Lyneham, *U.K.* **14** 51 30N 1 57W
Lynemouth, *U.K.* **21** 55 15N 1 29W
Lynmouth, *U.K.* **16** 51 14N 3 50W
Lynn Lake, *Canada* **88** 56 51N 101 3W
Lynton, *U.K.* **16** 51 14N 3 50W
Lyons, *Fr.* **35** 45 46N 4 50 E
Lytchett Minster, *U.K.* **14** 50 44N 2 3W
Lytham St. Anne's, *U.K.* **18** 53 45N 2 58W
Lythe, *U.K.* **19** 54 30N 0 40W

M

Ma'ān, *Jord.* **56** 30 12N 35 44 E
Maarianhamina, *Fin.* **45** 60 5N 19 55 E
Maastricht, *Neth.* **36** 50 50N 5 40 E
Mablethorpe, *U.K.* **19** 53 21N 0 14 E
Macapá, *Brazil* **101** 0 5N 51 4W
Macau ■, *Asia* **61** 22 16N 113 35 E
Macclesfield, *U.K.* **18** 53 16N 2 9W
McClure Str., *Canada* **103** 75 0N 119 0W
Macdonnell Ranges, *Austral.* **66** 23 40S 133 0 E
Macduff, *U.K.* **23** 57 40N 2 30W
Macedonia □, *Greece* **41** 40 39N 22 0 E
Macedonia □, *Yug.* **41** 41 53N 21 40 E
Maceió, *Brazil* **101** 9 40S 35 41W
Macgillycuddy's Reeks, *Ire.* **25** 52 2N 9 45W
Machakos, *Kenya* **80** 1 30S 37 15 E
Machala, *Ecuad.* **100** 3 20S 79 57W
Machars, The, *U.K.* **20** 54 46N 4 30W
Machrihanish, *U.K.* **20** 55 25N 5 42W
Machynlleth, *U.K.* **17** 52 36N 3 51W
Macintyre →, *Austral.* **67** 28 37S 150 47 E
Mackay, *Austral.* **67** 21 8S 149 11 E
Mackay, L., *Austral.* **66** 22 30S 129 0 E
McKeesport, *U.S.A.* **92** 40 21N 79 50W
Mackenzie →, *Austral.* **67** 23 38S 149 46 E
Mackenzie →, *Canada* **88** 69 10N 134 20W
Mackenzie Mts., *Canada* **88** 64 0N 130 0W
McKinley, Mt., *U.S.A.* **88** 63 2N 151 0W
M'Clintock Chan., *Canada* **88** 72 0N 102 0W
Macon, *U.S.A.* **91** 32 50N 83 37W
Macquarie →, *Austral.* **70** 30 5S 147 30 E
Macquarie Harbour, *Austral.* **67** 42 15S 145 23 E
Macquarie Is., *S. Oc.* **64** 54 36S 158 55 E
Macroom, *Ire.* **25** 51 54N 8 57W
Madadeni, *S. Afr.* **81** 27 43S 30 3 E
Madagascar ■, *Africa* **81** 20 0S 47 0 E
Madeira, *Atl. Oc.* **78** 32 50N 17 0W
Madeira →, *Brazil* **100** 3 22S 58 45W
Madeley, *Salop, U.K.* **14** 52 38N 2 28W
Madeley, *Staffs., U.K.* **18** 52 59N 2 20W
Madhya Pradesh □, *India* **59** 21 50N 81 0 E
Madīnat ash Sha'b, *S. Yem.* **56** 12 50N 45 0 E
Madison, *U.S.A.* **92** 43 5N 89 25W
Madiun, *Indon.* **63** 7 38S 111 32 E
Madley, *U.K.* **14** 52 3N 2 51W
Madras, *India* **58** 13 8N 80 19 E
Madre, L., *U.S.A.* **91** 26 0N 97 40W
Madre, Sierra, *Mex.* **94** 16 0N 93 0W
Madrid, *Sp.* **37** 40 25N 3 45W
Madurai, *India* **58** 9 55N 78 10 E
Maesteg, *U.K.* **17** 51 36N 3 40W
Magadan, *U.S.S.R.* **49** 59 38N 150 50 E
Magdalena →, *Col.* **100** 11 6N 74 51W
Magdeburg, *E. Ger.* **42** 52 8N 11 36 E
Magee, I., *U.K.* **24** 54 48N 5 44W
Magelang, *Indon.* **63** 7 29S 110 13 E
Magellan's Str., *Chile* **102** 52 30S 75 0W
Maggiore, L., *It.* **40** 46 0N 8 35 E
Magherafelt, *U.K.* **24** 54 44N 6 37W
Maghull, *U.K.* **18** 53 31N 2 56W
Magnitogorsk, *U.S.S.R.* **46** 53 27N 59 4 E
Mahajanga, *Madag.* **81** 17 0S 47 0 E
Maiden Bradley, *U.K.* **14** 51 9N 2 18W
Maiden Newton, *U.K.* **14** 50 46N 2 35W
Maidenhead, *U.K.* **15** 51 31N 0 42W
Maidstone, *U.K.* **15** 51 16N 0 31 E
Maiduguri, *Nig.* **79** 12 0N 13 20 E
Main →, *U.K.* **24** 54 49N 6 20W
Maine □, *U.S.A.* **93** 45 20N 69 0W
Maine →, *Ire.* **25** 52 10N 9 40W
Mainland, *Orkney, U.K.* **23** 59 0N 3 10W
Mainland, *Shetland, U.K.* **22** 60 15N 1 22W
Mainz, *W. Ger.* **36** 50 0N 8 17 E
Maitland, *Austral.* **70** 32 33S 151 36 E
Majorca, I. = Mallorca, *Sp.* **37** 39 30N 3 0 E
Makasar, Str. of, *Indon.* **63** 1 0S 118 20 E
Maker, *U.K.* **16** 50 20N 4 10W
Makeyevka, *U.S.S.R.* **47** 48 0N 38 0 E
Makhachkala, *U.S.S.R.* **47** 43 0N 47 30 E
Makran Coast Range, *Pak.* **58** 25 40N 64 0 E
Mal B., *Ire.* **25** 52 50N 9 30W
Malabar Coast, *India* **58** 11 0N 75 0 E
Malacca, Str. of, *Indon.* **63** 3 0N 101 0 E
Málaga, *Sp.* **37** 36 43N 4 23W
Malang, *Indon.* **63** 7 59S 112 45 E
Malanje, *Angola* **80** 9 36S 16 17 E
Mälaren, *Swed.* **45** 59 30N 17 10 E
Malatya, *Turk.* **47** 38 25N 38 20 E
Malawi ■, *Africa* **81** 13 0S 34 0 E
Malay Pen., *Asia* **63** 7 25N 100 0 E
Malaysia ■, *Asia* **63** 5 0N 110 0 E
Maldives ■, *Ind. Oc.* **129** 7 0N 73 0 E
Maldon, *U.K.* **15** 51 43N 0 41 E
Malham Tarn, *U.K.* **18** 54 6N 2 11W
Mali ■, *Africa* **78** 15 0N 2 0W
Mallaig, *U.K.* **22** 57 0N 5 50W
Mallorca, *Sp.* **37** 39 30N 3 0 E
Mallow, *Ire.* **25** 52 8N 8 40W
Malmédy, *Belg.* **36** 50 25N 6 2 E
Malmesbury, *U.K.* **14** 51 35N 2 5W
Malmö, *Swed.* **45** 55 36N 12 59 E
Malpas, *U.K.* **18** 53 3N 2 47W
Malta ■, *Europe* **40** 35 50N 14 30 E
Maltby, *U.K.* **19** 53 25N 1 12W
Malton, *U.K.* **19** 54 9N 0 48W
Malvern, *U.K.* **14** 52 7N 2 19W
Malvern Hills, *U.K.* **14** 52 0N 2 19W
Malvern Wells, *U.K.* **14** 52 4N 2 19W
Malvinas, Is. = Falkland Is., *Atl. Oc.* **102** 51 30S 59 0W
Man, I. of, *U.K.* **18** 54 15N 4 30W
Manaar, Gulf of, *Asia* **58** 8 30N 79 0 E
Manacles, The, *U.K.* **16** 50 3N 5 5W
Manado, *Indon.* **63** 1 29N 124 51 E
Managua, *Nic.* **94** 12 6N 86 20W
Manaus, *Brazil* **100** 3 0S 60 0W
Manby, *U.K.* **19** 53 22N 0 6 E
Manchester, *U.K.* **18** 53 30N 2 15W
Manchester, *U.S.A.* **93** 42 58N 71 29W
Manchuria, *China* **61** 42 0N 125 0 E
Mandalay, *Burma* **59** 22 0N 96 4 E
Manea, *U.K.* **15** 52 29N 0 10 E
Mangalore, *India* **58** 12 55N 74 47 E
Mangotsfield, *U.K.* **14** 51 29N 2 29W
Manila, *Phil.* **63** 14 40N 121 3 E
Manitoba □, *Canada* **88** 55 30N 97 0W
Manizales, *Col.* **100** 5 5N 75 32W
Manly, *Austral.* **70** 33 48S 151 17 E
Mannheim, *W. Ger.* **42** 49 28N 8 29 E
Manningtree, *U.K.* **15** 51 56N 1 3 E
Mans, Le, *Fr.* **34** 48 0N 0 10 E
Mansfield, *U.K.* **19** 53 8N 1 12W
Mansfield, *U.S.A.* **92** 40 45N 82 30W
Mansfield Woodhouse, *U.K.* **19** 53 11N 1 11W
Mantes-la-Jolie, *Fr.* **34** 49 0N 1 41 E
Manton, *U.K.* **15** 52 37N 0 41W
Mantua, *It.* **40** 45 20N 10 42 E
Manukau, *N.Z.* **71** 37 1S 174 55 E
Manzhouli, *China* **61** 49 35N 117 25 E
Maoming, *China* **61** 21 50N 110 54 E
Maputo, *Mozam.* **81** 25 58S 32 32 E
Mar del Plata, *Arg.* **102** 38 0S 57 30W
Maracaibo, *Ven.* **100** 10 40N 71 37W
Maracaibo, L., *Ven.* **100** 9 40N 71 30W
Maracay, *Ven.* **100** 10 15N 67 28W
Marajó, I. de, *Brazil* **101** 1 0S 49 30W
Maranhão = São Luís, *Brazil* **101** 2 39S 44 15W
Marañón →, *Peru* **100** 4 30S 73 35W
Marazion, *U.K.* **16** 50 8N 5 29W
March, *U.K.* **15** 52 33N 0 5 E
Marden, *U.K.* **14** 52 7N 2 42W
Maree L., *U.K.* **22** 57 40N 5 30W
Mareeba, *Austral.* **67** 16 59S 145 28 E
Mareham le Fen, *U.K.* **19** 53 7N 0 3W
Marfleet, *U.K.* **19** 53 45N 0 15W
Margarita I., *Ven.* **100** 11 0N 64 0W
Margate, *U.K.* **15** 51 23N 1 24 E
Maribor, *Yug.* **40** 46 36N 15 40 E
Maricourt, *Canada* **89** 56 34N 70 49W
Marie-Galante, *W. Ind.* **94** 15 56N 61 16W
Marília, *Brazil* **101** 22 13S 50 0W
Maringá, *Brazil* **102** 23 26S 52 2W
Mark, *U.K.* **20** 55 2N 5 1W
Market Bosworth, *U.K.* **14** 52 37N 1 24W
Market Deeping, *U.K.* **15** 52 40N 0 20W
Market Drayton, *U.K.* **18** 52 55N 2 30W
Market Harborough, *U.K.* **15** 52 29N 0 55W
Market Lavington, *U.K.* **14** 51 17N 1 59W
Market Rasen, *U.K.* **19** 53 24N 0 20W
Market Weighton, *U.K.* **19** 53 52N 0 40W
Markfield, *U.K.* **14** 52 42N 1 18W
Markinch, *U.K.* **21** 56 12N 3 9W
Marks Tey, *U.K.* **15** 51 53N 0 48 E
Marlborough, *U.K.* **14** 51 26N 1 44W
Marlborough □, *N.Z.* **71** 41 45S 173 33 E
Marlborough Downs, *U.K.* **14** 51 25N 1 55W
Marlow, *U.K.* **15** 51 34N 0 47W
Marmara, Sea of, *Turk.* **47** 40 45N 28 15 E
Marne →, *Fr.* **34** 48 48N 2 24 E
Marnhull, *U.K.* **14** 50 58N 2 20W
Maroua, *Cam.* **80** 10 40N 14 20 E
Marple, *U.K.* **18** 53 23N 2 5W
Marquesas Is., *Pac. Oc.* **65** 9 30S 140 0W
Marrakech, *Mor.* **78** 31 9N 8 0W
Marseilles, *Fr.* **35** 43 18N 5 23 E
Marshall Is., *Pac. Oc.* **64** 9 0N 171 0 E
Marshfield, *U.K.* **14** 51 27N 2 18W
Marske by the Sea, *U.K.* **19** 54 35N 1 0W
Marston Moor, *U.K.* **19** 53 58N 1 17W
Martaban, G. of, *Burma* **59** 16 5N 96 30 E
Martham, *U.K.* **15** 52 42N 1 38 E
Martinique, *W. Ind.* **94** 14 40N 61 0W
Martley, *U.K.* **14** 52 14N 2 22W
Martock, *U.K.* **14** 50 58N 2 47W
Mary Kathleen, *Austral.* **67** 20 44S 139 48 E
Maryborough, *Austral.* **67** 37 0S 143 44 E
Maryland □, *U.S.A.* **93** 39 10N 76 40W
Maryport, *U.K.* **18** 54 43N 3 30W
Marytavy, *U.K.* **16** 50 34N 4 6W
Masan, *S. Kor.* **61** 35 11N 128 32 E
Maseru, *Les.* **81** 29 18S 27 30 E
Masham, *U.K.* **19** 54 15N 1 40W
Mashhad, *Iran* **57** 36 20N 59 35 E
Mask, L., *Ire.* **24** 53 36N 9 24W
Massachusetts □, *U.S.A.* **93** 42 25N 72 0W
Massif Central, *Fr.* **35** 45 30N 3 0 E
Masterton, *N.Z.* **71** 40 56S 175 39 E
Masvingo, *Zimb.* **81** 20 8S 30 49 E
Matadi, *Zaïre* **80** 5 52S 13 31 E
Matamoros, *Mex.* **94** 25 33N 103 15W
Matera, *It.* **40** 40 40N 16 37 E
Matlock, *U.K.* **19** 53 8N 1 32W
Mato Grosso □, *Brazil* **101** 14 0S 55 0W
Matsue, *Jap.* **62** 35 25N 133 10 E
Matsuyama, *Jap.* **62** 33 45N 132 45 E
Matterhorn, *Switz.* **42** 45 58N 7 39 E
Maturín, *Ven.* **100** 9 45N 63 11W
Maubeuge, *Fr.* **34** 50 17N 3 57 E
Mauchline, *U.K.* **20** 55 31N 4 23W
Maughold, *U.K.* **18** 54 18N 4 17W
Maughold Hd., *U.K.* **18** 54 18N 4 17W
Maui, *U.S.A.* **90** 20 45N 156 20 E
Mauna Loa, *U.S.A.* **90** 21 8N 157 10W
Mauritania ■, *Africa* **78** 20 50N 10 0W
Mauritius ■, *Ind. Oc.* **129** 20 0S 57 0 E
Mawgan, *U.K.* **16** 50 4N 5 10W
Mawlaik, *Burma* **59** 23 40N 94 26 E
Maxwellheugh, *U.K.* **21** 55 35N 2 23W
May, I. of, *U.K.* **21** 56 11N 2 32W
May Pen, *Jam.* **94** 17 58N 77 15W
Maybole, *U.K.* **20** 55 21N 4 41W
Mayfield, *Derby, U.K.* **19** 53 1N 1 47W
Mayfield, *E. Sussex, U.K.* **15** 51 1N 0 17 E
Maynooth, *Ire.* **24** 53 22N 6 38W
Mayo □, *Ire.* **24** 53 47N 9 7W
Mazar-e Sharīf, *Afg.* **57** 36 41N 67 0 E
Mazatlán, *Mex.* **94** 23 13N 106 25W
Mbabane, *Swaz.* **81** 26 18S 31 6 E
Mbandaka, *Zaïre* **80** 0 1N 18 18 E
Mbanza Ngungu, *Zaïre* **80** 5 12S 14 53 E
Mbeya, *Tanz.* **80** 8 54S 33 29 E
Mbini □, *Eq. Guin.* **80** 1 30N 10 0 E
Mbuji-Mayi, *Zaïre* **80** 6 9S 23 40 E
Mdantsane, *S. Afr.* **81** 32 56S 27 46 E
Mealsgate, *U.K.* **18** 54 46N 3 14W
Measham, *U.K.* **14** 52 43N 1 30W
Meath □, *Ire.* **24** 53 32N 6 40W
Mecca, *Si. Arab.* **56** 21 30N 39 54 E
Mechelen, *Belg.* **36** 50 58N 5 41 E
Medan, *Indon.* **63** 3 40N 98 38 E
Medellín, *Col.* **100** 6 15N 75 35W
Medicine Hat, *Canada* **88** 50 0N 110 45W
Medina, *Si. Arab.* **56** 24 35N 39 52 E
Mediterranean Sea, *Europe* **38** 35 0N 15 0 E
Medley, *Canada* **88** 54 25N 110 16W
Medstead, *U.K.* **14** 51 7N 1 4W
Medway →, *U.K.* **15** 51 28N 0 45 E
Meekatharra, *Austral.* **66** 26 32S 118 29 E
Meerut, *India* **58** 29 1N 77 42 E
Mei Xian, *China* **61** 24 16N 116 6 E
Meknès, *Mor.* **78** 33 57N 5 33W
Mekong →, *Asia* **63** 9 30N 106 15 E
Melanesia, *Pac. Oc.* **64** 4 0S 155 0 E
Melbourn, *U.K.* **15** 52 5N 0 1 E
Melbourne, *Austral.* **70** 37 50S 145 0 E
Melbourne, *U.K.* **14** 52 50N 1 25W
Melfort, Loch, *U.K.* **20** 56 13N 5 33W
Melitopol, *U.S.S.R.* **47** 46 50N 35 22 E
Melksham, *U.K.* **14** 51 22N 2 9W
Melmerby, *U.K.* **18** 54 44N 2 35W
Melrose, *U.K.* **21** 55 35N 2 44W
Melsonby, *U.K.* **19** 54 28N 1 41W
Melton, *U.K.* **15** 52 6N 1 20 E
Melton Constable, *U.K.* **15** 52 52N 1 1 E
Melton Mowbray, *U.K.* **15** 52 46N 0 52W
Melvich, *U.K.* **23** 58 33N 3 55W
Melville I., *Austral.* **66** 11 30S 131 0 E
Melville Pen., *Canada* **89** 68 0N 84 0W
Memphis, *U.S.A.* **91** 35 7N 90 0W
Menai Bridge, *U.K.* **17** 53 14N 4 11W
Menai Strait, *U.K.* **17** 53 14N 4 10W
Menan = Chao Phraya →, *Thai.* **63** 13 32N 100 36 E
Mendip Hills, *U.K.* **14** 51 17N 2 40W
Mendlesham, *U.K.* **15** 52 15N 1 4 E
Mendoza, *Arg.* **102** 32 50S 68 52W
Menindee, *Austral.* **70** 32 20S 142 25 E
Menorca, *Sp.* **37** 40 0N 4 0 E
Mere, *U.K.* **14** 51 5N 2 16W
Mérida, *Mex.* **94** 20 58N 89 37W
Mérida, *Ven.* **100** 8 24N 71 8W
Meriden, *U.K.* **14** 52 27N 1 36W
Merrick, *U.K.* **20** 55 8N 4 30W
Merse, *U.K.* **21** 55 40N 2 30W
Mersea I., *U.K.* **15** 51 48N 0 55 E
Mersey →, *U.K.* **18** 53 20N 2 56W
Merseyside □, *U.K.* **18** 53 25N 2 55W
Mersin, *Turk.* **47** 36 51N 34 36 E
Merthyr Tydfil, *U.K.* **17** 51 45N 3 23W
Merton, *U.K.* **15** 51 25N 0 13W
Meru, *Tanz.* **80** 3 15S 36 46 E
Mesa, *U.S.A.* **90** 33 20N 111 56W
Mesopotamia, *Asia* **56** 33 30N 44 0 E
Messina, *It.* **40** 38 10N 15 32 E
Messina, Str. of, *It.* **40** 38 5N 15 35 E
Metheringham, *U.K.* **19** 53 9N 0 22W
Methil, *U.K.* **21** 56 10N 3 1W
Methven, *U.K.* **21** 56 25N 3 35W
Methwold, *U.K.* **15** 52 30N 0 33 E
Metz, *Fr.* **34** 49 8N 6 10 E
Meuse →, *Europe* **34** 50 45N 5 41 E
Mevagissey, *U.K.* **16** 50 16N 4 48W
Mevagissey Bay, *U.K.* **16** 50 15N 4 40W
Mexborough, *U.K.* **19** 53 29N 1 18W
Mexicali, *Mex.* **94** 32 40N 115 29W
México, *Mex.* **94** 19 20N 99 10W
Mexico ■, *Cent. Am.* **94** 20 0N 100 0W
Mexico, G. of, *Cent. Am.* **94** 25 0N 90 0W
Miami, *U.S.A.* **91** 25 45N 80 15W
Micheldever, *U.K.* **14** 51 7N 1 17W
Michigan □, *U.S.A.* **92** 44 40N 85 40W
Michigan, L., *U.S.A.* **92** 44 0N 87 0W
Mickle Fell, *U.K.* **18** 54 38N 2 16W
Mickleover, *U.K.* **19** 52 55N 1 32W
Mickleton, *Durham, U.K.* **18** 54 36N 2 3W
Mickleton, *Oxon., U.K.* **14** 52 5N 1 45W
Micronesia, *Pac. Oc.* **64** 11 0N 160 0 E
Mid Calder, *U.K.* **21** 55 53N 3 23W
Mid Glamorgan □, *U.K.* **17** 51 40N 3 25W
Middle Zoy, *U.K.* **14** 51 5N 2 54W
Middleham, *U.K.* **19** 54 17N 1 49W
Middlemarsh, *U.K.* **14** 50 51N 2 29W
Middlesbrough, *U.K.* **19** 54 35N 1 14W
Middleton, *Gr. Manchester, U.K.* **18** 53 33N 2 12W
Middleton, *Norfolk, U.K.* **15** 52 43N 0 29 E
Middleton Cheney, *U.K.* **14** 52 4N 1 17W
Middleton-in-Teesdale, *U.K.* **18** 54 38N 2 5W
Middleton on the Wolds, *U.K.* **19** 53 56N 0 35W
Middlewich, *U.K.* **18** 53 12N 2 28W
Midhurst, *U.K.* **15** 50 59N 0 44W
Midland, *U.S.A.* **90** 32 0N 102 3W
Midleton, *Ire.* **25** 51 52N 8 12W
Midsomer Norton, *U.K.* **14** 51 17N 2 29W
Midway Is., *Pac. Oc.* **64** 28 13N 177 22W
Mieres, *Sp.* **37** 43 18N 5 48W
Mikkeli, *Fin.* **44** 61 43N 27 15 E
Milan, *It.* **40** 45 28N 9 10 E
Milborne Port, *U.K.* **14** 50 58N 2 28W
Mildenhall, *U.K.* **15** 52 20N 0 30 E
Mildura, *Austral.* **70** 34 13S 142 9 E
Milford Haven, *U.K.* **17** 51 43N 5 2W
Milford Haven, B., *U.K.* **17** 51 40N 5 10W
Milford on Sea, *U.K.* **14** 50 44N 1 36W
Milk →, *U.S.A.* **90** 48 5N 106 15W
Millbrook, *U.K.* **16** 50 19N 4 12W
Milleur Pt., *U.K.* **20** 55 2N 5 5W
Millom, *U.K.* **18** 54 13N 3 16W
Millport, *U.K.* **20** 55 45N 4 55W
Milltown Malbay, *Ire.* **25** 52 51N 9 25W
Milnathort, *U.K.* **21** 56 14N 3 25W
Milngavie, *U.K.* **20** 55 57N 4 20W
Milnthorpe, *U.K.* **18** 54 14N 2 47W
Milton, *Dumf. & Gall., U.K.* **20** 55 18N 4 50W
Milton, *Hants., U.K.* **14** 50 45N 1 40W
Milton, *Highland, U.K.* **23** 57 18N 4 32W
Milton Abbot, *U.K.* **16** 50 35N 4 16W
Milton Keynes, *U.K.* **15** 52 3N 0 42W

Milverton, *U.K.* 14 51 2N 3 15W
Milwaukee, *U.S.A.* 92 43 9N 87 58W
Minas Gerais □, *Brazil* 101 18 50S 46 0W
Minatitlán, *Mex.* 94 17 59N 94 31W
Minchinghampton, *U.K.* 14 51 42N 2 10W
Mindanao, *Phil.* 63 8 0N 125 0 E
Mindoro, *Phil.* 63 13 0N 121 0 E
Minehead, *U.K.* 14 51 12N 3 29W
Minneapolis, *U.S.A.* 91 44 58N 93 20W
Minnesota □, *U.S.A.* 91 46 40N 94 0W
Minnigaff, *U.K.* 20 54 58N 4 30W
Minorca = Menorca, *Sp.* 37 40 0N 4 0 E
Minsk, *U.S.S.R.* 46 53 52N 27 30 E
Minster, *U.K.* 15 51 20N 1 20 E
Minster-on-Sea, *U.K.* 15 51 25N 0 50 E
Minsterley, *U.K.* 14 52 38N 2 56W
Mirfield, *U.K.* 19 53 37N 1 54W
Mirzapur, *India* 59 25 10N 82 34 E
Miskolc, *Hung.* 43 48 7N 20 50 E
Misrātah, *Libya* 79 32 24N 15 3 E
Mississippi □, *U.S.A.* 91 33 0N 90 0W
Mississippi →, *U.S.A.* 91 29 0N 89 15W
Mississippi, Delta of the, *U.S.A.* 91 29 15N 90 30W
Missouri □, *U.S.A.* 91 38 25N 92 30W
Missouri →, *U.S.A.* 91 38 50N 90 8W
Misterton, *Notts., U.K.* 19 53 27N 0 49W
Misterton, *Somerset, U.K.* 14 50 51N 2 46W
Mitcheldean, *U.K.* 14 51 51N 2 29W
Mitchell →, *Austral.* 67 15 12S 141 35 E
Mitchelstown, *Ire.* 25 52 16N 8 18W
Mittelland Kanal, *W. Ger.* 36 52 23N 7 45 E
Mitumba, Mts., *Zaïre* 80 6 0S 29 0 E
Miyazaki, *Jap.* 62 31 56N 131 30 E
Mizen Hd., *Cork, Ire.* 25 51 27N 9 50W
Mizen Hd., *Wicklow, Ire.* 25 52 52N 6 4W
Mizoram □, *India* 59 23 30N 92 40 E
Mmabatho, *S. Afr.* 81 25 49S 25 30 E
Mo i Rana, *Nor.* 44 66 15N 14 7 E
Mobile, *U.S.A.* 91 30 41N 88 3W
Mobutu Sese Seko, L., *Africa* 80 1 30N 31 0 E
Moçâmedes = Namibe, *Angola* 81 15 7S 12 11 E
Modbury, *U.K.* 16 50 21N 3 53W
Módena, *It.* 40 44 39N 10 55 E
Moe, *Austral.* 70 38 12S 146 19 E
Moffat, *U.K.* 21 55 20N 3 27W
Mogadishu, *Som.* 73 2 2N 45 25 E
Mogilev, *U.S.S.R.* 46 53 55N 30 18 E
Moidart, L., *U.K.* 22 56 47N 5 40W
Mojave Desert, *U.S.A.* 90 35 0N 116 30W
Mold, *U.K.* 17 53 10N 3 10W
Moldavia □, *U.S.S.R.* 47 47 0N 28 0 E
Mole →, *U.K.* 15 51 13N 0 15W
Mollendo, *Peru* 100 17 0S 72 0W
Mölndal, *Swed.* 45 57 40N 12 3 E
Molokai, *U.S.A.* 90 21 8N 157 0W
Moluccas, *Indon.* 63 1 0S 127 0 E
Mombasa, *Kenya* 80 4 2S 39 43 E
Mona Passage, *W. Ind.* 95 18 0N 67 40W
Monach Is., *U.K.* 22 57 32N 7 40W
Monaco ■, *Europe* 35 43 46N 7 23 E
Monadhliath Mts., *U.K.* 23 57 10N 4 4W
Monaghan, *Ire.* 24 54 15N 6 58W
Monaghan □, *Ire.* 24 54 10N 7 0W
Monastir = Bitola, *Yug.* 41 41 5N 21 10 E
Monclova, *Mex.* 94 26 50N 101 30W
Moncton, *Canada* 93 46 7N 64 51W
Moneymore, *U.K.* 24 54 42N 6 40W
Monghyr, *India* 59 25 23N 86 30 E
Mongolia ■, *Asia* 60 47 0N 103 0 E
Mongu, *Zam.* 81 15 16S 23 12 E
Moniaive, *U.K.* 21 55 11N 3 55W
Monifieth, *U.K.* 21 56 30N 2 48W
Monkton, *U.K.* 20 55 30N 4 37W
Monmouth, *U.K.* 17 51 48N 2 43W
Monnow →, *U.K.* 14 51 54N 2 48W
Monroe, *U.S.A.* 91 32 32N 92 4W
Monrovia, *Lib.* 78 6 18N 10 47W
Mons, *Belg.* 36 50 27N 3 58 E
Montana □, *U.S.A.* 90 47 0N 110 0W
Montbéliard, *Fr.* 34 47 31N 6 48 E
Montceau-les-Mines, *Fr.* 34 46 40N 4 23 E
Monte-Carlo, *Monaco* 35 43 46N 7 23 E
Montego Bay, *Jam.* 94 18 30N 78 0W
Montería, *Col.* 100 8 46N 75 53W
Monterrey, *Mex.* 94 25 40N 100 30W
Montes Claros, *Brazil* 101 16 30S 43 50W
Montevideo, *Urug.* 102 34 50S 56 11W
Montgomery, *U.K.* 17 52 34N 3 9W
Montgomery, *U.S.A.* 91 32 20N 86 20W
Montluçon, *Fr.* 35 46 22N 2 36 E
Montpelier, *U.S.A.* 93 44 15N 72 38W
Montpellier, *Fr.* 35 43 37N 3 52 E
Montréal, *Canada* 93 45 31N 73 34W
Montrose, *U.K.* 23 56 43N 2 28W
Montserrat, *W. Ind.* 94 16 40N 62 10W
Moonie →, *Austral.* 67 29 19S 148 43 E
Moorfoot Hills, *U.K.* 21 55 44N 3 8W
Moose Jaw, *Canada* 88 50 24N 105 30W
Moosehead L., *U.S.A.* 93 45 34N 69 40W
Mopti, *Mali* 78 14 30N 4 0W
Moradabad, *India* 58 28 50N 78 50 E
Morar L., *U.K.* 22 56 57N 5 40W
Moray Firth, *U.K.* 23 57 50N 3 30W
Morebattle, *U.K.* 21 55 30N 2 20W
Morecambe, *U.K.* 18 54 5N 2 52W
Morecambe B., *U.K.* 18 54 7N 3 0W
Morelia, *Mex.* 94 19 42N 101 7W
Morena, Sierra, *Sp.* 37 38 20N 4 0W
Moreton-in-Marsh, *U.K.* 14 51 59N 1 42W
Moretonhampstead, *U.K.* 16 50 39N 3 45W
Morley, *U.K.* 19 53 45N 1 36W
Morocco ■, *N. Afr.* 78 32 0N 5 50W
Morogoro, *Tanz.* 80 6 50S 37 40 E
Morpeth, *U.K.* 19 55 11N 1 41W
Morte Bay, *U.K.* 16 51 10N 4 13W
Morte Pt., *U.K.* 16 51 13N 4 14W
Mortehoe, *U.K.* 16 51 21N 4 12W
Mortimer's Cross, *U.K.* 14 52 17N 2 50W
Morton Fen, *U.K.* 15 52 45N 0 23W
Morvern, *U.K.* 22 56 38N 5 44W
Morwell, *Austral.* 70 38 10S 146 22 E
Morwenstow, *U.K.* 16 50 53N 4 32W
Moscow, *U.S.S.R.* 46 55 45N 37 35 E
Moselle →, *Europe* 34 50 22N 7 36 E
Moshi, *Tanz.* 80 3 22S 37 18 E
Mossley, *U.K.* 18 53 31N 2 1W
Mossoró, *Brazil* 101 5 10S 37 15W
Mostaganem, *Alg.* 78 35 54N 0 5 E
Mostar, *Yug.* 41 43 22N 17 50 E
Mosul, *Iraq* 56 36 15N 43 5 E
Motcombe, *U.K.* 14 51 1N 2 12W
Motherwell, *U.K.* 21 55 48N 4 0W
Mottisfont, *U.K.* 14 51 2N 1 32W
Moulmein, *Burma* 59 16 30N 97 40 E
Moulton, *U.K.* 15 52 17N 0 51W
Mount Barker, *Austral.* 66 34 38S 117 40 E
Mount Gambier, *Austral.* 70 37 50S 140 46 E
Mount Isa, *Austral.* 67 20 42S 139 26 E
Mount Lofty Ra., *Austral.* 67 34 35S 139 5 E
Mountain Ash, *U.K.* 17 51 42N 3 22W
Mountmellick, *Ire.* 25 53 7N 7 20W
Mounts Bay, *U.K.* 16 50 3N 5 27W
Mountsorrel, *U.K.* 14 52 43N 1 9W
Mourne →, *U.K.* 24 54 45N 7 39W
Mourne Mts., *U.K.* 24 54 10N 6 0W
Mouscron, *Belg.* 36 50 45N 3 12 E
Moville, *Ire.* 24 55 11N 7 3W
Moy →, *Ire.* 24 54 5N 8 50W
Moyle □, *U.K.* 24 55 10N 6 15W
Mozambique ■, *Africa* 81 19 0S 35 0 E
Mozambique Chan., *Africa* 81 20 0S 39 0 E
Mu Us Shamo, *China* 61 39 0N 109 0 E
Mubarraz, *Si. Arab.* 56 25 29N 49 40 E
Much Dewchurch, *U.K.* 14 51 58N 2 45W
Much Marcle, *U.K.* 14 51 59N 2 27W
Much Wenlock, *U.K.* 14 52 36N 2 34W
Muck, *U.K.* 22 56 50N 6 15W
Mudanjiang, *China* 61 44 38N 129 30 E
Mudgee, *Austral.* 70 32 32S 149 31 E
Mufulira, *Zam.* 81 12 32S 28 15 E
Muine Bheag, *Ire.* 25 52 42N 6 57W
Muir of Ord, *U.K.* 23 57 30N 4 35W
Muirdrum, *U.K.* 21 56 31N 2 40W
Muirhead, *U.K.* 21 55 54N 4 5W
Muirkirk, *U.K.* 21 55 31N 4 6W
Mülheim, *W. Ger.* 36 51 26N 6 53 E
Mulhouse, *Fr.* 34 47 40N 7 20 E
Mull, *U.K.* 20 56 27N 6 0W
Mull, Ross of, *U.K.* 20 56 20N 6 15W
Mull, Sound of, *U.K.* 20 56 30N 5 50W
Mullet Pen., *Ire.* 24 54 10N 10 2W
Mullingar, *Ire.* 24 53 31N 7 20W
Mullion, *U.K.* 16 50 1N 5 15W
Multan, *Pak.* 58 30 15N 71 36 E
Mumbles Hd., *U.K.* 17 51 33N 4 0W
Munchen-Gladbach, *W. Ger.* 36 51 12N 6 23 E
Mundesley, *U.K.* 15 52 53N 1 24 E
Munich, *W. Ger.* 42 48 8N 11 33 E
Münster, *W. Ger.* 36 51 58N 7 37 E
Munster □, *Ire.* 25 52 20N 8 40W
Murchison →, *Austral.* 66 27 45S 114 0 E
Murcia, *Sp.* 37 38 20N 1 10W
Mureş →, *Rom.* 43 46 15N 20 13 E
Murmansk, *U.S.S.R.* 46 68 57N 33 10 E
Murray →, *S. Austral., Austral.* 67 35 20S 139 22 E
Murrumbidgee →, *Austral.* 70 34 43S 143 12 E
Murton, *U.K.* 19 54 51N 1 22W
Murwillumbah, *Austral.* 67 28 18S 153 27 E
Muscat, *Oman* 57 23 40N 58 38 E
Musgrave Ras., *Austral.* 66 26 0S 132 0 E
Musselburgh, *U.K.* 21 55 57N 3 3W
Muswellbrook, *Austral.* 70 32 16S 150 56 E
Mutare, *Zimb.* 81 18 58S 32 38 E
Muthill, *U.K.* 21 56 20N 3 50W
Muzaffarpur, *India* 59 26 7N 85 23 E
Mwanza, *Tanz.* 80 2 30S 32 58 E
Mweelrea, *Ire.* 24 53 37N 9 48W
My Tho, *Viet.* 63 10 29N 106 23 E
Myanmar = Burma ■, *Asia* 59 21 0N 96 30 E
Myddle, *U.K.* 14 52 49N 2 47W
Myitkyina, *Burma* 59 25 24N 97 26 E
Mymensingh, *Bangla.* 59 24 45N 90 24 E
Mynydd Du, *U.K.* 17 51 45N 3 45W
Mynydd Prescelly, *U.K.* 17 51 57N 4 48W
Mysore, *India* 58 12 17N 76 41 E

N

Naas, *Ire.* 25 53 12N 6 40W
Nābulus, *Jord.* 57 32 14N 35 15 E
Nafferton, *U.K.* 19 54 1N 0 24W
Nagaland □, *India* 59 26 0N 94 30 E
Nagano, *Jap.* 62 36 40N 138 10 E
Nagaoka, *Jap.* 62 37 27N 138 51 E
Nagasaki, *Jap.* 62 32 47N 129 50 E
Nagoya, *Jap.* 62 35 10N 136 50 E
Nagpur, *India* 58 21 8N 79 10 E
Naha, *Jap.* 62 26 13N 127 42 E
Nailsea, *U.K.* 14 51 25N 2 44W
Nailsworth, *U.K.* 14 51 41N 2 12W
Nairn, *U.K.* 23 57 35N 3 54W
Nairobi, *Kenya* 80 1 17S 36 48 E
Nakuru, *Kenya* 80 0 15S 36 4 E
Nalchik, *U.S.S.R.* 47 43 30N 43 33 E
Nam Co, *China* 60 30 30N 90 45 E
Namangan, *U.S.S.R.* 48 41 0N 71 40 E
Namib Desert, *Nam.* 81 22 30S 15 0 E
Namibe, *Angola* 81 15 7S 12 11 E
Namibia ■, *Africa* 81 22 0S 18 9 E
Nampula, *Mozam.* 81 15 6N 39 15 E
Namur, *Belg.* 36 50 27N 4 52 E
Nan Shan, *China* 60 38 30N 99 0 E
Nanaimo, *Canada* 88 49 10N 124 0W
Nanchang, *China* 61 28 42N 115 55 E
Nanchong, *China* 60 30 43N 106 2 E
Nancy, *Fr.* 34 48 42N 6 12 E
Nanda Devi, *India* 58 30 23N 79 59 E
Nanjing = Nanking, *China* 61 32 2N 118 47 E
Nanking, *China* 61 32 2N 118 47 E
Nanning, *China* 60 22 48N 108 20 E
Nanping, *China* 61 26 38N 118 10 E
Nantes, *Fr.* 34 47 12N 1 33W
Nantong, *China* 61 32 1N 120 52 E
Nantucket Sd., *U.S.A.* 93 41 30N 70 15W
Nantwich, *U.K.* 18 53 5N 2 31W
Napier, *N.Z.* 71 39 30S 176 56 E
Naples, *It.* 40 40 50N 14 17 E
Nappa, *U.K.* 18 53 58N 2 14W
Nara, *Jap.* 62 34 40N 135 49 E
Narayanganj, *Bangla.* 59 23 40N 90 33 E
Narberth, *U.K.* 17 51 48N 4 45W
Narborough, *U.K.* 14 52 34N 1 12W
Nare Head, *U.K.* 16 50 12N 4 55W
Narmada →, *India* 58 21 38N 72 36 E
Narrandera, *Austral.* 70 34 42S 146 31 E
Narrogin, *Austral.* 66 32 58S 117 14 E
Narromine, *Austral.* 70 32 12S 148 12 E
Narvik, *Nor.* 44 68 28N 17 26 E
Naseby, *U.K.* 15 52 24N 0 59W
Nashua, *U.S.A.* 93 42 50N 71 25W
Nashville, *U.S.A.* 91 36 12N 86 46W
Nasik, *India* 58 19 58N 73 50 E
Nassau, *Baham.* 95 25 0N 77 20W
Nasser, L., *Egypt* 79 23 0N 32 30 E
Nässjö, *Swed.* 45 57 39N 14 42 E
Natal, *Brazil* 101 5 47S 35 13W
Natal □, *S. Afr.* 81 28 30S 30 30 E
Nauru ■, *Pac. Oc.* 64 1 0S 166 0 E
Navan = An Uaimh, *Ire.* 24 53 39N 6 40W
Navenby, *U.K.* 19 53 7N 0 32W
Naver →, *U.K.* 23 58 34N 4 15W
Náxos, *Greece* 41 37 8N 25 25 E
Nazareth, *Isr.* 57 32 42N 35 17 E
Naze, The, *U.K.* 15 51 53N 1 19 E
Ndjamena, *Chad* 79 12 10N 14 59 E
Ndola, *Zam.* 81 13 0S 28 34 E
Neagh, L., *U.K.* 24 54 35N 6 25W
Neath, *U.K.* 17 51 39N 3 49W
Nebraska □, *U.S.A.* 90 41 30N 100 0W
Needham Market, *U.K.* 15 52 9N 1 2 E
Needles, The, *U.K.* 14 50 39N 1 35W
Negro →, *Arg.* 102 41 2S 62 47W
Negro →, *Brazil* 100 3 0S 60 0W
Negros, *Phil.* 63 9 30N 122 40 E
Neijiang, *China* 60 29 35N 104 55 E
Neilston, *U.K.* 20 55 47N 4 27W
Neiva, *Col.* 100 2 56N 75 18W
Nellore, *India* 58 14 27N 79 59 E
Nelson, *N.Z.* 71 41 18S 173 16 E
Nelson, *U.K.* 18 53 50N 2 14W
Nelson →, *Canada* 88 54 33N 98 2W
Nelspruit, *S. Afr.* 81 25 29S 30 59 E
Nenagh, *Ire.* 25 52 52N 8 11W
Nene →, *U.K.* 15 52 38N 0 13 E
Nepal ■, *Asia* 59 28 0N 84 30 E
Nephin, *Ire.* 24 54 1N 9 21W
Ness, Loch, *U.K.* 23 57 15N 4 30W
Neston, *U.K.* 18 53 17N 3 3W
Netanya, *Isr.* 57 32 20N 34 51 E
Nether Stowey, *U.K.* 14 51 0N 3 10W
Netherbury, *U.K.* 14 50 46N 2 45W
Netherlands ■, *Europe* 36 52 0N 5 30 E
Netley, *U.K.* 14 50 53N 1 21W
Netley Marsh, *U.K.* 14 50 55N 1 32W
Nettlebed, *U.K.* 15 51 34N 0 54W
Nettleham, *U.K.* 19 53 15N 0 28W
Neuchâtel, *Switz.* 42 47 0N 6 55 E
Neukirchen, *W. Ger.* 36 54 52N 8 44 E
Neuss, *W. Ger.* 36 51 12N 6 39 E
Neustadt, *W. Ger.* 36 49 21N 8 10 E
Neuwied, *W. Ger.* 36 50 26N 7 29 E
Nevada □, *U.S.A.* 90 39 20N 117 0W
Nevada, Sierra, *Sp.* 37 37 3N 3 15W
Nevada, Sierra, *U.S.A.* 90 39 0N 120 30W
Nevers, *Fr.* 34 47 0N 3 9 E
New Abbey, *U.K.* 21 54 59N 3 38W
New Alresford, *U.K.* 14 51 6N 1 10W
New Amsterdam, *Guy.* 101 6 15N 57 36W
New Bedford, *U.S.A.* 93 41 40N 70 52W
New Brighton, *N.Z.* 71 43 29S 172 43 E
New Brighton, *U.K.* 18 53 27N 3 2W
New Brunswick □, *Canada* 93 46 50N 66 30W
New Caledonia, *Pac. Oc.* 64 21 0S 165 0 E
New Castile, *Sp.* 37 39 45N 3 20W
New Cumnock, *U.K.* 20 55 24N 4 13W
New Forest, *U.K.* 14 50 53N 1 40W
New Galloway, *U.K.* 21 55 4N 4 10W
New Guinea, *Pac. Oc.* 64 4 0S 136 0 E
New Hampshire □, *U.S.A.* 93 43 40N 71 40W
New Haven, *U.S.A.* 93 41 20N 72 54W
New Hebrides = Vanuatu ■, *Pac. Oc.* 64 15 0S 168 0 E
New Holland, *U.K.* 19 53 42N 0 22W
New Jersey □, *U.S.A.* 93 40 30N 74 10W
New London, *U.S.A.* 93 41 23N 72 8W
New Luce, *U.K.* 20 54 57N 4 50W
New Mexico □, *U.S.A.* 90 34 30N 106 0W
New Mills, *U.K.* 18 53 22N 2 0W
New Orleans, *U.S.A.* 91 30 0N 90 5W
New Plymouth, *N.Z.* 71 39 4S 174 5 E
New Quay, *U.K.* 17 52 13N 4 21W
New Radnor, *U.K.* 17 52 15N 3 10W
New Romney, *U.K.* 15 50 59N 0 57 E
New Ross, *Ire.* 25 52 24N 6 58W
New Rossington, *U.K.* 19 53 30N 1 4W
New Siberian Is., *U.S.S.R.* 49 75 0N 142 0 E
New South Wales □, *Austral.* 70 33 0S 146 0 E
New York □, *U.S.A.* 93 42 40N 76 0W
New York City, *U.S.A.* 93 40 45N 74 0W
New Zealand ■, *Pac. Oc.* 71 40 0S 176 0 E
Newark, *U.S.A.* 93 40 41N 74 12W
Newark-on-Trent, *U.K.* 19 53 6N 0 48W
Newbiggin-by-the-Sea, *U.K.* 21 55 12N 1 31W
Newbigging, *U.K.* 21 55 42N 3 33W
Newburgh, *U.K.* 21 56 21N 3 15W
Newburn, *U.K.* 21 54 57N 1 45W
Newbury, *U.K.* 14 51 24N 1 19W
Newby Bridge, *U.K.* 18 54 16N 2 59W
Newcastle, *Austral.* 70 33 0S 151 46 E
Newcastle, *U.K.* 24 54 13N 5 54W
Newcastle Emlyn, *U.K.* 17 52 2N 4 29W
Newcastle-under-Lyme, *U.K.* 18 53 2N 2 15W
Newcastle-upon-Tyne, *U.K.* 19 54 59N 1 37W
Newcastleton, *U.K.* 21 55 10N 2 50W
Newent, *U.K.* 14 51 56N 2 24W
Newfoundland □, *Canada* 89 53 0N 58 0W
Newham, *U.K.* 15 51 31N 0 2 E
Newhaven, *U.K.* 15 50 47N 0 4 E
Newington, *Kent, U.K.* 15 51 5N 1 8 E
Newington, *Kent, U.K.* 15 51 21N 0 40 E
Newlyn, *U.K.* 16 50 6N 5 33W
Newlyn East, *U.K.* 16 50 22N 5 3W
Newman, *Austral.* 66 23 18S 119 45 E
Newmarket, *Ire.* 25 52 13N 9 0W
Newmarket, *Lewis, U.K.* 22 58 14N 6 24W
Newmarket, *Suffolk, U.K.* 15 52 15N 0 23 E
Newmilns, *U.K.* 20 55 36N 4 20W
Newnham, *U.K.* 14 51 48N 2 27W
Newport, *Dyfed, U.K.* 17 52 1N 4 53W
Newport, *Essex, U.K.* 15 51 58N 0 13 E
Newport, *Gwent, U.K.* 17 51 35N 3 0W
Newport, *I. of W., U.K.* 14 50 42N 1 18W
Newport, *Salop, U.K.* 14 52 47N 2 22W
Newport News, *U.S.A.* 91 37 2N 76 30W
Newport on Tay, *U.K.* 21 56 27N 2 56W
Newport Pagnell, *U.K.* 15 52 5N 0 42W
Newquay, *U.K.* 16 50 24N 5 6W
Newry, *U.K.* 24 54 10N 6 20W
Newry & Mourne □, *U.K.* 24 54 10N 6 15W
Newton Abbot, *U.K.* 16 50 32N 3 37W
Newton Arlosh, *U.K.* 18 54 53N 3 15W
Newton-Aycliffe, *U.K.* 19 54 36N 1 33W
Newton Ferrers, *U.K.* 16 50 19N 4 3W
Newton le Willows, *U.K.* 18 53 28N 2 40W
Newton St. Cyres, *U.K.* 16 50 46N 3 35W
Newton Stewart, *U.K.* 20 54 57N 4 30W
Newtongrange, *U.K.* 21 55 52N 3 4W
Newtonmore, *U.K.* 23 57 4N 4 7W
Newtown, *Wales, U.K.* 17 52 31N 3 19W
Newtown St. Boswells, *Scotland, U.K.* 21 55 34N 2 38W
Newtownabbey, *Ire.* 24 54 40N 5 55W
Newtownabbey □, *U.K.* 24 54 45N 6 0W
Newtownards, *U.K.* 24 54 37N 5 40W
Nha Trang, *Viet.* 63 12 16N 109 10 E
Niagara Falls, *Canada* 92 43 7N 79 5W
Niagara Falls, *U.S.A.* 92 43 5N 79 0W
Niamey, *Niger* 78 13 27N 2 6 E
Nicaragua ■, *Cent. Am.* 94 11 40N 85 30W
Nicaragua, L., *Nic.* 94 12 0N 85 30W
Nice, *Fr.* 35 43 42N 7 14 E
Nicobar Is., *Ind. Oc.* 51 9 0N 93 0 E
Nicosia, *Cyprus* 47 35 10N 33 25 E
Nicoya, Pen. de, *C.R.* 94 9 45N 85 40W

Nidd →, *U.K.* **19** 54 1N 1 32W
Nidderdale, *U.K.* **19** 54 5N 1 46W
Niger ■, *W. Afr.* **78** 13 30N 10 0 E
Niger →, *W. Afr.* **78** 5 33N 6 33 E
Nigeria ■, *W. Afr.* **78** 8 30N 8 0 E
Niigata, *Jap.* **62** 37 58N 139 0 E
Niihau, *U.S.A.* **90** 21 55N 160 10W
Nijmegen, *Neth.* **36** 51 50N 5 52 E
Nikolayev, *U.S.S.R.* **47** 46 58N 32 0 E
Nikolayevsk, *U.S.S.R.* **49** 50 0N 45 35 E
Nile →, *Africa* **79** 30 10N 31 6 E
Nîmes, *Fr.* **35** 43 50N 4 23 E
Ninety Mile Beach, The, *Austral.* **70** 38 15S 147 24 E
Ninfield, *U.K.* **15** 50 53N 0 26 E
Ningbo, *China* **61** 29 51N 121 28 E
Ningxia Huizu Zizhiqu □, *China* **60** 38 0N 106 0 E
Niort, *Fr.* **35** 46 19N 0 29W
Nipigon, L., *Canada* **92** 49 50N 88 30W
Niš, *Yug.* **41** 43 19N 21 58 E
Niterói, *Brazil* **101** 22 52S 43 0W
Nith →, *U.K.* **21** 55 20N 3 5W
Nithsdale, *U.K.* **21** 55 14N 3 50W
Niton, *U.K.* **14** 50 35N 1 14W
Nizhniy Tagil, *U.S.S.R.* **46** 57 55N 59 57 E
Nkongsamba, *Cam.* **80** 4 55N 9 55 E
Nobeoka, *Jap.* **62** 32 36N 131 41 E
Nogales, *Mex.* **94** 31 20N 110 56W
Nordelph, *U.K.* **15** 52 34N 0 18 E
Nordhorn, *W. Ger.* **36** 52 27N 7 4 E
Nordvik, *U.S.S.R.* **49** 74 2N 111 32 E
Nore →, *Ire.* **25** 52 40N 7 20W
Norfolk, *U.S.A.* **91** 36 40N 76 15W
Norfolk □, *U.K.* **15** 52 39N 1 0 E
Norfolk Broads, *U.K.* **15** 52 30N 1 15 E
Norfolk I., *Pac. Oc.* **64** 28 58S 168 3 E
Norham, *U.K.* **21** 55 44N 2 9W
Norilsk, *U.S.S.R.* **49** 69 20N 88 6 E
Norman, *U.S.A.* **90** 35 12N 97 30W
Normandy, *Fr.* **34** 48 45N 0 10 E
Normanton, *U.K.* **19** 53 41N 1 26W
Norrbotten □, *Swed.* **44** 66 30N 22 30 E
Norrköping, *Swed.* **45** 58 37N 16 11 E
Norrland □, *Swed.* **44** 66 50N 18 0 E
Norseman, *Austral.* **66** 32 8S 121 43 E
North Battleford, *Canada* **88** 52 50N 108 17W
North Bay, *Canada* **92** 46 20N 79 30W
North Berwick, *U.K.* **21** 56 4N 2 44W
North Cape, *Nor.* **44** 71 15N 25 40 E
North Carolina □, *U.S.A.* **91** 35 30N 80 0W
North Cerney, *U.K.* **14** 51 45N 1 58W
North Channel, *U.K.* **20** 55 0N 5 30W
North Collingham, *U.K.* **19** 53 8N 0 46W
North Dakota □, *U.S.A.* **90** 47 30N 100 0W
North Dorset Downs, *U.K.* **14** 50 50N 2 30W
North Down □, *U.K.* **24** 54 40N 5 45W
North Downs, *U.K.* **15** 51 17N 0 30 E
North Esk →, *U.K.* **23** 56 44N 2 25W
North European Plain **26** 55 0N 20 0 E
North Foreland, *U.K.* **15** 51 22N 1 28 E
North Hill, *U.K.* **16** 50 33N 4 26W
North Hykeham, *U.K.* **19** 53 10N 0 35W
North I., *N.Z.* **71** 38 0S 175 0 E
North Minch, *U.K.* **22** 58 5N 5 55W
North Molton, *U.K.* **16** 51 3N 3 48W
North Petherton, *U.K.* **14** 51 6N 3 1W
North Pole, *Arctic* **103** 90 0N 0 0 E
North Queensferry, *U.K.* **21** 56 1N 3 22W
North Rhine Westphalia □, *W. Ger.* **42** 51 55N 7 0 E
North Ronaldsay, *U.K.* **23** 59 20N 2 30W
North Sea, *Europe* **26** 56 0N 4 0 E
North Somercotes, *U.K.* **19** 53 28N 0 9 E
North Sunderland, *U.K.* **21** 55 35N 1 40W
North Tawton, *U.K.* **16** 50 48N 3 55W
North Thoresby, *U.K.* **19** 53 27N 0 3W
North Tidworth, *U.K.* **14** 51 14N 1 40W
North Tyne →, *U.K.* **19** 54 59N 2 7W
North Uist, *U.K.* **22** 57 40N 7 15W
North Walsham, *U.K.* **15** 52 49N 1 22 E
North West Highlands, *U.K.* **22** 57 35N 5 2W
North West Territories □, *Canada* **88** 67 0N 110 0W
North York Moors, *U.K.* **19** 54 25N 0 50W
North Yorkshire □, *U.K.* **19** 54 15N 1 25W
Northallerton, *U.K.* **19** 54 20N 1 26W
Northam, *Austral.* **66** 31 35S 116 42 E
Northam, *U.K.* **16** 51 2N 4 13W
Northampton, *U.K.* **15** 52 14N 0 54W
Northampton □, *U.K.* **15** 52 16N 0 55W
Northern Ireland □, *U.K.* **24** 54 45N 7 0W
Northern Marianas, *Pac. Oc.* **64** 17 0N 145 0 E
Northern Territory □, *Austral.* **66** 16 0S 133 0 E
Northfleet, *U.K.* **15** 51 26N 0 20 E
Northiam, *U.K.* **15** 50 59N 0 39 E
Northland □, *N.Z.* **71** 35 30S 173 30 E
Northleach, *U.K.* **14** 51 49N 1 50W
Northrepps, *U.K.* **15** 52 53N 1 20 E
Northumberland □, *U.K.* **19** 55 12N 2 0W
Northumberland Str., *Canada* **93** 46 20N 64 0W
Northwich, *U.K.* **18** 53 16N 2 30W
Northwold, *U.K.* **15** 52 33N 0 37 E
Norton, *N. Yorks., U.K.* **19** 54 9N 0 48W
Norton, *Suffolk, U.K.* **15** 52 15N 0 52 E
Norton Fitzwarren, *U.K.* **14** 51 1N 3 10W
Norway ■, *Europe* **44** 63 0N 11 0 E
Norwegian Sea, *Atl. Oc.* **44** 66 0N 1 0 E
Norwich, *U.K.* **15** 52 38N 1 17 E
Noss Hd., *U.K.* **23** 58 29N 3 4W
Nottingham, *U.K.* **19** 52 57N 1 10W
Nottingham □, *U.K.* **19** 53 10N 1 0W
Nouâdhibou, *Maurit.* **78** 20 54N 17 0W
Nouakchott, *Maurit.* **78** 18 9N 15 58W
Nouméa, *N. Cal.* **64** 22 17S 166 30 E
Nova Scotia □, *Canada* **93** 45 10N 63 0W
Novara, *It.* **40** 45 27N 8 36 E
Novaya Zemlya, *U.S.S.R.* **48** 75 0N 56 0 E
Novi Sad, *Yug.* **41** 45 18N 19 52 E
Novocherkassk, *U.S.S.R.* **47** 47 27N 40 5 E
Novokuznetsk, *U.S.S.R.* **48** 53 45N 87 10 E
Novomoskovsk, *U.S.S.R.* **46** 54 5N 38 15 E
Novorossiysk, *U.S.S.R.* **47** 44 43N 37 46 E
Novoshakhtinsk, *U.S.S.R.* **47** 47 46N 39 58 E
Novosibirsk, *U.S.S.R.* **48** 55 0N 83 5 E
Nubian Desert, *Sudan* **79** 21 30N 33 30 E
Nuevo Laredo, *Mex.* **94** 27 30N 99 30W
Nullarbor Plain, *Austral.* **66** 30 45S 129 0 E
Nuneaton, *U.K.* **14** 52 32N 1 29W
Nunney, *U.K.* **14** 51 13N 2 20W
Nuremburg, *W. Ger.* **42** 49 26N 11 5 E
Nyasa, L., *Africa* **81** 12 30S 34 30 E
Nyíregyháza, *Hung.* **43** 47 58N 21 47 E
Nykøbing, *Den.* **45** 56 48N 8 51 E

O

Oa, Mull of, *U.K.* **20** 55 35N 6 20W
Oa, The, Pen., *U.K.* **20** 55 36N 6 17W
Oadby, *U.K.* **14** 52 37N 1 7W
Oahe L., *U.S.A.* **90** 45 30N 100 25W
Oahu, *U.S.A.* **90** 21 30N 158 0W
Oakengates, *U.K.* **14** 52 42N 2 29W
Oakham, *U.K.* **15** 52 40N 0 43W
Oakland, *U.S.A.* **90** 37 50N 122 18W
Oakleigh, *Austral.* **70** 37 54S 145 6 E
Oamaru, *N.Z.* **71** 45 5S 170 59 E
Oaxaca, *Mex.* **94** 17 2N 96 40W
Ob →, *U.S.S.R.* **48** 66 45N 69 30 E
Ob, G. of, *U.S.S.R.* **48** 70 0N 73 0 E
Oban, *U.K.* **20** 56 25N 5 30W
Oberhausen, *W. Ger.* **36** 51 28N 6 50 E
Ochil Hills, *U.K.* **21** 56 14N 3 40W
Ochiltree, *U.K.* **20** 55 26N 4 23W
October Revolution I., *U.S.S.R.* **49** 79 30N 97 0 E
Odense, *Den.* **45** 55 22N 10 23 E
Odessa, *U.S.A.* **90** 31 51N 102 23W
Odessa, *U.S.S.R.* **47** 46 30N 30 45 E
Odiham, *U.K.* **15** 51 16N 0 56W
Odra →, *Pol.* **42** 53 33N 14 38 E
Offaly □, *Ire.* **25** 53 15N 7 30W
Offenbach, *W. Ger.* **42** 50 6N 8 46 E
Ogbomosho, *Nig.* **78** 8 1N 4 11 E
Ogden, *U.S.A.* **90** 41 13N 112 1W
Ohio □, *U.S.A.* **92** 40 20N 14 10 E
Ohio →, *U.S.A.* **92** 38 0N 86 0W
Ōita, *Jap.* **62** 33 14N 131 36 E
Okavango Swamps, *Bots.* **81** 18 45S 22 45 E
Okayama, *Jap.* **62** 34 40N 133 54 E
Okazaki, *Jap.* **62** 34 57N 137 10 E
Okehampton, *U.K.* **16** 50 44N 4 1W
Okhotsk, *U.S.S.R.* **49** 59 20N 143 10 E
Okhotsk, Sea of, *Asia* **49** 55 0N 145 0 E
Oklahoma □, *U.S.A.* **90** 35 20N 97 30W
Oklahoma City, *U.S.A.* **91** 35 25N 97 30W
Ólafsfjörður, *Ice.* **44** 66 4N 18 39W
Öland, *Swed.* **45** 56 45N 16 38 E
Old Basing, *U.K.* **14** 51 16N 1 3W
Old Castile, *Sp.* **37** 41 55N 4 0W
Old Castle, *Ire.* **24** 53 46N 7 10W
Old Kilpatrick, *U.K.* **20** 55 56N 4 34W
Old Leake, *U.K.* **19** 53 2N 0 6 E
Oldbury, *Gloucs., U.K.* **14** 51 38N 2 30W
Oldbury, *W. Midlands, U.K.* **14** 52 30N 2 0W
Oldenburg, *W. Ger.* **36** 53 10N 8 10 E
Oldham, *U.K.* **18** 53 33N 2 8W
Oldmeldrum, *U.K.* **23** 57 20N 2 19W
Olekminsk, *U.S.S.R.* **49** 60 25N 120 30 E
Olinda, *Brazil* **101** 8 1S 34 51W
Ollerton, *U.K.* **19** 53 12N 1 1W
Olney, *U.K.* **15** 52 9N 0 42W
Olomouc, *Czech.* **42** 49 38N 17 12 E
Olsztyn, *Pol.* **43** 53 48N 20 29 E
Olympia, *Greece* **41** 37 39N 21 39 E
Olympus, Mt., *Greece* **41** 40 6N 22 23 E
Omagh, *U.K.* **24** 54 36N 7 20W
Omagh □, *U.K.* **24** 54 35N 7 15W
Omaha, *U.S.A.* **91** 41 15N 96 0W
Oman ■, *Si. Arab.* **57** 23 0N 58 0 E
Oman, G. of, *Asia* **57** 24 30N 58 30 E
Ombersley, *U.K.* **14** 52 17N 2 12W
Omdurmân, *Sudan* **79** 15 40N 32 28 E
Ōmiya, *Jap.* **62** 35 54N 139 38 E
Omsk, *U.S.S.R.* **48** 55 0N 73 12 E
Ōmuta, *Jap.* **62** 33 0N 130 26 E
Onchan, *U.K.* **18** 54 11N 4 27W
Onega →, *U.S.S.R.* **46** 63 58N 37 55 E
Onega, G. of, *U.S.S.R.* **46** 64 30N 37 0 E
Onega, L., *U.S.S.R.* **46** 62 0N 35 30 E
Onehunga, *N.Z.* **71** 36 55S 174 48 E
Onny →, *U.K.* **14** 52 30N 2 50W
Ontario □, *Canada* **88** 52 0N 88 10W
Ontario, L., *N. Am.* **92** 43 40N 78 0W
Opole, *Pol.* **43** 50 42N 17 58 E
Oporto, *Port.* **37** 41 8N 8 40W
Oradea, *Rom.* **43** 47 2N 21 58 E
Oran, *Alg.* **78** 35 45N 0 39W
Orange, *Austral.* **70** 33 15S 149 7 E
Orange →, *S. Afr.* **81** 28 41S 16 28 E
Orange Free State □, *S. Afr.* **81** 28 30S 27 0 E
Ord, Mt., *Austral.* **66** 17 20S 125 34 E
Ordos = Mu Us Shamo, *China* **61** 39 0N 109 0 E
Ordzhonikidze, *U.S.S.R.* **47** 43 0N 44 35 E
Örebro, *Swed.* **45** 59 20N 15 18 E
Oregon □, *U.S.A.* **90** 44 0N 121 0W
Orekhovo-Zuyevo, *U.S.S.R.* **46** 55 50N 38 55 E
Orel, *U.S.S.R.* **46** 52 57N 36 3 E
Orenburg, *U.S.S.R.* **46** 51 45N 55 6 E
Orense, *Sp.* **37** 42 19N 7 55W
Orford, *U.K.* **15** 52 6N 1 31 E
Orford Ness, *U.K.* **15** 52 6N 1 31 E
Orinoco →, *Ven.* **100** 9 15N 61 30W
Orissa □, *India* **59** 20 0N 84 0 E
Oristano, *It.* **40** 39 54N 8 35 E
Orizaba, *Mex.* **94** 18 51N 97 6W
Orkney □, *U.K.* **23** 59 0N 3 0W
Orkney Is., *U.K.* **23** 59 0N 3 0W
Orlando, *U.S.A.* **91** 28 30N 81 25W
Orléans, *Fr.* **34** 47 54N 1 52 E
Ormesby St. Margaret, *U.K.* **15** 52 39N 1 42 E
Ormskirk, *U.K.* **18** 53 35N 2 53W
Örnsköldsvik, *Swed.* **44** 63 17N 18 40 E
Oronsay, Pass of, *U.K.* **20** 56 0N 6 10W
Oronsay I., *U.K.* **20** 56 0N 6 14W
Orsk, *U.S.S.R.* **46** 51 12N 58 34 E
Orton Tebay, *U.K.* **18** 54 28N 2 35W
Oruro, *Bol.* **100** 18 0S 67 9W
Orwell →, *U.K.* **15** 52 2N 1 12 E
Ōsaka, *Jap.* **62** 34 40N 135 30 E
Osh, *U.S.S.R.* **48** 40 37N 72 49 E
Oshawa, *Canada* **92** 43 50N 78 50W
Oshogbo, *Nig.* **78** 7 48N 4 37 E
Osijek, *Yug.* **41** 45 34N 18 41 E
Osizweni, *S. Afr.* **81** 27 49S 30 7 E
Oslo, *Nor.* **45** 59 55N 10 45 E
Oslo Fjord, *Nor.* **45** 58 30N 10 0 E
Osmotherley, *U.K.* **19** 54 22N 1 18W
Osnabrück, *W. Ger.* **36** 52 16N 8 2 E
Osorno, *Chile* **102** 40 25S 73 0W
Ossett, *U.K.* **19** 53 40N 1 35W
Ostend, *Belg.* **36** 51 15N 2 50 E
Östersund, *Swed.* **44** 63 10N 14 38 E
Ostrava, *Czech.* **43** 49 51N 18 18 E
Osumi, Is., *Jap.* **62** 30 30N 130 45 E
Oswaldtwistle, *U.K.* **18** 53 44N 2 27W
Oswestry, *U.K.* **14** 52 52N 3 3W
Otago □, *N.Z.* **71** 44 44S 169 10 E
Otaru, *Jap.* **62** 43 10N 141 0 E
Otley, *U.K.* **19** 53 54N 1 41W
Otranto, Str. of, *It.* **41** 40 15N 18 40 E
Ōtsu, *Jap.* **62** 35 0N 135 50 E
Ottawa, *Canada* **93** 45 27N 75 42W
Ottawa →, *Canada* **93** 45 27N 74 8W
Otter →, *U.K.* **16** 50 47N 3 12W
Otter Ferry, *U.K.* **20** 56 1N 5 20W
Otterburn, *U.K.* **21** 55 14N 2 12W
Ottery St. Mary, *U.K.* **16** 50 45N 3 16W
Ouagadougou, *B. Faso* **78** 12 25N 1 30W
Oujda, *Mor.* **78** 34 41N 1 55W
Oulton, *U.K.* **15** 52 29N 1 40 E
Oulton Broad, *U.K.* **15** 52 28N 1 43 E
Oulu, *Fin.* **44** 65 1N 25 29 E
Oulu, L., *Fin.* **44** 64 25N 27 0 E
Oundle, *U.K.* **15** 52 28N 0 28W
Ouse →, *E. Sussex, U.K.* **15** 50 43N 0 3 E
Ouse →, *N. Yorks., U.K.* **19** 54 3N 0 7 E
Outer Hebrides, *U.K.* **22** 57 30N 7 40W
Outwell, *U.K.* **15** 52 36N 0 14 E
Over Wallop, *U.K.* **14** 51 9N 1 35W
Overstand, *U.K.* **15** 52 55N 1 20 E
Overton, *U.K.* **14** 51 14N 1 16W
Oviedo, *Sp.* **37** 43 25N 5 50W
Owston Ferry, *U.K.* **19** 53 28N 0 47W
Ox Mts., *Ire.* **24** 54 6N 9 0W
Oxford, *U.K.* **14** 51 45N 1 15W
Oxford □, *U.K.* **14** 51 45N 1 15W
Oykel →, *U.K.* **23** 57 55N 4 26W
Ozark Plateau, *U.S.A.* **91** 37 20N 91 40W

P

Paarl, *S. Afr.* **81** 33 45S 18 56 E
Pacaraima, Sierra, *Ven.* **100** 4 0N 62 30W
Pachuca, *Mex.* **94** 20 10N 98 40W
Pacific Ocean **64** 10 0N 140 0W
Padang, *Indon.* **63** 1 0S 100 20 E
Paddock Wood, *U.K.* **15** 51 13N 0 24 E
Padiham, *U.K.* **18** 53 48N 2 20W
Padstow, *U.K.* **14** 50 33N 4 57W
Padstow Bay, *U.K.* **16** 50 35N 4 58W
Padua, *It.* **40** 45 24N 11 52 E
Pagalu = Annobón, *Atl. Oc.* **73** 1 25S 5 36 E
Paignton, *U.K.* **16** 50 26N 3 33W
Painswick, *U.K.* **14** 51 47N 2 11W
Paisley, *U.K.* **20** 55 51N 4 27W
Pakistan ■, *Asia* **58** 30 0N 70 0 E
Palawan, *Phil.* **63** 9 30N 118 30 E
Palembang, *Indon.* **63** 3 0S 104 50 E
Palencia, *Sp.* **37** 42 1N 4 34W
Palermo, *It.* **40** 38 8N 13 20 E
Palgrave, *U.K.* **15** 52 22N 1 7 E
Palk Strait, *Asia* **58** 10 0N 79 45 E
Palma de Mallorca, *Sp.* **37** 39 35N 2 39 E
Palmer →, *Austral.* **66** 24 46S 133 25 E
Palmerston North, *N.Z.* **71** 40 21S 175 39 E
Palmira, *Col.* **100** 3 32N 76 16W
Pamirs, *U.S.S.R.* **48** 37 40N 73 0 E
Pamlico Sd., *U.S.A.* **91** 35 20N 76 0W
Pampas, *Arg.* **96** 35 0S 63 0W
Pamplona, *Sp.* **37** 42 48N 1 38W
Panamá, *Pan.* **94** 9 0N 79 25W
Panama ■, *Cent. Am.* **95** 8 48N 79 55W
Panamá, G. de, *Pan.* **95** 8 4N 79 20W
Panama Canal, *Pan.* **94** 9 10N 79 37W
Panay, *Phil.* **63** 11 10N 122 30 E
Pančevo, *Yug.* **41** 44 52N 20 41 E
Pangbourne, *U.K.* **14** 51 28N 1 5W
Pantelleria, *It.* **40** 36 52N 12 0 E
Papua New Guinea ■, *Oc.* **64** 8 0S 145 0 E
Pará □, *Brazil* **101** 3 20S 52 0W
Paraguay ■, *S. Am.* **102** 23 0S 57 0W
Paraguay →, *Par.* **102** 27 18S 58 38W
Paramaribo, *Surinam* **101** 5 50N 55 10W
Paraná, *Arg.* **102** 31 45S 60 30W
Paraná →, *Arg.* **102** 33 43S 59 15W
Parecis, Serra dos, *Brazil* **100** 13 0S 60 0W
Parepare, *Indon.* **63** 4 0S 119 40 E
Paris, *Fr.* **34** 48 50N 2 20 E
Parkes, *Austral.* **70** 33 9S 148 11 E
Parma, *It.* **40** 44 50N 10 20 E
Parnaíba →, *Brazil* **101** 3 0S 41 50W
Parracombe, *U.K.* **16** 51 11N 3 55W
Parramatta, *Austral.* **70** 33 48S 151 1 E
Parrett →, *U.K.* **14** 51 7N 2 58W
Partney, *U.K.* **19** 53 12N 0 7 E
Parton, *U.K.* **18** 54 34N 3 35W
Passage West, *Ire.* **25** 51 52N 8 20W
Pasto, *Col.* **100** 1 13N 77 17W
Patagonia, *Arg.* **102** 45 0S 69 0W
Patcham, *U.K.* **15** 50 52N 0 9W
Pateley Bridge, *U.K.* **19** 54 5N 1 45W
Paterson, *U.S.A.* **93** 40 55N 74 10W
Patna, *India* **59** 25 35N 85 12 E
Patna, *U.K.* **20** 55 21N 4 30W
Pátrai, *Greece* **41** 38 14N 21 47 E
Patrick, *U.K.* **18** 54 13N 4 41W
Patrington, *U.K.* **19** 53 41N 0 1W
Patterdale, *U.K.* **18** 54 33N 2 55W
Pau, *Fr.* **35** 43 19N 0 25W
Paull, *U.K.* **19** 53 42N 0 12W
Pavia, *It.* **40** 45 10N 9 10 E
Pavlodar, *U.S.S.R.* **48** 52 33N 77 0 E
Pawtucket, *U.S.A.* **93** 41 51N 71 22W
Paz, La, *Bol.* **100** 16 20S 68 10W
Pazardzhik, *Bulg.* **41** 42 12N 24 20 E
Peace →, *Canada* **88** 59 0N 111 25W
Peacehaven, *U.K.* **15** 50 47N 0 1 E
Peak, The, *U.K.* **18** 53 24N 1 53W
Peasenhall, *U.K.* **15** 52 17N 1 24 E
Pechora →, *U.S.S.R.* **46** 68 13N 54 15 E
Pécs, *Hung.* **43** 46 5N 18 15 E
Peebles, *U.K.* **21** 55 40N 3 12W
Peel, *U.K.* **18** 54 14N 4 40W
Peel Fell, *U.K.* **21** 55 17N 2 35W
Pegasus Bay, *N.Z.* **71** 43 20S 173 10 E
Pegswood, *U.K.* **21** 55 12N 1 38W
Pegu, *Burma* **59** 17 20N 96 29 E
Pegu Yoma, *Burma* **59** 19 0N 96 0 E
Pegwell Bay, *U.K.* **15** 51 18N 1 22 E
Pekanbaru, *Indon.* **63** 0 30N 101 15 E
Peking, *China* **61** 39 55N 116 20 E
Peloponnese □, *Greece* **41** 37 10N 22 0 E
Pelotas, *Brazil* **102** 31 42S 52 23W
Pelvoux, Massif de, *Fr.* **35** 44 52N 6 20 E
Pematangsiantar, *Indon.* **63** 2 57N 99 5 E
Pemba, *Tanz.* **80** 5 0S 39 45 E
Pembridge, *U.K.* **14** 52 13N 2 54W
Pembroke, *U.K.* **17** 51 41N 4 57W
Pembury, *U.K.* **15** 51 8N 0 20 E
Pen-y-Ghent, *U.K.* **18** 54 10N 2 15W
Pen-y-groes, *U.K.* **17** 53 3N 4 18W
Penang = Pinang, *Malay.* **63** 5 25N 100 15 E
Penarth, *U.K.* **17** 51 26N 3 11W
Pendeen, *U.K.* **16** 50 11N 5 39W
Pendle Hill, *U.K.* **18** 53 53N 2 18W
Penicuik, *U.K.* **21** 55 50N 3 14W
Peninsular Malaysia □, *Malay.* **63** 4 0N 102 0 E
Penistone, *U.K.* **19** 53 31N 1 38W
Penkridge, *U.K.* **14** 52 44N 2 8W
Pennines, *U.K.* **18** 54 50N 2 20W
Pennsylvania □, *U.S.A.* **92** 40 50N 78 0W
Penpont, *U.K.* **21** 55 14N 3 49W

Penrith, *Austral.* ..... **70** 33 43S 150 38 E
Penrith, *U.K.* **18** 54 40N 2 45W
Penryn, *U.K.* **16** 50 10N 5 7W
Pensacola, *U.S.A.* **91** 30 30N 87 10W
Penshurst, *U.K.* ...... **15** 51 10N 0 12 E
Pentire Pt., *U.K.* **16** 50 35N 4 57W
Pentland Firth, *U.K.* .. **23** 58 43N 3 10W
Pentland Hills, *U.K.* ... **21** 55 48N 3 25W
Penwortham, *U.K.* **18** 53 45N 2 44W
Penza, *U.S.S.R.* ...... **46** 53 15N 45 5 E
Penzance, *U.K.* **16** 50 7N 5 32W
Peoria, *U.S.A.* **92** 40 40N 89 40W
Pereira, *Col.* **100** 4 49N 75 43W
Perm, *U.S.S.R.* .... **46** 58 0N 57 10 E
Perouse Str., La, *Jap.* . **64** 45 40N 142 0 E
Perpignan, *Fr.* .... **35** 42 42N 2 53 E
Perranporth, *U.K.* **16** 50 21N 5 9W
Perranzabuloe, *U.K.* .. **16** 50 18N 5 7W
Pershore, *U.K.* **14** 52 7N 2 4W
Persian Gulf = Gulf, The, *Asia* .... **56** 27 0N 50 0 E
Perth, *Austral.* .... **66** 31 57S 115 52 E
Perth, *U.K.* **21** 56 24N 3 27W
Peru ■, *S. Am.* **100** 8 0S 75 0W
Perúgia, *It.* .... **40** 43 6N 12 24 E
Pescara, *It.* .... **40** 42 28N 14 13 E
Peshawar, *Pak.* ...... **58** 34 2N 71 37 E
Peterborough, *Canada* **92** 44 20N 78 20W
Peterborough, *U.K.* ... **15** 52 35N 0 14W
Peterchurch, *U.K.* **14** 52 3N 2 57W
Peterhead, *U.K.* **23** 57 30N 1 49W
Peterlee, *U.K.* **19** 54 45N 1 18W
Petersfield, *U.K.* **15** 51 0N 0 56W
Petropavlovsk, *U.S.S.R.* **48** 54 53N 69 13 E
Petropavlovsk-Kamchatskiy, *U.S.S.R.* .... **49** 53 3N 158 43 E
Petrópolis, *Brazil* **101** 22 33S 43 9W
Petrozavodsk, *U.S.S.R.* **46** 61 41N 34 20 E
Petworth, *U.K.* **15** 50 59N 0 37W
Pevensey, *U.K.* ...... **15** 50 49N 0 20 E
Pevensey Levels, *U.K.* **15** 50 50N 0 20 E
Pewsey, *U.K.* **14** 51 20N 1 46W
Pewsey, Vale of, *U.K.* . **14** 51 20N 1 46W
Pforzheim, *W. Ger.* ... **42** 48 53N 8 43 E
Philadelphia, *U.S.A.* .. **93** 40 0N 75 10W
Philippines ■, *Asia* ... **63** 12 0N 123 0 E
Phnom Penh, *Cambod.* **63** 11 33N 104 55 E
Phoenix, *U.S.A.* **90** 33 30N 112 10W
Phoenix Is., *Pac. Oc.* . **65** 3 30S 172 0W
Piacenza, *It.* .... **40** 45 2N 9 42 E
Piatra Neamţ, *Rom.* .. **43** 46 56N 26 21 E
Picardie, *Fr.* .... **34** 49 50N 3 0 E
Picardy = Picardie, *Fr.* **34** 49 50N 3 0 E
Pickering, *U.K.* **19** 54 15N 0 46W
Pickering, Vale of, *U.K.* **19** 54 0N 0 45W
Pidley, *U.K.* **15** 52 33N 0 4W
Piedmont □, *It.* ...... **40** 45 0N 7 30 E
Piedras Negras, *Mex.* . **94** 28 42N 100 31W
Pierowall, *U.K.* **23** 59 20N 3 0W
Pietermaritzburg, *S. Afr.* **81** 29 35S 30 25 E
Pilbara, *Austral.* ..... **66** 21 15S 118 16 E
Pilcomayo →, *Par.* .. **102** 25 21S 57 42W
Pilling, *U.K.* **18** 53 55N 2 54W
Pilton, *U.K.* **14** 51 0N 2 35W
Pinang, *Malay.* .... **63** 5 25N 100 15 E
Pinchbeck, *U.K.* **15** 52 48N 0 9W
Pindus Mts., *Greece* .. **41** 40 0N 21 0 E
Pine Bluff, *U.S.A.* **91** 34 10N 92 0W
Pingxiang, *China* ..... **60** 22 6N 106 46 E
Pinhoe, *U.K.* **16** 50 44N 3 29W
Pinjarra, *Austral.* ..... **66** 32 37S 115 52 E
Pinwherry, *U.K.* **20** 55 9N 4 50W
Piotrków Trybunalski, *Pol.* .... **43** 51 23N 19 43 E
Piracicaba, *Brazil* **102** 22 45S 47 40W
Piraiévs, *Greece* ..... **41** 37 57N 23 42 E
Pirbright, *U.K.* **15** 51 17N 0 40W
Pirmasens, *W. Ger.* ... **36** 49 12N 7 30 E
Pisa, *It.* .... **40** 43 43N 10 23 E
Pistóia, *It.* .... **40** 43 57N 10 53 E
Pitcairn I., *Pac. Oc.* ... **65** 25 5S 130 5W
Piteşti, *Rom.* .... **43** 44 52N 24 54 E
Pitlochry, *U.K.* **23** 56 43N 3 43W
Pittenweem, *U.K.* **21** 56 13N 2 43W
Pittsburgh, *U.S.A.* **92** 40 25N 79 55W
Pittsfield, *U.S.A.* **93** 42 28N 73 17W
Piura, *Peru* **100** 5 15S 80 38W
Pladda, I., *U.K.* **20** 55 25N 5 7W
Plata, La, *Arg.* **102** 35 0S 57 55W
Plata, Río de la, *S. Am.* **102** 34 45S 57 30W
Plauen, *E. Ger.* ...... **42** 50 29N 12 9 E
Plenty, Bay of, *N.Z.* ... **71** 37 45S 177 0 E
Pleven, *Bulg.* .... **41** 43 26N 24 37 E
Płock, *Pol.* .... **43** 52 32N 19 40 E
Ploieşti, *Rom.* .... **43** 44 57N 26 5 E
Plovdiv, *Bulg.* .... **41** 42 8N 24 44 E
Plymouth, *U.K.* **16** 50 23N 4 9W
Plymouth Sd., *U.K.* ... **16** 50 20N 4 10W
Plympton, *U.K.* **16** 50 24N 4 2W
Plymstock, *U.K.* **16** 50 22N 4 6W
Plynlimon = Pumlumon Fawr, *U.K.* **17** 52 29N 3 47W
Plzen, *Czech.* .... **42** 49 45N 13 22 E
Po →, *It.* .... **40** 44 57N 12 4 E
Pocklington, *U.K.* **19** 53 56N 0 48W
Podolsk, *U.S.S.R.* .... **46** 55 25N 37 30 E
Pointe-à-Pitre, *Guad.* . **94** 16 10N 61 30W
Pointe Noire, *Congo* .. **80** 4 48S 11 53 E
Poitiers, *Fr.* .... **34** 46 35N 0 20 E
Poland ■, *Europe* .... **43** 52 0N 20 0 E
Polden Hills, *U.K.* **14** 51 7N 2 50W
Polegate, *U.K.* .... **15** 50 49N 0 15 E
Polesworth, *U.K.* **14** 52 37N 1 37W
Polperro, *U.K.* **16** 50 19N 4 31W
Polruan, *U.K.* **16** 50 17N 4 36W
Poltava, *U.S.S.R.* ..... **47** 49 35N 34 35 E
Polynesia, *Pac. Oc.* ... **64** 10 0S 162 0W
Ponce, *P.R.* **95** 18 1N 66 37W
Pondicherry, *India* .... **58** 11 59N 79 50 E
Ponta Grossa, *Brazil* .. **102** 25 7S 50 10W
Pontardawe, *U.K.* **17** 51 43N 3 51W
Pontardulais, *U.K.* **17** 51 42N 4 3W
Pontchartrain, L., *U.S.A.* **91** 30 12N 90 0W
Pontefract, *U.K.* **19** 53 42N 1 19W
Ponteland, *U.K.* **21** 55 7N 1 45W
Pontevedra, *Sp.* **37** 42 26N 8 40W
Pontianak, *Indon.* .... **63** 0 3S 109 15 E
Pontrilas, *U.K.* **14** 51 56N 2 53W
Pontypool, *U.K.* **17** 51 42N 3 1W
Pontypridd, *U.K.* **17** 51 36N 3 21W
Poole, *U.K.* **14** 50 42N 1 58W
Poole Harbour, *U.K.* .. **14** 50 41N 2 0W
Pooley Bridge, *U.K.* .. **18** 54 37N 2 49W
Poona = Pune, *India* . **58** 18 29N 73 57 E
Poopó, L., *Bol.* **100** 18 30S 67 35W
Popayán, *Col.* **100** 2 27N 76 36W
Popocatépetl, Volcán, *Mex.* **94** 19 2N 98 38W
Pori, *Fin.* .... **45** 61 29N 21 48 E
Porirua, *N.Z.* .... **71** 41 8S 174 52 E
Porlock, *U.K.* **14** 51 13N 3 36W
Porlock B., *U.K.* **14** 51 14N 3 37W
Porlock Hill, *U.K.* **14** 51 12N 3 40W
Porsangen Fjord, *Nor.* **44** 70 45N 25 0 E
Port Antonio, *Jam.* ... **94** 18 10N 76 30W
Port Arthur, *U.S.A.* ... **91** 30 0N 94 0W
Port Askaig, *U.K.* **20** 55 51N 6 8W
Port-au-Prince, *Haiti* .. **95** 18 40N 72 20W
Port Augusta, *Austral.* **67** 32 30S 137 50 E
Port Bannatyne, *U.K.* . **20** 55 51N 5 4W
Port Carlisle, *U.K.* **18** 54 56N 3 12W
Port-Cartier, *Canada* .. **89** 50 2N 66 50W
Port Charlotte, *U.K.* .. **20** 55 44N 6 22W
Port Elizabeth, *S. Afr.* . **81** 33 58S 25 40 E
Port Ellen, *U.K.* **20** 55 38N 6 10W
Port Erin, *U.K.* **18** 54 5N 4 45W
Port-Gentil, *Gabon* ... **80** 0 40S 8 50 E
Port Glasgow, *U.K.* ... **20** 55 57N 4 40W
Port Harcourt, *Nig.* ... **78** 4 40N 7 10 E
Port Hedland, *Austral.* **66** 20 25S 118 35 E
Port Isaac, *U.K.* **16** 50 35N 4 50W
Port Isaac B., *U.K.* ... **16** 50 36N 4 50W
Port Laoise, *Ire.* **25** 53 2N 7 20W
Port Logan, *U.K.* **20** 54 42N 4 57W
Port Macquarie, *Austral.* **67** 31 25S 152 25 E
Port Moresby, *P.N.G.* . **64** 9 24S 147 8 E
Port of Spain, *Trin. & Tob.* **94** 10 40N 61 31W
Port Phillip B., *Austral.* **70** 38 10S 144 50 E
Port Pirie, *Austral.* .... **67** 33 10S 138 1 E
Port Said, *Egypt* ..... **79** 31 16N 32 18 E
Port St. Mary, *U.K.* ... **18** 54 5N 4 45W
Port Sudan, *Sudan* ... **79** 19 32N 37 9 E
Port Sunlight, *U.K.* ... **18** 53 22N 3 0W
Port Talbot, *U.K.* **17** 51 35N 3 48W
Port William, *U.K.* ... **20** 54 46N 4 35W
Portadown, *U.K.* **24** 54 27N 6 26W
Portaferry, *U.K.* **24** 54 23N 5 32W
Portage La Prairie, *Canada* **88** 49 58N 98 18W
Portarlington, *Ire.* **25** 53 10N 7 10W
Porthcawl, *U.K.* **17** 51 28N 3 42W
Porthleven, *U.K.* **16** 50 5N 5 19W
Porthmadog, *U.K.* **17** 52 55N 4 13W
Portishead, *U.K.* **14** 51 29N 2 46W
Portland, *Austral.* .... **70** 38 20S 141 35 E
Portland, *Maine, U.S.A.* **93** 43 40N 70 15W
Portland, *Oreg., U.S.A.* **90** 45 35N 122 40W
Portland Bill, *U.K.* ... **14** 50 31N 2 27W
Portland, I. of, *U.K.* ... **14** 50 32N 2 25W
Portnacroish, *U.K.* ... **20** 56 34N 5 24W
Portnahaven, *U.K.* ... **20** 55 40N 6 30W
Pôrto Alegre, *Brazil* ... **102** 30 5S 51 10W
Porto Novo, *Benin* ... **78** 6 23N 2 42 E
Pôrto Velho, *Brazil* ... **100** 8 46S 63 54W
Porton, *U.K.* **14** 51 8N 1 42W
Portoviejo, *Ecuad.* **100** 1 7S 80 28W
Portpatrick, *U.K.* **20** 54 50N 5 7W
Portree, *U.K.* **22** 57 25N 6 11W
Portrush, *U.K.* **24** 55 13N 6 40W
Portslade, *U.K.* **15** 50 50N 0 11W
Portsmouth, *U.K.* **14** 50 48N 1 6W
Portsmouth, *U.S.A.* ... **93** 43 5N 70 45W
Portsoy, *U.K.* **23** 57 41N 2 41W
Portstewart, *U.K.* **24** 55 12N 6 43W
Portugal ■, *Europe* ... **37** 40 0N 7 0W
Portumna, *Ire.* **25** 53 5N 8 12W
Posadas, *Arg.* **102** 27 30S 55 50W
Postbridge, *U.K.* **16** 50 36N 3 54W
Potchefstroom, *S. Afr.* **81** 26 41S 27 7 E
Potenza, *It.* .... **40** 40 40N 15 50 E
Potomac →, *U.S.A.* .. **92** 38 0N 76 23W
Potosí, *Bol.* **100** 19 38S 65 50W
Potsdam, *E. Ger.* .... **42** 52 23N 13 4 E
Potter Heigham, *U.K.* . **15** 52 44N 1 33 E
Potterne, *U.K.* **14** 51 19N 2 0W
Potters Bar, *U.K.* **15** 51 42N 0 11W
Potterspury, *U.K.* **15** 52 5N 0 52W
Poulaphouca Res., *Ire.* **25** 53 8N 6 30W
Poulton le Fylde, *U.K.* . **18** 53 51N 2 59W
Poundstock, *U.K.* **16** 50 44N 4 34W
Powell, L., *U.S.A.* **90** 37 25N 110 45W
Powick, *U.K.* **14** 52 9N 2 15W
Powys □, *U.K.* **17** 52 20N 3 20W
Poyang Hu, *China* .... **61** 29 10N 116 10 E
Poznań, *Pol.* .... **42** 52 25N 16 55 E
Prague, *Czech.* ...... **42** 50 5N 14 22 E
Prato, *It.* .... **40** 43 53N 11 5 E
Prawle Pt., *U.K.* **16** 50 13N 3 41W
Prees, *U.K.* **18** 52 54N 2 40W
Preesall, *U.K.* **18** 53 55N 2 58W
Prescot, *U.K.* **18** 53 27N 2 49W
Preshute, *U.K.* **14** 51 24N 1 45W
Presidente Prudente, *Brazil* **101** 22 5S 51 25W
Presque Isle, *U.S.A.* .. **93** 46 40N 68 0W
Prestatyn, *U.K.* **17** 53 20N 3 24W
Prestbury, *U.K.* **14** 51 54N 2 2W
Presteigne, *U.K.* **17** 52 17N 3 0W
Preston, *Borders, U.K.* **21** 55 48N 2 18W
Preston, *Dorset, U.K.* . **14** 50 38N 2 26W
Preston, *Lancs., U.K.* . **18** 53 46N 2 42W
Prestonpans, *U.K.* ... **21** 55 58N 3 0W
Prestwich, *U.K.* **18** 53 32N 2 18W
Prestwick, *U.K.* **20** 55 30N 4 38W
Pretoria, *S. Afr.* ..... **81** 25 44S 28 12 E
Prince Albert, *Canada* **88** 53 15N 105 50W
Prince Edward I. □, *Canada* **93** 46 20N 63 20W
Prince George, *Canada* **88** 53 55N 122 50W
Prince of Wales I., *Canada* **88** 73 0N 99 0W
Prince Rupert, *Canada* **88** 54 20N 130 20W
Princes Risborough, *U.K.* **15** 51 43N 0 50W
Princess Charlotte B., *Austral.* .... **67** 14 25S 144 0 E
Princetown, *U.K.* **16** 50 33N 4 0W
Pripyat Marshes, *U.S.S.R.* .... **46** 52 0N 28 10 E
Priština, *Yug.* .... **41** 42 40N 21 13 E
Prizren, *Yug.* .... **41** 42 13N 20 45 E
Probus, *U.K.* **16** 50 17N 4 55W
Prokopyevsk, *U.S.S.R.* **48** 54 0N 86 45 E
Prome, *Burma* .... **59** 18 49N 95 13 E
Provence, *Fr.* .... **35** 43 40N 5 46 E
Providence, *U.S.A.* ... **93** 41 50N 71 28W
Prudhoe, *U.K.* **21** 54 57N 1 52W
Prudhoe Bay, *U.S.A.* .. **88** 70 20N 148 20W
Prut →, *Rom.* ...... **41** 46 3N 28 10 E
Przemyśl, *Pol.* .... **43** 49 50N 22 45 E
Puddletown, *U.K.* **14** 50 45N 2 21W
Pudsey, *U.K.* **19** 53 47N 1 40W
Puebla, *Mex.* **94** 19 3N 98 12W
Pueblo, *U.S.A.* **90** 38 20N 104 40W
Puerto La Cruz, *Ven.* . **100** 10 13N 64 38W
Puerto Montt, *Chile* ... **102** 41 28S 73 0W
Puerto Rico ■, *W. Ind.* **95** 18 15N 66 45W
Pula, *It.* .... **40** 39 0N 9 0 E
Pulborough, *U.K.* **15** 50 58N 0 30W
Pulham Market, *U.K.* .. **15** 52 25N 1 15 E
Pulham St. Mary, *U.K.* **15** 52 25N 1 14 E
Pumlumon Fawr, *U.K.* . **17** 52 29N 3 47W
Pune, *India* .... **58** 18 29N 73 57 E
Punjab □, *India* ..... **58** 31 0N 76 0 E
Punjab □, *Pak.* ..... **58** 30 0N 72 0 E
Punta Arenas, *Chile* .. **102** 53 10S 71 0W
Punto Fijo, *Ven.* **100** 11 50N 70 13W
Purbeck, Isle of, *U.K.* . **14** 50 40N 2 5W
Purfleet, *U.K.* .... **15** 51 29N 0 15 E
Purley, *U.K.* **14** 51 29N 1 4W
Purnia, *India* .... **59** 25 45N 87 31 E
Purus →, *Brazil* **100** 3 42S 61 28W
Pusan, *S. Kor.* ...... **61** 35 5N 129 0 E
Puy-de-Dôme, *Fr.* .... **35** 45 46N 2 57 E
Pwllheli, *U.K.* **17** 52 54N 4 26W
Pyŏngyang, *N. Kor.* ... **61** 39 0N 125 30 E
Pyrenees, *Europe* .... **35** 42 45N 0 18 E

Q

Qandahār, *Afg.* ...... **57** 31 32N 65 30 E
Qatar ■, *Asia* ...... **56** 25 30N 51 15 E
Qattâra Depression, *Egypt* .... **79** 29 30N 27 30 E
Qazvin, *Iran* .... **56** 36 15N 50 0 E
Qena, *Egypt* .... **79** 26 10N 32 43 E
Qingdao, *China* ...... **61** 36 5N 120 20 E
Qinghai □, *China* .... **60** 36 0N 98 0 E
Qinghai Hu, *China* ... **60** 36 40N 100 10 E
Qingjiang, *China* .... **61** 33 30N 119 2 E
Qiqihar, *China* ...... **61** 47 26N 124 0 E
Qom, *Iran* .... **56** 34 40N 51 0 E
Quadring, *U.K.* **19** 52 53N 0 9W
Quainton, *U.K.* **15** 51 51N 0 53W
Quantock Hills, *U.K.* .. **14** 51 8N 3 10W
Queanbeyan, *Austral.* . **70** 35 17S 149 14 E
Québec, *Canada* **93** 46 52N 71 13W
Québec □, *Canada* ... **89** 50 0N 70 0W
Queen Charlotte Is., *Canada* **88** 53 20N 132 10W
Queen Elizabeth Is., *Canada* **103** 76 0N 95 0W
Queen Maud G., *Canada* **88** 68 15N 102 30W
Queenborough, *U.K.* .. **15** 51 24N 0 46 E
Queensbury, *U.K.* **18** 53 46N 1 50W
Queensferry, *U.K.* **21** 56 0N 3 25W
Queensland □, *Austral.* **67** 22 0S 142 0 E
Queenstown, *N.Z.* .... **71** 45 1S 168 40 E
Queenstown, *S. Afr.* .. **81** 31 52S 26 52 E
Querétaro, *Mex.* **94** 20 36N 100 23W
Quetta, *Pak.* .... **58** 30 15N 66 55 E
Quezon City, *Phil.* .... **63** 14 38N 121 0 E
Qui Nhon, *Viet.* ...... **63** 13 40N 109 13 E
Quimper, *Fr.* **34** 48 0N 4 9W
Quito, *Ecuad.* **100** 0 15S 78 35W
Quorndon, *U.K.* **14** 52 45N 1 10W

R

Raasay, *U.K.* **22** 57 25N 6 4W
Raasay, Sd. of, *U.K.* .. **22** 57 30N 6 8W
Rabat, *Malta* .... **40** 35 53N 14 25 E
Rabat, *Mor.* **78** 34 2N 6 48W
Rackheath, *U.K.* ..... **15** 52 41N 1 22 E
Radcliffe, *Gr. Manchester, U.K.* **18** 53 35N 2 19W
Radcliffe, *Notts., U.K.* . **19** 52 57N 1 3W
Radley, *U.K.* **14** 51 42N 1 14W
Radnor Forest, *U.K.* .. **17** 52 17N 3 10W
Radom, *Pol.* .... **43** 51 23N 21 12 E
Radstock, *U.K.* **14** 51 17N 2 25W
Ragusa, *It.* .... **40** 36 56N 14 42 E
Rainham, *U.K.* .... **15** 51 22N 0 36 E
Rainworth, *U.K.* **19** 53 8N 1 6W
Raipur, *India* .... **59** 21 17N 81 45 E
Rajahmundry, *India* ... **59** 17 1N 81 48 E
Rajasthan □, *India* ... **58** 26 45N 73 30 E
Rajkot, *India* .... **58** 22 15N 70 56 E
Raleigh, *U.S.A.* **91** 35 47N 78 39W
Rame Head, *U.K.* **16** 50 19N 4 14W
Rampside, *U.K.* **18** 54 6N 3 10W
Rampur, *India* .... **58** 28 50N 79 5 E
Ramree Kyun, *Burma* .. **59** 19 0N 94 0 E
Ramsbottom, *U.K.* ... **18** 53 36N 2 20W
Ramsbury, *U.K.* **14** 51 26N 1 37W
Ramsey, *Cambs., U.K.* **15** 52 27N 0 6W
Ramsey, *Essex, U.K.* . **15** 51 55N 1 12 E
Ramsey, *I. of M., U.K.* **18** 54 20N 4 21W
Ramsey Bay, *U.K.* ... **18** 54 23N 4 20W
Ramsgate, *U.K.* ..... **15** 51 20N 1 25 E
Rancagua, *Chile* **102** 34 10S 70 50W
Ranchi, *India* .... **59** 23 19N 85 27 E
Rangoon, *Burma* ..... **59** 16 45N 96 20 E
Rannoch, L., *U.K.* **23** 56 41N 4 20W
Rannoch Moor, *U.K.* .. **20** 56 38N 4 48W
Rasht, *Iran* .... **56** 37 20N 49 40 E
Rath Luirc, *Ire.* **25** 52 21N 8 40W
Rathdrum, *Ire.* **25** 52 57N 6 13W
Rathfriland, *U.K.* **24** 54 12N 6 12W
Rathkeale, *Ire.* **25** 52 32N 8 57W
Rathlin I., *U.K.* **24** 55 18N 6 14W
Rathlin O'Birne I., *Ire.* . **24** 54 40N 8 50W
Rattray Hd., *U.K.* **23** 57 38N 1 50W
Raukumara Ra., *N.Z.* . **71** 38 5S 177 55 E
Raunds, *U.K.* **15** 52 20N 0 32W
Raurkela, *India* ...... **59** 22 14N 84 50 E
Ravenglass, *U.K.* **18** 54 21N 3 25W
Ravenna, *It.* .... **40** 44 28N 12 15 E
Ravenstonedale, *U.K.* . **18** 54 26N 2 26W
Rawalpindi, *Pak.* ..... **58** 33 38N 73 8 E
Rawmarsh, *U.K.* **19** 53 27N 1 20W
Rawtenstall, *U.K.* **18** 53 42N 2 18W
Rayleigh, *U.K.* ...... **15** 51 36N 0 38 E
Reading, *U.K.* **15** 51 27N 0 57W
Reading, *U.S.A.* **93** 40 20N 75 53W
Recife, *Brazil* **101** 8 0S 35 0W
Reculver, *U.K.* ...... **15** 51 22N 1 12 E
Red → = Hong *Viet.* .... **60** 20 17N 106 34 E
Red →, *U.S.A.* **91** 31 0N 91 40W
Red Deer, *Canada* ... **88** 52 20N 113 50W
Red Dial, *U.K.* **18** 54 48N 3 9W
Red Sea, *Asia* .... **56** 25 0N 36 0 E
Redbridge, *U.K.* ..... **15** 51 35N 0 7 E
Redcar, *U.K.* **19** 54 37N 1 4W
Redditch, *U.K.* **14** 52 18N 1 57W
Rede →, *U.K.* **21** 55 8N 2 12W
Redesmouth, *U.K.* ... **21** 55 7N 2 12W
Redhill, *U.K.* **15** 51 14N 0 10W
Redlynch, *U.K.* **14** 50 59N 1 42W
Redmile, *U.K.* **19** 52 54N 0 48W
Redmire, *U.K.* **18** 54 19N 1 55W
Redruth, *U.K.* **16** 50 14N 5 14W
Ree, L., *Ire.* **24** 53 35N 8 0W
Reedham, *U.K.* ...... **15** 52 34N 1 33 E
Reepham, *U.K.* ...... **15** 52 46N 1 6 E
Reeth, *U.K.* **18** 54 23N 1 56W
Regensburg, *W. Ger.* . **42** 49 1N 12 7 E
Réggio di Calábria, *It.* . **40** 38 7N 15 38 E
Réggio nell' Emilia, *It.* . **40** 44 42N 10 38 E
Regina, *Canada* **88** 50 27N 104 35W
Reigate, *U.K.* **15** 51 14N 0 11W
Reims, *Fr.* .... **34** 49 15N 4 1 E
Reindeer L., *Canada* .. **88** 57 15N 102 15W
Remscheid, *W. Ger.* .. **36** 51 11N 7 12 E
Renfrew, *U.K.* **20** 55 52N 4 24W
Renmark, *Austral.* ... **67** 34 11S 140 43 E
Rennes, *Fr.* **34** 48 7N 1 41W
Reno, *U.S.A.* **90** 39 30N 119 50W
Repton, *U.K.* **14** 52 50N 1 32W
Resistencia, *Arg.* **102** 27 30S 59 0W
Reston, *U.K.* **21** 55 51N 2 11W
Réthímnon, *Greece* ... **41** 35 18N 24 30 E
Reykjavík, *Ice.* **44** 64 10N 21 57W
Reynosa, *Mex.* **94** 26 5N 98 18W

Rhayader, *U.K.* **17** 52 19N 3 30W
Rheidol →, *U.K.* **17** 52 25N 4 5W
Rhein →, *W. Ger.* **36** 51 52N 6 20 E
Rheine, *W. Ger.* **36** 52 17N 7 25 E
Rhine = Rhein →, *W. Ger.* **36** 51 52N 6 20 E
Rhineland-Palatinate □, *W. Ger.* **42** 50 0N 7 0 E
Rhins, The, *U.K.* **20** 54 52N 5 3W
Rhode Island □, *U.S.A.* **93** 41 38N 71 37W
Rhodes = Ródhos, *Greece* **41** 36 15N 28 10 E
Rhodesia = Zimbabwe ■, *Africa* **81** 20 0S 30 0 E
Rhodope Mts., *Bulg.* **41** 41 40N 24 20 E
Rhondda, *U.K.* **17** 51 39N 3 30W
Rhône →, *Fr.* **35** 43 28N 4 42 E
Rhosllanerchrugog, *U.K.* **17** 53 3N 3 4W
Rhossili, *U.K.* **17** 51 34N 4 18W
Rhum, *U.K.* **22** 57 0N 6 20W
Rhyl, *U.K.* **17** 53 19N 3 29W
Rhymney, *U.K.* **17** 51 32N 3 17W
Ribble →, *U.K.* **18** 54 13N 2 20W
Ribeirão Prêto, *Brazil* **101** 21 10S 47 50W
Riccall, *U.K.* **19** 53 50N 1 4W
Riccarton, *N.Z.* **71** 43 32S 172 37 E
Riccarton Junc., *U.K.* **21** 55 16N 2 43W
Richmond, *N. Yorks., U.K.* **19** 54 24N 1 43W
Richmond, *Surrey, U.K.* **15** 51 28N 0 18W
Richmond, *U.S.A.* **92** 37 33N 77 27W
Rickmansworth, *U.K.* **15** 51 38N 0 28W
Ridsdale, *U.K.* **21** 55 9N 2 8W
Rievaulx, *U.K.* **19** 54 16N 1 7W
Riga, *U.S.S.R.* **46** 56 53N 24 8 E
Riga, G. of, *U.S.S.R.* **46** 57 40N 23 45 E
Rijeka, *Yug.* **40** 45 20N 14 21 E
Rijswijk, *Neth.* **36** 52 4N 4 22 E
Rillington, *U.K.* **19** 54 10N 0 41W
Rimini, *It.* **40** 44 3N 12 33 E
Rîmnicu Vîlcea, *Rom.* **43** 45 9N 24 21 E
Rimouski, *Canada* **93** 48 27N 68 30W
Rineanna, *Ire.* **25** 52 42N 85 7W
Ringford, *U.K.* **21** 54 55N 4 3W
Ringmer, *U.K.* **15** 50 53N 0 5 E
Ringwood, *U.K.* **14** 50 50N 1 48W
Rio Branco, *Brazil* **100** 9 58S 67 49W
Río Cuarto, *Arg.* **102** 33 10S 64 25W
Rio de Janeiro, *Brazil* **101** 23 0S 43 12W
Río Gallegos, *Arg.* **102** 51 35S 69 15W
Río Grande, *Brazil* **102** 32 0S 52 20W
Rio Grande →, *U.S.A.* **90** 25 57N 97 9W
Rio Grande do Norte □, *Brazil* **94** 5 40S 36 0W
Río Muni = Mbini □, *Eq. Guin.* **80** 1 30N 10 0 E
Riobamba, *Ecuad.* **100** 1 50S 78 45W
Ripley, *Derby, U.K.* **19** 53 3N 1 24W
Ripley, *N. Yorks., U.K.* **19** 54 3N 1 34W
Ripon, *U.K.* **19** 54 8N 1 31W
Risca, *U.K.* **17** 51 36N 3 6W
Rishton, *U.K.* **18** 53 46N 2 26W
Riverside, *U.S.A.* **90** 34 0N 117 22W
Riyadh, *Si. Arab.* **56** 24 41N 46 42 E
Roade, *U.K.* **15** 52 10N 0 53W
Roadhead, *U.K.* **18** 55 4N 2 44W
Roag, L., *U.K.* **22** 58 10N 6 55W
Roanne, *Fr.* **35** 46 3N 4 4 E
Roanoke, *U.S.A.* **92** 37 19N 79 55W
Robe →, *Ire.* **24** 53 38N 9 10W
Roberton, *U.K.* **21** 55 24N 2 53W
Robin Hood's Bay, *U.K.* **19** 54 26N 0 31W
Rocester, *U.K.* **18** 52 56N 1 50W
Rochdale, *U.K.* **18** 53 36N 2 10W
Roche, *U.K.* **16** 50 24N 4 50W
Rochelle, La, *Fr.* **35** 46 10N 1 9W
Rochester, *Kent, U.K.* **15** 51 22N 0 30 E
Rochester, *Northumberland, U.K.* **21** 55 16N 2 16W
Rochester, *Minn., U.S.A.* **91** 44 1N 92 28W
Rochester, *N.Y., U.S.A.* **92** 43 10N 77 40W
Rochford, *U.K.* **15** 51 36N 0 42 E
Rockall, *Atl. Oc.* **26** 57 37N 13 42W
Rockcliffe, *U.K.* **18** 54 58N 3 0W
Rockford, *U.S.A.* **92** 42 20N 89 0W
Rockhampton, *Austral.* **67** 23 22S 150 32 E
Rockingham, *U.K.* **15** 52 32N 0 43W
Rockingham Forest, *U.K.* **15** 52 28N 0 42W
Rocky Mts., *N. Am.* **88** 55 0N 121 0W
Ródhos, *Greece* **41** 36 15N 28 10 E
Roding →, *U.K.* **15** 51 31N 0 7 E
Roe →, *U.K.* **24** 55 10N 6 59W
Roeselare, *Belg.* **36** 50 57N 3 7 E
Rogaland fylke □, *Nor.* **45** 59 12N 6 20 E
Rogans Seat, *U.K.* **18** 54 25N 2 10W
Rogate, *U.K.* **15** 51 0N 0 51W
Roma, *Austral.* **67** 26 32S 148 49 E
Roma = Rome, *It.* **40** 41 54N 12 30 E
Romania ■, *Europe* **43** 46 0N 25 0 E
Rome, *It.* **40** 41 54N 12 30 E
Romney Marsh, *U.K.* **15** 51 0N 1 0 E
Romsey, *U.K.* **14** 51 0N 1 29W
Rona, *U.K.* **22** 57 33N 6 0W
Ronse, *Belg.* **36** 50 45N 3 35 E
Roosendaal, *Neth.* **36** 51 32N 4 29 E
Roper →, *Austral.* **67** 14 43S 135 27 E
Ropsley, *U.K.* **19** 52 53N 0 31W
Roraima, Mt., *Ven.* **100** 5 10N 60 40W
Rosario, *Arg.* **102** 33 0S 60 40W
Roscommon, *Ire.* **24** 53 38N 8 11W
Roscommon □, *Ire.* **24** 53 40N 8 15W
Roscrea, *Ire.* **25** 52 58N 7 50W
Roseau, *Dom.* **94** 15 20N 61 24W
Rosedale Abbey, *U.K.* **19** 54 22N 0 51W
Roskilde, *Den.* **45** 55 38N 12 3 E
Rosneath, *U.K.* **20** 56 1N 4 49W
Ross Ice Shelf, *Ant.* **103** 80 0S 180 0 E
Ross on Wye, *U.K.* **14** 51 55N 2 34W
Ross Sea, *Ant.* **103** 74 0S 178 0 E
Rossall Pt., *U.K.* **18** 53 55N 3 2W
Rossan Pt., *Ire.* **24** 54 42N 8 47W
Rosslare, *Ire.* **25** 52 17N 6 23W
Rostock, *E. Ger.* **42** 54 4N 12 9 E
Rostov, *U.S.S.R.* **47** 47 15N 39 45 E
Rosyth, *U.K.* **21** 56 2N 3 26W
Rothbury, *U.K.* **21** 55 19N 1 55W
Rothbury Forest, *U.K.* **21** 55 19N 1 50W
Rother →, *U.K.* **15** 50 59N 0 40 E
Rotherham, *U.K.* **19** 53 26N 1 21W
Rothes, *U.K.* **23** 57 31N 3 12W
Rothesay, *U.K.* **20** 55 50N 5 3W
Rothwell, *Northants., U.K.* **15** 52 25N 0 48W
Rothwell, *W. Yorks., U.K.* **19** 53 46N 1 29W
Rotorua, *N.Z.* **71** 38 9S 176 16 E
Rotorua, L., *N.Z.* **71** 38 5S 176 18 E
Rotterdam, *Neth.* **36** 51 55N 4 30 E
Rottingdean, *U.K.* **15** 50 48N 0 3W
Roubaix, *Fr.* **34** 50 40N 3 10 E
Rouen, *Fr.* **34** 49 27N 1 4 E
Rousay, *U.K.* **23** 59 10N 3 2W
Rowanburn, *U.K.* **21** 55 5N 2 54W
Rowrah, *U.K.* **18** 54 34N 3 26W
Roxburgh, *U.K.* **21** 55 34N 2 30W
Roxby, *U.K.* **19** 53 38N 0 37W
Royston, *U.K.* **15** 52 3N 0 1W
Royton, *U.K.* **18** 53 34N 2 7W
Ruahine Ra., *N.Z.* **71** 39 55S 176 2 E
Rub' al Khali, *Si. Arab.* **56** 18 0N 48 0 E
Rubery, *U.K.* **14** 52 24N 1 59W
Rubh a' Mhail, *U.K.* **20** 55 55N 6 10W
Rubha Hunish, *U.K.* **22** 57 42N 6 20W
Rudgwick, *U.K.* **15** 51 7N 0 54W
Rudston, *U.K.* **19** 54 6N 0 19W
Rufford, *U.K.* **18** 53 37N 2 50W
Rugby, *U.K.* **14** 52 23N 1 16W
Rugeley, *U.K.* **14** 52 47N 1 56W
Rum Jungle, *Austral.* **66** 13 0S 130 59 E
Runcorn, *U.K.* **18** 53 20N 2 44W
Ruse, *Bulg.* **41** 43 48N 25 59 E
Rushden, *U.K.* **15** 52 17N 0 37W
Ruskington, *U.K.* **19** 53 5N 0 23W
Russian S.F.S.R. □, *U.S.S.R.* **46** 62 0N 105 0 E
Rutherglen, *U.K.* **20** 55 50N 4 11W
Ruthin, *U.K.* **17** 53 7N 3 20W
Ruthwell, *U.K.* **21** 55 0N 3 24W
Rwanda ■, *Africa* **80** 2 0S 30 0 E
Ryan, L., *U.K.* **20** 55 0N 5 2W
Ryazan, *U.S.S.R.* **46** 54 40N 39 40 E
Rybinsk = Andropov, *U.S.S.R.* **46** 58 5N 38 50 E
Rybinsk Res., *U.S.S.R.* **46** 58 30N 38 0 E
Rydal, *U.K.* **18** 54 28N 2 59W
Ryde, *U.K.* **14** 50 44N 1 9W
Rye, *U.K.* **15** 50 57N 0 46 E
Rye →, *U.K.* **19** 54 12N 0 53W
Rye Bay, *U.K.* **15** 50 50N 0 50 E
Ryhope, *U.K.* **21** 54 52N 1 22W
Ryton, *Tyne & Wear, U.K.* **21** 54 58N 1 44W
Ryton, *Warwick, U.K.* **14** 52 23N 1 25W
Ryūkyū Is., *Jap.* **62** 26 0N 128 0 E
Rzeszów, *Pol.* **43** 50 5N 21 58 E

S

Saarbrücken, *W. Ger.* **36** 49 15N 6 58 E
Saaremaa, *U.S.S.R.* **46** 58 30N 22 30 E
Saarland □, *W. Ger.* **36** 49 15N 7 0 E
Saba, *W. Ind.* **94** 17 42N 63 26W
Sabadell, *Sp.* **37** 41 28N 2 7 E
Sabah □, *Malay.* **63** 6 0N 117 0 E
Sabhah, *Libya* **79** 27 9N 14 29 E
Sacramento, *U.S.A.* **90** 38 33N 121 30 E
Sacriston, *U.K.* **19** 54 49N 1 38W
Saddell, *U.K.* **20** 55 31N 5 30W
Saffron Walden, *U.K.* **15** 52 2N 0 15 E
Safi, *Mor.* **78** 32 18N 9 20W
Sagar, *India* **58** 14 14N 75 6 E
Saginaw, *U.S.A.* **92** 43 26N 83 55W
Saginaw B., *U.S.A.* **92** 43 50N 83 40W
Sahara, *Africa* **78** 23 0N 5 0 E
Saharan Atlas, *Alg.* **78** 34 9N 3 29 E
Saharanpur, *India* **58** 29 58N 77 33 E
Saigon = Ho Chi Minh City, *Viet.* **63** 10 58N 106 40 E
St. Abb's, *U.K.* **21** 55 54N 2 7W
St. Abb's Head, *U.K.* **21** 55 55N 2 10W
St. Agnes, *U.K.* **16** 50 18N 5 13W
St. Agnes Hd., *U.K.* **16** 50 19N 5 14W
St. Agnes I., *U.K.* **16** 49 53N 6 20W
St. Albans, *U.K.* **15** 51 44N 0 19W
St. Alban's Head, *U.K.* **14** 50 34N 2 3W
St. Andrews, *U.K.* **21** 56 20N 2 48W
St. Ann's, *U.K.* **21** 55 14N 3 28W
St. Asaph, *U.K.* **17** 53 15N 3 27W
St. Austell, *U.K.* **16** 50 20N 4 48W
St. Bees, *U.K.* **18** 54 29N 3 36W
St. Bee's Hd., *U.K.* **18** 54 30N 3 38 E
St. Blazey, *U.K.* **16** 50 22N 4 48W
St. Boniface, *Canada* **88** 49 53N 97 5W
St. Boswells, *U.K.* **21** 55 34N 2 39W
St. Briavels, *U.K.* **14** 51 44N 2 39W
St. Brides B., *U.K.* **17** 51 48N 5 15W
St.-Brieuc, *Fr.* **34** 48 30N 2 46W
St. Budeaux, *U.K.* **16** 50 23N 4 10W
St. Buryan, *U.K.* **16** 50 4N 5 34W
St. Catharines, *Canada* **92** 43 10N 79 15W
St. Catherine's Pt., *U.K.* **14** 50 34N 1 18W
St. Christopher-Nevis ■, *W. Ind.* **94** 17 20N 62 40W
St. Clair, L., *Canada* **92** 42 30N 82 45W
St.-Claude, *Fr.* **35** 46 22N 5 52 E
St. Clears, *U.K.* **17** 51 48N 4 30W
St. Columb Major, *U.K.* **16** 50 26N 4 56W
St. David's, *U.K.* **17** 51 54N 5 16W
St. David's Head, *U.K.* **17** 51 55N 5 16W
St. Dennis, *U.K.* **16** 50 23N 4 53W
St. Dominick, *U.K.* **16** 50 28N 4 15W
St. Elias Mts., *Canada* **88** 60 33N 139 28W
St. Endellion, *U.K.* **16** 50 33N 4 49W
St. Enoder, *U.K.* **16** 50 22N 4 57W
St. Erth, *U.K.* **16** 50 10N 5 26W
St.-Étienne, *Fr.* **35** 45 27N 4 22 E
St. Fillans, *U.K.* **21** 56 25N 4 7W
St. Gallen, *Switz.* **42** 47 25N 9 20 E
St. George's, *Gren.* **94** 12 5N 61 43W
St. George's Channel, *U.K.* **25** 52 0N 6 0W
St. Germans, *U.K.* **16** 50 24N 4 19W
St. Helena, *Atl. Oc.* **128** 15 55S 5 44W
St. Helena B., *S. Afr.* **81** 32 40S 18 10 E
St. Helens, *I. of W., U.K.* **14** 50 42N 1 6W
St. Helens, *Merseyside, U.K.* **18** 53 28N 2 44W
St. Helier, *U.K.* **34** 49 11N 2 6W
St-Hyacinthe, *Canada* **93** 45 40N 72 58W
St. Issey, *U.K.* **16** 50 30N 4 55W
St. Ives, *Cambs., U.K.* **15** 52 20N 0 5W
St. Ives, *Cornwall, U.K.* **16** 50 13N 5 29W
St. Ives Bay, *U.K.* **16** 50 15N 5 27W
St-Jean, L., *Canada* **93** 48 40N 72 0W
St-Jérôme, *Canada* **93** 45 47N 74 0W
St. John, *Canada* **93** 45 20N 66 8W
St. John's, *Antigua* **94** 17 6N 61 51W
St. John's, *Canada* **89** 47 35N 52 40W
St. John's, *U.K.* **18** 54 13N 4 38W
St. Johns Chapel, *U.K.* **18** 54 43N 2 10W
St. Joseph, *U.S.A.* **91** 39 46N 94 50W
St. Just, *U.K.* **16** 50 7N 5 41W
St. Keverne, *U.K.* **16** 50 3N 5 5W
St. Kew, *U.K.* **16** 50 34N 4 48W
St. Lawrence →, *Canada* **93** 49 30N 66 0W
St. Lawrence, Gulf of, *Canada* **89** 48 25N 62 0W
St. Leonards, *U.K.* **15** 50 51N 0 34 E
St. Levan, *U.K.* **16** 50 3N 5 36W
St.-Lô, *Fr.* **34** 49 7N 1 5W
St-Louis, *Sene.* **78** 16 8N 16 27W
St. Louis, *U.S.A.* **92** 38 40N 90 12W
St. Lucia ■, *W. Ind.* **94** 14 0N 60 50W
St. Maarten, *W. Ind.* **94** 18 0N 63 5W
St. Mabyn, *U.K.* **16** 50 30N 4 45W
St.-Malo, *Fr.* **34** 48 39N 2 1W
St. Margaret's-at-Cliffe, *U.K.* **15** 51 10N 1 23 E
St. Margaret's Hope, *U.K.* **23** 58 49N 2 58W
St-Martin, I., *W. Ind.* **94** 18 0N 63 0W
St. Martin's I., *U.K.* **16** 49 58N 6 16W
St. Mary Bourne, *U.K.* **14** 51 16N 1 24W
St. Mary's, *U.K.* **16** 49 55N 6 17W
St. Mary's Sd., *U.K.* **16** 49 53N 6 19W
St. Mawes, *U.K.* **16** 50 10N 5 1W
St. Merryn, *U.K.* **16** 50 31N 4 58W
St. Michael's Mt., *U.K.* **16** 50 7N 5 30W
St. Minver, *U.K.* **16** 50 34N 4 52W
St. Monance, *U.K.* **21** 56 13N 2 46W
St.-Nazaire, *Fr.* **34** 47 17N 2 12W
St. Neots, *U.K.* **15** 52 14N 0 16W
St-Niklaas, *Belg.* **36** 51 10N 4 8 E
St. Osyth, *U.K.* **15** 51 47N 1 4 E
St. Paul, *U.S.A.* **91** 44 54N 93 5W
St. Peter Port, *U.K.* **34** 49 27N 2 31W
St. Petersburg, *U.S.A.* **91** 27 45N 82 40W
St.-Pierre et Miquelon □, *N. Am.* **89** 46 55N 56 10W
St.-Quentin, *Fr.* **34** 49 50N 3 16 E
St. Stephen, *U.K.* **16** 50 20N 4 52W
St. Teath, *U.K.* **16** 50 34N 4 45W
St.-Tropez, *Fr.* **35** 43 17N 6 38 E
St. Tudy, *U.K.* **16** 50 33N 4 45W
St. Vincent and the Grenadines ■, *W. Ind.* **94** 13 0N 61 10W
Saintfield, *U.K.* **24** 54 28N 5 50W
Sakai, *Jap.* **62** 34 30N 135 30 E
Sakhalin, *U.S.S.R.* **49** 51 0N 143 0 E
Salado →, *Arg.* **102** 31 40S 60 41W
Salamanca, *Sp.* **37** 40 58N 5 39W
Salcombe, *U.K.* **16** 50 14N 3 47W
Salcombe Regis, *U.K.* **16** 50 41N 3 11W
Sale, *Austral.* **70** 38 6S 147 6 E
Sale, *U.K.* **18** 53 26N 2 19W
Salem, *India* **58** 11 40N 78 11 E
Salen, *U.K.* **20** 56 31N 5 57W
Salerno, *It.* **40** 40 40N 14 44 E
Salford, *U.K.* **18** 53 30N 2 17W
Salford Priors, *U.K.* **14** 52 10N 1 52W
Salisbury = Harare, *Zimb.* **81** 17 43S 31 2 E
Salisbury, *U.K.* **14** 51 4N 1 48W
Salisbury Plain, *U.K.* **14** 51 13N 1 50W
Salonica = Thessaloníki, *Greece* **41** 40 38N 22 58 E
Salop = Shropshire □, *U.K.* **14** 52 36N 2 45W
Salt Lake City, *U.S.A.* **90** 40 45N 111 58W
Salta, *Arg.* **102** 24 57S 65 25W
Saltash, *U.K.* **16** 50 25N 4 13W
Saltburn by the Sea, *U.K.* **19** 54 35N 0 58W
Saltcoats, *U.K.* **20** 55 38N 4 47W
Saltee Is., *Ire.* **25** 52 7N 6 37W
Saltergate, *U.K.* **19** 54 20N 0 40W
Saltfleet, *U.K.* **19** 53 25N 0 11 E
Saltfleetby, *U.K.* **19** 53 23N 0 10 E
Saltillo, *Mex.* **94** 25 25N 101 0W
Salto, *Urug.* **102** 31 27S 57 50W
Saltwood, *U.K.* **15** 51 4N 1 5 E
Salvador, *Brazil* **101** 13 0S 38 30W
Salween →, *Burma* **59** 16 31N 97 37 E
Salzburg, *Austria* **42** 47 48N 13 2 E
Salzgitter, *W. Ger.* **42** 52 13N 10 22 E
Samarinda, *Indon.* **63** 0 30S 117 9 E
Samarkand, *U.S.S.R.* **48** 39 40N 66 55 E
Sámos, *Greece* **41** 37 45N 26 50 E
Sampford Courtenay, *U.K.* **16** 50 47N 3 58W
Samsun, *Turk.* **47** 41 15N 36 22 E
San Angelo, *U.S.A.* **90** 31 30N 100 30W
San Antonio, *U.S.A.* **90** 29 30N 98 30W
San Bernardino, *U.S.A.* **90** 34 7N 117 18W
San Carlos, *Phil.* **63** 15 55N 120 20 E
San Cristóbal, *Ven.* **100** 16 50N 92 40W
San Diego, *U.S.A.* **90** 32 43N 117 10W
San Fernando, *Mex.* **94** 30 0N 115 10W
San Francisco, *U.S.A.* **90** 37 47N 122 30W
San Jorge, G., *Arg.* **102** 46 0S 66 0W
San José, *C.R.* **95** 10 0N 84 2W
San Jose, *U.S.A.* **90** 37 20N 121 53W
San Juan, *Arg.* **102** 31 30S 68 30W
San Juan, *P.R.* **95** 18 28N 66 8W
San Luis Potosí, *Mex.* **94** 22 9N 100 59W
San Marino ■, *Europe* **40** 43 56N 12 25 E
San Matías, G., *Arg.* **102** 41 30S 64 0W
San Miguel de Tucumán, *Arg.* **102** 26 50S 65 20W
San Pedro Sula, *Hond.* **94** 15 30N 88 0W
San Salvador, *El Salv.* **94** 13 40N 89 10W
San Salvador de Jujuy, *Arg.* **102** 24 10S 64 48W
San Sebastián, *Sp.* **37** 43 17N 1 58W
Sana', *Yem.* **56** 15 27N 44 12 E
Sanda I., *U.K.* **20** 55 17N 5 35W
Sanday, *U.K.* **23** 59 15N 2 30W
Sandbach, *U.K.* **18** 53 9N 2 23W
Sandbank, *U.K.* **20** 55 58N 4 57W
Sandgate, *U.K.* **15** 51 5N 1 9 E
Sandhead, *U.K.* **20** 54 48N 4 58W
Sandhurst, *U.K.* **15** 51 21N 0 48W
Sandness, *U.K.* **22** 60 18N 1 38W
Sandown, *U.K.* **14** 50 39N 1 9W
Sandringham, *U.K.* **15** 52 50N 0 30 E
Sandwich, *U.K.* **15** 51 16N 1 21 E
Sandy, *U.K.* **15** 52 8N 0 18W
Sangli, *India* **58** 16 55N 74 33 E
Sanquhar, *U.K.* **21** 55 21N 3 56W
Santa Ana, *Mex.* **94** 30 33N 111 7W
Santa Ana, *U.S.A.* **90** 33 48N 117 55W
Santa Clara, *Cuba* **95** 22 20N 80 0W
Santa Cruz, *Bol.* **100** 17 43S 63 10W
Santa Cruz de Tenerife, *Can. Is.* **78** 28 28N 16 15W
Santa Fe, *Arg.* **102** 31 35S 60 41W
Santa Fe, *U.S.A.* **90** 35 40N 106 0W
Santa Maria, *Brazil* **102** 29 40S 53 48W
Santa Marta, *Col.* **100** 11 15N 74 13W
Santander, *Sp.* **37** 43 27N 3 51W
Santarém, *Brazil* **101** 2 25S 54 42W
Santarém, *Port.* **37** 39 12N 8 42W
Santiago, *Chile* **102** 33 24S 70 40W
Santiago de Compostela, *Sp.* **37** 42 52N 8 37W
Santiago de Cuba, *Cuba* **95** 20 0N 75 49W
Santiago de los Cabelleros, *Dom. Rep.* **95** 19 30N 70 40W
Santo André, *Brazil* **102** 23 39S 46 29W
Santo Domingo, *Dom. Rep.* **95** 18 30N 64 54W
Santos, *Brazil* **102** 24 0S 46 20W
São Francisco →, *Brazil* **101** 10 30S 36 24W
São José do Rio Prêto, *Brazil* **101** 20 50S 49 20W
São Luís, *Brazil* **101** 2 39S 44 15W
São Paulo, *Brazil* **102** 23 32S 46 37W
São Roque, C. de, *Brazil* **101** 5 30S 35 16W
São Tomé & Principe ■, *Africa* **73** 0 12N 6 39 E
Saône →, *Fr.* **35** 45 44N 4 50 E
Sapporo, *Jap.* **62** 43 0N 141 21 E

Sarajevo, Yug. 41 43 52N 18 26 E
Saransk, U.S.S.R. 46 54 10N 45 10 E
Saratov, U.S.S.R. 46 51 30N 46 2 E
Sarawak □, Malay. 63 2 0N 113 0 E
Sardinia, I., It. 40 40 0N 9 0 E
Sargodha, Pak. 58 32 10N 72 40 E
Sarh, Chad 79 9 5N 18 23 E
Sarnia, Canada 92 42 58N 82 23W
Sasebo, Jap. 62 33 10N 129 43 E
Saskatchewan □, Canada 88 54 40N 106 0W
Saskatchewan →, Canada 88 53 37N 100 40W
Saskatoon, Canada 88 52 10N 106 38W
Sássari, It. 40 40 44N 8 33 E
Satpura Ra., India 58 21 25N 76 10 E
Satu Mare, Rom. 43 47 46N 22 55 E
Sauðarkrókur, Ice. 44 65 45N 19 40W
Saudi Arabia ■, Asia 56 26 0N 44 0 E
Sault Ste. Marie, Canada 92 46 30N 84 20W
Saundersfoot, U.K. 17 51 43N 4 42W
Sava →, Yug. 41 44 50N 20 26 E
Savanna la Mar, Jam. 94 18 10N 78 10W
Savannah, U.S.A. 91 32 4N 81 4W
Savona, It. 40 44 19N 8 29 E
Savonlinna, Fin. 44 61 52N 28 53 E
Sawbridgeworth, U.K. 15 51 49N 0 10 E
Sawel, Mt., U.K. 24 54 48N 7 5W
Sawston, U.K. 15 52 7N 0 11 E
Sawtry, U.K. 15 52 26N 0 17W
Saxilby, U.K. 19 53 16N 0 40W
Saxlingham Nethergate, U.K. 15 52 33N 1 16 E
Saxmundham, U.K. 15 52 13N 1 29 E
Saydā, Leb. 57 33 35N 35 25 E
Scafell Pikes, U.K. 18 54 26N 3 14W
Scalasaig, U.K. 20 56 4N 6 10W
Scalby, U.K. 19 54 18N 0 26W
Scalby Ness, U.K. 19 54 18N 0 25W
Scalloway, U.K. 22 60 9N 1 16W
Scalpay, U.K. 22 57 51N 6 40W
Scamblesby, U.K. 19 53 17N 0 5W
Scandinavia, Europe 44 64 0N 12 0 E
Scapa Flow, U.K. 23 58 52N 3 6W
Scarba, I., U.K. 20 56 10N 5 42W
Scarborough, U.K. 19 54 17N 0 24W
Scarinish, U.K. 20 56 30N 6 48W
Scarning, U.K. 15 52 40N 0 53 E
Schefferville, Canada 89 54 48N 66 50W
Schenectady, U.S.A. 93 42 50N 73 58W
Schiedam, Neth. 36 51 55N 4 25 E
Schleswig-Holstein □, W. Ger. 42 54 10N 9 40 E
Schwerin, E. Ger. 42 53 37N 11 22 E
Scilly, Isles of, U.K. 16 49 55N 6 15W
Scole, U.K. 15 52 22N 1 10 E
Scone, U.K. 21 56 25N 3 26W
Scopwick, U.K. 19 53 6N 0 24W
Scotland □, U.K. 20 57 0N 4 0W
Scranton, U.S.A. 93 41 22N 75 41W
Scremerston, U.K. 21 55 44N 1 59W
Scridain, L., U.K. 20 56 23N 6 7W
Scunthorpe, U.K. 19 53 35N 0 38W
Seaford, U.K. 15 50 46N 0 8 E
Seaham, U.K. 21 54 51N 1 20W
Seahouses, U.K. 21 55 35N 1 39W
Seamer, U.K. 19 54 14N 0 27W
Seascale, U.K. 18 54 24N 3 29W
Seaton, Cumbria, U.K. 18 54 40N 3 31W
Seaton, Devon, U.K. 16 50 42N 3 3W
Seaton Delaval, U.K. 21 55 5N 1 33W
Seattle, U.S.A. 90 47 41N 122 15W
Sedbergh, U.K. 18 54 20N 2 31W
Sedgefield, U.K. 19 54 40N 1 27W
Seend, U.K. 14 51 20N 2 2W
Segovia, Sp. 37 40 57N 4 10W
Seil, I., U.K. 20 56 17N 5 37W
Seine →, Fr. 34 49 26N 0 26 E
Sekondi-Takoradi, Ghana 78 4 58N 1 45W
Selborne, U.K. 15 51 5N 0 55W
Selby, U.K. 19 53 47N 1 5W
Selkirk, U.K. 21 55 33N 2 50W
Selsey, U.K. 15 50 44N 0 47W
Selsey Bill, U.K. 15 50 44N 0 47W
Selvas, Brazil 100 6 30S 67 0W
Selwyn Ra., Austral. 67 21 10S 140 0 E
Semarang, Indon. 63 7 0S 110 26 E
Semipalatinsk, U.S.S.R. 48 50 30N 80 10 E
Sendai, Jap. 62 38 15N 140 53 E
Senegal ■, W. Afr. 78 14 30N 14 30W
Senegal →, W. Afr. 78 15 48N 16 32W
Sennen, U.K. 16 50 4N 5 42W
Seoul, S. Kor. 61 37 31N 126 58 E
Seph →, U.K. 19 54 17N 1 9W
Sequoia Nat. Park, U.S.A. 90 36 30N 118 30W
Serbia □, Yug. 41 43 30N 21 0 E
Seremban, Malay. 63 2 43N 101 53 E
Serena, La, Chile 102 29 55S 71 10W
Serpukhov, U.S.S.R. 46 54 55N 37 28 E
Sétif, Alg. 78 36 9N 5 26 E
Settat, Mor. 78 33 0N 7 40W
Settle, U.K. 18 54 5N 2 18W
Setúbal, Port. 37 38 30N 8 58W
Sevastopol, U.S.S.R. 47 44 35N 33 30 E
Seven →, U.K. 19 54 11N 0 51W
Sevenoaks, U.K. 15 51 16N 0 11 E
Severn →, U.K. 14 51 35N 2 38W
Severn Beach, U.K. 14 51 34N 2 39W
Severn Stoke, U.K. 14 52 5N 2 13W
Severnaya Zemlya, U.S.S.R. 49 79 0N 100 0 E
Seville, Sp. 37 37 23N 6 0W
Seward Pen., U.S.A. 88 65 0N 164 0W
Seychelles ■, Ind. Oc. 129 5 0S 56 0 E
Seyðisfjörður, Ice. 44 65 16N 14 0W
Sfax, Tunisia 79 34 49N 10 48 E
Shaanxi □, China 61 35 0N 109 0 E
Shache, China 60 38 20N 77 10 E
Shaftesbury, U.K. 14 51 0N 2 12W
Shahjahanpur, India 58 27 54N 79 57 E
Shakhty, U.S.S.R. 47 47 40N 40 16 E
Shaldon, U.K. 16 50 32N 3 31W
Shan □, Burma 59 21 30N 98 30 E
Shandong □, China 61 36 0N 118 0 E
Shanghai, China 61 31 15N 121 26 E
Shangrao, China 61 28 25N 117 59 E
Shanklin, U.K. 14 50 39N 1 9W
Shannon →, Ire. 25 52 35N 9 30W
Shantou, China 61 23 18N 116 40 E
Shanxi □, China 61 37 0N 112 0 E
Shaoguan, China 61 24 48N 113 35 E
Shaoyang, China 61 27 14N 111 25 E
Shap, U.K. 18 54 32N 2 40W
Shapinsay, U.K. 23 59 2N 2 50W
Shark B., Austral. 66 11 20S 130 30 E
Sharpness, U.K. 14 51 43N 2 28W
Shawbury, U.K. 14 52 48N 2 40W
Shawinigan, Canada 93 46 35N 72 50W
Shebbear, U.K. 16 50 52N 4 12W
Sheelin, Lough, Ire. 24 53 48N 7 20W
Sheep Haven, Ire. 24 55 12N 7 55W
Sheerness, U.K. 15 51 26N 0 47 E
Sheffield, U.K. 19 53 23N 1 28W
Shefford, U.K. 15 52 2N 0 20W
Shelekhov G., U.S.S.R. 49 59 30N 157 0 E
Shellharbour, Austral. 70 34 31S 150 51 E
Shelling Rocks, Ire. 25 51 45N 10 35W
Shenfield, U.K. 15 51 39N 0 21 E
Shenyang, China 61 41 50N 123 25 E
Shepparton, Austral. 70 36 23S 145 26 E
Sheppey, I. of, U.K. 15 51 23N 0 50 E
Shepshed, U.K. 14 52 47N 1 18W
Shepton Mallet, U.K. 14 51 11N 2 31W
Sherborne, U.K. 14 50 56N 2 31W
Sherborne St. John, U.K. 14 51 18N 1 7W
Sherbrooke, Canada 93 45 28N 71 57W
Sherburn, N. Yorks., U.K. 19 54 12N 0 32W
Sherburn, N. Yorks., U.K. 19 53 47N 1 15W
Shere, U.K. 15 51 13N 0 28W
Sherfield English, U.K. 14 51 1N 1 35W
Sheriff Hutton, U.K. 19 54 5N 1 0W
Sheriff Muir, U.K. 21 56 12N 3 53W
Sheringham, U.K. 15 52 56N 1 11 E
Sherston, U.K. 14 51 35N 2 13W
Sherwood Forest, U.K. 19 53 5N 1 5W
Shetland □, U.K. 22 60 30N 1 30W
Shetland Is., U.K. 22 60 30N 1 30W
Shiel, L., U.K. 22 56 48N 5 32W
Shieldaig, U.K. 22 57 31N 5 39W
Shifnal, U.K. 14 52 40N 2 23W
Shijiazhuang, China 61 38 2N 114 28 E
Shikoku, Jap. 62 33 30N 133 30 E
Shilbottle, U.K. 21 55 23N 1 42W
Shildon, U.K. 19 54 37N 1 39W
Shiliguri, India 59 26 45N 88 25 E
Shillelagh, Ire. 25 52 46N 6 32W
Shillingstone, U.K. 14 50 54N 2 15W
Shillong, India 59 25 35N 91 53 E
Shimonoseki, Jap. 62 33 58N 131 0 E
Shin, L., U.K. 23 58 7N 4 30W
Shipbourne, U.K. 15 51 13N 0 19 E
Shipdham, U.K. 15 52 38N 0 53 E
Shipley, U.K. 19 53 50N 1 47W
Shipston-on-Stour, U.K. 14 52 4N 1 38W
Shipton-under-Wychwood, U.K. 14 51 51N 1 35W
Shīrāz, Iran 56 29 42N 52 30 E
Shirebrook, U.K. 19 53 13N 1 11W
Shizuoka, Jap. 62 35 0N 138 24 E
Shkoder, Alb. 41 42 6N 19 20 E
Shoeburyness, U.K. 15 51 31N 0 49 E
Shoreham-by-Sea, U.K. 15 50 50N 0 17W
Shotts, U.K. 21 55 49N 3 47W
Shreveport, U.S.A. 91 32 30N 93 50W
Shrewsbury, U.K. 14 52 42N 2 45W
Shrewton, U.K. 14 51 11N 1 55W
Shrivenham, U.K. 14 51 36N 1 39W
Shropshire □, U.K. 14 52 36N 2 45W
Shuangyashan, China 61 46 28N 131 5 E
Siam = Thailand ■, Asia 63 16 0N 102 0 E
Sian, China 61 34 2N 109 0 E
Siberia, U.S.S.R. 50 60 0N 100 0 E
Sibiu, Rom. 43 45 45N 24 9 E
Sible Hedingham, U.K. 15 51 58N 0 37 E
Sibsey, U.K. 19 53 3N 0 1 E
Sichuan □, China 60 31 0N 104 0 E
Sicily, It. 40 37 30N 14 30 E
Sidbury, U.K. 16 50 43N 3 12W
Sidlaw Hills, U.K. 21 56 32N 3 10W
Sidlesham, U.K. 15 50 46N 0 46W
Sidmouth, U.K. 16 50 40N 3 13W
Sidon = Saydā, Leb. 57 33 35N 35 25 E
Siegen, W. Ger. 36 50 52N 8 2 E
Siena, It. 40 43 20N 11 20 E
Sierra Leone ■, W. Afr. 78 9 0N 12 0W
Sighty Crag, U.K. 21 55 8N 2 37W
Siglufjörður, Ice. 44 66 12N 18 55W
Sikhote Alin Ra., U.S.S.R. 49 46 0N 136 0 E
Sikkim □, India 59 27 50N 88 30 E
Silloth, U.K. 18 54 53N 3 25W
Silsden, U.K. 18 53 55N 1 55W
Silverstone, U.K. 14 52 5N 1 3W
Silverton, U.K. 16 50 49N 3 29W
Simferopol, U.S.S.R. 47 44 55N 34 3 E
Simonsbath, U.K. 14 51 8N 3 45W
Simonside, U.K. 21 55 17N 2 0W
Simpson Desert, Austral. 67 25 0S 137 0 E
Sinai Peninsula, Egypt 79 29 30N 34 0 E
Sind Sagar Doab, Pak. 58 32 0N 71 30 E
Singapore ■, Asia 63 1 17N 103 51 E
Singleton, U.K. 15 50 55N 0 45W
Sioux Falls, U.S.A. 91 43 35N 96 40W
Siping, China 61 33 25N 114 10 E
Siracusa, It. 40 37 4N 15 17 E
Sittingbourne, U.K. 15 51 20N 0 43 E
Sittwe, Bur. 59 20 18N 92 45 E
Sivas, Turk. 47 39 43N 36 58 E
Siwalik Range, Nepal 59 28 0N 83 0 E
Sizewell, U.K. 15 52 13N 1 38 E
Sjælland, Den. 45 55 30N 11 30 E
Skagerrak, Den. 45 57 30N 9 0 E
Skagway, U.S.A. 88 59 23N 135 20W
Skegness, U.K. 19 53 9N 0 20 E
Skellefteå, Swed. 44 64 45N 20 58 E
Skellingthorpe, U.K. 19 53 14N 0 37W
Skelmersdale, U.K. 18 53 34N 2 49W
Skelmorlie, U.K. 20 55 52N 4 53W
Skelton, Cleveland, U.K. 19 54 33N 0 59W
Skelton, Cumbria, U.K. 18 54 42N 2 50W
Skerries, The, U.K. 17 53 27N 4 40W
Skibbereen, Ire. 25 51 33N 9 16W
Skiddaw, U.K. 18 54 39N 3 9W
Skien, Nor. 45 59 12N 9 35 E
Skikda, Alg. 78 36 50N 6 58 E
Skipness, U.K. 20 55 46N 5 20W
Skipsea, U.K. 19 53 58N 0 13W
Skipton, U.K. 18 53 57N 2 1W
Skopje, Yug. 41 42 1N 21 32 E
Skull, Ire. 25 51 32N 9 40W
Skye, U.K. 22 57 15N 6 10W
Slaidburn, U.K. 18 53 57N 2 28W
Slaley, U.K. 21 54 55N 2 4W
Slaney →, Ire. 25 52 52N 6 45W
Sleaford, U.K. 19 53 0N 0 22W
Sleat, Sd. of, U.K. 22 57 5N 5 47W
Sledmere, U.K. 19 54 4N 0 35W
Sleights, U.K. 19 54 27N 0 40W
Slieve Aughty, Ire. 25 53 4N 8 30W
Slieve Bloom, Ire. 25 53 4N 7 40W
Slieve Donard, U.K. 24 54 10N 5 57W
Slieve Gullion, U.K. 24 54 8N 6 26W
Slieve Mish, Ire. 25 52 12N 9 50W
Slievenamon, Ire. 25 52 25N 7 37W
Sligo, Ire. 24 54 17N 8 28W
Sligo □, Ire. 24 54 10N 8 35W
Sligo B., Ire. 24 54 20N 8 40W
Sliven, Bulg. 41 42 42N 26 19 E
Slough, U.K. 15 51 30N 0 35W
Slovenská Socialisticka Republika □, Czech. 43 48 30N 20 0 E
Slyne Hd., Ire. 24 53 25N 10 10W
Smederevo, Yug. 41 44 40N 20 57 E
Smethwick, U.K. 14 52 29N 1 58W
Smithfield, U.K. 18 54 59N 2 51W
Smolensk, U.S.S.R. 46 54 45N 32 0 E
Snaefell, U.K. 18 54 18N 4 26W
Snainton, U.K. 19 54 14N 0 33W
Snaith, U.K. 19 53 42N 1 1W
Snake →, U.S.A. 90 46 12N 119 2W
Snape, U.K. 15 52 11N 1 29 E
Snettisham, U.K. 15 52 52N 0 30 E
Snizort, L., U.K. 22 57 33N 6 28W
Snowdon, U.K. 17 53 4N 4 8W
Snowy Mts., Austral. 70 36 30S 148 20 E
Sobral, Brazil 101 3 50S 40 20W
Sochi, U.S.S.R. 47 43 35N 39 40 E
Society Is., Pac. Oc. 65 17 0S 151 0W
Socotra, Ind. Oc. 57 12 30N 54 0 E
Söderhamn, Swed. 45 61 18N 17 10 E
Sofia, Bulg. 41 42 45N 23 20 E
Sogn og Fjordane fylke □, Nor. 44 61 40N 6 0 E
Sognefjorden, Nor. 45 61 10N 5 50 E
Sohâg, Egypt 79 26 33N 31 43 E
Soham, U.K. 15 52 20N 0 20 E
Sokoto, Nig. 78 13 2N 5 16 E
Solapur, India 58 17 43N 75 56 E
Solent, The, U.K. 14 50 45N 1 25W
Solihull, U.K. 14 52 26N 1 47W
Solimões → = Amazon →, S. Am. 100 0 5S 50 0W
Solingen, W. Ger. 36 51 10N 7 4 E
Solomon Is. ■, Oc. 64 6 0S 155 0 E
Solway Firth, U.K. 18 54 45N 3 38W
Somali Rep. ■, E. Afr. 73 7 0N 47 0 E
Somerby, U.K. 15 52 42N 0 49W
Somerset □, U.K. 14 51 9N 3 0W
Somersham, U.K. 15 52 24N 0 0 E
Somerton, U.K. 14 51 3N 2 45W
Sompting, U.K. 15 50 51N 0 20W
Søndre Strømfjord, Green. 89 66 59N 50 40W
Sonning, U.K. 15 51 28N 0 53W
Sorbie, U.K. 20 54 46N 4 26W
Soria, Sp. 37 41 43N 2 32W
Sorisdale, U.K. 20 56 40N 6 28W
Sorn, U.K. 20 55 31N 4 18W
Sorocaba, Brazil 102 23 31S 47 27W
Sosnowiec, Pol. 43 50 20N 19 10 E
Sousse, Tunisia 79 35 50N 10 38 E
South Africa, Rep. of ■, Africa 81 32 0S 17 0 E
South Australia □, Austral. 66 32 0S 139 0 E
South Barrule, U.K. 18 54 9N 4 36W
South Bend, U.S.A. 92 41 38N 86 20W
South Benfleet, U.K. 15 51 33N 0 34 E
South Brent, U.K. 16 50 26N 3 50W
South Carolina □, U.S.A. 91 33 45N 81 0W
South Cave, U.K. 19 53 46N 0 37W
South China Sea, Asia 63 10 0N 113 0 E
South Dakota □, U.S.A. 90 45 0N 100 0W
South Dorset Downs, U.K. 14 50 40N 2 26W
South Downs, U.K. 15 50 53N 0 10W
South Elkington, U.K. 19 53 22N 0 5W
South Esk →, U.K. 23 56 44N 3 3W
South Foreland, U.K. 15 51 7N 1 23 E
South Georgia, Atl. Oc. 102 54 30S 37 0W
South Glamorgan □, U.K. 17 51 30N 3 20W
South Hayling, U.K. 15 50 47N 0 56W
South I., N.Z. 71 44 0S 170 0 E
South Korea ■, Asia 61 36 0N 128 0 E
South Molton, U.K. 16 51 1N 3 50W
South Orkney Is., Ant. 103 63 0S 45 0W
South Petherton, U.K. 14 50 57N 2 49W
South Petherwin, U.K. 16 50 35N 4 22W
South Platte →, U.S.A. 90 41 7N 100 42W
South Pole, Ant. 103 90 0S 0 0 E
South Ronaldsay, U.K. 23 58 46N 2 58W
South Sandwich Is., Ant. 103 57 0S 27 0W
South Shetland Is., Ant. 103 62 0S 59 0W
South Shields, U.K. 19 54 59N 1 26W
South Tawton, U.K. 16 50 44N 3 55W
South Tyne →, U.K. 19 54 46N 2 25W
South Uist, U.K. 22 57 20N 7 15W
South West Africa = Namibia ■, Africa 81 22 0S 18 9 E
South Woodham Ferrers, U.K. 15 51 40N 0 37 E
South Yemen ■, Asia 56 15 0N 48 0 E
South Yorkshire □, U.K. 19 53 30N 1 20W
Southam, U.K. 14 52 16N 1 24W
Southampton, U.K. 14 50 54N 1 23W
Southampton I., Canada 89 64 30N 84 0W
Southampton Water, U.K. 14 50 52N 1 21W
Southborough, U.K. 15 51 10N 0 15 E
Southend, U.K. 20 55 18N 5 38W
Southend-on-Sea, U.K. 15 51 32N 0 42 E
Southern Alps, N.Z. 71 43 41S 170 11 E
Southern Ocean 103 62 0S 60 0 E
Southern Uplands, U.K. 21 55 30N 3 3W
Southery, U.K. 15 52 32N 0 23 E
Southland □, N.Z. 71 45 51S 168 13 E
Southminster, U.K. 15 51 40N 0 51 E
Southport, U.K. 18 53 38N 3 1W
Southwark, U.K. 15 51 29N 0 5W
Southwell, U.K. 19 53 4N 0 57W
Southwick, U.K. 15 50 50N 0 14W
Southwold, U.K. 15 52 19N 1 41 E
Sovetskaya Gavan, U.S.S.R. 49 48 50N 140 0 E
Soviet Union ■ = Union of Soviet Socialist Republics ■, Eurasia 48 60 0N 100 0 E
Sowerby, U.K. 19 54 13N 1 19W
Soweto, S. Afr. 81 26 14S 27 54 E
Spain ■, Europe 37 40 0N 5 0W
Spalding, U.K. 15 52 47N 0 9W
Spanish Town, Jam. 94 18 0N 76 57W
Sparkford, U.K. 14 51 2N 2 33W
Spean Bridge, U.K. 22 56 53N 4 55W
Speke, U.K. 18 53 21N 2 51W
Spelve, L., U.K. 20 56 22N 5 45W
Spencer G., Austral. 67 34 0S 137 20 E
Spennymoor, U.K. 19 54 43N 1 35W
Sperrin Mts., U.K. 24 54 50N 7 0W
Spey →, U.K. 23 57 26N 3 25W
Spézia, La, It. 40 44 8N 9 50 E
Spilsby, U.K. 19 53 10N 0 6 E
Spithead, U.K. 15 50 43N 1 5W
Spitzbergen = Svalbard, Arctic 103 78 0N 17 0 E
Split, Yug. 40 43 31N 16 26 E
Spofforth, U.K. 19 53 57N 1 28W
Spokane, U.S.A. 90 47 45N 117 25W
Springfield, Ill., U.S.A. 92 39 48N 89 40W
Springfield, Mass., U.S.A. 93 42 8N 72 37W
Springfield, Mo., U.S.A. 91 37 15N 93 20W
Springfield, Ohio, U.S.A. 92 39 58N 83 48W
Sproatley, U.K. 19 53 46N 0 9W
Spurn Hd., U.K. 19 53 34N 0 8 E
Sredinnyy Ra., U.S.S.R. 49 57 0N 160 0 E
Srednekolymsk, U.S.S.R. 49 67 27N 153 40 E
Sri Lanka ■, Asia 58 7 30N 80 50 E
Srinagar, India 58 34 5N 74 50 E

Staffa, U.K. 20 56 26N 6 21W
Stafford, U.K. 14 52 49N 2 9W
Stafford □, U.K. 14 52 53N 2 10W
Staindrop, U.K. 19 54 35N 1 49W
Staines, U.K. 15 51 26N 0 30W
Stainforth, U.K. 19 53 37N 0 59W
Stainmore For., U.K. 18 54 29N 2 5W
Stainton, U.K. 19 53 17N 0 23W
Staithes, U.K. 19 54 33N 0 47W
Stalbridge, U.K. 14 50 57N 2 22W
Stalham, U.K. 15 52 46N 1 31 E
Stalingrad = Volgograd, U.S.S.R. 47 48 40N 44 25 E
Stallingborough, U.K. 19 53 36N 0 11W
Stalybridge, U.K. 18 53 29N 2 4W
Stamford, U.K. 15 52 39N 0 29W
Stamford, U.S.A. 93 41 5N 73 30W
Stamford Bridge, U.K. 19 53 59N 0 53W
Stamfordham, U.K. 21 55 3N 1 53W
Standish, U.K. 18 53 35N 2 39W
Standon, U.K. 15 51 53N 0 2 E
Stanford on Teme, U.K. 14 52 17N 2 26W
Stanhope, U.K. 18 54 45N 2 0W
Stanley, Falk. 102 51 40S 59 51W
Stanley, Durham, U.K. 19 54 53N 1 42W
Stanley, Tayside, U.K. 21 56 29N 3 28W
Stannington, U.K. 21 55 7N 1 41W
Stanovoy Ra., U.S.S.R. 49 55 0N 130 0 E
Stansted Mountfitchet, U.K. 15 51 54N 0 13 E
Stanwix, U.K. 18 54 54N 2 56W
Stapleford, U.K. 19 52 56N 1 16W
Staplehurst, U.K. 15 51 9N 0 35 E
Stara Zagora, Bulg. 41 42 26N 25 39 E
Start Bay, U.K. 16 50 15N 3 35W
Start Pt., U.K. 16 50 13N 3 38W
Staunton, U.K. 14 51 58N 2 19W
Stavanger, Nor. 45 58 57N 5 40 E
Staveley, Cumbria, U.K. 18 54 24N 2 49W
Staveley, Derby, U.K. 19 53 16N 1 20W
Stavropol, U.S.S.R. 47 45 5N 42 0 E
Stenhousemuir, U.K. 21 56 2N 3 46W
Sterlitamak, U.S.S.R. 46 53 40N 56 0 E
Stevenage, U.K. 15 51 54N 0 11W
Stevenston, U.K. 20 55 38N 4 46W
Stewart I., N.Z. 71 46 58S 167 54 E
Stewarton, U.K. 20 55 40N 4 30W
Steyning, U.K. 15 50 54N 0 19W
Stillington, U.K. 19 54 7N 1 5W
Stinchar →, U.K. 20 55 10N 4 50W
Stiperstones Mt., U.K. 14 52 36N 2 57W
Stirling, U.K. 21 56 7N 3 57W
Stobo, U.K. 21 55 38N 3 18W
Stockbridge, U.K. 14 51 7N 1 30W
Stockholm, Swed. 45 59 20N 18 3 E
Stockport, U.K. 18 53 25N 2 11W
Stocksbridge, U.K. 19 53 30N 1 36W
Stockton, U.S.A. 90 38 0N 121 20W
Stockton-on-Tees, U.K. 19 54 34N 1 20W
Stoke, U.K. 15 51 26N 0 41 E
Stoke Ferry, U.K. 15 52 34N 0 31 E
Stoke Fleming, U.K. 16 50 19N 3 36W
Stoke Mandeville, U.K. 15 51 46N 0 47W
Stoke-on-Trent, U.K. 18 53 1N 2 11W
Stoke Prior, U.K. 14 52 18N 2 5W
Stokenham, U.K. 16 50 15N 3 40W
Stokesley, U.K. 19 54 27N 1 12W
Stone, Bucks., U.K. 15 51 48N 0 52W
Stone, Staffs., U.K. 18 52 55N 2 10W
Stonehaven, U.K. 23 56 58N 2 11W
Stonehouse, Gloucs., U.K. 14 51 45N 2 18W
Stonehouse, Strathclyde, U.K. 21 55 42N 4 0W
Stonham Aspall, U.K. 15 52 11N 1 7 E
Stony Stratford, U.K. 15 52 4N 0 51W
Storm B., Austral. 67 43 10S 147 30 E
Stornoway, U.K. 22 58 12N 6 23W
Stort →, U.K. 15 51 50N 0 7 E
Stotfold, U.K. 15 52 2N 0 13W
Stour →, Dorset, U.K. 14 50 48N 2 7W
Stour →, Hereford & Worcs., U.K. 14 52 25N 2 13W
Stour →, Kent, U.K. 15 51 15N 1 20 E
Stour →, Suffolk, U.K. 15 51 55N 1 5 E
Stourbridge, U.K. 14 52 28N 2 8W
Stourport, U.K. 14 52 21N 2 18W
Stow, U.K. 21 55 41N 2 50W
Stow Bardolph, U.K. 15 52 38N 0 24 E
Stow-on-the-Wold, U.K. 14 51 55N 1 42W
Stowmarket, U.K. 15 52 11N 1 0 E
Strabane, U.K. 24 54 50N 7 28W
Strabane □, U.K. 24 54 45N 7 25W
Strachur, U.K. 20 56 10N 5 5W
Stradbroke, U.K. 15 52 19N 1 16 E
Stralsund, E. Ger. 42 54 17N 13 5 E
Strangford, L., U.K. 24 54 30N 5 37W
Stranraer, U.K. 20 54 54N 5 0W
Strasbourg, Fr. 34 48 35N 7 42 E
Stratford-on-Avon, U.K. 14 52 12N 1 42W
Stratford St. Mary, U.K. 15 51 58N 0 59 E
Strath Earn, U.K. 21 56 20N 3 50W
Strath Spey, U.K. 23 57 15N 3 40W
Strathaven, U.K. 21 55 40N 4 4W
Strathclyde □, U.K. 20 56 0N 4 50W
Strathmore, U.K. 23 56 40N 3 4W
Strathpeffer, U.K. 23 57 35N 4 32W
Strathy Pt., U.K. 23 58 35N 4 0W
Strathyre, U.K. 20 56 14N 4 20W
Stratmiglo, U.K. 21 56 16N 3 15W
Stratton, Cornwall, U.K. 16 50 49N 4 31W
Stratton, Wilts., U.K. 14 51 41N 1 45W
Stratton St. Margaret, U.K. 14 51 35N 1 45W
Streatley, U.K. 14 51 31N 1 9W
Street, U.K. 14 51 7N 2 43W
Strensall, U.K. 19 54 3N 1 2W
Stretford, U.K. 18 53 27N 2 19W
Stretton, U.K. 18 53 21N 2 34W
Strichen, U.K. 23 57 35N 2 5W
Striven, L., U.K. 20 55 58N 5 9W
Stromeferry, U.K. 22 57 20N 5 33W
Stromness, U.K. 23 58 58N 3 18W
Stronachlachar, U.K. 20 56 15N 4 35W
Strone, U.K. 20 55 59N 4 54W
Stronsay, U.K. 23 59 8N 2 38W
Stroud, U.K. 14 51 44N 2 12W
Studland, U.K. 14 50 39N 1 58W
Studley, U.K. 14 52 16N 1 54W
Sturminster Marshall, U.K. 14 50 48N 2 4W
Sturminster Newton, U.K. 14 50 56N 2 18W
Sturt Cr. →, Austral. 66 20 8S 127 24 E
Sturton, U.K. 19 53 22N 0 39W
Stuttgart, W. Ger. 42 48 46N 9 10 E
Subotica, Yug. 41 46 6N 19 49 E
Suck →, Ire. 25 53 17N 8 18W
Sucre, Bol. 100 19 0S 65 15W
Sudan ■, Africa 78 15 0N 30 0 E
Sudbury, Canada 92 46 30N 81 0W
Sudbury, Derby, U.K. 19 52 53N 1 43W
Sudbury, Suffolk, U.K. 15 52 2N 0 44 E
Suez, Egypt 79 29 58N 32 31 E
Suffolk □, U.K. 15 52 16N 1 0 E
Suir →, Ire. 25 52 15N 7 10W
Sukkur, Pak. 58 27 42N 68 54 E
Sulawesi □, Indon. 63 2 0S 120 0 E
Sulby, U.K. 18 54 18N 4 29W
Sullom Voe, U.K. 22 60 30N 1 20W
Sulu Sea, E. Ind. 63 8 0N 120 0 E
Sumatra □, Indon. 63 0 40N 100 20 E
Sumbawa, Indon. 63 8 26S 117 30 E
Sumburgh Hd., U.K. 22 59 52N 1 17W
Summer Is., U.K. 22 58 0N 5 27W
Sumy, U.S.S.R. 47 50 57N 34 50 E
Sunart, L., U.K. 22 56 42N 5 43W
Sunda Str., Indon. 63 6 20S 105 30 E
Sundarbans, The, Asia 59 22 0N 89 0 E
Sunderland, U.K. 19 54 54N 1 22W
Sundsvall, Swed. 44 62 23N 17 17 E
Sunk Island, U.K. 19 53 38N 0 7W
Sunninghill, U.K. 15 51 25N 0 40W
Sunshine, Austral. 70 37 48S 144 52 E
Superior, L., N. Am. 92 47 40N 87 0W
Sūr, Leb. 57 33 19N 35 16 E
Surabaya, Indon. 63 7 17S 112 45 E
Surakarta, Indon. 63 7 35S 110 48 E
Surat, India 58 21 12N 72 55 E
Surgut, U.S.S.R. 48 61 14N 73 20 E
Surinam ■, S. Am. 101 4 0N 56 0W
Surrey □, U.K. 15 51 16N 0 30W
Surtsey, Ice. 44 63 20N 20 30W
Sutlej →, Pak. 58 29 23N 71 3 E
Sutterton, U.K. 19 52 54N 0 8W
Sutton, U.K. 15 51 22N 0 13W
Sutton Bridge, U.K. 15 52 46N 0 12 E
Sutton Coldfield, U.K. 14 52 33N 1 50W
Sutton Courtenay, U.K. 14 51 39N 1 16W
Sutton-in-Ashfield, U.K. 19 53 7N 1 20W
Sutton-on-Sea, U.K. 19 53 18N 0 18 E
Sutton Scotney, U.K. 14 51 9N 1 20W
Suva, Fiji 64 18 6S 178 30 E
Suzhou, China 61 31 19N 120 38 E
Svalbard, Arctic 103 78 0N 17 0 E
Svendborg, Den. 45 55 4N 10 35 E
Sverdlovsk, U.S.S.R. 46 56 50N 60 30 E
Sverdrup Is., Canada 103 79 0N 97 0W
Swadlincote, U.K. 14 52 47N 1 34W
Swaffham, U.K. 15 52 38N 0 42 E
Swale →, U.K. 19 54 5N 1 20W
Swan Hill, Austral. 70 35 20S 143 33 E
Swanage, U.K. 14 50 36N 1 59W
Swansea, U.K. 17 51 37N 3 57W
Swaziland ■, Africa 81 26 30S 31 30 E
Sweden ■, Europe 44 57 0N 15 0 E
Swift Current, Canada 88 50 20N 107 45W
Swilly, L., Ire. 24 55 12N 7 35W
Swindon, U.K. 15 51 33N 1 47W
Swineshead, U.K. 19 52 56N 0 11W
Swinton, Borders, U.K. 21 55 43N 2 14W
Swinton, Gr. Manchester, U.K. 18 53 31N 2 21W
Swinton, S. Yorks., U.K. 19 53 28N 1 20W
Switzerland ■, Europe 42 46 30N 8 0 E
Swords, Ire. 24 53 27N 6 15W
Sydney, Austral. 70 33 53S 151 10 E
Sydney, Canada 93 46 7N 60 7W
Syktyvkar, U.S.S.R. 46 61 45N 50 40 E
Symington, U.K. 21 55 35N 3 36W
Symonds Yat, U.K. 14 51 50N 2 38W
Syracuse, U.S.A. 93 43 4N 76 11W
Syrdarya →, U.S.S.R. 48 46 3N 61 0 E
Syria ■, Asia 56 35 0N 38 0 E
Syrian Desert, Asia 56 31 0N 40 0 E
Syston, U.K. 14 52 42N 1 5W
Syzran, U.S.S.R. 46 53 12N 48 30 E
Szczecin, Pol. 42 53 27N 14 27 E
Szeged, Hung. 43 46 16N 20 10 E
Székesfehérvár, Hung. 43 47 15N 18 25 E

T

Tabora, Tanz. 80 5 2S 32 50 E
Tabrīz, Iran 56 38 7N 46 20 E
Tabūk, Si. Arab. 56 28 23N 36 36 E
Tacna, Peru 100 18 0S 70 20W
Tacoma, U.S.A. 90 47 15N 122 30W
Tacuarembó, Urug. 102 31 45S 56 0W
Tadcaster, U.K. 19 53 53N 1 16W
Tadley, U.K. 14 51 21N 1 8W
Tadzhikistan □, U.S.S.R. 48 35 30N 70 0 E
Taegu, S. Kor. 61 35 50N 128 37 E
Taejŏn, S. Kor. 61 36 20N 127 28 E
Taganrog, U.S.S.R. 47 47 12N 38 50 E
Tagus = Tajo →, Sp. 37 38 40N 9 24W
Tahiti, Pac. Oc. 65 17 37S 149 27W
Taichung, Taiwan 61 24 10N 120 35 E
Taimyr Pen., U.S.S.R. 49 75 0N 100 0 E
Tain, U.K. 23 57 49N 4 4W
Tainan, Taiwan 61 23 17N 120 18 E
Taipei, Taiwan 61 25 2N 121 30 E
Taiwan ■, Asia 61 23 30N 121 0 E
Taiyuan, China 61 37 52N 112 33 E
Ta'izz, Yem. 56 13 35N 44 2 E
Tajo →, Sp. 37 38 40N 9 24W
Tak, Thai. 59 16 52N 99 8 E
Takamatsu, Jap. 62 34 20N 134 5 E
Takaoka, Jap. 62 36 47N 137 0 E
Takapuna, N.Z. 71 36 47S 174 47 E
Takasaki, Jap. 62 36 20N 139 0 E
Takeley, U.K. 15 51 52N 0 16 E
Takla Makan, China 60 39 0N 83 0 E
Talca, Chile 102 35 28S 71 40W
Talcahuano, Chile 102 36 40S 73 10W
Talgarth, U.K. 17 51 59N 3 15W
Tallahassee, U.S.A. 91 30 25N 84 15W
Tallinn, U.S.S.R. 46 59 22N 24 48 E
Tamar →, U.K. 16 50 33N 4 15W
Tambov, U.S.S.R. 46 52 45N 41 28 E
Tame →, U.K. 14 52 43N 1 45W
Tamerton Foliot, U.K. 16 50 25N 4 10W
Tamil Nadu □, India 58 11 0N 77 0 E
Tampa, U.S.A. 91 27 57N 82 38W
Tampere, Fin. 44 61 30N 23 50 E
Tampico, Mex. 94 22 20N 97 50W
Tamworth, Austral. 67 31 7S 150 58 E
Tamworth, U.K. 14 52 38N 1 41W
Tana, L., Eth. 79 13 5N 37 30 E
Tanami Desert, Austral. 66 18 50S 132 0 E
Tandragee, U.K. 24 54 22N 6 23W
Tanga, Tanz. 80 5 5S 39 2 E
Tanganyika, L., E. Afr. 80 6 40S 30 0 E
Tangier, Mor. 78 35 50N 5 49W
Tangshan, China 61 39 38N 118 10 E
Tanworth, U.K. 14 52 20N 1 50W
Tanzania ■, E. Afr. 80 6 40S 34 0 E
Tapajós →, Brazil 101 2 24S 54 41W
Tarābulus, Leb. 56 34 31N 35 50 E
Tarābulus, Libya 79 32 49N 13 7 E
Taranaki □, N.Z. 71 39 5S 174 51 E
Táranto, It. 40 40 30N 17 11 E
Táranto, G. di, It. 40 40 0N 17 15 E
Tarbat Ness, U.K. 23 57 52N 3 48W
Tarbert, Strathclyde, U.K. 20 55 55N 5 25W
Tarbert, W. Isles, U.K. 22 57 54N 6 49W
Tarbes, Fr. 35 43 15N 0 3 E
Tarbet, U.K. 20 56 13N 4 44W
Tarbolton, U.K. 20 55 30N 4 30W
Taree, Austral. 70 31 50S 152 30 E
Tarija, Bol. 100 21 30S 64 40W
Tarim Basin, China 60 40 0N 84 0 E
Tarleton, U.K. 18 53 41N 2 50W
Tarnów, Pol. 43 50 3N 21 0 E
Tarporley, U.K. 18 53 10N 2 42W
Tarragona, Sp. 37 41 5N 1 17 E
Tarrasa, Sp. 37 41 34N 2 1 E
Tashkent, U.S.S.R. 48 41 20N 69 10 E
Tasman B., N.Z. 71 40 59S 173 25 E
Tasman Sea, Pac. Oc. 71 36 0S 160 0 E
Tasmania □, Austral. 67 42 0S 146 30 E
Tatar A.S.S.R. □, U.S.S.R. 46 55 30N 51 30 E
Tattenhall, U.K. 18 53 7N 2 47W
Taunton, U.K. 14 51 1N 3 7W
Taupo, N.Z. 71 38 41S 176 7 E
Taupo, L., N.Z. 71 38 46S 175 55 E
Tauranga, N.Z. 71 37 42S 176 11 E
Taurus Mts., Turk. 47 37 0N 35 0 E
Tavistock, U.K. 16 50 33N 4 9W
Tavoy, Burma 59 14 2N 98 12 E
Taw →, U.K. 16 17 37S 177 55 E
Tay →, U.K. 21 56 37N 3 38W
Tay, Firth of, U.K. 21 56 25N 3 8W
Tay, L., U.K. 21 56 30N 4 10W
Tay Bridge, U.K. 21 56 28N 3 0W
Taynuilt, U.K. 20 56 25N 5 15W
Tayport, U.K. 21 56 27N 2 52W
Tayside □, U.K. 21 56 25N 3 30W
Tbilisi, U.S.S.R. 47 41 43N 44 50 E
Te Anau, L., N.Z. 71 45 15S 167 45 E
Te Aroha, N.Z. 71 37 32S 175 44 E
Tebay, U.K. 18 54 25N 2 35W
Tees →, U.K. 19 54 36N 1 25W
Teesdale, U.K. 18 54 37N 2 10W
Teesside, U.K. 19 54 37N 1 13W
Tegid, L., U.K. 17 52 53N 3 38W
Tegucigalpa, Hond. 94 14 5N 87 14W
Tehrān, Iran 56 35 44N 51 30 E
Tehuantepec, Gulf of, Mex. 94 15 50N 95 0W
Tehuantepec, Isthmus of, Mex. 94 17 0N 94 30W
Teifi →, U.K. 17 52 4N 4 14W
Teign →, U.K. 16 50 41N 3 42W
Teignmouth, U.K. 16 50 33N 3 30W
Tejo →, Port. 37 38 40N 9 24W
Tel Aviv-Jaffa, Isr. 57 32 4N 34 48 E
Telemark fylke □, Nor. 45 59 25N 8 30 E
Telford, U.K. 14 52 42N 2 31W
Teluk Betung, Indon. 63 5 20S 105 10 E
Tema, Ghana 78 5 41N 0 0 E
Teme →, U.K. 14 52 23N 2 15W
Temirtau, U.S.S.R. 48 50 5N 72 56 E
Temora, Austral. 70 34 30S 147 30 E
Temple Combe, U.K. 14 51 0N 2 25W
Temple Ewell, U.K. 15 51 9N 1 15 E
Temple Sowerby, U.K. 18 54 38N 2 33W
Templemore, Ire. 25 52 48N 7 50W
Tenbury, U.K. 14 52 18N 2 35W
Tenby, U.K. 17 51 40N 4 42W
Tenerife, Can. Is. 78 28 15N 16 35W
Tennessee □, U.S.A. 91 36 0N 86 30W
Tennessee →, U.S.A. 91 37 4N 88 34W
Tenterden, U.K. 15 51 4N 0 42 E
Teófilo Otoni, Brazil 101 17 50S 41 30W
Tepic, Mex. 94 21 30N 104 54W
Téramo, It. 40 42 40N 13 40 E
Teresina, Brazil 101 5 9S 42 45W
Terni, It. 40 42 34N 12 38 E
Terre Haute, U.S.A. 92 39 28N 87 24W
Teruel, Sp. 37 40 22N 1 8W
Test →, U.K. 14 51 7N 1 30W
Tetbury, U.K. 14 51 37N 2 9W
Tetlin, U.S.A. 88 63 14N 142 50W
Tetney, U.K. 19 53 30N 0 1W
Tétouan, Mor. 78 35 35N 5 21W
Tetovo, Yug. 41 42 1N 21 2 E
Tettenhall, U.K. 14 52 35N 2 7W
Teviot →, U.K. 21 55 21N 2 51W
Teviotdale, U.K. 21 55 25N 2 50W
Teviothead, U.K. 21 55 19N 2 55W
Tewkesbury, U.K. 14 51 59N 2 8W
Texas □, U.S.A. 90 31 40N 98 30W
Texel, Neth. 36 53 5N 4 50 E
Teynham, U.K. 15 51 19N 0 50 E
Thailand ■, Asia 63 16 0N 102 0 E
Thailand, G. of, Asia 63 11 30N 101 0 E
Thal Desert, Pak. 58 31 10N 71 30 E
Thame, U.K. 15 51 44N 0 58W
Thame →, U.K. 15 51 35N 1 8W
Thames →, U.K. 15 51 30N 0 35 E
Thanet, I. of, U.K. 15 51 21N 1 20 E
Thar Desert, India 58 28 0N 72 0 E
Thatcham, U.K. 14 51 24N 1 17W
Thaxted, U.K. 15 51 57N 0 20 E
The Entrance, Austral. 70 33 21S 151 30 E
The Grenadines, Is., W. Ind. 94 12 40N 61 20W
The Hague, Neth. 36 52 7N 4 17 E
The Pas, Canada 88 53 45N 101 15W
Theale, U.K. 14 51 26N 1 5W
Thessaloníki, Greece 41 40 38N 22 58 E
Thessaloníki, Gulf of, Greece 41 40 15N 22 45 E
Thessaly □, Greece 41 39 30N 22 0 E
Thetford, U.K. 15 52 25N 0 44 E
Thies, Sene. 78 14 50N 16 51W
Thimphu, Bhutan 59 27 31N 89 45 E
Thionville, Fr. 34 49 20N 6 10 E
Thirlmere, L., U.K. 18 54 32N 3 4W
Thirsk, U.K. 19 54 15N 1 20W
Thirston, U.K. 21 55 19N 1 34W
Thisted, Den. 45 56 58N 8 40 E
Thompson →, Canada 88 50 15N 121 24W
Thornaby on Tees, U.K. 19 54 36N 1 19W
Thornbury, U.K. 14 51 36N 2 31W
Thorndon, U.K. 15 52 16N 1 8 E
Thorne, U.K. 19 53 36N 0 56W
Thorney, U.K. 15 52 37N 0 8W
Thornham, U.K. 15 52 59N 0 35 E
Thornhill, U.K. 21 55 15N 3 46W
Thornthwaite, U.K. 18 54 36N 3 13W
Thornton, U.K. 18 53 52N 2 29W
Thornton Dale, U.K. 19 54 14N 0 41W
Thorpe, U.K. 15 52 38N 1 20 E
Thorpe le Soken, U.K. 15 51 50N 1 11 E
Thrace □, Greece 41 41 9N 25 30 E
Thrapston, U.K. 15 52 24N 0 32W
Threlkeld, U.K. 18 54 37N 3 2W
Threshfield, U.K. 18 54 5N 2 2W
Thule, Green. 103 77 40N 69 0W
Thunder Bay, Canada 92 48 20N 89 15W
Thurlby, U.K. 15 52 45N 0 21W
Thurles, Ire. 25 52 40N 7 53W
Thurmaston, U.K. 14 52 40N 1 8W
Thursby, U.K. 18 54 40N 3 3W
Thurso, U.K. 23 58 34N 3 31W
Tian Shan, China 60 43 0N 84 0 E
Tianshui, China 60 34 32N 105 40 E
Tiber →, It. 40 41 44N 12 14 E
Tiberias, Isr. 57 32 47N 35 32 E
Tibesti, Chad 79 21 0N 17 30 E
Ticehurst, U.K. 15 51 2N 0 23 E
Tickhill, U.K. 19 53 25N 1 8W
Tideswell, U.K. 19 53 17N 1 46W
Tientsin, China 61 39 10N 117 15 E
Tierra del Fuego □, Arg. 102 54 0S 67 45W
Tighnabruaich, U.K. 20 55 55N 5 13W
Tigris →, Iraq 56 37 0N 42 30 E

Tijuana, Mex. 94 32 30N 117 10W
Tiksi, U.S.S.R. 49 71 40N 128 45 E
Tilburg, Neth. 36 51 31N 5 6 E
Tilbury, U.K. 15 51 27N 0 24 E
Till →, U.K. 19 55 35N 2 3W
Tillicoultry, U.K. 21 56 9N 3 44W
Tilmanstone, U.K. 15 51 13N 1 18 E
Tilt →, U.K. 23 56 50N 3 50W
Timaru, N.Z. 71 44 23S 171 14 E
Timbuktu = Tombouctou, Mali 78 16 50N 3 0W
Timişoara, Rom. 43 45 43N 21 15 E
Timmins, Canada 92 48 28N 81 25W
Timor, Indon. 63 9 0S 125 0 E
Timor Sea, E. Ind. 66 10 0S 127 0 E
Tingewick, U.K. 14 51 59N 1 4W
Tintagel, U.K. 16 50 40N 4 45W
Tintagel Hd., U.K. 16 50 40N 4 46W
Tipperary, Ire. 25 52 28N 8 10W
Tipperary □, Ire. 25 52 37N 7 55W
Tipton, U.K. 14 52 32N 2 4W
Tiptree, U.K. 15 51 48N 0 46 E
Tiranë, Alb. 41 41 18N 19 49 E
Tiree, U.K. 20 56 31N 6 55W
Tiree, Passage of, U.K. 20 56 30N 6 30W
Tîrgu Mureş, Rom. 43 46 31N 24 38 E
Tiruchchirappalli, India 58 10 45N 78 45 E
Tisbury, U.K. 14 51 4N 2 4W
Tisza →, Hung. 43 46 8N 20 2 E
Titchfield, U.K. 14 50 51N 1 13W
Titicaca, L., Peru 100 15 30S 69 30W
Titograd, Yug. 41 42 30N 19 19 E
Tiverton, U.K. 16 50 54N 3 30W
Tizi-Ouzou, Alg. 78 36 42N 4 3 E
Toamasina, Madag. 81 18 10S 49 25 E
Tobago, W. Ind. 94 11 10N 60 30W
Tobermory, U.K. 20 56 37N 6 4W
Tobol →, U.S.S.R. 48 58 10N 68 12 E
Tocantins →, Brazil 101 1 45S 49 10W
Toddington, U.K. 15 51 57N 0 31W
Todmorden, U.K. 18 53 43N 2 7W
Togliatti, U.S.S.R. 46 53 32N 49 24 E
Togo ■, W. Afr. 78 6 15N 1 35 E
Tokelau Is., Pac. Oc. 64 9 0S 171 45W
Tōkyō, Jap. 62 35 45N 139 45 E
Tolageak, U.S.A. 88 70 2N 162 50W
Tolbukhin, Bulg. 41 43 37N 27 49 E
Toledo, Sp. 37 39 50N 4 2W
Toledo, U.S.A. 92 41 37N 83 33W
Toliara, Madag. 81 23 21S 43 40 E
Tollesbury, U.K. 15 51 46N 0 51 E
Toluca, Mex. 94 19 20N 99 40W
Tom Price, Austral. 66 22 40S 117 48 E
Tombouctou, Mali 78 16 50N 3 0W
Tomnavoulin, U.K. 23 57 19N 3 18W
Tomsk, U.S.S.R. 48 56 30N 85 5 E
Tonbridge, U.K. 15 51 12N 0 18 E
Tone →, U.K. 16 50 59N 3 15W
Tong, U.K. 14 52 39N 2 18W
Tonga ■, Pac. Oc. 64 19 50S 174 30W
Tonga Trench, Pac. Oc. 64 18 0S 175 0W
Tongue, U.K. 23 58 29N 4 25W
Tonkin, G. of, Asia 60 20 0N 108 0 E
Toowoomba, Austral. 67 27 32S 151 56 E
Topeka, U.S.A. 91 39 3N 95 40W
Topsham, U.K. 16 50 40N 3 27W
Tor Bay, U.K. 16 50 26N 3 31W
Torbay, U.K. 16 50 26N 3 31W
Torne älv →, Swed. 44 65 50N 24 12 E
Toronto, Canada 92 43 39N 79 20W
Torpoint, U.K. 16 50 23N 4 12W
Torquay, U.K. 16 50 27N 3 31W
Torran Rocks, U.K. 20 56 14N 6 24W
Torrens, L., Austral. 67 31 0S 137 50 E
Torreón, Mex. 94 25 33N 103 26W
Torridge →, U.K. 16 50 51N 4 10W
Torridon, L., U.K. 22 57 35N 5 50W
Torthorwald, U.K. 21 55 7N 3 30W
Tortosa, Sp. 37 40 49N 0 31 E
Toruń, Pol. 43 53 0N 18 39 E
Torver, U.K. 18 54 20N 3 7W
Tory I., Ire. 24 55 17N 8 12W
Totland, U.K. 14 50 41N 1 32W
Totley, U.K. 19 53 18N 1 32W
Totnes, U.K. 16 50 26N 3 41W
Totton, U.K. 14 50 55N 1 29W
Toulon, Fr. 35 43 10N 5 55 E
Toulouse, Fr. 35 43 37N 1 27 E
Tournai, Belg. 36 50 35N 3 25 E
Tours, Fr. 34 47 22N 0 40 E
Towcester, U.K. 15 52 7N 0 56W
Town Yetholm, U.K. 21 55 33N 2 19W
Townsville, Austral. 67 19 15S 146 45 E
Toyama, Jap. 62 36 40N 137 15 E
Toyohashi, Jap. 62 34 45N 137 25 E
Trabzon, Turk. 47 41 0N 39 45 E
Trail, Canada 88 49 5N 117 40W
Tralee, Ire. 25 52 16N 9 42W
Tralee B., Ire. 25 52 17N 9 55W
Tramore, Ire. 25 52 10N 7 10W
Tranent, U.K. 21 55 57N 2 58W
Transcaucasia, U.S.S.R. 47 42 0N 44 0 E
Transvaal □, S. Afr. 81 25 0S 29 0 E
Transylvanian Alps, Rom. 43 45 30N 25 0 E
Trápani, It. 40 38 1N 12 30 E
Traralgon, Austral. 70 38 12S 146 34 E
Trawsfynydd, U.K. 17 52 54N 3 55W
Tredegar, U.K. 17 51 47N 3 16W
Tregaron, U.K. 17 52 14N 3 56W
Trent →, U.K. 19 53 33N 0 44W
Trentham, U.K. 18 52 59N 2 12W
Trentino-Alto Adige □, It. 40 46 30N 11 0 E
Trento, It. 40 46 5N 11 8 E
Trenton, U.S.A. 93 40 15N 74 41W
Tresco I., U.K. 16 49 57N 6 20W
Treshnish Is., U.K. 20 56 30N 6 25W
Trevose Hd., U.K. 16 50 33N 5 3W
Trier, W. Ger. 36 49 45N 6 37 E
Trieste, It. 40 45 39N 13 45 E
Trim, Ire. 24 53 34N 6 48W
Trimdon, U.K. 19 54 43N 1 23W
Trimley, U.K. 15 51 59N 1 19 E
Trincomalee, Sri L. 58 8 38N 81 15 E
Trinidad, W. Ind. 94 10 30N 61 15W
Trinidad & Tobago ■, W. Ind. 94 10 30N 61 20W
Tripoli = Tarābulus, Leb. 56 34 31N 35 50 E
Tripoli = Tarābulus, Libya 79 32 49N 13 7 E
Tristan da Cunha, Atl. Oc. 128 37 6S 12 20W
Trivandrum, India 58 8 41N 77 0 E
Trois-Riviéres, Canada 93 46 25N 72 34W
Trollhättan, Swed. 45 58 17N 12 20 E
Troms fylke □, Nor. 44 68 56N 19 0 E
Tromsø, Nor. 44 69 40N 18 56 E
Trondheim, Nor. 44 63 36N 10 25 E
Troon, U.K. 20 55 33N 4 40W
Trossachs, The, U.K. 20 56 14N 4 24W
Trostan, U.K. 24 55 4N 6 10W
Trotternish, U.K. 22 57 32N 6 15W
Trowbridge, U.K. 14 51 18N 2 12W
Troy, U.S.A. 93 42 45N 73 39W
Troyes, Fr. 34 48 19N 4 3 E
Trujillo, Peru 100 8 6S 79 0W
Truk, Pac. Oc. 64 7 25N 151 46 E
Trull, U.K. 14 50 58N 3 8W
Trumpington, U.K. 15 52 11N 0 6 E
Truro, U.K. 16 50 17N 5 2W
Tselinograd, U.S.S.R. 48 51 10N 71 30 E
Tsimlyansk Res., U.S.S.R. 47 48 0N 43 0 E
Tsu, Jap. 62 34 45N 136 25 E
Tsugaru Str., Jap. 62 41 30N 140 30 E
Tuam, Ire. 24 53 30N 8 50W
Tuamotu Arch., Pac. Oc. 65 17 0S 144 0W
Tuath, Loch, U.K. 20 56 30N 6 15W
Tubuai Is., Pac. Oc. 65 25 0S 150 0W
Tucson, U.S.A. 90 32 14N 110 59W
Tula, U.S.S.R. 46 54 13N 37 38 E
Tulcán, Ecuad. 100 0 48N 77 43W
Tulla, L., U.K. 20 56 33N 4 47W
Tullamore, Ire. 25 53 17N 7 30W
Tullow, Ire. 25 52 48N 6 45W
Tulsa, U.S.A. 91 36 10N 96 0W
Tulua, Col. 100 4 6N 76 11W
Tumaco, Col. 100 1 50N 78 45W
Tummel, L., U.K. 23 56 43N 3 55W
Tunbridge Wells, U.K. 15 51 7N 0 16 E
Tuncurry, Austral. 70 32 17S 152 29 E
Tunis, Tunisia 78 36 50N 10 11 E
Tunisia ■, Africa 78 33 30N 9 10 E
Tunja, Col. 100 5 33N 73 25W
Tunstall, U.K. 15 52 7N 1 28 E
Tura, India 59 25 30N 90 16 E
Turfan Depression, China 50 42 40N 89 25 E
Turin, It. 40 45 4N 7 40 E
Turkana, L., Kenya 80 3 30N 36 5 E
Turkey ■, Eurasia 47 39 0N 36 0 E
Turkmenistan □, U.S.S.R. 48 39 0N 59 0 E
Turks Is., W. Ind. 95 21 20N 71 20W
Turku, Fin. 45 60 30N 22 19 E
Turnberry, U.K. 20 55 19N 4 50W
Turnu-Severin, Rom. 43 44 39N 22 41 E
Turriff, U.K. 23 57 32N 2 28W
Tuskar Rock, Ire. 25 52 12N 6 10W
Tutbury, U.K. 14 52 52N 1 41W
Tuticorin, India 58 8 50N 78 12 E
Tuvalu ■, Pac. Oc. 64 8 0S 178 0 E
Tuxford, U.K. 19 53 14N 0 52W
Tuxtla Gutiérrez, Mex. 94 16 50N 93 10W
Tuz Gölü, Turk. 47 38 45N 33 30 E
Tuzla, Yug. 41 44 34N 18 41 E
Twatt, U.K. 23 59 6N 3 15W
Tweed →, U.K. 21 55 42N 1 59W
Tweedmouth, U.K. 21 55 46N 2 1W
Tweedshawe, U.K. 21 55 26N 3 29W
Twenty, U.K. 15 52 43N 0 20W
Twyford, Berks., U.K. 15 51 29N 0 51W
Twyford, Hants., U.K. 14 51 1N 1 19W
Tychy, Pol. 43 50 9N 18 59 E
Tydd St. Mary, U.K. 15 52 45N 0 9 E
Tyldesley, U.K. 18 53 31N 2 29W
Tyler, U.S.A. 90 32 18N 95 18W
Tyndrum, U.K. 20 56 26N 4 41W
Tyne →, Tyne & Wear, U.K. 19 54 58N 1 28W
Tyne →, Lothian, U.K. 21 55 58N 2 45W
Tyne & Wear □, U.K. 19 54 55N 1 35W
Tynemouth, U.K. 19 55 1N 1 27W
Tyre = Sūr, Leb. 57 33 19N 35 16 E
Tyrol □, Austria 42 47 3N 10 43 E
Tyrrhenian Sea, Europe 40 40 0N 12 30 E
Tyumen, U.S.S.R. 48 57 11N 65 29 E
Tywardreath, U.K. 16 50 21N 4 40W
Tywi →, U.K. 17 51 48N 4 20W
Tywyn, U.K. 17 52 36N 4 5W

U

Ube, Jap. 62 33 56N 131 15 E
Uberaba, Brazil 101 19 50S 47 55W
Uberlândia, Brazil 101 19 0S 48 20W
Ucayali →, Peru 100 4 30S 73 30W
Uckfield, U.K. 15 50 58N 0 6 E
Udaipur, India 58 24 36N 73 44 E
Uddevalla, Swed. 45 58 21N 11 55 E
Uddingston, U.K. 21 55 50N 4 3W
Údine, It. 40 46 5N 13 10 E
Ufa, U.S.S.R. 46 54 45N 55 55 E
Uffculme, U.K. 16 50 54N 3 19W
Ufford, U.K. 15 52 6N 1 22 E
Uganda ■, E. Afr. 80 2 0N 32 0 E
Ugborough, U.K. 16 50 22N 3 53W
Uig, U.K. 22 57 35N 6 20W
Uitenhage, S. Afr. 81 33 40S 25 28 E
Ujung Pandang, Indon. 63 5 10S 119 20 E
Ukraine □, U.S.S.R. 47 49 0N 32 0 E
Ulan Bator, Mong. 60 47 55N 106 53 E
Ulan Ude, U.S.S.R. 49 51 45N 107 40 E
Ulceby Cross, U.K. 19 53 14N 0 6 E
Ulhasnagar, India 58 19 15N 73 10 E
Ullapool, U.K. 22 57 54N 5 10W
Ullswater, U.K. 18 54 35N 2 52W
Ulm, W. Ger. 42 48 23N 10 0 E
Ulster □, U.K. 24 54 35N 6 30W
Ulva, I., U.K. 20 56 30N 6 12W
Ulverston, U.K. 18 54 13N 3 7W
Ulyanovsk, U.S.S.R. 46 54 20N 48 25 E
Ulyasutay, Mong. 60 47 56N 97 28 E
Umbria □, It. 40 42 53N 12 30 E
Umeå, Swed. 44 63 45N 20 20 E
Umtata, S. Afr. 81 31 36S 28 49 E
Ungava B., Canada 89 59 30N 67 30W
Ungava Pen., Canada 89 60 0N 74 0W
Union of Soviet Socialist Republics ■, Eurasia 48 60 0N 100 0 E
United Arab Emirates ■, Asia 57 23 50N 54 0 E
United Kingdom ■, Europe 5 55 0N 3 0W
United States of America ■, N. Am. 90 37 0N 96 0W
United States Trust Terr. of the Pacific Is. □, Pac. Oc. 64 10 0N 160 0 E
Unst, U.K. 22 60 50N 0 55W
Upavon, U.K. 14 51 17N 1 49W
Upington, S. Afr. 81 28 25S 21 15 E
Upper Heyford, U.K. 14 51 54N 1 16W
Upper L. Erne, U.K. 24 54 14N 7 22W
Upper Volta ■ = Burkina Faso ■, Africa 78 12 0N 1 0W
Uppingham, U.K. 15 52 36N 0 43W
Uppsala, Swed. 45 59 53N 17 38 E
Upton, U.K. 18 53 14N 2 52W
Upton-upon-Severn, U.K. 14 52 4N 2 12W
Upwey, U.K. 14 50 40N 2 29W
Ural Mts., U.S.S.R. 46 60 0N 59 0 E
Uralsk, U.S.S.R. 46 51 20N 51 20 E
Uranium City, Canada 88 59 34N 108 37W
Ure →, U.K. 19 54 20N 1 25W
Urgench, U.S.S.R. 48 41 40N 60 41 E
Urmia, L., Iran 56 37 50N 45 30 E
Urmston, U.K. 18 53 28N 2 22W
Uruguay ■, S. Am. 102 32 30S 56 30W
Uruguay →, S. Am. 102 34 12S 58 18W
Ürümqi, China 60 43 45N 87 45 E
Usk →, U.K. 17 51 37N 2 56W
Üsküdar, Turk. 47 41 0N 29 5 E
Usselby, U.K. 19 53 25N 0 21W
Ust-Kamenogorsk, U.S.S.R. 48 50 0N 82 36 E
Ust Urt Plateau, U.S.S.R. 48 44 0N 55 0 E
Ustinov, U.S.S.R. 46 56 51N 53 14 E
Utah □, U.S.A. 90 39 30N 111 30W
Utica, U.S.A. 93 43 5N 75 18W
Utrecht, Neth. 36 52 5N 5 8 E
Utsunomiya, Jap. 62 36 30N 139 50 E
Uttar Pradesh □, India 58 27 0N 80 0 E
Uttoxeter, U.K. 18 52 53N 1 50W
Uzbekistan □, U.S.S.R. 48 41 30N 65 0 E

V

Vaasa, Fin. 44 63 6N 21 38 E
Vadodara, India 58 22 20N 73 10 E
Vadsø, Nor. 44 70 3N 29 50 E
Val d'Or, Canada 92 48 7N 77 47W
Valdez, U.S.A. 88 61 14N 146 17W
Valdivia, Chile 102 39 50S 73 14W
Valence, Fr. 35 44 57N 4 54 E
Valencia, Sp. 37 39 27N 0 23W
Valencia, Ven. 100 10 11N 68 0W
Valenciennes, Fr. 34 50 20N 3 34 E
Valentia Hr., Ire. 25 51 56N 10 17W
Valentia I., Ire. 25 51 54N 10 22W
Valladolid, Sp. 37 41 38N 4 43W
Valledupar, Col. 100 10 29N 73 15W
Valletta, Malta 40 35 54N 14 30 E
Valley, U.K. 17 53 17N 4 31W
Valparaíso, Chile 102 33 2S 71 40W
Van, L., Turk. 47 38 30N 43 0 E
Van Diemen G., Austral. 66 11 45S 132 0 E
Vancouver, Canada 88 49 15N 123 10W
Vancouver I., Canada 88 49 50N 126 0W
Vänern, Swed. 45 58 47N 13 30 E
Vanua Levu, Fiji 64 16 33S 179 15 E
Vanuatu ■, Pac. Oc. 64 15 0S 168 0 E
Varanasi, India 59 25 22N 83 0 E
Varangar Fjord, Nor. 44 70 3N 29 25 E
Vardar →, Yug. 41 40 35N 22 50 E
Värmlands län □, Swed. 45 60 0N 13 20 E
Varna, Bulg. 41 43 13N 27 56 E
Västerås, Swed. 45 59 37N 16 38 E
Västmanlands län □, Swed. 45 59 45N 16 20 E
Vatnajökull, Ice. 44 64 30N 16 48W
Vättern, Swed. 45 58 25N 14 30 E
Växjö, Swed. 45 56 52N 14 50 E
Vendée □, Fr. 34 46 50N 1 35W
Venezuela ■, S. Am. 100 8 0N 65 0W
Venice, It. 40 45 27N 12 20 E
Venlo, Neth. 36 51 22N 6 11 E
Ventnor, U.K. 14 50 35N 1 12W
Veracruz, Mex. 94 19 10N 96 10W
Vercelli, It. 40 45 19N 8 25 E
Vereeniging, S. Afr. 81 26 38S 27 57 E
Verkhoyansk, U.S.S.R. 49 67 35N 133 25 E
Verkhoyansk Ra., U.S.S.R. 49 66 0N 129 0 E
Vermont □, U.S.A. 93 43 40N 72 50W
Verona, It. 40 45 27N 11 0 E
Versailles, Fr. 34 48 48N 2 8 E
Verviers, Belg. 36 50 37N 5 52 E
Verwood, U.K. 14 50 53N 1 53W
Veryan, U.K. 16 50 13N 4 56W
Veryan Bay, U.K. 16 50 12N 4 51W
Vestmannaeyjar, Ice. 44 63 27N 20 15W
Vesuvius, Mt., It. 40 40 50N 14 22 E
Viborg, Den. 45 56 27N 9 23 E
Vickerstown, U.K. 18 54 8N 3 17W
Victoria, Canada 88 48 30N 123 25W
Victoria □, Austral. 70 37 0S 144 0 E
Victoria →, Austral. 66 15 10S 129 40 E
Victoria, L., Austral. 70 33 57S 141 15 E
Victoria, L., E. Afr. 80 1 0S 33 0 E
Victoria Falls, Zimb. 81 17 58S 25 52 E
Victoria I., Canada 88 71 0N 111 0W
Victoria Ld., Ant. 103 75 0S 160 0 E
Vienna, Austria 42 48 12N 16 22 E
Vientiane, Laos 51 17 58N 102 36 E
Vietnam ■, Asia 63 19 0N 106 0 E
Vigo, Sp. 37 42 12N 8 41W
Vijayawada, India 59 16 31N 80 39 E
Villahermosa, Mex. 94 17 59N 92 55W
Villefranche-sur-Saône, Fr. 35 45 59N 4 43 E
Vilnius, U.S.S.R. 46 54 38N 25 19 E
Vilyuysk, U.S.S.R. 49 63 40N 121 35 E
Viña del Mar, Chile 102 33 0S 71 30W
Vineland, U.S.A. 93 39 30N 75 0W
Vinnitsa, U.S.S.R. 47 49 15N 28 30 E
Virgin Is., W. Ind. 95 18 40N 64 30W
Virginia □, U.S.A. 91 37 45N 78 0W
Viscount Melville Sd., Canada 88 74 10N 108 0W
Vishakhapatnam, India 59 17 45N 83 20 E
Vistula = Wisła →, Pol. 43 54 22N 18 55 E
Vitebsk, U.S.S.R. 46 55 10N 30 15 E
Viterbo, It. 40 42 25N 12 8 E
Viti Levu, Fiji 64 17 30S 177 30 E
Vitim →, U.S.S.R. 49 59 26N 112 34 E
Vitória, Brazil 101 20 20S 40 22W
Vitoria, Sp. 37 42 50N 2 41W
Vitória da Conquista, Brazil 101 14 51S 40 51W
Vlaardingen, Neth. 36 51 55N 4 21 E
Vladimir, U.S.S.R. 46 56 15N 40 30 E
Vladivostok, U.S.S.R. 49 43 10N 131 53 E
Vlissingen, Neth. 36 51 26N 3 34 E
Vlórë, Alb. 41 40 32N 19 28 E
Voil, L., U.K. 20 56 20N 4 25W
Volga →, U.S.S.R. 47 48 30N 46 0 E
Volga Hts., U.S.S.R. 47 51 0N 46 0 E
Volgograd, U.S.S.R. 47 48 40N 44 25 E
Vologda, U.S.S.R. 46 59 10N 40 0 E
Vólos, Greece 41 39 24N 22 59 E
Volta, L., Ghana 78 7 30N 0 15 E
Volta Redonda, Brazil 101 22 31S 44 5W
Volzhskiy, U.S.S.R. 47 48 56N 44 46 E
Voorburg, Neth. 36 52 5N 4 24 E
Vorkuta, U.S.S.R. 46 67 48N 64 20 E
Voronezh, U.S.S.R. 46 51 40N 39 10 E
Voroshilovgrad, U.S.S.R. 47 48 38N 39 15 E
Vosges, Fr. 34 48 20N 7 10 E
Vryburg, S. Afr. 81 26 55S 24 45 E
Vyrnwy, L., U.K. 17 52 48N 3 30W

W

Waal →, Neth. 36 51 59N 4 30 E
Wabash →, U.S.A. 92 37 46N 88 2W
Waco, U.S.A. 91 31 33N 97 5W
Wâd Medanî, Sudan 79 14 28N 33 30 E
Waddenzee, Neth. 36 53 6N 5 10 E
Waddesdon, U.K. 15 51 50N 0 54W

Waddingham, *U.K.* **19** 53 28N 0 31W
Waddington, *U.K.* **19** 53 10N 0 31W
Waddington, Mt., *Canada* **88** 51 23N 125 15W
Wadebridge, *U.K.* **16** 50 31N 4 51W
Wadhurst, *U.K.* **15** 51 3N 0 21 E
Wagga Wagga, *Austral.* **70** 35 7S 147 24 E
Wagin, *Austral.* **66** 33 17S 117 25 E
Wainfleet All Saints, *U.K.* **19** 53 7N 0 16 E
Waipara, *N.Z.* **71** 43 3S 172 46 E
Waitaki →, *N.Z.* **71** 44 56S 171 7 E
Wakatipu, L., *N.Z.* **71** 45 5S 168 33 E
Wakayama, *Jap.* **62** 34 15N 135 15 E
Wakefield, *U.K.* **19** 53 41N 1 31W
Walberswick, *U.K.* **15** 52 18N 1 39 E
Wałbrzych, *Pol.* **42** 50 45N 16 18 E
Walbury Hill, *U.K.* **14** 51 22N 1 28W
Waldron, *U.K.* **15** 50 56N 0 13 E
Wales □, *U.K.* **17** 52 30N 3 30W
Walgett, *Austral.* **67** 30 0S 148 5 E
Wallachia, *Rom.* **43** 44 35N 25 0 E
Wallasey, *U.K.* **18** 53 26N 3 2W
Wallingford, *U.K.* **14** 51 40N 1 15W
Wallis & Futuna, *Pac. Oc.* **64** 13 18S 176 10W
Wallsend, *U.K.* **19** 54 59N 1 30W
Walmer, *U.K.* **15** 51 12N 1 23 E
Walney, Isle of, *U.K.* **18** 54 5N 3 15W
Walpole, *U.K.* **15** 52 44N 0 13 E
Walsall, *U.K.* **14** 52 36N 1 59W
Walsoken, *U.K.* **15** 52 41N 0 12 E
Waltham, *U.K.* **19** 53 32N 0 6W
Waltham Abbey, *U.K.* **15** 51 40N 0 1 E
Waltham Forest, *U.K.* **15** 51 37N 0 2 E
Waltham on the Wolds, *U.K.* **15** 52 49N 0 48W
Walton-on-the-Naze, *U.K.* **15** 51 52N 1 17 E
Walvis Bay, *S. Afr.* **81** 23 0S 14 28 E
Wanborough, *U.K.* **14** 51 33N 1 40W
Wandsworth, *U.K.* **15** 51 28N 0 15W
Wanganui, *N.Z.* **71** 39 56S 175 3 E
Wangaratta, *Austral.* **70** 36 21S 146 19 E
Wansbeck, *U.K.* **21** 55 12N 1 28W
Wantage, *U.K.* **14** 51 35N 1 25W
Warboys, *U.K.* **15** 52 25N 0 5W
Warburton →, *Austral.* **67** 28 4S 137 28 E
Wardington, *U.K.* **14** 52 8N 1 17W
Wardle, *U.K.* **18** 53 7N 2 35W
Ward's Stone, *U.K.* **18** 54 2N 2 39W
Ware, *U.K.* **15** 51 48N 0 2W
Wareham, *U.K.* **14** 50 41N 2 8W
Wark, *U.K.* **21** 55 5N 2 14W
Warkworth, *U.K.* **21** 55 22N 1 38W
Warley, *U.K.* **14** 52 30N 2 0W
Warminster, *U.K.* **14** 51 12N 2 11W
Warracknabeal, *Austral.* **70** 36 9S 142 26 E
Warrego →, *Austral.* **67** 30 24S 145 21 E
Warrenpoint, *U.K.* **24** 54 7N 6 15W
Warrington, *U.K.* **18** 53 25N 2 38W
Warrnambool, *Austral.* **70** 38 25S 142 30 E
Warsaw, *Pol.* **43** 52 13N 21 0 E
Warsop, *U.K.* **19** 53 13N 1 9W
Warta →, *Pol.* **42** 52 35N 14 39 E
Warthe = Warta →, *Pol.* **43** 52 35N 14 39 E
Warwick, *Austral.* **67** 28 10S 152 1 E
Warwick, *U.K.* **14** 52 17N 1 36W
Warwick □, *U.K.* **14** 52 20N 1 30W
Wasatch Ra., *U.S.A.* **90** 40 30N 111 15W
Wash, The, *U.K.* **19** 52 58N 0 20 E
Washford, *U.K.* **14** 51 9N 3 22W
Washington, *U.K.* **21** 54 55N 1 30W
Washington, *U.S.A.* **92** 38 52N 77 0W
Washington □, *U.S.A.* **90** 47 45N 120 30W
Wast Water, L., *U.K.* **18** 54 26N 3 18W
Watchet, *U.K.* **14** 51 10N 3 20W
Waterbeach, *U.K.* **15** 52 16N 0 11 E
Waterbury, *U.S.A.* **93** 41 32N 73 0W
Waterford, *Ire.* **25** 52 16N 7 8W
Waterford □, *Ire.* **25** 52 10N 7 40W
Waterford Harb., *Ire.* **25** 52 10N 6 58W
Watergate Bay, *U.K.* **16** 50 26N 5 4W
Waterloo, *U.K.* **18** 53 29N 3 2W
Watford, *U.K.* **15** 51 38N 0 23W
Wath, *U.K.* **19** 53 29N 1 20W
Watlington, *Norfolk, U.K.* **15** 52 40N 0 24 E
Watlington, *Oxon., U.K.* **15** 51 38N 1 0W
Watton, *U.K.* **15** 52 35N 0 50 E
Waveney →, *U.K.* **15** 52 24N 1 20 E
Waver →, *U.K.* **18** 54 50N 3 15W
Weald, The, *U.K.* **15** 51 7N 0 9 E
Wear →, *U.K.* **19** 54 55N 1 22W
Weardale, *U.K.* **18** 54 44N 2 5W
Wearhead, *U.K.* **18** 54 45N 2 14W
Weaver →, *U.K.* **18** 53 17N 2 35W
Weaverham, *U.K.* **18** 53 15N 2 30W
Weddell Sea, *Ant.* **103** 72 30S 40 0W
Wedmore, *U.K.* **14** 51 14N 2 50W
Wednesbury, *U.K.* **14** 52 33N 2 1W
Wednesfield, *U.K.* **14** 52 36N 2 3W
Weedon Bec, *U.K.* **14** 52 14N 1 6W
Weifang, *China* **61** 36 47N 119 10 E
Weldon, *U.K.* **21** 55 16N 1 46W
Welford, *Berks., U.K.* **14** 51 28N 1 24W
Welford, *Northants., U.K.* **14** 52 26N 1 5W
Welkom, *S. Afr.* **81** 28 0S 26 50 E
Welland →, *U.K.* **15** 52 43N 0 10W
Wellesley Is., *Austral.* **67** 16 42S 139 30 E
Wellingborough, *U.K.* **15** 52 18N 0 41W
Wellington, *Austral.* **70** 32 35S 148 59 E
Wellington, *N.Z.* **71** 41 19S 174 46 E
Wellington, *Salop, U.K.* **14** 52 42N 2 31W
Wellington, *Somerset, U.K.* **14** 50 58N 3 13W
Wellow, *U.K.* **14** 51 20N 2 22W
Wells, *Norfolk, U.K.* **15** 52 57N 0 51 E
Wells, *Somerset, U.K.* **14** 51 12N 2 39W
Welney, *U.K.* **15** 52 31N 0 15 E
Wels, *Austria* **42** 48 9N 14 1 E
Welshpool, *U.K.* **17** 52 40N 3 9W
Welton, *U.K.* **19** 53 19N 0 29W
Welwyn Garden City, *U.K.* **15** 51 49N 0 11W
Wem, *U.K.* **14** 52 52N 2 45W
Wembury, *U.K.* **16** 50 19N 4 6W
Wemyss Bay, *U.K.* **20** 55 52N 4 54W
Wendover, *U.K.* **15** 51 46N 0 45W
Wenhaston, *U.K.* **15** 52 17N 1 35 E
Wenlock Edge, *U.K.* **14** 52 30N 2 43W
Wensleydale, *U.K.* **18** 54 18N 2 0W
Wensum →, *U.K.* **15** 52 35N 1 20 E
Wenzhou, *China* **61** 28 0N 120 38 E
Weobley, *U.K.* **14** 52 9N 2 52W
Werribee, *Austral.* **70** 37 54S 144 40 E
Werrington, *U.K.* **16** 50 40N 4 22W
Weser →, *W. Ger.* **42** 53 33N 8 30 E
West Auckland, *U.K.* **19** 54 38N 1 42W
West Bengal □, *India* **59** 23 0N 88 0 E
West Bridgford, *U.K.* **19** 52 56N 1 8W
West Bromwich, *U.K.* **14** 52 32N 2 1W
West Calder, *U.K.* **21** 55 51N 3 34W
West Coker, *U.K.* **14** 50 55N 2 40W
West Fen, *U.K.* **19** 53 5N 0 5W
West Germany ■, *Europe* **42** 52 0N 9 0 E
West Glamorgan □, *U.K.* **17** 51 40N 3 55W
West Grinstead, *U.K.* **15** 50 58N 0 19W
West Haddon, *U.K.* **14** 52 21N 1 5W
West Kilbride, *U.K.* **20** 55 41N 4 50W
West Kirby, *U.K.* **18** 53 22N 3 11W
West Linton, *U.K.* **21** 55 45N 3 24W
West Lulworth, *U.K.* **14** 50 37N 2 14W
West Malling, *U.K.* **15** 51 16N 0 25 E
West Meon, *U.K.* **14** 51 2N 1 3W
West Mersea, *U.K.* **15** 51 46N 0 55 E
West Midlands □, *U.K.* **14** 52 30N 1 55W
West Moors, *U.K.* **14** 50 49N 1 50W
West Parley, *U.K.* **14** 50 46N 1 52W
West Rasen, *U.K.* **19** 53 23N 0 23W
West Schelde →, *Neth.* **36** 51 23N 3 50 E
West Siberian Plain, *U.S.S.R.* **48** 62 0N 75 0 E
West Sussex □, *U.K.* **15** 50 55N 0 30W
West Tarbert, L., *U.K.* **20** 55 58N 5 30W
West Virginia □, *U.S.A.* **92** 39 0N 81 0W
West Wyalong, *Austral.* **70** 33 56S 147 10 E
West Yorkshire □, *U.K.* **19** 53 45N 1 40W
Westbourne, *U.K.* **15** 50 53N 0 55W
Westbury, *Salop, U.K.* **14** 52 40N 2 57W
Westbury, *Wilts., U.K.* **14** 51 16N 2 11W
Westbury-on-Severn, *U.K.* **14** 51 49N 2 24W
Westerham, *U.K.* **15** 51 16N 0 5 E
Western Australia □, *Austral.* **66** 25 0S 118 0 E
Western Ghats, *India* **58** 14 0N 75 0 E
Western Isles □, *U.K.* **22** 57 30N 7 10W
Western Sahara ■, *Africa* **78** 25 0N 13 0W
Western Samoa ■, *Pac. Oc.* **64** 14 0S 172 0W
Westfield, *U.K.* **15** 50 53N 0 30 E
Westhoughton, *U.K.* **18** 53 34N 2 30W
Westland Bight, *N.Z.* **71** 42 55S 170 5 E
Westmeath □, *Ire.* **24** 53 30N 7 30W
Weston, *U.K.* **14** 52 51N 2 2W
Weston-super-Mare, *U.K.* **14** 51 20N 2 59W
Westport, *Ire.* **24** 53 44N 9 31W
Westport, *N.Z.* **71** 41 46S 171 37 E
Westray, *U.K.* **23** 59 18N 3 0W
Westruther, *U.K.* **21** 55 45N 2 34W
Westward Ho!, *U.K.* **16** 51 2N 4 16W
Wetherby, *U.K.* **19** 53 56N 1 23W
Wetwang, *U.K.* **19** 54 2N 0 35W
Wexford, *Ire.* **25** 52 20N 6 28W
Wexford □, *Ire.* **25** 52 20N 6 25W
Wexford Harb., *Ire.* **25** 52 20N 6 25W
Wey →, *U.K.* **15** 51 19N 0 29W
Weybourne, *U.K.* **15** 52 57N 1 9 E
Weybridge, *U.K.* **15** 51 22N 0 28W
Weymouth, *U.K.* **14** 50 36N 2 28W
Whakatane, *N.Z.* **71** 37 57S 177 1 E
Whaley Bridge, *U.K.* **18** 53 20N 2 0W
Whalley, *U.K.* **18** 53 49N 2 25W
Whalsay, *U.K.* **22** 60 22N 1 0W
Whalton, *U.K.* **21** 55 7N 1 46W
Whangarei, *N.Z.* **71** 35 43S 174 21 E
Whaplode, *U.K.* **15** 52 42N 0 3W
Wharfe →, *U.K.* **19** 53 55N 1 30W
Wharfedale, *U.K.* **18** 54 7N 2 4W
Whauphill, *U.K.* **20** 54 48N 4 31W
Wheatley Hill, *U.K.* **19** 54 45N 1 23W
Whernside, *U.K.* **18** 54 14N 2 24W
Whichham, *U.K.* **18** 54 14N 3 22W
Whimple, *U.K.* **16** 50 46N 3 21W
Whipsnade, *U.K.* **15** 51 51N 0 32W
Whissendine, *U.K.* **15** 52 43N 0 46W
Whiston, *U.K.* **18** 53 25N 2 45W
Whitburn, *U.K.* **21** 55 52N 3 41W
Whitby, *U.K.* **19** 54 29N 0 37W
Whitchurch, *Devon, U.K.* **16** 50 31N 4 7W
Whitchurch, *Hants., U.K.* **14** 51 14N 1 20W
Whitchurch, *Hereford & Worcs., U.K.* **14** 51 51N 2 41W
Whitchurch, *Salop, U.K.* **18** 52 58N 2 42W
White Esk →, *U.K.* **21** 55 14N 3 11W
White Horse Hill, *U.K.* **14** 51 35N 1 35W
White Nile →, *Sudan* **79** 15 38N 32 31 E
White Russia □, *U.S.S.R.* **46** 53 30N 27 0 E
White Sea, *U.S.S.R.* **46** 66 30N 38 0 E
Whiteadder Water →, *U.K.* **21** 55 47N 2 20W
Whitehaven, *U.K.* **18** 54 33N 3 35W
Whitehead, *U.K.* **24** 54 45N 5 42W
Whitehorse, *Canada* **88** 60 43N 135 3W
Whitehorse, Vale of, *U.K.* **14** 51 37N 1 30W
Whitekirk, *U.K.* **21** 56 2N 2 36W
Whitesand B., *U.K.* **16** 50 18N 4 20W
Whithorn, *U.K.* **20** 54 44N 4 25W
Whitley Bay, *U.K.* **21** 55 4N 1 28W
Whitney, Mt., *U.S.A.* **90** 36 35N 118 14W
Whitstable, *U.K.* **15** 51 21N 1 2 E
Whittington, *Derby, U.K.* **19** 53 17N 1 26W
Whittington, *Salop, U.K.* **14** 52 53N 3 0W
Whittlesey, *U.K.* **15** 52 34N 0 8W
Whittlesford, *U.K.* **15** 52 6N 0 9 E
Whitton, *U.K.* **19** 53 42N 0 39W
Whitwell, *Derby, U.K.* **19** 53 16N 1 11W
Whitwell, *I. of W., U.K.* **14** 50 35N 1 19W
Whitwick, *U.K.* **14** 52 45N 1 23W
Whitworth, *U.K.* **18** 53 40N 2 11W
Whixley, *U.K.* **19** 54 2N 1 19W
Whyalla, *Austral.* **67** 33 2S 137 30 E
Wichita, *U.S.A.* **91** 37 40N 97 20W
Wichita Falls, *U.S.A.* **90** 33 57N 98 30W
Wick, *U.K.* **23** 58 26N 3 5W
Wickford, *U.K.* **15** 51 37N 0 31 E
Wickham, *U.K.* **14** 50 54N 1 11W
Wickham Market, *U.K.* **15** 52 9N 1 21 E
Wicklow, *Ire.* **25** 53 0N 6 2W
Wicklow □, *Ire.* **25** 52 59N 6 25W
Wicklow Mts., *Ire.* **25** 53 0N 6 30W
Wickwar, *U.K.* **14** 51 35N 2 23W
Widdrington, *U.K.* **21** 55 15N 1 35W
Widecombe, *U.K.* **16** 50 34N 3 48W
Widemouth, *U.K.* **16** 50 45N 4 34W
Widnes, *U.K.* **18** 53 22N 2 44W
Wiesbaden, *W. Ger.* **36** 50 7N 8 17 E
Wigan, *U.K.* **18** 53 33N 2 38W
Wight, I. of, *U.K.* **14** 50 40N 1 20W
Wigmore, *U.K.* **14** 52 19N 2 51W
Wigston, *U.K.* **14** 52 35N 1 6W
Wigton, *U.K.* **18** 54 50N 3 9W
Wigtown, *U.K.* **20** 54 52N 4 27W
Wigtown B., *U.K.* **20** 54 46N 4 15W
Wilhelm II Land, *Ant.* **103** 68 0S 90 0 E
Wilhelmshaven, *W. Ger.* **42** 53 30N 8 9 E
Wilkes Barre, *U.S.A.* **93** 41 15N 75 52W
Wilkes Land, *Ant.* **103** 69 0S 120 0 E
Willemstad, *Cur.* **94** 12 5N 69 0W
Willenhall, *U.K.* **14** 52 36N 2 3W
Willesborough, *U.K.* **15** 51 8N 0 55 E
Williamstown, *Austral.* **70** 37 51S 144 52 E
Willingdon, *U.K.* **15** 50 47N 0 17 E
Williton, *U.K.* **14** 51 9N 3 20W
Willoughby, *U.K.* **19** 53 14N 0 12 E
Wilmington, *U.K.* **16** 50 46N 3 8W
Wilmington, *U.S.A.* **93** 39 45N 75 32W
Wilmslow, *U.K.* **18** 53 19N 2 14W
Wilnecote, *U.K.* **14** 52 36N 1 40W
Wilsons Promontory, *Austral.* **70** 38 55S 146 25 E
Wilton, *U.K.* **14** 51 5N 1 52W
Wiltshire □, *U.K.* **14** 51 20N 2 0W
Wimblington, *U.K.* **15** 52 31N 0 5 E
Wimborne Minster, *U.K.* **14** 50 48N 2 0W
Wimmera →, *Austral.* **70** 36 8S 141 56 E
Wincanton, *U.K.* **14** 51 3N 2 24W
Winchelsea, *U.K.* **15** 50 55N 0 43 E
Winchester, *U.K.* **14** 51 4N 1 19W
Windermere, *U.K.* **18** 54 24N 2 56W
Windermere, L., *U.K.* **18** 54 20N 2 57W
Windhoek, *Nam.* **81** 22 35S 17 4 E
Windrush →, *U.K.* **14** 51 48N 1 35W
Windsor, *Canada* **92** 42 18N 83 0W
Windsor, *U.K.* **15** 51 28N 0 36W
Windward Passage, *W. Ind.* **95** 20 0N 74 0W
Windygates, *U.K.* **21** 56 12N 3 1W
Wing, *U.K.* **15** 51 54N 0 41W
Wingham, *Austral.* **70** 31 48S 152 22 E
Wingham, *U.K.* **15** 51 16N 1 12 E
Winkleigh, *U.K.* **16** 50 49N 3 57W
Winnipeg, *Canada* **88** 49 54N 97 9W
Winnipeg, L., *Canada* **88** 52 0N 97 0W
Winsford, *U.K.* **18** 53 12N 2 31W
Winslow, *U.K.* **15** 51 57N 0 52W
Winster, *U.K.* **19** 53 9N 1 42W
Winston-Salem, *U.S.A.* **91** 36 7N 80 15W
Winterborne Abbas, *U.K.* **14** 50 43N 2 30W
Winterthur, *Switz.* **42** 47 30N 8 44 E
Winterton, *Humberside, U.K.* **19** 53 39N 0 37W
Winterton, *Norfolk, U.K.* **15** 52 43N 1 43 E
Wirksworth, *U.K.* **19** 53 5N 1 34W
Wirral, *U.K.* **18** 53 25N 3 0W
Wisbech, *U.K.* **15** 52 39N 0 10 E
Wisborough Green, *U.K.* **15** 51 2N 0 30W
Wisconsin □, *U.S.A.* **92** 44 30N 90 0W
Wishaw, *U.K.* **21** 55 46N 3 55W
Wiske →, *U.K.* **19** 54 26N 1 27W
Wisła →, *Pol.* **43** 54 22N 18 55 E
Witbank, *S. Afr.* **81** 25 51S 29 14 E
Witham, *U.K.* **15** 51 48N 0 39 E
Witham →, *U.K.* **19** 53 3N 0 8W
Withern, *U.K.* **19** 53 19N 0 9 E
Withernsea, *U.K.* **19** 53 43N 0 2 E
Witley, *U.K.* **15** 51 9N 0 39W
Witney, *U.K.* **14** 51 47N 1 29W
Witten, *W. Ger.* **36** 51 26N 7 19 E
Wittersham, *U.K.* **15** 51 1N 0 42 E
Wiveliscombe, *U.K.* **14** 51 2N 3 20W
Wivenhoe, *U.K.* **15** 51 51N 0 59 E
Włocławek, *Pol.* **43** 52 40N 19 3 E
Woburn, *U.K.* **15** 51 59N 0 37W
Woburn Sands, *U.K.* **15** 52 1N 0 38W
Wodonga, *Austral.* **70** 36 5S 146 50 E
Woking, *U.K.* **15** 51 18N 0 33W
Wokingham, *U.K.* **15** 51 25N 0 50W
Wolf Rock, *U.K.* **16** 49 56N 5 50W
Wolfsburg, *W. Ger.* **42** 52 27N 10 49 E
Wollongong, *Austral.* **70** 34 25S 150 54 E
Wolsingham, *U.K.* **18** 54 44N 1 52W
Wolverhampton, *U.K.* **14** 52 35N 2 6W
Wolverton, *U.K.* **15** 52 3N 0 48W
Wolviston, *U.K.* **19** 54 39N 1 25W
Wombwell, *U.K.* **19** 53 31N 1 23W
Wŏnsan, *N. Kor.* **61** 39 11N 127 27 E
Wonston, *U.K.* **14** 51 9N 1 18W
Woodbridge, *U.K.* **15** 52 6N 1 19 E
Woodbury, *U.K.* **16** 50 40N 3 24W
Woodhall Spa, *U.K.* **19** 53 10N 0 12W
Woodhouse, *U.K.* **19** 53 23N 1 21W
Woodley, *U.K.* **15** 51 26N 0 54W
Woods, L. of the, *Canada* **88** 49 15N 94 45W
Woodstock, *U.K.* **14** 51 51N 1 20W
Wookey, *U.K.* **14** 51 13N 2 41W
Wookey Hole, *U.K.* **14** 51 13N 2 41W
Wool, *U.K.* **14** 50 41N 2 13W
Woolacombe, *U.K.* **16** 51 10N 4 12W
Wooler, *U.K.* **21** 55 33N 2 0W
Wootton Bassett, *U.K.* **14** 51 32N 1 55W
Wootton Wawen, *U.K.* **14** 52 16N 1 47W
Worcester, *S. Afr.* **81** 33 39S 19 27 E
Worcester, *U.K.* **14** 52 12N 2 12W
Worcester, *U.S.A.* **93** 42 14N 71 49W
Worfield, *U.K.* **14** 52 34N 2 22W
Workington, *U.K.* **18** 54 39N 3 34W
Worksop, *U.K.* **19** 53 19N 1 9W
Wormit, *U.K.* **21** 56 26N 2 59W
Worms, *W. Ger.* **42** 49 37N 8 21 E
Worplesdon, *U.K.* **15** 51 16N 0 36W
Wortham, *U.K.* **15** 52 22N 1 3 E
Worthing, *U.K.* **15** 50 49N 0 21W
Wotton-under-Edge, *U.K.* **14** 51 37N 2 20W
Woy Woy, *Austral.* **70** 33 30S 151 19 E
Wragby, *U.K.* **19** 53 17N 0 18W
Wrangel I., *U.S.S.R.* **49** 71 0N 180 0 E
Wrangle, *U.K.* **19** 53 3N 0 9 E
Wrath, C., *U.K.* **22** 58 38N 5 0W
Wrekin, The, *U.K.* **14** 52 41N 2 35W
Wrentham, *U.K.* **15** 52 24N 1 39 E
Wrexham, *U.K.* **17** 53 5N 3 0W
Writtle, *U.K.* **15** 51 44N 0 27 E
Wrocław, *Pol.* **43** 51 5N 17 5 E
Wrotham, *U.K.* **15** 51 18N 0 20 E
Wroughton, *U.K.* **14** 51 31N 1 47W
Wroxham, *U.K.* **15** 52 42N 1 23 E
Wuhan, *China* **61** 30 31N 114 18 E
Wuhu, *China* **61** 31 22N 118 21 E
Wuppertal, *W. Ger.* **36** 51 15N 7 8 E
Würzburg, *W. Ger.* **42** 49 46N 9 55 E
Wutongqiao, *China* **60** 29 22N 103 50 E
Wuxi, *China* **61** 31 30N 120 30 E
Wuzhou, *China* **61** 23 30N 111 18 E
Wye, *U.K.* **15** 51 11N 0 56 E
Wye →, *U.K.* **14** 51 36N 2 40W
Wylye →, *U.K.* **14** 51 8N 1 53W
Wymondham, *Leics., U.K.* **15** 52 45N 0 42W
Wymondham, *Norfolk, U.K.* **15** 52 34N 1 7 E
Wyndham, *Austral.* **66** 15 33S 128 3 E
Wyoming □, *U.S.A.* **90** 42 48N 109 0W
Wyre →, *U.K.* **18** 53 52N 2 57W
Wyre Forest, *U.K.* **14** 52 24N 2 24W

X

Xiaguan, *China* **60** 25 32N 100 16 E
Xiamen, *China* **61** 24 25N 118 4 E
Xiangfan, *China* **61** 32 2N 112 8 E
Xiangtan, *China* **61** 27 51N 112 54 E
Xiangyang, *China* **61** 32 1N 112 8 E
Xingu →, *Brazil* **101** 1 30S 51 53W
Xining, *China* **60** 36 34N 101 40 E
Xinjiang Uygur Zizhiqu □, *China* **60** 42 0N 86 0 E
Xuzhou, *China* **61** 34 18N 117 10 E

Y

Yablonovy Ra., *U.S.S.R.* **49** 53 0N 114 0 E
Yakut A.S.S.R. □, *U.S.S.R.* **49** 62 0N 130 0 E
Yakutsk, *U.S.S.R.* **49** 62 5N 129 50 E
Yamagata, *Jap.* **62** 38 15N 140 15 E
Yamal, Peninsula, *U.S.S.R.* **48** 71 0N 70 0 E
Yambol, *Bulg.* **41** 42 30N 26 36 E
Yamuna →, *India* **59** 25 30N 81 53 E
Yana →, *U.S.S.R.* **49** 71 30N 136 0 E
Yangtze Kiang →, *China* **60** 31 40N 122 0 E
Yanji, *China* **61** 42 59N 129 30 E
Yantai, *China* **61** 37 34N 121 22 E
Yaoundé, *Cam.* **80** 3 50N 11 35 E
Yarcombe, *U.K.* **16** 50 51N 3 6W
Yare →, *U.K.* **15** 52 36N 1 28 E
Yarm, *U.K.* **19** 54 31N 1 21W
Yarmouth, *U.K.* **14** 50 42N 1 29W
Yaroslavl, *U.S.S.R.* **46** 57 35N 39 55 E
Yarrow, *U.K.* **21** 55 32N 3 0W
Yate, *U.K.* **14** 51 32N 2 26W
Yatsushiro, *Jap.* **62** 32 30N 130 40 E
Yatton, *U.K.* **14** 51 23N 2 50W
Yaxley, *U.K.* **15** 52 31N 0 14W
Yazd, *Iran* **56** 31 55N 54 27 E
Yealmpton, *U.K.* **16** 50 21N 4 0W
Yell, *U.K.* **22** 60 35N 1 5W
Yell Sd., *U.K.* **22** 60 33N 1 15W
Yellow Sea, *China* **61** 35 0N 123 0 E
Yellowknife, *Canada* **88** 62 27N 114 29W
Yellowstone →, *U.S.A.* **90** 47 58N 103 59W
Yellowstone National Park, *U.S.A.* **90** 44 35N 110 0W
Yemen ■, *Si. Arab.* **56** 15 0N 44 0 E
Yenisey →, *U.S.S.R.* **48** 71 50N 82 40 E
Yeo →, *U.K.* **14** 51 10N 3 0W
Yeovil, *U.K.* **14** 50 57N 2 38W
Yerevan, *U.S.S.R.* **47** 40 10N 44 31 E
Yes Tor, *U.K.* **16** 50 41N 3 59W
Yibin, *China* **60** 28 45N 104 32 E
Yichang, *China* **61** 30 40N 111 20 E
Yichuan, *China* **60** 36 2N 110 10 E
Yining, *China* **60** 43 58N 81 10 E
Yogyakarta, *Indon.* **63** 7 49S 110 22 E
Yokkaichi, *Jap.* **62** 35 0N 136 38 E
Yokohama, *Jap.* **62** 35 27N 139 28 E
Yokosuka, *Jap.* **62** 35 20N 139 40 E
Yonkers, *U.S.A.* **93** 40 57N 73 51W
York, *U.K.* **19** 53 58N 1 7W
York, *U.S.A.* **92** 39 57N 76 43W
York, Vale of, *U.K.* **19** 54 15N 1 25W
Yorkshire Wolds, *U.K.* **19** 54 0N 0 30W
Yosemite National Park, *U.S.A.* **90** 38 0N 119 30W
Yoshkar Ola, *U.S.S.R.* **46** 56 38N 47 55 E
Youghal, *Ire.* **25** 51 58N 7 51W
Youghal B., *Ire.* **25** 51 55N 7 50W
Youlgreave, *U.K.* **19** 53 12N 1 50W
Youngstown, *U.S.A.* **92** 41 7N 80 41W
Yoxall, *U.K.* **14** 52 45N 1 49W
Yoxford, *U.K.* **15** 52 16N 1 30 E
Ypres, *Belg.* **36** 50 51N 2 53 E
Ystalyfera, *U.K.* **17** 51 46N 3 48W
Ythan →, *U.K.* **23** 57 26N 2 0W
Yuan Jiang →, *China* **61** 28 55N 111 50 E
Yucatán, Península de, *Mex.* **94** 19 30N 89 0W
Yucatan Str., *Carib.* **94** 22 0N 86 30W
Yugoslavia ■, *Europe* **41** 44 0N 20 0 E
Yukon →, *N. Am.* **88** 65 30N 150 0W
Yukon Territory □, *Canada* **88** 63 0N 135 0W
Yunnan □, *China* **60** 25 0N 102 30 E
Yuzhno-Sakhalinsk, *U.S.S.R.* **49** 46 58N 142 45 E

Z

Zaandam, *Neth.* **36** 52 26N 4 49 E
Zabrze, *Pol.* **43** 50 18N 18 50 E
Zagorsk, *U.S.S.R.* **46** 56 20N 38 10 E
Zagreb, *Yug.* **40** 45 50N 16 0 E
Zagros Mts., *Iran* **56** 33 45N 47 0 E
Zahlah, *Leb.* **57** 33 52N 35 50 E
Zaïre ■, *Africa* **80** 3 0S 23 0 E
Zaïre →, *Africa* **80** 6 4S 12 24 E
Zákinthos, *Greece* **41** 37 47N 20 57 E
Zambezi →, *Africa* **81** 18 55S 36 4 E
Zambia ■, *Africa* **81** 15 0S 28 0 E
Zamboanga, *Phil.* **63** 6 59N 122 3 E
Zamora, *Sp.* **37** 41 30N 5 45W
Zante = Zákinthos, *Greece* **41** 37 47N 20 57 E
Zanzibar, *Tanz.* **80** 6 12S 39 12 E
Zaporozhye, *U.S.S.R.* **47** 47 50N 35 10 E
Zaragoza, *Sp.* **37** 41 39N 0 53W
Zaria, *Nig.* **78** 11 0N 7 40 E
Zeebrugge, *Belg.* **36** 51 19N 3 12 E
Zeist, *Neth.* **36** 52 5N 5 15 E
Zhangjiakou, *China* **61** 40 48N 114 55 E
Zhangzhou, *China* **61** 24 30N 117 35 E
Zhanjiang, *China* **61** 21 15N 110 20 E
Zhdanov, *U.S.S.R.* **47** 47 5N 37 31 E
Zhejiang □, *China* **61** 29 0N 120 0 E
Zhengzhou, *China* **61** 34 45N 113 34 E
Zhitomir, *U.S.S.R.* **47** 50 20N 28 40 E
Zibo, *China* **61** 36 47N 118 3 E
Zielona Góra □, *Pol.* **42** 51 57N 15 30 E
Zigong, *China* **60** 29 15N 104 48 E
Ziguinchor, *Sene.* **78** 12 35N 16 20W
Žilina, *Czech.* **43** 49 12N 18 42 E
Zimbabwe ■, *Africa* **81** 20 0S 30 0 E
Zion Nat. Park, *U.S.A.* **90** 37 25N 112 50W
Zlatoust, *U.S.S.R.* **46** 55 10N 59 40 E
Zonguldak, *Turk.* **47** 41 28N 31 50 E
Zrenjanin, *Yug.* **41** 45 22N 20 23 E
Zug, *Switz.* **42** 47 10N 8 31 E

MAP PROJECTIONS

MAP PROJECTIONS

A map projection is the systematic depiction on a plane surface of the imaginary lines of latitude or longitude from a globe of the earth. This network of lines is called the graticule and forms the framework upon which an accurate depiction of the earth is made. The map graticule, which is the basis of any map, is constructed sometimes by graphical means, but often by using mathematical formulae to give the intersections of the graticule plotted as x and y co-ordinates. The choice between projections is based upon which properties the cartographer wishes the map to possess, the map scale and also the extent of the area to be mapped. Since the globe is three dimensional, it is not possible to depict its surface on a two dimensional plane without distortion. Preservation of one of the basic properties listed below can only be secured at the expense of the others and the choice of projection is often a compromise solution.

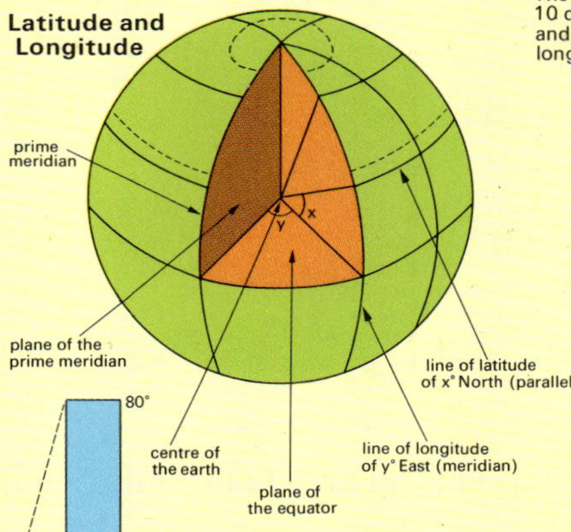

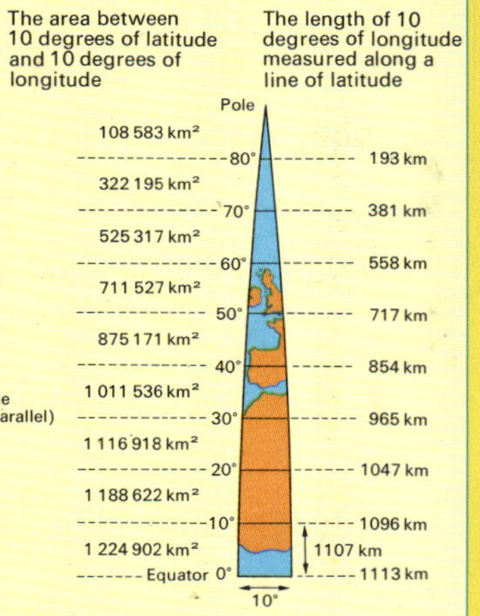

Correct Area

In these projections the areas from the globe are to scale on the map. For example, if you look at the diagram at the top right, areas of 10° x 10° are shown from the equator to the poles. The proportion of this area at the extremities are approximately 11:1. An equal area projection will retain that proportion in its portrayal of those areas. This is particularly useful in the mapping of densities and distributions. Projections with this property are termed **Equal Area, Equivalent or Homolographic.**

Correct Distance

In these projections the scale is correct along the meridians, or in the case of the Azimuthal Equidistant scale is true along any line drawn from the centre of the projection. They are called **Equidistant**.

Correct Shape

This property can only be true within small areas as it is achieved only by having a uniform scale distortion along both x and y axes of the projection. The projections are called **Conformal** or **Orthomorphic.**

In order to minimise the distortions at the edges of some projections, central portions of them are often selected for atlas maps. Below are listed some of the major types of projection.

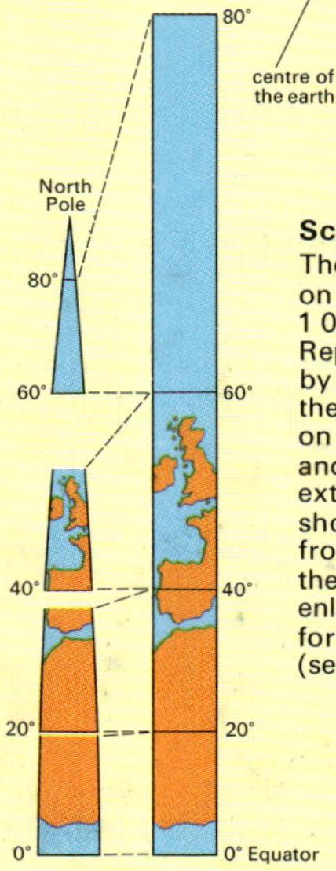

Scale Measurement

The **Representative Fraction** 1:1 000 000 means that 1 unit on the map represents 1 million on the earth. So 1 cm = 1 000 000 cm or 10 km. In SI units (the metric system) the Representative Fraction can be converted to the scale of 1 cm by moving the decimal point through five places, usually deleting the last five zeros thus :- 1: 20 000 000 – 1cm = 200 km. Scale on map projections can only be correct along specific meridians and parallels or from one or two specific points. To take an extreme example of scale distortion, the diagram on the left shows how a portion of the earth's surface, when unwrapped from around a globe (**a gore**) compares with the same area at the same equatorial scale but on Mercator's Projection. The enlargement of scale away from the equator is considerable and for this reason a variable scale for each line of latitude is given (see below).

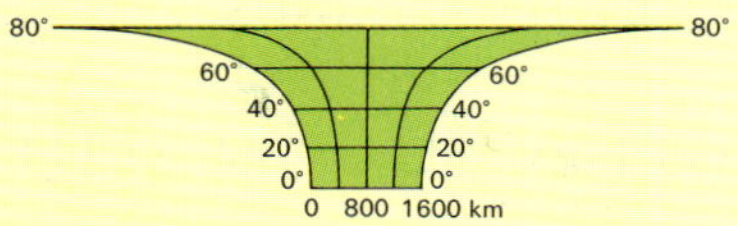

AZIMUTHAL OR ZENITHAL PROJECTIONS

These are constructed by the projection of part of the graticule from the globe onto a plane tangential to any single point on it. This plane may be tangential to the equator (**equatorial case**), the poles (**polar case**) or any other point (**oblique case**). Any straight line drawn from the point at which the plane touches the globe is the shortest distance from that point and is known as a **great circle**. In its **Gnomonic** construction *any* straight line on the map is a great circle, but there is great exaggeration towards the edges and this reduces its general uses. There are five different ways of transferring the graticule onto the plane and these are shown on the right. The central diagram below shows how the graticules vary, using the polar case as the example.

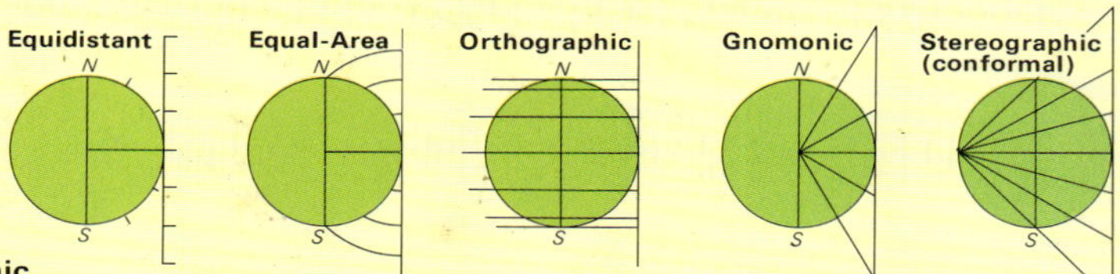

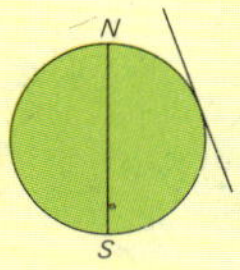

Oblique Case

The plane touches the globe at any point between the equator and poles. The oblique orthographic uses the distortion in azimuthal projections away from the centre to give a graphic depiction of the earth as seen from any desired point in space. It can also be used in both Polar and Equatorial cases. It is used not only for the earth but also for the moon and planets.

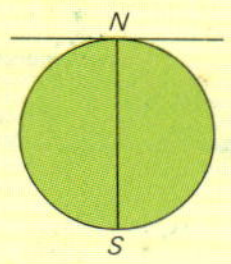

Polar Case

The polar case is the simplest to construct and the diagram below shows the differing effects of all five methods of construction comparing their coverage, distortion etc., using North America as the example.

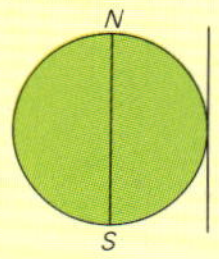

Equatorial Case

The example shown here is Lambert's Equivalent Azimuthal. It is the only projection which is both equal area and where bearing is true from the centre.

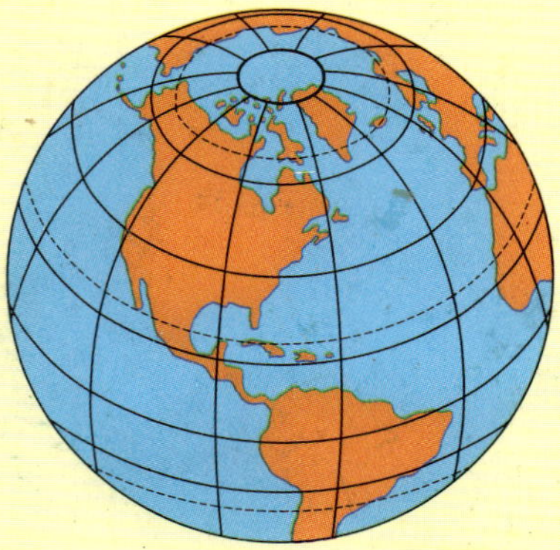

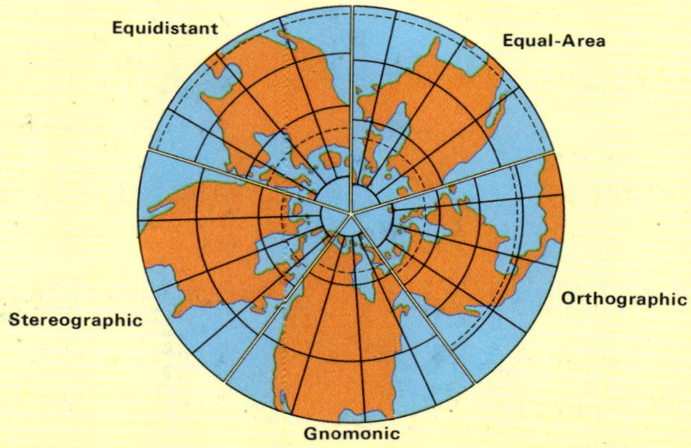

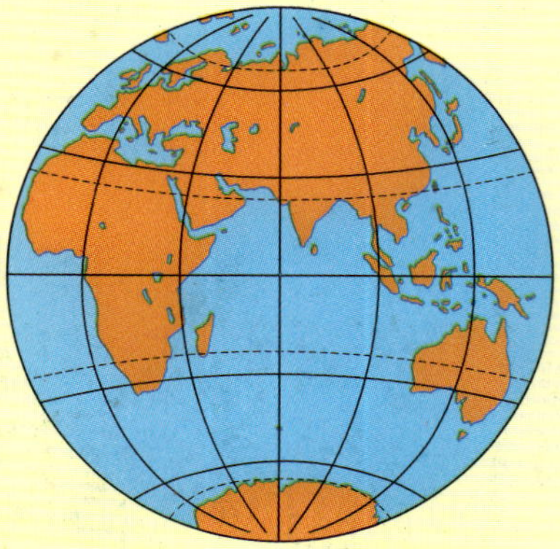